Contributors

Ryan Abbott is Professor of Law and Health Sciences, School of Law, University of Surrey, Guildford, Surrey, UK, and Adjunct Assistant Professor, David Geffen School of Medicine, University of California, Los Angeles.

Mary Acri is Research Assistant Professor, Department of Child and Adolescent Psychiatry, New York University School of Medicine, New York.

Rhiannon Adams was a researcher with the School of Public Health, University of Alberta, Edmonton, Alberta, Canada.

Stefan Bechtold is Professor of Intellectual Property at ETH Zurich, Switzerland.

Andrea Boggio is Associate Professor of Legal Studies, Bryant University, Smithfield, Rhode Island.

Tania Bubela is Professor and Dean at the Faculty of Health Sciences, Simon Fraser University, Burnaby, British Columbia, Canada. At the time this work was completed, she was Professor at the School of Public Health, University of Alberta, Edmonton, Alberta, Canada.

Helena Canhão is Professor, Nova Medical School, Nova University, Lisbon, Portugal.

Shubha Chandrasekharan is Assistant Research Professor, Duke Global Health Institute, Duke University, Durham, North Carolina.

Margaret Chon is Donald and Lynda Horowitz Professor for the Pursuit of Justice, Seattle University School of Law, Seattle, Washington.

Jorge L. Contreras is Professor, University of Utah S. J. Quinney College of Law, Adjunct Associate Professor, University of Utah School of Medicine, Department of Human Genetics, Salt Lake City, Utah; Senior Policy Fellow, Program on Intellectual Property and Information Justice, American University Washington College of Law, Washington, DC.

Barbara J. Evans is Alumae College Professor of Law and Director of the Center for Biotechnology and Law at the University of Houston Law Center, Houston, Texas, and is Professor of Electrical and Computer Engineering at the Cullen College of Engineering, University of Houston, Houston, Texas.

Stephen Flowers is Professor of Management (Innovation), Kent Business School, University of Kent, Canterbury, Kent, UK.

Brett M. Frischmann is Charles Widger Endowed University Professor in Law, Business and Economics at Villanova University Charles Widger School of Law, Charles Widger School of Law, Villanova, Pennsylvania.

Maja Larson is General Counsel, Allen Institute (formerly Allen Institute for Brain Science), Seattle, Washington.

Peter Lee is Professor of Law at University of California Davis School of Law, Davis, California.

Songyan Liu is a researcher in bioinformatics at the Research Institute in Oncology and Hematology, University of Manitoba and Cancer Care Manitoba, Winnipeg, Manitoba, Canada.

Michael J. Madison is Professor of Law and Faculty Director of the Innovation Practice Institute at the University of Pittsburgh School of Law, Pittsburgh, Pennsylvania.

Michael Mattioli is Associate Professor of Law at the Indiana University Bloomington Maurer School of Law, Bloomington, Indiana.

Amrita Mishra was a researcher at the School of Public Health, University of Alberta, Edmonton, Alberta, Canada.

Pedro Oliveira is an associate professor at the Católica Lisbon School of Business and Economics, Lisbon, Portugal.

Laura G. Pedraza-Fariña is Assistant Professor of Law at Northwestern University Pritzker School of Law, Chicago, Illinois.

Glenn Saxe is the Arnold Simon Professor and Chair of the Department of Child and Adolescent Psychiatry at New York University School of Medicine and the Director of the Child Study Center at NYU Langone Medical Center, New York.

Katherine J. Strandburg is the Alfred B. Engelberg Professor of Law and Faculty Director of the Engelberg Center for Innovation Law and Policy at the New York University School of Law, New York.

Andrew W. Torrance is Earl B. Shurtz a research professor at the University of Kansas School of Law, Lawrence, Kansas.

Leid Zejnilović is an assistant professor at Nova School of Business and Economics, Nova University, Lisbon, Portugal.

Knowledge Commons and the Road to Medical Commons

Katherine J. Strandburg, Brett M. Frischmann, and Michael J. Madison

This book picks up where *Governing Knowledge Commons*, our 2014 collection of perspectives and case studies of knowledge commons governance, left off. *Governing Knowledge Commons* (GKC) laid down a research program that contributes to evidence-based policymaking about innovation and creative knowledge production, as well as the creation, preservation, and uses of existing and new knowledge. The cases presented in GKC are, in a word, diverse. They range from arts to sciences, from the professions to popular culture, from historical to contemporary. *Governing Medical Knowledge Commons* sustains that research program but with a specific, thematic focus. This book collects and presents a series of case studies of knowledge commons centered on recent and emerging experience in the life sciences, medical research, and medical practice.

FOUNDATIONS

We reiterate anew some key, foundational themes and principles that underlie the research program and the expanding set of cases that implement and illustrate it. First is the proposition that both "commons" as a general concept and "knowledge commons" as the particular concept that frames this work describe modes of governance of resources – sustained, systematized sharing – rather than a place (such as a literal or metaphorical open ground) or a political or philosophical commitment (such as unregulated openness, use, or access). Our intuition, shared by many, is that commons governance has much to offer society in terms of innovation, growth, and other

Katherine J. Strandburg is the Alfred B. Engelberg Professor of Law and a Faculty Director of the Engelberg Center for Innovation Law and Policy at the New York University School of Law, New York. Brett M. Frischmann is The Charles Widger Endowed University Professor in Law, Business and Economics at Villanova University Charles Widger School of Law, Villanova, Pennsylvania. Michael J. Madison is Professor of Law and Faculty Director of the Innovation Practice Institute at the University of Pittsburgh School of Law, Pittsburgh, Pennsylvania. Professor Strandburg acknowledges the generous support of the Filomen D'Agostino and Max E. Greenberg Research Fund.

forms of social welfare but also that knowledge commons is no panacea. The tough work of systematized research is needed to understand the strengths and weaknesses of knowledge commons at different times and in different contexts.

Second is the proposition that knowledge commons research takes an explicitly institutional perspective on the challenges of understanding processes of innovation; creativity; and knowledge and information production, preservation, and consumption. A great deal of intellectual property law and policy analysis and decision making adopts the perspective of the individual actor or firm, and the individual invention, creative work, or specific item of knowledge or information. We argue that this important work can only be effectively understood and applied if it is situated in the larger context of institutions, which include both formal entities and informal but regular patterns of economic and other social interaction. Knowledge production is ecological and environmental.

As in GKC, therefore, we embrace the analogy between the cultural environment and the natural environment (Boyle 2008; Frischmann 2007) to explore the proposition that just as natural resources often are governed by commons rather than being managed as either public or private property, the production and sharing of knowledge often are sustained by commons governance. We continue to borrow from researchers of the natural resource environment who have developed successful methods for studying commons arrangements systematically and in detail. Our knowledge commons research framework adopts the style of and begins with the Institutional Analysis and Development (IAD) framework developed and used by Elinor Ostrom and others. Our GKC framework adapts the IAD framework to speak to the unique attributes of knowledge and information.

The third foundational proposition underlying our work is that knowledge commons governance involves both law and other modes of governance. This is more than "law in action" or "law in society"; it is attempting to understand the actual role that law plays in constructing and sustaining effective resource governance – or, at times, in failing to sustain it. In some contexts, intellectual property law and other formal law play critical roles in ensuring the continued supply of new knowledge and other innovation. In other contexts, either intellectual property law or other law or both are all but invisible and absent. And in many contexts, knowledge production depends on distinct blends of law and other norms, both formal and informal.

Our fourth and final starting point is that the knowledge commons research program is intentionally designed as a learning exercise, so that the results of each iteration of knowledge commons research informs and helps refine the structure of the next round. The conclusion of GKC teaches that the research framework as initially specified did not quite capture aspects of knowledge commons that appeared repeatedly in GKC's collection of case studies (Frischmann, Madison, and Strandburg 2014, at 469–84). The framework as applied and described in this book has been updated as a result, and we anticipate further revisions and refinements in the future.

BUILDING THE FRAMEWORK

This project grew initially out of our shared interest in the functioning of systems of intellectual property rights – patent, copyright, and related bodies of law – and how those systems relate to now-abundant examples of institutions that support collaborative creativity and innovation. Wikipedia is a canonical, almost trite example, but we recognize that collaborative production of new knowledge is neither truly novel (though modern computer networks appear to have increased its power and visibility dramatically) nor rare. Whether one looks at online encyclopedias, or patent pools as they began to emerge during the nineteenth century, or the system of correspondence known as the Republic of Letters that energized scientific discovery during the seventeenth and eighteenth centuries (Mokyr 2002), it appears to be clear that systems of collaborative production have been critical parts of knowledge production for centuries, in both arts and sciences. The research questions that these raise consist not merely of "why would people contribute?" but more importantly "in cultural, economic, and legal terms, how do such institutions function, how have they evolved, and how are they likely to evolve in the future?"

The existence, indeed abundance, of knowledge commons institutions challenges the traditional perspective of many intellectual property law scholars, who divide the world of innovation and creativity production into two default categories: innovation systems organized around markets, supported by intellectual property rights directed to exclusivity and ownership, and innovation systems organized around governments, which intervene in markets (or avoid markets) in various ways to sponsor and subsidize innovation. A third approach, commons-based *sharing* of knowledge and information resources to produce innovation and creativity, had typically been omitted – though, through GKC and other research, it is increasingly acknowledged. We aim to continue to move that third approach beyond the conceptual, and beyond its occasional positioning as a rhetorical device imposed to stifle the expansion of intellectual property protection (Hyde 2010). Empirical study of norm- and custom-based innovation communities, sometimes collected under the label "IP [Intellectual Production] without IP [Intellectual Property]," often is developed in opposition to (and therefore in reliance on) market-based presumptions of the need for exclusivity, substituting norm-based exclusivity for legally defined intellectual property (Perzanowski and Darling 2017). Our knowledge commons research program and the IP without IP strand of IP scholarship share an interest in detailed empirical investigation in innovation and creativity institutions and practices, an interest in understanding the roles and limits of formal IP systems, and a desire to break free of the exclusive rights in markets vs. government intervention duality that has long characterized policy discussions regarding innovation and knowledge production. But our research program is distinct in adopting a particular framework for systematizing that research and in its expansive view of governance dilemmas and institutions.

One of our continuing goals, in other words, is to stake out knowledge commons governance as an independent, affirmative means for producing innovation and creativity and an important domain for research. In our view, commons are not wholly independent of or opposed to markets based on exclusive rights (whether formal or informal), neither are they subordinate to them.

Our perspective is inspired by the comparative institutional analysis approach of the Nobel Prize–winning research of the late Elinor Ostrom, who was best known for her lifetime of research into the functioning of commons governance, especially in the natural resources context. Ostrom was far from the first scholar to examine resource systems and governance using an institutionalist lens. But her work and that of her collaborators and successors highlighted commons as an object of study in a way that no scholar had done before. Ostrom also approached the topic with an extraordinary humility and disciplinary generosity, recognizing that understanding this complex area could only be achieved through the contributions of researchers from many fields, aligned via a shared research framework that could accommodate a variety of disciplines and methods. Her impact was magnified by her emphasis on a shared research framework accessible to and usable by numerous disciplines and throughout the world. In all of our work on knowledge commons, we have tried to adopt both the spirit and style of Ostrom's work.

Toward the end of Ostrom's career, she and her colleagues recognized the emerging importance of knowledge commons as an area for sustained research and began to apply the IAD framework to them (Ostrom and Hess 2006; Hess 2012). In 2010, we developed a research framework inspired by the IAD framework but specifically tailored to the properties that distinguish knowledge and information from natural resources (Madison, Frischmann, and Strandburg 2010). That framework, with some elaborations and clarifications, follows this introduction as Chapter 1 of this book.

ORGANIZATION OF THE BOOK

The knowledge commons research framework is presented in Chapter 1. We provide both a thorough explanation of the framework and a short, almost "pocket-sized" version, anticipating that additional researchers may want to use the framework and improve on it in their own studies of knowledge commons. Both the framework and overviews of both this book and GKC are available at a dedicated website, http://knowledge-commons.net, for the benefit of researchers developing new case studies and data analyses.

After the framework come 15 case studies of knowledge commons in the medical context, which we characterize as cases of "medical commons," from a group of interdisciplinary researchers. These cases continue the detailed exploration of how knowledge commons function, the place they occupy in the cultural environment, the specific benefits they offer, the costs and risks they create, and their relationships to other institutional structures. The case study authors come from a variety of research traditions, offering a variety of perspectives on life sciences, health, and medicine but unified via their shared application of the knowledge commons framework. GKC offered an initial demonstration of the value of studying knowledge commons carefully, in a comparative fashion, to develop evidence of the details of their purposes and operations. This book drills down to study knowledge commons in a particular subject area. In time, the data collected in these and other knowledge commons case studies should provide insights into how to design and/or harness knowledge commons for broad public benefit.

Scientific research and medical research are domains in which knowledge commons governance has long been a primary institutional approach. Researchers often share resources and infrastructure that include background scientific and medical information, data, techniques, materials, and devices. The first cluster of case studies, in Chapters 2 through 8, develops and applies the knowledge commons research framework to commons arrangements for pooling and governing biological data, biomedical data, and scientific research data in the life sciences and medicine. Traditional intellectual property rights are unlikely to play important roles in governing data sharing by virtue of the weak IP rights that ordinarily apply to data, data sets, and collections of data. Yet researchers have strong interests in data production, coordination, and sharing, which prompt the formation of robust modes of commons-based institutional governance. In Chapter 2, Jorge Contreras addresses the development of several different collections of human genomic data. Peter Lee's Chapter 3 explores the management of the genomic data commons via the tools and techniques deployed in its construction and analysis. In Chapter 4, Barbara Evans further discusses the use of genomic data for genetic testing. Andrea Boggio follows that chapter with a case study addressing biobanks and their associated data collections, particularly population-level biobanks. In Chapter 6, Ryan Abbott describes commons governance attributes of the U.S. Food and Drug Administration's Sentinel Initiative, an effort to collect and analyze public health data associated with the safety of medical products. Michael Mattioli follows that chapter with a case study of a collaborative of institutions focused on the collection and analysis of oncology treatment data. This section of the book concludes in Chapter 8 with a case study by Maja Larson and Margaret Chon of the open neuroscience movement and its efforts to collect and distribute research data.

Research-related and therapeutic tools, materials, and techniques may be governed as commons either in spite of or by building alongside traditional or conventional intellectual property regimes. Chapters 9 and 10 describe knowledge commons governance of innovations in the production of health and medicine-related devices and clinical therapies. In Chapter 9, Andrew Torrance reviews knowledge commons institutions that are constructing the emerging field of synthetic biology, or the production of engineered human tissues. In Chapter 10,

Tania Bubela and her colleagues describe commons governance of the production of research tools, engineered mice, that are critical to the translation of laboratory and clinical science to medically useful therapies.

Clinical research and clinical care are the subjects of the final group of case studies, in which traditional intellectual property systems may be absent, on historical or ethical grounds, or insufficient in other respects. Some of these case studies focus on commons governance by providers of medical care and some focus on governance by or including patients themselves. In Chapter 11, Laura Pedraza-Fariña provides a case study of the collaborative production of techniques for fertility care for oncology patients. In Chapter 12, Glenn Saxe and Mary Acri describe a case of knowledge commons governance of the delivery of mental health services, drawing not only on the knowledge commons research framework but also on existing research on user innovation. Pedro Oliveira and his colleagues follow in Chapter 13 with a description of a project for pooling patient and caregiver innovations in medical care. Again, user innovation perspectives are usefully combined with the knowledge commons framework. In Chapter 14, Stephen Flowers describes a group of patients creating and sharing innovation at the "outlaw" edge of standard medical research. Chapters 15 and 16 present the findings of case studies of two consortia operating under the umbrella of the Rare Diseases Clinical Research Network at the National Institutes of Health in the United States. In Chapter 15, Brett Frischmann and Katherine Strandburg describe the knowledge commons governance of the North American Mitochondrial Disease Consortium. In Chapter 16, Katherine Strandburg and Stefan Bechtold describe the knowledge commons governance of the Consortium for Eosinophilic Gastroinstestinal Disease Research.

As in GKC, a concluding chapter in this book highlights commonalities and differences among the knowledge commons studied here, draws relevant lessons with respect to knowledge commons research and knowledge commons in general, and looks forward to future studies. Knowledge commons do important work in the medical arena. The case studies in this book move us closer to understanding how and why.

ACKNOWLEDGMENTS

Our knowledge commons research efforts are now roughly a decade old. We are proud to note that on account of this long gestation, those efforts are now yielding more and more useful research products. The collaboration that underlies this book began in conversations among the editors about cultural commons and knowledge commons in 2006 and 2007. It took root with the publication of Madison, Frischmann, and Strandburg (2010) and with responses to that article from a group of generous scholars (Eggertson 2010; Gordon 2010; Macey 2010; Merges 2010; Ostrom 2010; Solum 2010). The collaboration continued in September 2011 as a number of researchers from around the world gathered at the Engelberg Center for Innovation Law and Policy at New York University School of Law for a workshop titled *Convening Cultural Commons*; many of the chapters in GKC were shared in early form in that setting. The case studies in this volume were shared in early form at a second workshop at the Engelberg Center in May 2014 that joined communities of researchers with backgrounds in intellectual property law and policy, on the one hand, and researchers with expertise in the domain of user innovation, a field pioneered by Eric von Hippel at MIT. As noted earlier, several of the chapters in this book suggest fruitful complements between knowledge commons research and user innovation research.

Each of us, as editors of this volume and participants in an emerging global enterprise for the study of knowledge commons, is grateful to the Engelberg Center for its continuing hospitality and support. We are also grateful for the openness with which the work has been received so far, for the generous critiques and conversations that our colleagues (both old and new) have shared, and for what we hope is a long, continuing discussion of this important topic.

REFERENCES

Boyle, James, *The Public Domain: Enclosing the Commons of the Mind* (Yale University Press 2008).

Eggertsson, Thráinn, Response: Mapping Social Technologies in the Cultural Commons, 95 *Cornell L. Rev*. 711 (2010).

Frischmann, Brett M., Cultural Environmentalism and *The Wealth of Networks*, 74 *U. Chi. L. Rev*. 1083 (2007).

Frischmann, Brett M., Michael J. Madison, and Katherine J. Strandburg (eds.), *Governing Knowledge Commons* (Oxford University Press 2014).

Gordon, Wendy J., Response: Discipline and Nourish: On Constructing Commons, 95 *Cornell L. Rev*. 733 (2010).

Hess, Charlotte, Constructing a New Research Agenda for Cultural Commons, in *Cultural Commons: A New Perspective on the Production and Evolution of Cultures* 19 (Enrico Bertacchini et al. eds., Edward Elgar Publishing 2012).

Hyde, Lewis, *Common as Air: Revolution, Art, and Ownership* (Farrar, Straus and Giroux 2010).

Macey, Gregg P., Response: Cooperative Institutions in Cultural Commons, 95 *Cornell L. Rev*. 757 (2010).

Madison, Michael J., Brett M. Frischmann, and Katherine J. Strandburg, Constructing Commons in the Cultural Environment, 95 *Cornell L. Rev*. 657 (2010).

Merges, Robert P., Response: Individual Creators in the Cultural Commons, 95 *Cornell L. Rev*. 793 (2010).

Mokyr, Joel, *The Gifts of Athena: Historical Origins of the Knowledge Economy* (Princeton University Press 2002).

Ostrom, Elinor, Response: The Institutional Analysis and Development Framework and the Commons, 95 *Cornell L. Rev*. 807 (2010).

Ostrom, Elinor, and Charlotte Hess, A Framework for Analyzing the Knowledge Commons, in *Understanding Knowledge as a Commons: From Theory to Practice* (Charlotte Hess and Elinor Ostrom eds., MIT Press 2006).
Perzanowski, Aaron, and Kate Darling (eds.), *Creativity without Law: Challenging the Assumptions of Intellectual Property* (New York University Press 2017).
Solum, Lawrence B., Response: Questioning Cultural Commons, 95 *Cornell L. Rev*. 817 (2010).

1

The Knowledge Commons Framework

Katherine J. Strandburg, Brett M. Frischmann, and Michael J. Madison

1.1 INTRODUCTION

This chapter sets out the knowledge commons framework that forms the foundation for the case study chapters that follow.[1] The framework is inspired by and builds in part on the Institutional Analysis and Development (IAD) approach pioneered by Elinor Ostrom and her collaborators for studying commons arrangements in the natural environment (Ostrom 1990). The version of the framework set out in this chapter closely tracks the version published as chap. 1 of *Governing Knowledge Commons* (Frischmann, Madison, and Strandburg 2014), and in an earlier paper (Madison, Frischmann, and Strandburg 2010a), with some important updates and revisions added to reflect lessons learned in the course of conducting the case studies published in that book. By reproducing and further refining the framework here, we hope to inspire future researchers to adopt, extend, and continue to refine it.

The systematic approach to case study design and analysis provided by the knowledge commons framework aims to structure individual case studies in a useful and productive way and to make it possible eventually to produce generalizable results. Comparing and aggregating case studies performed according to the knowledge commons framework should enable an inventory of the structural similarities and differences between

Katherine J. Strandburg is the Alfred B. Engelberg Professor of Law and a Faculty Director of the Engelberg Center for Innovation Law and Policy at the New York University School of Law, New York, New York. Brett M. Frischmann is The Charles Widger Endowed University Professor in Law, Business and Economics at Villanova University Charles Widger School of Law, Villanova, Pennsylvania. Michael J. Madison is Professor of Law and Faculty Director of the Innovation Practice Institute at the University of Pittsburgh School of Law, Pittsburgh, Pennsylvania. Professor Strandburg acknowledges the generous support of the Filomen D'Agostino and Max E. Greenberg Research Fund.

[1] In prior work, we explained in substantial detail the need for a research framework for systematically studying knowledge commons; *Governing Knowledge Commons* (Frischmann, Madison, and Strandburg 2014) was a successful proof of concept. *Governing Medical Knowledge Commons* builds upon that work. This chapter does not aim to justify the GKC framework or research program; instead, it only provides an abbreviated discussion of the framework itself. For motivations, justifications, and comprehensive discussion of how the GKC framework relates to Ostrom's work and especially the IAD framework, please refer to our prior work.

commons in different industries, disciplines, and knowledge domains and shed light on the underlying contextual reasons for the differences. This structured inquiry provides a basis for developing theories to explain the emergence, form, and stability of the observed variety of knowledge commons and, eventually, for designing models to explicate and inform institutional design. In addition, an improved understanding of knowledge commons should facilitate a more complete perspective on intellectual property (IP) law and policy and its interactions with other legal and social mechanisms for governing creativity and innovation.

1.1.1 *What Do We Mean by Knowledge Commons?*

"Knowledge commons" is shorthand. It refers to an institutional approach (commons) to governing the management or production of a particular type of resource (knowledge).

Commons refers to a form of community management or governance. It applies to resources and involves a group or community of people, but it does not denote the resources, the community, a place, or a thing. Commons is the institutional arrangement of these elements: "The basic characteristic that distinguishes commons from noncommons is institutionalized sharing of resources among members of a community" (Madison, Frischmann, and Strandburg 2010b: 841). Critically, commons governance is used by a wide variety of communities to manage many types of resources. Commons governance confronts various obstacles to sustainable sharing and cooperation. Some of those obstacles derive from the nature of the resources and others derive from other factors, such as the nature of the community or external influences. Communities can and often do overcome obstacles through constructed as well as emergent commons. Importantly, while commons-governed institutions generally offer substantial openness regarding both informational content and community membership, they usually impose some limits relating, for example, to who contributes, what contributions are incorporated into the shared pool, who may use the pooled knowledge, or how it may be used. The limitations imposed by a knowledge commons often reflect and help resolve the obstacles to sharing encountered in its particular context.

Knowledge refers to a broad set of intellectual and cultural resources. In prior work, we used the term "cultural environment" to invoke the various cultural, intellectual, scientific, and social resources (and resource systems) that we inherit, use, experience, interact with, change, and pass on to future generations. To limit ambiguity and potential confusion, and to preserve the wide applicability of the framework, we currently use the term "knowledge." We emphasize that we cast a wide net and that we group together information, science, knowledge, creative works, data, and so on.

Knowledge commons is thus shorthand for the institutionalized community governance of the sharing and, in many cases, creation of information, science, knowledge, data, and other types of intellectual and cultural resources. Demand for governance institutions arises from a community's need to overcome various social dilemmas associated with producing, preserving, sharing, and using information, innovative technology, and creative works.

Some initial illustrations of knowledge commons illustrate the variety of institutional arrangements that may be usefully studied using the GKC framework. Consider the following examples from the *Governing Knowledge Commons* book:

- Nineteenth-century journalism commons
- Astronomical data commons
- Early airplane invention commons
- Entrepreneurial/user innovation commons
- Genomic data commons
- Intellectual property pools
- Legispedia (a legislative commons)
- Military invention commons
- News reporting wire services,
- Online creation communities
- Open source software
- Rare disease research consortia
- Roller derby naming commons
- Wikipedia

At first glance, these examples may appear to be disparate and unrelated. Yet we believe that a systematic, comprehensive, and theoretically informed research framework offers significant potential to produce generalizable insights into these commons phenomena. Comparative institutional investigation of knowledge commons is relevant to understanding social ordering and institutional governance generally, including via intellectual property law and policy.

1.2 INTELLECTUAL PROPERTY, FREE RIDING, COMMONS, AND THE GKC FRAMEWORK FOR EMPIRICAL STUDY

As discussed in more detail in our earlier work, our approach to the study of knowledge commons governance is founded on three basic propositions, which we simply state here, having elaborated upon them in detail in our earlier work: First, traditional intellectual property "free rider" theory fails to account for cooperative institutions for creating and sharing knowledge that are prevalent (and perhaps increasingly so) in society. Policy based solely on this traditional view is thus likely to fail to promote socially valuable creative work that is best governed by a commons approach and may, at least in some circumstances, impede such work. Second, the widespread recognition of certain well-known successes of the commons approach, such as open source software, can itself be problematic when it ignores the significant governance challenges that often arise for such institutions. A more nuanced appreciation of the benefits and challenges of knowledge commons governance is necessary for wise policy choices. Third, the development of a more sophisticated approach to knowledge commons governance will require systematic empirical study of knowledge commons governance "in the wild."

1.2.1 *The IAD Framework for Studying Natural Resource Commons*

To develop a systematic empirical approach for studying knowledge commons governance, we turned to the work of Elinor Ostrom and collaborators, who faced a similar scholarly challenge in understanding natural resource commons, such as lakes and forests. There, simplistic "tragedy of the commons" models suggested a policy space bifurcated between private property and government subsidy or top-down regulation. Real-world observation of well-functioning commons governance arrangements exposed the inadequacies of such a simplistic theoretical approach to the variety and complexity of social and natural contexts involved.

In response, Ostrom and her collaborators developed the Institutional Analysis and Development (IAD) framework for structuring and analyzing case studies of natural resource commons and situating them with respect to private property and government subsidy or regulation. A framework approach is pre-theoretical, in that it "helps to identify the elements (and the relationships among these elements) that one needs to consider for institutional analysis. Frameworks … provide the most general set of variables that should be used to analyze all types of settings relevant for the framework … They attempt to identify the universal elements that any relevant theory would need to include" (Ostrom 2005: 28–29). It thus avoids the myopia (and mistakes) that can result from forcing the complexity of real-world social behavior into a single theory or model (such as "tragedy of the commons" or "free riding") and opens up the theoretical space so that researchers can identify salient factors and social dilemmas that should drive theoretical understanding. A framework approach also systematizes the development of general observations that can be of use both for policymaking and for understanding how to craft and apply more specific theories and models for particular cases.

The IAD framework centers on the concept of an "action arena," in which relevant actors interact with one another to deal with the social dilemmas associated with sharing and sustaining a particular natural resource in light of its characteristics and the environment and community in which it is situated. Interactions within an action arena are governed by "rules-in-use," which may be formal or informal, to produce particular outcomes.

Structuring a case study according to the IAD framework involves asking specific questions about the resources, actors, environment, rules-in-use, and other aspects of a particular commons arrangement that assist the researcher in drilling down into the facts of a particular case (Ostrom 2005: 13–14). The IAD framework thus allows researchers to move beyond the overly general assumptions of the "tragedy of the commons" story to investigate how resources actually are governed, structuring the empirical inquiry so that comparisons are possible, while avoiding unwarranted assumptions related to particular theories or models. Using the information obtained by applying the IAD framework to structured case studies, natural resources researchers developed theories and models for particular commons situations, designed experiments to test those theories, and used statistical methods to look for regularities across cases. Based on this empirical work, Ostrom advanced a set of design principles for successful natural resource commons (Ostrom et al. 2007: 15181–82).

1.2.2 *Developing a Framework for the Study of Knowledge Commons Governance*

Several years ago, Ostrom and her colleagues began to apply the IAD framework to investigate the management of collections of existing knowledge resources (Ostrom and Hess 2007). A direct application of the IAD framework to knowledge commons had its limitations, however. In particular, it neglected (or, at least, did not emphasize) certain ways in which knowledge resources and their associated communities differ from natural resources and the communities that use and manage them. In creating the *Governing Knowledge Commons* (GKC) framework, we identified several important distinctions and modified and extended the IAD framework to better account for the distinctive character of knowledge commons.

First, knowledge resources must be created before they can be shared. Individual motivations for participating in knowledge creation are many and various, ranging from the intrinsic to the pecuniary. Motivations may also be social and thus interwoven with the character of the community. Therefore, knowledge commons often must manage both resource production and resource use within and potentially beyond the commons community.

Second, those who participate in knowledge production necessarily borrow from and share with others – and not in any fixed or small number of ways. Indeed, it may be impossible to divest oneself of knowledge to which one has been exposed. Inevitably, the intellectual products of past and contemporary knowledge producers serve as inputs into later knowledge production. As a result, knowledge commons must cope with challenges in coordinating and combining preexisting resources to create new knowledge.

Third, because knowledge is nonrivalrous once created, there is often social value in sharing it beyond the bounds of the community that created it. The public goods character of knowledge resources necessitates consideration not only of dynamics internal to a commons community but also of relationships between those communities and outsiders. Knowledge commons must confront questions of openness that may generate additional social dilemmas (Madison, Frischmann, and Strandburg 2009: 368–69).

Fourth, intangible knowledge resources are not naturally defined by boundaries that limit their use. Depending upon the knowledge at issue and the circumstances of its creation, creators may or may not be able to limit use by others as a practical matter, for example, through secrecy. In essence, the boundaries of knowledge resources are built rather than found. Boundaries come from at least two sources. Intangible knowledge resources often are embodied in tangible forms, which may create boundaries around the embedded knowledge as a practical matter. Additionally, law and other social practices may create boundaries around knowledge resources, as, for example, in the case of the "claims" of a patent. The creation of boundaries is partly within and partly outside the control of the members of a knowledge commons community and generates a series of social dilemmas to be resolved.

Fifth, the nonrivalry of knowledge and information resources often rides on top of various rivalrous inputs (such as time or money) and may provide a foundation for various rivalrous outputs (such as money or fame). Knowledge commons must confront the social dilemmas associated with obtaining and distributing these rivalrous resources.

Sixth, knowledge commons frequently must define and manage not only these resources but also the make-up of the community itself. Knowledge commons members often come together for the very purpose of creating particular kinds of knowledge resources. The relevant community thus is determined not by geographical proximity to an existing resource, but by some connection – perhaps of interest or of expertise – to the knowledge resources to be created. Moreover, the characteristics of the knowledge created by a given community ordinarily are determined, at least to some extent, by the community itself. Thus, neatly separating the attributes of the managed resources from the attributes and rules-in-use of the community that produces and uses them is impossible.

Finally, because of the way in which knowledge resources and communities are co-created, both tend to evolve over time. Thus, to understand knowledge commons governance, it is often crucial to engage with the particular narratives of the community, which may be grounded in storytelling, metaphor, history, and analogy. The property scholar Carol Rose emphasizes the role of narratives, especially of origin stories, in explaining features of property regimes that are not determinable strictly on theoretical or functional grounds, particularly if one assumes that everyone begins from a position of rational self-interest (Rose 1994: 35–42). The stories that are told about knowledge commons, and by those who participate in them, are instructive with respect to understanding the construction, consumption, and coordination of knowledge resources. Particular histories, stories, and self-understandings may be important in constructing the social dilemmas that arise and in determining why a particular knowledge commons approaches them in a particular way.

The GKC framework for conducting case-based research and collecting and comparing cases is intended to be inclusive, in that various disciplinary perspectives, including law, economics, sociology, and history, may be relevant to applying it to particular cases. By design, and in light of our still-nascent understanding of knowledge commons governance, the GKC framework remains a work in progress, which will be most valuable if it is developed and honed as more examples are studied. Indeed, the description here already reflects some reorganization and fine-tuning of our initial take on the framework as presented in earlier work (Madison, Frischmann, and Strandburg 2010a).

We illustrate the GKC framework and its relationship to the IAD framework with the flow charts in Figures 1.1 and 1.2.

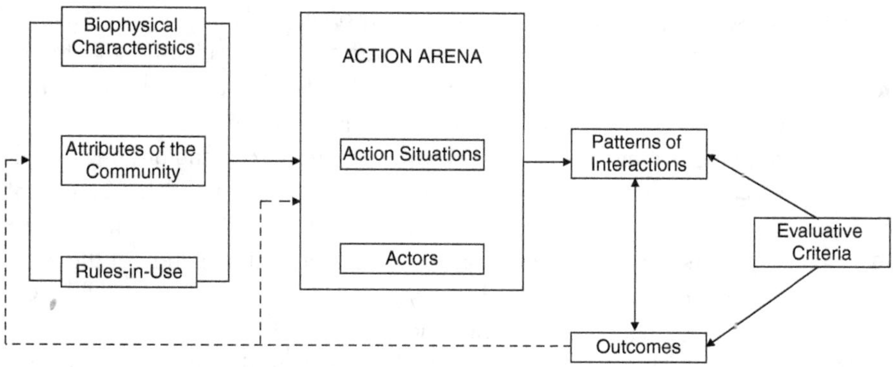

FIGURE 1.1 Based on a flow chart used to illustrate the IAD framework (Ostrom 2005: 15). It pictures the way in which relevant variables, including the biophysical characteristics of the natural resource, the attributes of the community, and the rules-in-use in the community influence the way in which actors interact in particular action situations to produce patterns of interactions and outcomes, which may be evaluated from a social perspective through evaluative criteria. The dotted lines illustrate the way in which the outcomes from a given pattern of interactions can influence the input variables, for example, by leading to destruction or sustainability of the resource or to modifications of the rules-in-use because the community is dissatisfied with the outcomes.

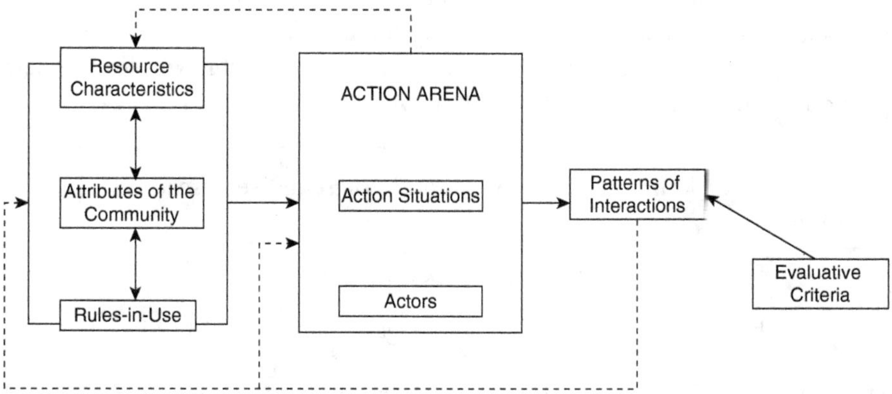

FIGURE 1.2 The GKC framework. Because of the more complex relationships among resources, participants, and governance structures in knowledge commons, relevant attributes may not divide as neatly into categories as they do when one is describing a pool of natural resources. Thus, in the leftmost part of the chart, we connect the resources characteristics, community attributes, and rule-in-use to emphasize their interrelated and contingent character. The dotted line leading directly from the action arena to resource characteristics illustrates the way in which interactions in the action arena, by creating intellectual resources, feed directly back into resource characteristics without being mediated by ongoing patterns of interactions.

Figure 1.2 also collapses a distinction made in the original IAD framework between "patterns of interactions" that follow from the action arena and outcomes that follow from the patterns of interaction. The patterns of interactions generated by the formal and informal rules systems of a knowledge commons are often inseparable from the outcomes it produces. How people interact with rules, resources, and one another, in other words, is itself an outcome that is inextricably linked with and determinative of the form and content of the knowledge or informational output of the commons. In an open source software project, for example, the existence and operation of the open source development collaborative, the identity of the dynamic thing called the open source software program and the existence and operation of the relevant open source software license and other governance mechanisms are constitutive of one another.

With this general picture in mind, we now lay out the GKC framework for empirical study of knowledge commons in the box, "Knowledge Commons Framework and Representative Research Questions." More detail about the various aspects of the framework is provided in our earlier work and illustrated in the case studies in this book.

During the course of a case study, the framework of questions summarized in the box is used in two ways. First, it is used as a guide in planning interviews with relevant actors, documentary research, and so forth. Second, it is used as a framework for organizing and analyzing the information gained from interviews, relevant documents, and so forth. Though we list the various "buckets" of questions in the framework sequentially, in practice the inquiry is likely to be iterative. Learning more about goals and objectives is likely to result in the identification of additional shared resources; understanding the makeup of the community will lead to new questions about general governance, and so forth.

Knowledge Commons Framework and Representative Research Questions

BACKGROUND ENVIRONMENT

- What is the background context (legal, cultural, etc.) of this particular commons?
- What is the "default" status, in that background context, of the sorts of resources involved in the commons (patented, copyrighted, open, or other)?

ATTRIBUTES

Resources

- What resources are pooled and how are they created or obtained?
- What are the characteristics of the resources? Are they rival or nonrival, tangible or intangible? Is there shared infrastructure?

- What technologies and skills are needed to create, obtain, maintain, and use the resources?

Community Members

- Who are the community members and what are their roles?
- What are the degree and nature of openness with respect to each type of community member and the general public?

Goals and Objectives

- What are the goals and objectives of the commons and its members, including obstacles or dilemmas to be overcome?
- What are the history and narrative of the commons?

GOVERNANCE

- What are the relevant action arenas and how do they relate to the goals and objective of the commons and the relationships among various types of participants and with the general public?
- What are the governance mechanisms (e.g., membership rules, resource contribution or extraction standards and requirements, conflict resolution mechanisms, sanctions for rule violation)?
- Who are the decision makers and how are they selected?
- What are the institutions and technological infrastructures that structure and govern decision making?
- What informal norms govern the commons?
- How do nonmembers interact with the commons? What institutions govern those interactions?
- What legal structures (e.g., intellectual property, subsidies, contract, licensing, tax, antitrust) apply?

PATTERNS AND OUTCOMES

- What benefits are delivered to members and to others (e.g., innovations and creative output, production, sharing, and dissemination to a broader audience, and social interactions that emerge from the commons)?
- What costs and risks are associated with the commons, including any negative externalities?

REFERENCES

Boyle, James, *The Public Domain: Enclosing the Commons of the Mind* (Yale University Press 2008).

Eggertsson, Thráinn, Response: Mapping Social Technologies in the Cultural Commons, 95 *Cornell L. Rev.* 711 (2010).

Frischmann, Brett M., Cultural Environmentalism and *The Wealth of Networks*, 74 *U. Chi. L. Rev.* 1083 (2007).

Frischmann, Brett M., Madison, Michael J., and Strandburg, Katherine J. (eds.), *Governing Knowledge Commons* (Oxford University Press 2014).

Gordon, Wendy J., Response: Discipline and Nourish: On Constructing Commons, 95 *Cornell L. Rev.* 733 (2010).

Hess, Charlotte, Constructing a New Research Agenda for Cultural Commons, in *Cultural Commons: A New Perspective on the Production and Evolution of Cultures* 19 (Enrico Bertacchini et al. eds., Edward Elgar Publishing 2012).

Hyde, Lewis, *Common as Air: Revolution, Art, and Ownership* (Farrar, Straus and Giroux 2010).

Macey, Gregg P., Response: Cooperative Institutions in Cultural Commons, 95 *Cornell L. Rev.* 757 (2010).

Madison, Michael J., Frischmann, Brett M., and Strandburg, Katherine J., Constructing Commons in the Cultural Environment, 95 *Cornell L. Rev.* 657 (2010).

Merges, Robert P., Response: Individual Creators in the Cultural Commons, 95 *Cornell L. Rev.* 793 (2010).

Mokyr, Joel, *The Gifts of Athena: Historical Origins of the Knowledge Economy* (Princeton University Press 2002).

Ostrom, Elinor, Response: The Institutional Analysis and Development Framework and the Commons, 95 *Cornell L. Rev.* 807 (2010).

Ostrom, Elinor, and Charlotte Hess, A *Framework for Analyzing the Knowledge Commons*, in *Understanding Knowledge as a Commons: From Theory to Practice* (Charlotte Hess and Elinor Ostrom eds., MIT Press 2007).

Perzanowski, Aaron, and Kate Darling (eds.), *Creativity without Law: Challenging the Assumptions of Intellectual Property* (New York University Press 2017).

Solum, Lawrence B., Response: Questioning Cultural Commons, 95 *Cornell L. Rev.* 817 (2010).

2

Leviathan in the Commons: Biomedical Data and the State

Jorge L. Contreras

The US federal government's 2017 budget allocated $72.4 billion to non-defense-related research and development (Holdren 2016: 3). This significant level of government-funded research generates vast amounts of data every year. In accordance with their public missions, many federal agencies have long made much of this data accessible to the public. It is widely acknowledged that the public release of data can have significant spillover effects promoting scientific discovery, technological development, and economic growth (OECD 2015: 38; Frischmann 2012).

During the Obama administration, the federal government adopted a strong commitment to the public dissemination of federally funded data in the United States (Holdren 2013; White House 2013). As explained in a 2014 White House report, "treating government data as an asset and making it available, discoverable, and usable – in a word, open – strengthens democracy, drives economic opportunity, and improves citizens' quality of life" (Exec. Off. President 2014: 11). Accordingly, the US government appears ready to foster the growth of public data resources on an unprecedented scale. But how can it do so most effectively, sustainably, and with the greatest scientific impact?

This chapter analyzes the role that the state has played with respect to the generation and management of scientific data repositories, situating it within the context of commons theory and the organization of common pool resources. Analyzing the functional roles that the state plays in data-generating research can yield a number of insights. First, the state's role in fostering innovation and scientific advancement is often analyzed in terms of incentives that the state may offer to private actors. These incentives include tax credits, intellectual property protection, grant awards, and

Jorge Contreras is Professor, University of Utah S.J. Quinney College of Law, Adjunct Professor, University of Utah School of Medicine, Department of Human Genetics; Senior Policy Fellow, Program on Intellectual Property and Information Justice, American University Washington College of Law. This chapter benefited substantially from feedback and discussion at the 2014 NYU Workshop on Medical User Innovation and Knowledge Commons. Research assistance by Michael Eixenberger is gratefully acknowledged. The author discloses that he served as legal counsel to the SNP Consortium and the International SAE Consortium, and as a member of the advisory councils of NIH's National Human Genome Research Institute (NHGRI) and National Center for Advancing Translational Science (NCATS). He currently serves on NIH's Council of Councils.

prizes (NRC 2014: 53–56; Sarnoff 2013; Scotchmer 2004: 31–58). The functional analysis presented in this chapter reconceptualizes the state's role from that of an external actor seeking to incentivize behavior within an innovation system to that of one actor/stakeholder among many within that system.

Analyzing the functional roles of the state in the context of particular data-generating projects also highlights areas in which the state's involvement may be inefficient or ineffective in achieving its ends. As a result, suggestions may be made for improvement, both in terms of efficiency and the pursuit of specified goals. The analytical framework described in this chapter offers a means by which state engagement with data-intensive research projects may be compared across agencies, fields, and national borders. This framework can then be used to assess the effectiveness of state engagement in such research and to improve planning for future research endeavors.

2.1 COMMONS THEORY AND THE ROLE OF THE STATE

2.1.1 *Physical Resource Commons and the State*

Garrett Hardin and contemporary theorists, responding to the threat of a "tragedy of the commons," believed that the most reliable way to avoid over-consumption of finite environmental resources was through governmental intervention (Hardin 1968: 1244; Ostrom 1990: 8–12). In particular, they argued that state control and allocation of scarce resources was the only way to ensure efficient consumption and avoid environmental collapse. As explained by David Ehrenfeld, if "private interests cannot be expected to protect the public domain then external regulation by public agencies, governments, or international authorities is needed" (Ehrenfeld 1972: 322).

In contrast, theorists such as Harold Demsetz and Robert J. Smith favored an approach rooted in principles of private property. They argued that the creation of property rights in limited resources such as land would motivate property owners, acting in their own self-interest, to make the most efficient use of those resources (Demsetz 1967: 347). As Smith argues, "the only way to avoid the tragedy of the commons in natural resources and wildlife is to end the common-property system by creating a system of private property rights" (Smith 1981: 467).

Both of these approaches were challenged beginning in the 1970s by Elinor Ostrom and others, who observed numerous arrangements in which local populations made use of common resources without destroying them, and without recourse either to centralized state control or privatization (Benkler 2013: 1508; Ostrom 1990: 18–19). Ostrom's principal insight, based on these observations, was that self-governing, self-organizing systems for common property management frequently arose to address problems of scarcity, without a need for state or market-driven intervention (Ostrom 1990: 10; Rose 1986: 719–20).

Ostrom was not, however, insensitive to the participation of state actors in the management, governance, and usage of common pool resources. Under her well-known adaptation of the Institutional Analysis and Development (IAD) framework, state actors may interact with other stakeholder communities in various action arenas, and they may influence rule making with respect to common resources. For example, she describes the positive role played by "large-scale supportive institutions" such as the US Geological Survey (USGS) (Ostrom 2005: 278–79). The USGS, she explains, is uniquely positioned to offer expert technical services to local groups to assist them with the management of local resources. It would be impossible for individual groups to replicate the expertise and resources of the USGS, suggesting that the functions performed by such an agency are ideally situated within a centralized and far-reaching governmental organization.

2.1.2 *The State and Knowledge Commons*

In the mid-1990s, scholars began to apply commons theory to intangible shared resources and information (Hess and Ostrom 2007; Scotchmer 2004: 31–40). Since then, much has been written about so-called information or knowledge commons of resources such as open source software, network capacity, artistic content, academic scholarship, and scientific data (Benkler 2013: 1509, 1513–18; Madison, Frischmann, and Strandburg 2010; Hess and Ostrom 2007; Boyle 2003: 44–49). But unlike finite physical resources, information may be consumed by an unlimited number of individuals without being depleted: it is "nonrivalrous." Thus, Hardin's "tragedy of the commons," which arises from self-interested over-consumption of a finite resource, is unlikely to occur within the context of information commons. Likewise, the resource scarcity that drives theorists toward state-centric and market-centric solutions does not arise naturally in knowledge commons.[1] What role, then, can and should the state play in the creation and maintenance of knowledge commons? The next section turns to the growth of public repositories of scientific data, and the roles that the state has played in creating and maintaining these repositories.

2.1.3 *Beyond the Big Science Paradigm: Nine Roles for the State*

Since the end of World War II, the US federal government has funded scientific research projects that have generated large quantities of data. These projects, typically involving large-scale, resource-intensive, multiyear undertakings, have been made possible by government investment in advanced instruments and facilities such as particle accelerators, telescopes, and spacecraft (Scotchmer 2004: 16–26; IOM 2003: 29–79; Galison 1992). The substantial bodies of data generated by these projects have

1 But see Frischmann (2013: 397–400), analogizing free rider problems, incentive deficits and underproduction affecting knowledge commons to the resource depleting tragedies to which physical resource commons are susceptible.

often been made available to the public, either directly by governmental agencies (NASA's National Space Science Data Center, the National Center for Atmospheric Research (NCAR), and the US Geological Survey's Earth Resources Observation Systems (EROS) Data Center) or by government-funded repositories at private institutions (the Space Telescope Science Institute at Johns Hopkins University) (Scotchmer 2004: 240–42; NAS 2002).

The conventional "big science" account of governmental engagement in research portrays the state as either the direct generator of data or the principal funder and procurer of data from institutional researchers (Scotchmer 2004: 16–22, 228–35, 240–42; Galison 1992). Much of the policy and economics literature that considers the state's role in scientific research often focuses on this procurement function and how governmental policy can incentivize research output to maximize social welfare (Bozeman 2000: 627–55; Loiter and Norberg-Bohm 1999: 85–97).

In recent years, however, the government's role with respect to the creation and maintenance of large scientific data pools has evolved and diversified, particularly in the area of biomedical research. As a result, the traditional big science model of state research sponsorship is incomplete. As Mazzucato observes, the modern state has at its disposal a range of tools including procurement, commissioning, and regulation that it can use "to shape markets and drive technological advance" (2013: 74). This section explores the evolving role of the state in biomedical research data commons, both to improve the theoretical understanding of institutional commons structures and to inform the discussion around structuring future biomedical data commons.

First, it is necessary to identify the different roles that state actors may play in the formation and maintenance of data commons. The following nine categories offer a functional breakdown of these roles:

1 ***Creator*** The state itself, through the use of government-owned and -operated instruments, facilities, and resources, collects and generates data. This role reflects the traditional "big science" model of state-sponsored research and the many important data-centric projects historically led by national laboratories and agencies such as DARPA, NASA, and NOAA (Scotchmer 2004: 16–22; IOM 2003: 29–79).
2 ***Funder*** The state funds the collection and generation of data by academic and other non-state institutions either through grant-based funding, direct contract, or other procurement mechanisms (Scotchmer 2004: 247; IOM 2003: 82–115). The funding agency may exert varying degrees of control over the activity of the researcher and the data generated. The National Institutes of Health (NIH) is currently the largest public funder of biomedical research in the world, with an annual research budget in excess of US$30 billion (NIH 2017).
3 ***Convenor*** The state facilitates the formation of collaborative activities among private sector actors and/or governmental agencies. These "public-private partnerships" have become the focus of growing scholarly and policy attention, given their potential to harness private sector resources and expertise to solve

scientific problems prioritized by governmental agencies (Vertinsky 2015: 110; Strandburg, Frischmann, and Cui 2014). For example, the Foundation for the National Institutes of Health (FNIH), a Congressionally chartered nonprofit organization, is expressly authorized to serve as a "neutral convenor of NIH and other partners" for the purpose of encouraging dialog and collaboration between government and the private sector (FNIH 2015).

4 ***Collaborator*** The state, acting through a research-based agency such as NIH, DOE, or NASA, is an active participant in a research project that is led principally by private actors. These arrangements often arise in the context of the public-private partnerships described in the previous category but may also arise independently through interaction between researchers at government laboratories and academic institutions or private firms, or as conditions of government grants (Strandburg, Frischmann, and Cui 2014: 175–76).

5 ***Endorser*** The state is a nonparticipant that encourages a particular private sector research activity, either explicitly, by association of a state agency with the announcements and achievements of the activity, or through the implicit (and nonbinding) promise of favorable regulatory treatment for private sector participants in the activity. In this manner, the state promotes social and organizational norms (such as broad data sharing) without direct rule making or the expenditure of significant governmental resources (Rai 1999: 147–51). Through such endorsements, the state also encourages private sector behavior that is consistent with governmental goals and attitudes, with the incipient threat of greater state regulation or intervention if the private sector fails to comply.

6 ***Curator*** A state agency acts as the host and manager of data resulting from a research project and often oversees its dissemination to the public. Knowledge curation can include a range of activities including quality control, validation, preservation, collection, evaluation, and distribution (OECD 2015: 194–95; Madison 2011: 1963). An agency engaged in active curation may verify, correct, annotate, organize, and recombine data that is deposited in a repository, whereas a more passive curator may simply offer a publicly accessible location from which data may be viewed and accessed in more or less its original form (Contreras and Reichman 2015).

7 ***Regulator*** The state develops and implements policies and rules governing access to and use of a pool of scientific data (i.e., the "rules-in-use" modeled by Ostrom and others (Ostrom 1990: 50–54)). These rules may include both exogenous laws and regulations enacted by governmental authorities, as well as endogenous norms and policies imposed through the private governance mechanisms of the community.[2] Exogenous rules (e.g., laws governing intellectual property and data privacy) generally have effects beyond a single

[2] Madison, Frischmann, and Strandburg (2010: 684–88) consider the background legal regime affecting a commons to be part of the "natural" environment in which the commons exists. Their reasoning is that for intellectual resources, such as data, the legal regime often delineates the resources themselves

resource,[3] whereas endogenous rules are typically directed to the use, maintenance, and governance of the specific resource at hand.

8 ***Enforcer*** The state may police compliance with both endogenous and exogenous rules and issue formal and informal sanctions against violators. While this function is to a large degree inherent to the state apparatus, Ostrom, Rose, and others have expressed skepticism regarding central enforcement mechanisms for common pool resources (Ostrom 1990: 10; Rose 1986: 719–20). Specifically, Ostrom observed that for the state to enforce rules accurately and effectively, it must possess the capabilities to gather and evaluate large quantities of information, to monitor compliance by multiple actors, and to impose sanctions reliably and fairly. Needless to say, these criteria are not always met in practice.

9 ***Consumer*** State agencies may utilize the data found in a repository for their internal research purposes or in support of their regulatory, enforcement, and other missions. For example, as discussed in Section 2.3.2.4, the US Food and Drug Administration (FDA) utilizes data provided by applicants and clinical trial sites in assessing the safety and efficacy of drugs and medical devices submitted for regulatory approval.

Table 2.1 summarizes the nine functional roles of the state in creating and maintaining scientific data commons.

TABLE 2.1 *Roles of the state in scientific data commons*

State Role	Description
1. Creator	Generator of data through government-owned or -operated instruments
2. Funder	Funder of academic or private sector research institutions that generate data
3. Convenor	Convenor of private sector actors and governmental agencies for the purpose of engaging in collaborative research activities
4. Collaborator	Active participant in a research project involving private sector actors
5. Endorser	Nonparticipant encouraging particular private sector research activities, either explicitly or implicitly
6. Curator	Host and manager of scientific data repositories
7. Regulator	Drafter and implementer of policies and legal rules governing access to and use of scientific data
8. Enforcer	Enforcer of the above policies and rules
9. Consumer	User of data for governmental regulatory and other purposes

and their relation to the contextual environment. This differs from the natural resource context examined by Ostrom.

3 Depending on the size and nature of a common pool resource, some exogenous rules may target it exclusively. For example, governmental permitting requirements, land use regulations, zoning ordinances, and the like may be narrowly tailored to affect specific properties or resources to the exclusion of others (Ostrom 1990: 50–54).

The existence of these overlapping and complementary state roles, while underappreciated in the literature of scientific research, is not surprising when data and public repositories of scientific data in particular are viewed as elements of the scientific research infrastructure. Generally speaking, infrastructural resources such as roads, communication systems, and utilities provide the "underlying foundation or basic framework" needed to support a wide range of downstream productive activities (Frischmann 2012; NRC 1987). As such, scientific data repositories that are broadly accessible may be considered key elements of the scientific research infrastructure (OECD 2015: 179).

The state plays a number of well-understood roles with respect to the planning, provisioning, and maintenance of publicly owned infrastructure resources such as highways, prisons, and public utilities. Likewise, the state is often involved in the oversight, regulation, and operation of private and public-private infrastructural resources such as airports and telecommunications networks. Why then should the same types of complementary and overlapping relationships not arise with respect to data resources that form an integral part of the research infrastructure?

In the case studies that follow, the evolution of the state's role from big science provisioner to the more multifaceted relationships described earlier is analyzed.

2.2 NIH AND THE GENOME COMMONS

The multiple roles of the state described in the preceding section are illustrated by the US federal government's involvement in the creation, growth, and ongoing maintenance of the large body of public data concerning the human genome. This aggregation of data, which has been referred to as the "genome commons" (Contreras 2011, 2014) presents a useful case study for several reasons. First, the genome commons, which was initiated in the late 1990s with the Human Genome Project (HGP), has had a long and well-documented history (McElheny 2010; Contreras 2011). Over the two decades of its existence, it has adapted to accommodate a range of organizational and institutional changes, within both the government and the larger biomedical research community. The genome commons, which today includes data from a broad range of public, private, and public-private research efforts, can also be characterized as a common pool resource of the type described by commons theorists. That is, the genomic and associated data contained within the commons is provisioned and governed through a set of polycentric, multi-stakeholder mechanisms (Contreras 2014: 107–08).[4]

[4] The focus of this chapter is on biomedical data resources. For the sake of brevity, it does not seek to address the constellation of related issues surrounding physical biological samples held in hospitals, laboratories, biobanks, and repositories around the world. For a comprehensive discussion of these issues, see, e.g., Reichman, Uhlir, and Dedeurwaerdere (2016) and Rhodes (2013).

2.2.1 *Beginnings: The Human Genome Project*

Though researchers began to identify bits and pieces of the human genetic code in the mid-twentieth century, the creation of a complete sequence map of the human genome was not seriously proposed until 1985. At that time, leading genetic researchers, encouraged by the emergence of improved DNA sequencing technologies, first outlined a proposal to sequence the entire 3.2 billion DNA base pairs constituting the human genome. Doing this, they argued, would lead to significant improvements in understanding the genetic bases of disease (McElheny 2010: 17–33; Cook-Deegan 1994: 79–91). These efforts opened the door for the largest biomedical research endeavor of its day, the HGP.

Two US federal agencies initially led the HGP: the NIH, the funder of most disease-focused research in the United States, and the Department of Energy (DOE), whose expertise in genetics arose from studying the effects of radiation on atom bomb survivors (Cook-Deegan 1994: 97–104). These two agencies joined forces in 1990 to co-lead the project with additional support from the UK-based Wellcome Trust and funding agencies in the United Kingdom, France, Germany, and Japan. The massive research effort was compared to the Manhattan Project and the Apollo lunar landing program, among other projects. Yet even at an early stage, the role of the state in the HGP was more complex and multifaceted than it had been in these previous "big science" endeavors.

State as Convenor Unlike earlier large-scale scientific projects relating to national defense and space exploration, the proposal to map the human genome originated with academic researchers rather than government officials. From an early stage, leaders at NIH and DOE interacted closely with the scientists who proposed the project and who would eventually carry it out. As the HGP coalesced, governmental actors worked closely with academic investigators not only to develop a scientific roadmap for the project but also to establish rules regarding the sharing and release of data generated by the project (see later discussion of "State as Regulator").

Moreover, rather than assign career bureaucrats to oversee the HGP, NIH recruited prominent scientists to lead the project. Chief among these was James Watson, Nobel laureate and co-discoverer of the structure of the DNA molecule, who was appointed to oversee the newly formed National Center for Human Genome Research. Watson was succeeded in 1992 by Francis Collins, a prominent genetic researcher from the University of Michigan who was best known for his leading role in discovering a gene closely associated with cystic fibrosis. A host of other prominent researchers, in the United States, the UK, and elsewhere, were active in the leadership of the HGP, facilitating the close interaction of government and academia during the long project (Contreras 2011: 76–77; n.60). In this sense, NIH acted as a *convenor* of the scientific community, bringing it together to collaborate on planning and executing the most ambitious scientific undertaking of its day. Without the engagement of the broader scientific community, the HGP would never have been possible.

State as Funder/Creator The HGP is estimated to have cost more than $2 billion to complete, the bulk of which the NIH funded. NIH's research funding is typically allocated through grant awards. These awards are based on the agency's evaluation of competitive research proposals submitted by academic and other investigators.[5] Award recipients are expected to complete the projects that they have proposed, but the agency seldom intervenes in the conduct of the research program itself.

The HGP was organized differently. Rather than act as a passive research funder, NIH led planning efforts and solicited bids from research institutions to carry out specific components of the project (IOM 2003: 31–40). Three academic centers were selected to perform DNA sequencing: Washington University in St. Louis, the Whitehead Institute at MIT, and the Sanger Centre in Cambridge, England. Thus, even though NIH did not carry out the sequencing work using government-owned or -operated resources, it assumed a leading role with respect to the data generated by the HGP that could characterize it as a *creator* as much as a *funder*.

State as Curator Although the sequencing work of the HGP was carried out by academic research institutions funded by NIH and the other project sponsors, hosting and maintenance (curation) of the massive (for the time) quantities of data generated by the project fell to NIH itself.[6] This curatorial role was not unique to the HGP. Over the years, governmental projects in fields such as astronomy, earth science, and particle physics made large quantities of observational and experimental data available to the public. This data was often hosted at federally managed facilities such as the National Center for Atmospheric Research (NCAR) and the US. Geological Survey's Earth Resources Observation Systems (EROS) Data Center, and at private institutions contracted by the federal government, such as the Space Telescope Science Institute at Johns Hopkins University (NAS 2002). The HGP was distinctive, however, in that the data being curated by the state was not generated by government-owned and -operated instruments, but by academic institutions supported by governmental funding. Thus, in the case of HGP data, the state's role as curator diverges from the role it typically assumed in big science projects.

The HGP elected to utilize the existing GenBank database, administered by the National Center for Biotechnology Information (NCBI), a division of the NIH's National Library of Medicine, for the deposit and public release of genomic sequence data. GenBank originated with the Los Alamos Sequence Library operated by Los Alamos National Laboratory since 1979 (Hilgartner 1995: 243). NIH contracted with Los Alamos in 1982 to create GenBank as a publicly accessible repository for DNA sequences (Strasser 2008: 538). It has been operated by NCBI

5 An example of such grant-funding mechanisms is discussed in Strandburg, Frischmann, and Cui (2014).

6 The European Molecular Biology Library (EMBL) and DNA Data Bank of Japan maintain comparable repositories that are synchronized with NCBI's GenBank on a daily basis (Strasser 2008).

since 1992, making it one of the longest-running state-operated repositories of scientific data (Ankeny and Leonelli 2015: 128–29; Benson, Lipman, and Ostell 1993: 2963).

In addition, given its pre-HGP origins, GenBank is, and has always been, open to deposits of DNA sequence information from sources other than NIH-funded research projects. Underscoring this source-neutral policy, GenBank even accepted the human genome sequence data generated by privately held Celera Genomics, which competed fiercely with the HGP to sequence the human genome from 1998 to 2000 (Kaiser 2005: 775).

State as Regulator From an early date, NIH's involvement in the HGP included the creation of both exogenous legal regulations and endogenous rules-in-use. One of the most important sets of exogenous rules affecting the HGP concerned the ability of private parties to obtain patents covering DNA sequence information. By the mid-1990s, many commentators feared that allowing patents on DNA sequences of unknown function would stymie biomedical research (Heller and Eisenberg 1998: 698; Cook-Deegan 1994: 308–11). This perceived threat was one of the most hotly contested legal issues in the emerging field of genomics and "became the main focus of a cottage industry of biotechnology patenting articles in law reviews and scientific journals" (Demaine and Fellmeth 2002: 326).

NIH's position, which it solidified only after a contentious attempt to obtain its own patents covering DNA sequences, strongly disfavored the patenting of genetic material. Beginning in the mid-1990s, the agency engaged in an unofficial campaign to persuade the US Patent and Trademark Office (USPTO) to stop issuing such patents (NRC 2006: 52–53). Based on this and other input, in 1999 the USPTO adopted a policy that disallowed the patenting of DNA sequences of unknown function because they lack the required "utility" for patent protection (USPTO 1999: 714–40).

Perhaps even more significantly, NIH led the development of the endogenous rules-in-use that governed the deposit and release of genomic data generated by the HGP. NIH's 1996 data release policy for the HGP was largely based on the so-called Bermuda Principles, a set of guidelines developed by a group of prominent researchers and policymakers (Bermuda Principles 1996). The Bermuda Principles were revolutionary in that they established, for the first time, that data from public genomic projects should be released to the public almost immediately after being generated, rather than after a waiting period of 6 to 18 months, as was the norm for federal projects at the time (Contreras 2011: 84–85; Bermuda Principles 1996; NHGRI 1996). These rapid data release requirements were intended to promote three NIH policy goals: achieving coordination among the many independent sequencing centers working on the HGP, accelerating scientific advancement, and limiting third parties' ability to patent data first generated by the HGP (Contreras 2011: 86).

2.2.2 *The State's Evolving Role in Post-HGP Genomics Projects*

The HGP published its first draft of the full human genomic sequence in 2001 and announced its completion in 2003. As the lengthy public project drew to a close, researchers began to plan a number of follow-on activities designed to build on and make use of the basic sequence data generated by the HGP. These projects included both NIH grant-funded projects along the lines of the original HGP (these projects included the Encyclopedia of DNA Elements (ENCODE) (2003), the Cancer Genome Atlas (TCGA) (2006), and the Human Microbiome Project (HMP) (2007)), as well as projects in which NIH partnered with a range of public and private sector funders, both from the United States and abroad (Contreras 2011: 97–107, 2014: 123–27). Particularly in this later category of projects, NIH's role shifted from that of a typical big science *creator* and *funder* to that of a *convenor*.

Expansion of the Convenor Role Shortly after the HGP released its initial draft sequence in 2001, a group of researchers led by Eric Lander at the Whitehead Institute proposed a project that would chart the ways in which markers along the human genome recurred in groups (haplotypes) (Int'l HapMap Consortium 2003: 789). Though NIH participated in funding the resulting "HapMap" project, additional funding came from state agencies in Japan, the United Kingdom, Canada, China, and Nigeria. The HapMap project was in no sense "led" by NIH or the US government. Rather, NIH served, to a degree, as a convenor of other parties, both governmental and academic, that were interested in the project.

Curation as an Independent Function The GenBank database maintained by NCBI served as one of the principal repositories for DNA data generated by the HGP. NCBI's curatorial role with respect to this data was similar to that played by other governmental agencies that maintained large data sets that they created or funded. At a high level, the genomic data managed by NCBI was not so different from radio telescope data managed by NASA or atmospheric data managed by NOAA.

But following the conclusion of the HGP, as the cost of gene sequencing began to decrease, more and more human and nonhuman genomic data was produced by researchers around the world. Though many of these researchers were unaffiliated with NIH's large-scale data-generation projects, they, too, were welcome to deposit genomic data in GenBank at no charge. GenBank thus became a global repository for DNA sequences and related data, irrespective of their origin, and NCBI became the de facto curator of this data from sources around the world.

Far from being a passive role, curation of genomic data requires not only suitable computing and networking resources but also significant technical and scientific expertise in data selection, quality control, formatting, display, and visualization (Ankeny and Leonelli 2015: 133–34; OECD 2015: 194–95; Madison 2011: 1982–87). Academic research groups curate many important scientific databases, and governmental agencies stepping into this role have comparable requirements. For example, the DNA sequence data uploaded by researchers to GenBank may at times be duplicative, incomplete, or corrupted. Researchers wishing to download the complete genome of a particular organism would be hard pressed to identify and assemble all the necessary elements from GenBank deposits. NCBI addressed this issue with the introduction of the RefSeq (reference sequence) database in 2000. RefSeq contains a "reference" genome for each organism (and particular strains of organisms) that is compiled by NCBI staff from GenBank records. RefSeq genomes are continually updated and refined as higher-quality data is added to GenBank (Lee, Chapter 3, this volume; NCBI 2013).

Another significant aspect of curation in the area of biomedical data involves the protection of individual health information. Like astronomical and atmospheric data, it was once thought that DNA sequence data divorced from its donors' identities (de-identified) carried little risk to individuals. But as genomic research evolved and researchers began to explore the associations between genes and health, they began to link genomic sequence data with physiological, demographic, and clinical data (phenotypic data). While genome-wide association studies (GWAS) have shed substantial light on the interactions between genes and human health, they also give rise to increased risks that the identities of DNA donors can be determined from disclosed data. Today, in fact, many researchers believe that it is virtually impossible to de-identify genetic data with absolute assurance (e.g., Couzin-Frankel 2015: 502).

To address the risks of re-identification of data subjects and to accommodate the linkage of DNA sequence data with phenotypic data, NCBI created the Database of Genotypes and Phenotypes (dbGaP). NCBI's curatorial role with respect to dbGaP is significantly greater than it is with respect to GenBank: dbGaP has a two-tiered structure that allows access to potentially identifying information to be authorized on a case-by-case basis by a standing Data Access Committee (DAC) composed of NIH personnel (Paltoo et al. 2014: 936). Through this approval function, NIH acts not only as a technological curator of data but also as the guardian of personally sensitive information that may be gleaned from the data stored within its repositories.

While the state, through the curatorial role played by NCBI and other NIH divisions, provides an invaluable service to the global scientific community, this service is not without cost. NCBI, which operates GenBank and a number of more specialized data resources, had an annual budget in 2016 of approximately $54.3 million (NLM 2016). Other NIH divisions support a wide range of biomedical research databases. It has been estimated that the annual budget for NIH data resources excluding NCBI and other NLM divisions is approximately $110 million (Kaiser 2016). At these funding levels, NIH has been under pressure to reduce its support for more specialized data resources, including genomic repositories for various microorganisms and model organism systems (Kaiser 2016). Thus, even in the area of genomics, where the state has been a leader in developing and curating valuable data resources, the pendulum may be swinging back toward a more modest role for state actors, both in terms of fewer supported data resources and a lower level of curation and maintenance for those data resources that remain (Kaiser 2016; Mishra, Schofield, and Bubela 2016 284; Contreras and Reichman 2015: 1312).

Increasing Regulation Following the HGP, both the expanding types of data housed within genomic data repositories and the privacy risks associated with individual health data led to increasingly detailed and complex endogenous rules governing genomic data resources. NIH's policies grew from relatively simple Bermuda-based requirements regarding the timing of data deposits to comprehensive regulations, exemplified by NIH's 2007 GWAS policy, regarding data security, access, and usage, as well as the ability of investigators to publish discoveries made using genomic data and to seek patents claiming those discoveries (Contreras 2014: 123–29).

The growth in policy length and complexity, however, does not necessarily indicate a shift in NIH's role from collaborator to regulator. As I have described previously, the development of NIH's policies regarding genomic data resulted from an open and consultative process among multiple stakeholders including researchers, patient advocacy groups, and private industry (Contreras 2014: 107–11, 127). Moreover, as noted earlier, many of the NIH officials involved in policymaking are themselves respected scientific researchers with significant and ongoing research programs. Thus, NIH's increasing codification of the rules-in-use of the genome commons does not necessarily detract from its role as collaborator. The same may not be true, however, with respect to the agency's role as "enforcer," discussed next.

State as Enforcer As the developer and implementer of rules governing the deposit, access, and use of genomic data housed in NIH repositories, NIH stands in a unique position to monitor and enforce compliance with those rules. Thus, if an NIH-funded sequencing center failed to upload its data to GenBank within the required time period, NIH could take a number of enforcement steps including discussing the deficiency with the delinquent center; developing a remedial plan; and if repeated violations occurred, withholding or reducing the funding to that center.

Many NIH rules-in-use, however, are phrased as "encouragements" rather than "requirements" (sometimes referred to as "norms" or "soft" rules) (Contreras 2011: 87–88; Ostrom 2005: 121–27; Rai and Eisenberg 2003: 293–94). NIH's policy discouraging the patenting of DNA sequences is one example of such "soft" rules. This policy warns that the agency "will monitor grantee activity . . . to learn whether or not attempts are being made to patent large blocks of primary human genomic DNA sequence" (NIH 1996). With respect to its dbGaP database, NIH catalogs the types and frequency of policy violations that it discovers, including data submission errors, inappropriate use or dissemination of data, data security lapses, and violations of publication embargoes (NIH 2015).

Yet it is not clear how effective NIH's policing function has been, even with respect to dbGaP. The agency claims that with more than 20,000 data access requests between 2007 and 2015, it has identified only 27 policy violations, all of which it has managed to a satisfactory resolution (NIH 2015). Several of the 27 incidents were reported to NIH by the violators themselves; others were caused by bugs in the dbGaP software and procedural errors. This low rate (less than 0.1% of total data access requests) could indicate either a low incidence of noncompliance or, more likely, a low incidence of *detection*. The handful of disclosed noncompliance incidents offer little indication that the agency has implemented an effective program to monitor and police the use of genomic data.

Moreover, unlike other federal enforcement agencies that make their investigations and conclusions public, NIH, despite its rhetoric of openness, does not publicly disclose the names of parties or individuals implicated in its reported policy violations. This hesitancy may offer a clue as to the underlying causes of NIH's weak enforcement of its genomic data policies. Ironically, it is the very diversity of roles played by the agency in the research enterprise that may hamper its desire or ability to enforce its rules vigorously. That is, unlike a neutral state enforcement agency such as the Department of Justice, NIH has numerous institutional ties to its funded researchers: NIH officials are drawn from NIH-funded research institutions; NIH has convened many of the relevant research groups, tying its reputation to the success of the project; NIH staff (intramural researchers) collaborate closely with extramural NIH-funded researchers; and NIH eventually holds and curates the data produced by the research effort. These close ties may make NIH officials reluctant to enforce the agency's rules against familiar research institutions and researchers, leading perhaps to more informal (and possibly less effective) enforcement after the occurrence of actual and suspected violations.

2.2.3 *Public-Private Genomics*

In addition to the federally funded genomics projects described above, a number of significant private sector genomic research projects emerged during and after the HGP. However, unlike typical industrial research programs, many of these initiatives publicly released large quantities of genomic data, to both governmental and privately operated repositories.

Convenor and Collaborator Even though the federal government is not the primary funder or planner of private sector research initiatives, it may engage with them in several ways. NIH in particular has an active program of collaborating with the private sector through public-private partnerships, and through its National Center for Advancing Translational Sciences (NCATS) (NCATS 2015; NIH 2010). The US Food and Drug Administration (FDA) also encourages and participates in collaborations with the private sector through its Critical Path Initiative, among other programs (FDA 2017).

One example of a successful public-private collaboration in the area of genomics data was the Genetic Association Information Network (GAIN). GAIN was launched in 2006 as a public-private partnership among commercial firms (Pfizer, Affymetrix, Perlegen Sciences, and Abbott), academic institutions (the Broad Institute), NCBI, and FNIH (GAIN 2007: 1045–46). The goal of the project was to use genome-wide association studies (GWAS) to study the genetic basis for six common diseases. GAIN involved both FNIH's role as a *convenor* and NIH/NCBI itself as a *collaborator*, a combination of roles that is not uncommon.

Endorser The SNP Consortium Ltd. was formed in 1999 by a group of pharmaceutical and information technology firms with additional financial support from the Wellcome Trust (Holden 2002: 22–26). The consortium's goal was to identify and map genetic markers known as "single nucleotide polymorphisms" (SNPs) during the concluding years of the HGP. Though NIH did not formally join or fund the SNP Consortium, it actively monitored its activities and helped coordinate the consortium's research with the data being produced by the HGP. Given the HGP's highly publicized race with Celera Genomics, NIH welcomed and publicly supported private sector research activities that worked in concert with, and did not oppose, the public HGP. In this sense, NIH acted as a significant *endorser* of the SNP Consortium and similar efforts (McElheny 2010: 143; Shreeve 2004: 294).

The state's endorser role was more recently exemplified by the FDA's interaction with the International Serious Adverse Events Consortium (iSAEC), a group of pharmaceutical and health care companies organized in 2007 to identify DNA markers associated with serious adverse drug reactions (Holden et al. 2014: 795). The FDA helped generate industry support for the iSAEC and its mission, which is in line with recent FDA initiatives relating to drug safety (Holden et al. 2014: 795). Though no formal relationship exists between the FDA and iSAEC, the agency sends representatives to iSAEC meetings and jointly announces research milestones with iSAEC (US Food and Drug Admin. 2010). As a result, iSAEC's activities are portrayed to the public as aligned with the FDA, thereby validating the organization and its activities. The FDA likewise benefits from association with a research program that has generated significant data in a field that is important to the agency's mission.

Curator In addition to interactions with the state in the conduct of research programs, private sector researchers often submit genomic data to federally supported databases such as GenBank and dbGaP. NCBI will accept and curate this data at no charge to the submitter while offering substantial technical expertise and oversight. As a result, NCBI plays a significant *curatorial* role with respect to privately sourced data. As noted earlier, even Celera Genomics eventually deposited its entire human and mouse genome sequences in GenBank (Kaiser 2005: 775). The SNP Consortium, which made its data available through a privately operated website, also uploaded this data to GenBank, as did a significant genomic research effort sponsored by the pharmaceutical firm Merck (Contreras 2011: 95; Holden 2002: 25–26). GAIN, along with other public-private research collaborations, also deposited its data in dbGaP (GAIN 2007).

Thus, while many private sector researchers retain their data within corporate repositories, those that release data to the public often do so through state-supported facilities such as GenBank and dbGaP. It is likely that this route is attractive to private sector researchers, as NCBI conducts its massive data curation program at taxpayer expense, while providing substantial bioinformatics and data curation expertise. It is in the state's interest to offer this service to maximize the likelihood that data will be utilized by a broad range of researchers, thus advancing scientific progress, and also ensuring that the data generated by private sector researchers will be subject to the same data quality, privacy, and security restrictions as data generated by state-funded projects. As a result, a symbiotic relationship is fostered between private sector and state actors in the area of data curation.

Nevertheless, as noted earlier, the cost of maintaining an ever-expanding set of data resources has already begun to strain federal budgets. As a result, the future may see a shift back toward privately curated data collections in some areas. The hope, from a social welfare standpoint, is that the custodians of these private resources will continue to make them broadly accessible to the public, even with reduced state support.

Limited State Regulation and Enforcement Though exogenous laws and regulations impact private sector research to much the same degree as they impact state-funded research, NIH did not play a direct role in formulating the endogenous rules-in-use of private sector genomic data projects. Rather, these rules have typically been created by the institutions and firms involved in a project, based on their internal goals, requirements, and policies. Nevertheless, the influence that NIH rules regarding data access and use have on private sector policies is significant. First, NIH's data policies have become norms in the field of genomics, if not the broader biomedical arena. Researchers in the private sector have often been educated and trained at academic institutions and have thus become accustomed to the requirements of such policies, internalizing these norms in their standard scientific practices. Moreover, most academic institutions are recipients of federal research funding, and many have officially or unofficially adopted internal rules and policies for data sharing that conform to federal standards. As such, the state has acted as a norm setter, even in these private sector research projects.

2.2.4 *Assessing the State's Roles in Genomics Research Projects*

Table 2.2 illustrates the roles played by the state in genomic research projects that have resulted in the contribution of data to the public, including the HGP, post-HGP federally funded genomic research projects, and private sector projects that have contributed genomic data to the public.

TABLE 2.2 *Roles of the state (NIH) in genomic data generation projects*

State Role	HGP	Post-HGP (NIH)	Private Sector
Convenor	Yes	Sometimes	Sometimes
Funder	Yes	Yes	No
Creator	Partially	Partially	No
Collaborator	Yes	Sometimes	Sometimes
Endorser	Yes	Yes	Sometimes
Curator	Yes	Yes, but declining	Sometimes
Regulator	Yes	Yes	Yes, if data is state curated
Enforcer	Yes (though never exercised)	Yes (though rarely exercised)	Yes, if data is state curated
Consumer	No	No	No

As Table 2.2 illustrates, NIH has played a range of roles in these projects, going well beyond that of either passive funder or big science creator. These additional state roles have added substantial value to data-generating research projects. In some cases, research may not have been possible, or would have had a less significant impact, were it not for the supporting roles played by the state. Accordingly, to maximize the effectiveness of a government-funded data-generating project, planners should take into account the different potential roles of state actors over the life cycle of the data.

Even more interesting are the many potential roles that the state may play in public-private or private sector data-generating projects. The genome commons provides several examples in which substantial benefits have accrued from the state's convening of multiple independent actors, its collaboration with academic and industrial researchers, and its curation of large data sets in existing or new data repositories.

Despite these benefits, as discussed in Section 2.2.2, NIH's enforcement of its data access and usage rules has been weak, possibly as a result of a failure to detect violations or a failure to initiate enforcement measures against violators. Thus, to the extent that either governmental or private sector planners wish to implement a robust set of rules-in-use relating to their data commons, they could explore policing and enforcement options beyond those offered by NIH's current model.

2.3 SHAPING THE ROLE OF THE STATE IN FUTURE DATA COMMONS: CLINICAL TRIALS DATA

As illustrated by the genome commons, the state may play a range of roles in the generation and maintenance of scientific data commons. These roles extend well beyond the traditional big science model of state-sponsored resource creation and provisioning. However, there is little detailed analysis of state roles at the outset of commons formation. This section suggests ways in which the analytical framework developed here may be used by policymakers and project planners to model the engagement of state agencies in new public aggregations of scientific data.

2.3.1 *Sharing Clinical Trials Data*

Clinical trials are health interventions designed to assess the safety or efficacy of a drug or medical device. Clinical trials are required by the FDA to obtain regulatory approval to market a new drug or medical device in the United States (IOM 2015: 68–69).[7] Such trials are often sponsored by a pharmaceutical or medical device company, which contracts with one or more academic research institutions to conduct the trials. More than 200,000 clinical trials have been conducted worldwide since 2000 (ClinicalTrials.gov 2015).

Many clinical trials involve thousands of individuals observed over long periods of time. In addition to data regarding the intervention being studied (e.g., the chemical composition and other characteristics of the drug, device or procedure, the experimental protocol, data analysis methods, and analytic code), data is collected regarding the study participants' health history, demographic profile, phenotypic traits, clinical diagnosis, adverse reactions, and post-intervention prognosis (IOM 2015: 97–105). Much of this data is submitted to the FDA in support of new drug or device applications. The Food and Drug Administration Amendments Act of 2007 (FDAAA) requires that summary data be disclosed to the public via the NIH-operated ClinicalTrials.gov website, but this data is limited to major outcomes and adverse events. Moreover, data from trials that were deemed unsuccessful and did not result in an approved drug or device are typically not required to be disclosed. As a result, the vast majority of clinical trials data that is generated remains nonpublic (IOM 2015: 113).

In view of this situation, many have argued that more clinical trials data should be made available to the public. Between 2012 and 2015, the Institute of Medicine (IOM) conducted a series of workshops that explored issues relating to the sharing of clinical trials data. It summarized the substantial public benefits of sharing this data as follows:

> From the perspective of society as a whole, sharing of data from clinical trials could provide a more comprehensive picture of the benefits and risks of an intervention and allow health care professionals and patients to make more informed decisions about clinical care. Moreover, sharing clinical trial data could potentially lead to enhanced efficiency and safety of the clinical research process by, for example, reducing unnecessary duplication of effort and the costs of future studies, reducing

7 The focus of this section is US law and regulation. However, similar regulatory regimes exist in most developed countries. According to the OECD (2015: 339), at least 10 countries have planned to implement systems for systematically analyzing clinical trials data for public health and other purposes.

> exposure of participants in future trials to avoidable harms identified through the data sharing, and providing a deeper knowledge base for regulatory decisions.
>
> In the long run, sharing clinical trial data could potentially improve public health and patient outcomes, reduce the incidence of adverse effects from therapies, and decrease expenditures for medical interventions that are ineffective or less effective than alternatives. In addition, data sharing could open up opportunities for exploratory research that might lead to new hypotheses about the mechanisms of disease, more effective therapies, or alternative uses of existing or abandoned therapies that could then be tested in additional research. (IOM 2015: 32)

Offsetting these benefits, of course, are risks that may arise from data sharing, including compromising the privacy and confidentiality of trial participants, inadvertently disclosing sponsor companies' trade secrets, fueling spurious liability suits, and deterring the use of potentially beneficial therapies (IOM 2015: 33–34). As a result, the IOM has recommended a balancing of interests, with a goal of maximizing the benefits of sharing clinical trial data while minimizing its potential harms (IOM 2015: 34). Some private firms, together with academic institutions, have already taken steps toward broader data sharing, but these early efforts remain tentative (IOM 2015: 20–21).

Were more clinical trial data to be publicly disclosed, as envisioned by the IOM and others, this data would contribute to a substantial knowledge commons. Like the genome commons, a clinical trials data commons would most likely be governed through polycentric mechanisms involving stakeholder groups including study participants, funders and sponsors, advocacy groups, regulatory agencies, researchers, research institutions, scientific journals, and professional societies (IOM 2015: 4–6). Existing rules-in-use would need to be expanded to establish the scope of public access to such data, and the terms on which it could be utilized (IOM 2015: chap. 5).

2.3.2 *Potential Roles of the State in a Clinical Trials Data Commons*

2.3.2.1 State Actors and Primary Roles: NIH as Funder, FDA as Regulator

NIH and FDA are the two primary federal agencies involved in the conduct of clinical trials in the United States, although their roles differ significantly. NIH financially supports numerous clinical trials.[8] As of 2015, this support covered more than 3,000 active clinical trials in the United States (IOM 2015: 59). Unlike the HGP and the broader genome commons, however, NIH plays little role in the planning and conduct of clinical trials or the generation of clinical trials data. As such, its role with respect to clinical trials data is closer to that of a typical grant-based funding agency than the funder-creator role that it assumed in genomics projects.

[8] In addition to receiving support from NIH, clinical trials are supported by private industry, charities such as the Wellcome Trust and the Bill and Melinda Gates Foundation, as well as disease advocacy groups (IOM 2015: 58).

The FDA, on the other hand, serves as the principal US regulator of new drugs and medical devices. The FDA requires that applicants for approval of these new interventions conduct clinical trials to establish their safety and efficacy. As noted earlier, the FDA also requires that summary data generated by clinical trials be released to the public and is engaged in an ongoing public discussion regarding the potential expansion of the scope of data to be publicly released (IOM 2015: 173–76; Hudson and Collins 2014: 365).

2.3.2.2 Clinical Trials Data Curation

The principal public repository of summary clinical trials data today is housed at NIH's National Library of Medicine (NLM) and is accessible through the ClinicalTrials.gov website.[9] Thus, as it does with genomic data, NIH serves a curatorial function for clinical trials data. However, unlike the data stored in repositories such as GenBank and dbGaP, clinical trials data is generated by researchers without direct NIH involvement. Because clinical trial data is central to the FDA regulatory approval process and forms the basis on which FDA evaluates applicants' new drugs and devices, NIH does not validate, annotate, or enhance clinical trial data, as it does genomic data (e.g., in creating the RefSeq database). Moreover, because the types of data that are made accessible through ClinicalTrials.gov are mandated by statute, NIH does not maintain a data access committee (DAC) to review and approve applications to access clinical trial data, as it does with genomic data stored in dbGaP. Thus, while NIH performs a curatorial function with respect to both clinical trial and genomic data, its role with respect to clinical trial data is more passive and mechanical than it is with respect to genomic data.

Moreover, ClinialTrials.gov today houses only the summary data required by the FDAAA. If more substantial clinical trials data were to be released in a systematic manner, some observers fear that NCBI's current platform is inadequate and far greater computing resources and infrastructure will be required (IOM 2015: 15). As a result, substantial investments will need to be made in data infrastructure, and the role of the state in this infrastructure development, as well as ongoing data curation, will need to be clarified.

Given these considerations, planners may wish to consider alternatives to state curation of clinical trials data beyond ClinicalTrials.gov. For example, outsourcing this function to a private sector contractor may result in a lower-cost and more

[9] The statutory mandate for ClinicalTrials.gov is found in Section 113 of the Food and Drug Administration Modernization Act of 1997, which required NIH to create a public resource including information about federally and privately funded clinical trials conducted under investigational new drug applications (INDs) being prepared for submission to the FDA. Congress enhanced the requirements for submission to ClinicalTrials.gov in Section 801 of the Food and Drug Administration Amendments Act of 2007. The amendment expanded the number and types of trials requiring registration, as well as the amount and type of summary data to be disclosed.

streamlined system that does not otherwise drain resources from the budget-constrained NIH/NCBI. While such an approach could have drawbacks in the highly technical realm of genomics data, it may be a preferable solution in the case of a data system that requires only hosting and open access. Such privatized data hosting systems have been successfully implemented by agencies such as the Securities and Exchange Commission[10] and may be worth consideration as larger bodies of clinical trials data become available for public release.

2.3.2.3 Enforcement of Data Policies

Rules regarding the deposit, access, and use of data within an expanded clinical trials database will likely be promulgated by the FDA and/or Congress. As noted earlier, the FDAAA today requires that clinical trial sponsors submit summary data to ClinicalTrials.gov and imposes stiff penalties for noncompliance (fines for reporting violations can reach $10,000 per day) (ClinicalTrials.gov 2012). Nevertheless, compliance with these requirements has been referred to as "disappointing" (Hudson and Collins 2014: 355). According to IOM, only 46 percent of NIH-funded clinical trials publish their results within 30 months of completion (IOM 2015: 59). One study found that even after four years, the results from 30 percent of a sample of 400 clinical trials had neither been published nor reported on ClinicalTrials.gov (Saito and Gill 2014).

These findings suggest that current enforcement of the rules governing clinical trials data is not being managed effectively. There are several possible reasons for the enforcement gaps in this area. First, the agencies responsible for policing compliance with the rules, NIH and FDA, may lack the resources to undertake necessary compliance-monitoring measures. While a lack of resources is a perennial issue with governmental agencies, more systemic issues likely hinder effective enforcement of data-related rules. NIH, in particular, acts as a *collaborator* with the institutions conducting clinical trials, which, as discussed in Section 2.2.2, may make agency personnel reluctant to enforce rules too harshly against them. This risk is particularly acute if the same agency personnel are responsible for both collaborative activity and compliance monitoring and enforcement (i.e., both because of the greater potential sympathy that agency personnel may have for their colleagues and because agency personnel who are actively collaborating in the conduct of trials may have less need for access to data through public means, making its unavailability less noticeable and inconvenient to them). Accordingly, if the state wishes to mandate the disclosure of expanded clinical trials data, it will need to develop more robust approaches to enforcing its disclosure requirements.

10 In 1997, the US Securities and Exchange Commission (SEC) privatized its Electronic Data Gathering, Analysis, and Retrieval (EDGAR) Public Dissemination Service (PDS) (US Securities and Exchange Comm. 1997).

2.3.2.4 State as Consumer

One distinct role that the state plays with respect to clinical trials data, but which it does not significantly play in the genome commons, is that of a *consumer* or user of the data for its internal purposes. The FDA in particular utilizes clinical trials data submitted by researchers in its regulatory capacity, as it evaluates applications for new drug and device approvals. The character of this role is distinct from other roles played by the state as it places the state in a position similar to other private and public sector users of data within the commons. Yet there are also differences between the state's use of clinical trials data and, say, an academic or industrial researcher's use of genomic data. Whereas the latter researchers typically access and use data to advance their own research, the FDA's utilization of clinical trial data supports a regulatory function that ultimately inures to the benefit of the data submitter (if the drug or device application is approved), and to society more broadly (Abbott, Chapter 6, this volume).

But while the new drug or device applicant benefits from the FDA's review of its data (assuming that review is favorable), the applicant does *not* benefit from the disclosure of its data to the public (which includes not only interested citizens but also the applicant's competitors and potential litigants over safety and other claims). The FDA, however, reviews all the applicant's trials data, whether or not the data is made public. As discussed in Section 2.3.1, the question for policymakers is how much of the applicant's data should be disclosed to the public, and the degree to which social welfare gains from disclosure outweigh potential prejudice to the applicant and privacy risks to individual trial participants (IOM 2015: 32–34). As a consumer of the data, the agency itself is relatively unaffected by the amount of data publicly disclosed.[11]

2.3.3 *Assessing State Roles: Genomics and Clinical Trials*

Table 2.3 offers a comparison of the roles of the state in the genome commons and its potential roles in a clinical trials data commons. Consideration of the different roles played by the state in these two contexts suggests ways that state involvement may be configured in new data commons that may enhance the efficiency and effectiveness of data-sharing arrangements and improve overall social welfare.

As illustrated, NIH plays a lead or strong collaborative role in many genomics data generation projects. The agency's role is less active with respect to clinical trials, however, tending more toward that of an external funder. There may, however, be opportunities for NIH to use its substantial internal expertise in support of clinical trials and data generation. Such opportunities may arise, for example, through the work of the National Center for Advancing Translational Sciences (NCATS), which

[11] One could even argue that the agency could open its own decisions and judgment to greater public scrutiny and challenge to the extent that more data is disclosed and made available to the public.

TABLE 2.3 *Comparison of state roles: genomics and clinical trials*

State Role	HGP	Post-HGP (NIH)	Private Sector	Clinical Trials
Convenor	Yes	Sometimes	Sometimes	No
Funder	Yes	Yes	No	Sometimes
Creator	Partially	Partially	No	No
Collaborator	Yes	Sometimes	Sometimes	Sometimes
Endorser	Yes	Yes	Sometimes	No
Curator	Yes	Yes, but declining	Sometimes	Limited
Regulator	Yes	Yes	Yes, if data is state-curated	Yes (FDA)
Enforcer	Yes (though never exercised)	Yes (though rarely exercised)	Yes, if data is state-curated	Yes, though not vigorously
Consumer	No	No	No	Yes (FDA)

has demonstrated a propensity for engaging in successful collaborative activity with private sector firms. This trend may be worth encouraging further in the area of clinical trials data.

The same may not be true with respect to the curatorial function. NIH through NCBI currently acts as the curator of summary clinical trials data submitted to ClinicalTrials.gov. Unlike NCBI's value-adding role with respect to genomic data, the agency adds little to clinical trials data, for the reasons discussed earlier. Thus, it is not clear that NCBI's substantial expertise is necessary to host and manage a clinical trials data commons. Particularly in view of federal budgetary constraints, it may be worth considering whether other options, such as outsourcing the curatorial function to a private sector contractor selected through competitive bidding, may result in greater efficiencies and cost savings.

Finally, as the previous examples illustrate, NIH's enforcement of rules relating to both genomics data and clinical trials data has been lackluster, at best. This failure of enforcement may arise from the close collaborative relationships between NIH and its funded researchers. To improve the effectiveness of rules enforcement, planners may wish to consider moving enforcement responsibilities away from NIH and to a different agency. With respect to clinical trials data, FDA may be a more logical choice, as it already exists in an arm's length, if not adversarial, relationship to the pharmaceutical and medical device firms that it regulates. It may also be possible to designate a different governmental agency to fill the enforcement role, either an existing agency more accustomed to policing and enforcement activity (such as the Federal Trade Commission or Department of Justice) or a new agency or subagency within NIH or FDA. Any of these approaches would sever the potential ties of loyalty and familiarity between the research-focused arm of NIH and the researchers whom it seeks to police.

CONCLUSIONS

This chapter has shown that the state plays a multiplicity of roles in the formation and management of large repositories of biomedical research data, extending well beyond the traditional big science model of the state as a creator/provisioner of data commons. The nine discrete state roles and the analytical framework described in this chapter offer a means by which state engagement with data-intensive research projects may be compared across agencies, fields, and national borders. This framework may be used to assess the effectiveness of state engagement in such research programs.

In particular, a number of lessons may be learned from NIH's evolving role in the genome commons, from funder and primary overseer of the HGP to convenor, collaborator, and curator. One such lesson suggests that the state may be a good curator of research data, whether governmental laboratories, grant-funded academic institutions, or the private sector generated that data. So long as data is intended to be disseminated to the public in a uniform manner, a state actor with requisite expertise may be the most logical candidate for that curation role. Nevertheless, extensive and expert data curation comes at a significant cost, and as the body of available scientific data continues to grow, the state's ability to offer curation services at no cost to the public may become strained.

Additional inefficiencies may arise from comingling the state's collaboration and enforcement roles. NIH's lackluster enforcement record as to both the genome commons and ClinicalTrials.gov suggests that alternative enforcement mechanisms should be considered for future data commons.

The state's engagement with the genome commons offers insights to planners of future research data commons, including the proposed clinical trials data commons. But while NIH's achievements in the area of genomics data should be applauded, they may not always translate directly to other research domains. For example, there may be more cost-effective or streamlined mechanisms for sharing research data that mandate less active curation and updating than the substantial NCBI resources devoted to genomic data.

In general, it is hoped that the analytical framework developed in this chapter will help researchers and policymakers configure state engagement in new data commons in a manner that will enhance the efficiency and effectiveness of data-sharing arrangements and improve overall social welfare.

REFERENCES

Ankeny, Rachel A. and Sabina Leonelli, Valuing Data in Postgenomic Biology: How Data Donation and Curation Practices Challenge the Scientific Publication System, in *Postgenomics: Perspectives on Biology after the Genome* 126 (Sarah S. Richardson and Hallam Stevens eds., Duke University Press 2015).

Benkler, Yochai, Review: Commons and Growth: The Essential Role of Open Commons in Market Economies, 80 *U. Chicago L. Rev.* 1499 (2013).

Benson, Dennis, David J. Lipman, and Jams Ostell, GenBank, 21 *Nucleic Acids Research* 2963 (1993).

Bermuda Principles, Summary of Principles Agreed at the First International Strategy Meeting on Human Genome Sequencing (1996), www.ornl.gov/sci/techresources/Human_Genome/research/bermuda.shtml

Boyle, James, The Second Enclosure Movement and the Construction of the Public Domain, 66 *Law & Contemp. Probs.* (2003).

Bozeman, Barry, Technology Transfer and Public Policy: A Review of Research and Theory, 29 *Research Policy* 627 (2000).

ClinicalTrials.gov, Overview of FDAAA and Other Trial Registration (2012), https://prsinfo.clinicaltrials.gov/trainTrainer/Overview-FDAAA-Other-Regist-Policies.pdf

ClinicalTrials.gov, Trends, Charts, and Maps (2015), https://clinicaltrials.gov/ct2/resources/trends

Contreras, Jorge L., Constructing the Genome Commons in *Governing Knowledge Commons* 99 (Brett M. Frischmann, Michael J. Madison, and Katherine J. Strandburg eds., Oxford University Press 2014).

Contreras, Jorge L., Bermuda's Legacy: Policy, Patents, and the Design of the Genome Commons, 12 *Minn. J.L. Sci. & Tech.* 61 (2011).

Contreras, Jorge L. and Jerome H. Reichman, Sharing by Design: Data and Decentralized Commons, 350 *Science* 1312 (2015).

Cook-Deegan, Robert, *The Gene Wars – Science, Politics, and the Human Genome* (Norton 1994).

Couzin-Frankel, Jennifer, Trust Me, I'm a Medical Researcher, 347 *Science* 501 (2015).

Demaine, Linda J. and Aaron Xavier Fellmeth, Reinventing the Double Helix. A Novel and Nonobvious Reconceptualization of the Biotechnology Patent, 55 *Stanford Law Review* 303 (2002).

Demsetz, Harold, Toward a Theory of Property Rights, 57 *Am. Econ. Rev.* 347 (1967).

Ehrenfeld, David W., *Conserving Life on Earth* (Oxford University Press 1972).

Exec. Off. President, Big Data: Seizing Opportunities, Preserving Values (2014).

Food and Drug Administration Amendments Act of 2007 (FDAAA).

Fndn. for the Natl. Inst. Health (FNIH), How We Work (2015), http://fnih.org/about/how-we-work.

Frischmann, Brett M., *Infrastructure: The Social Value of Shared Resources* (Oxford University Press 2012).

Frischmann, Brett M., Two Enduring Lessons from Elinor Ostrom, 9 *J. Institutional Econ.* 387 (2013).

Galison, Peter, The Many Faces of Big Science in *Big Science: The Growth of Large-Scale Research* 1 (Peter Galison and Bruce Hevly eds., Stanford University Press 1992).

The GAIN Collaborative Research Group (GAIN), New Models of Collaboration in Genome-Wide Association Studies: The Genetic Association Information Network, 39 *Nature Genetics* 1045 (2007).

Hardin, Garrett, The Tragedy of the Commons, 162 *Science* 1243 (1968).

Heller, Michael A. and Rebecca S. Eisenberg, Can Patents Deter Innovation? The Anticommons in Biomedical Research, 280 *Science* 698 (1998).

Hess, Charlotte and Elinor Ostrom, Introduction: An Overview of the Knowledge Commons in *Understanding Knowledge as a Commons: From Theory to Practice* 4 (Charlotte Hess and Elinor Ostrom eds., MIT Press 2007).

Hilgartner, Stephen, Biomolecular Databases – New Communication Regimes for Biology? 17 *Science Communication* 240 (1995).

Holden, Arthur, The SNP Consortium: Summary of a Private Consortium Effort to Develop an Applied Map of the Human Genome, 32 *BioTechniques* 22–26 (2002).

Holden, Arthur L. et al., The International Serious Adverse Events Consortium, 13 *Nat. Rev. Drug Discovery* 795 (2014).

Holdren, John P., Director, Off. Sci. Tech. Policy, Memorandum for the Heads of Executive Departments and Agencies: Increasing Access to the Results of Federally Funded Scientific Research (2013).

Holdren, John P., The 2017 Budget: Investing in American Innovation (2016), www.whitehouse.gov/sites/default/files/microsites/ostp/fy_17_ostp_slide_deck.pdf

Hudson, Kathy L. and Francis S. Collins, Sharing and Reporting the Results of Clinical Trials, 313 *J. Am. Med. Assn.* 355 (2014).

Inst. of Med. (IOM) and National Research Council, Large-Scale Biomedical Science (National Research Council 2003).

Inst. of Med. (IOM), Sharing Clinical Trial Data: Maximizing Benefits, Minimizing Risk (National Research Council 2015).

Int'l HapMap Consortium, The International HapMap Project, 426 *Nature* 789 (2003).

Kaiser, Jocelyn, Celera to End Subscriptions and Give Data to Public GenBank, 308 *Science* 775 (2005).

Kaiser, Jocelyn, Funding for Key Data Resources in Jeopardy, 351 *Science* 14 (2016).

Loiter, Jeffrey M. and Vicky Norberg-Bohm, Technology Policy and Renewable Energy: Public Roles in the Development of New Energy Technologies, 37 *Energy Policy* 85 (1999).

Madison, Michael J., Knowledge Curation, 86 *Notre Dame L. Rev.* 1957 (2011).

Madison, Michael J., Brett M. Frischmann, and Katherine J. Strandburg, Constructing Commons in the Cultural Environment, 95 *Cornell L. Rev.* 657 (2010).

Mazzucato, Mariana, *The Entrepreneurial State: Debunking Public vs. Private Sector Myths* (Public Affairs 2013).

Mcelheny, Victor K., *Drawing the Map of Life – Inside the Human Genome Project* (Basic Books 2010).

Mishra, A., P. N. Schofield, and T. M. Bubela, Sustaining Large-Scale Infrastructure to Promote Pre-Competitive Biomedical Research: Lessons from Mouse Genomics, 33 *New Biotechnology* 280 (2016).

Nat'l. Acad. Sci., Eng. and Med. (NAS), Assessment of the Usefulness and Availability of NASA's Earth and Space Science Mission Data (2002), http://sites.nationalacademies.org/cs/groups/ssbsite/documents/webpage/ssb_051716.pdf.

Nat'l. Center for Advancing Translational Sciences (NCATS), Alliances at NCATS (2015), https://ncats.nih.gov/alliances/about.

Nat'l Center for Biotechnology Info. (NCBI), *The NCBI Handbook* (2nd ed.) (2013).

Nat'l Human Genome Research Inst. (NHGRI), NHGRI Policy Regarding Intellectual Property of Human Genomic Sequence (1996), www.genome.gov/10000926.

Nat'l. Inst. Health (NIH), Genomic Data Sharing (GDS) – Categories, Statistics, and Summary Information on Policy Violations (2015), https://gds.nih.gov/20ComplianceStatistics_dbGap.html.

Nat'l. Inst. Health (NIH), NIH Public-Private Partnership Program – Partnership Examples (2010), http://ppp.od.nih.gov/pppinfo/examples.asp.

Nat'l Inst. Health (NIH), Budget (2017), https://www.nih.gov/about-nih/what-we-do/budget

Nat'l Library Medicine (NLM), Congressional Justification FY 2016, www.nlm.nih.gov/about/2016CJ.html#Justification.

Nat'l. Research Council (NRC), Rising to the Challenge: US Innovation Policy for the Global Economy (National Research Council 2014).

Nat'l. Research Council (NRC), Reaping the Benefits of Genomic and Proteomic Research (National Research Council: 2006), www.nap.edu/catalog/798/infrastructure-for-the-21st-century-framework-for-a-research-agenda

OECD, Data-Driven Innovation: Big Data for Growth and Well-Being (OECD Publishing 2015).

Ostrom, Elinor, *Governing the Commons: The Evolution of Institutions for Collective Action* (Cambridge University Press 1990).

Ostrom, Elinor, *Understanding Institutional Diversity* (Princeton University Press 2005).

Paltoo, Dina N. et al., Data Use under the NIH GWAS Data Sharing Policy and Future Directions, 46 *Nature Genetics* 934 (2014).

Rai, Arti Kaur, Regulating Scientific Research: Intellectual Property Rights and the Norms of Science, 94 *Northwestern U. L. Rev.* 77 (1999).

Rai, Arti K. and Rebecca S. Eisenberg, Bayh-Dole Reform and the Progress of Biomedicine, 66 *Law & Contemp. Probs.* 289 (2003).

Reichman, Jerome H., Paul F. Uhlir, and Tom Dedeurwaerdere, *Governing Digitally Integrated Genetic Resources, Data, and Literature: Globally Intellectual Property Strategies for a Redesigned Microbial Research Commons* (Cambridge University Press 2016).

Rhodes, Catherine, *Governance of Genetic Resources: A Guide to Navigating the Complex Global Landscape* (Edward Elgar 2013).

Rose, Carol M., The Comedy of the Commons: Commerce, Custom, and Inherently Public Property, 53 *U. Chicago L. Rev.* 711 (1986).

Saito, Hiroki and Christopher J. Gill, How Frequently Do the Results from Completed US Clinical Trials Enter the Public Domain? A Statistical Analysis of the Clinicaltrials.Gov Database, 9 *PLoS One* (2014).

Sarnoff, Joshua D., Government Choices in Innovation Funding (With Reference to Climate Change), 62 *Emory L. Rev.* 1087 (2013).

Scotchmer, Suzanne, *Innovation and Incentives* (MIT Press 2004).

Shreeve, James, *The Genome War* (Knopf 2004).

Smith, Robert J., Resolving the Tragedy of the Commons by Creating Private Property Rights in Wildlife, 1 *CATO J.* 439 (1981).

Strandburg, Katherine J., Brett M. Frischmann, and Can Cui, The Rare Diseases Clinical Research Network and the Urea Cycle Disorders Consortium as Nested Knowledge Commons, in *Governing Knowledge Commons* 155 (Brett M. Frischmann, Michael J. Madison, and Katherine J. Strandburg eds., Oxford University Press 2014).

Strasser, Bruno J., GenBank – Natural History in the 21st Century? 322 *Science* 537 (2008).

US Food & Drug Admin., *Critical Path Initiative* (2017), http://www.fda.gov/ScienceResearch/SpecialTopics/CriticalPathInitiative/.

US Food and Drug Admin., FDA News Release: FDA and International Serious Adverse Events Consortium Complete Third Data Release (2010), www.fda.gov/NewsEvents/Newsroom/PressAnnouncements/ucm201286.htm.

US Patent and Trademark Office, Revised Utility Examination Guidelines; Request for Comments, 64 *Fed. Reg.* 71440 (1999).

US Securities and Exchange Comm., Report to the Congress on Section 107 of the National Securities Markets Improvement Act of 1996 – Privatization of EDGAR (1997), https://www.sec.gov/news/studies/edgpriv.htm.

Vertinsky, Liza S., Patents, Partnerships, and the Pre-Competitive Collaboration Myth in Pharmaceutical Innovation, 48 *U.C. Davis L. Rev.* 101 (2015).

White House, Exec. Order 13642, Making Open and Machine Readable the New Default for Government Information (2013).

3

Centralization, Fragmentation, and Replication in the Genomic Data Commons

Peter Lee

INTRODUCTION

Genomics – the study of organisms' genomes – holds great promise to advance biological knowledge and facilitate the development of new diagnostics and therapeutics. Genomics research has benefited greatly from various policies requiring rapid disclosure of nucleotide sequence data in public databases. Such disclosure has helped create a genomic data commons, a repository of information widely accessible to all members of the scientific community. Notably, this commons operates almost completely outside the strictures of formal intellectual property law through a combination of public funding, agency policy, and communal norms. The genomic data commons has attracted significant scholarly interest because of both its great potential to facilitate biomedical research and its broader lessons about the nature of commons-based production systems (Frischmann et al. 2014; Contreras 2014; Van Overwalle 2014). For instance, recent data release policies by governmental and nongovernmental entities have helped shift the genomic data commons from a more open structure toward a governance regime of selective access and exclusivity. This chapter builds on this rich literature to provide a more granular analysis of the genomic data commons, exploring less appreciated but highly significant challenges of managing existing information in the commons. In so doing, it seeks to shed greater light on the nature of commons in general.

In particular, this chapter focuses on the governance challenges of correcting, updating, and annotating vast amounts of sequence data in the commons. Most legal accounts of the genomic data commons focus on researchers' initial provisioning of data and its use by the scientific community. These accounts implicitly assume that

Peter Lee is Professor of Law at the University of California, Davis, School of Law, Davis, California.
Professor Lee would like to thank Janice Ahn, Martin Bobrow, Liza Vertinsky, and workshop participants at Yale Law School, NYU School of Law, and the US Patent and Trademark Office for comments on earlier versions of this chapter. Special thanks to Brett Frischmann, Michael Madison, and Kathy Strandburg for organizing and editing this volume.

the data is largely "correct" and that the most significant governance challenges involve managing access to that data. Delving into the science of genome sequencing, assembly, and annotation, however, this chapter highlights the indeterminate nature of sequence data and related information, thus giving rise to a strong need to correct, complete, and update existing data. This chapter draws on the Institutional Analysis and Development (IAD) methodological framework developed by Elinor Ostrom and refined by Michael Madison, Brett Frischmann, and Katherine Strandburg (Ostrom and Hess 2007; Madison et al. 2010) to examine four approaches for rendering the genomic data commons more accurate and intelligible: third-party biocuration, contributor-centric data management, community-based wikification, and specialized databases and genome browsers. It argues that these approaches reveal deep tensions between centralization and fragmentation of control over data modification within the genomic data commons, a tension that can be mitigated through a strategy of replicating information.

On the one hand, third-party biocuration and contributor-centric data management tend to consolidate and centralize control over data. On the other hand, wiki-based annotation fragments control throughout the community, exploiting the power of peer production and parallel data analysis to modify existing data records. Both centralization and fragmentation have their strengths and weaknesses, and this chapter argues that stakeholders can capture the best of both worlds through exploiting the nonrivalrous nature of information, which can be consumed without diminishing its availability for other uses. In particular, researchers are engaged in a strategy of replicating and reproducing multiple views of sequence data, employing specialized databases and genome browsers that combine centralized, archival data and widespread community input to provide more textured, value-added renderings of genomic information.[1] Among other advantages, this approach has important epistemological implications as it both reflects and reveals that genomic knowledge is the product of social consensus.

This analysis sheds new light on the dynamic structure of the genomic data commons. Within a conventional perspective, the commons represents a repository of land, information, or other assets that is open to a particular community (Smith 2000). Perhaps because of analogies to physical resources, commentators often characterize the commons' constituent resource units – such as fish, oil, or bits of information – as largely static and fixed. While the overall number of units may change, such as when fish are caught or additional bits of information enter the commons, the underlying resource does not change. However, the genomic data commons reveals that communal efforts may change the nature of the constituent resource units themselves. Contributors to the commons not only provide and use

[1] Notably, community-based wikification as well as specialized databases and genome browsers also represent significant forms of user innovation. Users develop knowledge and tools to advance their own research interests and freely share them, thus benefiting the research community at large (Strandburg 2008, 2009; von Hippel 1976).

data; they also fundamentally transform the nature of that data. In this sense, as Frischmann et al. describe, the commons plays an active role in refining and producing knowledge (Frischmann et al. 2014: 11).

Furthermore, although the genomic data commons has been lauded as accelerating research, closer examination complicates the question of how and to what extent it truly operates as a commons. This chapter reveals that the genomic data commons is both less and more of a commons than previously thought. On the one hand, it features a highly centralized data architecture. The efforts of thousands of genomic researchers around the world feed into a consortium of three publicly sponsored databases, which members of the community may not modify directly. On the other hand, it may be more accurate to characterize this knowledge system as a set of commons on top of a commons. On one level, it is an archival data repository emerging from a global community of scientists. On another level, the genomic data commons also encompasses many subcommunities (often organized around model organisms) that develop their own specialized databases and nomenclatures. Additionally, user groups develop infrastructural meta-tools such as genome browsers and freely distribute them throughout the community. In this sense, the genomic data commons represents a nested set of commons (Strandburg et al. 2014: 156). To simply refer to this as a genomic data commons is to miss some of the nuance and complexity of this knowledge management construct.

Finally and relatedly, this chapter highlights the strong role of centralization and standardization in the effective operation of a commons. The commons is often perceived as an open space free of government intervention and insulated from market demands (Dagan and Heller 2001: 555). Indeed, the genomic data commons has been structured quite conscientiously to operate outside the legal and financial influence of patents. However, the genomic data commons reveals that commons-based productivity systems are not simply free-for-alls lacking order or regulation (Rose 1986: 713). Too much control, and the power of parallel processing and peer production goes unrealized. Too little control, and the commons simply dissipates into chaos and entropy. Truly effective commons function at the balance of centralization and fragmentation.

Section 3.1 reviews the history of genomic data release policies and their implications for commons scholarship. Section 3.2 builds on this foundation by exploring the underappreciated challenges of correcting, updating, and annotating genomic data. Applying the IAD framework, this section examines in greater detail the contingent nature of the information at the heart of the genomic data commons. Delving into the science of genome sequencing, assembly, and annotation, this section shows that genomic information is much less determinate and complete than generally perceived and is constantly in need of updating and refinement. Section 3.3 continues to apply the IAD framework, this time focusing on issues of openness, control, and governance. Drawing on the scientific discussion in Section 3.2, it explores third-party biocuration, contributor-centric data management, community-based wikification, and specialized databases and genome browsers as mechanisms for adding value to existing information. In particular, it explores deep tensions between centralized and fragmented control of data modification in the genomic data commons and attempts to revolve these tensions by exploiting non-rivalry and replication. Section 3.4 considers the deeper implications of these observations for the genomic data commons as well as commons in general.

3.1 THE EVOLUTION OF GENOMIC DATA POLICIES

The genomic data commons represents an illuminating case study of the promise and challenges of commons-based production. As early as the 1970s, molecular biologists and computer scientists recognized the need for a centralized, computerized database for DNA sequence data (Strasser 2008: 537). The National Institutes of Health (NIH) solicited various proposals and ultimately adopted the submission from Los Alamos National Laboratory in significant part because of its open design; the database operators structured it to be accessible through ARPANET and disavowed any proprietary interest in the data (Strasser 2008: 538). In 1982, NIH moved the Los Alamos database to the National Center for Biotechnology Information (NCBI) and renamed it GenBank (Lathe et al. 2008). In the years leading up to the Human Genome Project, the National Research Council recommended that all data generated by the project "be provided in an accessible form to the general research community worldwide" (Nat'l Res. Council 1988: 8). Based largely on its open design, GenBank ultimately became one of the primary databases of the Human Genome Project.

NIH and the Department of Energy (DOE) launched the Human Genome Project in 1990. Initially, researchers participating in the project released sequence data only upon publishing their findings in a peer-reviewed journal, consistent with scientific norms (Contreras 2011: 65; Nat'l Human Genome Res. Inst. 2000). Early on, however, NIH and DOE recognized the importance of sharing data even *before* publication to promote progress and avoid duplicative effort (Nat'l Inst. of Health and Dept. of Energy 1991). Accordingly, in 1992, NIH and DOE adopted a policy requiring publicly funded researchers to deposit sequence data into a public database, such as GenBank, the European Molecular Biology Laboratory (EMBL)–Bank, or the DNA Databank of Japan (DDBJ)[2] within *six months* of data generation, which may be long before publication in a scientific journal (Nat'l Inst. of Health and Dept. of Energy 1991).

However, the demand for even faster, prepublication data release soon led to another policy revision. At a 1996 conference in Bermuda, leaders of the biomedical research community agreed that all DNA sequence assemblies greater than 1 kilobase (kb) should be deposited in publicly accessible databases within *24 hours* after

[2] These databases comprise the central repositories of the International Nucleotide Sequence Database Collaboration (INSDC).

generation (Dept. of Energy 1996).[3] In addition to facilitating rapid scientific advance, the so-called Bermuda Principles also preempted patents on genomic sequences (Contreras 2010: 393; Eisenberg 2000: 72). As Jorge Contreras observes, the Bermuda Principles "represent a significant achievement of private ordering in shaping the practices of an entire industry and establishing a global knowledge resource for the advancement of science" (Contreras 2011: 65). As will be a consistent theme, policymakers played a catalytic role in both recognizing and solidifying community consensus, which ultimately became formalized as agency policy. In 1997, the National Human Genome Research Institute (NHGRI) officially adopted the Bermuda Principles in its funding policy (Nat'l Human Genome Res. Inst. 1997).

Although the Bermuda Principles garnered praise for accelerating collective research, concerns arose that rapid access to sequence data might compromise other interests. For example, researchers often had to release data well before they could publish their findings, thus allowing other scientists to "scoop" them by publishing first (Eisenberg 2006: 1021; Marshall 2002: 1206). To address these concerns as well as complications arising from new sequencing technology, in 2000 NHGRI revised its data release policy (Nat'l Human Genome Res. Inst. 2000). The new policy prohibited users from utilizing public data "for the initial publication of the complete genome sequence assembly or other large-scale analyses." The policy further stated that minor changes in sequence assemblies need not be subject to the 24-hour release policy of the Bermuda Principles and also noted the difficulty of applying the Bermuda Principles to the more recent technological development of "whole genome shotgun sequencing." For this high-throughput sequencing technique, a significant amount of time typically elapsed between generating initial sequence reads and assembling a clean sequence. While there was scientific value to releasing individual sequence reads immediately, such early release put data generators at a potential disadvantage. The policy thus encouraged other scientists to wait to allow data generators to first publish sequence assemblies and large-scale analyses, thus imposing restraints on data users (Contreras 2011: 89).

Soon, however, the balance shifted slightly back toward less constrained use of genomic data. In 2003, a high-profile gathering of sequence producers and users in Fort Lauderdale, Florida, reconsidered existing data release policies. The attendees enthusiastically "reaffirmed"[4] the 1996 Bermuda Principles, and they recommended extending this policy to all sequence data, including raw traces and whole genome shotgun assemblies (The Wellcome Trust 2003: 2). The attendees also agreed that rapid data release policies should apply to so-called community resource projects (CRPs), which are "specifically devised and implemented to create a set of data,

[3] The Bermuda Principles applied to sequence assemblies of 1 kb or greater.

[4] Although the text of the Fort Lauderdale Principles states that it "reaffirm[s] the 1996 Bermuda Principles," the Bermuda Principles require immediate release of sequence assemblies larger than 1 kb, while the Fort Lauderdale Principles require immediate release of sequence assemblies larger than 2 kb.

reagents or other material whose primary utility will be as a resource for the broad scientific community" (The Wellcome Trust 2003: 2). Significantly, the rules eliminated any formal restriction preventing users from publishing whole genome analyses before the sequencers' initial publication of the complete genome (Dennis 2003: 877). Nonetheless, the Fort Lauderdale Principles included hortatory language emphasizing that users should recognize and respect data generators' interest in publishing the first analyses of this data. A few months after the Fort Lauderdale meeting, NHGRI adopted several elements of the Fort Lauderdale Principles in a formal policy statement (Nat'l Human Genome Res. Inst. 2003).[5] Although somewhat mitigated, the Fort Lauderdale Principles reflected an intuition that some proprietary interest in data may be valuable to maintain incentives to conduct research.

In addition to protecting scientific credit, concerns over privacy also led to greater pockets of exclusivity in the genomic data commons. Privacy concerns are particularly relevant for genome-wide association studies (GWAS) that discern how genetic patterns may contribute to disease (Kaye 2012: 417–18). Such studies produce data sets that link individual genotypes to phenotypes, thus raising the specter of associating individual test subjects with a genetic predisposition for a particular disease. Indeed, privacy issues have led researchers to remove large data sets from public databases (Lathe et al. 2008; Kaye 2012: 419). Concerns over privacy, particularly in the context of GWAS, motivated a "second generation" of data release policies (Contreras 2011: 97). Such policy evolution is evident in the Genetic Association Information Network (GAIN), a public-private partnership aimed at elucidating the genetic basis of various diseases (Contreras 2011: 97–99). Researchers participating in GAIN deposit their data in the database of Genotypes and Phenotypes (dbGaP), a database housed at the National Library of Medicine that links sequence and phenotype data for test subjects. As Contreras describes, dbGaP features a two-level system of both open and controlled access to data. Although the general public enjoys open access to summary, nonsensitive data, researchers seeking controlled access must register with the GAIN Data Access Committee (DAC) (Kaye 2012: 418, 424). Among other considerations, researchers must agree to utilize the data only for research purposes and not identify or contact research participants or make intellectual property claims derived directly from the data sets (Genetic Assoc. Info. Network 2010).

This interest in controlling access and protecting privacy is further reflected in broader NIH policies governing GWAS. In 2007, NIH released a policy emphasizing that "[r]apid and broad data access is particularly important for GWAS" (Nat'l Inst. of Health 2007). However, the policy establishes that an NIH DAC will regulate prospective users' access to the data. Among other conditions, users may only use

5 There are some differences between the Fort Lauderdale Principles and NHGRI policy nominally adopting them. The NHGRI policy diverges from the Fort Lauderdale Principles in holding that sequence traces, including those from whole genome shotgun projects, should be deposited in a trace archive within *one week* of production.

data for approved research, and they must protect confidentiality, follow appropriate data security protections, and not identify individuals from whom data was collected. Additionally, although the policy requires rapid data release for federally funded researchers, it imposes a 12-month publication and presentation "embargo" on users to allow original data generators to publish their findings.

Government agencies and the scientific community have applied these policies to an evermore complex set of sequencing initiatives. Soon after the draft of the human genome was published in 2001, researchers launched the International HapMap Project, an ambitious initiative to create a haplotype map of the human genome that locates sets of statistically associated single-nucleotide polymorphisms (SNPs).[6] Participants in the HapMap Project adopted a data release policy similar to the Fort Lauderdale Principles, and they characterized their initiative as a CRP (Contreras 2011: 92). The 1000 Genomes Project builds off the International HapMap Project and GWAS "to discover, genotype and provide accurate haplotype information on all forms of human DNA polymorphism in multiple human populations" (The 1000 Genomes Project Consortium 2010). Similarly, NHGRI launched the Encyclopedia of DNA Elements (ENCODE) pilot project in 2003 to "elucidate the biological functions of various genetic elements" (Contreras 2011: 93). In so doing, NHGRI also adopted a data release policy modeled on the Fort Lauderdale Principles and designated ENCODE as a CRP (Contreras 2011: 94).[7] Additionally, NIH is sponsoring an ambitious project to sequence the genomes of the huge numbers of microbes that inhabit the human body (McGuire et al. 2008). NIH designated the data producing elements of the Human Microbiome Project as a CRP, and it has endorsed rapid data disclosure (Nat'l Inst. of Health 2013). NIH recently issued a new policy that requires researchers to deposit large-scale human genomic data in a public repository but embargoes data access for up to six months to allow the depositors to publish related findings (Nat'l Inst. of Health 2014).[8] Increasing complexity, including tensions between open and regulated access to data, will be a consistent theme of ongoing genome sequencing projects.

Not surprisingly, the emergence and evolution of the genomic data commons has attracted significant scholarly attention. In particular, Contreras and Van Overwalle have fruitfully applied a modified version of Ostrom's IAD framework to evaluate this socially constructed commons. These policies reflect a significant shift: "Whereas the initial HGP required the rapid release of genomic data to the public,

[6] An SNP arises when the DNA sequences of two organisms from the same species vary by a single nucleotide.

[7] Efforts to extend rapid-release policies beyond Bermuda and Fort Lauderdale have continued in the context of whole-genome association studies, microarray surveys, epigenomics scans, protein structures, screening of small molecules for biological activity, and functional genomics data (Pennisi 2009: 1000).

[8] Additionally, the new policy requires researchers to include a Genomic Data Sharing Plan in applications for funding and establishes a tiered system in which a Data Access Committee differentiates between data that is available on a controlled or unrestricted basis (Nat'l Inst. of Health 2014).

effecting what might be considered a *public good* in economic terms, later projects added increasingly complex rules governing human subject protection and publication priority" (Contreras 2014: 123). Indeed, these constraints have led Van Overwalle to reject characterizing the genomic data commons as a truly open knowledge commons, instead describing it as a limited "genome *research* commons" (Van Overwalle 2014: 150).

From the perspective of commons scholarship, this transition reflects an evolution from a largely open structure to a more tightly regulated "governance" model in which various actors manage access to data. Scholars have noted that governance regimes incur high information costs as decision makers must determine what parties have access to what resources under what circumstances (Smith 2002: S453). Many stakeholders are involved: government agencies that fund projects and define data policies, data generators who "populate" the genomic data commons, users who are expected to delay certain publications, and centralized data access committees that screen access to sensitive information. Far from a simple model in which data generators produce vast amounts of information for the public at large, the genomic data commons has assumed much greater complexity in its rules and operation. This chapter continues this theme of complexity by examining the challenges of correcting, updating, and annotating the data residing in the genomic commons. To do so, it must first examine in greater depth the kinds of information at the heart of this commons.

3.2 RESOURCE ATTRIBUTES: GENOME SEQUENCING, ASSEMBLY, AND ANNOTATION

As Frischmann et al. observe, an important characteristic of any commons is the resource that is the subject of communal pooling and sharing (Frischmann et al. 2014: 24). This section examines the information – or, more precisely, the multiple kinds of information – at the heart of the genomic data commons. Commentators generally describe this resource as "genomic data," but that phrase includes a multiplicity of types of information, including raw sequence reads, sequence assemblies, and annotated genomes as well as phenotypic and demographic data related to research subjects. To elucidate some of this complexity, this section delves into the science of genome sequencing, assembly, and annotation. While commons scholarship to date has focused largely on "upstream" functions such as sequencing and related analyses, this chapter looks more closely at the "downstream" functions of sequence assembly and genome annotation. Ultimately, these "value-added" functions represent additional vantage points from which to evaluate the structure, governance, and operation of the genomic data commons.

Traditional accounts of the Human Genome Project and its progeny focus on genome *sequencing*, an activity that is more complex than commonly perceived. At a conceptual level, sequencing involves determining the nucleotide sequence of particular segments of DNA. Thus, it is popularly understood that the Human Genome Project determined the nucleotide sequence for the human genome, and subsequent initiatives aim to determine the nucleotide sequence of various model organisms and other entities of interest. Mainstream conceptions of sequencing imply a high degree of determinism; one might conceive of scientists taking DNA samples and simply sequencing chromosomes from one end to the other, thus revealing a definitive series of As, Ts, Cs, and Gs that constitutes an organism's genome.

For a variety of technical reasons, however, DNA sequencing is far from determinate. For instance, researchers cannot sequence extremely long strips of DNA in one fell swoop. Conventional sequencing utilizing the chain-termination method (also known as Sanger sequencing) (Price 2012: 1619; Sanger et al. 1977) is rather limited and can only directly sequence relatively short nucleotide fragments (up to 1000 nucleotides long) in a single reaction (Nelson et al. 2011: 7.0.3). Chromosomes and other strips of DNA of interest, however, can be hundreds of thousands of nucleotides long. Scientists have utilized a technique known as "primer walking" to painstakingly sequence contiguous fragments one at a time until they can combine them to ascertain a sequence of interest.

In particular, "whole genome shotgun sequencing" has accentuated the indeterminate nature of genome sequencing and the extent to which researchers *assemble* sequences rather than simply discover them (Salzberg 2007). Whole genome shotgun sequencing utilizes the basic Sanger method but transcends some of its limitations by utilizing massive parallel processing. With the advent of commercial automated sequencing machines in the 1980s, this method of "high-throughput" sequencing became the norm (Nelson et al. 2011: 7.0.2). In this technique, researchers first purify the DNA of interest and then shear it into a huge number of small fragments.[9] Researchers then clone and sequence these small fragments in parallel, thus greatly accelerating the pace of sequencing. These sequenced fragments are called "traces,"[10] and fitting traces together into the natural genomic sequence is not a straightforward task. Researchers utilize complex software programs to analyze sequence overlaps and assemble these fragments into what is believed to be their natural order. Assembly can proceed *de novo*, similar to fitting the pieces of a jigsaw puzzle based on their edges, or based on a reference sequence that provides a guide (Price 2012: 1620). These assemblies consist of contiguous DNA sequences (contigs) held together by scaffolds.

[9] Sequencing traditionally used DNA purified from a pool of cells, which created more "noise." The current trend is to perform single-cell sequencing, particularly for RNA (interview with Dr. Janice Ahn, March 3, 2015).

[10] NIH's 2003 policy (following the Fort Lauderdale Principles) requires depositing traces from whole genome shotgun projects in an archive such as the NCBI Trace Repository or Ensembl Trace Server within one week of production (Nat'l Human Genome Res. Inst. 2003).

A crucial knowledge-enhancing step following sequencing and assembly is genome *annotation*. Such annotation involves "mapping" the location and function of genes on (what is perceived to be) a particular segment of DNA (Claverie 2000: 12).[11] Starting with the raw DNA sequences, annotation involves "adding the layers of analysis and interpretation necessary to extract its biological significance and place it into the context of our understanding of biological processes" (Stein 2001: 493). To this end, researchers might start by utilizing gene-finding software such as GlimmerM, which identifies sequences that are characteristic of protein-coding strands of nucleotides. This initial analysis provides the basis for a series of programs called Basic Local Alignment Search Tool (BLAST), a bioinformatics algorithm that enables researchers to compare a query sequence with a database of known sequences to correlated proteins (Benson et al. 2014: D36). Researchers utilize BLAST in cross-species comparisons to identify new genes. For example, a researcher who has discovered a new mouse gene may use BLAST to compare that nucleotide sequence with a human genome database to determine if humans have a similar gene. Once genes have been identified and mapped, researchers attempt to relate them to biological processes through functional annotation (Stein 2001: 500). Within this process, researchers often compare proteins (as well as messenger RNA) between species to determine process-level annotation (Stein 2001: 499). Ultimately, "customized annotation programs are used to decide what name and function to assign to each protein, leading to the final annotated genome" (Salzberg 2007: 102.2 fig. 1).

Genome sequencing, assembly, and annotation are far from precise sciences, and there is uncertainty and indeterminacy in each step. Whole genome shotgun sequencing generates enormous amounts of data, and the likelihood of errors is relatively high (Pennisi 2009: 1000). For example, sequencing techniques can introduce contaminants that get sequenced along with the DNA of interest (Pennisi 1999: 447). As mentioned, assembly is an indeterminate exercise that fits traces together based on probabilities, not certainties. Annotation may also produce errors. Pseudogenes may complicate gene-finding efforts, gene fragments may be contaminated, and complementary DNA (cDNA) sequences often contain repetitive sequences, which may cause incorrect genomic matches (Stein 2001: 495). Annotation often proceeds on the "draft" form of a genome, which may be problematic if a gene "runs off" the end of a contig; in such cases, the annotation protocol may assign the same gene to two different locations (Salzberg 2007: 102.3). Additionally, the accuracy of BLAST analysis depends on the quality of the annotation software as well as

[11] This section includes a basic overview of genome annotation. For a more comprehensive discussion, see Stein 2001. Genome annotation can be split into various subtasks. For example, some commentators distinguish between nucleotide-level, protein-level, and process-level annotation. Others distinguish between structural annotation, which encompasses identifying genomic elements, and functional annotation, which involves attaching biological information to genomic elements. Researchers utilize comprehensive data "warehouses" such as Microbiogenomics and querying modules such as GenoQuery to aid in functional annotation (Lemoine et al. 2008).

how up to date its reference databases of known sequences are (Salzberg 2007: 102.2). Given that annotation software finds genes based on probabilistic algorithms, even the best programs can produce errors, thus accentuating the need for manual oversight and verification by biologists with relevant expertise in the species in question. Not surprisingly, many researchers complain of flaws in GenBank annotations, and inaccuracies regarding gene structure and function "plague" GenBank and related databases (Bidartondo et al. 2008: 1616; Bridge et al. 2003: 44; Claverie 2000: 12; Lathe et al. 2008; Nilsson et al. 2006: e59; Pennisi 2008: 1598; Salzberg 2007: 102.1, 102.3).

This cursory examination of sequencing, assembly, and annotation sheds new light on the information at the heart of the genomic data commons. First, it illustrates that genomic information varies along a value-added continuum from raw sequence data to assemblies to annotated genomes identifying the location and function of specific genes. Second, it illustrates that these resources are not necessarily determinate or complete. Although lists of As, Ts, Cs, and Gs may suggest that genomic sequences are precise and apprehensible, many sequence assemblies and annotations are incorrect and incomplete. Put simply, "GenBank is full of mistakes" (Pennisi 1999: 448). Correcting and updating information, and thus adding value to existing data records, remain critical challenges to maintaining the integrity of the genomic data commons. The question of how to accomplish these functions, moreover, involves underappreciated governance challenges and sheds new light on the deep structure of the genomic commons, a topic to which this chapter now turns.

3.3 MAKING SENSE OF THE GENOMIC DATA COMMONS

Controlling access to data to safeguard scientific authorship and privacy is far from the only governance challenge facing the genomic data commons. The objective of correcting, updating, and adding greater intelligence to existing data, thus facilitating the transition from data to information to knowledge (Machlup 1983: 641), raises difficult questions of *who* should perform these functions and *how*. As we will see, a variety of players, including biocurators, data submitters, and the research community at large, have various strengths and weaknesses in managing this data. A background complicating factor, of course, is the sheer amount of data in the commons and its rapid expansion. To address these challenges, this section draws on the IAD framework derived from Ostrom and Madison et al. to examine additional dimensions of the genomic data commons, namely its degree of openness as well as the "rules in use" of community participants (Madison et al. 2010: 694–703; Van Overwalle 2014: 138). This analysis reveals that the genomic data commons features an ongoing tension between openness and control and has developed a variety of rules and institutions to govern knowledge-enhancing functions.

As Madison et al. (2010: 694) observe, "Commons regimes are defined both by the *degree of openness and control* that they exhibit with respect to contributors, users, and resources, and by the *assignment of control, or custody of the power to administer access*." Openness, of course, has many dimensions. Most accounts of the genomic data commons focus on *access* and *use* of data. Thus, data policies have evolved from a largely open system to one in which concerns over scientific credit and privacy have constrained researchers' ability to use data. This section, however, focuses on another type of openness, one that deals with the deeper architecture of the genomic data commons. In particular, it observes a deep tension between centralization and fragmentation of *control* over data, including the ability to modify existing data records. This tension is endemic to many commons-based production systems, such as Wikipedia. Regarding governance and rules in use, Madison et al. (2010: 701) emphasize the importance of "the identities and roles of . . . institutions and how their functions relate to the pool and its members." A variety of formal and informal institutions, from government agencies to loosely connected communities to temporary, project-specific groups, play important roles in correcting, updating, and annotating genomic data.

Although the open nature of the genomic data commons has greatly accelerated biomedical research, there are ways in which it is quite closed and centralized. This tension is evident in the very genesis of the Human Genome Project, in which decentralized teams of scientists working around the globe deposited nucleotide sequences in a highly centralized system of databases. The tension between centralization and fragmentation is particularly germane to efforts to render the genomic data commons more accurate, complete, and intelligible. These functions span basic (but important) biocuration functions such as standardizing data and nomenclature (Standardizing Data 2008) as well as higher valued-added processes such as genome annotation. This chapter now examines several approaches that are currently playing a prominent role in enhancing the accuracy, richness, and intelligibility of genomic data (Figure 3.1). It contrasts more centralized models of control, such as third-party biocuration and contributor-centric data management, with highly fragmented approaches, such as community-based wikification. Finally, it turns to specialized databases and genome browsers to illustrate how nonrivalry and replication may allow researchers to obtain the best of both approaches.

Third-Party Biocuration

At the centralized end of the spectrum is third-party biocuration (Howe et al. 2008: 47; Salimi and Vita 2006). Biocuration, which is performed both by professional scientists and automated processes, involves collecting, validating, annotating, and organizing biological information. Biocuration entails several functions, including "extracting, tagging with controlled vocabularies, and representing data from the literature" (Howe et al. 2008: 47). Such standardization renders information more coherent, intelligible, and useful given that "[t]he value of data is only as good as its annotation and accessibility: it must be properly curated and stored in machine-

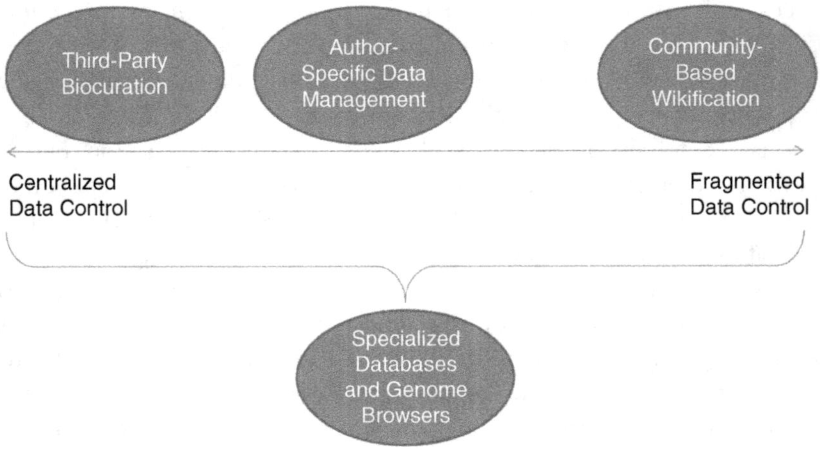

FIGURE 3.1 Continuum of data modification governance models.

readable form in public databases" (Standardizing Data 2008: 1123). Centralized, professional biocuration can help establish a single standard annotation for the genomes of model organisms, thus greatly facilitating research in those fields. Although biocuration generally focuses on such basic functions, it sometimes ventures into higher-level data analysis. For instance, one of the potential functions of centralized biocurators is to recompute genome annotations using the most up-to-date software and reference databases (Salzberg 2007: 102.4).

One set of stakeholders that is well positioned to perform biocuration is database operators themselves. For example, GenBank standardizes data formats (Standardizing Data 2008: 1123)[12] and assigns unique accession numbers to sequences and annotations upon intake. These accession numbers are shared with EMBL-Bank and DDBJ and represent "the most efficient and reliable way to cite a sequence record in publications" (Benson et al. 2014: D33–34). More ambitiously, NCBI maintains and actively curates the Reference Sequence (RefSeq) database, which links information in nucleotide and protein databases. RefSeq identifies a single "best" sequence for each protein-coding region of DNA and dynamically culls and updates the best information available on each segment of DNA (Pennisi 1999: 450). Among other functions, NCBI staff members coordinate with other database operators to maximize consistency between databases (Pruitt et al. 2012: D132). Additionally, journals also perform biocuration by requiring that contributing authors submit data to the appropriate public database in standardized formats (Walsh et al. 2003: 329). Interestingly, the operators of DNA databases originally helped convince journal editors to make electronic data submission a condition for publication (Strasser 2008: 538).

12 For instance, NCBI checks for proper strandedness and chimeric sequences for submissions of prokaryotic ribosomal RNA data (Benson et al. 2014: D32).

Although it adds significant value, third-party biocuration is somewhat limited in its ability to enhance the knowledge content of the genomic data commons. Almost by definition, biocuration focuses on lower-level functions such as standardization of data formats rather than more complex functions such as genome annotation. Furthermore, even if biocurators perform annotation, their distance from the original data and lack of familiarity with particular species may compromise outcomes. Biocuration may involve automated processes, and centralized recomputation of genomic annotations may overwrite manually annotated genomes that are even more accurate (Salzberg 2007: 102.4). Another limitation of third-party biocuration is inherent in its centralized nature: such efforts do not take advantage of the enormous community of users who can help correct and add value to existing data records. There has been increasing interest in harnessing commons-like mechanisms to take advantage of user-generated correction and annotation of genomic data.

3.3.1 *Contributor-Centric Data Management*

Beyond third-party biocuration, a slightly less centralized model of data management involves original data contributors exercising exclusive control over particular data records. Of course, in many ways, it makes logical sense for a data generator to take the lead in curating and annotating "her" data; she has intimate, perhaps tacit (Lee 2012), knowledge of the data and has personal and professional incentives to ensure its quality and completeness. Contributors can do much to enhance the value of existing data. They can label their data with standardized tags to facilitate subsequent studies[13] as well as recompute raw sequence data with newer software and more up-to-date reference databases to yield newer (and presumably more accurate) assemblies. Similarly, newer software and reference databases can produce more accurate annotations.

Notably, a centralized, contributor-centric approach to data modification is hardwired in the structure of GenBank. The rules and structure of that database establish that a scientist who contributes a sequence is the designated "author" of that entry, and only she can update the data record. Although data is free for *use* by members of the community (subject to constraints imposed by various policies discussed earlier), they may not modify it. The guiding metaphor for GenBank is that of a library: authors contribute books, which others can check out and access, but only original authors can revise the text of their volumes with new information. Interestingly, in a system built on openness and designed to avoid intellectual property claims, this centralized structure establishes something of a proprietary interest in the data on the part of the contributing researcher. Indeed, this sense of ownership and exclusive

[13] These tags include the National Center for Biotechnology Information (NCBI) Taxon IDs, the Gene Ontology (GO) IDs, and Enzyme Commission (EC) numbers (Howe et al. 2008: 48).

control over modifying data may help motivate widespread contributions to GenBank (Salzberg 2007: 102.3).

Although data contributors are well positioned to manage "their" data records, GenBank's centralized approach features some limitations. Empirically, data contributors seldom revise their records; in the busy life of academic science, researchers submitting sequence data often simply move on to other projects (Pennisi 1999: 448, 2008: 1598). Furthermore, although disclosing tacit information may greatly benefit the research community, data generators have little incentive to do so since such disclosure does not increase the value of existing data (Howe et al. 2008: 48). In a broader sense, strict control of data records by original contributors prevents other members of the community from updating and adding value to such data, a phenomenon to which this chapter now turns.

3.3.2 *Community-Based Wikification*

At the opposite end of the spectrum from third-party biocuration and contributor-centric data management are approaches to data management based on fragmentation of control. In particular, community-based wikification represents a very different model for correcting and annotating genomic data. As the name implies, this model involves wide swaths of independent researchers annotating and re-annotating existing sequences in a manner analogous to peer editing of Wikipedia (Pennisi 2008: 1598; Salzberg 2007: 102.5). Unlike centralized or contributor-centric data management systems, wikification is highly decentralized and requires data modification capabilities to be open to the broader user community (Madison et al. 2010: 694–96). Community-based wikification holds great promise for enhancing the knowledge content of genomic data. After all, subsequent users of GenBank "often learn more about the data than the initial depositors or curation staff" (Chu et al. 2008: 1289). As noted, although data generators are well positioned to correct and augment their data, they seldom do so. Community-based wikification enables huge numbers of subsequent data users to incorporate their experience and knowledge to improve data records. In many ways, wikification reflects Eric Raymond's observation that "[g]iven enough eyeballs, all bugs are shallow" (Raymond 1999: 30).

This distributed model of wikification has already facilitated valuable community-based genome annotation. For example, communal efforts to annotate genomic data for the Daphnia Genomics Consortium, the International Glossina Genomics Initiative, and PortEco (a hub for researchers studying *E. coli*) have greatly enhanced the value of these communal resources (Chu et al. 2008: 1289; Howe et al. 2008: 48). Indeed, community-based annotation has gained significant support (Hubbard and Birney 2000: 825), and researcher-edited wiki-type websites have proliferated (Waldrop 2008: 22). Commentators speculate that open-content databases modeled on Wikipedia might render GenBank, EMBL-Bank, and DDBJ obsolete in the same way that Wikipedia has done for the *Encyclopedia Britannica* (Strasser 2008: 538).

Not surprisingly, researchers have integrated wiki-based gene annotation directly into Wikipedia. The Gene Wiki project utilizes software to automatically generate thousands of Wikipedia stubs for human genes, thus inviting communal updating of such pages (Howe et al. 2008: 48; Huss et al. 2008; Waldrop 2008: 24). Its founders explicitly sought to exploit the "long tail" of incorporating small contributions from large numbers of contributors (Huss et al. 2008: 1398). Early results indicate that automated creation of "stubs" has "roughly doubled the amount of mammalian gene annotation activity in Wikipedia" (Huss et al. 2008: 1400). Although an important resource, the organizers of Gene Wiki recognize its uniqueness and limitations. Gene Wiki pages utilize an unstructured format of free text, images, and diagrams rather than the more structured (and easier-to-analyze) organization of gene portals. Gene Wiki organizers, moreover, recognize that it is not meant to substitute for more authoritative sources like gene portals and model organism databases, nor is it intended to be a source for citation in traditional peer-reviewed articles (Huss et al. 2008: 1401). Indeed, many researchers do not place citation-level confidence in wiki pages because of their open, decentralized nature.

In subtle ways, community-based wikification has even crystallized into more formal, government-run databases. For instance, NCBI maintains a Third Party Annotation (TPA) database, which includes sequences, assemblies, and annotations based on information already contained in an INSDC database. The TPA database represents a location where parties other than the contributor of the primary sequence record can submit data and analyses building off the primary source material (Benson et al. 2014: D36). In some ways, the TPA operates as a bridge between GenBank and RefSeq, allowing third parties to re-annotate sequences already existing in public databases. However, TPA records are distinct from original data records.

Though a potentially powerful source of annotation and curation, wikification has raised concerns about the degree to which it fragments control over genomic data. Indeed, one of the reasons why NCBI developed the TPA database is that it has resisted direct modification of GenBank records by third parties. Though scientists have argued for direct access to GenBank data (Salzberg 2007: 102.3), NCBI has consistently opposed wikification as undermining a structure where data records "belong" to the original contributor (Pennisi 2008: 1598). Along these lines, some worry that providing editorial access to GenBank records may "quickly destroy the archival function of GenBank, as original entries would be erased over time" (Salzberg 2007: 102.3). Interestingly, although GenBank maintains that only contributors themselves can modify sequence data or annotations, it provides an email address for feedback from the user community, and "all users are encouraged to report lags in releasing data or possible errors or omissions to GenBank" (Benson et al. 2014: D34).

As with other instances of peer production, wikification of genome correction and annotation faces challenges of motivation and accuracy (Benkler 2006).

Community-based wikification relies on broad-based participation and voluntary contributions, which may not necessarily materialize (Waldrop 2008: 23; Mons et al. 2008: 89.8). For instance, researchers rarely submit records to the TPA database, presumably because of lack of incentive (Standardizing Data 2008: 1123). Recall that in the evolution of data release policies concerns over scientific credit motivated policy reforms to limit "scooping" by data users, thus maintaining incentives for original data generators to perform research and publish their findings. A similar motivational challenge faces wikification, and providing scientific credit for third-party annotation can accelerate such activity (Stein 2001: 502; Waldrop 2008: 25). Indeed, technical measures can address this concern. Thus, for instance, WikiGenes tracks – and allocates credit for – every contribution made (Waldrop 2008: 23, 25).[14] Even in a data commons, "attribution of scholarly contributions can be tracked and acknowledged" (It's Not About the Data 2012: 111). In a broader sense, cultural and institutional norms may need to change so that community-based contributions provide credit in university tenure and promotion decisions. In addition to challenges of motivation, the open and anonymous nature of wikification raises concerns about accuracy. Here, however, decentralization can not only help generate information but can also help ensure its quality: "[a] sizable population of readers then serves simultaneously as consumers, reviewers, and editors of content" (Huss et al. 2008: 1401). Thus, concerns that wikification leads to overlapping, duplicative work (Claverie 2000: 12) may be overstated, as such duplication and rechecking can ensure the accuracy of community-based annotations.

More subtly, certain aspects of genome sequencing, assembly, and annotation may more naturally lend themselves to wikification than others. The initial phases of annotation, which involve finding genes, mapping variations, and locating landmarks, lend themselves to brute force automation (Stein 2001: 500–01). Interpreting their functional roles, however, may be better suited for centralized biocuration by specialists in the field. Biocurators, perhaps working for model organism databases, may be well positioned to systematically catalog and classify genomes, correcting the mistakes of computational annotation (Stein 2001: 501). At this stage, community-based annotation may also be helpful, and some research communities have even organized "jamborees" to annotate parts of model organism genomes in a short period of time (Stein 2001: 501).

Ultimately, community-based wikification represents a powerful, decentralized model of knowledge production and verification that shows promise within genomics as well as other fields. For instance, SNPedia is a wiki resource wherein users contribute information relating to the functional consequences of human genetic information (Cariaso and Lennon 2011). Moving to proteomics, PDBWiki is a system for annotating protein structures deposited in the Protein Data Bank (PDB) (Stehr et al. 2010). This

[14] WikiGenes, which is separate from Gene Wiki, is an online platform by which scientists can contribute to particular research topics, including but not limited to genes.

database operates in parallel to central archives, and PDB is synchronized with PDBWiki every week (Stehr et al. 2010: 2). Similarly, WikiProteins is a "web-based, interactive and semantically supported workspace based on Wiki pages" that allows community members to annotate protein-related data (Mons et al. 2008: 89.2). Moving beyond annotation, wikification can help organize scientific knowledge more broadly. For example, the WikiProject Molecular and Cellular Biology initiative is a community of Wikipedia users committed to organizing and improving scientifically relevant articles; it hosts several subcommunities, including the RNA WikiProject (Daub et al. 2008: 1–2). At an even more distributed level, the general public could be involved in annotating genomic (and other scientific) data (Howe et al. 2008: 49).[15] Ultimately, "[c]ommunity data curation promises to be a solution to the problem of coping with the increasing size and complexity of biological data. The challenge is to make use of the 'wisdom of the many' without compromising the advantages of central, trusted and manually curated databases" (Stehr et al. 2010: 6).

3.3.3 *Specialized Databases and Genome Browsers*

A promising method for harmonizing the perceived trade-offs of centralized data management and community-based wikification is to pursue both simultaneously. This approach manifests in several forms. First, parallel databases have emerged alongside GenBank that draw from GenBank's data while also providing flexibility for community-based annotation and curation. In this fashion, GenBank remains the "archival" resource, but more specialized, value-added databases – which are also widely accessible within research communities – build off its contents.[16] Second, "genome browsers" have emerged that find, aggregate, filter, and present all information about a particular DNA sequence, thus offering the user both original, archival data as well as alternate views and additional layers of annotation. Perhaps the best approach to balancing centralization and fragmentation is to embrace both approaches through exploiting replication and the nonrivalry of data. In this manner, data represents an infrastructural resource that facilitates many downstream uses and is not itself subject to scarcity once created (Frischmann 2012: 62; OECD 2015: 178).

Based partly on the constraints of GenBank, various communities have developed specialized databases that replicate archival data while augmenting it with additional input and modification. Databases organized around model organisms have become particularly important (Salzberg 2007: 102.5). Resources such as FlyBase for the fruit fly and TAIR for *Arabidopsis* both incorporate GenBank data as well as clean up mistakes in sequence information (Pennisi 2008: 1599). The Daphnia

[15] However, some members of the scientific community oppose such a movement because of a lack of quality control and standardization (interview with Dr. Janice Ahn, March 3, 2015).

[16] It should be noted that Entrez, the retrieval system for accessing data in GenBank, links to other informational sources, such as academic articles in PubMed and PubMed Central that discuss particular sequences (Benson et al. 2014: D36).

Genomics Consortium performs a similar function for its community members (Lathe et al. 2008). Notably, many of these specialized databases incorporate wiki-based annotation (Galperin and Fernandez-Suarez 2012: D4). Hundreds of species- and taxa-specific genome databases exist that integrate archival and value-added data to serve specific research needs (Lathe et al. 2008). Even NCBI, which has resisted community-based annotation and modification of data records in GenBank, has embraced a system of parallel databases. As mentioned, NCBI maintains both GenBank, an "archival" resource, and RefSeq, an actively curated database that combines original data with value-added information (Pennisi 2008: 1599). Ultimately, an "ecosystem of databases" has emerged with replication, synchronization, and cross-linking of data (Galperin and Fernandez-Suarez 2012: D6). These resources take advantage of the inherent nonrivalry of information by copying and modifying archival data while leaving the original data unchanged.

Another resource that exploits accretive and overlapping information is genome browsers, sometimes referred to as gene portals (Furey 2006: 266). Such browsers "repackage genome and gene annotation data sets from GenBank and other subject-specific databases to provide a genomic context for individual genome features, such as genes or disease loci" (Lathe et al. 2008). In essence, they collect, aggregate, and display desired data from multiple sources, including central databases such as GenBank, wikified community pages, and specialized databases (Furey 2006: 266; Hubbard and Birney 2000: 825). This information often integrates value-added information, such as the location of clones from bacterial artificial chromosomes (BAC) libraries, expressed sequence tags (ESTs), sequence-tagged site (STS) markers from genetic maps, and boundaries of cytogenetic bands, all of which aid in mapping genomes (Furey 2006: 266). Among other virtues, genome browsers allow researchers to select only data sources that they seek to view (Hubbard and Birney 2000: 825). Such data aggregation and visualization can greatly enhance data analysis (Cline and Kent 2009: 153).

Just as genome browsers provide a multiplicity of views, there is a multiplicity of genome browsers that differ in their presentation, content, and functionality (Furey 2006: 266–69). Prominent examples include UCSC's genome browser, EBI's Ensembl, and NCBI's MapViewer (Lathe et al. 2008). The multitude of options allows researchers to pick the particular tool that best suits their needs (Furey 2006: 269). There are now more than 3000 distinct genomic resources, tools, and databases publicly available on the Internet (Lathe 2008).

Contrary to conventional views, genome browsers more realistically depict the messiness and indeterminateness of genome sequencing, assembly, and annotation. A common format is to present several parallel "tracks" showing various depictions of the same nucleotide sequence from different sources, often with different standards of evidence and confidence intervals (Cline and Kent 2009: 153). As Cline and Kent (2009: 153) observe, "Virtually any genomic data can be erroneous, and one should be wary of data suggested by only a single observation." Genome browsers more faithfully represent the indeterminacy of genomics, aggregating multiple views to aid the researcher in her particular pursuit. While the guiding metaphor for GenBank may be a library that lends out archival resources, the guiding metaphor for genome browsers may be something like BitTorrent, wherein a user, perhaps with the aid of a central registry, can obtain, aggregate, and filter any and all information related to a particular genome sequence.[17] In some ways, this system resembles whole genome shotgun sequencing as a mechanism for building genomic knowledge. Decentralized, massively parallel efforts to process data – including community-based wikification – are aggregated and assembled, thus rendering the genomes of various organisms more intelligible.

A system of "replicative" specialized databases and genome browsers seeks to combine the virtues of centralization and fragmentation. They maintain the archival status of contributor-centric and professionally curated databases such as GenBank, thus shoring up authorial incentives to submit to such databases because other members of the community cannot modify data records directly. However, these resources also take advantage of wikification by giving users access to both original data sets and community-based annotation. In so doing, they exploit the inherent nonrivalry of information to powerful effect; specialized databases can "consume" and modify all of the data in GenBank without depleting or altering the original data records at all.

Drawing on the theme of fragmentation versus centralization, however, this multiplicity of data resources gives rise to a strong need for standardization. The specialized nature of community-specific databases is both a feature and a bug. Because such databases are tailored to the unique nomenclature and practices of biological subfields, they may represent the same information differently in different contexts. As a result of fragmentation, organism-specific communities and databases often utilize their own unique nomenclature for genes and their products (The Gene Ontology Consortium 2000: 25). Data is not completely consistent between species and research projects, thus making cross-species comparisons difficult (Lathe et al. 2008). This proliferation of alternate names undermines database interoperability and complicates the process of finding related genes and gene products across different species (The Gene Ontology Consortium 2000: 25). Ironically, while standardization within communities has helped make information more internally coherent (Field and Sansone 2006: 85), it has exacerbated incommensurabilities between communities, as one group's standards may be incompatible with those of another (Field and Sansone 2006: 90).

Genomics thus faces the significant challenge of adopting a standardized classification system that can account for myriad biological functions across diverse species while maintaining the particularity to distinguish subtle nuances within a given

[17] I am indebted to Jonathan Eisen for this metaphor (interview with Dr. Jonathan Eisen, UC Davis Genome Center, March 17, 2014).

species (Stein 2001: 500). Various user communities have led standardization efforts to help bridge these gaps, thus bringing some degree of centralization to the fragmented realm of community-specific nomenclature, practices, and databases. In a sense, a metacommons has emerged to mediate among different communities utilizing different standards and nomenclatures. For example, the Generic Model Organism Database (GMOD) has collaboratively developed a standardized set of tools and database schema (Lathe et al. 2008).

Perhaps most ambitiously, several model organism databases formed the Gene Ontology (GO) consortium to standardize annotation conventions across all species (Contreras 2013: 116).[18] The GO aims to "produce a structured, precisely defined, common, controlled vocabulary for describing the roles of genes and gene products in any organism" (The Gene Ontology Consortium 2000: 26). Within this structure, "[d]ata can be annotated to varying levels depending on the amount and completeness of available information" (The Gene Ontology Consortium 2000: 27). While GO may sacrifice some species-specific conventions, it ultimately serves the broader purpose of standardizing the accumulation of knowledge and facilitating cross-species comparisons. Particularly amid such multiplicity, standardization and centralization remain highly valuable.

At a more fundamental level, the multiplicity of databases and the power of genome browsers to aggregate all relevant information on a particular nucleotide sequence hold important epistemological implications for genomic knowledge. Neat rows of As, Ts, Cs, and Gs, suggest that the genome of any organism is completely knowable, an objective fact just waiting to be discovered. However, genome sequencing, assembly, and annotation are imprecise sciences, and different methodologies, technologies, equipment, and techniques can yield different results. Even the same or related gene may be represented quite differently in different databases or systems of nomenclature. Genome browsers are sensitive to this multiplicity by providing a wide array of views of the "same" physical phenomenon. And, of course, human subjectivity informs both the various processes that create data as well as the perspectives that interpret it. Just as Thomas Kuhn postulated that scientific theory reflects more social consensus than objective fact (Kuhn 1962), perhaps "true" genomic knowledge only arises from gathering, comparing, and reconciling a multiplicity of competing perspectives. The genomic data commons certainly *holds* knowledge in the sense that it encompasses an enormous repository of data. But it also *produces* knowledge by allowing social consensus to coalesce around particular epistemological paradigms.

[18] As Field and Sansone describe, "An ontology is an explicit formal representation of the knowledge in a subject area, which includes controlled vocabularies referring to the concepts and logical statements that describe what the concepts are and how they can or cannot be related to each other" (Field and Sansone 2006: 87).

3.4 BROADER IMPLICATIONS FOR THE GENOMIC DATA COMMONS AND COMMONS IN GENERAL

In a variety of ways, this chapter sheds new light on the genomic data commons. Applying the IAD framework, it reveals the indeterminate nature of the shared and pooled resource at the heart of the commons – genomic data and related information. Popular views of gene sequencing envision an orderly and determinate process of discerning the As, Ts, Cs, and Gs that make up an organism's genome. However, genome sequencing, assembly, and annotation are probabilistic sciences, and data records in GenBank are rife with errors and incompleteness. These technological limitations exacerbate tensions between centralization and fragmentation of control over data. Data contributors and professional biocurators can add significant value to existing data, but their efforts are necessarily limited. The research community represents an enormous resource for annotating and updating genomic data, but disaggregated control over information threatens the "purity" and provenance of archival data records. In various contexts, the genomic data commons features centralized control over data modification, wide community participation in data modification, and information replication as a structural strategy for harmonizing these competing approaches.

More subtly, this chapter also sheds new light on the concept of the commons itself. The commons is often understood as a repository of ontologically determinate resources. Although the commons may grow or shrink in size, each individual resource unit has a particular identity that is largely fixed. However, at least in a knowledge commons, members of the community can change the fundamental nature of these constituent elements, as when a user corrects or annotates an existing data record. Thus, the community is responsible for not only provisioning and extracting resources but also fundamentally changing the character of those resources along the way. Far from being a passive repository, the commons is a teeming, dynamic entity continually subject to human intervention and manipulation. Derived from the Human Genome Project, the genomic data commons is an indelibly *human* commons not only in the DNA sequences that constitute its subject matter but also in the social and communal processes that modify data and produce knowledge.

This chapter also reveals that the genomic data commons is both less and more of a commons than previously appreciated. On one level, the genomic data commons certainly reflects a social construct where wide access to pooled, shared resources – sequence data and related information – has greatly accelerated biomedical research. Through a complex ecosystem of public funding, agency policy, enabling infrastructure, and communal norms, a practice has emerged in which researchers routinely submit highly valuable sequence and related information to public databases well before publication. As scholars have fruitfully explored, the genomic data commons has evolved from a largely open structure to a more complex governance regime that constrains the use of genomic data to preserve scientific credit and research subject privacy. Notwithstanding these complexities, the genomic data commons reflects the power and potential for widely shared resources to advance productivity.

Upon closer inspection, however, some aspects of the genomic data commons are highly centralized and do not function as a commons at all. Although the Human Genome Project involved large numbers of researchers around the world, it required data release into a synchronized network of three centralized databases. While GenBank receives data from many parties and provides access to the entire scientific community, certain aspects of data control are highly centralized; it is designed so that only original data contributors can modify "their" data records. NCBI has consistently resisted community-based wikification of GenBank, thus preserving the archival nature of data records rather than making them truly open. The evolution of data release policies has limited how researchers can use sequence data, and the structure of GenBank flatly prohibits directly modifying such data, even when it is incorrect. In this fashion, the structure of GenBank propagates a property-like interest on the part of data generators, which seems contrary to the character of a true commons.

At the same time, however, data users have built multiple commons on top of a commons with a proliferation of peer-based wikification, specialized databases, and genome browsers. Harnessing the power of distributed, parallel processing, researchers around the world are adding greater intelligence to existing data records in the form of wiki-based correction, updating, and annotation, and they are making such value-added knowledge widely available to others. Model organism communities are creating their own commons, crafting openly accessible, specialized databases to serve their needs. And innovative users are creating genome browsers and freely distributing them to aid in aggregating and representing enormous amounts of data. This study of the genomic data commons reveals that it actually represents a collection of multiple, overlapping commons operating at several levels.

Along related lines, these multiple commons also reflect a high degree of user innovation (Strandburg 2008, 2009). Users have coordinated formal wikification initiatives such as Gene Wiki as well as more informal annotation "jamborees." Model organism communities have developed specialized databases, combining archival as well as more recent data to advance their research. In doing so, they have created a communal resource with significant spillovers. Similarly, users have developed genome browsers to serve their own needs for enhanced data visualization and analysis, which are now available for all to use. Such user innovations have significantly enhanced the value of the underlying sequence information in the genomic data commons.

Finally, this chapter reveals the enduring importance of standardization and centralization to unleash the creative power of a commons. The commons is lauded for its openness and fluidity, but an effective commons is not a free-for-all where anything goes. Just as a physical commons may benefit from centralized governance

(Rose 1986: 719), the genomic data commons requires some degree of standardization and centralization to function effectively. Community-based wikification represents a powerful resource for annotating genomes, but it requires centralized coordination. Furthermore, the proliferation of model organism databases provides a high degree of specialization for particular communities, but it creates a strong need for an overarching, standardized system for referring to genomic elements to facilitate cross-species comparisons and interoperability. Balance between the competing forces of centralization and fragmentation is critical to effective operation of this commons.

CONCLUSION

The genomic data commons has rightly attracted significant attention both as a formidable resource for advancing biomedical research as well as an exemplar of commons-based management systems. This chapter has built upon prior studies by further applying the IAD framework to assess underappreciated facets of this knowledge commons. In particular, it has focused on annotating, curating, and rendering intelligible the vast amounts of genomic information produced around the world. In some ways, the genomic data commons is highly centralized, with institutionalized data curation and exclusive authorial rights in GenBank data records. In other ways, the genomic data commons is actually a metacommons in which communal annotation and curation help enhance the value of communally accessible data. In an innovative fashion, users have developed specialized databases and genome browsers to draw from and build upon centralized resources, thus exploiting the inherent nonrivalry of information to render genomic data more intelligible. These dynamics have enormous practical impact, for it is only by transforming data to information to knowledge that the promise of the Human Genome Project and its progeny will be fully realized. More broadly, these dynamics reflect that massively fragmented productivity must be subject to some level of centralized coordination to maximize the creative potential of a commons.

REFERENCES

Benkler, Yochai, *The Wealth of Networks* (Yale University Press 2006).

Benson, Dennis A. et al., GenBank, 42 *Nucleic Acids Res.* D32 (2014).

Bidartondo, M. I. et al., Preserving Accuracy in GenBank, 319 *Science* 1616 (2008).

Bridge, Paul D. et al., On the Unreliability of Published DNA Sequences, 160 *New Phytologist* 43 (2003).

Cariaso, Michael, and Greg Lennon, SNPedia: A Wiki Supporting Personal Genome Annotation, Interpretation, and Analysis, 40 *Nucleic Acids Res.* D1308 (2011).

Chu, James C. et al., The Emerging World of Wikis, 320 *Science* 1289 (2008).

Claverie, Jean-Michel, Do We Need a Huge New Centre to Annotate the Human Genome? 403 *Nature* 12 (2000).

Cline, Melissa S. and W. James Kent, Understanding Genome Browsing, 2 *Nature Biotechnology* 153 (2009).

Contreras, Jorge L., Prepublication Data Release, Latency, and Genome Commons, 329 *Science* 393 (2010).

Contreras, Jorge L., Bermuda's Legacy: Policy, Patents and the Design of the Genome Commons, 12 *Minnesota J.L. Sci. & Tech.* 1 (2011).

Contreras, Jorge L., Technical Standards and Bioinformatics, in *Bioinformatics Law: Legal Issues for Computational Biology in the Post-Genome Era* (Jorge L. Contreras and A. James Cuticchia eds., ABA Book Publishing 2013).

Contreras, Jorge L., Constructing the Genome Commons, *in Governing Knowledge Commons* (Brett M. Frischmann, Michael J. Madison, and Katherine J. Strandburg eds., Oxford University Press 2014).

Dagan, Hanoch and Michael A. Heller, The Liberal Commons, 110 *Yale L.J.* 549 (2001).

Daub, Jennifer et al., The RNA WikiProject: Community Annotation of RNA Families, 14 *RNA* 1 (2008).

Dennis, Carina, Draft Guidelines Ease Restrictions on Use of Genome Sequence Data, 421 *Nature* 877 (2003).

Dept. of Energy, Summary of Principles Agreed Upon at the First International Strategy Meeting on Human Genome Sequencing (Bermuda, 25–28 February 1996) as Reported by HUGO, http://web.ornl.gov/sci/techresources/Human_Genome/research/bermuda.shtml

Eisenberg, Rebecca S., Genomics in the Public Domain: Strategy and Policy, 1 *Nature Rev. Genetics* 70 (2000).

Eisenberg, Rebecca S., Patents and Data-Sharing in Public Science, 15 *Indus. & Corp. Change* 1013 (2006).

Field, Dawn and Susanna-Assunta Sansone, A Special Issue on Data Standards, 10 *OMICS* 84 (2006).

Frischmann, Brett M., *Infrastructure: The Social Value of Shared Resources* (Oxford University Press 2012).

Frischmann, Brett M. et al., Governing Knowledge Commons, in *Governing Knowledge Commons* (Brett M. Frischmann, Michael J. Madison, and Katherine J. Strandburg eds., Oxford University Press 2014).

Furey, Terrence S., Comparison of Human (and Other) Genome Browsers, 2 *Hum. Genomics* 266 (2006).

Galperin, Michael Y. and Xose M. Fernandez-Suarez, The 2012 Nucleic Acids Research Database Issue and the Online Molecular Database Collection, 40 *Nucleic Acids Res.* D1 (2012).

Genetic Assoc. Info. Network (GAIN), Data Use Certification Agreement (March 1, 2010), https://dbgap.ncbi.nlm.nih.gov/aa/wga.cgi?view_pdf&stacc=phs000016.v1.p1.

Howe, Doug et al., The Future of Biocuration, 455 *Nature* 47 (2008).

Hubbard, Tim and Ewan Birney, Open Annotation Offers a Democratic Solution to Genome Sequencing, 403 *Nature* 825 (2000).
Huss, Jon W. III et al., A Gene Wiki for Community Annotation of Gene Function, 6 *PLoS Biology* 1398 (2008).
It's Not About the Data, 2 *Nature Genetics* 111 (2012).
Kaye, Jane, The Tension between Data Sharing and the Protection of Privacy in Genomics Research, 13 *Ann. Rev. Genomics & Hum. Genetics* 415 (2012).
Kuhn, Thomas, *The Structure of Scientific Revolutions* (University of Chicago Press 1962).
Lathe, Warren C. III et al., Genomic Data Resources: Challenges and Promises, 2 *Nature Educ.* 1 (2008).
Lee, Peter, Transcending the Tacit Dimension, 100 *California L. Rev.* 1503 (2012).
Lemoine, Frederic et al., GenoQuery: A New Querying Module for Functional Annotation in a Genomic Warehouse, 24 *Bioinformatics* i322 (2008).
Machlup, Fritz, Semantic Quirks in Studies of Information, in *The Study of Information: Interdisciplinary Messages* (Fritz Machlup and Una Mansfield eds., Wiley 1983).
Madison, Michael J. et al., Constructing Commons in the Cultural Environment, 95 *Cornell L. Rev.* 657 (2010).
Marshall, Eliot, DNA Sequencer Protests Being Scooped with His Own Data, 295 *Science* 1206 (2002).
McGuire, Amy L. et al., Ethical, Legal, and Social Considerations in Conducting the Human Microbiome Project, 18 *Genome Res.* 1861 (2008).
Mons, Barend et al., Calling on a Million Minds for Community Annotation in Wiki Proteins, 9 *Genome Biology* R. 89 (2008).
Nat'l Human Genome Res. Inst., Current NHGRI Policy for Release and Data Deposit of Sequence Data (March 7, 1997), https://www.genome.gov/10000910#old.
Nat'l Human Genome Res. Inst., NHGRI Policy for Release and Database Deposition of Sequence Data (Dec. 21, 2000), www.genome.gov/pfv.cfm?pageID=10000910
Nat'l Human Genome Res. Inst., Reaffirmation and Extension of NHGRI Rapid Data Release Policies: Large-Scale Sequencing and Other Community Resource Projects (Feb. 2003), www.genome.gov/pfv.cfm?pageID=10506537
Nat'l Inst. of Health, Policy for Sharing of Data Obtained in NIH Supported or Conducted Genome-Wide Association Studies (GWAS) (Aug. 28, 2007), http://grants.nih.gov/grants/guide/notice-files/NOT-OD-07–088.html
Nat'l Inst. of Health, HMP Data Release and Resource Sharing Guidelines for Human Microbiome Project Data Production Grants (last updated Aug 27, 2013), http://commonfund.nih.gov/hmp/datareleaseguidelines
Nat'l Inst. of Health, Final NIH Genomic Data Sharing Policy, 79 *Fed. Reg.* 51345 (Aug. 28, 2014).
Nat'l Inst. of Health and Dept. of Energy, Guidelines for Access to Mapping and Sequence Data and Material Resources (1991), www.genome.gov/10000925.
Nat'l Res. Council, Mapping and Sequencing the Human Genome (1988).

Nelson, F. Kenneth et al., Introduction and Historical Overview of DNA Sequencing, *Current Protocols in Molecular Biology*, 7.0.1 (Oct. 2011).
Nilsson, R. Henrik et al., Taxonomic Reliability of DNA Sequences in Public Sequence Databases: A Fungal Perspective, 1 *PLoS One* e59 (2006).
OECD, Data-Driven Innovation: Big Data for Growth and Well-Being (2015).
Ostrom, Elinor and Charlotte Hess, A Framework for Analyzing the Knowledge Commons, in *Understanding Knowledge as a Commons: From Theory to Practice* (Charlotte Hess and Elinor Ostrom eds., MIT Press 2007).
Pennisi, Elizabeth, Keeping Genome Databases Clean and Up to Date, 289 *Science* 447 (1999).
Pennisi, Elizabeth, Proposal to "Wikify" GenBank Meets Stiff Resistance, 319 *Science* 1598 (2008).
Pennisi, Elizabeth, Group Calls for Rapid Release of More Genomics Data, 324 *Science* 1000 (2009).
Price, W. Nicholson II, Unblocked Future: Why Gene Patents Won't Hinder Whole Genome Sequencing and Personalized Medicine, 33 *Cardozo L. Rev.* 1601 (2012).
Pruitt, Kim D. et al., NCBI Reference Sequences (RefSeq): Current Status, New Features and Genome Annotation Policy, 40 *Nucleic Acids Res.* D130 (2012).
Raymond, Eric S., *The Cathedral and the Bazaar* (O'Reilly Media, Inc. 1999).
Rose, Carol, The Comedy of the Commons: Custom, Commerce, and Inherently Public Property, 53 *U. Chicago L. Rev.* 711 (1986).
Salimi, Nima, and Randi Vita, The Biocurator: Connecting and Enhancing Scientific Data, 2 *PLoS Computational Biology* 1190 (2006).
Salzberg, Steven L., Genome Re-annotation: A Wiki Solution, 8 *Genome Biology* 102 (2007).
Sanger, F. et al., DNA Sequencing with Chain-Terminating Inhibitors, 74 *Proc. Nat'l Acad. Sci.* 5463 (1977).
Smith, Henry E., Semicommon Property Rights and Scattering in the Open Fields, 29 *J. Leg. Stud.* 131 (2000).
Smith, Henry E., Exclusion versus Governance: Two Strategies for Delineating Property Rights, 31 *J. Leg. Stud.* S453 (2002).
Standardizing Data (Editorial), 10 *Nature Cell Biology* 1123 (2008).
Stehr, Henning et al., PDBWiki: Added Value through Community Annotation of the Protein Data Bank, 1 *Database* (2010).
Stein, Lincoln, Genome Annotation: From Sequence to Biology, 2 *Nature Rev. Genetics* 493 (2001).
Strandburg, Katherine J., Users as Innovators: Implications for Patent Doctrine, 79 *U. Colo. L. Rev.* 467 (2008).
Strandburg, Katherine J., User Innovator Community Norms: At the Boundary between Academic and Industry Research, 77 *Fordham L. Rev.* 2237 (2009).
Strandburg, Katherine J. et al., The Rare Diseases Clinical Research Network and the Urea Cycle Disorders Consortium as Nested Knowledge Commons, in *Governing Knowledge Commons* (Brett M. Frischmann, Michael J. Madison, and Katherine J. Strandburg eds., Oxford University Press 2014).

Strasser, Bruno J., GenBank – Natural History in the 21st Century? 322 *Science* 537 (2008).

The 1000 Genomes Project Consortium, A Map of Human Genome Variation from Population-Scale Sequencing, 467 *Nature* 1061 (2010).

The Gene Ontology Consortium, Gene Ontology: Tool for the Unification of Biology, 24 *Nature Genetics* 24 (2000).

The Wellcome Trust, Sharing Data from Large-Scale Biological Research Projects: A System of Tripartite Responsibility 2 (2003), www.genome.gov/pages/research/wellcomereport0303.pdf

Van Overwalle, Geertrui, Governing Genomic Data: Plea for an "Open Commons," in *Governing Knowledge Commons* (Brett M. Frischmann, Michael J. Madison, and Katherine J. Strandburg eds., Oxford University Press 2014).

von Hippel, Eric, The Dominant Role of Users in the Scientific Instrument Innovation Process, 5 *Res. Policy* 212 (1976).

Waldrop, Mitch, Wikiomics, 455 *Nature* 22 (2008).

Walsh, John P. et al., Effects of Research Tool Patents and Licensing on Biomedical Innovation, in *Patents in the Knowledge-Based Economy* (Wesley M. Cohen and Stephen A. Merrill eds., National Academies Press 2003).

4

Genomic Data Commons

Barbara J. Evans

INTRODUCTION

Understanding the clinical impact of genetic variants is one of the grand scientific challenges of the twenty-first century. A typical person has around 3 to 3.5 million variants, or little changes that distinguish the individual's genome from an idealized human reference genome (Kohane et al. 2012; US Dep't of HHS/FDA 2014c). The role, if any, that most variants play in human health has not yet been discovered. As many as half a million of a person's detected variants may be novel or at least rare (Kohane et al. 2012), which means scientists may have had little opportunity to study the variants and infer their effects on health.

A 2014 study concluded that fewer than 200 variants were well enough understood at that time to merit further scrutiny for potential medical significance after a person undergoes genomic testing (Dewey et al. 2014). As for the rest of the variants that a test detects, their clinical validity is uncertain or unknown. Clinical validity "addresses whether there is a strong and well validated association between having a particular gene variant and having a particular health condition and whether knowing that a person has the gene variant offers meaningful insight into the person's health or reproductive risks" (Secretary's Advisory Committee on Genetic Testing 2000). Once a variant has an "established" clinical meaning, a test that detects that variant is said to have clinical validity for purposes of diagnosing the associated health condition (Fabsitz et al. 2010).

Modern genomic tests provide a practical way to identify the many genetic variants that people have, but interpreting the meaning of those variants depends on an external body of knowledge: cumulative discoveries about the associations between genotype (the specific gene variants a person has) and phenotype (physical characteristics in which those gene variants may have played a role). For most of the

Barbara J. Evans is Alumnae College Professor of Law and Director of the Center for Biotechnology and Law at the University of Houston Law Center, Houston, Texas, and is Professor of Electrical and Computer Engineering at the Cullen College of Engineering, University of Houston, Houston, Texas.
This work received support from NIH/NHGRI/NCI grants U01HG006507 and U01HG007307 and from the Robert Wood Johnson Foundation's Health Data Exploration Project (K. Patrick, PI), with additional support provided by NIH/NHGRI awards R01HG008918 and R01HG008605.

variants that tests can detect, the tests lack clinical validity because these associations are not yet known.

This chapter focuses on genomic tests, which differ both in technology and in scale from the traditional genetic tests of the past. Traditional genetic tests – including many still used today – typically focus on one or a few specific genes and are designed to detect a predetermined list of variants that were known in advance to be pathogenic – that is, variants already known to have a negative impact on health (US Dep't of HHS/FDA 2014c). Polymerase chain reaction (PCR) and single-nucleotide polymorphism (SNP) arrays are examples of these older genetic-testing technologies. In contrast, genomic tests include next generation sequencing (NGS) assays that can detect any variant present in a specific group of genes; whole genome sequencing (WGS) tests that detect variants in virtually the entirety of a person's genome; whole exome sequencing (WES) tests that detect variants in the roughly 1.5 percent of the genome that contains the person's genes; and copy number variant arrays (Evans, Burke, and Jarvik 2015).

The US Food and Drug Administration (FDA) notes that genomic tests can produce large volumes of information that may include novel variants never seen before and variants that, while previously seen in other people, have unknown clinical impact (US Dep't of HHS/FDA 2014c). This state of affairs creates concern about the safety of patients, research subjects, and other consumers (together, "consumers") who undergo genomic testing. The FDA has expressed concern that consumers may pursue irreversible medical treatments – such as prophylactic surgeries to mitigate a suspected susceptibility to cancer – based on findings that later prove to have lacked any clinical validity (US Dep't of HHS/FDA 2014a). Late in 2014, the agency sought comments on two Draft Guidances that proposed to regulate laboratory developed tests (LDTs) as medical devices; doing so would reverse a long-standing policy of using FDA's enforcement discretion to avoid regulating most LDTs (US Dep't of HHS/FDA 2014a, 2014b). FDA ultimately chose not to finalize the Draft Guidances, but identified a set of unresolved issues likely to reemerge as focuses of FDA regulatory attention in the future.

The two Draft Guidances defined a test's safety and effectiveness in terms of two parameters: analytic validity (whether the test accurately detects the variants it purports to detect) and clinical validity (whether the detected variants have a well-established association with specific clinical conditions that can be diagnosed or predicted based on the test results) (US Dep't of HHS/FDA 2014a). It was apparent that FDA's traditional premarket review process for medical devices was not well suited to the task of evaluating the safety and effectiveness of genomic tests: how can test sponsors be required to prove – in advance – the clinical validity of the many millions of genetic variants that a test may detect, when the full range of variants that exists in the human population only becomes known after the test is approved and moves into wide clinical use?

In response to this dilemma, FDA published a discussion paper proposing to rely on high-quality, curated genetic databases to establish the clinical validity of genomic tests (US Dep't of HHS/FDA 2014c). This approach would draw on an external body of cumulative knowledge – all that is known about the genome, as reflected in well-curated, external databases at any given time – rather than requiring test manufacturers to generate from scratch the entire body of evidence needed to support FDA's review of a new test. The agency convened a workshop in February 2015 to discuss this proposal and subsequently held two further public workshops in November 2015 to explore analytical performance standards for NGS tests and ways to harness databases to ensure their clinical validity (US Dep't of HHS/FDA 2015c, 2015d).

As FDA and other policymakers continue to develop approaches for regulating genomic tests, one thing seems clear: to make genomic testing safe and effective for consumers, it will be necessary to develop large-scale genomic data resources. This chapter draws on the work of Elinor Ostrom to explore whether the human genome can be modeled as a common-pool resource (CPR). It concludes that this analogy is strong, at least at this time. The strength of the analogy may, however, be an artifact of the technologies – and the costs of those technologies – currently used to test the human genome. So long as the CPR analogy remains apt – and it may remain so for a period of years or even decades – lessons learned in managing other types of CPRs may shed light on how best to organize collective efforts to create and sustain genomic data resources and help maximize their productivity in terms of new discoveries and clinically useful insights that improve human health.

4.1 THE HUMAN GENOME AS A NATURAL RESOURCE

Ostrom warned about the perils of using natural resource commons as an analogy for unrelated phenomena (Ostrom 1990), yet the human genome is a natural resource in a very real sense. Like all other natural resources, the human genome is "found in nature and is necessary or useful to humans" (American Heritage Science Dictionary 2005). Naturally occurring gene sequences are not "made by man" but rather are "manifestations of . . . nature," akin to a "new mineral discovered in the earth or a new plant found in the wild" (*Diamond v. Chakrabarty*, 447 US 303, 309 (1980); *Funk Brothers Seed Co. v. Kalo Inoculant Co.*, 333 US 127, 130 (1948)). The Supreme Court's 2013 decision in *Association for Molecular Pathology (AMP) v. Myriad Genetics* rightly characterized isolated gene sequences as non-patentable subject matter because they are products of nature (133 S.Ct. 2107 (2013)). Medical genetics can be modeled as an extractive industry that creates infrastructure – such as genomic testing instruments, laboratories, databases, and computer algorithms – to mine these natural resources and process the extracted raw commodity (information about the specific genetic variants detected in tested individuals) into useful products and services that improve human health (Evans 2014a).

The fact that the human genome is a natural resource does not necessarily imply it is a CPR, as conceptualized in Ostrom's work (Ostrom 1990: 30). The relevant aspect of a CPR, for the present discussion, is that it is a resource system whose ultimate productivity can be optimized through coordinated action and sound governance. In the classic CPR context, the natural resources include fisheries, mineral deposits, or grazing areas – some renewable, some nonrenewable, depending on whether they can be replenished on a time scale relevant to humans. These resources are subject to congestion or depletion, and careful coordination is needed to manage those problems. In the genomic context, the challenge is somewhat different: coordination is necessary in order to create data infrastructures that make it possible to extract useful knowledge by testing people's genomes. People have a vast supply of copies of their own genomes, which are replicated in every one of the cells of their bodies, but extracting useful information from this raw genetic material requires coordination with other people.

Ostrom defines a resource system as a stock that is "capable, under favorable conditions, of producing a maximum quantity of a flow variable without harming the stock or the resource system itself" (Ostrom 1990: 30). As users appropriate "resource units" – for example, by harvesting fish from a fishery or withdrawing oil from a reservoir – their actions may affect the ultimate productivity of the resource system itself, for example, by collapsing the sustainability of a renewable system or by failing to optimize the total recovery from a nonrenewable one. When multiple individuals or firms jointly use a resource system, failure to coordinate their activities may diminish the ultimate flow of beneficial resource units for all. This aspect of CPR systems is highly relevant to genomics.

The unique genomes buried beneath the skins of human beings are a stock that can yield a flow of valuable resource units, but only in an environment of sustainable knowledge and data sharing. Individuals who undergo genomic testing – assuming each person acts in isolation and no data sharing occurs – would learn the configuration of nucleotides in their respective genomes, but they would have no basis to infer what this configuration implies about their present and future health. These latter inferences – in other words, useful knowledge about the clinical meaning of particular genetic variants – can only be made by pooling genetic and other types of health data for large samples of the human population and then drawing statistical inferences based on which variants and health conditions appear to occur together in the same individuals: for example, people with genetic variant X also tend to manifest disease Y, whereas the people without variant X seem not to develop disease Y as often.

The valuable resource units in genomics are discoveries establishing the clinical validity of specific gene variants, as well as clinically useful individual diagnoses based on those discoveries. Humankind's collective stock of genomic material is a natural resource, but extracting value from it requires data infrastructure to study additional variants beyond those understood today. Each statistically valid inference that uncovers a new association between a specific gene variant and a specific health condition is one resource unit, in Ostrom's terminology. The number and pace of these discoveries can be maximized under favorable conditions. What are those conditions, and can Ostrom's work on other types of CPRs help identify them?

In principle, the genomic resource system that can be studied includes the genomes of all living people plus any deceased individuals for which genomic data (or biospecimens that could be tested to derive genomic data) still exist (Evans 2014a). In practice, genomes become part of the useable resource system only when people undergo genomic testing. Testing is the act that causes a person's variants to come to light, like gold nuggets uncovered in the sand, so that their possible clinical impacts can be explored. Most people living in the early twenty-first century will never undergo genomic testing. As of 2014, only about 228,000 human genomes had been fully or partly sequenced worldwide, mostly in research settings because genomic testing has only recently begun to move into wider clinical use (Regalado 2014). The Precision Medicine Initiative announced by President Obama early in 2015 envisions testing a 1-million-person cohort of volunteers (The White House 2015; Collins and Varmus 2015). One million is an impressive figure but still a mere 14 thousandths of 1 percent of the entire human population. Shirts et al. (2014) note that many of the genetic variants detected during evaluations of familial cancer risk have uncertain clinical significance, and very large sample sizes – hundreds of thousands to millions of individuals – may be required to ascertain the impact of these variants.

Discovering the clinical significance of not-yet-understood gene variants will require a much larger data infrastructure than exists today. The requisite data resources would include genome sequencing data for very large samples of the human population along with detailed phenotypic information – that is, data reflecting their past and present health conditions, environmental exposures, and lifestyle habits (Evans, Burke, and Jarvik 2015). These data resources must be large scale (in the sense of including data for many individuals) and deeply descriptive (in the sense of containing much or all of the available health-related information for each of them) (Evans 2016a).

Public research budgets – that is, funds available from governmental agencies such as the National Institutes of Health and its counterparts in other nations – will not suffice to sequence the needed number of genomes. The genomic data resource system needs to capture not just the genomes tested under grants of NIH research funding (Evans 2016a). It also needs to include genomes sequenced in clinical settings as part of regular health care financed by public and private payers such as Medicare and health insurers, as payers begin covering clinical genomic testing (Evans 2016a). Also important – potentially, very important – are the direct-to-consumer genomic test results of financially capable, curious consumers who take matters into their own hands when payers fail to cover the genomic tests consumers need or desire. These respective data streams are under radically different legal and regulatory regimes: federal research regulations and privacy laws for data generated during research; federal privacy law and a web of state privacy and medical records laws for the clinical data; and corporate privacy policies, including click-through contractual agreements, and state laws that address access to data from direct-to-consumer personal health services (Evans 2016a).

The resource units to be extracted from this resource system include both broadly generalizable knowledge such as discoveries about the clinical impact of a human gene variant, as well as context-specific insights that improve the well-being of individuals (e.g., a more accurate interpretation of one patient's genomic test) (OECD 2015: 29). This distinction is expressed in US regulations as the difference between generalizable knowledge that has the potential to benefit many people in the future ("research") versus patient-specific inferences drawn during clinical care ("treatment") (see, e.g., 45 C.F.R. § 164.501). Extracting value from this resource system involves four basic steps: (1) conducting individual genomic tests to detect which variants each individual has; (2) linking each tested individual's genomic data to detailed phenotypic information such as longitudinal health records from the person's encounters with the health care system as well as available environmental and lifestyle data, such as data from wearable fitness sensing devices; (3) pooling these linked genomic and health records for large populations of individuals; and (4) searching for statistically significant associations between specific gene variants and specific health conditions.

In step 1, NGS tests are an efficient way to identify the range of genetic variants each individual carries. While the cost of gene sequencing has dropped significantly in recent years, the cost of NGS testing is still high enough that, at this time, a person whose genetic variants are detected by one laboratory is unlikely to repeat the testing at a different laboratory (Evans 2014a). In this respect, genomic testing differs from blood typing and many other common diagnostic tests that are easily repeated whenever a different physician or researcher needs to know the same information. This fact may change over time as the cost of gene sequencing drops, but, for now, a laboratory that detects a person's variants in effect captures the resulting information.

Individual genomic test results – or more precisely, opportunities to conduct genomic testing – are, in effect, a nonrenewable resource: production of a person's gene variant data by one laboratory effectively precludes production of those same data by a different laboratory. A vast collective human gene pool consists of two unique genomes (one from mom, one from dad) for each member of the human species. When a laboratory tests an individual, it appropriates that person's genomic information, which is unlikely ever to be sampled again. Thereafter, the person's genomic information is unavailable for others to study unless shared beyond the initial laboratory.

This remains true even in clinical settings, where a physician orders genomic testing to guide a patient's health care. Clinical laboratories typically report only a tiny fraction of the variants genomic tests identify back to the physician for inclusion in the patient's medical record. Yet the testing generates a massive amount of underlying data that, once generated, could be reused, repurposed, copied, and/or shared at a relatively modest marginal cost. The marginal cost of data sharing is not, however, zero (Evans 2014b). It includes various items that HIPAA characterizes as costs of "data preparation and transmittal" (42 U.S.C. § 17935(d)(2)(B); 45 C.F.R. § 164.502(a)(5)(ii)(B)(2)(ii)). Examples include the costs of paying skilled personnel and tying up capital (such as information systems and software) to locate data responsive to a particular request; to convert those data into a consistent, machine-readable format that allows information from one source to be compared with data from external sources; to comply with legal and regulatory requirements, such as review by an Institutional Review Board, that may be necessary to effect a lawful data transfer, and to convey the data securely to the requesting party (Evans 2014b). The fact that the marginal costs of data preparation and transmittal are nonzero has important implications for the development of large-scale genomic data resources. It means that designing a workable revenue model is essential to the task of developing sustainable genomic data resources, as discussed further later, in Section 4.4.

As for the types of "underlying" data that may be on file at a genomic testing laboratory, the initial step of genome sequencing produces image files and base call (BCL) files. These files are so large that laboratories process them in real time and almost immediately discard them because of data storage constraints (Evans et al. 2014). The follow-on data analysis generates, in order: (1) FASTQ files containing raw sequences for fragments of the person's genome, along with quality scores bearing on how reliable the information is; (2) BAM (binary alignment/map) files that map these raw sequences onto the reference human genome; and (3) a VCF (variant call format) file that summarizes the individual's sequence variants, sorted by their positions in the genome (Evans et al., 2014). Only a handful of the variants in the VCF file will have a known relevance to the particular medical condition that caused the patient to undergo genomic testing. Laboratories typically interpret only the medically relevant variants for reporting to the physician and patient. The remaining variants – 3 million or so in a patient undergoing whole genome sequencing – often remain in the laboratory's files. Clinical laboratories are subject to data retention requirements under the Clinical Laboratory Improvement Amendments of 1988 (CLIA) (42 U.S.C. § 263a; 42 C.F.R. § 493.1105). There are no direct regulatory instructions on how to apply these requirements to the various files genomic testing generates, but recent studies recommend retaining a patient's VCF file and – if storage permits – the BAM and FASTQ files (Gargis et al. 2012; Rehm et al. 2013).

To extract resource units (discoveries) from these individual genomic data files, they would need to be linked to the person's other health data (step 2 of the discovery process) and studied alongside similar records for many other individuals (steps 3 and 4). This second step – linking an individual's data files that have been stored by multiple data holders – requires at least some identifying information to verify that the files being linked all relate to the same individual (Evans 2011: 93–94). The need for identifiers potentially adds to the transaction cost of assembling genomic data resources because, under the existing US federal regulations discussed in the next section, the sharing of identifiers may trigger the need to procure individual informed consents and/or privacy authorizations before data holders can share data (see discussion infra later in Section 4.2). If an individual's FASTQ, BAM, and VCF files stay siloed at the clinical laboratory that ran the test, their full scientific value cannot be harvested. Fragmentation of genomic and health care data resources creates dilemmas that threaten to impede or block genomic discovery if collective action fails.

4.2 THE DATA ACCESS CHALLENGE

The existence of stored genomic and clinical data offers a major opportunity to develop immensely valuable public infrastructure in the form of large-scale data resources to support new discoveries about the clinical significance of human gene variants. There are, however, a number of barriers and obstacles to overcome – most notably, collective action and governance dilemmas that bear a familial resemblance to CPR and other shared resource contexts.

At present, each patient's data – any available genomic test results as well as other health records – are scattered among many data holders such as physicians, hospitals, laboratories, and insurers with which the person has done business. Recent efforts to promote interoperable electronic health records have not injected order or consistency. The President's Council of Advisors on Science and Technology (P-CAST), surveying the situation in 2010, despaired that a standard data format would ever emerge: "Any attempt to create a national health IT ecosystem based on standardized record formats is doomed to failure . . . With so many vested interests behind each historical system of recording health data, achieving a natural consolidation around one record format . . . would be difficult, if not impossible" (P-CAST 2010: 39). Even if data holders shared a common data format that enabled them to communicate with one another, they often do not want to do so: a study funded by the National Human Genome Research Institute surveyed a diverse group of genomics industry insiders who ranked data holders' resistance to data sharing as the most important but least tractable policy challenge (McGuire et al. 2016).

Health data sharing has been characterized as a tragedy of the anticommons (Hall 2010; Rodwin 2010). Rodwin adds that, in reality, there are two distinct tragedies: the first reflects the fragmentation of genomic and other health data resources at the level of institutional and commercial data holders, such as hospitals, laboratories, and research institutions. The second tragedy unfolds at the level of individual patients and consumers, who can block the sharing of their data under a web of privacy and human subject protection regulations that, in many instances, condition data access on individual consent (Rodwin 2010: 606). This two-tiered tragedy of the anticommons is the challenge to be overcome.

Individual / Data holder	consents to data use	consent not available
willing to share data	**Quadrant 1** Data accessible for the use	**Quadrant 2** No access unless use fits in consent exception.
not willing to share data	**Quadrant 3** Individual's wish to share data is thwarted, without access-forcing mechanism	**Quadrant 4** Data not accessible unless law requires access (e.g., public health, judicial subpoena)

FIGURE 4.1 The challenge of access to commercially held clinical data (adapted from Evans 2016a: 668, Figure 1).

Elsewhere, I have analyzed this problem using the analytical framework for governing knowledge commons outlined by Frischmann, Madison, and Strandburg (2014). Key points can be summarized as follows: there have been persistent calls for individual ownership of health data, but the legal reality is that neither the individual nor the data holder has exclusive ownership of stored health data; the two parties share control (Evans 2016a: 661–64; OECD 2015). Their shared control creates four possible pathways for assembling large-scale data resources, as portrayed in Figure 4.1.

In the best of all possible data-sharing worlds, there would be consent alignment, with the individual and the data holder both willing to share data (see Quadrant 1 in Figure 4.1). Both parties would facilitate flows of data to create a national genomic infrastructure. In theory, consent alignment could arise spontaneously or, perhaps, in response to educational stimuli such as a public information campaign highlighting the many benefits that large data resources could offer. To date, however, consent alignment has not emerged in our society at the level required to create multi-million-person genomic data resources. A variant of Quadrant 1 is incentivized consent alignment, in which a fiscally empowered entity – such as a government or a public research funding agency – uses conditional grants (offers of money that are contingent on the recipients' agreement to share data). Related options would be to create tax incentives for data sharing or to condition a desired benefit (such as an FDA approval or a Medicare reimbursement) on data sharing (Evans 2016a: 18).

The National Institutes of Health (NIH) and research funding agencies in other nations have made effective use of conditional spending and have fostered data sharing through policies that obligate grantee research organizations to deposit certain kinds of data generated using grant funds into shared databases (Contreras 2014; Evans et al. 2015). Examples of this approach include the genomic data resources curated by NIH's ClinGen program and deposited in ClinVar (Rehm et al. 2015). Depositing de-identified data does not require consent of the individual research subjects under current regulations; when identifiable data do need to be shared, the requisite consents can be obtained at the time individuals consent more broadly to participate in the grant-funded research. Another example of incentivized consent alignment is the million-person research cohort under President Obama's Precision Medicine Initiative, later renamed the NIH All of Us research program, which envisions using a combination of conditional NIH grants to secure cooperation of data-holding research institutions and individual consents/privacy authorization from a cohort of volunteers (Patil, Williams, and Devaney 2016).

Publicly funded efforts of this sort have launched the long process of developing national genomic data infrastructure, but they are costly and ultimately not scalable to the task of creating several-hundred-million-person genomic data infrastructures (Evans 2016a: 19). To date, the genomic data resources assembled using incentivized consent alignment are small in two respects: first, they include data for only a sliver of the genetic variants that the included individuals have. The NIH ClinVar database just described only holds variants of interest – that is, specific variants that were the focus of a research study or that were related to a disease that led a doctor to order genomic testing. Many and indeed most of the detected variants – such as the variants recorded in individuals' entire VCF files – are not reported. Existing data resources illuminate small, already explored spaces of the human genome but do little to illuminate the vast dark spaces beyond.

A second problem is that the existing databases are small in the sense of not including data for many people. The FDA's 2014 discussion paper on NGS proposed the use of databases, including the one "curated by NIH's ClinGen program and deposited in ClinVar," to infer the clinical validity of genomic tests (US Dep't of HHS/FDA 2014c). As of November 2015, despite rapid progress, ClinVar only contained about 130,000 variants that had interpretations of their clinical significance (US Dep't of HHS/FDA 2015d: 27). For some of those variants, the available "interpretation" consists of a statement that the variant's clinical significance is unknown (Rehm et al. 2015). To reflect a truly large sample of the population, it ultimately will be necessary to harness data from clinical genetic testing as well as from research studies. The NIH policies that incentivize deposits of data into ClinGen and ClinVar are mandatory only with respect to research data generated using NIH funds. Some commercial clinical laboratories voluntarily contribute data about variants they detect in the course of conducting clinical genomic tests, but others decline to contribute (Evans et al. 2015).

Even if all available genomic data were reported into shared data resources such as ClinVar, the reality is that genomic data – by themselves – are of limited scientific use unless detailed phenotypic data also are available for the same individuals. "Making discoveries" means inferring verifiable associations between gene variants and health conditions, and verifiability means not only that the final scientific conclusion is shared – for example, by sharing a finding that a specific genotype-phenotype association has been detected. It also means that the underlying data that supports the conclusion is available for further inspection and analysis (Cook-Deegan et al. 2013; National Research Council 2003). Existing genomic data commons such as ClinVar typically do not capture detailed phenotypic data, such as a patient's longitudinal health record or information about lifestyle and environmental factors. Such data would need to come from clinical health care providers, insurers, fitness device manufacturers, and others beyond the reach of NIH's funding incentives. Moreover, patients would need to consent to the sharing of their entire health histories. Research participants may be willing to allow sharing of specific research data when consenting to a specific research project, but many if not most people would balk at consenting to share their entire cradle-to-grave health histories as a condition of participating in a research project.

4.3 WHEN CONSENT ALIGNMENT FAILS

Consent alignment can fail in three ways, if either the individual or the data holder is reluctant to share data or perhaps both are unwilling to share (Evans 2016a: 669–74). This section explores existing regulatory and legal pathways that help foster data sharing in these situations. It also identifies key limitations of these approaches.

Quadrant 2 of Figure 4.1 portrays the situation wherein a data holder is willing to share data in its possession, but the data pertains to an individual who does not wish to share (or perhaps cannot be located at the time consent is needed). The Health Insurance Portability and Accountability Act of 1996 (HIPAA, Pub. L. No. 104–191, 1996) Privacy Rule (45 C.F.R. pts. 160, 164) provides pathways that enable sharing data in this situation. The Privacy Rule has various exceptions to its baseline requirement that individuals must authorize disclosures of their data. One of the exceptions is that data holders may share de-identified data without the individual's authorization (45 C.F.R. § 164.502(d)(2)). Data holders also do not need individual authorization to supply data for use by public health authorities (45 C.F.R. § 164.512(b)(1)(i)). The Privacy Rule also has a waiver provision that lets an Institutional Review Board or Privacy Board (together, IRB) approve the sharing of data for use in research without individual authorization (45 C.F.R. § 164.512(i)).

The Common Rule (45 C.F.R. pt. 46) governs federally funded research and, at some academic institutions, covers all of their research, including privately funded studies. The Common Rule has a waiver mechanism (45 C.F.R. § 46.116(d) of the current regulation that is functionally similar to the one in the HIPAA Privacy Rule. The Common Rule also has definitional nuances that mimic HIPAA's pathways for supplying data, without consent, in de-identified form or for use in some types of public health activities (Evans 2011). The FDA research regulations (21 C.F.R. pts. 50, 56), which apply mainly to commercial research that aims to develop new medical products, resemble the Common Rule in many respects but, importantly, lack a waiver provision. When regulations allow consent waivers or other exceptions to individual consent, these provisions facilitate data sharing in the Quadrant 2 situation. A willing data holder, using these provisions, may contribute data into the genomic data commons on its own initiative, without individual consent.

In the past, these regulatory mechanisms have provided workable access to data for research and public health. Large data holders such as insurers and hospitals often possess data for hundreds, thousands, or even millions of individuals. The regulatory consent exceptions empower data holders to overcome the collective action problems that otherwise would exist at the level of individuals. Each data holder can act as an aggregator of a large data set that includes all of the individuals with which the data holder does business, and the data holder becomes a single point of contact for those seeking data access. The regulatory consent exceptions spell out a narrow set of circumstances (e.g., de-identification of data, public health uses of data, and IRB-approved waivers for research) in which the data holder is granted discretion to share data without individual consents or privacy authorizations. These regulations enable a scheme of data-holder-driven access, in which data holders are the prime movers in assembling large-scale data resources for research and public health.

A classic example data-holder-driven access is FDA's Mini-Sentinel/Sentinel System, which has been extensively described in the past and is covered in Ryan Abbott's chapter in this volume (Chapter 6) (Evans 2009, 2010a, 2010b; Mini-Sentinel Coordinating Center 2016; Pharmacoepidemiology and Drug Safety 2012;). As of October 2014, this system had entered voluntary partnerships with 19 data partners – mostly large health insurers and health systems – enabling access to data for 178 million individuals (US Dep't of HHS/FDA 2015a: 4). Pursuant to the public health exceptions available under the HIPAA Privacy Rule and Common Rule, which applied because Congress authorized FDA to develop this data infrastructure for post-marketing drug safety surveillance, a mere 19 large data holders were able to mobilize data for more than half the individuals in the United States. This demonstrates the power of the traditional, twentieth-century data-holder-driven access scheme, which empowers data holders to act as aggregators to avoid the collective action problems and transaction costs of having to mobilize 180 million people to contribute their data.

Looking to the future, unfortunately, this traditional data-holder-driven scheme is breaking down for reasons explored in detail elsewhere (Evans 2016a: 670–71). To summarize the problems, genomic science requires deeply descriptive data sets that link genotypic, phenotypic, lifestyle, and environmental data for each included individual. A single data holder, such as a hospital or insurer, holds data for many individuals, but it only has a small portion of the available data about each of them – for example, a hospital would only have complete records of *its own* treatment encounters with each individual, and a private health insurer would hold data only for the brief period (on average, about 3 years) that it insures an individual before the individual (or the individual's employer) shifts to a different plan. Data holders, while well positioned to aggregate data across many individuals, are not well positioned to aggregate data across the multitude of data holders with which each individual has done business.

Another problem is that deeply descriptive data sets – for example, rich data sets that include much of a person's health history along with genomic and other data – are inherently re-identifiable (see, e.g., Federal Trade Commission 2012). This fact undermines the credibility of traditional regulatory consent exceptions that rely on de-identification as a pretext for unconsented sharing of data. The resulting privacy concerns make it ever more difficult for IRBs to justify the approval of consent waivers, which have been a major pathway of research data access in the past. The traditional scheme of data-holder-driven formation of research data commons, grounded on HIPAA and Common Rule individual consent exceptions that are growing increasingly implausible, functioned fairly well in the past, but it will not suffice as a way to assemble the large-scale, deeply descriptive data resources that the future requires (Evans 2016a).

An even more fundamental problem with data-holder-driven access is that commercial data holders, such as clinical laboratories and private health care providers, have various incentives not to share data that they hold (Cook-Deegan et al. 2013). Research laboratories also may hoard data in the hope of preserving their leadership in future discoveries based on the data. The HIPAA and Common Rule consent exceptions allow data holders to share data but do not require them to do so. Commercial clinical laboratories may regard data they generated in the course of their past testing activities as a valuable proprietary asset. In the environment of weakened patent protection after the 2013 *Myriad* case (133 S.Ct. 2107 (2013)), laboratories may not be able to maintain exclusivity over test administration (the business of offering the test itself). They may, however, be able to maintain a strong competitive advantage if they have previously amassed rich stores of genomic data that enable them to interpret test results more accurately than their competitors are able to do (Cook-Deegan et al. 2013; Evans 2014c).

Another commercial concern is that data holders face nonzero marginal costs of data preparation and transmittal, as discussed earlier. A 2014 survey by the Health Data Exploration Project found that many mobile and wearable sensor device data holders view the advancement of research as a worthy goal but not their primary business priority (Health Data Exploration Project 2014). Particularly in the genomics and advanced diagnostics industries, innovative companies that hold valuable stores of data sometimes are thinly capitalized start-ups that can ill afford to donate the labor and investments that it would take to link their respective data sets into a shared data infrastructure for research. Data holders also may harbor genuine concerns about patient privacy. Unfortunately, data holders sometimes cite patient privacy concerns as a pretext for hoarding data, even when regulations such as the HIPAA Privacy Rule would allow data to be shared, or, in the alternative, patients might be quite willing to authorize the sharing if asked (but the data holders do not ask them).

Balky data holders create the situation shown Quadrant 3 of Figure 4.1 (Evans 2016a: 671–73). Here, the individual may be willing to share her data for use in research, but an uncooperative data holder blocks sharing. The bioethical literature is asymmetrical, evincing deep concern about unconsented data uses (Quadrant 2) while failing to register ethical objections when data holders (or their IRBs) deny access to data for uses of which the individual would have approved (Quadrant 3). In one study, IRBs refused to supply about 5 percent of the requested medical records for a well-documented, congressionally authorized public health purpose, thwarting not only the will of Congress but also of any individuals who may have preferred to participate in the study (Cutrona et al. 2010).

The HIPAA Privacy Rule provides an access-forcing mechanism that helps address the problem in Quadrant 3. HIPAA grants individuals a broad right of access to their own data held by data holders, such as insurers and most health care providers, that are covered by the Privacy Rule (45 C.F.R. § 164.524). This individual access right is the only provision in the Privacy Rule that *requires* a HIPAA-covered data holder to disclose data – all other provisions, such as HIPAA's waiver provision, are permissive (allowing an entity to disclose data when certain conditions are met) but not mandatory. By invoking their Section 164.524 access rights, patients can obtain access to their data, which they then would be free to contribute for research if they so desire.

This important HIPAA access right has recently been extended to cover laboratory-held genomic and other diagnostic information. In 2014, the US Department of Health and Human Services (HHS) amended the Privacy Rule and the CLIA regulations to apply the Section 154.524 access right to HIPAA-covered laboratories, which had not previously been required to comply with it (US Dep't of HHS/OCR 2014: 7292). An early legal analysis suggested that at genomic testing laboratories, these amendments would allow individuals to obtain not only their final genomic testing reports but also any underlying data that the laboratory maintains in VCF, BAM, or FASTQ files (Evans et al. 2014). During the first year after this new right went into effect, patients reported difficulty obtaining their underlying genomic data from genomic testing laboratories. Early in 2016, however, HHS issued guidance confirming that patients are indeed entitled to receive their underlying genomic data from HIPAA-covered laboratories (US Dep't of HHS/OCR 2016). HIPAA's access-forcing mechanism thus can help free genomic data held by uncooperative data holders.

A defect of the Common Rule (including its recent revision) is that it provides no similar access-forcing mechanism to help research subjects obtain access to data about themselves generated during research. Fortunately, many genomic research laboratories are HIPAA-covered entities as a result of being affiliated with larger academic medical centers that have HIPAA-covered status (Evans et al. 2014). If a research laboratory is HIPAA covered, the Section 164.524 access right applies to it, and research subjects should be able to access their data under HIPAA, even though the Common Rule does not respect their right of access to their own data.

By empowering individuals with the power to force access to their own data, the Privacy Rule is positioning them as a force that potentially can drive the formation of genomic data infrastructure in the future. The experience of some disease-specific patient advocacy groups suggests that at least some consumers may be motivated to do so. In general, however, a consumer access right is only a partial solution: once consumers obtain their data, there remains a collective action problem in getting them to work together to develop large-scale genomic data resources. The HIPAA access right thus is only a first step, although it is a crucial one: it can liberate data from uncooperative data holders. The second step – developing institutional arrangements to empower groups of individuals to collaborate to assemble powerful, large-scale health data resources for use in scientific research – presents a different kind of challenge: how to form and operate consumer-driven knowledge commons (see Frischmann, Madison, and Strandburg 2014). This second step is the one where Ostrom's work on CPRs and other shared resources becomes relevant, as discussed further in the next section.

Before moving on, however, one last failure of consent alignment deserves discussion. In Quadrant 4 of Figure 4.1, neither the data holder nor the individual is willing to share data, leading some commentators to recommend coercive, legislative approaches that would simply place health data into the public domain (see, e.g., Rodwin 2010). As already noted, the Privacy Rule and Common Rule contain no provisions mandating access to data for research or public health studies. Authority to compel data access must come from other law, such as court orders or state and federal public health laws that require specific types of data to be reported to governmental agencies for particular purposes (Evans 2016a: 673–74). One possible alternative would be for Congress to enact legislation requiring a broader program of compulsory data collection to support specific types of genomic research.

With compulsory data-sharing legislation in place, the HIPAA Privacy Rule's public health exception (45 C.F.R. Section 164.512(b)(1)(i)) would allow covered entities to share data with public health authorities (i.e., to state or federal public health agencies such as the FDA, or to private entities working under contracts with these governmental agencies). HIPAA's public health exception is broadly worded and allows release of data for a list of activities that includes public health "investigations." This phrasing suggests public health research as well as routine public health practice activities are permissible grounds for data disclosure (Evans 2011). Discovering the clinical significance of the public's genetic variants clearly would serve an important public health purpose.

All the HIPAA-covered data holder must do is verify three things: (1) that the person requesting the data truly is a public health official (who works for, or is under contract to, a public health authority); (2) that the public health authority really does have legislative authorization to collect the data; and (3) that the data requested is the "minimal necessary" to fulfill the legislatively authorized task – that is, that the official has not requested more data than actually is required for the public health purpose (45 C.F.R. § 164.514). In verifying these three things, a HIPAA-covered entity may rely on the public health authority's representations. For example, if a public health agency states that it has legislative authorization, the data holder is not required to second-guess that statement. Reliance is permitted so long as it is "reasonable." Thus, if a person claiming to be a public health official presented a fake-looking badge and credentials, it would be unreasonable to rely on that information and the data holder could face administrative sanctions for releasing the data. If the credentials appear facially reasonable, however, the data holder may respond to a public health official's request for data without fear of violating the HIPAA Privacy Rule.

A problem with public health legislation of this sort is that compulsory data access raises ancillary legal and ethical issues (Evans 2016a: 674). Members of the public have strong feelings about the privacy of their genomic and other health data, and it would be difficult for elected legislators to ignore these strong public sentiments and mandate that all health sector data holders must share people's data for broad, unspecified genomic research purposes. When legislators pass laws that require health data to be shared, this is usually limited to narrow purposes where the need to gather the data is compelling: for example, tracking epidemics or detecting domestic violence. There arguably is a strong public health rationale for developing large-scale genomic data infrastructure, because genetic diseases – including cancer – potentially affect every member of the public. To date, however, our society has not reached a consensus that the need to unlock the secrets of the human genome is so compelling that it overrides the individual's interest in data privacy.

Another problem is that forcing private sector data holders to disclose their data holdings may raise takings issues under the Fifth and Fourteenth Amendments to the Constitution, which provide that the government cannot take a person's property for public use without just compensation (Evans 2011). Who owns data held in genomic and health databases is a question of state property law. In most instances, the consumer and the data holder both have various legal interests in the data but, in most states, neither enjoys outright ownership (Evans 2011: 73–74). Thus, data holders usually do not have property interests in the data that could support a takings claim. However, data holders may have made significant capital investments and investments of labor to curate and format the data, to convert data into an accessible format, and to develop information systems that render the data useful for clinical and research purposes (Evans 2011: 106–07; Evans 2014a). Legislation forcing a data holder to share data could diminish the value of those investments, generating takings claims. Even if the government ultimately prevailed on the takings questions, litigation could drag on and delay formation of genomic data commons.

A final point is that compulsory sharing of data would not, in reality, ensure the development of useful genomic data resources. Developing useful data resources requires access not only to data but also to ancillary services that the data holders would need to provide – for example, data preparation services to convert their data into an interoperable format so that it can be analyzed together with data from other sources (Evans 2011: 106–7). The government has little power to force unwilling private entities to contribute services (Brenner and Clarke 2010), even if data holders could be forced to part with their data. The necessary services can only be procured through consensual methods, such as entering contracts with the data holders or requiring their services as a condition of a grant (Beam and Conlan 2002; Kelman 2002). Such methods all would require substantial funding. These considerations all seem to disfavor compulsory data sharing and point to a need for voluntary, incentives-based arrangements (Evans 2014a). Ryan Abbott (Chapter 6, this volume) describes the FDA's use of voluntary approaches in developing its Sentinel System.

The options for developing large-scale genomic data resources can be summarized as follows: consent alignment is a lovely thing when it occurs, but, to date, it has not occurred at the level required to create the massively scaled data infrastructures now needed to move genomic science forward. Incentivized consent alignment, where funding agencies such as the NIH promote data sharing through conditional grants, can jump-start efforts to create genomic data infrastructure, but this approach ultimately is not scalable (Evans 2016a: 668–69). Existing regulations such as the HIPAA Privacy Rule and Common Rule enable a scheme of data-holder-driven creation of research data resources that has functioned well in the past but is ill adapted to the challenge of creating large-scale, deeply descriptive data resources to support genomic science (Evans 2016a: 669–71). Into this breach, recent amendments to the HIPAA Privacy Rule have expanded individuals' access to their own data, and this opens a possible new pathway: consumer-driven data commons (Evans 2016a: 671–73. However, the success of this pathway will require systematic work to overcome the collective action and governance challenges of getting millions of people to cooperate to create and sustain useful genomic data resources (Evans 2016b). A final alternative – legislatively imposed mandatory data sharing – has so many legal drawbacks that it is unlikely to offer meaningful solutions (Evans 2016a: 673–74). Surveying this landscape, consumer-driven data commons emerge as the most attractive – albeit far from easy – solution.

4.4 THE EMERGENCE OF CONSUMER-DRIVEN DATA COMMONS

A fundamental question is how to conceive the aims of genomic data infrastructure and the role regulatory agencies should play in relation to this infrastructure. One possibility is for genomic data systems to serve as a repository that compiles authoritative records of already discovered associations between genetic variants and health conditions. The database operators would collect discoveries made externally and curate the reported information to reconcile conflicts, if multiple laboratories have assigned divergent clinical meanings to particular genetic variants. The role of a consumer safety regulator, such as FDA, would be limited to certifying the quality of information stored in the database, to assure it provides an authoritative snapshot of what is known about the clinical significance of the genetic variants included at a particular point in time. When approving the safety and effectiveness of new genomic tests, the regulator would allow test manufacturers to make claims about the clinical validity of genomic tests if the database provides support for such claims, and the regulator would block claims that lack database support. This scheme corresponds to the approach FDA proposed in its December 2014 NGS discussion paper (US Dep't of HHS/FDA 2014c). Such a scheme treats genomic uncertainty as "static" in the sense that the regulator ultimately has no control over it. The regulator can block clinical claims that external sources indicate are too uncertain at a given moment but has no power to hasten the pace at which uncertainty is resolved (Evans et al. 2015).

An alternative view is that genomic data commons should be interoperable information systems capable of supporting fresh discoveries of as-yet-unknown associations between genetic variants and human health. By this view, genomic databases are not mere repositories of externally discovered associations but instead should serve as critical resources to fuel an active, ongoing, continuous discovery process involving a wide range of academic, commercial, and public health researchers, all of whom contribute to the grand challenge of deciphering the clinical meaning of the human genome. This scheme would treat uncertainty about the clinical significance of gene variants as "dynamic" in the sense of being a parameter that regulatory policies can influence. One of the regulator's major responsibilities would be to implement policies that hasten the pace at which uncertainty shrinks through the discovery of new, statistically significant relationships between genotypes and phenotypes (Evans et al. 2015). In this scheme, the regulator is not merely an information taker but instead is an information steward. Jorge Contreras (Chapter 2, this volume) explores the regulator's role in further detail.

Existing genomic data infrastructures, such as ClinGen/ClinVar and the cohort planned as part of the Precision Medicine Initiative/All of Us research program, are moves in the right direction, but they have not yet achieved the scale and the level of detail that ultimately will be required. Financial sustainability is a major concern with systems such as these, financed with limited-term grants and other sources of federal funding (Evans et al. 2015). Sustainability will require a workable revenue model to cover system costs, including such items as the costs data holders incur as they prepare and transmit data to the system, costs of developing and maintaining the system's information infrastructure, and costs of ensuring data security protections and rigorous ethical/legal compliance.

The United States has a long history, dating back to the late 1800s, of mobilizing private capital to help develop major national infrastructure such as railroads, high-voltage power transmission grids, natural gas pipeline networks, and telecommunications infrastructure (Frischmann 2012). Similar voluntary, incentive-based approaches may offer promise in genomics (Evans 2014a, 2014c). The genomic data resource system should be viewed as one of a long line of national infrastructure challenges that many nations have faced in the past and continue to face in the twenty-first century (Frischmann 2012).

Before policymakers embrace any approach, however, a crucial decision node often goes unacknowledged. Any voluntary, incentive-based approach must first establish who are the volunteers it seeks to incentivize. Control of genomic and other relevant health data, as portrayed in Figure 4.1, is fragmented at two levels: at the level of data holders and at the level of individual data subjects. One alternative – for convenience, a data-holder-driven strategy – would direct incentives toward institutional data holders who can, if suitably motivated, invoke various consent exceptions in privacy and human-subject protection regulations to facilitate flows of individual data into genomic data commons. The other alternative – a consumer-driven strategy – would direct incentives toward individual data subjects, who can invoke the access-forcing mechanism in existing privacy law to free their data from recalcitrant data holders and contribute the data to form useful genomic data infrastructures. For reasons outlined in the previous section, this latter approach appears to be the last strategy standing that has a potential to work, but it will require considerable effort going forward, because institutional arrangements are not yet in place to orchestrate the required levels of collective action.

An important point to emphasize is that data-holder-driven and consumer-driven strategies are equally viable from a legal standpoint. Policymaking efforts of the past – and most recent proposals – have focused on data-holder-driven strategies that treat data holders as the prime movers of data infrastructure development, while dismissing consumer-driven strategies. The idea of engaging individuals in the creation of genomic data commons was raised at FDA's November 2015 Public Workshop exploring use of databases to establish clinical validity of genomic tests:

> Across the country and the various states patients are getting more and more access to not only their clinical tests, their medical records but also their lab test records. Quite often in many cases it is the patient that is most incentivized to find out what they can about their condition. What does the panel think about taking crowd sourcing to patient level? (US Dep't of HHS/FDA 2015d: 40)

This suggestion drew skepticism, primarily reflecting concerns that patient-handled data would be prone to errors and inconsistencies (US Dep't of HHS/FDA 2015d: 40–43). One response to such concerns is that data from *all* health care sources is prone to errors and inconsistencies; scrubbing and reformatting data into a common data format is always one of the most challenging and time-consuming components of any effort to create useful health data systems, regardless of the data source (Evans 2011; P-CAST 2010: 39). Information in electronic health records held by health care providers and payers is often directed toward billing, which introduces its own biases and inaccuracies (US Dep't of HHS/FDA 2015d: 71), such as a tendency to overstate the gravity of a patient's symptoms to qualify for a higher insurance reimbursement, or the tendency to record that a diagnostic test was performed without bothering to note what the test discovered (Evans 2010b: 483). Another response is that HIPAA's Section 164.524 access right, which allows individuals to free their data held by HIPAA-covered laboratories and health care providers, also allows them to direct that the data be transmitted directly on their behalf to a third party, which could be a qualified data infrastructure operator. Thus, data do not need to pass through individuals' hands while being conveyed, at their instruction, to the genomic data resource system. This could help allay concerns that individuals may alter or corrupt information that passes through their hands.

Despite the skepticism expressed at FDA's Public Workshop, the idea of involving consumers in genomic data infrastructure development gained some support, with experienced geneticists noting that patients often have phenotypic information beyond what is in their medical and insurance records, and that this information is "incredibly accurate in many cases" (US Dep't of HHS/FDA 2015d: 70). The discussion ended with suggestions to "embrace" patient-driven strategies more (US Dep't of HHS/FDA 2015d: 71).

How to mobilize consumer-driven strategies is the unanswered question, and this is not a question that this chapter can fully answer, except by noting that early work already is under way (Evans 2016a, 2016b) to position consumer-driven genomic data commons in the analytical framework associated with Elinor Ostrom and her modern interpreters (Frischmann, Madison, and Strandburg 2014; Hess and Ostrom 2006; Ostrom 1990). This framework offers intriguing insights. To cite one example, Ostrom's exploration of self-organizing and self-governing CPRs suggests principles, such as the use of nested enterprises involving small groups that elicit trust (Ostrom 1990: 189). This approach for overcoming collective action problems evokes a pattern of activity already observed among disease-specific patient advocacy groups that have created disease-specific data resources, such as a cystic fibrosis genetic database that already is supplying reliable data to support FDA review of genomic tests (US Dep't of HHS/FDA 2015d: 16). The Precision Medicine Initiative apparently has embraced a centralized data architecture for its one-million-person cohort study, and a centralized database is a feasible alternative at such a small scale – and make no mistake: one million is small scale in the context of genomic research. Genomic data resource systems ultimately must attain a much larger scale, and a distributed network-of-networks architecture, such as the nested enterprise model Ostrom suggests, may have merit, particularly in overcoming the reluctance of individuals to cede their data to a centralized network operated by strangers.

Early work on consumer-driven data commons conceives these entities as institutional arrangements to empower groups of consenting individuals to collaborate to assemble powerful, large-scale health data resources for use in scientific research, on terms the group members themselves would set (Evans 2016a, 2016b). The consumer-driven data commons movement is, above all, a critique of the atomistic vision of individual autonomy that pervaded twentieth-century bioethics: a presumption that patients, research subjects, and consumers of direct-to-consumer health-related services are fundamentally alone, individualistic, disorganized, weak, and vulnerable (Tauber 2005: 13, 117) and in need of paternalistic protectors – concerned bioethicists and dedicated IRBs – to look after their interests. This presumption of human disempowerment pervades federal regulations such as the HIPAA Privacy Rule and Common Rule, which reject the approach of organizing individual consumers to protect themselves, for example, by unionizing them to protect their own interests through collective bargaining with researchers who want to use their data (Evans 2016b). The federal regulatory framework that set out to protect individuals ultimately disempowered the very patients and research subjects it sought to protect, empowering them to make decisions as individuals, but only as individuals, and lacking a roadmap for collective action (Evans 2016b: 248).

Edmund S. Morgan has chronicled developments, in the 1600s and 1700s, that erupted in the history-altering concept that individual British subjects are not fundamentally alone and limited to one-on-one autonomous interactions with the king in whose presence they are weak and disempowered. Instead, individuals can interact with one another to create a larger fictional construct, *The People*, which exudes "a certain majesty [that] could be placed in the scales against the divinity of the king" (Morgan 1988: 24). Consumer-driven data commons are institutional arrangements to bring about a similar moment of truth for traditional bioethics: those whose data populate large-scale health data networks are awakening from the condition Thomas Hobbes referred to as "the confusion of a disunited multitude," unifying into a *People* that rejects the privacy and access standards of the past and demands new standards of the people, by the people, and for the people (Evans 2016b: 252; Hobbes 1952).

Surveys show that a majority – up to 80 percent –of consumers have a positive attitude about health-related research and support the concept that their health data should be used to advance research (Health Data Exploration Project 2014; Kish and Topol 2015; Topol 2015). Yet very few people actually volunteer their data for research (Evans 2016a: 683; Evans 2016b: 247). The inescapable conclusion is that people are not comfortable with the ethical and privacy frameworks that bioethical experts and regulators have devised, top-down, to protect them. Consumer-driven data commons would engage consenting individuals in the task of designing better ethical and privacy frameworks to govern access to *their* data.

Twentieth-century genomic science requires large data sets aggregated across many individuals and many data holders. Traditional data-holder-driven data access mechanisms are good at aggregating data across people, but not across data holders. Individual health care consumers now have the power to aggregate data about themselves across many data holders by using their HIPAA access rights. But can they work together to aggregate their data across large, diverse groups of individuals? That is the question.

The vision of consumer-driven data commons is that individuals would obtain their own health data by exercising their HIPAA Section 164.524 access rights and voluntarily deposit their data into one or more consumer-driven data commons (Evans 2016b: 262–64). No individual would be required to join such a group. Each consumer-driven commons would announce transparent rules addressing how to become a member of the group, the duties of membership, and the terms of exit from the group. Members of each commons would decide, through self-governance processes, which research uses of their collective data resources are permissible and which are not. These collective decisions would be binding on the members for so long as they choose to remain in the commons. Thus, commons groups would be able to offer high-valued, aggregated data sets that incorporate deeply descriptive longitudinal data for their entire membership (Evans 2016b: 262-64).

Individual members, when joining a consumer-driven commons, would cede their right of traditional, individualized informed consent. Instead, they would agree to be governed by the collective decision-making processes of the group, in which they would have a meaningful voice. Thus, each individual's right of informed consent would be exercised at the point of making a decision to join, stay in, or leave a particular consumer-driven data commons group. While in it, individuals in effect would appoint the group's decision-making body to act as their personal representative (as is allowed by the HIPAA Privacy Rule and Common Rule) to consent to specific uses of their data on their behalf. These commons-forming groups could be membership organizations organized by data-contributing individuals themselves, or they could be organized by disease advocacy groups or by commercial data management companies that agree to manage members' collective data resources according to rules the members themselves would set (Evans 2016b: 262–64).

What are the advantages of consumer-driven data commons? The greatest advantage is the power of data aggregation and collective decision making. An individual, acting alone, can almost never (unless she has an incredibly bizarre and fascinating medical condition) offer a data resource that is sufficiently attractive to place the individual in a position to set terms and conditions about how the data can be used, what privacy protections should apply, and what data security protections are expected. The right of individual informed consent granted by regulations such as the Privacy Rule and Common Rule is basically a useless, take-it-or-leave-it right: individuals can consent to privacy and ethical practices *defined by regulations and by the data user*, or they can take their data and go home, but they cannot negotiate the terms on which their data can be used (Evans 2016b: 248). The aim of consumer-driven data commons is to place groups of like-minded individuals in a position to insist that their collective, well-considered privacy and ethical preferences be given weight. A large group of individuals who deposit their data into a consumer-driven data commons can amass a sufficiently attractive data resource to make demands.

As commons-forming groups enunciate their respective visions of ethical data access, a "marketplace" of ethical and privacy policies would emerge (Evans 2016b: 264). Individuals could compare these policies when choosing which consumer-driven data commons to join. Successful consumer-driven commons would be the ones that offer policies that address the concerns that data-contributing individuals feel, while still making data available for useful lines of research that benefit their members and the public at large. As these successful consumer-driven data commons expand, their policies would inform the policies of other commons-forming groups, leading to a possible convergence of consumer-driven bioethical standards to replace the top-down, expert-driven bioethical standards in place today (Evans 2016a: 683).

Another crucial advantage of consumer-driven data commons is that they may be better positioned to achieve financial sustainability than data-holder-driven commons are under current US law. Federal regulations such as the HIPAA Privacy Rule do not restrict individuals' ability to sell their own data (Evans 2016a: 681). Consumer-driven data commons – assuming their members are comfortable with the ethics of data commodification – would be able to charge data access fees to cover the costs of engaging suitably skilled consultants to convert their members' data into interoperable formats, to develop system infrastructure, and to operate their collective data resources on an ongoing basis.

In contrast, institutional data holders are subject to restrictions under the 2009 Health Information Technology for Economic and Clinical Health (HITECH) Act (Pub. L. 111–5, Div. A, Title XIII, Div. B, Title IV, 123 Stat. 226, 467 (Feb. 17, 2009)). HITECH inserted data sales restrictions into the HIPAA Privacy Rule that do not allow HIPAA-covered entities to sell data (42 U.S.C. § 17935(d)(1); 45 C.F.R. §164.502 (a)(5)(ii)). They can, however, charge a reasonable, cost-based fee for data preparation and transmittal services when they share data for research under the Privacy Rule's waiver provision (45 C.F.R. §164.502(a)(5)(ii)(B)(2)(ii)). This cost-based fee, had it been implemented properly, could have supported robust data sharing, just as cost-of-service utility rates have successfully supported the development of major national infrastructures in many industrial sectors (Evans 2014a, 2014b). Unfortunately, the 2013 Privacy Rule revisions implementing the cost-based fee set it so low that it denies data holders a reasonable rate of return on capital they invest in data development and system infrastructure (US Dep't of HHS/OCR 2013). This limits data holders' potential to lead the charge in developing the genomic data resources that twenty-first-century science needs. As explained elsewhere, the current regulations have the unintended consequence of virtually forcing data holders to embrace distributed network architectures if they wish to earn a reasonable rate of return on their invested capital (Evans 2014a: 508, col. 2). Distributed data architectures have many merits, but decisions about system architecture should be guided by system performance objectives rather than turning on accidents in regulated pricing formulas. Consumer-driven data commons, unburdened by the current restrictions on cost recovery, appear better positioned to pioneer financially sustainable data sharing solutions.

CONCLUSION

Consumer-driven genomic data commons, at this point, are in the earliest phases of conceptualization and should be viewed "not as a panacea, but as a grand experiment in democratic data self-governance, perhaps worth trying at a time when existing mechanisms of data access seem destined not to meet the challenges that lie ahead" (Evans 2016a: 684). The goal of this chapter was to describe the legal obstacles that stand in the way of developing large-scale genomic data resources and to invite the community of commons scholars to get involved with overcoming them.

The ultimate value of Ostrom's work, in the context of genomic testing, may lie in its potential to reframe the human genome as a shared resource that can and should be managed through collective efforts of the people whose data are involved. Genetic information is often characterized as deeply personal and private, but this is a mistake: to test one's genome is to enter a public space where one discovers what one has in common with other people. Gene variants that are unique can never have an established clinical validity because clinical validity can be inferred only by comparing an individual's variants to those of other people. We shall "crack" the human genome and discover its meaning together, or not do so at all.

The appropriate norm, as we undertake this challenge, is the norm of "common purpose" recently enunciated by Ruth Faden and her coauthors (Faden et al. 2013). They acknowledged that the moral framework for twenty-first-century science may differ in significant respects from traditional conceptions of clinical and research ethics" and may include an obligation for individuals to participate in knowledge-generating activities (Faden et al. 2013: S16, S18). They see this as a bounded obligation that would vary with the degree of risk and burden involved, so that individuals would not be obligated to participate in clinical trials that pose physical risks but may have an obligation to contribute their data to studies that offer the prospect of useful scientific advances (Faden et al. 2013: S23). They suggest that this obligation is grounded in a "norm of common purpose . . . a principle presiding over matters that affect the interests of everyone" (Faden et al. 2013: S16): "Securing these common interests is a shared social purpose that we cannot as individuals achieve" (Faden et al. 2013: S16).

The unanswered questions with this common purpose ethical framework are how to operationalize it, monitor it, and overcome the collective action and governance problems it presents. Ostrom's case studies of community efforts to create self-organized and self-governing commons in other contexts may provide the missing piece that bioethicists have as yet been unable to supply: a set of principles drawn from how real people in real circumstances have been able to create sustainable commons.

REFERENCES

American Heritage Science Dictionary (Boston, MA: Houghton Mifflin Company, 2005).

Beam, D. R. and T. J. Conlan, Grants, in *The Tools of Government* 340, 341 (Lester M. Salamon ed., Oxford University Press, 2002).

Brenner, S. W. and L. L. Clarke, Civilians in Cyberwarfare: Conscripts, 43 *Vanderbilt Journal of Transnational Law* 1011–76, at 1056–57 (2010).

Collins, F. S. and H. Varmus, A New Initiative on Precision Medicine, 372 *New England Journal of Medicine* 793–95 (2015).

Contreras, J. L., Constructing the Genome Commons, in *Governing Knowledge Commons* 99–119 (Brett M. Frischmann, Michael J. Madison, and Katherine J. Strandburg eds., Oxford University Press, 2014).

Cook-Deegan, R., J. M. Conley, J. P. Evans et al., The Next Controversy in Genetic Testing: Clinical Data as Trade Secrets?, 21 *European Journal of Human Genetics* 585–588 (2013).

Cutrona S. L. et al., Mini-Sentinel Systematic Validation of Health Outcome of Interest: Acute Myocardial Infarction Case Report (2010), www.mini-sentinel.org/work_products/Validation_HealthOutcomes/Mini-Sentinel-Validation-of-AMI-Cases.pdf, at 10, 12.

Dewey, F. E., M. E. Grove, C. Pan et al., Clinical Interpretation and Implications of Whole-Genome Sequencing, 311 *JAMA* 1035–45 (2014).

Evans, B. J., Congress' New Infrastructural Model of Medical Privacy, 84 *Notre Dame Law Review* 585–654 (2009).

Evans, B. J., Authority of the Food and Drug Administration to Require Data Access and Control Use Rights in the Sentinel Data Network, 65 *Food & Drug Law Journal* 67–112 (2010a).

Evans, B. J., Seven Pillars of a New Evidentiary Paradigm: The Food, Drug, and Cosmetic Act Enters the Genomic Era, 85 *Notre Dame Law Review* 519–624 (2010b).

Evans, B. J., Much Ado about Data Ownership, 25 *Harvard Journal of Law & Technology* 69–130 (2011).

Evans, B. J., Mining the Human Genome after Association for Molecular Pathology v. Myriad Genetics, 6 *Genetics in Medicine* 504–8 (2014a).

Evans, B. J., Sustainable Access to Data for Postmarketing Medical Product Safety Surveillance under the Amended HIPAA Privacy Rule, in Symposium: Balancing Privacy, Autonomy and Scientific Progress: Patients' Rights and the Use of Electronic Medical Records for Non-Treatment Purposes, *Health Matrix* 2411–47 (2014b).

Evans, B. J., Economic Regulation of Next-Generation Sequencing, in *Special Issue: Clinical Integration of Next-Generation Sequencing: A Policy Analysis* (Amy L. McGuire, David J. Kaufman, and Margaret A. Curnutte eds.), 42 *Journal of Law, Medicine, and Ethics* 51–66 (2014c).

Evans, B. J., Barbarians at the Gate: Consumer-Driven Data Commons and the Transformation of Citizen Science, 42 *American Journal of Law & Medicine* 651–85 (2016a).

Evans, B. J., Power to the People: Data Citizens in the Age of Precision Medicine, 19 *Vanderbilt Journal of Entertainment & Technology Law* 243–65 (2016b).

Evans, B. J., M. O. Dorschner, W. Burke, and G. P. Jarvik, Regulatory Changes Raise Troubling Questions for Genomic Testing, 16 *Genetics in Medicine* 799–803 (2014).

Evans, B. J., W. Burke, and G. P. Jarvik, The FDA and Genomic Tests – Getting Regulation Right, 372 *New England Journal of Medicine* 2258–64 (2015).

Fabsitz, R. R., A. McGuire, R. R. Sharp et al., Ethical and Practical Guidelines for Reporting Genetic Research Results to Study Participants: Updated Guidelines from a National Heart, Lung, and Blood Institute Working Group, 3 *Circulation Cardiovascular Genetics* 574–80 (2010).

Fabsitz, R. R., N. E. Kass, S. N. Goodman et al., An Ethics Framework for a Learning Health Care System: A Departure from Traditional Research Ethics and Clinical Ethics, *The Hastings Center Report* 2013 Special Issue: S16–27, at S16 (2013).

Federal Trade Commission, Protecting Consumer Privacy in an Era of Rapid Change: A Proposed Framework for Businesses and Policymakers, at 19-20 (US Federal Trade Commission, 2012), available at www.ftc.gov/sites/default/files/documents/reports/federal-trade-commission-report-protecting-consumer-privacy-era-rapid-change-recommendations/120326privacyreport.pdf.

Frischmann, B. M. *Infrastructure: The Social Value of Shared Resources* (Oxford University Press, 2012).

Frischmann, B. M., M. J. Madison, and K. J. Strandburg, Governing Knowledge Commons in *Governing Knowledge Commons* (Brett M. Frischmann, Michael J. Madison, and Katherine J. Strandburg eds., Oxford University Press, 2014).

Gargis, A. S., L. Kalman, M. W. Berry et al., Assuring the Quality of Next-Generation Sequencing in Clinical Laboratory Practice, 30 *Nature Biotechnolology* 1033–36 (2012).

Hall, M. A., Property, Privacy, and the Pursuit of Interconnected Electronic Medical Records, 95 *Iowa Law Review* 631–63, at 647–48 (2010).

Health Data Exploration Project, Personal Data for the Public Good: New Opportunities to Enrich Understanding of Individual and Population Health (March), http://hdexplore.calit2.net/wp/project/personal-data-for-the-public-good-report/, at 12 (2014).

Hess, C. and E. Ostrom (eds.), *Understanding Knowledge as a Commons* (MIT Press, 2006).

Hobbes, T., *Leviathan* (William Benton/Encyclopedia Britannica, Inc.), at 101 (1952).

Kelman, S. J., Contracting, in *The Tools of Government* 282, 283–85 (Lester M. Salamon ed., Oxford University Press, 2002).

Kish, L. J. and E. J. Topol, Unpatients – Why Patients Should Own Their Medical Data, 11 *Nature Biotechnology* 921–24 (2015).

Kohane, I. S., M. Hsing, and S. W. Kong, Taxonomizing, Sizing, and Overcoming the Incidentalome, 14 *Genetics in Medicine* 399–404 (2012).

McGuire, A. L. et al., NIH/NHGRI Project R01 HG006460 (communication on file with author) (2016).

Mini-Sentinel Coordinating Center, www.mini-sentinel.org/default.aspx (2016).

Morgan, E. S., Inventing the People: The Rise of Popular Sovereignty in England and America, at 24 (1988).

National Research Council, Sharing Publication-Related Data and Materials: Responsibility of Authorship in the Life Sciences (National Academies Press, 2003).

OECD, Data-Driven Innovation: Big Data for Growth and Wellbeing (Organization for Economic Cooperation and Development, 2015) available at www.oecd.org/sti/data-driven-innovation-9789264229358-en.htm

Ostrom, E., *Governing the Commons: The Evolution of Institutions for Collective Action* (Cambridge University Press, 1990).

Patil, D. J., C. Williams, and S. Devaney, Your Data in Your Hands: Enabling Access to Health Information (Mar. 10), https://medium.com/@WhiteHouse/your-data-in-your-hands-enabling-access-to-health-information-6fce6da976cb#.60242uv2i (2016).

Pharmacoepidemiology and Drug Safety, Special Issue: The US Food and Drug Administration's Mini-Sentinel Program, 21, Issue Supplement S-1, 1–302 (January), http://onlinelibrary.wiley.com/doi/10.1002/pds.v21.S1/issuetoc (2012).

P-CAST (President's Council of Advisors on Science and Technology, Exec. Office of the President), Report to the President: Realizing the Full Potential of Health Information Technology to Improve Healthcare for Americans: The Path Forward, at 39 (2010).

Regalago, A., EmTech: Illumina Says 228,000 Human Genomes Will Be Sequenced This Year, *MIT Technology Review* (September 24, 2014).

Rehm, H. L., S. J. Bale, P. Bayrak-Toydemir et al., Working Group of the American College of Medical Genetics and Genomics Laboratory Quality Assurance Committee. ACMG Clinical Laboratory Standards for Next-Generation Sequencing, 15 *Genetics in Medicine* 733–47 (2013).

Rehm, H. L., J. S. Berg, L. D. Brooks et al., ClinGen – The Clinical Genome Resource, 372 *New England Journal of Medicine* 2235–42 (2015).

Rodwin, M. A., Patient Data: Property, Privacy & the Public Interest, 36 *American Journal of Law & Medicine* 586–618, at 606 (2010).

Secretary's Advisory Committee on Genetic Testing, Enhancing the Oversight of Genetic Tests: Recommendations of the SACGT(2000), available at http://osp.od.nih.gov/sites/default/files/oversight_report.pdf.

Shirts, B. H., A. Jacobson, G. P. Jarvik, and B. L. Browning, Large Numbers of Individuals are Required to Classify and Define Risk for Rare Variants in Known Cancer Risk Genes, 16 *Genetics in Medicine* 529–34 (2014).

Tauber, A. I., *Patient Autonomy and the Ethics of Responsibility*, at 13, 117 (MIT Press, 2005).

Topol, E., The Big Medical Data Miss: Challenges in Establishing an Open Medical Resource, 16 *Nature Reviews Genetics* 253–54 (2015).

US Dep't of HHS/OCR, Modifications to the HIPAA Privacy, Security, Enforcement, and Breach Notification Rules under the Health Information Technology for Economic and Clinical Health Act and the Genetic Information Nondiscrimination Act; Other Modifications to the HIPAA Rules, *Federal Register* (Jan. 25), 78:5566–702 (2013).
US Dep't of HHS/OCR, CLIA Program and HIPAA Privacy Rule; Patients' Access to Test Reports, 79 *Federal Register* (Feb. 6) (25): 7290–316 (2014).
US Dep't of HHS/OCR, Individuals' Right under HIPAA to Access Their Health Information 45 CFR § 164.524 (2016), www.hhs.gov/hipaa/for-professionals/privacy/guidance/access/index.html.
US Dep't of HHA/FDA, Draft Guidance for Industry, Food and Drug Administration Staff, and Clinical Laboratories: Framework for Regulatory Oversight of Laboratory Developed Tests (LDTs) (October 3, 2014a), www.fda.gov/downloads/medicaldevices/deviceregulationandguidance/guidancedocuments/ucm416685.pdf
US Dep't of HHS/FDA, Draft Guidance for Industry, Food and Drug Administration Staff, and Clinical Laboratories: FDA Notification and Medical Device Reporting for Laboratory Developed Tests (October 3, 2014b), www.fda.gov/downloads/medicaldevices/deviceregulationandguidance/guidancedocuments/ucm416684.pdf
US Dep't of HHA/FDA, Optimizing FDA's Regulatory Oversight of Next Generation Sequencing Diagnostic Tests – Preliminary Discussion Paper (December 29, 2014c.), www.fda.gov/downloads/medicaldevices/newsevents/workshopsconferences/ucm427869.pdf
US Dep't of HHS/FDA, Sentinel Program Interim Assessment (FY 15) (September 24, 2015a), www.fda.gov/downloads/ForIndustry/UserFees/PrescriptionDrugUserFee/UCM464043.pdf, at 4.
US Dep't of HHS/FDA, Public Workshop – Standards Based Approach to Analytical Performance Evaluation of Next Generation Sequencing In Vitro Diagnostic Tests (November 12, 2015b), www.fda.gov/MedicalDevices/NewsEvents/WorkshopsConferences/ucm459449.htm.
US Dep't of HHS/FDA, Public Workshop – Use of Databases for Establishing the Clinical Relevance of Human Genetic Variants (November 13, 2015c), www.fda.gov/medicaldevices/newsevents/workshopsconferences/ucm459450.htm.
US Dep't of HHS/FDA, Transcript: Use of Databases for Establishing Clinical Relevance of Human Genetic Variants: Public Meeting (November 13, 2015d), www.fda.gov/downloads/MedicalDevices/NewsEvents/WorkshopsConferences/UCM478844.pdf, at 40.
The White House, Office of the Press Secretary, Fact Sheet: President Obama's Precision Medicine Initiative (January 30, 2015), www.whitehouse.gov/precision-medicine

5

Population Biobanks' Governance: A Case Study of Knowledge Commons

Andrea Boggio

The term "biobank" refers to a variety of research infrastructures that involve the collection, storage, and analysis of genetics samples that are linked to data regarding the health and lifestyle of the sample sources. Population biobanks are a particular type of biobank as they focus primarily on a population or a large subset of a population and permit research to explore the relationship between genes, environment, and lifestyle on large cohorts. Population biobanks are also an emerging knowledge commons: they are infrastructures made of pooled resources that researchers from all over the world can access for uses that are not predetermined by the biobank managers. In this chapter, I discuss how population biobanks are increasingly managed as commons, what role biobank governance experts have played in overcoming regulatory obstacles and in managing negative externalities, and areas of governance that need further refinement for population biobanks to be fully managed as commons. The case study traces the history of biobanking governance and discusses the process that has led to a convergence toward a commons approach. My analysis draws from the literature on biobank governance and on knowledge commons theory as well as my experience as a scholar who participated in the governance shift toward a commons approach to biobank governance. This case study provides important lessons to scholars of knowledge commons as it shows the importance of expertise in managing pooled resources as commons.

5.1 DEFINING POPULATION BIOBANKS

A biobank is "an organized collection of human biological material and associated information stored for one or more research purposes" (Public Population Project in Genomics and Society (P3G), 27). The classes of biobanks that are included in this definition are heterogeneous in terms of scope, geographical presence, cohort characteristics, size, scientific aims, nature of the samples collected, duration, type

Andrea Boggio is Professor of Legal Studies, Bryant University, Smithfield, Rhode Island.

of data, level of security, institutional setting, and funding (Dove et al. 2012). The term is of relatively recent usage. For years, various terms, such as genetic databases or tissues and data collections, were used to refer to projects combining genotype and phenotype data. Its usage has been increasingly prevalent from the mid-2000s.

The term "biobank" is now widely used as umbrella concept to refer to diverse structural arrangements with a research common core. In this chapter, I focus my attention primarily on population biobanks, which are "collections of biological material and the associated data and information stored in an organized system for a population or a large subset of a population" (Organisation for Economic Co-operation and Development 2006). UK Biobank constitutes a textbook example of a population biobank. This biobank was established in the mid-2000s with public funds, which have been supplemented with private money from organizations such as the British Heart Foundation and Diabetes UK. The vision of the promoters of UK Biobank was to establish a long-term research infrastructure for the study of the interactions between genes, environment, and health. To achieve this goal, the biobank has collected samples (blood, urine, and saliva) and detailed information from half a million UK residents between the ages of 40 and 69 from across the UK recruited between 2006 and 2010 (Sudlow et al. 2015). Genotypic data are linked to data on blood pressure, lung function and grip strength, height, weight and body mass, arterial stiffness, vision, hearing, family history of common diseases, bone density, diet, and fitness. At the recruitment stage, participants were asked to consent to their samples and data being used in "a diverse range of research intended to improve the prevention, diagnosis and treatment of illness, and the promotion of health throughout society" (UK Biobank 2006). UK Biobank has conducted its own research project as a nonprofit charity under the direction of a principal investigator who has management authority both as a scientist and as the director of the Coordinating Centre. Since its inception, researchers from all over the world have been able to access the collection since 2012 (Sudlow et al. 2015). Between 2012 and 2014, "over 1,000 researchers successfully registered, and over 200 applications were submitted" (Sudlow et al. 2015).

UK Biobanks is not the only population biobank in operation. Population biobanks have been established throughout the world since the mid-2000s. The Public Population Project in Genomics (P3G), which is an international consortium that is a leader in genomics and biobanking governance, provides an excellent source to map out which population biobanks are active and where they are located. In fact, P3G maintains various "catalogues" providing information on population projects in genomics. The Study Catalogue (www.p3gobservatory.org/studylist.htm) lists 164 population-based studies in genomics. All of them are infrastructures that collect samples and/or data. The Network Catalogue (www.p3gobservatory.org/network/populationBased.htm) is composed of 16 networks involving two or more institutions conducting population-based studies in genomics. Some are based in a country (Canada, Italy, Norway, Latvia, Finland, Singapore, Sweden); some are regional (Danube River and in neighboring regions); some are international.

5.2 POPULATION BIOBANKS AND KNOWLEDGE COMMONS

This chapter focuses on population biobanks, even though some of the insights are applicable to other types of biobanks. This choice is based on the fact that population biobanks are increasingly managed as commons – and more so than other kinds of biobanks – and, as a result, are more relevant to the study of knowledge commons. Knowledge commons, which includes commons involving informational, scientific, cultural, and other types of intellectual resources, refers to governance regimes for shared resources in the cultural environment (Frischmann 2012; Frischmann et al. 2014a). Scholarly interest in knowledge commons stems from the study of commons involving natural resources that are shared by a group of people and are subject to the dilemmas of collective action (Ostrom 1990, 2002) and on the preliminary work by Ostrom and Hess in the area of knowledge commons (Hess 2012; Hess and Ostrom 2007). The two authors conceptualized these commons as possessing three dimensions – information facilities (in which information is stored), artifacts (the physical units that flow from a facility), and ideas (nonphysical units that flow from artifacts and the content of artifacts).

Building on these insights, scholars of knowledge commons have developed an analytical framework that applies some of the ideas developed for the governance of natural resources to cultural resources. The framework deploys multiple variables that are specific to a particular commons, including attribute variables (resources, community members, and goals and objective of the commons), governance variables (mechanisms, decision makers, institutions, formal and informal norms), and variables associated with patterns of use and outcomes (benefits, costs, and risk) (Frischmann 2013; Frischmann et al. 2014a). A commons management approach for resources entails some degree of openness of the resources to contributors and users on nondiscriminatory terms and some degree of freedom that users enjoy when accessing the resource. They must be able to use it "as they see fit" (Frischmann 2012: 92). A commons approach does not imply the right to use the resource for free or without any terms and conditions. What it implies is that the choices that users make upon accessing the resource are not predetermined or prioritized by the resource managers (Frischmann 2012). Because of their characteristics, population biobanks can be construed as knowledge commons. They involve a set of resources that are *pooled* – stored samples and associated data – *with a purpose* – the goal of population biobanks is to produce valuable data and knowledge by enabling genomics research that advances our understanding of how genes and environment affect health – that can be best achieved when the resource is *shared by a community of users* – researchers in the biomedical field.[1]

Population biobanks also share another feature with knowledge commons: they contribute to solving social dilemmas of three kinds: overcoming financial barriers that are insurmountable for the average researcher, balancing access to the resources with the risk of depletion and pollution, and management of negative externalities. The first dilemma is one of cost. The costs involved with setting up and maintaining a biobank are substantial and unaffordable for the average researcher or institution. Population biobanks are vehicles to pool resources that researchers would not have at their disposal if they were acting individually. In the absence of biobanks, the collective loss would be tangible because it would reduce opportunities for conducting genomics research and producing genomics knowledge. Population biobanks solve the dilemma by pooling sufficient resources and allowing researchers to use the infrastructure on a discriminatory basis.

The second dilemma is one of depletion and pollution of the resources through use. The dilemma stems from the fact that biobanks are only valuable if they are accessed and used, but access and use can diminish or pollute the resource and create negative externalities in the form of risk of harm (invasion of privacy, discrimination, social stigma, or distress) for those who have consented to the storage of their samples and personal data. Depletion is inherent to the nature of some of the collected resources. Research with human tissue, for example, naturally consumes a certain quantity of the resource whenever it is studied. To perform certain analyses, researchers must have access to tissue, cut a slice out, and analyze in their lab. This is a classic example of a social dilemma: the resource is diminished as a result of being used. More use means increasing social value but also diminishing the resource. With regard to pollution, data is valuable if it can be read and used by the scientific community. If there were a risk that a researcher could, perhaps negligently, destroy some data, change the format, add irrelevant and confusing information, and so forth, the social utility of the resource would be diminished. To solve this dilemma, biobanks are set up with governance bodies and policies that require them to act in the public interest as stewards of the resource. Biobanks thus only grant access to tissue and data if users agree to use the resources in a way that does not compromise them for future uses. To this end, biobanks monitor access and use by ensuring that tissue is used in research that is scientifically sound and in the public interest.

Finally, the third dilemma concerns the negative externalities associated with the use (and misuse) of the samples and data stored at a biobank. Access to these resources could harm those who agreed to tissue and personal information being

[1] According to Hess and Ostrom (2003), data and knowledge can be respectively labeled as artifacts and ideas. In the case of population biobanks, artifacts consist of the physical stream of data that flow from the research conducted using the biobank and include articles, research notes, books, databases, computer files, and webpages. Ideas are the nonphysical flow units that collectively constitute the body of genomics knowledge.

stored. Third parties could use genotypic and phenotypic data as well as other personal information to identify the person linked to this data and engage in harmful behavior against that person. Further, those who access a biobank could make incidental discoveries (regarding predisposition to disease, paternity, and similar situations) that could have negative consequences for participants or family members. To solve this dilemma, biobanks also act as trusted protectors of the interests of participants, being set up in a way that ensures that the resource is used without compromising the interests of the donors. This is done through record de-identification, data encryption, and other security measures.

To resolve these social dilemmas, biobanks have been increasingly managed as stewards of samples and data, acting as trusted mediators between the interests of participants and the public interest in pursuing research and arbiters among scientists competing for the use of the resource. The commons approach naturally constitutes a governance framework that ensures that the social value of the resource is maximized while the types of social dilemmas that I describe are solved.

5.3 POPULATION BIOBANKS ARE INCREASINGLY MANAGED AS KNOWLEDGE COMMONS

According to Frischmann (2012), an infrastructure is managed as a commons if it grants access to the resource to a certain community of users on a nondiscriminatory basis, that is, independently from the identity of the user and for a wide range of uses that are not predetermined by the infrastructure managers. Normatively, nondiscriminatory sharing is a desirable management principle as infrastructure uses are likely to generate positive externalities or "spillovers" (Frischmann and Lemley 2007) consisting of artifacts and ideas that are produced by the very fact that the infrastructure is constantly used in novel and creative ways. When applied to population biobanks, nondiscriminatory sharing entails making the research platform accessible by members of the scientific community with regard to their identity and for a wide variety of researches.

A review of current access and use policies of population biobanks reveals that nondiscriminatory sharing has been adopted by many organizations. According to the P3G catalogues, which are maintained by the international consortium Public Population Project in Genomics (P3G), 66 of the 164 collections of human tissue included in the database grant some sort of access to external researchers. These collections include large population biobanks (with tissue collected from more than 100,000 participants) in Malaysia, Denmark, Australia, the Netherlands, the United States, Saudi Arabia, Taiwan, France, Norway, China, and the United Kingdom.[2] The database also includes an Access Catalogue (www.p3gobservatory.org/access/list.htm)

[2] The results were retrieved by submitting a query to www.p3gobservatory.org/ and selecting "Allow access to biological samples to external researchers."

with detailed information on data and samples for 42 biobanks. The information concerns (1) whether data or samples can be accessed by researchers outside the study/biobank; (2) whether data/samples can leave the study/biobank facility/country under the policies and regulations of the proposed study; (3) restriction to the category/type of investigator requesting access to the study; and (4) limitations regarding the scientific scope of the projects that can use the study's data/sample. An analysis of this data shows that researchers outside the study/biobank can access data and/or samples of all 42 studies. Thirty-six biobanks allow for samples to be transported to a different research facility (domestic and foreign) for analysis. Twenty-seven biobanks allow all kinds of scientific uses of samples and data. Of the 15 biobanks that restrict use, the most commons restrictions involve limiting research to certain diseases or for the uses that are expressly listed in the informed consent. In four cases, the restriction consists merely in approval by an ethics committee.

One of the organizations that has adopted nondiscriminatory sharing is UK Biobank. Researchers from all over the world can access data and tissue stored by UK Biobank on a nondiscriminatory basis. The Access Procedures make the resource accessible to users who are registered and agree to respect certain terms and conditions as long as their research proposals are properly submitted and approved by the biobank. Access is granted "without preferential or exclusive access for any person" and all proposals are subject "to the same application process and approval criteria" (UK Biobank 2011). Moreover, access is granted for a wide range of research projects. Sample and data were in fact collected upon sample sources consenting to any kind of research as long as it is "intended to improve the prevention, diagnosis and treatment of illness, and the promotion of health throughout society" (UK Biobank 2006).

Upon submitting a research proposal detailing what the researcher intends to access (data, sample, tissues and/or recontacting participants) and the scientific rational supporting the study, the biobank managers – the principal investigator and UK Biobank Coordinating Centre – review the proposal. Since the proposals are purposely heterogeneous, the level of scrutiny and requirements vary depending on the nature of the proposal. If researchers request access to data only, the scrutiny is minimal. The level of review is higher for research proposals aiming at accessing stored tissues or involving the recontact of participants, and that are potentially controversial: "Following initial assessment by the executive team, all applications are assessed and either approved or rejected (with right of appeal) by an independent Access Subcommittee" (Sudlow et al. 2015). Occasionally proposals are referred to the University of Oxford's Ethox Centre and the biobanks' Ethics and Governance Council for review in the event the proposed research raises ethical issues.

Data on researchers' access to UK Biobank confirm that the resource has been managed as a commons. Since 2012, more than 1,000 researchers successfully registered to access the resource (Sudlow et al. 2015), and many have been able to ultimately access the biobank with the intent to pursue a wide range of research uses.

According to a summary posted on the UK Biobank's website, research conducted since 2012 has involved 39 topics, ranging from genetics and genotyping studies (not surprisingly the most popular category with 253 proposals), cancer, and cardiovascular disease, to pain, asthma, mental health, and sleep (UK Biobank 2015).

What is also typical of (and perhaps unique to) research infrastructures is that the resource grows through use. In fact, accessing users agree to feed back to UK Biobank the results of their research. Section C11.4 of the Access Procedures provides that "within 6 months of publication or 12 months of when the research project was to be completed, the Applicant PI is required to provide the results of the research, and the raw data behind them, for inclusion in the Resource in such detail and format as UK Biobank reasonably requires" (UK Biobank 2011). Accessing researchers are also under the obligation "to use their best endeavours to publish the findings of any research deriving from the Resource in an academic journal or on an open source publication site within 6 months after the date when it was agreed that the research would be completed" (UK Biobank 2011).

5.4 THE ROLE OF EXPERTS IN SOLVING REGULATORY OBSTACLES AND NEGATIVE EXTERNALITIES

As this survey of policies on access shows, biobanks are increasingly managed as commons, permitting external researchers to access the collection, to extract data and samples from the platform, and to perform scientifically and ethically sound research without predetermined aims. This has not always been the case. In fact, when biobanks emerged as new platforms, the existing regulatory framework – composed of both legal rules and rules-in-use – and a widely popular narrative that genetics was exceptional, and therefore needed special handling, were preconditions for contesting and opposing a commons approach to biobank management. As Frischmann et al. (2014b) point out, the "narratives of creation and operation and [the] history" matter in shaping the attributes of a knowledge commons. This is certainly the case with the emergence of population biobanks. In this section, I explore the evolutionary shift of biobank governance from a non-commons approach to a commons one in some detail. I discuss the regulatory and discursive obstacles to the emergence of biobanks as knowledge commons and argue that biobanking governance experts played a crucial role in reorienting the debate toward a commons approach.

When population biobanks emerged in the 1990s as new research resources, the governance framework that was applied to them by default was composed of traditional principles of scientific research governance. The existing legal rules (international and domestic instruments) (Council for International Organizations of Medical Sciences 2002; World Medical Association 2013) and rules-in-fact (professional guidelines and informal norms) emphasized protections of research subjects through a stringent conception of the requirement of informed consent, recognized the right of researchers and institutions to control collections, and discouraged resource sharing with external researchers and institutions. This regulatory framework was consequential as it made it difficult for advocates of nondiscriminatory sharing to defend a commons approach to biobank governance.

Two rules were particularly problematic. First, the requirement of informed consent to research was understood as demanding that samples and data could be used only if research subjects disclosed all foreseeable uses in some detail and consented to all of them. This reading of informed consent was a clear obstacle to the emergence of biobanks as research infrastructures for science that was not hypothesis driven. It was an obstacle to establishing both retrospective and prospective biobanks. Retrospective biobanks entailed converting existing collections of samples and data that hospitals, pathology departments, and university labs had maintained for decades before the advent of DNA sequencing. The informed consent taken at that time did not contemplate genetic studies. Many commentators criticized the plan to set up biobanks arguing that a conventional readings of key research ethics governance instruments (Council for International Organizations of Medical Sciences 2002; World Medical Association 2013) prohibited the use of stored samples when intended uses were not foreseen at the time participants had given consent unless every participant was recontacted and agreed to the new uses (Ayme 2003). Unfortunately, recontacting is not a viable option because many of the participants have likely died or moved or, if found, could decline to consent to the new uses. In addition, some argued that the requirement of informed consent inherently prohibits establishing prospective biobanks because research platforms are based on the premise that uses cannot be predicted at the time research participants consent to the storage of samples and data. Informed consent, some argued, was valid only for expressly identified uses (Ghosh 2003). The second obstacle came from the prevailing norm among scientists and clinicians that collections are deemed to be the "property" of the researcher or institution that had established them. This implied the right to exclude other researchers from using the resource, a right that is clearly at odds with nondiscriminatory sharing (Reilly 1999).

In addition to regulatory obstacles, a popular narrative (genetics exceptionalism) fed the discourse that genetic resources presented unique risks and opening access to them would have been unwise and unreasonably dangerous to research subjects and their relatives (Murray 1997; Reilly 1999). According to this narrative, which gained traction in the 1990s, genetic data is qualitatively different from other health-related information in at least three aspects:

> Firstly, genetic tests can provide more accurate data on the likelihood of an individual developing a particular medical condition. Secondly, genetics tests can provide information about the family members of the individuals who is tested, and conversely, the health status of family members can provide information about the

> genetic and future health of the individual. Thirdly, genetic (test) information is more profoundly personal than non-genetic medical information, and one's essential identity is largely determined by one's genetic makeup. (Launis 2003: 90)

Genetic exceptionalism scholars viewed genetic data as "future diaries" (Murray 1997) and maintained that third parties who were given access to this data would read our future lives. This raised concerns that access could result in discrimination against research subjects (Council for Responsible Genetics 1990). Genetic exceptionalism thus represented a powerful narrative against the idea of nondiscriminatory sharing of genetic data stored in biobanks.

In the face of these regulatory and ideological challenges, the community of scholars and policymakers working on biobank governance played a key role in shifting the debate from models that were anchored on protecting research subjects and researcher's ownership of collection to a commons approach. The conceptual shift became possible when members of this community began developing expertise specifically tailored to biobanks. Before the emergence of biobank-tailored expertise, scholars and practitioners had deployed ideas generated in their specific fields (research ethics, health and intellectual property (IP) laws, science management, or basic research) and tended to the existing governance models that I discussed earlier. Many were maintaining an almost dogmatic approach to research subjects' autonomy, which was often deployed as a conceptual tool to restrict the wide range of uses that biobanks were enabling. This was compounded by the then widely shared norm that human tissue collections were "owned" by a certain researcher or lab and not open for sharing with the scientific community. This intellectual posture slowly faded in the background as biobank-specific expertise began emerging in the mid-2000s. Scholars started thinking about and publishing on biobanks' unique characteristics and issues. They participated in policy discussions at the institutional, local, and international levels (Capron et al. 2009). Funding agencies allocated money to study the ethical, legal, and social implications of genomics (also known as ELSI programs), and doctoral and postdoctoral programs began training younger scholars in biobanking governance.

It is thus important to acknowledge the role of experts in breaking path dependency set by existing regulations and professional expertise in reshaping narratives and patterns of interaction around this emerging knowledge commons. Initially both sets of rules generated resistance to the demands for innovation embodied in emerging biobanks. It is through the interventions of resource-specific experts, working in partnership with the scientific community, that the tension between innovation and preservation was mediated and resolved by creating innovative governance paths. These paths have not only enabled innovation but also reformed those rules-in-use in the scientific community and built renewed interest in cooperation among scientists. It was the active role of community members, especially scientists and funders, who pushed biobanking through its initial stages and shaped its identity as a common pool resource and as a source of knowledge to be widely shared. Policy development was very much driven from the bottom up by practice, where "practice" should be read both as the practice of science (and scientific research) and the practice of governing the resource. Actors with different viewpoints were able to contribute to the discussion as a community and define and redefine governance objectives as the practices evolved as a direct result of technological and scientific change and reflectively as a result of changes in the governance mechanisms.

Since the emergence of resource-specific expertise, the governance debate became enriched with new ideas and approaches. Guided by "practical wisdom" (Knoppers 2004), experts developed a consensus that existing collections and databases could be merged into biobanks (Helgesson et al. 2007) and that participants' consent could be broad enough to encompass future, unknown uses of samples and data (Petrini 2010). A 2012 review of major biobanks' practices shows that 8 out of 11 adopted a broad consent approach and that the other 3 rejected specific consent (Master et al. 2014). In 2013, Steinsbekk et al. (2013: 897) noted that broad consent had been adopted "by many current biobank projects, like UK Biobank, CARTaGENE ... and the Norwegian HUNT study." Furthermore, consensus emerged that biobanks were more valuable resources if a multitude of researchers could access them to pursue a variety of studies (Kaye 2011). Finally, in the United States, proposed changes to the regulatory process for research with human samples would permit biobanks to collect samples using a "brief standard consent form" in which prospective donors agree "to generally permit future research" (Office for Human Research Protections 2011).

Biobanking governance experts thus shifted the narrative from the risks of research subjects to the social value of these nascent infrastructures, opening new opportunities for biobanking. The emerging consensus was that biobanks needed to be purposely designed as versatile resources for open-ended inquiries rather than hypothesis-driven science (Bush and Moore 2012). Regulatory models were refined and focused on issues of data and sample ownership and access, on acceptable levels of risk of traceability of the sample sources, on patentability and benefit-sharing arrangements (Cambon-Thomsen et al. 2007; Capron et al. 2009; Elger et al. 2008; Greely 2007).[3] As a result, *de novo*, large-scale population biobanks were established:[4] they were funded by public money, storing samples collected from scratch and linked to personal information (including medical records, family histories, and other personal data) in ways that protected the identity of the sample source, and meant to be the research community for a wide variety of uses.

[3] The concept of benefit sharing is rooted in the 1992 Rio Convention on Biological Diversity. Although purposely made not applicable to human genetic resources, biobanking scholars used to frame discussions of social value and social justice (Andrews 2005).

[4] These were proposed primarily as tool to study genomics at the population level in Iceland, the United Kingdom, Estonia, Latvia, Sweden, Singapore, and Quebec, Canada (Austin et al. 2003).

5.5 THE SUCCESS OF BIOBANKS AS KNOWLEDGE COMMONS

In March 2009, *Time Magazine* picked biobanking as one of the top 10 ideas changing the world (Park 2009). In 2014, at least 330 biobanks were located in 29 European countries (Kuhn et al. 2015). These and other biobanks are increasingly managed as commons. They are managed as research infrastructures for the study of a broad range of scientific questions that are not precisely determined at the moment the resources are set up and participants consent to the storage of samples and data (Austin et al. 2003: Hansson et al. 2006). They enable basic research that is not always hypothesis driven but rather is often an open-ended inquiry looking for associations between genetic traits and major diseases. Researchers from all over the world can request access. Ordinarily they must submit a proposal to the biobank, which reviews it to make sure it is scientifically and ethically sound and fulfills a public interest in the form of generating knowledge. Users are required to feed data back to the bank so that the resource is enriched by use.

The interactions between users and resources over the past 20 years have led to an impressive degree of maturity in governance approaches. Consistent with other examples within the commons literature, biobanking governance provides a clear example of nested governance (Ostrom 1990). Nested institutions imply an institutional continuum from local to global. Biobanks are governed by multilevel, interacting, nested layers of institutions – from the governing bodies of the resource itself to international law. Governance instruments include informed consent forms, tissue access protocols, material transfer agreements, technology transfer agreements, research agreements among institutions, rules set by consortia, professional organization guidelines, and national and international statutes.

The case study of population biobanks further confirms that bottom-up approaches are effective in governing shared resources. Akin to physical resources, knowledge commons can be organized effectively in nested structures with multiple layers of activities with a regulatory priority of community-based institutions. These layers are organized around the primacy of the local level and an emphasis on rules that are being developed to bind members of a community of practice around a biobank or a consortium. Formal law and the government are increasingly assuming a position of subsidiarity, providing regulatory support for interactions of members of the biobanking community rather than regulating the interactions directly.

While experts should receive credit for the success of population biobanks, endogenous forces have also contribute to the rise of this resource. Technological and scientific developments have reshaped the action arena, to use commons scholars' language (Frischmann et al. 2014a: 35), in ways that favored the use of biobanks by multiple researchers in cooperation. Technological developments include progress in data encryption and database security which have significantly reduced privacy and confidentiality concerns and have increased opportunity for research exchanges among scientists. The advent of big data and cloud computing facilitated the scaling up of biobanks and also made international collaborations a feasible, efficient, and appealing mode of operation of genomics science. Scientific advancements injected complexity into our understanding of genomics information and their role in explaining health and disease. Most diseases escaped simplistic explanations but required sophisticated conceptual tools to unravel the complexities of the gene/environment interactions as explanatory bases of disease. This change in perspective "normalized" genomics knowledge and took away some of the concerns that had been captured by the concept of genetic exceptionalism. With a less "exceptional" view of genes and more complex and nuanced conceptual models to capture genetic contribution to human health, genomics is now a more layered field in which biobanks play a strategic role as infrastructures that mediate among a vast array of data, forms of knowledge, and expertise. Population biobanks are now strategic infrastructures, established scientifically, and increasingly used by research networks to perform genomics research.

The success of biobanks stems also from their ability to coproduce innovation in science. Biobanks have in fact benefited from macrolevel trends in science and medicine and, in turn, have acted as infrastructures enabling innovation. They contributed to the reduction in cost and time needed generate genomics knowledge, to the rise of data intensive science (Critchlow et al. 2013; Schofield et al. 2010), to the growth of research collaborations among scientists of different countries, and to generating knowledge that is at the root of the paradigm shift toward more personalized forms of health care. As a result, biobanks are now ideally positioned as strategic research infrastructures that facilitate knowledge commons building.

5.6 THE NEXT CHALLENGES IN BIOBANKING GOVERNANCE

Since these resources have been in operation, biobanking governance experts have kept debating and refining their understanding on how to maximize their social value. New governance challenges have also emerged from practice as more researchers are accessing data. For instance, using biobanks in international collaborations (Harris et al. 2012; Kaye 2011) is problematic because of the lack of data-sharing standardization (Knoppers et al. 2011), poor coordination among investigators (Fransson et al. 2015), and legal restriction to the circulation of samples and data (Schulte in den Bäumen, Paci, and Ibarreta 2010). Much governance work has thus focused on (1) improving data and protocol standardization (Hudson et al. 2010; Joly et al. 2012), (2) expanding access for external researchers (Knoppers 2013), (3) harmonizing data privacy regulation (Dove 2015), and (4) identifying the proper way to handle incidental and non-incidental findings that have clinical relevance (Bledsoe et al. 2013; Wolf 2013a, 2013b, Wolf et al. 2012). Biobanks should develop systems for monitoring those who are accessing data as well as explicit sanctions and dispute resolution strategies (Joly et al.

2011). The role of commercial interests in relation to publicly funded biobanks is also being debated (Caulfield et al. 2014; Nilstun et al. 2006; Turner et al. 2013). Rules are being developed in the area of authorship and attribution of work for those who contribute to the management of the infrastructure but are not knowledge generators (in the form of generating research ideas or drafting manuscripts for publication) (Colledge et al. 2013).

While substantial steps have been made in the right direction, the nested institution model for biobank governance lacks key elements. Governance is "thick" at the local level and at the international level but lacking in between. At the local level, governance is robust because of the requirements imposed by research ethics, institutional review of protocols, and the use of contract law to solve issues that include sample and data ownership, data access, funding, and authorship. At the national or international level, laws, declarations, treaties, and judicial opinions also provide a rational (yet contested) governance framework that, with gaps, for the support of biobanks. Moving forward, governance-building work needs to focus on the levels in between. A layer of institutional governance that fosters sharing, collaboration, and sustainability to this important resource needs to be built for biobanks to become effectively embedded in our health systems. The lessons developed by scholars and practitioners of the commons are helpful in identifying the goals and objectives of new governance arrangements, offering suggestions on how the authority vacuum can be filled and contributing to the cultural shift of construing biobanking not only as research infrastructure but also as a public health resource.

Further governance work needs to be done in harmonizing biobanks to guarantee full resource exploitation and minimizing resource pollution and degradation (Karimi-Busheri et al. 2015). Policies were developed at the biobank level or at the level of consortia of research and then spilled over into the field and became norms for more biobanks and consortia. Questions of harmonization, sharing protocols, and quality control became progressively the focus of debates pushing questions of ownership, consent, and confidentiality away from the center of the debate.

Further work also needs to be done toward incorporating patients' views of biobank governance and providing feedback mechanisms to research participants. With regard to patients, a recent study of the cancer patient community in the United Kingdom by Wilcox et al. (2015: 182) concludes that "mutual respect and effective collaboration between lay members and professionals is essential for biobanks to achieve their potential value in health research and thus for future patient benefit." The authors points out that "the consent and willingness of patients and the public to participate in this research will be vital and their involvement will help ensure that the trust and transparency, which is needed, can be maintained (Wilcox et al. 2015: 183). Another recent study, also among patient in the United

Kingdom, shows that participants would welcome a more interactive engagement with the biobank and that they would welcome more information through an online interface (Teare et al. 2015).

A particularly thorny issue is the problem of feeding results back to individuals who decide to participate in a population biobank. It is an issue that has been a contested and complex one to resolve (Wolf et al. 2015).

With regard to the future of population biobanks, my hope is that they will become fully integrated in the public health system and eventually in clinical practice as infrastructures generating knowledge that contributes to assessing health outcomes. With the practice of medicine becoming more "personalized" (Davies 2015), clinicians will increasingly incorporate biobank-generated data into the analysis of a patient's health record. This will close the benefits loop, enhance the collective value of this commons, and reinforce patients' willingness to consent to their tissue and data being stored and used in biobanking. Furthermore, genomics knowledge produced by biobanks will be part, hopefully, of everyday medicine in which patients are treated based on a layered approach to disease (not a full personalized one), driven by an integrated analysis of genotype and phenotype data. Funding will be ensured by the recognition of biobanks as pillars of the public health system. Data will be increasingly shared across borders with members obtaining access based on the promise to respect the terms of agreement of the genomics consortia that make the data available to the community of scientists and clinicians. This way, biobanking will truly spread its wings and achieve its potential as a knowledge commons.

Overall, the case study of biobanking governance reinforces the merits of the framework proposed by Frischmann et al. (2014a: 470) and its usefulness in capturing "the complexity of the interplay among characteristics of particular resources; various communities and groups; and the social, political, economic, and institutional attributes of governance." Biobanking struggled to become a resource with an identity connected to but distinct from traditional biomedical research with human subjects. Its role is, to some extent, still contested and debated as part of the persistent fixation on research subjects' risk and ethics review practices that are not attuned to data-intensive science. A challenge for the future is to overcome one of the weaknesses of the current biobanking governance system, that is, the mid-level governance gap or "authority vacuum," as argued by Jerry Menikoff (2010), the director of the US federal government's Office for Human Research Protections, and developed in the context of biobanks by Dove et al. (2014). Resource governance arrangements must be developed to connect local governance levels with national and international policies. This governance gap is slowing down biobanking growth and eventually could hinder this resource from expressing its full potential as a knowledge commons.

REFERENCES

Andrews, Lori B., Harnessing the Benefits of Biobanks. 33 *Journal of Law, Medicine and Ethics* (1):22–30 (2005).

Austin, M. A., S. Harding, and C. McElroy, Genebanks: A Comparison of Eight Proposed International Genetic Databases. 6 *Public Health Genomics* (1):37–45 (2003).

Ayme, Ségolène, Data Storage and DNA Banking for Biomedical Research: Technical, Social and Ethical Issues. 11 *European Journal Human Genetics* (12):906–8 (2003).

Bledsoe, Marianna J., Ellen Wright Clayton, Amy L. McGuire, William E. Grizzle, P. Pearl O'Rourke, and Nikolajs Zeps, Return of Research Results from Genomic Biobanks: A Call for Data. 15 *Genetics in Medicine* (2):159–60 (2013).

Bush, William S., and Jason H. Moore, 8 Genome-Wide Association Studies. *PLoS Computational Biology* (12):e1002822 (2012).

Cambon-Thomsen, Anne, Emmanuelle Rial-Sebbag, and Bartha M. Knoppers, Trends in Ethical and Legal Frameworks for the Use of Human Biobanks. 30 *European Respiratory Journal* (2):373–82 (2007).

Capron, Alexander Morgan, Alexandre Mauron, Bernice Simone Elger, Andrea Boggio, Agomoni Ganguli-Mitra, and Nikola Biller-Andorno, Ethical Norms and the International Governance of Genetic Databases and Biobanks: Findings from an International Study. 19 *Kennedy Institute of Ethics Journal* (2):101–24 (2009).

Caulfield, Timothy, Sarah Burningham, Yann Joly, Zubin Master, Mahsa Shabani, Pascal Borry, Allan Becker, Michael Burgess, Kathryn Calder, Christine Critchley, Kelly Edwards, Stephanie M. Fullerton, Herbert Gottweis, Robyn Hyde-Lay, Judy Illes, Rosario Isasi, Kazuto Kato, Jane Kaye, Bartha M. Knoppers, John Lynch, Amy McGuire, Eric Meslin, Dianne Nicol, Kieran O'Doherty, Ubaka Ogbogu, Margaret Otlowski, Daryl Pullman, Nola Ries, Chris Scott, Malcolm Sears, Helen Wallace, and Ma'n H. Zawati, A Review of the Key Issues Associated with the Commercialization of Biobanks. 1 *Journal of Law and the Biosciences* (1):94–110 (2014). doi: 10.1093/jlb/lst004.

Colledge, Flora M. A., Bernice S. Elger, and David M. Shaw, "Conferring Authorship": Biobank Stakeholders' Experiences with Publication Credit in Collaborative Research. 8 *PloS ONE* (9):e76686 (2013).

Council for International Organizations of Medical Sciences, International Ethical Guidelines for Biomedical Research Involving Human Subjects (2002). www.cioms.ch/publications/layout_guide2002.pdf

Council for Responsible Genetics, Position Paper on Genetic Discrimination. Position Paper on Human Genome Initiative. 3 *Issues in Reproductive and Genetic Engineering: Journal of International Feminist Analysis* (3):287 (1990).

Critchlow, Terence and Kerstin Kleese Van Dam, *Data-Intensive Science*, Chapman & Hall/CRC Computational Science Series (Boca Raton, FL: CRC 2013).

Davies, Kevin, *The $1,000 Genome: The Revolution in DNA Sequencing and the New Era of Personalized Medicine* (New York: Simon and Schuster 2015).

Dove, Edward S., Biobanks, Data Sharing, and the Drive for a Global Privacy Governance Framework. 43 *Journal of Law, Medicine & Ethics* (4):675–89 (2015). doi: 10.1111/jlme.12311.

Dove, Edward S., Yann Joly, Bartha M. Knoppers, V. Ozdemir, Y. Joly, E. Kirby, and D. Avard, Power to the People: A Wiki-Governance Model for Biobanks. 1 *Genome Biology* 158 (2012).

Dove, Edward S., Bartha M. Knoppers, and Ma'n H. Zawati, Toward an Ethics Safe Harbor for Global Biomedical Research. 1 *Journal of Law and the Biosciences* (1):3–51 (2014). doi: 10.1093/jlb/lst002.

Elger, Bernice S., Nikola Biller-Andorno, Alex Mauron, and Alexander Capron, *Ethical Issues in Governing Biobanks: Global Perspectives* (London: Ashgate 2008).

Fransson, Martin N., Emmanuelle Rial-Sebbag, Mathias Brochhausen, and Jan-Eric Litton, Toward a Common Language for Biobanking. 23 *European Journal Human Genetics* (1):22–28 (2015). doi: 10.1038/ejhg.2014.45.

Frischmann, Brett M., *Infrastructure: The Social Value of Shared Resources* (New York: Oxford University Press 2012).

Frischmann, Brett M., Two Enduring Lessons from Elinor Ostrom. 9 *Journal of Institutional Economics* (4):387–406 (2013).

Frischmann, Brett M., and Mark A. Lemley, Spillovers. 107 *Columbia Law Review* (1):257–301 (2007).

Frischmann, Brett M., Michael J. Madison, and Katherine J. Strandburg (eds.), *Governing Knowledge Commons* (New York: Oxford University Press 2014a).

Frischmann, Brett M., Michael J. Madison, and Katherine J. Strandburg, Governing Knowledge Commons. In *Governing Knowledge Commons* (Brett M. Frischmann, Michael J. Madison, and Katherine J. Strandburg, eds., 1–43. Oxford University Press 2014b).

Ghosh, Pallab, Will Biobank Pay Off? Last modified September 24, 2003. http://news.bbc.co.uk/2/hi/health/3134622.stm

Greely, Henry T., The Uneasy Ethical and Legal Underpinnings of Large-Scale Genomic Biobanks. 8 *Annual Review of Genomics and Human Genetics* 343–64 (2007).

Hansson, Mats G., Joakim Dillner, Claus R. Bartram, Joyce A. Carlson, and Gert Helgesson, Should Donors Be Allowed to Give Broad Consent to Future Biobank Research? 7 *The Lancet Oncology* (3):266–69 (2006).

Harris, Jennifer R., Paul Burton, Bartha M. Knoppers, Klaus Lindpaintner, Marianna Bledsoe, Anthony J. Brookes, Isabelle Budin-Ljosne, Rex Chisholm, David Cox, Mylene Deschenes, Isabel Fortier, Pierre Hainaut, Robert Hewitt, Jane Kaye, Jan-Eric Litton, Andres Metspalu, Bill Ollier, Lyle J. Palmer, Aarno Palotie, Markus Pasterk, Markus Perola, Peter H. J. Riegman, Gert-Jan van Ommen, Martin Yuille, and Kurt Zatloukal, Toward a Roadmap in Global Biobanking for Health. 20 *European Journal Human Genetics* (11):1105–11 (2012).

Helgesson, Gert, Joakim Dillner, Joyce Carlson, Claus R. Bartram, and Mats G. Hansson, Ethical Framework for Previously Collected Biobank Samples. 25 *Nature Biotechnology* (9):973–76 (2007).

Hess, Charlotte, The Unfolding of the Knowledge Commons. 8 *St Antony's International Review* (1):13–24 (2012).

Hess, Charlotte, and Elinor Ostrom, Ideas, Artifacts, and Facilities: Information as a Common-Pool Resource. 66 *Law and Contemporary Problems* (1/2):111–45 (2003).

Hess, Charlotte, and Elinor Ostrom, *Understanding Knowledge as a Commons: From Theory to Practice* (Cambridge, MA: MIT Press 2007).

Hudson, Thomas J., Warwick Anderson, Axel Aretz, Anna D. Barker, Cindy Bell, Rosa R. Bernabé, M. K. Bhan, Fabien Calvo, Iiro Eerola, and Daniela S. Gerhard, International Network of Cancer Genome Projects. 464 *Nature* (7291):993–98 (2010).

Joly, Yann, Edward S. Dove, Bartha M. Knoppers, Martin Bobrow, and Don Chalmers, Data Sharing in the Post-Genomic World: The Experience of the International Cancer Genome Consortium (ICGC) Data Access Compliance Office (DACO). 8 *PLoS Computational Biology* (7):e1002549 (2012).

Joly, Yann, Nik Zeps, and Bartha M. Knoppers, Genomic Databases Access Agreements: Legal Validity and Possible Sanctions. 130 *Human Genetics* (3):441–49 (2011).

Karimi-Busheri, Feridoun and Aghdass Rasouli-Nia, Integration, Networking, and Global Biobanking in the Age of New Biology. In *Biobanking in the 21st Century* (Feridoun Karimi-Busheri, 1–9, Cham: Springer International Publishing 2015).

Kaye, Jane, From Single Biobanks to International Networks: Developing e-Governance. 130 *Human Genetics* (3):377–82 (2011).

Knoppers, Bartha M., Ethics Watch. 5 *Nature Reviews Genetics* (7):485 (2004).

Knoppers, Bartha M., Genomics: From Persons to Populations and Back Again. 56 *Genome* (10):537–39 (2013). doi: 10.1139/gen-2013–0148.

Knoppers, Bartha M., Jennifer R. Harris, Anne Marie Tassé, Isabelle Budin-Ljøsne, Jane Kaye, Mylène Deschênes, and Ma'n H Zawati, Toward a Data Sharing Code of Conduct for International Genomic Research. 3 *Genome Medicine* (7):46 (2011).

Kuhn, Klaus, Raffael Bild, and Helmut Spengler, BBMRI Catalogue. 5 *Journal of Clinical Bioinformatics* (Suppl 1):S19 (2015).

Launis, Veikko, Solidarity, Genetic Discrimination, and Insurance: A Defense of Weak Genetic Exceptionalism. 29 *Social Theory and Practice* (1):87–111 (2003).

Master, Zubin, Lisa Campo-Engelstein, and Timothy Caulfield, Scientists' Perspectives on Consent in the Context of Biobanking Research. 23 *European Journal of Human Genetics* (5):569–74 (2015). doi: 10.1038/ejhg.2014.143.

Menikoff, Jerry, The Paradoxical Problem with Multiple-IRB Review. 363 *New England Journal of Medicine* (17):1591–93 (2010). doi: 10.1056/NEJMp1005101.

Murray, Thomas H., Genetic Exceptionalism and "Future Diaries": Is Genetic Information Different from Other Medical Information. In *Genetic Secrets: Protecting Privacy and Confidentiality in the Genetic Era* (Mark A. Rothstein, ed., 60–73, Yale University Press 1997).

Nilstun, Tore and Göran Hermerén, Human Tissue Samples and Ethics – Attitudes of the General Public in Sweden to Biobank Research. 9 *Medicine, Health Care and Philosophy* (1):81–86 (2006). doi: 10.1007/s11019-005-7984-4.

Office for Human Research Protections, ANPRM for Revision to Common Rule. Accessed June 6, 2011. www.hhs.gov/ohrp/humansubjects/anprm2011page.html.

Organisation for Economic Co-operation and Development, *Creation and Governance of Human Genetic Research Databases* (Paris: OECD 2006).

Ostrom, Elinor, *Governing the Commons: The Evolution of Institutions for Collective Action* (Cambridge: Cambridge University Press 1990).

Ostrom, Elinor, *The Drama of the Commons* (Washington, DC: National Academy Press 2002).

Park, Alice, 10 Ideas Changing the World Right Now: Biobanks. *Time*, 63 (2009).

Petrini, Carlo, "Broad" Consent, Exceptions to Consent and the Question of Using Biological Samples for Research Purposes Different from the Initial Collection Purpose. 70 *Social Science & Medicine* (2):217–20 (2010). doi: 10.1016/j.socscimed.2009.10.004.

Public Population Project in Genomics and Society (P3G), Biobank Lexicon. www.p3g.org/biobank-lexicon.

Reilly, Philip R., Efforts to Regulate the Collection and Use of Genetic Information. 123 *Archives of Pathology & Laboratory Medicine* (11):1066–70 (1999). doi:10.1043/0003–9985(1999)123<066:ETRTCA>2.0.CO;2.

Schofield, Paul N., Janan Eppig, Eva Huala, Martin Hrabe de Angelis, Mark Harvey, Duncan Davidson, Tom Weaver, Steve Brown, Damian Smedley, Nadia Rosenthal, Klaus Schughart, Vassilis Aidinis, Glauco Tocchini-Valentini, and John M. Hancock, Sustaining the Data and Bioresource Commons. 330 *Science* (6004):592–93 (2010). doi: 10.1126/science.1191506.

Schulte in den Bäumen, Tobias, Daniele Paci, and Dolores Ibarreta, Data Protection and Sample Management in Biobanking – A Legal Dichotomy. 6 *Genomics, Society and Policy* (1):1–14 (2010). doi: 10.1186/1746–5354-6–1-33.

Steinsbekk, Kristin Solum, Bjorn Kare Myskja, and Berge Solberg, Broad Consent versus Dynamic Consent in Biobank Research: Is Passive Participation an Ethical Problem? 21 *European Journal of Human Genetics* (9):897–902 (2013). doi: 10.1038/ejhg.2012.282.

Sudlow, Cathie, John Gallacher, Naomi Allen, Valerie Beral, Paul Burton, John Danesh, Paul Downey, Paul Elliott, Jane Green, Martin Landray, Bette Liu, Paul Matthews, Giok Ong, Jill Pell, Alan Silman, Alan Young, Tim Sprosen, Tim Peakman, and Rory Collins, UK Biobank: An Open Access Resource for Identifying the Causes of a Wide Range of Complex Diseases of Middle and Old Age. 12 *PLoS Med* (3):e1001779 (2015). doi: 10.1371/journal.pmed.1001779.

Teare, Harriet J. A., Michael Morrison, Edgar A. Whitley, and Jane Kaye, Toward "Engagement 2.0": Insights from a Study of Dynamic Consent with Biobank Participants. 1 *Digital Health* 1 (2015). doi: 10.1177/2055207615605644.

Turner, Andrew, Clara Dallaire-Fortier, and Madeleine J. Murtagh, Biobank Economics and the "Commercialization Problem." 7 *Spontaneous Generations: A Journal for the History and Philosophy of Science* (1):69–80 (2013).

UK Biobank, Consent Form (2006). www.ukbiobank.ac.uk/wp-content/uploads/2011/06/Consent_form.pdf

UK Biobank, Access Procedures: Application and Review Procedures for Access to the UK Biobank Resource (2011). www.ukbiobank.ac.uk/wp-content/uploads/2012/09/Access-Procedures-2011.pdf

UK Biobank, Submitted Access Applications by Areas of Interest, Submitted between 30.3.12 and 21.10.15 (2015). www.ukbiobank.ac.uk/wp-content/uploads/2014/12/Approved-areas-of-interest-graph-october-15.png

Wilcox, Maggie, Margaret Grayson, Mairead MacKenzie, Hilary Stobart, Helen Bulbeck, and Robert Flavel, The Importance of Quality Patient Advocacy to Biobanks: A Lay Perspective from Independent Cancer Patients Voice (ICPV), Based in the United Kingdom. In *Biobanking in the 21st Century* (171–83, Springer 2015).

Wolf, Susan M., Return of Individual Research Results and Incidental Findings: Facing the Challenges of Translational Science. 14 *Annual Review of Genomics and Human Genetics* 557–77 (2013a).

Wolf, Susan M., Return of Results in Genomic Biobank Research: Ethics Matters. 15 *Genetics in Medicine* (2):157–59 (2013b).

Wolf, Susan M., Brittney N. Crock, Brian Van Ness, Frances Lawrenz, Jeffrey P. Kahn, Laura M. Beskow, Mildred K. Cho, Michael F. Christman, Robert C. Green, and Ralph Hall, Managing Incidental Findings and Research Results in Genomic Research Involving Biobanks and Archived Data Sets. 14 *Genetics in Medicine* (4):361–84 (2012).

Wolf, Susan M., Rebecca Branum, Barbara A. Koenig, Gloria M. Petersen, Susan A. Berry, Laura M. Beskow, Mary B. Daly, Conrad V. Fernandez, Robert C. Green, and Bonnie S. LeRoy, Returning a Research Participant's Genomic Results to Relatives: Analysis and Recommendations. 43 *Journal of Law, Medicine & Ethics* (3):440–63 (2015).

World Medical Association, World Medical Association Declaration of Helsinki: Ethical Principles for Medical Research Involving Human Subjects. 310 *JAMA* (20):2191–94 (2013). doi: 10.1001/jama.2013.281053.

6

The Sentinel Initiative as a Knowledge Commons

Ryan Abbott

INTRODUCTION

The Sentinel System (Sentinel) is a national electronic safety-monitoring system for post-market evaluation of drugs and devices created by the US Food and Drug Administration ("FDA" or the "Agency"). Sentinel now has the ability to access data on more than 178 million individuals by tapping into existing databases maintained largely by private health care insurers and providers (Health Affairs 2015: 3). Unlike other post-market surveillance tools that primarily rely on third parties to submit reports of adverse events to FDA, Sentinel allows FDA to proactively monitor for safety issues in near real time. Sentinel is one of many initiatives designed to use electronic health records (EHRs) for purposes other than patient care (secondary use), and it may be the most successful domestic example of secondary use (Anonymous interviewee). Janet Woodcock, the director of the FDA's Center for Drug Evaluation and Research (CDER), has argued that Sentinel could "revolutionize" product safety (Abbott 2013: 239).

Sentinel came about as a result of a congressional mandate in the wake of the controversy over Vioxx's withdrawal. In September 2007, Congress passed the Food and Drug Administration Amendments Act (FDAAA), which, among other things, called for the Agency to develop an active surveillance system capable of accessing data from 25 million individuals by July 2010, and 100 million individuals by July 2012.[1] But FDAAA did not provide the Agency with much guidance in terms of how to build the system, and it did not provide FDA with any funding. Nor did Congress require the primary holders of this data (largely insurers and health care providers) to share data with FDA.

Ryan Abbott is Professor of Law and Health Sciences, School of Law, University of Surrey, Guildford, Surrey, UK, and Adjunct Assistant Professor, David Geffen School of Medicine, University of California, Los Angeles.

[1] Food and Drug Administration Amendments Act of 2007, Pub. L. No. 110–85, 121 Stat. 823 (2007).

After FDAAA was passed, a small group at FDA (the FDA Team) took ownership of the project and began making key decisions that would dictate the system's structure and governance (Anonymous interviewee). The group elected to operate Sentinel by contracting and self-regulation rather than through notice-and-comment rule making. That meant the Agency had to convince data holders to voluntarily share data. To do that, the Sentinel team engaged in an extensive and successful campaign to engage data holders by giving them the opportunity to participate in Sentinel's creation. The end result was that Sentinel was structured as a primarily distributed model, meaning that data holders almost entirely maintain control over their own data and only share aggregated results with FDA. However, the Agency did require data holders to translate their data into a common data format to allow FDA to analyze different data sets using common software. The Agency also elected to contract with a private entity to operate Sentinel, and to focus the system exclusively on safety research.

These strategic decisions were likely responsible for Sentinel achieving widespread data holder participation and for meeting (and exceeding) all of FDAAA's requirements. By that measure, Sentinel has certainly been a success. Until recently the Agency had no meaningful active surveillance tool, and now it has Sentinel – already answering queries from FDA on a regular basis and contributing to regulatory actions. Yet these strategic decisions limited the ability of Sentinel to be used by third parties and for non-safety queries.

6.1 METHODOLOGY

This case study followed the modified version of the Institutional Analysis and Development (IAD) framework (Frischmann et al. 2014). First, a literature review was conducted to search for published articles about Sentinel using medical, legal, and sociological databases including JSTOR, LexisNexis, PubMed, Scopus, and Westlaw. Relevant articles were reviewed and used to generate interview questions. Second, a series of semi-structured interviews were conducted with a range of stakeholders involved with the Sentinel Initiative (the larger program in which the Sentinel System is housed). The interviews ranged in length from 30 minutes to 60 minutes, with an average duration of about 45 minutes. Each interview was structured according to the modified IAD framework, using both generic and interviewee-specific interview questions. Information obtained from the interviewees was organized according to the IAD framework.

The following persons were interviewed for this case study:

- Richard Platt, Professor and Chair of the Department of Population Medicine, Harvard Pilgrim Health Care Institute. Dr. Platt was the Principal Investigator of the FDA Mini-Sentinel program and is now the Principal Investigator of Sentinel.

- Rachel Sherman, Deputy Commissioner for Medical Products and Tobacco. At the time of the interview, Dr. Sherman had recently retired from a 25-year career at FDA. She had been previously responsible for implementing Sentinel as Director of the Center for Drug Evaluation and Research's (CDER) Office of Medical Policy and Associate Center Director for Medical Policy.
- CDR Carlos Bell, USPHS, Senior Program Manager, Office of Medical Policy, FDA. CDR Bell is responsible for the program's day-to-day management.
- Marsha Raebel, Senior Investigator at Kaiser Permanente Colorado. Dr. Raebel leads the Sentinel program at Kaiser Permanente, one of the data partners participating in Sentinel.
- Barbara Evans, Alumnae College Professor of Law at the University of Houston. Professor Evans served as a consultant on privacy issues related to Sentinel for FDA.

Additional parties were interviewed and spoke on the condition of anonymity. Several data partners declined to be interviewed for this study.

6.2 SENTINEL'S BACKGROUND ENVIRONMENT

The use of electronic health records (EHRs) is booming, driven by ever-improving information technology, pro-EHR government policies, and the promise of EHR utilization resulting in better patient care with reduced costs (Hsiao et al. 2014). Yet widespread adoption of EHRs has the potential to do more than improve patient care (primary use); it may also be useful for a variety of non-direct patient care functions (secondary use).[2] For example, EHRs can be used in medical research for new drugs and devices, to evaluate health care providers, to compare hospital facilities, and to help insurance companies make utilization decisions (Safran et al. 2007). In fact, EHR use is even more prevalent among health insurance companies than health providers.[3]

Another obvious application for secondary use of EHRs is in the context of post-market drug and device surveillance, which is to say the ongoing evaluation of the safety and efficacy of medical products that are already being sold to the public (Abbott, 2014a). Unfortunately, the use of EHRs in post-market surveillance has been slow to develop. In part, this may be due to challenges in working with EHR data, which often suffers from quality problems, and EHRs often struggle

[2] "Secondary use of health data can enhance healthcare experiences for individuals, expand knowledge about disease and appropriate treatments, strengthen understanding about the effectiveness and efficiency of our healthcare systems, support public health and security goals, and aid businesses in meeting the needs of their customers" (Safran et al. 2007: 3).

[3] This chapter uses the term "electronic health records" to refer to electronic databases of patient information maintained by both providers and insurers, even though the term is not always used to refer to insurance company databases. Insurer databases generally do not contain the same sorts of patient information as provider databases.

(sometimes by design) with interoperability (meaning different EHR systems do not communicate well) (Weiskopf et al. 2013).

More importantly, access to EHR data is usually tightly restricted. EHRs are used primarily by insurance companies and health care providers, and these entities have good reason to avoid sharing access to their data. Chief among those reasons are privacy concerns and the risk of civil and criminal liability for unauthorized disclosure of patient data. Patient privacy is largely protected under the Health Insurance Portability and Accountability Act of 1996 (HIPAA), but also under a hodgepodge of state laws and less important federal regulations. Stakeholders are also concerned about the perception of privacy. Providers and insurers want consumers to believe their data is secure.

Stakeholders have reasons other than privacy and the perception of privacy to restrict access to their data. EHR data may have substantial financial value. For example, the data can be used by organizations to monitor their providers and promote or discourage unprofitable practices, by biotechnology companies to identify new uses for their existing products, and by insurance companies to inform contract negotiations. Sharing EHR data may reduce its value by eliminating its comparative advantage to a stakeholder. Data sharing may also be harmful because it may reveal stakeholder deficiencies. For example, a hospital may find that it has higher than average complication rates for a particular procedure or an insurer may find it has a higher percentage of inappropriately denied claims. In sum, while the public health benefits of using EHR data to conduct post-market surveillance are obvious, so are the numerous barriers to data holders actually sharing data. It is not surprising that a meaningful post-market surveillance system based on secondary use of EHR did not arise before Sentinel.

Some interviewees expressed the opinion that Sentinel's development was facilitated by the post-market withdrawal of Vioxx (rofecoxib) in 2004, the largest drug withdrawal in history (Health Affairs 2015: 3). The drug's withdrawal and ensuing controversy resulted in a series of congressional hearings on the safety of FDA-approved drugs, and criticism was leveled at the Agency for not withdrawing Vioxx sooner. In September 2005, the US Department of Health and Human Services (HHS) secretary asked FDA to expand its system for post-market monitoring.[4] In part, the secretary asked the Agency to evaluate building on the capabilities of existing data systems and creating a public-private collaboration framework for such an effort.[5] FDA also commissioned a report from the Institute of Medicine (IOM) on methods to improve the safety of marketed medicines.[6] That report,

4 US Dep't of Health and Hum. Svcs., The Sentinel Initiative: National Strategy for Monitoring Medical Product Safety (2008), www.fda.gov/downloads/Safety/FDAsSentinelInitiative/UCM124701.pdf

5 Ibid.

6 See The Future of Drug Safety: Promoting and Protecting the Health of the Public, 17 *Inst. of Med. of the Nat'l Acads.* 1, 1–2 (2007), http://books.nap.edu/openbook.php?record_id=11750&page=R1

issued in 2006, made several recommendations for improving post-market surveillance, including recommendations that FDA should "(a) increase their intramural and extramural programs that access and study data from large automated healthcare databases and (b) include in these programs studies on drug utilization patterns and background incident rates for adverse events of interest, and (c) develop and implement active surveillance of specific drugs and diseases as needed in a variety of settings."[7] The IOM report was followed by an FDA workshop with a diverse group of stakeholders to explore the feasibility of creating a *national electronic system for monitoring medical product safety*.[8] The general consensus in that workshop was that FDA could develop such a system by tapping into existing resources, which covered more than 100 million people (Platt interview 2014).

In September 2007, Congress passed the Food and Drug Administration Amendments Act of 2007 (FDAAA), which called for active post-market risk identification and analysis.[9] That was "either a great coincidence or someone was paying attention" (Platt interview 2014). Specifically, Section 905 of FDAAA required the HHS secretary to "develop validated methods for the establishment of a post-market risk identification and analysis system to link and analyze safety data from multiple sources."[10] FDAAA set a goal of accessing data from 25 million individuals by July 2010, and 100 million individuals by July 2012.[11] The law also required FDA to work closely with partners from public, academic, and private entities.[12] Section 905 was, like many of FDA's mandates, unfunded (Bell interview 2014).

FDAAA was a "vague piece of legislation" (Anonymous interviewee) with few hard requirements for Sentinel. One of those requirements was to create an "active" surveillance system. Most of FDA's tools for post-market evaluation are passive, meaning that they depend on third parties to recognize and report suspected adverse events in order for the Agency to be aware of potential problems.[13] Passive tools include the CDER's Adverse Event Reporting System (AERS), which is a system that receives reports of suspected adverse drug reactions and medical errors.[14] FDA can receive reports through passive systems such as AERS from the drug and device industries (for which reporting is mandatory), as well as from providers and

[7] Ibid. [8] US Dep't of Health and Hum. Svcs. (2008).

[9] Food and Drug Administration Amendments Act of 2007. [10] Ibid. [11] Ibid. [12] Ibid.

[13] US Dept. of Health and Human Services, Office of Medical Policy, The Sentinel Initiative: Access to Electronic Healthcare Data for More Than 25 Million Lives, Achieving FDAAA Section 905 Goal One 1–3 (2010), www.fda.gov/downloads/Safety/FDAsSentinelInitiative/UCM233360.pdf; see also Health Affairs 2015: 1–2.

[14] Ibid. Other passive surveillance systems include FDA's Center for Biologics Evaluation and Research's (CBER's) Vaccine Adverse Event Reporting System (VAERS), a database that captures reports of suspected vaccine-related adverse reactions, and FDA's Center for Devices and Radiological Health's (CDRH's) Manufacturer and User Facility Device Experience (MAUDE) that captures reports of suspected medical device–related adverse reactions. In addition to mandatory reporting by industry, FDA receives reports submitted through FDA's MedWatch program, which enables health care professionals and consumers (i.e., patients, family members, caregivers) to voluntarily report suspected adverse drug reactions and medication errors" Ibid.

consumers (for whom reporting is voluntary).[15] Even before FDAAA, the medical community has been critical of reliance on passive surveillance, which suffers from underreporting of adverse events (it has been estimated that only about 10 percent of adverse events are reported) (Health Affairs 2015: 2). By contrast, active surveillance systems such as Sentinel enable FDA to query data in near real time, using large data sets to evaluate broad swaths of the population.[16] Prior to Sentinel, the Agency did some active surveillance, for example, by utilizing claim databases to investigate safety questions, but this was done on an ad hoc basis (Woodcock 2008: 2).[17] For such investigations, the Agency had to identify specific systems it wanted data from and then it had to arrange access (Woodcock 2008: 2). Sentinel was the first effort to create a linked, sustainable network to continuously evaluate post-market safety questions in near real time (Woodcock 2008: 2).

6.3 ATTRIBUTES AND GOVERNANCE

This section explores Sentinel's structure and function. It begins by discussing how a small team of administrators at FDA (the FDA Team) started the program based on a congressional mandate, and how that team elected to finance Sentinel with general Agency funds. The project's financial structure limited the resources available for Sentinel and constrained its governance structure, but in ways desirable to the FDA Team. The section continues to discuss how the FDA Team engaged community members by conducting a protracted stakeholder outreach program. Based on the feedback from stakeholder outreach, FDA made a series of key decisions about Sentinel's structure designed to make the system useful to the Agency, convince insurers and health care organizations to share their data, and alleviate community concerns (largely related to privacy). As discussed in further detail later in this section, that involved contracting with a private entity for Sentinel's operations; designing Sentinel as a partially distributed, common data model; financing data partner participation; and focusing exclusively on safety research. Finally, the section provides some illustrative examples of Sentinel's outcomes and its impact on Agency decision making.

6.3.1 *Financing*

While there had been talk about a Sentinel-like program for some time at FDA, FDAAA was a turning point in actually creating a program. Even though FDAAA did not provide financial support for Sentinel, "Congressional mandates help even if they're unfunded" (Anonymous interviewee). After FDAAA, the FDA Team took control of the project and began making key decisions. Richard Platt believes the

[15] Ibid. [16] Ibid.
[17] The FDA also sometimes requires pharmaceutical companies to conduct post-market studies.

Agency did a "masterful job" of acting on the mandate (Platt interview 2014). He credited Rachel Sherman with being the person at FDA who "owned" Sentinel at a senior level, and who made many of the pivotal decisions (Platt interview 2014).

One of the first questions facing the FDA Team was how to finance the initiative. FDA is chronically underfunded,[18] and soon after the act was passed the US economy took a downturn in the fall of 2008. The FDA Team made a conscious decision not to seek dedicated money from Congress or money associated with the Recovery Act (The American Recovery and Reinvestment Act of 2009 (ARRA)) (Anonymous interviewee). Although Congress might have been willing to earmark funds for Sentinel, there was a perception that any money would have come with an expectation for a "quick, splashy outcome" (Anonymous interviewee). Instead, the FDA Team skillfully navigated FDA's internal budgeting process to finance the project with general funds from the Center for Drug Evaluation and Research (CDER) (Anonymous interviewee). That gave the group the ability to do what it believed was right from a scientific and programmatic perspective with minimal outside interference (Anonymous interviewee). Sentinel stayed out of the limelight, and the FDA Team had the opportunity to "crawl before we walked" (Anonymous interviewee).

The recession may have also facilitated a greater reliance on external collaborators. FDAAA required FDA to work closely with private partners, but there was pushback within the Agency about abrogating important functions to private entities (Anonymous interviewee). Those protests dwindled as money was short and people became more receptive to outsourcing. It would likely have been substantially more expensive to manage Sentinel entirely in-house (and potentially less effective) (Anonymous interviewee). Sentinel remains intramurally funded by FDA.

6.3.2 *Community Members*

The Sentinel Team had to engage a number of constituencies – "the biggest challenge was getting people to buy into this" (Bell interview 2014). Sentinel's primary users are the various FDA Centers (primarily CDER, where the initiative already had strong support), and Sentinel had to be constructed in such a way that it would provide valuable information to the Agency. Critically, the FDA Team also had to convince EHR data holders to participate in the program. This was necessary because Sentinel relies entirely on private entities voluntarily sharing their data – there is no mandated data sharing (Bell interview 2014). The EHR data holders who elect to share data with Sentinel are referred to as "data partners" in the initiative.

18 See, e.g., Ryan Abbott, Big Data and Pharmacovigilance: Using Health Information Exchanges to Revolutionize Drug Safety, 99 *Iowa L. Rev.* 225, 245–46 (2013).

For the most part, data partners are insurers and provider organizations (although other data sources can contribute such as disease and medical device registries) (Brown et al. 2009: 6). Provider databases generally contain more useful data than insurance databases, but most individuals lacked provider EHRs at the time Sentinel was being developed (Brown et al. 2009). By contrast, some large insurers had data on more than million individuals each (Moore et al. 2008). It was thought that combining several of these insurance databases could yield a data set of more than 100 million individuals (Brown et al. 2009: 6). Also, Sentinel did not require access to all of the data in provider EHRs (Brown et al. 2009: 6). It primarily needs data on exposures (with dates), outcomes, and comorbidities, as well as enrollment and demographic information (Brown et al. 2009: 6). This data can be used to calculate rates of use and complications. It is also helpful to be able to link data sets (cross-sectionally (e.g., different insurers), and longitudinally (e.g., different time points)) (Brown et al. 2009: 6).[19]

Interviewees also reported that the Agency wanted to get other community members to support Sentinel, including other government agencies, academic researchers, patient advocacy groups, and the public at large. Yet while support from a diverse group of stakeholders was important, support from data partners was critical. Without data partner participation, the Agency would not be able to fulfill FDAAA's mandate and Sentinel would have limited functionality. Given the imperative to recruit data partners, and the significant barriers to data sharing, FDA focused most of its outreach efforts on courting data holders: "A lot of time went in upfront to make sure everything was well thought out, all of the policy issues, how partners would interact with FDA, what you can and can't do with the data ... it doesn't usually happen like that ... communication was the key" (Bell interview 2014).

FDA conducted a series of stakeholder workshops, meetings, conferences, and webinars about Sentinel, including an annual public meeting at the Brookings Institution. Stakeholders were given numerous opportunities to express their thoughts about the project and preferences for Sentinel's structure. Major data partner concerns centered on protecting patient privacy (and the perception of privacy), protecting proprietary and valuable data, protecting institutional interests, evaluating opportunity costs, and ensuring appropriate professional rewards for personnel involved in the project: "What will bring them to the table, keep them,

[19] Access to this data on a large enough scale (ideally more than 100 million people) would allow the agency to use Sentinel for adverse event augment surveillance and signal strengthening, confirmatory safety studies, monitoring adoption and diffusion, registry information, calculation of background incident rates, better information regarding appropriate use of electronic data/validity of coding, and so on. Jeffrey Brown, Defining and Evaluating Possible Database Models to Implements the FDA Sentinel Initiative, Second Annual Sentinel Initiative Public Workshop, *Dept. of Population Medicine Harvard Medical School and Harvard Pilgrim Health Care* 5 (Jan. 11, 2010), www.brookings.edu/~/media/events/2010/1/11-sentinel-workshop/03_brown.pdf

or drive them away? . . . We needed to give them a voice and to understand them" (Anonymous interviewee).

Along with these meetings, FDA issued a series of contracts to generate white papers on issues including governance, privacy, data and infrastructure, scientific operations, and outreach (Woodcock 2008: 17–18).[20] Contractors solicited opinions from FDA Centers as well as other agencies, individuals who had attended FDA's Sentinel workshops and members of the International Society for Pharmacoepidemiology (Brown et al. 2009: 2). They also surveyed academics, data holders, biopharma industry representatives, patient advocates, and private firms (Brown et al. 2009: 3).

According to interviewees, all of these efforts created enthusiasm and thoughtful discussion: "Every organization felt it couldn't be left behind" (Platt interview 2014). It created a "culture of shared goals and sense of trust that the program will work on the things that are of mutual interest" (Platt interview 2014). The stakeholder feedback helped determine Sentinel's structure: "Partners are the ones driving this, the system was modeled after feedback from partners" (Bell interview 2014). Stakeholders provided guidance on what structures would encourage data sharing as well as how to make the system useful to FDA from a technical perspective: "This was new territory, we realized it was essential to get good feedback upfront to make this a success" (Bell interview 2014). This level of public engagement was time consuming, but the FDA Team believed it was critical foundational work: "Getting partnerships in place, doing the necessary work on privacy and security was not sexy or exciting, but it had to get done . . . staying under the radar really made us possible" (Bell interview 2014). FDAAA had given FDA a few years before any deliverables were due.

The stakeholder outreach sessions allowed FDA to identify objectives and potential obstacles to cooperation, to evaluate them, and to proactively design governance solutions. A similar process of stakeholder outreach sessions could be useful in other contexts where similarly diverse groups of constituencies, interests, and resources exist.

6.3.3 *Governance*

Sentinel functions as a collaboration between FDA, Sentinel's Coordinating Center (Harvard Pilgrim, a nonprofit health insurer based in Massachusetts), and around 18 data partners. It was clear early on that the Agency needed to operate a portion of Sentinel – FDA would never cede its core decision-making position (Anonymous interviewee). But the Agency elected to contract with a private organization in a

[20] These included defining and evaluating possible database models (Harvard Pilgrim); evaluating existing methods for safety, signal identification for Sentinel (Group Health Cooperative Center); evaluation of timeliness of medical uptake for surveillance and healthcare databases (IMS Government Solutions), and evaluation of potential data sources for the Sentinel Initiative (Booz Allen Hamilton) (Woodcock 2008: 17–18).

competitive process to manage most of Sentinel's operational functions. The Agency released a request for proposal (RFP) for a Coordinating Center, and the resulting contract went to Harvard Pilgrim for a five-year term with Platt as principal investigator. Platt considered it "the opportunity of a lifetime to help FDA develop this new capability." During FDA's first five-year contract with Harvard Pilgrim from 2009 to 2014 (a US$120 million pilot project), the Sentinel System was named "Mini-Sentinel." In 2014, Harvard Pilgrim's contract was renewed for an additional five years (in a contract for up to US$150 million), and the program was renamed the "Sentinel System." At the moment Harvard Pilgrim was awarded the initial contract, "there were four of us involved in this activity [at Harvard Pilgrim] now there are sixty of us" (Platt interview 2014).

Prior to winning the contract to serve as Coordinating Center, Harvard Pilgrim was one of the contractors that worked with the Agency to help design Sentinel's structure. Creating numerous smaller contracts not only helped develop Sentinel, it was also an important step in "getting this out of government ... Once the small contracts had been successful, it built momentum for larger contacts, and everything really took off with the contract to Harvard Pilgrim" (Anonymous interviewee).[21]

6.3.4 *A Partially Distributed, Common Data Model with Centralized Analysis*

Sentinel utilizes a partially distributed network and common data model with centralized (single analytic program) analysis (Platt interview 2014). The network is referred to as distributed because the data partners maintain physical and operational control over their own electronic data (Platt interview 2014). In other words, partners maintain and analyze their own data without sharing it with FDA (Platt interview 2014). FDA sends requests to partners for partners to analyze their own data, which partners do behind firewalls (a network security system that protects the resources of a private network from users of other networks). Partners then send the aggregate results of their analysis (e.g., days of exposure) to FDA (Platt interview 2014). Platt estimated that in the vast majority of cases, and thousands of protocols have already been run, partners only send de-identified data to FDA in the form of counts or pooled data (Platt interview 2014).

Data storage is not fully distributed (Platt interview 2014). In some cases, person-level or even personally identifiable information is deliberately shared, although these can generally be de-identified before they are sent to FDA (Platt interview 2014). Of potential concern, it may be possible to re-identify de-identified data, particularly when a data set is very small or when it involves an uncommon event (Abbott 2013). Still, these data sets fully meet de-identified standards, and the risks

[21] A list of contracts granted by FDA is available at www.fda.gov/Safety/FDAsSentinelInitiative/ucm149343.htm

of re-identification should be minimal given that Harvard Pilgrim and FDA usually maintain this information internally (Platt interview 2014). As one of the data partners commented, there are "generally enough layers of de-identification that [re-identification] is a theoretical but not a realistic concern" (Raebel interview 2014). On rare occasions, it may be necessary for partners to share actual source-level patient data with FDA, for example, to confirm that an adverse event has occurred (Platt interview 2014). Platt estimated that in the vast majority of cases, only de-identified data is transferred to the Agency. In the protocols in which individual medical record review is necessary, FDA requests only the minimum amount of directly identifiable information necessary (Platt interview 2014). This does make the model "partially" rather than "fully" distributed, even though in most cases the model functions in a fully distributed manner (Platt interview 2014). The decision to make the network *partially* distributed results in FDA having greater access to patient data, but it comes at the expense of allowing FDA to claim the model is *fully* distributed (one of the Agency's goals) (Platt interview 2014).

Even though data partners maintain their own electronic health data and do analysis behind firewalls, they are required to translate their data into a common format. This is largely to ensure that a single program can be used to analyze every partner's data (Brown et al. 2009: 23). The common data format is thought to be a critical element of Sentinel's structure, along with the centralized analysis it facilitates (Platt interview 2014). As one interviewee stated, "Why did Baltimore burn at the end of the century? Not because they didn't send fire trucks, but because the hoses didn't connect . . . the common data model allows the hoses to connect" (Anonymous interviewee). For each Sentinel query, expert programmers at the Sentinel Operations Center (at Harvard Pilgrim) write software that they send to data partners for the partners to execute against their databases (Platt interview 2014).[22] When partners receive software, the partners (should) already have a copy of the data in the common format (Platt interview 2014). "When all goes well," the programs run without modification (Platt interview 2014). This is a centralized analysis model (the Sentinel Operations Center develops the analysis software) as opposed to a decentralized analysis model (e.g., each partner develops its own analysis software) (Curtis et al. 2012). A centralized model reduces the potential for inconsistency associated with each data partner implementing FDA's protocols in their own way and makes it more likely that complex approaches are implemented identically across data sets. In other words, it helps ensure that the results from different partners can be compared apples to apples. A decentralized analysis could result in a lack of compatibility for results, complex programming requirements, and redundant effort (Brown et al. 2009: 23).

[22] Raebel did note there have been instances with site-specific questions where programmers at that site have written software instead of programmers at Harvard Pilgrim (Raebel email communication 2009).

The downside to requiring a common data model is largely that it is burdensome to data partners to translate their existing data into a new format.

A distributed, common data model was not the only option for Sentinel. In May 2009, Harvard Pilgrim prepared a report commissioned by FDA to evaluate possible database models to implement Sentinel (Brown 2010). That report discussed a number of possible configurations, depending on whether data storage was distributed or centralized, whether a common data model was used, and whether analysis was centralized or decentralized (Brown et al. 2009: 23). Harvard Pilgrim recommended a distributed, common data model with centralized analysis, and this was the model requested by FDA in its RFP for a Coordinating Center (Platt interview 2014).[23] From an analytical perspective, there would have been benefits to a centralized data storage model (e.g., at FDA or Harvard Pilgrim), but both the Agency and Harvard Pilgrim endorsed the distributed model because it would be more acceptable to data holders, alleviate privacy concerns, and could in principle accomplish all the same things as a centralized model. A distributed system "allows partners to have more control over their databases and work behind their firewalls" (Bell interview 2014). Requiring partners to share their data might have resulted in less partner participation (Brown et al. 2009: 23). Distributed data storage also makes it easier for FDA to tap into partner expertise with their own data and may result in cost savings (Platt interview 2014). Platt stated that he cannot recall any data partner deferring a query for which it had relevant data (only for queries involving data it did not have access to such as non-formulary drugs) (Platt interview 2014).

Another interviewee added that from his perspective a distributed network had important advantages. As he put it, every data set is "different and quirky," and the data partners understand their data better than FDA could (Anonymous interviewee). Partner data is crucial to their business, and "taking them out of the equation" would make them feel unimportant and discourage participation (Anonymous interviewee). Early feedback from two of FDA's contractors on legal issues also suggested that a distributed network would be less appealing to plaintiffs' attorneys, who might otherwise attempt to use Sentinel to support malpractice claims.

Marsha Raebel reported that for Kaiser a centralized system would have been a nonstarter (Raebel interview 2014). The risks of privacy loss, HIPAA violations, and the perception of privacy loss would have outweighed the benefits of participation

[23] There were numerous antecedent distributed models for Sentinel to model itself after, including the Electronic Primary Care Research Network (ePCRN), the Informatics for Integrating Biology and the Bedside (i2b2), the Shared Health Research Network (SHRINE), the HMO Research Network Virtual Data Warehouse (HMORN VDW), the Vaccine Safety Datalink (VSD), the Menengococcal Vaccine Study, and the Robert Wood Johnson Foundation Quality and Cost Project (Brown et al. 2009: 19–20).

(Raebel interview 2014). A distributed model was the only option where the burden of current laws and privacy concerns would allow Kaiser to participate.

The burden on Kaiser to translate its data into the common data model is modest (Raebel interview 2014). As a result of its internal research and data sharing, Kaiser already maintains its data in a standard data model, which allows data to be extracted and translated into alternate formats (Raebel interview 2014). Kaiser has substantial experience with data sharing and associated infrastructure. It has several regions with research institutions and a history of data sharing across these regions and with other collaborating organizations. Kaiser has maintained a "virtual data warehouse" for nearly two decades (Raebel interview 2014). In fact, Sentinel's common data model has many similarities to Kaiser's model (Raebel interview 2014). That may be because Harvard Pilgrim, which proposed the common data model, was familiar with Kaiser's model (Raebel interview 2014). In some respects, Sentinel improved the Kaiser model, and Kaiser subsequently incorporated those improvements into its own model (Raebel interview 2014). There is still a financial burden associated with Kaiser translating and refreshing data for Sentinel, but it is likely more burdensome for other data partners (Raebel interview 2014).

6.3.5 *Privacy*

The FDA Team believed that laws governing privacy and security were relatively simple compared to dealing with expectations about privacy. Indeed, the Agency is exempt from compliance with HIPAA as a public health entity, and it does not need to comply with state privacy laws. Data partners have to remain compliant with HIPAA and state laws, but they are permitted to share information with public health agencies, and data partners are already knowledgeable about relevant state privacy laws. Still, early in the process, FDA commissioned a multi-state privacy study, and the Agency worked closely with contracted privacy experts to ensure any legal requirements related to handling protected health information were complied with (Evans 2010).

More important to FDA than dealing with privacy as a legal issue was dealing with stakeholder expectations related to privacy. The most important action the FDA Team took to deal with privacy expectations was to structure Sentinel in a distributed fashion. Sentinel's lack of a centralized data repository assuaged data partners that their confidential data would be safe, because the data stays with the original owner almost exclusively. Data partners also directly guard against transmission of re-identifiable data (e.g., someone with a rare disease in a remote geographical area). In addition, one interviewee believed that for issues of perception, it was helpful that FDA already had a reputation for strongly protecting privacy (Anonymous interviewee). All of the interviewees believed that FDA had robust protections in place and that Sentinel's structure adequately addressed privacy concerns. Sentinel has not yet experienced a data breach.

3.3.6 *Safety vs. Effectiveness*

At present, Sentinel is only used to evaluate post-market safety issues (Health Affairs 2015: 3).[24] But the system could also be used for a variety of other purposes: for example, to aid in translational research (as the National Center for Advancing Translational Sciences (NCATS) is attempting to do with its own resources) or comparative effectiveness research (CER) (as the Patient-Centered Outcomes Research Institute (PCORI) is attempting to do with PCORnet) (www.pcori.org/research-results/pcornet-national-patient-centered-clinical-research-network).[25]

Safety surveillance was the only use mandated by FDAAA, but FDA's attorneys expressed the opinion that the Agency could have attempted to use Sentinel for other purposes (Anonymous interviewee). Sentinel's objective was narrowed for political reasons – FDA wanted to have stakeholder support for the initiative: "Easy to get everyone on board with safety. Easy to start talking about death panels when you start talking about comparative effectiveness research" (Anonymous interviewee). As Platt noted, "Sentinel is 15 percent technical and 85 percent governance. I'm on the governance side where there is a culture of shared goals and sense of trust that the program will work on things that are of mutual interest and not to the disadvantage of parties" (Platt interview 2014). Sentinel could easily be used to compare organizations and to create the impression that some partners are not delivering the highest quality care (Etheredge 2010). That could be used in competitive marketing (Abbott 2014b).

6.3.7 *Related Efforts to Pool EHRs*

While Sentinel relies entirely on data from privately insured patients, FDA has also worked to develop active surveillance tools in collaboration with other government entities (the Federal Partners' Collaboration). As part of the Federal Partners' Collaboration, FDA has interagency agreements with the Centers for Medicare and Medicaid Services (CMS), the Veteran's Administration (VA), and the Department of Defense (DOD) to share data. Like Sentinel, this initiative's model is distributed with each partner operating its own unique data infrastructure. Unlike Sentinel, no common data model is utilized (Bell interview 2014). The Federal Partners' Collaboration is "not nearly" to the scale of Sentinel (Bell interview 2014). FDA also operates the Safe RX Project in collaboration with CMS. That project was launched in 2008 when Medicare Part D data became available and evolved from

[24] Though as Platt noted, with some safety queries, such as comparing warfarin to newer anticoagulants where complications of interest are related to warfarin's very narrow therapeutic index, it may be difficult to separate safety from efficacy (Platt interview 2014).

[25] However, as Platt noted, concerns about using observational data for safety analysis may be magnified in CER. For example, clinicians may decide between treatments on the basis of data not available in EHRs. There are scientific reasons to potentially limit analysis to safety issues.

earlier collaborations between CMS and FDA primarily related to products covered by Medicare Part B.

Some of the stakeholders involved in Sentinel are involved in other efforts to pool EHR data for secondary use. For example, Kaiser does not sell data, but it does share data with numerous initiatives including the Clinical Data Research Networks (CDRNs) and the HMO Research Network. Platt is independently working with PCORI as the principal investigator of the Coordinating Center for PCORnet. PCORI is an organization created by the Affordable Care Act to focus on CER. Among its other initiatives, PCORI is trying to develop PCORnet as a Sentinel-like system focused on CER by pooling data largely from large clinical networks. Platt stated that Sentinel and PCORnet are complementary systems and that they could be used together.

6.3.8 *Data Partner Participation*

Enlisting data partners was very much a "back and forth process" (Anonymous interviewee). Platt initially identified the potential data partners that he believed might have useful data. In the case of Kaiser, Raebel reported that Platt approached her directly to inquire about Kaiser participating, as the two knew each other professionally (Raebel interview 2014). Kaiser was a particularly attractive potential data partner for Sentinel as one of the largest nonprofit integrated health systems with extensive EHR utilization.

Data partners are paid for their participation; however, the amount is generally only enough to make participation cost neutral. One interviewee reported that price was largely not an obstacle to FDA working with data partners, although the Agency did not work with some potential partners that wanted "a lot of money" without bringing new data to the table (Anonymous interviewee). Sentinel now costs around $10 million a year to operate, with the majority of funding still coming from CDER general funds (Bell interview 2014). FDA has a contract with each data partner requiring a certain level of performance and requiring queries to be returned within a certain amount of time. Yet the Agency did not have enough money to drive participation on a financial basis. Although it was important to provide enough funding to make partner participation cost neutral, the FDA Team believed that funding alone could not overcome partner objections to alternate Sentinel structures. Indeed, none of the interviewees thought that a direct financial benefit was motivating any of the data partners.

Data partners seem to have non-financial motivations for participation. As Platt reported, Janet Woodcock and FDA were masterful in setting the stage for Sentinel such that partners were "lined up to participate." One interviewee expressed the opinion that data partners largely chose to participate because it was the "right thing to do" (Anonymous interviewee). Other interviewees echoed the sentiment that everyone involved with Sentinel is excited about improving safety (but that some entities are opposed to addressing issues such as effectiveness).

Sentinel was a natural fit for Kaiser because the nonprofit organization is mission driven to benefit the community. Indeed, revenue generated by Kaiser that exceeds expenses is reinvested into member or community services. After being contacted by Platt, Raebel worked with health plan leaders and research directors across all of Kaiser's regions to drum up grassroots interest as well as leadership endorsement. Raebel stated that Kaiser is in this for improving safety and to help learn how to best avoid adverse events. Kaiser "looks outside the financial for benefits" (Raebel interview 2014). FDA covers Kaiser's costs for data sharing, but Kaiser does not financially profit for participation. Kaiser budgets based on expected work and invoices based on work actually performed. Ultimately, six of the seven Kaiser regions decided to participate in Sentinel (Raebel interview 2014).

Raebel notes that while Sentinel has entirely focused on safety, she believes that focus is likely to broaden. From Kaiser's perspective, it is important that participation does not financially burden member premiums, but the organization would be open to other uses of Sentinel that fit in from a member and organizational perspective. Raebel argued that Sentinel has become a "huge resource," and that it would not be appropriate to limit the system to safety (Raebel interview 2014). As for using Sentinel in CER, each project would have to be evaluated on its merits.

Platt noted that it was also important to provide appropriate professional rewards for individuals working for data partners. That often took the form of coauthorship of academic articles, but sometimes it simply involved providing individualized materials such as a letter from Janet Woodcock stating that a report was helpful, or providing evidence that Sentinel produced useful results for a federal advisory committee meeting.

6.3.9 *Outcomes*

Sentinel answers queries submitted by the various FDA Centers, and the results provided by Sentinel help the Agency protect public health. FDA also releases some of the results of Sentinel's analyses and that information may be useful to other entities such as academic researchers or pharmaceutical sales teams.[26] Data partners who have not previously translated their data into a common data model may also realize some positive externalities as translated data may facilitate internal statistical analysis or commercialization (e.g., data sale to pharmaceutical companies).

[26] Press Release Archive, FDA Mini-Sentinel Assessment Reinforces Safety Data of Pradaxa (dabigatran etexilate mesylate), *Boehringer Ingelheim* (Nov. 2, 2012), http://us.boehringer-ingelheim.com/news_events/press_releases/press_release_archive/2012/11-02-12-FDA-Mini-Sentinel-Assessment-Safety-Data-Pradaxa-dabigatran-etexilate-mesylate.html

Sentinel has already proved useful to the Agency. The Mini-Sentinel phase alone assessed 137 drugs (Health Affairs 2015: 4). For example, the use of Sentinel contributed to a label change for rotovirus vaccines, contributed to a label change for the anti–high blood pressure drug olmesartan, provided insight into the use of prasugrel (a drug approved in 2009 for acute coronary syndrome but contraindicated in patients with a history of stroke or transient ischemic attack (TIA)), and helped resolve concerns related to dabigatran (Southworth et al. 2013).

Dabigatran (Pradaxa) is an oral anticoagulant (blood thinner) drug developed by Boehringer Ingelheim and approved by FDA on October 19, 2010. The drug was approved to prevent strokes in patients with atrial fibrillation (an abnormal heartbeat that increases the risk of stroke). Dabigatran is used as an alternative to warfarin (coumadin), which has been used since 1954. While warfarin has been the anticoagulant of choice for most physicians for about 60 years, it requires careful monitoring and maintenance of drug blood levels. Dabigatran does not require the same monitoring. However, both drugs (and for that matter all blood thinners) create a risk of excessive bleeding. The effects of warfarin can be reversed if drug blood levels get too high or if a patient has a bleeding event, but there is no similar way to reverse the effects of dabigatran. The clinical trials submitted to FDA for dabigatran's approval showed the drug had a similar bleeding risk to warfarin.

After dabigatran was approved, the Agency received an unexpectedly high level of reports of patients on dabigatran experiencing severe bleeding events. Of course, as a known side effect, it was inevitable that some patients would experience severe bleeding events. However, it would have been a serious concern if dabigratan turned out to be riskier than warfarin. The reason for the reports was unclear: the approval studies might have been inaccurate; new (off-label) uses, dosages, or durations of the drug might be occurring; new populations (e.g., children) might be receiving the drug; there might be a reporting bias because of the drug's novelty or media coverage; physicians might be improperly adjusting for kidney function; and so on. The reports had limited information, but they did not appear to reveal an unrecognized risk factor for bleeding or off-label use. The AERS reports prompted the Agency to issue a drug safety communication in November 2011, regarding dabigatran's bleeding risk.

FDA used Sentinel (then Mini-Sentinel) to supplement the AERS analysis. Sentinel looked at bleeding rates from the time of the drug's approval until December 31, 2011, and found that bleeding rates associated with dabigatran were not higher than bleeding rates associated with warfarin (Southworth et al. 2013). Those results were consistent with the results of the drug's clinical trials. Sentinel's analysis was limited by a difficulty of adjusting for confounders and a lack of detailed medical record review to confirm actual bleeding occurred. Still, the Agency's analysis with Sentinel helped interpret a safety signal that could have resulted in dabigatran's withdrawal or a labeling change. A subsequent article in the journal

Nature Reviews Drug Discovery heralded that "Mini-Sentinel saves dabigatran" (*Nature Reviews Drug Discovery* 2013: 333).[27]

As one interviewee reported, Sentinel has been very effective at rapidly resolving the question of whether an emergency exists (Anonymous interviewee). Potential emergencies are expensive for the Agency because they pull staff off other projects, and most of the time there is no emergency. Before Sentinel, a large number of personnel had to "stop, look, and see ... are there 747s of patients falling to the ground?" (Anonymous interviewee). Now Sentinel can prevent a significant disruption to the Agency's workflow.

6.4 EVALUATION

The commentary on Sentinel has been mixed (Avorn 2013; Carnahan and Moores 2012; Carnahan et al. 2014). Some observers have praised the initiative, for example, as an "impressive achievement that deserves ongoing support" (Psaty and Breckenridge 2014). Others have argued that most of the data fueling Sentinel was never meant to be used for pharmacovigilance, and that "the biggest danger is that people will get a false reassurance about safety" (Thomas Moore, senior scientist at the Institute for Safe Medication Practices, qtd. in Greenfieldboyce 2014). Critics have also argued that Sentinel's results "may contradict the gold-standard clinical evidence from [randomized controlled trials]" (Sipahi et al. 2014). A 2015 article in Health Affairs claimed, "Sentinel has not yet become a tool for the rapid assessment of potential drug safety problems, which was one initial vision for the system. That's in large part because of persistent technical and methodological challenges ... And conflicting findings from different databases and studies can still lead to confusion and slow action, despite the power of Sentinel's database" (Health Affairs 2015: 4). On the whole, however, there has been relatively little praise or criticism of Sentinel. Several interviewees have been surprised by the relative dearth of academic and industry commentary on what one interviewee described as a "paradigm change" (Anonymous interviewee).

One obvious measure of success is with regard to Congress's mandate to the Agency in FDAAA. On that front FDA has certainly been successful. Sentinel meets all of FDAAA's requirements; in fact, it exceeds by about 78 million the number of patients FDAAA required. Compliance with FDAAA (and timely compliance) is a

[27] It should be noted that Sentinel's dabigatran findings were controversial. Some experts disagreed with the analysis and subsequent studies produced conflicting results (Health Affairs 2015: 4). Yet FDA's most recent update on dabigatran in May 2014 notes the Agency completed an observational cohort study of Medicare beneficiaries comparing dabigatran and warfarin that largely supported the findings of dabigatran's approval studies (FDA Drug Safety Communication: FDA Study of Medicare Patients Finds Risks Lower For Stroke and Death But Higher for Gastrointestinal Bleeding with Pradaxa (Dabigatran) Compared to Warfarin, *US Food & Drug Admin.*, http://www.fda.gov/Drugs/DrugSafety/ucm396470.htm (last visited May 18, 2016).

substantial accomplishment, particularly given FDAAA's ambition, a lack of funding, and a requirement to rely on voluntary participation by data holders. The Agency's success in meeting FDAAA's goals should not be undervalued.

Indeed, in 2008 when the HHS Secretary Mike Leavitt pledged "a national, integrated, electronic system for monitoring medical product safety," he also said it would be tied to another initiative, the Nationwide Health Information Network (NHIH), which would "connect clinicians across the health care system and enable the sharing of data as necessary with public health agencies" (Health Affairs 2015: 3). Like most efforts at secondary use of EHRs, NHIH never materialized. Sentinel, by contrast, now has access to 358 million person-years of data, including 4 billion prescriptions, 4.1 billion doctor or lab visits and hospital stays, and 42 million acute inpatient (hospital) stays (Health Affairs 2015: 3).

All of the individuals interviewed believed that Sentinel is an unqualified success (although all of these individuals have been involved in the program). They noted that seven years ago there was no active surveillance system to speak of, and now FDA has Sentinel. The Agency also has "solid, ethical policies" in place and strong privacy protections (Anonymous interviewee). Sentinel has become a valuable and regular resource to FDA, and it is poised to "prevent the next Vioxx" (Anonymous interviewee). To the extent that Sentinel was not used earlier or more prominently, this likely reflects Agency caution and the FDA Team's deliberate decision to proceed slowly and methodically.

One interviewee argued that FDAAA made bold demands without a roadmap of how to achieve them. Sentinel was the most difficult project he worked on professionally, and every effort was a new challenge. He attributes Sentinel's success to working methodically; taking care to worry about patient safety, security, and stakeholder engagement; awarding contracts to the best contractors; and never losing sight of the focus that Sentinel was designed as a "new tool for the Agency" (Anonymous interviewee). That interviewee believed that the biggest risk to sustainability is that only FDA has access to Sentinel, and he believes that access should be expanded to other users and uses.

Platt notes that five years into Sentinel, "people are comfortable." Specifically, and critically, data partners remain engaged. Bell believes that Sentinel is the biggest success story of secondary use, and that FDA is the only entity that has been able to get so many people to stay at the table. "Participation is voluntary; our collaborators participate on their own accord. And that's a major part of the success of the Sentinel program" (Bell interview 2014).

Raebel stated, "the overall philosophy and approach is totally in the right direction." She believes the only areas for improvement are small technical issues where greater efficiencies could be built in, and that there is a need to ensure data quality. For example, some critics have argued that claims data from insurers may poorly align with actual patient outcomes (Greenfieldboyce 2014). Raebel also mentioned it was critical to adjust for confounders, and that FDA has previously released nonadjusted results, although she added that the Agency often has to act on incomplete information. For example, Sentinel's analysis for dabigatran found a lower risk of GI bleeding compared to warfarin, while FDA's subsequent trial with Medicare data found an increased risk of bleeding. That may have been because of age differences between the populations examined and an inability to rigorously adjust for confounding variables with Sentinel's data.[28] The issue with age differences was specific to the case of dabigatran, but the inability to rigorously adjust for confounding variables is likely a function of Sentinel's design.

Sentinel might have been more successful as an analytic tool if it incorporated a centralized data repository. It might also have provided greater public health benefits if non-FDA parties had access, and if Sentinel was used for more than safety research. Those things did not occur for a variety of reasons, in large part because the Agency did not want to alienate data partners. Indeed, it seems likely that at least some data partners would not want to provide data to a centralized data repository, and that others would not want to participate in non-safety queries. Catering to data partners is necessary given that Sentinel operates by contracting and self-regulation rather than through notice-and-comment rule making.

Reliance on voluntary participation was not the only option. For example, England, which has the largest and the oldest single-payer health care system in the world (the National Health Service (NHS)), has a single, comprehensive repository for patient-level health care data known as the Secondary Uses Service (SUS). Although there are restrictions on access, the SUS can be accessed by multiple actors for a variety of purposes, including tracking referral treatment timelines, supporting payment by results (the hospital payment system in England), improving public health, or developing national policy.[29] The system de-identifies personal data at the point of entry and refers to such data as "pseudonymized." SUS has around 10 billion pseudonymized records and it is built to support more than 9,000 concurrent users.[30] Single-payer systems in the EU generally have significantly more developed patient databases for longitudinal study.

Congress and the Agency could have elected to mandate data sharing by data partners. Of course, that would have been logistically challenging given that EHR data in the United States is very different than it is from that in England. More importantly, it may not have been possible politically given the resistance to government intervention in health care. Mandating sharing almost certainly would have

28 FDA Drug Safety Communication: FDA Study of Medicare Patients Finds Risks Lower For Stroke and Death But Higher for Gastrointestinal Bleeding with Pradaxa (Dabigatran) Compared to Warfarin, *US Food & Drug Admin.*, www.fda.gov/Drugs/DrugSafety/ucm396470.htm (last visited May 18, 2016).

29 Secondary Uses Service (SUS), *Health & Social Care Information Centre*, www.hscic.gov.uk/sus (last visited May 18, 2016).

30 NHS Secondary Uses Service: Using the Power of Information to Improve Healthcare, *BT.com*, www.globalservices.bt.com/uk/en/casestudy/nhs_sus (last visited May 18, 2016).

generated substantial pushback (and legal challenges) from the health care industry. It might also have generated public backlash if there was a perception that such sharing might result in privacy violations. In any case, the decision to rely on contracting and self-regulation reflects a particular governance philosophy that ended up dictating Sentinel's structure. It may have resulted in a system with less utility and one that requires duplicated effort to share data in other contexts. On the other hand, increased government regulation has not always proved the best solution to a public health challenge, and mandating data sharing might have excluded the expertise of data partners, created new burdens on industry that would harm innovation, and resulted in privacy violations.

CONCLUSION

That Sentinel exists at all is a testament to the work of its architects in identifying stakeholders, objectives, potential barriers and solutions, and to their ability to navigate complex bureaucracies and political environments. And Sentinel does more than exist – it has been entirely successful at meeting FDAAA's mandate and at engaging data partners. In the future, Sentinel may remain a distributed network that solely focuses on safety. Non-safety queries may have to occur thorough other efforts at secondary use of EHR such as PCORnet.

Yet Sentinel still has the freedom to evolve within its current framework to incorporate a centralized data repository and non-safety queries: "Ideally our vision would be to have the infrastructure be a national resource" (Bell interview 2014). Woodcock has written that it is FDA's hope to allow other users to access Sentinel for multiple purposes (Woodcock 2014), and such access may help sustain Sentinel. It is possible that a critical mass of existing data partners would continue to participate in the program if it evolves. Alternately, new laws or regulations mandating data partner participation or providing dedicated funding for Sentinel might facilitate its expansion. Now that Sentinel is established, there is likely less risk to the system from accepting earmarks. Legislation mandating data sharing may now be less controversial given that Sentinel's feasibility has been demonstrated and there have been no privacy violations.

The FDA Team hypothesized that Sentinel could only be successful with an exclusive focus on safety and a distributed data model. To investigate whether this hypothesis is valid with similarly situated medical research knowledge commons, future case studies should investigate whether voluntary health data-sharing projects that are not exclusively focused on safety issues, such as PCORnet, are able to achieve sufficient third-party data contribution to function effectively. Similarly, it will be important to investigate whether voluntary health data-sharing projects that utilize centralized data repositories are able to achieve sufficient contributions.

REFERENCES AND SUGGESTED ADDITIONAL READING

Abbott, Ryan, Big Data and Pharmacovigilance: Using Health Information Exchanges to Revolutionize Drug Safety, 99 *Iowa L. Rev.* 225, 239 (2013).

Abbott, Ryan and Ian Ayres, Evidence and Extrapolation: Mechanisms for Regulating Off-Label Uses of Drugs and Devices, 64 *Duke L.J.* 377 (2014a).

Abbott, Ryan and Carl Stevens, Redefining Medical Necessity: A Consumer-Driven Solution to the US Health Care Crisis, 47 *Loy. L.A. L. Rev.* 943 (2014b).

Avorn, Jerry, The Promise of Pharmacoepidemiology in Helping Clinicians Assess Drug Risk, 128 *Circulation* 745 (2013).

Brown Jeffrey et al., *Defining and Evaluating Possible Database Models to Implement the FDA Sentinel Initiative*. Dept. of Ambulatory Care and Prevention Harvard Medical School and Harvard Pilgrim Health Care (2009), www.pharmamedtechbi.com/~/media/Images/Publications/Archive/The%20Pink%20Sheet/71/020/00710200015/sentinel_database_models_05_09.pdf

Brown, Jeffrey, Defining and Evaluating Possible Database Models to Implements the FDA Sentinel Initiative, *Second Annual Sentinel Initiative Public Workshop, Dept. of Population Medicine Harvard Medical School and Harvard Pilgrim Health Care* 5 (Jan. 11, 2010), www.brookings.edu/~/media/events/2010/1/11-sentinel-workshop/03_brown.pdf

Carnahan, Ryan M., Carlos J. Bell, and Richard Platt, Active Surveillance: The United States Food and Drug Administration's Sentinel Initiative, in *Mann's Pharmacovigilance*, 3rd ed. (Elizabeth B. Andrews and Nicholas Moore, eds., Wiley-Blackwell 2014).

Carnahan, Ryan M. and Kevin G. Moores, Mini-Sentinel's Systematic Reviews of Validated Methods for Identifying Health Outcomes Using Administrative Claims Data: Methods and Lessons Learned, 21 *Pharmacoepidemiology & Drug Safety* 82 (2012).

Curtis, Lesley H. et al., Design Considerations, Architecture, and Use of the Mini-Sentinel Distributed Data System, 21 *Pharmacoepidemiology & Drug Safety* 23 (2012).

Etheredge, Lynn M., Creating a High-Performance System for Comparative Effectiveness Research, 29 *Health Affairs* 1761 (2010), http://content.healthaffairs.org/content/29/10/1761.full.pdf+html

Evans, Barbara J., Authority of the Food and Drug Administration to Require Data Access and Control Use Rights in the Sentinel Data Network, 65 *Food & Drug L. J.* 67 (2010).

Food & Drug Administration Amendments Act of 2007, Pub. L. No. 110–85, 121 Stat. 823 (2007).

FDA Drug Safety Communication: FDA Study of Medicare Patients Finds Risks Lower for Stroke and Death But Higher for Gastrointestinal Bleeding with Pradaxa (Dabigatran) Compared to Warfarin, *US Food & Drug Admin.*, http://www.fda.gov/Drugs/DrugSafety/ucm396470.htm (last visited May 18, 2016).

Frischmann Brett M. et al., Governing Knowledge Commons in *Governing Knowledge Commons* 1 (Brett M. Frischmann, Michael J. Madison, and Katherine J. Strandburg eds., Oxford University Press 2014).

Greenfieldboyce, Nell, Big Data Peeps at Your Medical Records to Find Drug Problems, NPR (July 21, 2014), www.npr.org/sections/health-shots/2014/07/21/332290342/big-data-peeps-at-your-medical-records-to-find-drug-problems

Health Affairs, *Health Policy Brief: The FDA's Sentinel Initiative* (2015), http://healthaffairs.org/healthpolicybriefs/brief_pdfs/healthpolicybrief_139.pdf

Hsiao Chun-Ju et al., Trends in Electronic Health Record System Use among Office-Based Physicians: United States, 2007–2012. 75 *Nat'l Health Stat. Rep.* (May 20, 2014).

Mini-Sentinel Saves Dabigatran, *Nature Reviews Drug Discovery*, May 2013, at 333.

Moore, K. M. et al., Potential Population-Based Electronic Data Sources for Rapid Pandemic Influenza Vaccine Adverse Event Detection: A Survey of Health Plans, 17 *Pharmacoepidemiology and Drug Safety* 1137 (Sept. 2008).

Psaty Bruce M. and Alasdair M. Breckenridge, Mini-Sentinel and Regulatory Science – Big Data Rendered Fit and Functional, 370 N. *England J. Med.* 2165 (June 2014).

Safran, C. et al., Toward a National Framework for the Secondary Use of Health Data: An American Medical Informatics Association White Paper, 14 *J. Am. Med. Informatics Assoc.* 1 (2007).

Sipahi, Iike et al., A Comparison of Results of the US Food and Drug Administration's Mini-Sentinel Program with Randomized Clinical Trials, 174 *JAMA Internal Medicine* 150 (2014).

Southworth, Mary Ross et al., Dabigatran and Postmarketing Reports of Bleeding, 368 *New Eng. J. Med.* 1272 (2013).

US Dep't of Health and Hum. Svcs., The Sentinel Initiative: National Strategy for Monitoring Medical Product Safety. 2 (2008), www.fda.gov/downloads/Safety/FDAsSentinelInitiative/UCM124701.pdf

US Food and Drug Admin., FDA Drug Safety Communication: Safety Review of Post-Market Reports of Serious Bleeding Events with the Anticoagulant Pradaxa (Dabigatran Etexilate Mesylate) (2011), www.fda.gov/Drugs/DrugSafety/ucm282724.htm

Weiskopf, Nicole G. et al., Defining and Measuring Completeness of Electronic Health Records for Secondary Use, 46 *J. Biomedical Informatics* 830 (Oct. 2013).

Woodcock, Janet, Another Important Step in FDA's Journey towards Enhanced Safety through Full-Scale "Active Surveillance," US Food & Drug Admin. DA (Dec. 30, 2014), http://blogs.fda.gov/fdavoice/index.php/2014/12/another-important-step-in-fdas-journey-towards-enhanced-safety-through-full-scale-active-surveillance/

Woodcock, Janet, Sentinel Initiative: Structure, Function and Scope. The Meeting of the Food and Drug Administration and eHealth Foundation, in cooperation with the Brookings Institute 2 (Dec. 16, 2008), www.fda.gov/downloads/ScienceResearch/SpecialTopics/CriticalPathInitiative/PastEventsonCPI/UCM113469.pdf

7

Cancer: From a Kingdom to a Commons

Michael Mattioli

INTRODUCTION

In the late 1970s, decades before leukemia ended her life, the American writer Susan Sontag wrote, "Everyone who is born holds dual citizenship, in the kingdom of the well and in the kingdom of the sick."[1] We prefer to spend our days in the good country, but sooner or later, said Sontag, "we are all obliged to identify as citizens of that other place." In his 2010 Pulitzer Prize–winning book on cancer, Dr. Sidhartha Mukherjee invoked a similar geographic metaphor when he referred to the disease as a vast "empire."[2] In a letter to a friend, the novelist Thomas Wolfe once called his cancer "a strange country." By describing illness as a passport, these commentators conveyed the sense of dislocation that a cancer diagnosis can bring. But what if our doctors – our guides to this "other place," such as it is – could, by working together, redefine its national character? What if the sick were not subjects of a sovereign, but instead, members of a commons that heals itself? This possibility is at the heart of a new and hopeful movement in cancer research.

This chapter explores a privately governed collaborative composed of doctors and hospitals that seeks to aggregate, manage access to, and draw insights from oncology treatment data.[3] The thesis behind this collaboration is simple: if cancer treatment

Michael Mattioli is Associate Professor of Law at the Indiana University Bloomington Maurer School of Law, Bloomington, Indiana.

[1] Susan Sontag, *Illness as Metaphor* 3 (McGraw Hill 1977).

[2] Siddhartha Mukherjee, 9 *The Emperor of All Maladies: A Biography of Cancer* (Scribner 2010).

[3] In a companion law journal article, I explore the implications of health data pooling on innovation policy more generally. Michael Mattioli, The Data Pooling Problem, 32 *Berkeley Tech. L.J.* (2017). This study builds upon the earlier work of commentators from diverse fields of expertise, including law, medicine, and political science. See, e.g., Louise Trubek et al., Improving Cancer Outcomes Through Strong Networks and Regulatory Frameworks: Lessons From the United States and the European Union, 14 *Journal of Health Care Law & Policy* 119 (2011). Although this chapter focuses on private data-pooling, other commentators have recently written on public-private partnerships designed to facilitate cancer data-sharing. See Jacob S. Sherkow, Cancer's IP, 96 *North Carolina L. Rev.* (2018).

data could be aggregated on a large scale, scientists believe they would be able to select more effective treatments for particular cancers, and even for particular patients. Over time, this cooperative process could theoretically spur a "virtuous cycle" of medical advancement: more effective treatments would encourage more doctors, hospitals, and care centers to contribute even more data, which, in turn, would improve the quality of care, and so on.

This data-intensive approach to cancer treatment draws heavily upon the surprising power of correlations. For centuries, researchers have used the scientific method to grasp the *how* and *why* behind poorly understood phenomena – the underlying genetic or biochemical causes of an illness, for instance. While this approach can lead to useful treatments, it is not a particularly efficient or effective way to treat a single sick individual. It is often enough, rather, to understand and act upon a set of factors that *correlate with* a disease.[4] As two commentators from the field of computer science recently explained, "If millions of electronic medical records reveal that cancer sufferers who take a certain combination of aspirin and orange juice see their disease go into remission, then the exact cause for the improvement in health may be less important than the fact that they lived."[5] Cancer research and treatment is an endeavor in which, to quote Voltaire, "the perfect is the enemy of the good."[6]

Physicians have long embraced the power of correlations. Sidney Farber, the Boston physician and "grandfather" of cancer research, once stated in a congressional hearing that, "The history of Medicine is replete with examples of cures obtained years, decades, and even centuries before the mechanism of action was understood for these cures."[7] In 1854 London, the physician John Snow noticed a correlation between the home addresses of cholera victims and the location of a community water pump. Snow could not prove exactly *how* cholera spread through the water – Louis Pasteur would not develop "germ theory" until the following decade – but he urged officials to remove the handle from the pump and the spread of the disease halted soon after. In the 1950s, the English researchers Austin Bradford Hill and Richard Doll similarly drew upon correlations to conclude that cigarette smoking causes lung cancer. The two men compared a data set of English physicians who reported that they regularly smoked against a national registry that listed the causes of death of English physicians. This comparison revealed a strong correlation between smoking and lung cancer.

4 Some commentators offer a different, more descriptive term for these methods: "data-intensive science." Tony Hey et al. (eds.), *The Fourth Paradigm: Data-Intensive Scientific Discovery* (Microsoft Research 2009).

5 Victor Mayer-Schönberger and Kenneth Cukier, *Big Data: A Revolution That Will Transform How We Live, Work, and Think* (Houghton Mifflin Harcourt 2013).

6 This aphorism is widely attributed to Voltaire. Susan Ratcliffe (ed.), *Concise Oxford Dictionary of Quotations* 389 (Oxford University Press 2011).

7 Hearings before the Subcommittee on Public Health and Environment of the Committee on Interstate and Foreign Commerce, House of Representatives, Ninety-Second Congress, First Session, on the National Cancer Attack Act of 1971, H.R. 8843, H.R. 10681, S. 1828, Serial No. 92–40, at 271.

Correlations in health data allow doctors to effectively treat diseases they do not yet fully understand.

Today, health data is at once more detailed and more scattered than it was in Snow's time. This diffusion of information is particularly pronounced in the field of oncology. One commentator characterized the entire corpus of cancer data recorded in the United States as "utterly fragmented."[8] Health care providers – from small practices to large hospitals – are primary sources of patient treatment data. (As described in Section 7.4, such data may include machine readings, the results of physical exams and chemical tests, a doctor's subjective observations, etc.) Hospitals typically send this data to outside electronic health record (EHR) vendors that store and manage access to it. Shadows of the same information could be reflected in other places, though, such as in a hospital's billing department or in a medical insurance provider's database.[9] Some individual patients also retain their own private treatment records.[10] Pharmaceutical companies maintain troves of records related to clinical trials performed on human subjects; academic researchers store (and often jealously guard) valuable scientific data sets related to their work; online services store health data generated by fitness and health gadgets and smartphone apps. The list of oncology data stewards goes on – from drugstores to social networks.

This fragmented informational landscape presents a collective action problem that necessarily precedes the search for useful correlations: how to aggregate health data from the many institutions that hold it. Today, a researcher who wishes to search for correlations between, say, oncology data held by two hospitals in different states faces significant difficulties. The researcher would need to first learn which hospitals hold the data she wished to analyze – a potentially costly and time-consuming project in itself. She would then need to negotiate with each hospital to obtain access to the data. This, too, could impose upfront costs, including the time and money involved with negotiations, drafting contracts, and the high likelihood that either hospital (or both) simply will not agree to share their data. (As discussed in Sections 7.2.2 and 7.6.3, institutions that hold useful data often have strong practical disincentives to disclose it.)

A recent effort led by the government of the United Kingdom to aggregate the health data of its citizens brought these challenges vividly to light. Launched in 2013, the UK National Health Services' National Programme for IT (nicknamed "care. data") aimed to centralize patient records stored by general practitioners and hospitals across England. The project's stated goal was to "assess hospital safety,

8 Clifton Leaf, Why We're Losing the War on Cancer, *Fortune* (Mar. 22, 2004).

9 For more on the data held by insurance companies, and the potential this data holds, see Rebecca S. Eisenberg and W. Nicholson Price II, Promoting Healthcare Innovation on the Demand Side, 4 *Journal of Law and the BioSciences* 49 (2017).

10 The *New York Times* recently reported on an MIT doctoral student and cancer survivor who, through great effort, collected and published a wealth of data generated on his treatment. Steve Lohr, The Healing Power of Your Own Medical Records, *New York Times* (Mar. 31, 2015).

monitor trends in various diseases and treatments, and plan new health services."[11] The plan was beset with problems from the outset. Press reports and an academic study describe several causes of trouble, including gross mismanagement and conflicting interests: politicians and project managers pressed doctors across England for their patients' data without giving them sufficient time – just two months – to provide their patients with an opportunity to opt out, and without giving enough thought to the legal implications for patient privacy.[12] Unsurprisingly, this led to a strong public backlash. Meanwhile, physicians widely opposed the plan for reasons that were more cultural. As one academic study explained, "General practitioners view the medical record as a reflection of their professional relationship with the patient and their status as protectors of the record. The record is sacrosanct."[13] As a result of this widespread backlash, the project stalled and shows no signs of resuming operations.

During the same time period that the care data episode unfolded, several private initiatives formed in the United States with similar goals. Among these are CancerLinQ (the American Society of Clinical Oncology), Project Data Sphere (Celgene and Pfizer), Cancer Commons (a nonprofit group), and the Data Alliance Collaborative (Premier Healthcare). These collaboratives differ somewhat in their approaches, but they share seemingly elegant goals: to mediate the pooling of oncology data from various sources, to organize this information for research, and to provision access to it. In theory, institutions and individuals who contribute data to these groups could benefit by enjoying access to shared insights about how best to treat cancer. Meanwhile, outside researchers could benefit by having a "one-stop shop" for the data they need. It is a compelling institutional model reminiscent (if only superficially) of a patent pool or a copyright licensing collective.

These private data-gathering groups appear to be "commons" in the traditional sense that Nobelist Elinor Ostrom used that term. In her path-breaking book, *Governing the Commons*, Ostrom defined commons as institutions "governed by collective action whereby a group of participants can organize themselves voluntarily to retain the residuals of their efforts."[14] Ostrom inspired a generation of scholars from many domains – this author included – to study how commons govern production and access to valuable intangible assets, such as patents and data. Ostrom and her intellectual followers have showcased the economic, political, and social advantages of these collaboratives, in particular, how they can dramatically reduce

11 NHS England. Privacy Impact Assessment: Care.data (2014), www.england.nhs.uk/wp-content/uploads/2014/04/cd-pia.pdf

12 Abandoned NHS IT system has cost 10bn so far, *The Guardian* (Sept. 13, 2013), www.theguardian.com/society/2013/sep/18/nhs-records-system-10bn

13 Presser L., Hruskova M., Rowbottom H. and Kancir J., Care.data and Access to UK Health Records: Patient Privacy and Public Trust, *Technology Science* (Aug. 11, 2015), http://techscience.org/a/2015081103.

14 Elinor Ostrom, *Governing the Commons: The Evolution of Institutions for Collective Action* 24 (Cambridge University Press 1990).

transaction costs and barriers to aggregation of complementary assets. As private cooperatives, commons also operate free from "the leviathan" of direct governmental control and the temptations for opportunistic behavior created in market environments. This body of scholarship suggests that oncology data commons may offer a practical solution to a pressing public health problem.

Drawing upon the knowledge commons analytical framework, this chapter presents an ethnographic study of CancerLinQ – an early-stage oncology data commons created by the American Society of Clinical Oncology (ASCO).[15] The purpose of this study is to explore, through a single deep case study, the extent to which privately governed medical commons may be able to solve the increasingly urgent problem of aggregating oncology data for large-scale analysis, and along the way learn more about the challenges they face, and how well they are poised to advance the state of cancer treatment.[16] These are urgent questions that merit deep study.[17]

Section 7.1 explains the methodology of this case study. Section 7.2 describes the background contexts that define the world of oncology data, including the nature of cancer itself, the institutions that generate oncology data, the recent ascendancy of data-intensive science ("Big Data"), and relevant laws and regulations. Section 7.3 describes the type of data aggregated by CancerLinQ, including how this data is generated, where it is typically stored, and what legal rules apply to its use. Section 7.4 explains the variety of institutions involved with CancerLinQ. Section 7. 5 lays out the goals and objectives of the initiative, and some of the challenges that appear to lay ahead. A brief conclusion follows. These are still early days for efforts to aggregate privately held cancer treatment data; as such, this chapter's primary goal is not to cast judgment on CancerLinQ but rather to identify the broad challenges and opportunities that this effort and others like it may face.

7.1 METHODOLOGY

This chapter's approach follows Elinor Ostrom's Institutional Analysis and Development (IAD) framework, as adapted by Strandburg, Frischmann, and Madison for the study of knowledge commons.[18] This involved the following:

- ***A literature review***. To identify likely interview candidates and to gather general information about the state of data-intensive cancer research, I

[15] http://cancerlinq.org

[16] For a wider-angle view of data pooling as it relates to innovation policy generally, and for the results of my analysis of different health data commons, see Michael Mattioli, The Data Pooling Problem, 32 *Berkeley Tech. L.J.* (2017).

[17] Miguel Helft, Can Big Data Cure Cancer? *Fortune* (July 24, 2014), http://fortune.com/2014/07/24/can-big-data-cure-cancer/

[18] Brett M. Frischmann, Michael J. Madison, and Katherine J. Strandburg (eds.), *Governing Knowledge Commons* (Oxford University Press 2014).

surveyed recently published books, newspaper articles, and academic works related to this topic. This research also covered general interest publications on the so-called Big Data phenomenon and on cancer. From these sources, I identified private efforts designed to pool privately held oncology data, and the names of individuals involved with these efforts.

- ***Semi-structured interviews***. I interviewed 10 professionals currently or formerly involved with ASCO's CancerLinQ project or with significant knowledge of it through related work in the field of oncology care. In keeping with the knowledge commons framework, these interviews were semi-structured and organized around the following topics: (1) the scientific, technological, and social contexts in which the project has taken form; (2) the various types of data and related informational assets the group seeks to aggregate and organize access to; (3) the "default" status of these assets; (4) the players involved, including corporations and health care institutions; (5) the project's goals; (6) rules and related internal governance mechanisms; (7) the technological infrastructure supporting the project.

All interviews were conducted by telephone, recorded with the permission of the interview subjects, and professionally transcribed. The average duration of the interviews was 45 minutes. Some interviews were supplemented with brief follow-up email exchanges. In keeping with Internal Review Board procedures, subjects were furnished with an information sheet describing the goals of this study. With the help of a research assistant, I reviewed and flagged portions of each transcript to identify common themes and topics.

7.2 BACKGROUND ENVIRONMENT: CONTEXTS

It is helpful to begin the study of any knowledge commons by surveying the environment in which it has formed. This section focuses on the most prominent landmarks in the oncology data landscape: cancer itself, the people and institutions that generate data in the pursuit of treating it, the recent ascendance of Big Data, the legal rules and regulations that apply to oncology data, and at the center of it all, patients.

7.2.1 *The Biological Context*

In his bestselling book, *The Emperor of All Maladies*, Dr. Siddhartha Mukherjee defines cancer with plainspoken eloquence: "Cancer is not one disease but many diseases," he writes, "We call them all 'cancer' because they share a fundamental feature: the abnormal growth of cells."[19] In practical terms, the *kind* of abnormal

[19] Mukherjee, *The Emperor of All Maladies* xiii (Author's note).

growth that we call "cancer" involves cells proliferating uncontrollably through parts of the body where they do not belong, and interfering with vital internal processes along the way. Cancerous cells may develop into tumors, and even more treacherously, they may spread widely throughout the body and mutate into different forms as they go. This process is called "metastasis."

The problem's cause is genetic. Francis Crick and James Watson's discovery of DNA in the 1950s revealed that every cell of the human body contains a set of chemical blueprints for the entire organism. In simplified terms, every cell in the body divides according to what its local, internal copy of the blueprint says. When a healthy cell within, say, a human lung divides, it creates a duplicate of itself. Under normal circumstances, the original cell and its offspring both contain "correct" instructions and, as such, stop replicating when new lung cells are not needed. Cancerous cells, by contrast, contain mutated DNA that gives incorrect instructions on when cells should stop dividing. The result is runaway cell growth. The bulk of cancer research over the past 30 years has focused on understanding what causes DNA to mutate in this dangerous way, and what drugs and therapies can halt the process.

Cancer presents a puzzle of uncertainties to doctors who endeavor to treat it. As cancerous cells spread through the human body, they often become increasingly heterogeneous – that is, one mutation develops into *many* mutations, affecting different cells. Because different mutations may respond well to different drugs, cancer patients are often prescribed cocktails of therapies. For researchers who seek to understand which drugs work best and why, these combinational treatments present, in a sense, equations with too many unknown variables. If a patient responds well to a particular cocktail of therapies, this may be because one drug in the mix worked well, because several drugs worked well independently, or because there was a beneficial interaction between two or more of the drugs. The unknowns multiply when one considers that each patient's unique physiology can also play a role, and that some cancers can evolve to resist certain therapies. As a subject interviewed for this chapter put it, "you are dealing with thousands of cancers and hundreds of therapies, and often times you have to use multiple therapies in combinations or else the cancer will just evolve around the therapy ... you just can't test all of the variations and combinations in large trials."[20]

As explained in greater depth in Section 7.2.3, a vast collection of treatment data could make this puzzle solvable. Although it may, for now, still be impossible to understand *why* a particular drug or a combination of drugs works well for a single patient, it may be possible to learn which kinds of patients (i.e., what shared characteristics) respond well to certain treatments through statistical analysis of large sets of treatment data. To make that possible, it is necessary to first pool treatment data from many patients.

[20] Marty Tenenbaum, CEO, Cancer Commons.

7.2.2 *The Oncology Data Context*

Health providers, academic research institutions, and pharmaceutical companies: if cancer is a kingdom, these institutions are its counties, towns, and precincts – the points of contact between "the emperor" and its subjects. For CancerLinQ and similar projects seeking to pool treatment data, these institutions are where the data is generated.

Oncologists routinely collect and generate a wealth of useful treatment data. Approximately 13,000 board-certified clinical oncologists practice in the United States today.[21] They treat patients in group practices, medical schools, hospitals, specialty cancer treatment centers, and other clinical settings. Most oncologists are members of the American Society of Clinical Oncology (ASCO) – a professional organization founded in the 1960s, which holds conferences and workshops and publishes journals and books related to oncology practice. Oncologists interviewed for this chapter explained that cancer care is a relatively small and close-knit community, and most doctors interact regularly through professional meetings, conferences, and symposia. Of course, these statements reflect the subjective perceptions of only the relatively small set of individuals interviewed for this study. As an empirical matter, it is difficult to gauge just how close-knit the oncology profession as a whole truly is.

Academic researchers also generate and maintain access to sets of oncology data.[22] For these experts, scholarly publications represent a pathway to future grants, wider recognition, and tenure. As Jorge Contreras has astutely observed, however, "journal publication has proven to be inadequate for the dissemination of genomic data."[23] In part, this has led federal grant-awarding agencies such as the National Cancer Institute, which is part of the National Institutes of Health (NIH) to require the scholars they fund to release their data publicly. While such data research requirements may have sped the dissemination of data in some fields of medical science, experts interviewed for this study reported that this is not the case in the field of oncology. One prominent professor of medicine commented that in practice, academic researchers obligated to disclose their data often obfuscate useful data in a deluge of ancillary information. "When the NIH promotes sharing," the expert explained, "people will share but then they make it really hard for anybody else to

21 This chapter was written in 2015 and 2016. Key Trends in Tracking Supply of and Demand for Oncologists, ASCO (Jan. 2013), www.asco.org/practice-research/facts-and-figures-diversity-oncology (reporting the precise figure as 13,084 oncologists). See also *The State of Cancer Care in America: 2015*, www.asco.org/sites/www.asco.org/files/2015ascostateofcancercare.pdf (reporting additional relevant statistics and a census of the oncology workforce).

22 It is helpful to appreciate that there is a great deal of overlap between the foregoing domains: many practicing oncologists hold professorships at major universities and frequently publish in academic journals, for instance.

23 Jorge L. Contreras, Constructing the Genome Commons, in *Governing Knowledge Commons* (Brett M. Frischmann, Michael J. Madison and Katherine J. Strandburg eds., Oxford University Press 2014), at 103.

figure out what the hell to do with it."[24] The expert went on to broadly characterize academic researchers as reluctant to share data. "You'd think that the places that have the least interest in sharing are the ones that are for profit or commercial, but actually, it's just the opposite," the subject said, adding "It's the nonprofits – especially academic institutions – where the only incentive is nonfinancial and completely competitive." As discussed in Section 7.6.2, such disincentives to share data appear to pose a challenge for nascent data-pooling efforts.

Pharmaceutical companies also generate and manage a wealth of oncology data. They do so most often in the course of developing and testing new commercial drugs, diagnostic tools, and related methods. Because this information often has commercial value, pharmaceutical companies typically exert their dominion over it as much as possible by, for instance, restricting access through physical and digital barriers; nondisclosure agreements; asserting trade secret protection; and when possible and advantageous, patenting new methods and molecules.[25]

7.2.3 *The Big Data Context*

The recent ascendance of Big Data has introduced new types of workers and institutions to oncology research. The most publicly visible among these are technologists and entrepreneurs, who today are applying a Silicon Valley–style ethos to cancer research. In 2014, for instance, Netflix's chief product officer presented a public lecture exploring how the same algorithms that recommend films to consumers could one day suggest useful treatments to cancer patients.[26] Marty Tenenbaum, an engineer and entrepreneur who helped bring the Netscape web browser into existence in the 1990s, recently founded "Cancer Commons" – a data-pooling effort with goals similar to those of ASCO's CancerLinQ. In 2013, Bill Gates invested heavily in a Cambridge-based company that uses DNA sequencing to recommend more effective cancer treatments.[27] Verily, a subsidiary of Alphabet Inc. founded in 2015, is attempting to compose a detailed data-based portrait of the traits of a healthy human.[28]

Less visible but equally significant are many new technology companies helping to generate and mediate access to health data. Today, a variety of smartphone apps help cancer patients chart their treatments and vital statistics, for instance. The San Francisco–based technology company 23andMe is one of several companies to offer genetic screening for certain genetic health risks, and has furnished consumers with

[24] Interview Subject 42.

[25] The FDA publishes a helpful summary of its drug review policies on its website. See *The FDA's Drug Review Process: Ensuring Drugs Are Safe and Effective*, www.fda.gov/drugs/resourcesforyou/consumers/ucm143534.htm

[26] Neil Hunt, Big Data Meets Cancer (video), *TedXBeaconStreet*, https://youtu.be/IWu6XWzbPBs

[27] Matthew Herper, Bill Gates Invests in Cancer DNA Sequencing Firm, *Forbes* (Jan. 8, 2013), www.forbes.com/sites/matthewherper/2013/01/08/bill-gates-invests-in-cancer-dna-sequencing-firm/

[28] Verily Inc., www.verily.com (discussing "The Baseline Study").

portions of their "raw" DNA code, which may reveal still undiscovered health information in the future. Individual companies typically govern this consumer-oriented data through the use of form contracts ("end-user-license agreements") that govern how consumer data may be used and, in some scenarios, shared.[29]

These new services have introduced a new class of professionals to the world of oncology data: data scientists. While this job title is not well defined, data scientists typically hold degrees in computer science, engineering, and mathematics, and they are often hired by companies to help organize, manage, and analyze data. A data scientist hired by ASCO to assist with CancerLinQ explained in an interview for this chapter that his expertise involves removing any personally identifying information from patient treatment records ("anonymizing" or "de-identifying"), cleaning minor errors from data that was recorded incorrectly or incompletely, transcribing data into common formats to aid analysis, grouping data into useful clusters based on its characteristics, and finally, divining useful patterns from statistical noise.

7.2.4 *The Legal and Regulatory Environment*

The sources and stewards of oncology data described in the foregoing paragraphs – health care providers, academic research institutions, pharmaceutical companies, and technology companies – operate in a complex legal and regulatory environment that influences how oncology data can be collectively governed.

At the outset, it is helpful to appreciate that oncology data is often stored in computer databases protected by technological barriers that are difficult to circumvent, such as passwords and encryption mechanisms. A patchwork of federal and state laws prohibits gaining unauthorized access to such databases. The institutions that generate and store oncology data also typically contractually forbid their employees, partners, and customers from disseminating it. Because patent and copyright protection for data is generally quite thin, those two bodies of law do not represent a significant deterrent to its dissemination.[30] Trade secret law may, however, offer some recourse for data-holding firms. Unlike copyright and patent law, which apply to carefully defined categories of subject matter, trade secret protection can apply to many types of information. In simplified terms, the requirements for protection are typically that the information is valuable because it has been the subject of reasonable efforts to keep it secret. In theory, this could include many types of oncology treatment data and related information. (Leading legal

[29] See US experience with doctors and patients sharing clinical notes, *BMJ* 2015; 350:g7785, www.bmj.com/content/350/bmj.g7785. Another new project gaining traction in the health care community called OpenNotes provides new ways for doctors to share their notes and related data directly with patients through the Internet.

[30] Copyright protection may sometimes apply to compilations of data or data classifications, but such protection does not represent a significant barrier to unauthorized copying in this context.

commentators have noted, however, the challenges of maintaining secrecy over such information as well as the policy challenges presented by trade secrecy as applied to clinical information.)[31] In addition to longstanding state laws designed to protect trade secrets, the recent passage of the Defend Trade Secrets Act of 2016 provides a federal cause of action for misappropriation of trade secrets.[32] Ultimately though, perhaps the laws most important to oncology data are not those that forbid outsiders from taking it, but rather, those that govern its voluntary disclosure.

The Health Insurance Portability and Accountability Act of 1996 (HIPAA) prohibits hospitals from disclosing patient names, zip codes, treatment dates, and other pieces of potentially identifying information.[33] Some state and federal privacy laws provide similar protections to patients by imposing civil liability on those who disclose patient information without permission.[34] As a result, before a health care provider can contribute its data to a commons such as CancerLinQ, it will typically need to remove identifying information prior to disclosure.

In theory, antitrust law could also potentially discourage the formation and operations of oncology data pools. Antitrust authorities have long recognized that certain types of information-sharing arrangements between commercial firms can have anticompetitive effects that violate the Sherman and Clayton Acts.[35] Historically, such exchanges involved patents and other forms of organizational knowledge, but a data-sharing commons focused on commercially valuable health information could raise similar concerns, depending on how it was structured – if it conditioned access to one set of data on the licensing of substitutive data, for instance. While this possibility is interesting to consider, it seems remote in the case of efforts like CancerLinQ. If potential members and partners of a cancer data-pooling group *perceived* antitrust liability as a risk, however, that could present a challenge for group organizers to overcome.

Policymakers have recently taken some important steps to encourage controlled and limited disclosures of privately held health data. The 2010 Patient Protection and Affordable Care Act has helped to encourage the development of "accountable care organizations" (ACOs) across the country.[36] These hospitals and care centers

[31] Rebecca S. Eisenberg, Proprietary Rights and the Norms of Science in Biotechnology Research, 97 *Yale L.J.* 177, 194 (1987); J. H. Reichman and Pamela Samuelson, Intellectual Property Rights in Data?, 50 *Vand. L. Rev.* 51, 60 (1997).

[32] 18 U.S.C. §1836 et seq. [33] 45 C.F.R. § 164.514(e) (2013).

[34] An interesting reflection of the stigma that cancer once carried is the 1966 Freedom of Information Act's specific exemption for "treatment for cancer," describing disclosure of the fact of treatment as "an unwarranted invasion of personal privacy." 1966 Freedom of Information Act. 5 U.S.C. § 552 et seq.

[35] As David J. Teece has written, "meetings and exchanges of technical information … can cause antitrust suspicion." Teece, Information Sharing, Innovation, and Antitrust, 62 *Antitrust L.J.* 465, 474 (1994). The central concern is that some forms of information sharing may dampen competition for products and services.

[36] A helpful summary and map displaying these organizations is available at www.oliverwyman.com/content/dam/oliver-wyman/global/en/files/archive/2013/OW_HLS_ACO_maps.pdf

beneficially flip the traditional economics of patient care: private insurance companies or Medicare make higher payments to ACO doctors with strong track records for high-quality patient treatment. The quality of treatment may be measured by, for instance, how often a doctor's patient visits the hospital or an emergency room following treatment.[37] This payment model necessarily requires hospitals to report on the rates of success they have with treating patients. While the accountable care system involves such data being shared between the care provider and an insurance company, several subjects interviewed for this chapter expressed the hope that this shift could make hospitals more willing to share patient treatment data more generally – including with promising projects such as CancerLinQ.

The Department of Health and Human Services (HHS) has also recently advanced a number of projects to facilitate widespread health data sharing. One project, called the Blue Button Initiative, is designed to help patients gain easier access to their personal health records.[38] Beginning in 2014, the Health IT Policy Committee (a public advisory body on health-related information technology organized by the HHS) has regularly held workshops on health data sharing. Experts from government, private industry, and academia have participated in these workshops. The topics they have examined include health data information exchanges, personal privacy, and national security. Oncologists interviewed for this chapter expressed optimism that these recent steps might help get more clinical data available for oncology pooling efforts such as CancerLinQ.

7.2.5 *The Patient Context*

In 2014, there were approximately 14.7 million cancer patients in the United States and 1.6 million new patients per year.[39] These people are at the very core of oncology research, and yet they remain largely disconnected from the processes and systems that gather and use their data. As a cancer patient interviewed in the *New York Times* recently commented, "The person with the least access to the data in the system is the patient."[40] The reasons are partly cultural and partly financial. Traditionally, doctors simply did not regard cancer patients as people who needed to understand their situation in great detail. Not long ago, doctors typically reported bad news not to patients but, instead, to their families. A sick person's role was more or less passive. Only recently has a cultural shift occurred in which patients expect to be active participants in their care. Although that change has occurred, an important economic reality remains: because doctors profit from treating patients, sharing data

37 Patient Protection and Affordable Care Act § 2706 (March 23, 2010).

38 The Blue Button Initiative at www.healthit.gov/patients-families/your-health-data; see also www.hhs.gov/news/press/2014pres/02/20140203a.html

39 National Cancer Institution webpage, at seer.cancer.gov/statfacts/html/all.html (last accessed June 6, 2017).

40 Steve Lohr, The Healing Power of Your Own Medical Records, *New York Times* (Mar. 31, 2015).

with a patient makes it easier for that patient to go elsewhere. Subjects interviewed for this chapter explained that, as a result, medical culture is highly resistant to information sharing and the burden to obtain information (data or otherwise) remains squarely on patients. This may change, however, under plans such as the Blue Button initiative, and the accountable care reimbursement payment system, under which some hospitals and treatment centers will be unable to function without sharing treatment data more broadly.

7.3 GOALS, OBJECTIVES, AND HISTORY

Subjects interviewed for this chapter traced the genesis of CancerLinQ to a 2010 report published by Institute of Medicine (IOM) that explores the idea of a "Rapid Learning System for Cancer Care."[41] Drawing heavily upon the published work of leading oncologists, the report defines such a system as follows:[42]

> A rapid learning healthcare system (RLHS) is one that uses advances in information technology to continually and automatically collect and compile from clinical practice, disease registries, clinical trials, and other sources of information, the evidence needed to deliver the best, most up-to-date care that is personalized for each patient. The evidence is made available as rapidly as possible to the users of a RLHS, which include patients, physicians, academic institutions, hospitals, insurers, and public health agencies. A RLHS ensures that this data-rich system learns routinely and iteratively by analyzing captured data, generating evidence, and implementing new insights into subsequent care.[43]

The report discusses how an RLHS might work in practice, including how data could be collected from various sources, such as hospitals, and meaningfully analyzed.[44] A former president of ASCO explained that the IOM report was a watershed moment for CancerLinQ:

> The IOM report was a clarion call that [ASCO] really should be looking at this because it was a definable public good to bring together data from a broad array of sources and use them to both help instruct the care of the individual patients and to use that data collectively as a way to improve the overall health care of the nation. So it was clearly partially the fact that technically it was no longer possible to do, but also just because we thought it was the right thing to do for patients – individually and collectively.[45]

41 IOM (Institute of Medicine), *A Foundation for Evidence-Driven Practice: A Rapid Learning System for Cancer Care: Workshop Summary: Workshop Summary* (National Academies Press 2010).

42 See Amy P. Abernethy et al., Rapid-Learning System for Cancer Care, *J. Clinical Oncology* 28(27): 4268 (Sept. 2010).

43 Abernethy et al., Rapid-Learning System for Cancer Care.

44 Paul Howard, Can We Build a Kickstarter for Cancer? *Forbes* (Aug. 1, 2013), www.forbes.com/sites/theapothecary/2013/08/01/can-we-build-a-kickstarter-for-cancer/

45 George Sledge, Stanford.

The interview subject added that around the same time the report was published, experts at ASCO were growing aware that such a system was feasible. "We looked at [the report] and realized," he recalled, "that ... there may well be capacity in the system to link together a lot of these databases from a technical standpoint in a way that we would not have been able to do previously."[46]

CancerLinQ has two goals: first, to mediate among sources of oncology treatment data – primarily hospitals and cancer treatment centers – and second, to act as a central location for the storage, analysis, and distribution of shared informational resources – that is, treatment guidance and quality metrics. As the chief medical officer at ASCO explained, "The overarching goal for CancerLinQ is to allow doctors to learn from every clinical counsel with every cancer patient, so that they can be better informed for the management of all cancer patients."[47] When asked what ASCO would need to do to reach this goal, the subject focused more on technological tasks than institutional challenges:

> Setting up the health IT platform that enables us to actually capture information from the clinical care of every cancer patient, and then using that much larger experiential database to try to develop insights, assess trends, make inferences, hypotheses, that can then be pursued or could even result in immediate changes in clinical care, depending upon how robust the observation is.[48]

One subject said he believed that ASCO is well suited to coordinate the activities of an oncology data pool because it is less influenced by factors that could lead corporate institutions to behave opportunistically. "Pharmaceutical companies are very interested in having information about how people are using their drugs," he stated, adding that,

> insurers of course are very interested in having their hands on all of the information because it allows them to know rates to charge ... There is nothing wrong with those things, but they are not things that are necessarily going to improve patient care, so from a public good standpoint we viewed this as something important to have an honest broker, and we viewed ASCO as an honest broker.[49]

CancerLinQ has developed its technological infrastructure swiftly. In 2012, ASCO began work on a prototype designed to demonstrate the technological feasibility of aggregating treatment data from multiple care centers.[50] The prototype was completed soon after, and ASCO demonstrated the system publicly on March 27, 2013, at the National Press Club.[51] The demonstration was a proof-of-concept in which an

[46] George Sledge, Stanford. [47] Richard Shilsky, ASCO. [48] Richard Shilsky, ASCO.

[49] George Sledge, Stanford.

[50] http://cancerlinq.org/about ("2012: Prototype development begins /Aims to demonstrate the feasibility of CancerLinQ and obtain insights for the full system").

[51] Press Release, ASCO, ASCO Completes Prototype for CancerLinQ, Marking First Demonstration of a "Learning Health System" to Transform Cancer Care, www.asco.org/about-asco/press-center/news-releases/asco-completes-prototype-cancerlinq%E2%84%A2-marking-first (Mar. 31, 2013).

ASCO director searched and analyzed a set of records of more than 100,000 breast cancer patients originating from four cancer centers – Maine Center for Cancer Medicine, Marin Specialty Care and Marin General Hospital (California), Space Coast Cancer Center (Florida), and Tennessee Oncology – before an audience.[52] Following this demonstration, the project garnered significant attention in the national press, including reports in the Wall Street Journal and the LA Times, and accolades in a White House press release on the important role that Big Data can play in solving national problems.[53]

As of this writing, CancerLinQ is swiftly progressing. In early 2015, ASCO's president, Peter P. Yu, announced that CancerLinQ would go into operation later in the year with the support of eight community oncology practices and, possibly, seven large cancer centers. Yu stated that, thanks to these commitments, CancerLinQ will house 500,000 patient records at launch.[54] In a May 2015 press release, ASCO announced that the number of committed member institutions had expanded to fifteen.[55] According to another 2015 press report, ASCO is investing heavily in the project's future, having allocated funds in its budget in the "eight-figure" range over the next five years.[56] As of this writing, the CancerLinQ website indicates that the project is operational and overseen by CancerLinQ LLC, a subsidiary of ASCO.[57]

In addition to reporting on how CancerLinQ has developed and what its goals are, this brief history revealed the central members of the CancerLinQ community – a key element of the knowledge commons analytical framework. The key actors are ASCO personnel, oncologists at hospitals and universities who sit on the project's

52 The video can be viewed at www.asco.org/quality-guidelines/transforming-cancer-care-through-big-data-asco-unveils-cancerlinq-prototype; Jo Cavallo, Building CancerLinQ: The Road to Faster, More Efficient Treatment Delivery, *The ASCP Post* (Mar. 15, 2013), www.ascopost.com/issues/march-15,-2013/building-cancerlinq-the-road-to-faster,-more-efficient-treatment-delivery.aspx

53 Ron Winslow, Big Data for Cancer Care – Vast Storehouse of Patient Records Will Let Doctors Search for Effective Treatment, *Wall St. J.* (Mar. 27, 2013); Melissa Healy, Cancer trials aim to shore up 'precision medicine's' base of evidence, *L.A. Times* (June 1, 2015), www.latimes.com/science/sciencenow/la-sci-sn-trials-precision-medicine-20150601-story.html; Press Release, "Data to Knowledge to Action" Event Highlights Innovative Collaborations to Benefit Americans, *White House Office of Science and Technology Policy* (Nov. 12, 2013), www.whitehouse.gov/sites/default/files/microsites/ostp/Data2Action%20Press%20Release.pdf

54 Tony Berberabe, CancerLinQ to be Rolled Out to 15 Community Practices, Large Cancer Centers, *OncLive* (Jan. 21, 2015), www.onclive.com/web-exclusives/CancerLinQ-To-Be-Rolled-Out-to-15-Community-Practices-Large-Cancer-Centers. Centers include Inova Comprehensive Cancer & Research Institute (Virginia), South Coast Centers for Cancer Care (Massachusetts), New England Cancer Specialists (Maine), Medical Oncology Hematology Consultants (Delaware), Cancer Treatment Centers of America (Pennsylvania), Marin Cancer Care (California), Space Coast Cancer Center (Florida), and Michiana Hematology-Oncology (Indiana).

55 CancerLinQ™ Takes a Big Leap Forward (May 29, 2015), https://am.asco.org/cancerlinq™-takes-big-leap-forward

56 Nick Mulcahy, ASCO: "High-Risk" Project "Must Be Done": Tech Platform Is Best Known in Finance, *Medscape* (Jan. 22, 2015), www.medscape.com/viewarticle/838543

57 http://cancerlinq.org (last visited June 20, 2017).

various advisory boards, and the practices that have committed to donate their data to the project. The group's decision not to solicit data contributions from other potential sources mentioned in the original IOM report, such as pharmaceutical companies, academic researchers, or individual patients, may reflect how relatively closed off those domains are to health data transactions as compared to the clinical environment. This is perhaps the broadest way that the environment in which the project formed appears to have shaped its goals.[58]

7.4 ATTRIBUTES: THE CHARACTERISTICS OF ONCOLOGY DATA

The primary resource relevant to CancerLinQ is oncology treatment data from doctors, hospitals, and other care providers. An interview subject involved with the project helpfully divided this resource into two types: structured data and unstructured data. Structured patient treatment data includes objective, machine-recorded information such as "laboratory test results or the dosages of medicines prescribed, or patient vital signs," he explained, as well as medical history data, laboratory data, and imaging data from radiological studies, whereas unstructured data is generated and recorded more casually and based upon more subjective observations – a clinical physician's handwritten notes, for instance.[59]

Structured data is typically incorporated into a patient's electronic health record, which, at most hospitals, is digitally stored and managed by an outside vendor.[60] Unstructured data, meanwhile, is sometimes stored locally within a hospital or may be appended to a patient's EHR as a digital image. This data is often replicated in other places as well, such as a hospital's billing department or an insurance provider's customer database. "If the doctor bills for their services, all that sort of information gets converted, if you will, into a lot of different kinds of codes that are used to submit the claim to insurance," one subject explained. Another subject explained that one of the most important types of data in this area, patient mortality information, can be found in the social security death index, as well as newspaper obituaries, and sometimes even copies of handwritten condolence notes stored in patient files. In summary, oncology patient treatment data is scattered, but most of it resides in a patient's EHR maintained by a company on contract with the patient's care provider.

58 There are other data-pooling efforts that seek contributions of data from individual patients, however. The largest of these is Cancer Commons.

59 Dr. Richard Shilsky, ASCO.

60 According to a recent federal study conducted by the Office of the National Coordinator for Health Information Technology, about three out of four non-federal acute care hospitals have a basic EHR system. Office of the National Coordinator for Health Information Technology, Adoption of Electronic Health Record Systems among US NonFederal Acute Care Hospitals: 2008–2014, *ONC Data Brief No. 23* (Apr. 2015), www.healthit.gov/sites/default/files/data-brief/2014HospitalAdoptionDataBrief.pdf

CancerLinQ intends to use the treatment data it collects to generate a secondary asset: comparative assessments of the quality that member hospitals and doctors provide. As explained earlier (Section 7.2.4), such "quality metrics" can play an important role in how some hospitals and insurance companies reimburse doctors. As a result, hospitals may find CancerLinQ's metrics valuable, both to track their quality internally and for reporting purposes. The next section contains more information about how the project intends to use these metrics as an incentive to potential data contributors.

7.5 GOVERNANCE

7.5.1 *Formal Governance Structure*

CancerLinQ is governed by ASCO directors and by a collection of advisory boards populated by oncologists; academic researchers; and, perhaps surprisingly, employees of several large pharmaceutical companies.[61] A cursory look at these boards and their membership reveals the project's far-reaching constituency. The Board of Governors (the core leadership of CancerLinQ) includes ASCO's president and the president of a major cancer research center; a Business Strategy Committee includes employees of GlaxoSmithKline and Novartis; a committee designed to offer advice on interactions with physicians includes physicians who work at several cancer care centers around the country; another committee geared toward technology includes a professor from Harvard Medical School and a doctor employed at Merck Research Laboratories. More committees advising on regulatory compliance, patient outcomes, and more subjects include professors from the University of Pennsylvania, the University of Michigan, Duke, and leading cancer centers. ASCO's chief medical officers briefly listed several key challenges these boards expect to grapple with in the months leading up to CancerLinQ's official launch: "data quality, privacy, and security."[62]

7.5.2 *Incentives*

A central part of ASCO's vision for CancerLinQ is delivering useful information back to the members who contribute data. As explained throughout this chapter, this will include information that can be used to make treatment recommendations. A second enticement to join will be reports or "metrics" describing the quality of a contributor's medical services. Especially in light of the growth of the accountable

61 Office of the National Coordinator for Health Information Technology, Adoption of Electronic Health Record Systems ("Leading thinkers from an array of relevant fields engaged to advise on design and implementation. Advisors include leading oncologists, patient advocates, privacy advocates, health outcomes researchers, ethicists, health IT experts, and many others.")

62 Richard Shilsky, ASCO.

care business model, such data may hold great value. As ASCO's chief medical officer explained, "We think that one of the big incentives is going to be that . . . in order to optimize their reimbursement [doctors] are going to have to be able to demonstrate that they provide quality care and that they continuously improve their quality. And so one of the major focuses of CancerLinQ will be to develop and provide useful metrics on quality of care to clinicians and to federal government and other agencies."[63] In this sense, the subject explained, CancerLinQ acts as an information exchange between its members: "We will be able to return to the physician on a regular basis a dashboard report that shows what is the quality of their performance against . . . standard measures and [how] they can use that information to report to . . . their private insurers what their quality is, how it compares to other physicians."[64] Another subject explained that such data "could be used by the insurers or the government as a way of judging quality as we migrate . . . to payments based upon outcomes and quality. You know, having these sort of process measures in place will be very important."[65] The president of a member cancer care center said he believed this could be a powerful incentive to join the effort.[66]

7.5.3 *Openness*

Interview subjects reported that CancerLinQ has thoughtfully addressed difficult questions of openness and access from its earliest days. A former leader at ASCO who co-chaired a committee on the project provided examples of such questions:

> Governance is important at multiple levels. At one level, if you are getting data from an institution, or from an individual doctor, or from a group practice somewhere, who has access to that data? Is access given just in access to CancerLinQ staff who are aggregating and putting the data together? Do physicians have access to other physicians' data? How does ASCO give out access to health-services researchers who are interested in looking at important questions? At the end of the day, if ASCO has data that would be of interest to an insurer or a pharmaceutical company, what level of data do you allow access to? . . . So I actually view the governance issues as the most important issues surrounding CancerLinQ.[67]

Such concerns prompted the organizers of CancerLinQ to set up the Data Governance Committee very early on in the project's history. "It was one of the first things we did when we set up CancerLinQ," he stated. "And CancerLinQ actually has a full-time staff member who does nothing but Governance."[68] The committee is composed of oncologists at leading hospitals and universities around the country.[69]

At the time of this writing, ASCO has elected not to publicize its policies and rules governing who may join CancerLinQ as a contributor of data and who may join as a

[63] Richard Shilsky, ASCO. [64] Richard Shilsky, ASCO. [65] George Sledge, Stanford.
[66] Interview Subject 21 (commented on condition of anonymity). [67] George Sledge, Stanford.
[68] George Sledge, Stanford. [69] www.cancerlinq.org.

user of data. As a result, one can only infer these policies from ASCO's public statements and from the comments of others in the oncology community: CancerLinQ project leaders have consistently stated that their ultimate goal is to include the data from "all cancer patients in the United States" in its pool, for instance. These statements support an inference that the group is open to any and all cancer care providers who wish to donate useful data.

The more nebulous question at this time is who may join CancerLinQ purely as a *data user* – that is, a user who gains access to the anonymous oncology data contributed by member institutions. According to materials ASCO has published on the CancerLinQ website, the project's organizers anticipate providing access to outside researchers, but there are no specifics on the steps that such a researcher would need to take once CancerLinQ launches. A researcher (and CEO of a patient-centered oncology data pool) stated that he had requested access to the data that the project's organizers had gathered for its 2013 proof-of-concept to no avail. Commenting generally, he added, "[Many organizations] that you may think will share data are really silos."[70] Because CancerLinQ is still in early days, however, it seems appropriate to withhold any judgment with respect to this issue.

Perhaps the foregoing discussion of openness is most useful as a provocation – an impetus to speculate about the position ASCO may soon be in as a data pool administrator. There are, is seems, prudent reasons for ASCO to be reluctant to share patient treatment data very broadly. For one thing, it is becoming increasingly possible to re-identify patient records that have been made anonymous.[71] It could be problematic legally and professionally if the identities of patients represented in the pool of data were ever uncovered. (HIPAA, discussed in Section 7.6, represents one such risk.) Then again, tools are available – both legal and technological – that would permit data pools such as CancerLinQ to provide access while guarding against such risks. End user license agreements could forbid researchers from attempting to de-identify health data, for instance. Likewise, the data pool could decide to share only highly generalized information (i.e., trends, analytics, and summaries rather than individual records) with certain researchers in positions of lower trust.

7.6 CHALLENGES

7.6.1 *Legal and Regulatory Challenges*

In light of CancerLinQ's early stage, this chapter's primary goal is not to assess or evaluate it, but rather, to identify potential challenges that this group and other

[70] Marty Tenenbaum, Cancer Commons.

[71] See, e.g., Paul Ohm, Broken Promises of Privacy: Responding to the Surprising Failure of Anonymization, 57 *UCLA L. Rev*. 1701 (2010).

efforts like it may face. While several areas of law and regulation are relevant to CancerLinQ, the one that appears to present the greatest costs and risks is HIPAA. As explained earlier in this chapter, this law requires institutions to remove personally identifying information from health records before disclosing them. A patchwork of state and federal privacy laws impose similar requirements on health care institutions that seek to share data as well.

While it would be a simple matter to redact patient treatment records of names, dates of treatment, home addresses, and other identifiers, removing this information also removes a wealth of the useful underlying data – the period of time over which a patient was treated, or state of residence for instance. To remedy this problem at the proof-of-concept stage, ASCO employed a data scientist to creatively modify patient data without removing its underlying utility. Commenting for this chapter, the data scientist explained that these steps involved shifting treatment dates by a consistent offset (e.g., 27 days), replacing a zip code with the zip code of an adjacent community, or altering a patient's birthdate by a year or two. Importantly, patient names are frequently replaced with numerical identifiers, permitting the same patient to be recognized within the system and examined over the entire treatment period. Manipulating data in this way is costly and difficult to automate because it often requires the skills and judgment of a human data expert. (Mattioli 2014). It remains unclear who will bear these costs when CancerLinQ is no longer in the prototype stage.

7.6.2 *Cultural Challenges*

Although doctors and hospitals may be more likely than pharmaceutical companies or academic researchers to part with useful data, the medical culture remains largely antithetical to data sharing. As an editorial in *Genome Magazine* recently explained, there are "longstanding institutional barriers to gathering patient data, ranging from patient privacy to competition for patients to the idea the data has proprietary value."[72] Subjects interviewed for this chapter painted a consistent picture: "We have approached many, many medical institutions, large cancer centers, especially the big ones," explained the CEO of one data-pooling project, "They are very, very protective of their data. Because they think they are big enough to be able to not need anyone else's data, so they will not share their data. And they will argue strongly that competing strongly is the best way to move science forward. It is strongly in the culture."[73] Another subject summarized the culture of medical data in one word: "dysfunctional."

72 Eric Celeste, Collective Action, *Genome Magazine* (Aug. 24, 2014) available at http://genomemag.com/collective-action/#.WTcIwxPytE4 (last visited June 6, 2017).

73 Marty Tenenbaum, CEO Cancer Commons.

7.6.3 *Commercial Challenges*

Alongside the institutional reluctance woven in the culture of medical cancer care are challenges related to EHR vendors who act as stewards over most of the data in which CancerLinQ is interested.[74] "You need to have an EHR vendor or an institution that is willing to share the data," stated an ASCO director, adding that they are "notoriously proprietary" and poor at sharing useful data even within their own organizations. According to interviewees, this practice is strategic: it benefits EHR vendors to keep data in specialized formats that do not integrate well with other systems because this tends to discourage hospitals from moving to competing vendors. This problem is aggravated, the subject explained, by the fact that hospitals have few choices when selecting EHR vendors to work with. "A fairly small number of corporations that are responsible for the electronic health records in the United States," he said, adding, "none of them will speak to each other." Other subjects made consistent comments about the difficulty of obtaining data from EHR vendors and some explained that even when data is obtainable, it may not be immediately usable because it is in a proprietary digital format.

The president of a cancer treatment institution that is a CancerLinQ member explained that the difficulty of working with large EHRs and hospitals is why CancerLinQ has pursued smaller cancer care centers: ASCO "looked at private practices to start this project rather than academic institutions [because] the data's probably more easily extractable from the private practice EHRs and trying to get discrete information out of a big hospital system can be very tedious."[75] Other subjects interviewed consistently reported that data held by smaller private practices is typically subject to fewer institutional barriers.

CONCLUSION

The analysis of patient treatment data culled from hospitals, practices, and other private institutions across the country could profoundly improve how successfully cancer is treated. This possibility is, in part, a product of new developments in technology – the mass digitization of health information, advances in digital storage, and the new methods of organizing and analyzing information that go by the name Big Data. It is puzzling, however, that most accounts of this phenomenon focus on technology when the more significant story to be told is about institutions.

This chapter has focused on the early years of a prominent data pool that is still taking form. As such, it has centered on early-stage issues, such as gathering buy-in from potential contributors in a challenging regulatory and competitive environment. If one

74 Some of the information reported in this discussion also appears in a law review article that serves, in part, as a counterpart to this chapter. There, the information is placed in a broader context with respect to innovation policy. Michael Mattioli, The Data-Pooling Problem, 32 *Berkeley Tech. L. J.* (2017).

75 Interview Subject 21 (commented on condition of anonymity).

were to study CancerLinQ longitudinally, other sets of important institutional issues would likely arise. These could include resolving conflicts between members; establishing a framework for collective decision making; rules governing ownership of, and royalties generated by, intellectual property developed from the data pool; and so forth. Other issues and challenges still unknown rest on the horizon.

For now, it is helpful to consider today's challenges. This chapter has shown that medical data is not an abstract resource that can simply be gathered and mined; rather, it is the product of human effort and insight, scattered and stewarded by different organizations, each of which is motivated by different incentives, beholden to different interests, and averse to varying risks. Convincing these organizations to aggregate their data and to collectively govern access to it despite legal, competitive, and cultural pressures not to: this is the true challenge that CancerLinQ and projects like it face. There is a basis for optimism: if more care centers move to the accountable care payment model, the performance information that CancerLinQ will share with its members could offer a powerful incentive to contribute data. In addition, efforts such as the Blue Button Initiative could help create a cultural shift within the world of medicine, making care providers more comfortable with sharing properly de-identified patient data. Perhaps most importantly (although hardest to quantify) is the sense of forward inertia and excitement surrounding the idea of pooling medical data. There appears to be a widespread consensus among oncologists that access to a vast pool of patient treatment data would spur meaningful improvements in patient care. Perhaps this is a reflection of the fact that most doctors understand that medical advances have often emerged not from traditional scientific models of understanding, but from the statistical wisdom found in correlations. If enough care providers can be convinced to join together, the kingdom of cancer may one day become a true commons – a new country defined by data, governed collectively, and most importantly, a place from which more visitors return.

8

The Greatest Generational Impact: Open Neuroscience as an Emerging Knowledge Commons

Maja Larson and Margaret Chon

INTRODUCTION

> Neuroscience is transforming. Brain data collected in multitudes of individuals and institutions around the world are being openly shared, moved from office desks and personal storage devices to institutionally supported cloud systems and public repositories – effectively bringing Neuroscience into the era of Big Data. This is an important evolution in Neuroscience, since the value of open data sharing has not always been recognized.[1]

It is "truth" commonly asserted that research scientists participate in an ethos of knowledge sharing by virtue of customary norms and practices within the scientific community.[2] However, the reality in many scientific research settings can be quite different. The area of neuroscience research provides a timely case study of an incipient knowledge commons in the process of formation against a background of sometimes fierce competition for reputational rewards and results. Partly because of new large-scale intergovernmental

Maja Larson is General Counsel, Allen Institute (formerly Allen Institute for Brain Science), Seattle, Washington. Margaret Chon is Donald and Lynda Horowitz Professor for the Pursuit of Justice, Seattle University School of Law, Seattle, Washington. The authors are indebted to Maria Therese Fujiye (Seattle University School of Law class of 2016), who provided crucial research assistance at early stages of this project and collected the interview data with Ms. Larson, as well as to Natasha Khanna (Seattle University School of Law class of 2017) and Elizabeth O'Brien (Seattle University School of Law class of 2015) for their cite-checking assistance. They also acknowledge the many people who took time to share their observations, summarized and paraphrased here, and take responsibility for any inadvertent misrepresentation of the interview information. Participants in the NYU Law School Medical Commons Workshop and the Georgetown University Law Center IP/Tech Colloquium provided helpful feedback on earlier drafts. Last but not least, the authors thank the editors for the invitation to participate in the Medical Knowledge Commons project.

[1] Franco Pestilli, Test-retest measurements and digital validation for in vivo neuroscience, 2 *Sci. Data* 1 (2015).

[2] David Bollier, The Growth of the Commons Paradigm, in *Understanding Knowledge as a Commons: From Theory to Practice* 27 (Charlotte Hess and Elinor Ostrom eds., MIT Press 2006), at 37

initiatives[3] and sources of funding, it is fair to state that the neuroscience research community is in a process of active institutional change on local, regional and global levels.

This chapter describes what some in the neuroscience research community are calling the "open neuroscience movement."[4] It situates this case study within the intersecting scholarly literatures on knowledge infrastructure[5] and knowledge commons,[6] both of which are related to open innovation research.[7] By focusing on how institutional actors cooperate (or not) to form a knowledge commons and under what circumstances cooperation can occur,[8] this case study of sharing neuroscience data can shed light on enabling conditions for the emergence of these types of governance arrangements. It may be particularly useful in illuminating the dynamics in research environments dominated by an ethos of competitive, individual lab-based achievement.

According to Ostrom and Hess, the so-called action arena that is "at the heart of the [Institutional Analysis and Development [IAD] framework] . . . is an appropriate place to start when trying to think through the challenges of creating a new form of commons."[9] The open neuroscience movement is characterized by disparate institutional actors who have a common recognition: the importance of sharing data. Yet even when this acknowledgement is accompanied by a commitment to open access

3 Press Release, Office of the Press Secretary, The White House, Fact Sheet: BRAIN Initiative (Apr. 2, 2013), /www.whitehouse.gov/the-press-office/2013/04/02/fact-sheet-brain-initiative; Press Release, European Commission, Graphene and Human Brain Project Win Largest Research Excellence Award in History, as Battle for Sustained Science Funding Continues (Jan. 28, 2013), http://europa.eu/rapid/press-release_IP-13-54_en.htm); Press Release, RIKEN Brain Science Institute, Japan Brain/MINDS Project Launches at the RIKEN Brain Science Institute (Nov. 11, 2014), www.brain.riken.jp/en/announcements/20141029.html); David Cyranoski, "Neuroscience in China: growth factor," *Nature* 476, 22–24 (Aug. 3, 2011); David Cyranoski, "Chinese science gets mass transformation," *Nature* (Sept. 23, 2015), www.nature.com/news/chinese-science-gets-mass-transformation-1.15984.

4 Suparna Choudhury et al., Big data, open science and the brain: lessons learned from genomics, 8 *Frontiers in Human Neurosci.* 1, 3 (May 16, 2014), www.ncbi.nlm.nih.gov/pmc/articles/PMC4032989/; see also Kate Murphy, Should all research papers be free? *New York Times* (Mar. 12, 2016), www.nytimes.com/2016/03/13/opinion/sunday/should-all-research-papers-be-free.html; Taking the online medicine, *Economist* (Mar. 19, 2016), www.economist.com/news/science-and-technology/21694990-old-fashioned-ways-reporting-new-discoveries-are-holding-back-medical-research; Brian Owens, Montreal institute going "open" to accelerate science, *Science* (Jan. 21, 2016), www.sciencemag.org/news/2016/01/montreal-institute-going-open-accel-erate-science

5 Brett M. Frischmann, *Infrastructure: The Social Value of Shared Resources* (Oxford University Press 2012).

6 Brett M. Frischmann, Michael J. Madison, and Katherine J. Strandburg (eds.), *Governing Knowledge Commons* (Oxford University Press 2014); Bollier, note 2.

7 Jeremy De Beer, *"Open" innovation policy frameworks: Intellectual property, competition, investment and other market governance issues* ("Table 2: Various terms describing open innovation concepts") (Report prepared for Industry Canada, 2015).

8 Elinor Ostrom and Charlotte Hess, A Framework for Analyzing the Knowledge Commons, in *Understanding Knowledge as a Commons: From Theory to Practice* 34 (Charlotte Hess and Elinor Ostrom eds., MIT Press 2007).

9 Ibid. at 44–45, 53–57.

to research data by major actors, many impediments to the formation of a widely available, accessible and comprehensive neuroscience data commons still exist. By focusing primarily on action situations and actors within this particular action arena, this chapter also addresses why (despite prevailing disincentives) there is growing impetus for broader participation in a neuroscience data commons.

As noted elsewhere in this chapter, the primary actors (or stakeholders) in a knowledge commons include the individual scientists who both generate and use data, the institutions they work for or with, the research funders, and those representing the public who benefit from (and as taxpayers sometimes indirectly fund) the research.[10] Methodologically, this chapter buttresses its observations with interviews of selected actors within key institutions that are attempting to bring forward this emerging knowledge commons; the interviewees include representatives of the stakeholder groups.[11] The chapter first outlines some of the benefits of and then some of the primary obstacles to participation in the desideratum of a neuroscience data commons. It concludes with some suggestions about how to expand a neuroscience data commons that will allow scientists to share data more optimally than current institutional arrangements permit.

8.1 OVERVIEW OF THE EMERGING NEUROSCIENCE DATA COMMONS

> In spite of the vigorous development of neuroinformatics, and the many techniques for data collation, archiving, annotation, and distribution developed over the last decade, the amount of neuroscience data available is only a small fraction of the total. The solution depends upon commitments from both data providers across neuroscience and funding agencies to encourage the open archiving and sharing of data.[12]

Brett Frischmann, Michael Madison and Katherine Strandburg define a "knowledge commons" as arrangements for overcoming social dilemmas related to sharing and producing information, innovation and creative works,[13] and they further define the term "knowledge" as a set of intellectual and cultural resources.[14] These scholars characterize a knowledge commons as an institutional arrangement of resources "involving a group or community of people."[15] The governance of a commons addresses obstacles related to sustainable sharing[16] and is based upon the foundational recognition that multiple uses do not always lead to depletion or scarcity of

[10] Jorge L. Contreras, Data Sharing, Latency Variables, and the Science Commons, 25 *Berkeley Tech. L. J.* 1601, 1629 (2010).

[11] See Appendix ("App.") for a brief description of methodology.

[12] Daniel Gardner et al., The Neuroscience Information Framework: A Data and Knowledge Environment for Neuroscience, 6 *Neuroimform.* 149, 154 (2008).

[13] Brett M. Frischmann, Michael J. Madison and Katherine J. Strandburg, Governing Knowledge Commons, in *Governing Knowledge Commons* 1 (Brett M. Frischmann, Michael J. Madison, and Katherine J. Strandburg eds., Oxford University Press 2014), at 1.

[14] Ibid. at 2. [15] Ibid. [16] Ibid.

those resources.[17] The research on knowledge commons is a subset of the large body of scholarship on open innovation.[18]

To be sure, some intellectual resources can be affected negatively by those who free-ride on the ideas and efforts of others. This behavior can undermine creativity and innovation by making it more difficult for individual artists and inventors to benefit from their efforts. And of course this policy concern forms the rationale for exclusive rights such as copyrights and patents, as well as other forms of intellectual property. However, unlike biologist Garrett Hardin who forecast only tragic results from over-use of shared resources,[19] other scholars see myriad consequences, not all of which are negative. For example, legal scholar Carol Rose sees many "surprises" in commons-based arrangements for resource management, especially in the area of knowledge resources. Tragic examples such as acid rain are counterbalanced by surprising examples such as neglected disease consortiums[20] or Wikipedia.[21] And unlike the late political scientist Elinor Ostrom, who tended to view a commons of shared resources management as involving a limited community of participants with rather defined membership,[22] Rose views some resource-sharing arrangements as having porous rather than fixed boundaries for participation.[23]

Rose's perspective on commons-based resource management aligns well with the definition of openness propounded by Frischmann et al. as "the capacity to relate to a resource by accessing and using it. In other words, the openness of a resource corresponds to the extent to which there are barriers to possession or use."[24] Thus the IAD framework originally created by Ostrom can be adapted to analyze not only emerging rather than pre-existing collaborative arrangements but also "open science" initiatives such as the open neuroscience movement discussed here.

8.1.1 *The Open Neuroscience Movement*

The Human Genome Project (HGP) demonstrated the power of sharing research results. Jorge Contreras has noted that "according to one recent study, the U.S. economic output attributable to advances made by the HGP and follow-on projects

[17] See generally Carol M. Rose, Surprising Commons, 2014 *BYU L. Rev.* 1257 (2015).

[18] De Beer, note 7, at 27 ("Table 2: Various terms describing open innovation concepts").

[19] Garrett Hardin, The Tragedy of the Commons, 162 *Science* 1243 (Dec. 1968).

[20] Katherine J. Strandburg et al., The Rare Diseases Clinical Research Network and the Urea Cycle Disorders Consortium as a Nested Knowledge Commons, in *Governing Knowledge Commons* 155 (Brett M. Frischmann, Michael J. Madison, and Katherine J. Strandburg eds., Oxford University Press 2014).

[21] Rose, note 17, at 27.

[22] Elinor Ostrom, *Governing the Commons: The Evolution of Institutions for Collective Actions* (Cambridge University Press 1990).

[23] Rose, note 17, at 28.

[24] Frischmann et al., note 13, at 29.

totaled $65 billion in 2012 alone"[25] – demonstrating the powerful effect of knowledge infrastructure in generating economic and innovative activity. As he also documents:

> The fact that the genome commons is today a global, public resource owes much to a 1996 accord reached in Bermuda by scientific leaders and policy makers. The groundbreaking "Bermuda Principles" required that all DNA sequences generated by the HGP be released to the public a mere twenty-four hours after generation, a stark contrast to the months or years that usually preceded the release of scientific data (Bermuda Principles 1996). The Bermuda Principles arose from early recognition by scientists and policy makers that rapid and efficient sharing of data was necessary to coordinate activity among the geographically dispersed laboratories working on the massive project.[26]

Likewise, recent calls to make the growing banks of brain data, analytic tools and protocols publicly and freely accessible have been increasing in strength and visibility. They pervade the texts released by the committee for the U.S.-funded BRAIN Initiative[27] and other Big Data projects emerging in neuroscience.[28]

The ethos of the open neuroscience movement is to disseminate the data quickly – in a format that is accessible, useful and unrestricted – and encourage others to use it. This type of collaborative, large-scale basic scientific research has precedents outside of biology including the CERN particle accelerator project[29] and the Hubble Telescope. Certainly, the success of the HGP, which was biology's first large-scale project, stemmed from "strong leadership from the funders; the shared sense of the importance of the task; and the willingness of the researchers involved to cede individual achievements for the collective good."[30] In addition to government agencies funding neuroscience research, this era of Big Data is notable for the involvement of nonprofit organizations (NPOs), including private foundations, public charities, and other newer entrants into the science arena – colloquially dubbed "big philanthropy."[31]

[25] Jorge L. Contreras, Constructing the Genome Commons, in *Governing Knowledge Commons* 99 (Brett M. Frischmann, Michael J. Madison, and Katherine J. Strandburg eds., Oxford University Press 2014), at 100.

[26] Ibid. at 101.

[27] Advisory Committee to the Director, *Interim Report: Brain research through advancing innovative neurotechnologies* 47–51 (September 16, 2013), http://www.braininitiative.nih.gov/pdf/09162013_interim_report_508C.pdf.

[28] Choudhury et al., note 4, at 2.

[29] Peter Galison, The Collective Author, in *Scientific Authorship: Credit and Intellectual Property in Science* 325 (Mario Biagioli and Peter Galison eds., Routledge 2d ed. 2013), at 327. CERN is the acronym for the French Conseil Européen pour la Recherche Nucléaire.

[30] Eric Green, Francis Collins, James Watson, Human Genome Project: twenty-five years of big biology, 526 *Nature* 29, 30 (2015).

[31] William J. Broad, Billionaires with big ideas are privatizing American science, *New York Times* (Mar. 15, 2014),www.nytimes.com/2014/03/16/science/billionaires-with-big-ideas-are-privatizing-american-science.html

Openly accessible neuroscience data is valuable. As several open neuroscience advocates have asserted:

> Datasets from neuroimaging studies generally contain more information than one lab has the methodological and interpretive expertise to extract; data sharing therefore maximizes the utility of data and skills of researchers, accelerating the pace of investigations around particular questions [and is therefore a] crucial imperative from a scientific point of view to increase statistical rigor and open up interpretive possibilities.[32]

Interview participant Dana Bostrom, executive director, Orbis Cascade Alliance and former executive director of Data Commons LLC, observed that openly accessible data also provides an opportunity to generate bigger data sets through a combination of studies.[33] Open neuroscience advocates claim furthermore that

> neuroscience research yields enormous quantities of complex data at various levels of study and open access to data in shared repositories offers the potential to integrate, re-use and re-analyze data[;]... [thus d]ata-sharing not only affords much greater sample sizes and therefore better quality of data, correcting for effects of noise or other errors; [but] it also becomes an economic imperative at a moment in which funding institutions and universities have limited resources.[34]

Interviewee Michael Hawrylycz, PhD, investigator at the Allen Institute, asserted that open data sharing allows a more valid historical record to be created of work that has been done – essentially, an archive of what is available and what is completed.[35] Data sets stored in laboratory archives suggest the absence of appreciation for the potential value of the data beyond the aim of the first study and are sometimes lost to the scientific community forever.[36] This is particularly true with "long tail dark data," which is "unpublished data that includes results from failed experiments and records that are viewed as ancillary to published studies."[37] When this dark data is not made accessible to other researchers, it leaves an incomplete and possibly biased record, needless duplication of scientific efforts and contributes to failures in scientific replication and translation.[38]

Furthermore, to facilitate reproducibility of the research, scientific data must be shared to help mitigate issues related to fraud and perceptions of misconduct.[39] Interviewee Craig Wegner, PhD, executive director and head, Boston Emerging Innovations Unit, Scientific Partnering & Alliances at AstraZeneca IMED Biotech Unit stated that participation in the neuroscience data commons for organizations

32 Choudhury et al., note 4, at 2. 33 See App. (interview with Dana Bostrom).

34 Choudhury et al., note 4, at 2. 35 See App. (interview with Michael Hawrylycz).

36 Michael Peter Milham, Open neuroscience solutions for the connectome-wide association era, 73 *Neuron* 214 (2012).

37 Adam R. Ferguson, Big data from small data: data sharing in the "long tail" of neuroscience, 17 *Nature Neurosci.* 1442, 1443 (2014).

38 Ibid. 39 Ibid.

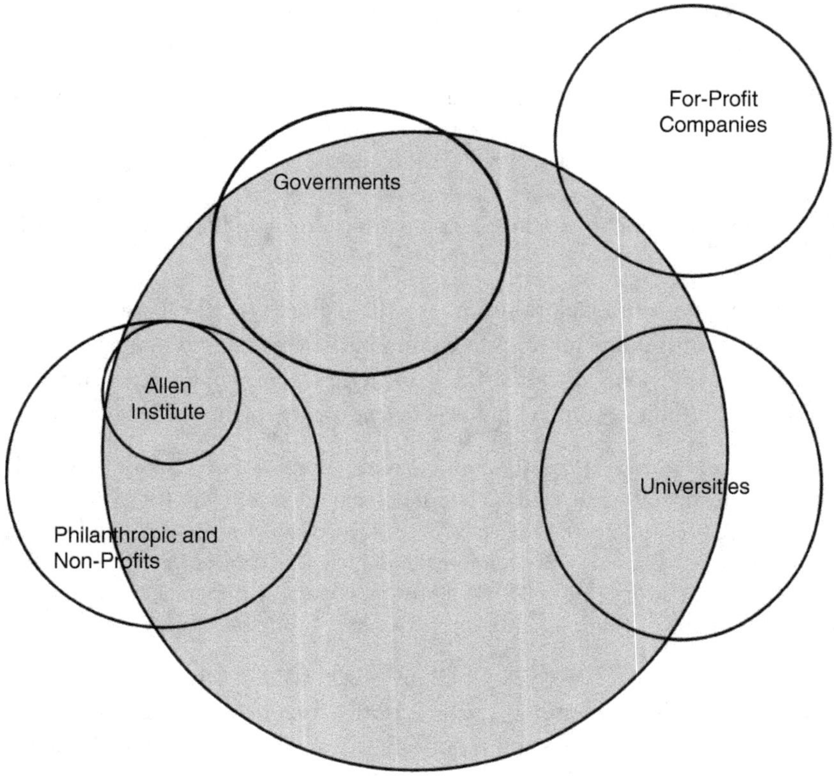

FIGURE 8.1 Actors in the neuroscience data action arena.

involved in clinical research can allay fears that the organization only publishes the positive research results and hides the adverse effects or negative results that are important for patients to know.[40] This openness can gain greater trust of patients and doctors for the research.[41]

Nonprofit research institutes, public and private universities and colleges, and for-profit biotechnology and pharmaceutical companies all have the ability to participate in a neuroscience data commons, yet not every organization chooses to participate as fully as it could, if at all (Figure 8.1). The next section explores some of the reasons affecting participation.

8.1.2 *Institutional Incentives to Participate in the Neuroscience Data Commons*

Three important organizational factors can incentivize (or de-incentivize) participation in the neuroscience data commons: (1) the mission of the organization, (2)

[40] See App. (interview with Craig Wegner). [41] Ibid.

primary funding for the organization's research, and (3) the focus of the organization's research within the research and development (R&D) cycle.

8.1.1.1 Mission

An organization's mission and core values are critical to its willingness to participate in open data sharing. For example, participating and contributing to open science is key to the mission of the Allen Institute – a 501(c)(3) medical research organization formerly known as the Allen Institute for Brain Science. The original mission statement for the Allen Institute for Brain Science asserts that it exists "to accelerate the understanding of how the human brain works in health and disease [and generate] useful public resources."[42] The mission statement of another nonprofit research institute involved in neuroscience research – the Eli and Edythe L. Broad Institute of Harvard and MIT (Broad Institute) – is to "propel progress in biomedicine through research aimed at the understanding and treatment of disease, and the dissemination of scientific knowledge for the public good."[43] Janelia Research Campus, also a neuroscience research institute, "believes that the more collaborative and open it can be, the greater will be its ability to move science forward."[44] The missions of all three of these nonprofit organizations go hand in hand with active participation in a neuroscience data commons.

Research universities also have missions that allow for broad participation in the neuroscience data commons. For example, Colorado State University (CSU) is "committed to excellence, setting the standard for public research universities in teaching, research, service and extension for the benefit of the citizens of Colorado, the United States and the world."[45] According to interviewee Kathryn Partin, PhD, director, Office of Research Integrity and former assistant vice president for research and a professor of biomedical sciences at CSU, the university's mission – focused on education, service, and outreach – is consistent with data sharing since it is dedicated to applying new knowledge to real-world problems, and to translating that new knowledge economically and/or to the benefit of humanity.[46]

[42] Allen Institute, https://alleninstitute.org/our-science/brain-science/about/vision-mission/ (last visited Dec. 26, 2015).

[43] Broad Institute, www.broadinstitute.org/. Eli and Edythe L. Broad Institute of Harvard and MIT (Broad Institute), is a Boston-based collaborative research institute funded primarily via a nonprofit foundation.

[44] Janelia Research Campus, founded by Howard Hughes Medical Institute in 2005, is a collaborative research center in Ashbury, Virginia. Janelia Research Campus, www.janelia.org/about-us (last visited Dec. 26, 2015).

[45] Colo. State University, http://csu-cvmbs.colostate.edu/academics/bms/Pages/default.aspx (last visited Dec. 26, 2015).

[46] See App. (interview with Kathryn Partin).

And while it may be counter-intuitive that a for-profit company would participate in open data sharing, the pharmaceutical industry is moving toward this model.[47] As Wegner stated, by participating at some level in open data sharing and increased transparency, these for-profit actors are also contributing to a change in culture for the research industry.[48] For example, AstraZeneca wants to make publicly accessible in an appropriate format all raw data that is generated in its clinical studies (rather than just a summary of results) so that the scientific community can look for trends and commonalities across multiple clinical studies and avoid duplication in future studies.[49] According to Wegner, AstraZeneca shares this data without fear of financial repercussion because by the time something is published, AstroZeneca is far ahead of a competitor who could reproduce the research.[50] The purpose of this is not just to advance science but also (as stated in the previous section) "to allay the fear that pharmaceutical companies will not just publish and show positive results while hiding adverse effects and other results important for patients to know."[51] By becoming more transparent, pharmaceutical companies hope to gain additional trust.[52]

8.1.2.2 Funding

Sharing data and other research results is expensive and time consuming. It requires a commitment from funders, researchers, and their institutions. Many funders of neuroscience research understand the importance of participation in the data commons. And as funders, they are in the position to strongly encourage participation as a prerequisite for receiving funding. But while some grants include funding to make the research data openly available, that funding does not generally include the cost of long-term maintenance of that data in the commons. To address this need, there has been a steady increase of initiatives for openness by national and international, public and private funders in recent years.

8.1.2.2.1 GOVERNMENT FUNDING

The National Institutes of Health (NIH) is one of the largest funders of neuroscience research in the world. According to it, "The era of 'Big Data' has arrived, and it is vital that the NIH play a major role in coordinating access to and analysis of many different data types that make up this revolution in biological information."[53] Through financial support, the NIH seeks to enable scientific research that improves

[47] Jeff Tolvin, Data sharing in pharmaceutical industry shows progress, *Rutgers Today* (Oct. 16, 2014), http://news.rutgers.edu/qa/data-sharing-pharmaceutical-industry-shows-progress/20141015.

[48] See App. (interview with Craig Wegner). [49] Ibid. [50] Ibid. [51] Ibid. [52] Ibid.

[53] Press Release, Francis S. Collins, Director, Nat'l Institutes of Health, *NIH Names Dr. Philip E. Bourne First Associate Director for Data Science* (Dec. 9, 2013), www.nih.gov/news-events/news-releases/nih-names-dr-philip-e-bourne-first-associate-director-data-science.

health and mitigates the burden of illness or disability.[54] In 2003, the NIH announced its broad data-sharing policy that applies to all data resulting from, among other things, basic and clinical research.[55] This policy encourages researchers to make their data as widely and freely accessible as feasible.[56] The NIH also encourages openness through its public access policy, which requires all publications funded by the NIH to be made publicly available within 12 months.[57] In 2007, the National Science Foundation (NSF) announced similar guidelines, encouraging open data sharing and allowing the costs of such data sharing to be allowable charges against an NSF grant.[58] And in 2013, the Office of Science and Technology Policy (OSTP) reiterated the U.S. government's commitment to transparency of scientific data.[59] On the heels of this commitment was the Obama administration's announcement of its BRAIN Initiative: a large-scale initiative designed to revolutionize the understanding of the human brain.[60] Data funded by the BRAIN Initiative is subject to OSTP's memorandum. The Defense Advanced Research Project Agency (DARPA) is another U.S. government agency that supports the BRAIN Initiative and has an open data initiative. DARPA's Open Catalog was launched in 2014 and is meant as an open resource for publicly accessible research results that are funded by DARPA.[61]

Other national government funders have also increased attention toward open data sharing. The Engineering and Physical Sciences Research Council (EPSRC), which is a main UK government agency for funding research and training in engineering and the physical sciences, is committed to open data sharing. In May 2015, the EPSRC announced its policy, which is founded on seven core principles, the first being that "EPSRC-funded research data is a public good produced in the public interest and should be made freely and openly available with as few restrictions as possible in a

54 Nat'l Institutes of Health, *Grants & Funding* (Sept. 24, 2015), http://grants.nih.gov/grants/grant_basics.htm.

55 Nat'l Institutes of Health, *NIH Data Sharing Policy and Implementation Guidance* (March 5, 2003), http://grants.nih.gov/grants/policy/data_sharing/data_sharing_guidance.htm.

56 Ibid. ("There are many reasons to share data from NIH-supported studies. Sharing data reinforces open scientific inquiry, encourages diversity of analysis and opinion, promotes new research, makes possible the testing of new or alternative hypotheses and methods of analysis, supports studies on data collection methods and measurement, facilitates the education of new researchers, enables the exploration of topics not envisioned by the initial investigators, and permits the creation of new datasets when data from multiple sources are combined. In NIH's view, all data should be considered for data sharing. *Data should be made as widely and freely available as possible while safeguarding the privacy of participants, and protecting confidential and proprietary data*" (emphasis in the original).

57 *NIH Data Sharing Policy and Implementation Guidance*, see note 55.

58 Nat'l Science Foundation, *Award and Admin. Guide* Chapter IV, Nat'l Sci. Found., www.nsf.gov/pubs/policydocs/pappguide/nsf11001/aag_6.jsp (last visited Oct. 15, 2015).

59 Memorandum from Office of Sci. & Tech. Policy, Exec. Office of the President on Increasing Access to the Results of Federally Funded Scientific Research (Feb 22, 2013) (on file with White House).

60 Office of The Press Sec'y, The White House, Fact Sheet: Brain Initiative (April 2, 2013), www.whitehouse.gov/the-press-office/2013/04/02/fact-sheet-brain-initiative.

61 Defense Advanced Research Project Agency, Our Research, www.darpa mil/our-research (last visited Dec. 26, 2015).

timely and responsible manner."[62] The European Commission also has indicated its support of open access to scientific information in its Europe 2020 Initiative.[63] In this initiative, similar to the NIH, the European Commission required a data management plan for funded projects under the Guidelines for Data Management in Horizon 2020.[64] The Organisation for Economic Co-operation and Development (OECD) added its voice with a policy report on the benefits of Big Data.[65]

8.1.2.2.2 PHILANTHROPIC FUNDING

This push for data sharing of publicly funded research comes when government funding for such research has been in decline. During the same period of time, however, philanthropic funding has been on the rise.[66] Individual philanthropists and foundations can provide a research organization with the funding needed to participate in the neuroscience data commons. Some examples of nonprofit organizations that participate in the neuroscience data commons are the Wellcome Trust, One Mind, and the Allen Institute.

The Wellcome Trust is a global charitable foundation supporting biomedical science, innovations, public engagement, and humanities and social sciences.[67] More than £700 million (or approximately US$900 million) are provided annually to support these research areas.[68] Its open access policy ensures that the research that it funds will ultimately foster a richer research culture by maximizing the distribution of these publications.[69] One Mind is a nonprofit organization dedicated to "benefiting all affected by brain illness and injury through fostering fundamental changes that will radically accelerate the development and implementation of improved diagnostics, treatments and cures – while eliminating the stigma that comes with mental illness."[70] One Mind published several principles on open science for projects it funds:

1. Provide informed consents for collection of medical data obtained from patients, which should permit use of their de-identified (anonymous) data for research

62 Engineering and Physical Sciences Research Council, ERSC policy framework on research data, www.epsrc.ac.uk/about/standards/researchdata/principles/ (last visited Sept. 24, 2015).

63 European Commission, Open Access to Scientific Information, https://ec.europa.eu/digital-agenda/en/open-access-scientific-information (last visited Dec. 26, 2015).

64 European Commission, Guidelines on Data Management in Horizon 2020 (Feb. 15, 2016), http://ec.europa.eu/research/participants/data/ref/h2020/grants_manual/hi/oa_pilot/h2020-hi-oa-data-mgt_en.pdf

65 OECD Policy Note, Data-driven Innovation: Big Data for Growth and Well-Being: What Implications for Governments and Businesses? (Oct. 2015), http://oe.cd/bigdata4

66 Our Approach, *Broad Inst.*, www.broadinstitute.org/what-broad/our-approach/our-approach (last visited Oct. 15, 2015).

67 Funding, *Wellcome Trust*, www.wellcome.ac.uk/funding/ (last visited Sept. 24, 2015).

68 Ibid.

69 Policy and Position Statements, *Wellcome Trust* www.wellcome.ac.uk/About-us/Policy/Policy-and-position-statements/WTX035043.htm (last visited Sept. 24, 2015).

70 About Us, *One Mind*, www.onemind.org/About-Us (last visited Dec. 2, 2015).

related to a broad range of conditions – this is consistent with protecting patient privacy.

2. Use widely accepted common data elements and conform to the highest possible standards when clinical data is collected. This enables it to be used by the widest possible array of users, whether academic, medical, clinical or commercial.
3. Make data available to the research community as soon as possible after study completion, with the goal of opening data access within 6 months whenever possible.
4. Make data accessible to external researchers during the course of a study (subject to relevant data use agreements).
5. Give data generators proper attribution & credit from those who use their data.
6. Do not delay the publication of findings, as it may affect patient care. Intellectual property should not stand in the way of research, but be used to incentivize material participation.[71]

Within the neuroscience data commons, the Allen Institute provides a prime example of data sharing by virtue of its ongoing open science policy and practices, which are strongly encouraged by its primary philanthropic funder.[72] In an article published in *Nature*, for example, the initial scientists involved in the inaugural Allen Institute for Brain Science project that mapped the mouse brain wrote the following:

> The Allen Brain Atlas project has taken a global approach to understanding the genetic structural and cellular architecture of the mouse brain by generating a genome-scale collection of cellular resolution gene expression profiles using ISH ... These methods enable global analysis and mining for detailed expression patterns in the brain. *The entire Allen Brain Atlas data set and associated informatics tools are available through an unrestricted web-based viewing application (emphasis added)* (*www.brain-map.org*).

This published research paper considers the data dissemination component to be integral to its scientific purpose. Thus these particular actors seem to be acutely aware of their role in the larger neuroscience and data-sharing commons within which the Allen Institute is nested,[73] illustrating that an institution's commitment to data sharing can permeate organizational culture and advance norms of open science. In 2014, the funding for neuroscience research done by the Allen Institute

[71] Our Solutions, *One Mind*, http://onemind.org/Our-Solutions/Open-Science (last visited Sept. 24, 2015).

[72] Paul Allen, Commentary: why we chose open science, *Wall St. J.* (Nov. 30, 2011), www.wsj.com/articles/SB10001424052970204630904577058162033028028

[73] Jonah Lehrer, Scientists map the brain, gene by gene, *Wired Magazine* (Mar. 28, 2009), http://archive.wired.com/medtech/health/magazine/17-04/ff_brainatlas

(approximately US$60 million) rivaled government funding by the NIH (approximately US$46 million) in the BRAIN Initiative's first year (2014).[74]

While it has a greater emphasis on infectious diseases than on neuroscience, the Bill & Melinda Gates Foundation (Gates Foundation) is a private foundation that makes enormous investments in global health[75] and thus has influenced the acceptance of open data access more generally through its global access policy.[76] This policy has been in effect for the past decade and requires that information (including data) arising from its funding be made rapidly accessible.[77] In 2012, it started a pilot project for grants in excess of US$500,000 and required grantees to provide a data access plan.[78] Since 2013, the Gates Foundation shifted its focus from dissemination of data to access to data. The Gates Foundation has an interest in data access for at least three reasons: (1) the data around early stage development of a drug, for example, to treat malaria, is relevant to showing scientific achievement or recognition that a particular drug is safe and effective; (2) the global, national, and local case data (e.g., mortality/morbidity granular data) is relevant to showing a reduction in the burden of disease, and to the extent that data can be overlaid with an introduction of new therapies, it helps make the case that the new therapy was the one that caused the reduction in burden and disease; and (3) the data that reflects the global level of effort in attacking a problem is important to ensure that the R&D spent by all funders – government, industry, private foundations – is funding work that is not duplication of effort but instead is complementary and consistent.[79]

8.1.2.2.3 RESEARCH AND DEVELOPMENT CYCLE

The extent to which an organization participates in the neuroscience data commons may also depend on its research focus. The typical R&D cycle for scientific research starts with basic research and moves to clinical and/or translational research. The research categories are not fixed or rigid and an organization may be involved in

74 Press Release, Nat'l Institutes of Health, NIH awards initial $46 million for BRAIN Initiative research (Sept. 30, 2014), www.nih.gov/news-events/news-releases/nih-awards-initial-46-million-brain-initiative-research; Valerie Bauman, Allen Institute a key research partner in Obama's BRAIN initiative, *Puget Sound Business J.* (Apr. 2, 2013), www.bizjournals.com/seattle/blog/techflash/2013/04/allen-institute-a-key-research-partner.html.

75 Bill and Melinda Gates Foundation, www.gatesfoundation.org/ (last visited Oct. 13, 2015).

76 See App. (interview with Richard Wilder).

77 Gates Foundation announces open access policy for grantees, *Philanthropy News Digest* (Nov. 28, 2014), http://philanthropynewsdigest.org/news/gates-foundation-announces-open-access-policy-for-grantees. ("Open-access policy to enable[s] unrestricted access to and reuse of all peer-reviewed published research, including underlying data sets, that it funds in whole or in part.").

78 See App. (interview with Richard Wilder). As a funder, the Gates Foundation generally does not have restrictions that potentially affect data sharing for the organizations it funds; rather, from a global access policy perspective, the overarching desire is to broadly and rapidly disseminate in an open fashion.

79 Ibid.

categories at varying points along the continuum.[80] The cost to move research from the bench to the bedside is very high, and few funders are willing to invest in that research without knowing that they will be able to reap the financial benefits of commercialization. Therefore, it is intuitive that an institution that focuses primarily on basic research would be more inclined to participate in the neuroscience data commons than an institution that works on translational and/or clinical research. Perhaps one outlier in terms of data sharing is the rare disease context, which typically falls under translational and clinical research and where open approaches may be more attractive because of the small numbers and geographical dispersion of potential research participants, as well as the inapplicability of the "blockbuster drug" business model.[81]

It is not intuitive, however, that a for-profit pharmaceutical company would participate in the neuroscience data commons at any level, but if it did, one would expect it to also participate with its basic research. Pharmaceutical companies may improve research and development efficacy by making the process transparent, such that researchers can have access to data on a certain molecule or compound or other limited situations such as for rare diseases that have more limited commercial interest. Indeed, the industry has adopted a "hybrid mode" whereby a pharmaceutical developer still owns the patent rights on a drug and retains the associated trade secrets but can still freely share study protocols, data analysis techniques, results, communications with regulatory agencies, and interactions with insurance companies.[82] At least one pharmaceutical company, AstraZeneca, has gone even further and is more likely to share data in a translational state as opposed to basic science.[83] Interviewee Wegner believes that its competitive edge rests is in coming up with a novel target and pursuing it with hypothesis testing.[84]

8.2 OBSTACLES TO FORMING A NEUROSCIENCE DATA COMMONS

> A recent survey about data-sharing practices among scientists revealed considerable unwillingness to disclose whether or not they share data. Nearly half of the respondents said they do not share data, citing reasons of lack of time, underdeveloped standards, and inadequate infrastructure. Interestingly, 85% of these respondents indicated an interest in having access to other researchers" datasets.[85]

The obstacles to participation in a neuroscience data commons are nontrivial. While any organization *can* participate in the neuroscience data commons at some level, the neuroscience organizations (and the scientists within the

[80] See generally Donald Stokes, *Pasteur"s Quadrant: Basic Science and Technological Innovation* (Brookings (Institution Press 1997); Steven H. Woolf, The Meaning of Translational Research and Why it Matters, 299 *JAMA* 211 (2008).

[81] Strandburg et al., note 20; Chapters 15 and 16, this volume.

[82] Timothy King, Can open science help patients and save pharma? OpenSource.com, (June 19, 2014), http://opensource.com/health/14/6/can-open-science-help-patients-and-save-pharma.

[83] See App. (interview with Craig D. Wegner). [84] Ibid. [85] Choudhury et al., note 4, at 4.

organizations) must be convinced that it is in their best interest to do so. Many of the barriers to access of routinely collected public health data are also relevant to the challenges in participation in the neuroscience data commons:(1) technical, (2) motivational, and (3) legal considerations.[86]

8.2.1 *Technical*

In the past, it was not logistically feasible to publish raw data. Now that data sharing is possible through the power of digital and network technologies, the concern is to ensure quality and integrity of the data and to have the data in a useful format. Definitions of "open data" vary, but they all have the same characteristics: it must be accessible, free of restrictions, and interoperable among systems.[87]

Scholars have defined data quality as "the extent to which a database accurately represents the essential properties of the intended application, and has three distinct properties: 1) data reliability, 2) logical or semantic integrity, and 3) physical integrity (the correctness of implementation details)."[88] While seemingly straightforward, the need for high-quality data has been a long-standing issue among users of organizational databases that put out data of poor quality.[89] An organization can practice open data sharing, but if it lacks standards, including interchangeability and a common language, the data it shares will not be useful to (or used by) other organizations.

Furthermore, as others have noted, common standards require time to understand and implement.[90] The potential for reuse for certain types of data varies.[91] Moreover, a lack of consensus on the data quality standards, which puts quality control in the hands of the users,[92] makes the data less useful. There are also issues of cleanliness in data production. As Bostrom observed, if the data is not interesting or clean enough, people will be unable to interpret it, and this will generate more questions or work that people do not want to spend time doing.[93] It can take a significant amount of time to annotate or detail the data to make it ready for

86 Willem G. van Panhuis et al., A systematic review of barriers to data sharing in public health, 14 *BMC Pub. Health* (2014), www.biomedcentral.com/content/pdf/1471–2458-14–1144.pdf

87 See, e.g., UK Minister of State for the Cabinet Office and Paymaster General, *White Paper on Open Data*, (June 2012), https://data.gov.uk/sites/default/files/Open_data_White_Paper.pdf; What is Open Data? *Open Data Handbook*, http://opendatahandbook.org/guide/en/what-is-open-data/ (last visited Nov. 22, 2015). See also OECD Policy Note, note 65, at 2 ("Obstacles to the reuse and sharing of data should be examined carefully with an eye to enhancing the benefits that can be reaped from data. Non-discriminatory access regimes, including data commons or open access regimes, should be explored, as a means to support the production of public and social goods without requiring governments or businesses to pick winners (either users or applications).").

88 Richard Y. Wang, A framework for analysis of data quality research, 7 *IEEE Trans. on Knowledge & Data Eng'g* 623, 629 (1995).

89 Ibid. at 623.

90 Strandburg et al., note 20, at 196.

91 Russell A. Poldrack and Krzysztof J. Gorgolewski, Making big data open: data sharing in neuroimaging, 17 *Nature Neurosci.* 1511 (2014).

92 Ibid.

93 See App. (interview with Dana Bostrom).

someone else to use and access.[94] The need to address the computational and logistical difficulties involved in moving around and analyzing these large amounts of data is resulting in the rapid increase in the use of cloud computing and new resources such as data commons.[95]

8.2.2 *Motivational*

Open neuroscience advocates have noted that the reward system for neuroscientists is not conducive to participation in the neuroscience data commons. As observed by Choudhury and others, "individual researchers' lack of motivation to share is considered a key obstacle to wider change in data sharing practices."[96] Indeed, a primary factor blocking broad participation in the neuroscience data commons is the desire among neuroscientists to be the first to analyze their data, and to be recognized for findings from their data. This is such a widespread issue that it deserves to be termed the "first to analyze data" problem. Generally, when neuroscientists are conducting science, they are not necessarily thinking about making it accessible for the public good – they are thinking about working on their hypotheses and getting credit for their hard work: "In an academic context where funding is increasingly competitive, and data are relatively expensive to generate, anxieties about being 'scooped,' or undercut, by other data collectors constitute a very real challenge to the cultural reform envisaged by open neuroscience advocates."[97]

Interviewee Hawrylycz stated that within the biological and medical sciences, organizations spend money to generate data, and this data is both precious and important to people's careers.[98] Thus, neuroscience researchers may want to hold data back until the professional glory is fully extracted from it.[99] Others have noted a similar lack of motivation for researchers to cooperate and contribute to a common data pool, in the context of research on neglected diseases.[100]

Hawrylycz added that organizations do not want to squelch the innovative spirit of their scientists; since innovation strives for something new that stretches boundaries, the data that is collected in pursuit of the innovation might contain inaccuracies or be misinterpreted in the absence of context.[101] In addition to the race to be the first to present new results, "neuroscientists may also . . . fear being scrutinized publicly for inadequate paradigms or data collection methods, particularly after the very public forms of criticism of neuroimaging analysis . . . which initially used freely accessible online forums for criticism rather than peer-reviewed academic journals."[102]

In many environments, individual neuroscientists "must meet tenure, promotion and grant criteria that fail to incent or reward sharing, but rather encourage

94 Ibid. at 4; Chapter 3, this volume. 95 Green et al., note 30.

96 Choudhury et al., note 4, at 4. See also Jean-Baptiste Poline et al., Data sharing in neuroimaging research, 6 *Frontiers in Neuroinformatics* 1 (2012).

97 Ibid. 98 See App. (interview with Michael Hawrylycz). 99 Ibid.

100 Strandburg et al., note 20, at 195. 101 See note 89. 102 Choudhury et al., note 4, at 4.

data retention as a basis for multiple publications."[103] Scientists are rewarded for their publications but not for making their data openly available. To be successful, participating in data sharing must be legitimized as a form of scholarly work, similar to publishing a scientific article. Philip Bourne, former associate director of data science at the NIH, has discussed this imperative in his talks around the NIH's commitment to data.[104]

And while putting neuroscience data into the neuroscience data commons might inform the scientific community about discoveries, accomplishments, and breakthroughs in research, data sharing presents challenges even in public research university settings. Interviewee Kathryn Partin stated that, while CSU has a strong culture for openness and transparency along with a taxpayer expectation for data to be shared for both ethical and financial reasons, its researchers may be hesitant to share raw data for no other reason outside of data integrity.[105] With raw data, uncertainty exists as to whether the data set contains inaccuracies. However, she noted that exclusion criteria are applied to published data, to ensure that the sample is what it says it is, thereby making it a shareable data set in which people can study the data without fear of misinterpretation.[106]

Unfortunately, no standard acknowledgment mechanisms exist for neuroscientists who practice team science; rather, the current knowledge ecosystem incentivizes individual accomplishments.[107] While the existing rewards may work fine for easy problems, the difficult questions that neuroscientists are trying to answer will not be answered without collaborative team science.[108] And even when there is collaboration and team science, there are tensions with being the first and last author on the publication.[109] Interesting differences among nonprofit organizations are apparent. For university-based researchers, the prevailing rules of academic scholarship, promotion, and tenure can reinforce the existing motivational barriers to sharing. On the other hand, 501(c)(3) organizations such as the Allen Institute are not bound as tightly to such imperatives. Many research scientists have migrated from prestigious research institutions such as CalTech, Harvard, and MIT, and some have given up tenure to participate in a nonprofit model of science that is not contingent upon the reward structures prevailing at academic institutions.

In addition to reputational and prestige motivations, economic motivations may militate against data sharing: "The process of data sharing requires human and technical resources for data preparation, annotation, communication with recipients, internet connectivity, etc."[110] Open neuroscience is expensive if done right; it is also

[103] Accelerating Open Science, *One Mind 3rd Annual Summit White Paper* 6 (May 2014), www.onemind.org/ckfinder/userfiles/files/One%20Mind%202014%20Summit%20White%20Paper_FINAL_for%20website_2_05_15.pdf

[104] Philip E. Bourne, Associate Director for Data Science, Nat'l Institutes of Health, Presentation at the University of Georgia: Data Science in Biomedicine – Where Are We Headed? (Oct. 12, 2015), www.slideshare.net/pebourne/data-science-in-biomedicine-where-are-we-headed.

[105] See App. (interview with Kathryn Partin). [106] Ibid. [107] Ibid. [108] Ibid. [109] Ibid.

[110] van Panhuis et al., note 86, at 5.

expensive to maintain. As stated earlier, the NIH requires a data-sharing plan for any research funded with more than $5,000; however, future maintenance costs are not generally included in the funding. Additionally, at least part of any innovators' motivation is financial; for those neuroscientists who are entrepreneurial, there is an inherent conflict between financial benefit and providing one's innovations openly. Thus the incentives to hoard data can be as strong as the incentives to share it. Furthermore, the Bayh-Dole Act of 1980, which established a uniform policy for patent rights in inventions made with federally funded research, can affect the mission of research universities by making potential commercialization an important goal of scientific research.[111]

8.2.3 *Legal*

At least three kinds of rules-in-use[112] present themselves in the neuroscience research field with respect to intellectual property: (1) the absence of intellectual property, (2) intellectual property with offensive downstream licensing (to enforce exclusive rights), and (3) intellectual property with defensive downstream licensing (to ensure freedom to operate).[113] These approaches are not mutually exclusive, and their common long-term goal is the diffusion of knowledge.[114] For individual neuroscientists and neuroscience organizations alike, the need to protect intellectual property rights, which are exclusive rights to the individual or institution, can quash any desire or ability to participate in the neuroscience data commons. When launching One Mind's open science principles, for example, the interaction between openness and protection of intellectual property was one of the biggest issues impeding full participation in open data sharing, according to interviewee General Chiarelli.[115]

[111] See generally Arti K. Rai and Rebecca S. Eisenberg, Bayh-Dole Reform and the Progress of Biomedicine, 66 *Law & Contemp. Probs.* 289 (2003).

[112] Ostrom and Hess, note 8, at 52–53.

[113] Cf. De Beer, see note 7, at 57–60 (describing offensive and defensive IP management strategies in the context of open innovation); see also Colleen V. Chien, Opening up the Patent System: Exclusionary and Diffusionary Levers in Patent Law, 89 *Southern California L. Rev.* 4 (2016) (defining "Defensive patenting – holding patents in order to facilitate freedom to operate – is practiced by an estimated half or more of patent holders" and stating further that "[w]hile it often seems that there are only two approaches for supporting innovation with patents – to opt-in and exclude, or to opt-out and share, intellectual property, a widely-used approach between them is to acquire patents *in order to share*, or "defensive patenting.").

[114] Chien, note 113 ("It is widely recognized that different industries use patents differently, and that patents support a diversity of business models. Allowing innovators to individually tailor patent rights, and in some cases, to change these options over the lifetime of the patent, would provide finer grained controls to those in the best position to know the right balance between exclusion and diffusion with respect to a particular invention.")

[115] See App. (interview with General Chiarelli). This suggests that the neuroscience research area may be plagued with the "anti-commons" problem suggested by Heller and Eisenberg regarding the role of patents in biomedical research, a topic that is beyond the scope of this chapter. See Michael A. Heller and Rebecca S. Eisenberg, Can patents deter innovation? the anticommons in biomedical research, 280 *Science* 698 (1998).

Intellectual property rules are also relevant for NPOs participating in the neuroscience data commons. For example, in contrast to the Allen Institute, which, to date, is not focused on building a patent portfolio, the Broad Institute has a wide patent portfolio. Both the Allen Institute and the Broad Institute have common origins in the successes of the HGP, and both are committed to openness of research results. Nonetheless they currently have different intellectual property management positions in pursuing their respective missions. The Allen Institute's full range of knowledge resources includes not only data but also software, hardware, biological materials such as transgenic mice, methods, models, algorithms, publications, and other tools. While the Allen Institute does not have a fully developed program to license out (i.e., provide others with materials on a royalty basis), it does license in for some of its research in order to use materials provided by others. It also has developed terms of use for downstream use of its data and images found on its website, with three requirements: (1) attribution to the Allen Institute of the data and/or images used, (2) prohibition of repackaging the data and/or images for profit, and (3) respect for the Allen Institute's freedom to continue innovation.[116] Thus the downstream out-licensing approach of the Allen Institute for its data and images preserves freedom to operate, or defensive downstream licensing.[117] The Allen Institute and others affiliated with big philanthropy such as the Gates Foundation have been informal advocates for a less revenue-driven view of technology licensing within nonprofit-based technology transfer forums such as the Association of University Technology Managers (AUTM), which is an organization supporting the global academic technology transfer profession.

In the context of collaborative research, no actor is completely closed off from the licensing impacts of intellectual property ownership.[118] As Colleen Chien observed with respect to the patent system:

> Declines in the cost of communication and computing, and increases in product complexity make it an opportune time for a pivot toward collaboration in the patent system. The patent system should pay more attention to supporting the rights of patentees to enable rather than to forbid, others from practicing patentable inventions, and to sell or waive certain patent rights or rights among certain populations. For example, if a patent holder wants to retain only rights to exclude larger competitors, or to waive all but defensive rights, enabling free use by green, humanitarian, educational, or start-up projects, for examples, it should be possible to do so. But presently, there are no easy ways to do so.[119]

116 See Terms of Use, *Allen Institute*, http://alleninstitute.org/terms-of-use/. As Paul Allen put it, "[o]ur terms-of-use agreement is about 10% as long as the one governing iTunes." Allen, note 72.

117 Chien, note 113.

118 Esther van Zimmeren et al., Patent pools and clearinghouses in the life sciences, 29 *Trends in Biotechnology* 569, 570 (2011).

119 Colleen Chien, Why it's time to open up our patent system, *Wall St. J.* (June 30, 2015), www.washingtonpost.com/news/innovations/wp/2015/06/30/why-its-time-to-open-up-our-patent-system/; see also Chien, note 114; De Beer, see note 7, at 57-60.

Analogously, neuroscience research does not have large-scale mechanisms that would allow for a more efficient exchange or sharing of biological materials, tools and data used in neuroscience research.

In addition to intellectual property issues, privacy issues are significant: "Researchers' willingness to share data can also be constrained by concerns for the privacy of the human research participants who are the data sources, and the data sharing permissions they have granted in consenting to participate."[120] With genomic data, there is a concern of re-identifiability once the data is released.[121] While privacy considerations are very important, evidenced by current efforts allowing for presentation and anonymization of brain imaging data that will allow others to access and reanalyze these results,[122] it is beyond the scope of this chapter to investigate their impact in greater detail.

8.3 TOWARD THE FORMATION OF A NEUROSCIENCE DATA COMMONS

> Data sharing is a common requirement of funding or publication, though this obligation may come as a surprise to some authors – and to their colleagues who have had trouble acquiring data from other laboratories. Many granting agencies, including the Wellcome Trust in the United Kingdom and the National Institutes of Health and the Howard Hughes Medical Institute in the United States, require grantees to share data whenever possible, so as to maximize the usefulness of the data whose collection they have funded.[123]

The previous sections summarize the importance of open neuroscience and some of the primary obstacles to participation. This part summarizes some possible solutions to these obstacles without attempting to assess or evaluate any efforts of the institutions discussed.

Open neuroscience advocates have welcomed more coordinated efforts among public and private organizations to advance more open data sharing in neuroscience. However, it is well documented that these types of partnerships were not as successful as had been hoped in the context of the HGP. The challenges faced by the public-private partnership model of the HGP caution the neuroscience research community that there may be some incompatibility in the goals of different types of institutions when they endeavor to share large-scale data.[124] That being said,

120 Choudhury et al., note 4, at 4. 121 Ibid.

122 Russel A. Poldrack et al., Toward open sharing of task-based fMRI data: the Open fMRI Project, 7 *Front Neuroinform.* 12 (Jul. 8, 2013).

123 Got Data?, 10 *Nature Neurosci.* 931 (2007).

124 Choudhury et al., note 4, at 5 ("Recognizing significant interest from both public and private entities in achieving its goals, promoters of the HGP argued that sequencing the human genome would be greatly accelerated through collaboration and sharing of technological and financial resources. A coordinated public/private partnership involving the United States' NIH and Department of Energy, The Wellcome Trust, and the private corporation of Celera was proposed to generate a draft

a number of public-private partnerships have emerged in the neuroscience research area, including Pistoia Alliance and Sage Bionetworks.[125]

Researchers have observed that "neuroscience does not at present have a central, general source for relevant data. Because there is no site that directly addresses their needs, neuroscientists by default make use of a variety of search engines (e.g., Google, Google Scholar, and PubMed) that are largely literature oriented."[126] To address the lack of a framework or standards to properly archive open neuroscience data, as part of the Blueprint for Neuroscience Research, the NIH funded the Neuroscience Information Framework, which "presents neuroscientists with a single starting point for their searches, one that can be a portal that students start using at the dawn of their training and continue to utilize as their primary access to multiple and complex sets of data accessible from a growing number of neuroscience-specific databases."[127] The NIH is also piloting projects enveloped under the commons framework[128] that, if fully implemented, would solve many of the technical issues addressed earlier. But, according to Philip Bourne, it will require more than the commitment from the NIH to be successful.[129]

Another more recent initiative aimed at working on ways to process and share big amounts of data is the Neurodata without Borders – Cellular Neurophysiology initiative,[130] in which researchers around the world can deposit their data, which would then be converted into a standardized format for use by other scientists. This pilot project, aimed at developing a common integrated data format for neurophysiology, was developed by private funding partners: the Kavli Foundation, the Howard Hughes Medical Institute (HHMI), and the Allen Institute.[131] The beta version of its Neurophysiology Data Format was released on June 9, 2016. Karel

sequence of the human genome using composites of 17 individuals. The hopes were that this partnership would reduce duplicative efforts and allow both private industry and public scientists to reap the rewards of efforts to sequence the genome with open access to data deposited in the GenBank public repository, though with some intellectual property rights in the data retained (Jasny, 2013). Despite a public face of coordinated effort, in reality the race to sequence the human genome was more like a competition between public and private interests in which neither side achieved their goals of a clean and complete publicly available sequence or a profitable private sequence in which all users would pay to view the results (Jasny, 2013)").

125 Allen, note 72 ("Private nonprofits like the Pistoia Alliance and Sage Bionetworks are curating their own open-source repositories.").

126 Gardner et al., note 12, at 157.

127 Ibid.

128 Philip E. Bourne, ADDS current vision statement, *PEBOURNE* (Oct. 31, 2014), https://pebourne.wordpress.com/ ("[W]hile it will take much more than one person to change a deeply ingrained culture centered around specific diseases and organs; the complexity of disease and the value of sharing data across institutional boundaries, will drive us forward.").

129 Philip E. Bourne, The commons, *PEBOURNE* (Oct. 7, 2014), https://pebourne.wordpress.com/2014/10/07/the-commons/

130 Neurodata Without Borders, www.nwb.org/ (last visited Dec. 28, 2015). The founding scientific partners include the Allen Institute, the Svoboda Lab at the Janelia Research Campus of HHMI, the Meister Lab at the California Institute of Technology, the Buzsáki Lab at New York University School of Medicine and the University of California.

131 Ibid.

Svoboda, one of the original scientists in the initiative, has stated, "Some of these data are incredibly hard won and then just die . . . This is an effort to get ahead of the problem and solve it from the bottom up."[132]

While the best motivations may come from agreement among significant actors that researchers will benefit from involvement in the neuroscience data commons, interviewee Hawrylycz noted a trade-off between individual credit, the need for funding, and doing good.[133] Therefore, the movement for openness is more likely to be realized with the increased acceptance and push from universities and funders, which are probably in the best position to strongly encourage participation in the neuroscience data commons. Even so, technical and incentive issues need to be addressed so that the funds that are provided are being used in the most efficient and effective way. And brute force by funders is not effective or sustainable given other institutional constraints.

Among the major commonly acknowledged hurdles to data sharing is the "crucial issue of academic credit, and [therefore the need to] devise methods that recognize and reward data sharing and encourage a culture of openness. This will include considerations about how best to reflect academic output and avenues for academic publication that encourage data acquisition and sharing as important contributions to the literature."[134] Choudhury suggests a possible solution in the form of

> "data papers," which, while common to other fields such as genetics, robotics, and earth sciences, are lacking in neuroscience. These data papers, which would serve to detail the experimental protocol and data specification without covering analysis or interpretation, might provide a mechanism for citable professional credit to the data generators . . . [D]ata papers solve the problem of motivation for individuals to share data while "making it count" in the university system of merit, and at the same time allow different data users to draw on the same data sets for different interpretations, consistent with a central epistemological goal of open neuroscience.[135]

To address the "first to analyze data" problem within the scientific community, interviewee General Chiarelli suggested that the Nobel Prize for medicine be abolished because it causes people to work as individuals, does not force people into team science, and therefore reinforces the barriers faced by open neuroscience advocates.[136] He adamantly recommended that the incentive system must move away from individual accomplishment and toward team accomplishment. One suggestion is a change in the publication process such that authors are published in alphabetical order rather than the traditional last author/first author system.[137]

[132] Ibid. [133] See App. (interview with Michael Hawrylycz).

[134] Choudhury et al., note 4, at 7. ("It has been suggested that h-indices, metrics of publication citation, as measures of performance, are already a useful way to capture a result of data sharing, as long as a system is ensured for citing data from repositories that are used for analysis and re-analysis by authors other than the data generators.")

[135] Ibid. [136] See App. (interview with General Peter Chiarelli). [137] Ibid.

Indeed, he went so far as to suggest that one year, the A's become Z's and the next year Z's become A's.[138]

In 2007, the editors of *Nature Neuroscience* wrote:

> If data sharing is to become a routine part of academic life, universities and funding agencies will need to make further efforts to encourage it. One major step forward would be universities to give credit for good citizenship, as reflected in data sharing, during hiring and promotion decisions. This process would be facilitated by a system to track the downloading and use of shared data. Similarly, funding agencies may give preference in awarding grants to scientists who can demonstrate that they have provided easy access to their data collected in connection with previous grants.[139]

While the Allen Institute does not generally track unique visitors to its brain atlas data portal (www.brain-map.org) individually, it measures impact in a number of ways to optimize the reach and impact of the Allen Institute resources. It tracks the number and IP address of its unique visitors in the aggregate and compares the visitor count against its public data releases and publications. It also tracks the number of primary publications citing Allen Institute data on the data portal – both published by Allen Institute scientists and by other scientists using Allen Institute data pulled from the data portal – as well as citations to these primary publications that are made as part of the Allen Institute's data portal terms of use. Additionally, it collects use-case scenarios on what people do with the data. Under its citation policy in the terms of use on the data portal, the Allen Institute asks users to give the organization credit with the appropriate citation. In this way, some interesting impact measures can be glimpsed. For example, starting with the problem that "neuroscience is data rich but theory poor," two scientists developed an innovative model for generating hypotheses for proof-of-concept, based on a text/data mining of the neuroscience literature.[140] They counted word pairs that appeared most frequently together in neuroscience articles and integrated them with the Allen Institute brain atlas, to find brain regions that strongly express a neurotransmitter gene but are understudied. For example, they found that serotonin and striatum were found together in 4782 neuroscience articles, and serotonin and migraine in 2943 articles; however, striatum and migraine were found in only 16. They also checked and verified that these perceived and presumed relationships correlate significantly with areas of real gene expression, as indicated by the Allen Institute's atlas. This single example illustrates a broader principle. One fundamental driver for

138 Ibid.

139 Got Data?, note 123. Since this observation, these editors have begun an initiative called Scientific Data, www.nature.com/sdata/, which is an open data publication resource, where authors in their other journals are encouraged to publish their data.

140 Jessica B. Voytek and Bradley Voytek, Automated cognome construction and semi-automated hypothesis generation, 208 *J. Neurosci. Methods* 6 (2012).

open neuroscience is that the neuroscience literature is too vast for any one researcher to integrate.

From these examples, it appears that the limited commons in individual laboratories are giving way to a spectrum of larger commons pools described by Jorge Contreras and Jerome Reichman.[141] The NIH Neuroscience Information Framework could be viewed as a type of intermediate distributed commons (independent data pools integrated via a central access point or portal).[142] The Neurodata without Borders initiative is an effort to construct a fully distributed commons (maintained locally and integrated by a common legal and policy framework that authorizes users to access individual nodes under terms and conditions – or legal interoperability).[143] As more neuroscience researchers are drawn to Big Data questions such as the one illustrated by the follow-on research based upon the Allen Brain Atlas, momentum will be created to increase participation in data knowledge commons through both small and dramatic changes in institutional arrangements and collaborative agreements.

CONCLUSION

> As with openness applied to resources, openness with regard to community describes an individual's capacity to relate to that community as a contributor, manager, or user of resources that comprise the knowledge commons.[144]

Several ambitious collaborative neuroscience initiatives have been announced recently,[145] indicating that it takes a global research village to make progress in neuroscience. Profound external as well as internal forces are pushing the neuroscience research community to come up with creative solutions and work-arounds to institutional dilemmas around sharing data. This chapter sets forth the context for encouraging participation in such a commons within an emergent open neuroscience movement. Its key observations include the following:

- The widespread desire in the neuroscience research community to engage more in collaborative data sharing to further the progress of science more efficiently.
- The identification of impediments, such as the existing reward structure for being first to analyze data rather than first to share.
- The convergence toward possible solutions, such as the formation of larger commons pools.

141 Jorge L. Contreras and Jerome H. Reichman, Sharing by design: data and decentralized commons – overcoming legal and policy obstacles, 350 *Science* 1312 (2015); see also Jerome H. Reichman and Ruth Okediji, When Copyright Law and Science Collide: Empowering Digitally Integrated Research Methods on a Global Scale, 96 *Minnesota L. Rev.* 1362 (2012).

142 Ibid. 143 Ibid. 144 Frischmann et al., note 13, at 29. 145 See note 3.

Arguably, every neuroscientist and neuroscience research organization could have greater impact by participating in the neuroscience data commons on some level. For example, the Allen Institute's "commitment to open science is rooted in [its] conviction to make an impact on science on a global scale."[146] To use the Ostrom and Hess terminology, the Allen Institute is an example of a relevant actor contributing toward action situation, with the goal of encouraging the formation of an open neuroscience ethos rather than participating uncritically in an ethos of individual competition. This chapter describes why many in this field believe the current level of data sharing is suboptimal, why this is an important moment to increase participation in a neuroscience data commons, and what some key actors intend to do about it.

APPENDIX: METHODOLOGY

With the assistance of Maria Therese Fujiye, the authors performed a literature search to identify the key questions in neuroscience research that related to open access, open data, and open science. Based upon the published literature, the authors formed a general outline for the research, followed by interviews with stakeholders, conducted by Maja Larson and Maria Fujiye. Interviewees were drawn from the following actors and action groups: individual scientists who both generate and use neuroscience data, representatives of institutions and companies that manage the dissemination of neuroscience research, research funders, and finally stakeholders representing the public who benefit from (and as taxpayers sometimes indirectly fund) the research.

Interviews Conducted for This Study:

- Telephone interview with General Peter Chiarelli, CEO, One Mind, August 20, 2015.
- Telephone interview with Michael Hawrylycz, PhD, Investigator, Allen Institute, August 14, 2015.
- Telephone interview with James Zanewicz, Chief Business Officer, Tulane University School of Medicine and Tulane National Primate Research Center & Instructor, Tulane University School of Medicine, July 29, 2015.
- Telephone interview with Richard Wilder, Associate General Counsel, Bill and Melinda Gates Foundation, July 30, 2015.
- Telephone interview with Kathryn Partin, PhD, Director of the federal Office of Research Integrity and former Assistant Vice President for Research and Professor, Department of Biomedical Sciences, Program of Molecular, Cellular and Integrative Neurosciences, Colorado State

[146] Global Impact, *Allen Institute*, http://alleninstitute.org/about/global-impact/ (last visited Jan. 12, 2016).

University, Daniel Draper, Digital Services Librarian, Colorado State University, and Nicole Kaplin, Information Manager, Natural Resource Ecology Lab, July 31, 2015.

- Telephone interview with Craig D. Wegner, PhD, Executive Director, Head, Boston Emerging Innovations Unit, Scientific Partnering & Alliances, AstraZeneca IMED Biotech Unit, August 3, 2015.
- Telephone interview with Dana Bostrom, Executive Director, Orbis Cascade Alliance and former Executive Director, Data Commons LLC, August 7, 2015.

9

Better to Give Than to Receive: An Uncommon Commons in Synthetic Biology

Andrew W. Torrance

INTRODUCTION

The ubiquity of the phrase "tragedy of the commons" signals its wide, and often uncritical, acceptance.[1] Without predictable and enforceable property rights, who will maintain or improve their land? Elinor Ostrom offered an eloquent answer to this question, suggesting that governance of commons may occur on the basis of informal rules that can be effective when stakeholders believe they are fairly adaptable to changing conditions.[2] Intellectual property has attracted a similar assumption that in the absence of exclusionary rights to prevent others from copying, making, or using inventions without permission, owners will no longer engage in innovative or creative endeavors.[3] However, as Frischmann, Madison, and Strandburg have demonstrated, socially beneficial governance of intangible, intellectual resources too may be effective without recourse to traditional intellectual property, via norms, community standards, and democratized participation.[4] The assumption that commons tend to descend into tragedy is difficult to test empirically, which has made it challenging to evaluate claims concerning that assumption. This chapter presents a case study that offers a rare opportunity to evaluate what can happen to rates of innovation in the absence of intellectual property protection.

Andrew W. Torrance is Earl B. Shurtz Research Professor at the University of Kansas School of Law, Lawrence, Kansas, and Visiting Scientist, MIT Sloan School of Management, Cambridge, Massachusetts.

1 See, e.g., Garrett Hardin, The Tragedy of the Commons, 162 *Science* 1243 (1968).

2 Elinor Ostrom and Charlotte Hess, Private and Common Property Rights, https://ssrn.com/abstract=1304699 (2007).

3 IP: Imperative for Innovation, *Biotechnology Industry Organization* (Mar. 29, 2011, 10:02 AM) ("Patent systems can provide an advantage to society by rewarding the development of new inventions, promoting the advancement of technology and protecting the investor."), www.bio.org/articles/ip-imperative-innovation.

4 Brett M. Frischmann, Michael J. Madison, and Katherine J. Strandburg, Governing Knowledge Commons, in *Governing Knowledge Commons* 1, 20–21 (Brett M. Frischmann, Michael J. Madison, and Katherine J. Strandburg eds., 2014).

The emerging scientific field of synthetic biology offers an array of technical and scientific approaches new to the biological sciences. In addition, the community of scientists leading synthetic biology tends to agree on an ethos of openness and collaboration that marks a departure from the previous proprietary norm predominant in biology. While traditional biologists have long relied upon the patent system to protect and foster commercialization of their inventions, the synthetic biology community has tended to promote the very different ethos of open innovation and has created knowledge commons governance institutions to support that ethos.[5] In fact, many in the field suspect patents of chilling research and believe that patenting ought to be avoided.[6] Instead, many synthetic biologists prefer to contribute the new strands of DNA that they create to a commons, whose contents are available to all. This chapter first provides some background on the field of synthetic biology. It next describes some of the institutions that synthetic biologists have put in place to create and maintain a synthetic biology commons. It then shares the first empirical evidence from synthetic biology that in the synthetic biology commons, giving behavior is overwhelmingly more frequent than taking behavior. In other words, instead of being dominated by free riders, the synthetic biology knowledge commons appears to offer free rides.

9.1 SYNTHETIC BIOLOGY: A HYBRID OF SCIENCE AND ENGINEERING

Over the past decade synthetic biology has emerged as a distinctive scientific discipline. A hybrid of biology and engineering, synthetic biology has grown rapidly in terms of its institutions, its adherents, and its scientific output. Understanding the foundations and growth of the field of synthetic biology provides historical and institutional context for understanding the empirical results presented in this chapter.

Synthetic biology may be understood in both weaker and stronger senses. Until now the weaker sense has predominated, largely involving the redesign and fabrication of existing biological components and systems. Here, living organisms and their constituent genes, proteins, and other biochemicals serve as templates for improvements in structure or function, leading to modifications, rather than creations made from scratch.[7] The stronger sense of synthetic biology focuses on the *de novo* design and fabrication of biological components and systems that do not already exist in the

[5] Obviously, this is a generalization. There are, of course, synthetic biologists who support robust patent rights, just as there are traditional biologists who eschew them. However, as explained in this chapter, the very founding of synthetic biology as a field was influenced by a strong skein of support for an open, rather than closed (i.e., proprietary), model of innovation.

[6] Bryn Nelson, Synthetic Biology: Cultural Divide, 509 *Nature* 152 (2014) ("[T]he patent-heavy intellectual-property model of biotechnology is hopelessly broken").

[7] *Synthetic Biology* ("Synthetic biology is the re-design of existing, natural biological systems for useful purposes"), http://syntheticbiology.org/

natural world.[8] Limited by current technology, current practitioners of synthetic biology generally hope to use advances developed while pursuing the weaker sense of synthetic biology as springboards eventually to achieve the strong sense.

In 1958, Edward L. Tatum used his speech accepting the Nobel Prize in Physiology or Medicine to articulate an optimistic vision of how the focus of biology might be transformed from description to modification. As he explained,

> It does not seem unrealistic to expect that as more is learned about control of cell machinery and heredity, we will see the complete conquering of many of man's ills, including hereditary defects in metabolism, and the momentarily more obscure conditions such as cancer and the degenerative diseases, just as disease of bacterial and viral etiology are now being conquered.
>
> With a more complete understanding of the functioning and regulation of gene activity in development and differentiation, these processes may be more efficiently controlled and regulated, not only to avoid structural or metabolic errors in the developing organism, but also to produce better organisms.
>
> Perhaps within the lifetime of some of us here, the code of life processes tied up in the molecular structure of proteins and nucleic acids will be broken. This may permit the improvement of all living organisms by processes which we might call *biological engineering*. [Emphasis added.][9]

By suggesting a future in which biology might emerge as an engineering science, Tatum presaged the development of synthetic biology.

It was not long after Tatum's Nobel speech that powerful and precise methods were developed for transferring DNA from one organism or species to another. In 1973, Stanley Cohen and Herbert Boyer successfully transferred DNA from one species to another, yielding "recombinant" organisms capable of replicating their recombinant genomes.[10] The turn of the millennium witnessed the successful completion of the Human Genome Project (HGP), when public and private research initiatives revealed the specific nucleotide sequences of nearly complete human genomes.[11] Only eight years later, in 2008, Craig Venter and his colleagues announced not only the *de novo* synthesis of a complete *Mycoplasma genitalium* genome, but also its insertion, to the astonishment of many, into the cell of a different species of *Mycoplasma*, whose own genome had been removed. The combined cell was then exposed to electrochemical stimuli to "boot up" what was largely a synthetic cell.[12]

8 Ibid. (Synthetic biology is also "the design and construction of new biological parts, devices, and systems.")

9 Edward Tatum, *Nobel Lecture* (Dec. 11, 1958), www.nobelprize.org/nobel_prizes/medicine/laureates/1958/tatum-lecture.html

10 *Genetics and Genomics Timeline*, www.genomenewsnetwork.org/resources/timeline/1973_Boyer.php

11 *Genetics and Genomics Timeline*, www.genomenewsnetwork.org/resources/timeline/2000_human.php

12 Smith et al., Generating a Synthetic Genome by Whole Genome Assembly: Phix174 Bacteriophage from Synthetic Oligonucleotides, 100 *Proc. Nat'l Acad. Sci. USA* 15440 (2003).

Meanwhile, a group of University of California, Berkeley, researchers, led by Jay Keasling, used synthetic biological approaches to produce artemisinin.[13] This chemical, a sesquiterpene lactone, acts as a potent treatment for malaria but had previously only been available as an expensive tree bark extract.[14] Keasling and his group, in cooperation with the Bill and Melinda Gates Foundation, developed a process for synthetic production of a precursor of artemisinin useful for making a relatively inexpensive synthesized version of the drug.[15] Another, more quixotic, advance occurred when George Church encoded the entire text of his 2012 book *Regenesis: How Synthetic Biology Will Reinvent Nature and Ourselves* in 5.3 Mb of synthetic DNA sequence.[16] Since the hopeful vision of Edward Tatum, accelerating advances in biological engineering have increasingly been realized by synthetic biology.

The field of synthetic biology also draws inspiration from the field of engineering, and in particular from the field of software engineering. This conscious reliance on engineering approaches includes widespread adoption of the principles of (1) standardization, (2) decoupling, and (3) abstraction.[17] Just as software engineers compose large modules of algorithmic code capable of carrying out specified functions, synthetic biologists synthesize large DNA molecules whose specified nucleotide sequences encode functional or structural polypeptides, which, in turn, express physical, physiological, or behavioral characteristics in host cells or organisms. Comprehensive software programs usually include many algorithmic modules that work together to accomplish complex tasks. Similarly, one of the aims of synthetic biology is to design and implement genetic circuits constructed from basic genetic components composed of discrete DNA molecules.

9.2 SYNTHETIC BIOLOGY, OPEN SOURCE, AND KNOWLEDGE COMMONS GOVERNANCE

The open source software movement has frequently been invoked by those within the synthetic biology community not only as a metaphor but also as a practical model for the field to emulate. It is no coincidence that many leading synthetic biologists are relatively recent converts to biology, whose academic and professional origins lie within engineering and computer science.[18] Their comfort with, and even affirmative preference for, open source software has strengthened the ethos of openness that pervades synthetic biology.

13 Ro et al., Production of the Antimalarial Drug Precursor Artemisinic Acid in Engineered Yeast, 440 *Nature* 940 (2006).

14 Ibid. 15 Ibid.

16 George Church and Ed Regis, *Regenesis: How Synthetic Biology Will Reinvent Nature and Ourselves* (2012).

17 Drew Endy, Foundations for Engineering Biology, 438 *Nature* 449 (2005).

18 See Olivia Solon, BioBricks Founder on His Shift from Computer Science to Synthetic Biology, *Wired* (Mar. 6, 2013).

Early in its development as a field, synthetic biology was fostered by the deliberate creation of formal supporting institutions aimed at fostering and facilitating an open commons–based approach. These institutions include, most notably, the BioBricks Foundation (BBF), the Registry of Standard Biological Parts (the Registry), and the annual International Genetically Modified Machines (iGEM) competition. Each member of this trio is discussed in more detail later. These three institutions have adopted a common standard for describing synthetic biology parts, or BioBricks, that serve as an important infrastructure for a commons-based approach. Although not discussed further in this chapter, several additional institutions merit mention, notably the Synthetic Biology Engineering Research Center (SynBERC), the International Open Facility Advancing Biotechnology (BIOFAB), the Synthetic Biology Open Language Team (SBOL), the International Association of Synthetic Biology (IASB), the International Consortium for Polynucleotide Synthesis (ICPS), and the semiannual International Meeting on Synthetic Biology conference series (e.g., SB1.0, SB2.0). This embarrassment of institutional richness at the foundation of a field is unique.

Perhaps also because of its roots in open source software, the field of synthetic biology has been unusually open to contributions from amateur participants, in addition to credentialed researchers. This push for democratization of biological innovation, *sensu* von Hippel,[19] has encouraged open disclosure of scientific results, free availability of basic genetic parts through the Registry, and enthusiastic sharing of information during the annual iGEM jamborees. In a notable and amusing first for any scientific field, synthetic biology was featured in the leading scientific journal *Nature*, both on its cover and in a lengthy feature article within, in the form of a comic strip designed to be accessible and attractive to readers spanning many levels of technical sophistication.[20]

9.2.1 *The Biobricks Standard*

The BBF, the Registry, and iGEM all specify BioBricks as the standard for genetic parts. Researchers have suggested other standards,[21] but BioBricks have become the most popular format of DNA parts because of their universality, compatibility, and ease of use.[22] In an analogous manner to how Lego® bricks click together predictably, BioBricks designs are standardized so as to allow multiple BioBrick parts to be linked together in a relatively straightforward manner.[23] Just as the former plug into

[19] Eric von Hippel, *Democratizing Innovation* (2005).

[20] *Nature* (Nov. 2005) ("Synthetic Biology – Life Is What We Make It").

[21] See generally Dimitri Rebatchouk, Nikolai Daraselia, and Jonathon ONarita, NOMAD: A Versatile Strategy for in vitro DNA Manipulation Applied to Promoter Analysis and Vector Design, 93 *Proc. Nat'l Acad. Sci. USA* 10891 (1996) (developing a generic strategy for cloning nucleic acid fragments); Adam P. Arkin and Drew Endy, A Standard Parts List for Biological Circuitry, *DARPA White Paper* (1999), http://hdl.handle.net/1721.1/ 29794 (listing a collection of useful biological parts).

[22] Reshma P. Shetty, Drew Endy, and Thomas F. Knight Jr., Engineering BioBrick Vectors from BioBrick Parts, 2 *J. Bio. Engineering* 1 (2008).

[23] Given the complexities of living systems, results tend to be somewhat more complicated for BioBricks than for Lego bricks.

each other physically, BioBricks that conform to the intended standard can be linked together via chemical bonds and coupled functionally with other BioBricks.[24] There has been a profusion of proposed standards for the physical composition, units of measurement, and functional composition of DNA parts, as well as relating to data exchange, software tools, and legal standards governing the use and contribution of parts, proposed by various researchers and institutions.[25] Interestingly, the most successful proposed standards in synthetic biology have concerned biosafety and biosecurity and resulted in large part because of pressure from the US government.[26]

Each conforming BioBrick is a standardized, continuous DNA sequence encoding a basic biological function.[27] Each individual BioBrick part is defined by its unique DNA sequence.[28] If two genetic parts having identical DNA sequences are designed independently, the standard requires that they be synonymized to avoid duplication and confusion. Composite BioBricks are composed of linear arrays of individual BioBrick parts separated by intervening chemical "scars" produced by their interlinkage. Proper BioBrick standard biological parts should conform to the BioBrick part assembly standard.

One example of a BioBrick from the Registry is Part:BBa_CO179.[29] This part is functionally categorized as a lasR activator.[30] A lasR activator is a 781 basepair transcriptional activator of an elastase structural gene that binds to the PAI autoinducer.[31] Figure 9.1 shows its DNA sequence.

Using its precise DNA sequence and functional description, researchers, do-it-yourself bio hobbyists (DIYbio), and even iGEM teams can synthesize, insert, express, and even modify this BioBrick using standard molecular biological techniques.

9.2.2 *BioBricks Foundation*

The BBF began its existence in 2005 as an informal group of leading synthetic biologists intent on fostering the success of their nascent field.[32] Given the ambitious, but somewhat unorthodox, aims and methods of synthetic biology, the group sought to promote two goals that are sometimes in tension: (1) scientific and technical advances and (2) ethical and responsible practices.[33] One purpose of their strategy was to avoid the sorts of controversy that bedeviled early recombinant DNA research,

24 See *iGEM*, http://parts.igem.org/Assembly:Standard_assembly (last visited Dec. 3, 2015).

25 See generally A. W. Torrance and L. J. Kahl, Bringing Standards to Life: Synthetic Biology Standards and Intellectual Property, 30 *Santa Clara High Tech. L.J.* 200 (2014) (especially Tables 1 and 2).

26 Ibid. at 218–20.

27 *BitesizeBio*, http://bitesizebio.com/20013/biobricks-lego-for-scientists/ (last visited Dec. 3, 2015).

28 Ibid. 29 *iGEM*, http://parts.igem.org/Part:BBa_C0179 (last visited Dec. 3, 2015). 30 Ibid.

31 www.uniprot.org/uniprot/P25084; http://parts.igem.org/Protein_coding_sequences/Transcriptional_regulators.

32 Board of Directors, *BioBricks Foundation*, https://biobricks.org/about-foundation/board-of-directors/ (last visited Apr. 6, 2016).

33 About, *BioBricks Foundation*, http://biobricks.org/about-foundation/ (last visited Apr. 6, 2016).

atggccttgg ttgacggttt tcttgagctg gaacgctcaa gtggaaaatt ggagtggagc
gccatcctcc agaagatggc gagcgacctt ggattctcga taccggaacc aactgccaaa
agaactcgac cttgcgagtt cacctttaa cctcacctcg cggtaggagg tcttctaccg
ctcgctggaa cctaagagct agatcctgtt cggcctgttg cctaaggaca gccaggacta
cgagaacgcc ttcatcgtcg gcaactaccc ggccgcctgg cgcgagcatt acgaccgggc
tctaggacaa gccggacaac ggattcctgt cggtcctgat gctcttgcgg aagtagcagc
cgttgatggg ccggcggacc gcgctcgtaa tgctggcccg tggctacgcg cgggtcgacc
cgacggtcag tcactgtacc cagagcgtac tgccgatttt ctgggaaccg tccatctacc
agacgcgaaa gcagcacgag accgatgcgc gcccagctgg gctgccagtc agtga-
catgg gtctcgcatg acggctaaaa gacccttggc aggtagatgg tctgcgcttt
cgtcgtgctc ttcttcgagg aagcctcggc cgccggcctg gtgtatgggc tgaccatgcc
gctgcatggt gctcgcggcg aactcggcgc gctgagcctc agcgtggaag aagaagctcc
ttcggagccg gcggccggac cacatacccg actggtacgg cgacgtacca cgagcgccgc
ttgagccgcg cgactcggag tcgcaccttc cggaaaaccg ggccgaggcc aaccgtttca
tagagtcggt cctgccgacc ctgtggatgc tcaaggacta cgcactgcaa agcggtgccg
gactggcctt gccttttggc ccggctccgg ttggcaaagt atctcagcca ggacggctgg
gacacctacg agttcctgat gcgtgacgtt tcgccacggc ctgaccggaa cgaacatccg
gtcagcaaac cggtggttct gaccagccgg gagaaggaag tgttgcagtg gtgcgccatc
ggcaagacca gttgggagat atcggttatc gcttgtaggc cagtcgtttg gccaccaaga
ctggtcggcc ctcttccttc acaacgtcac cacgcggtag ccgttctggt caaccctcta
tagccaata tgcaactgct cggaagccaa tgtgaacttc catatgggaa atattcggcg
gaagttcggt gtgacctccc gccgcgtagc ggccattatg gccgttaatt acgttgacga
gccttcggtt acacttgaag gtataccctt tataagccgc cttcaagcca cactggaggg
cggcgcatcg ccggtaatac cggcaattaa tgggtcttat tactctctaa taa

FIGURE 9.1 Part:BBa_C0179 (lasR activator).

ultimately necessitating the Asilomar Conference and the self-regulatory measures adopted there by members of the biological science community.[34]

In addition to fostering interest in synthetic biology in general, the BBF undertook two specific practical roles. It managed the Registry, which was originally housed in a hallway at MIT, which both accepted and disbursed BioBrick standard parts.[35] It also organized and ran the annual iGEM competition, which quickly became a highly successful venue for encouraging and expanding participation in synthetic biology research.

The iGEM competition and the BBF both grew out of intercession classes taught by MIT professors in January 2003 and 2004.[36] The professors quickly learned that students were spending too much time recreating simple parts, which inspired the creation of a parts registry.[37] Furthermore, popularity of these classes quickly outgrew their month-long format, leading synthetic biology leaders to form the BBF and

[34] Paul Berg, David Baltimore, Sydney Brenner, Richard O. Roblin III, and Maxine F. Singer, Summary Statement of the Asilomar Conference on Recombinant DNA Molecules, 72 *Proc. Natl. Acad. Sci.* 1981 (1975).

[35] See *BioBricks Foundation*, http://biobricks.org/programs/ (last visited Dec. 3, 2015).

[36] Christina D. Smolke, Building Outside of the Box: iGEM and the BioBricks Foundation, 27 *Nature Biotechnology* 1099 (2009).

[37] Ibid.

iGEM competition to allow more students at more universities to participate in the field.[38] In 2006, the BBF formally became an independent foundation, complete with a charter, officers, board of directors, headquarters, and endowment.[39] The board of directors currently includes MIT and Stanford University professors, various other synthetic biology scholars, and biotechnology industry leaders.[40] The BBF is funded by industry partners, individual donations, and grants from the National Science Foundation.[41] However, its ethos remains similar to the founding ethos of the field of synthetic biology: open works better than proprietary, especially for basic DNA building blocks and methods.[42] To quote from the front page of the BBF website, "The BBF's mission is to ensure that the engineering of biology is conducted in an open and ethical manner to benefit all people and the planet. We believe fundamental scientific knowledge belongs to all of us and must be freely available for ethical, open innovation. This is a new paradigm."[43]

9.2.3 *Registry of Standard Biological Parts*

The Registry originated informally in 2003, as a repository for the standard biological parts, or BioBricks, contributed and used by students and researchers.[44] Later, participants in iGEM began to make use of the existing Registry as well.[45] The Registry facilitated the progress of synthetic biology because it provided a central site for making previously designed and characterized parts, along with related documentation, available to other researchers in a standardized form. The early rules governing access to these parts were relatively informal, and largely entailed following professors' instructions and putting DNA samples into, and taking them out of, a freezer located in an easily accessible corridor in a building at MIT.[46] As the popularity of the Registry grew, the BBF was formed to adopt more formal policies and establish the iGEM competition that helped spread access to, and awareness of, the Registry beyond MIT.

Policies established by the BBF, iGEM, and the Registry included an official submission standard so that each part works with every other part, as well as the "Get & Give" philosophy.[47] The iGem competition formally enforces the Get & Give philosophy by requiring that each team submit a sample of its parts along with

38 Ibid. 39 *BioBricks Foundation*, http://biobricks.org/about-foundation/ (last visited Dec. 3, 2015).

40 Board of Directors, *BioBricks Foundation*, https://biobricks.org/about-foundation/board-of-directors/ (last visited Apr. 6, 2015).

41 Smolke, note 36, at 1099–1100; Donate, *BioBrick Foundation*, https://biobricks.org/donate/ (last visited Apr. 6, 2016).

42 Smolke, note 36, at 1099–100.

43 See *Biobricks Foundation*, http://biobricks.org/ (last visited May 20, 2016).

44 See *iGEM*, http://igem.org/Registry (last visited Dec. 3, 2015). 45 Ibid.

46 It is likely that, at the institutional level, MIT was unaware of the existence of the Registry freezer until long after it began storing Biobricks. What is clear is that MIT formally asked the Registry to remove their samples from MIT property in 2009.

47 Labs Program, *iGEM*, http://igem.org/Labs (last visited Apr. 6, 2016).

information such as their origin, function, and experimental information.[48] Outside of the context of the iGEM competition, academic research labs can also access the Registry, but they are not bound formally by the Get & Give philosophy.[49] Instead, they are supposed to be guided by the admonishment, on the Registry's "Labs Program" homepage, that "the Registry depends on the contributions of its users to increase the quality of its samples and information."[50]

From its inception in 2003, the Registry has grown rapidly in size and sophistication, with the number of BioBricks in its catalog having grown from fewer than 1000 parts in 2004 to more than 20,000 parts in 2015.[51] These parts can be mixed, matched, and modified to build synthetic biological "devices" and "systems." The Registry has provided a valuable and rapidly growing resource of free genetic parts to iGEM teams and academic research laboratories. The Registry supports a website, from which parts are easily searchable, and considerable data about each part is available on the part's Registry webpage, including its name, DNA sequence, classification category, year created, year submitted to the Registry, creators, and the number of times the part has been used.

The guiding philosophy of the Registry has always been Get & Give.[52] This philosophy is similar to the "viral" General Public License (GPL) of open source software, which ensures that users can change all aspects of a software program and that any work derived using the GPL will itself remain open source. Correspondingly, the Get & Give principle was designed to encourage synthetic biologists to use and reuse what others had already created, and then to give back to the community any new genetic variations they subsequently created.[53] Similarly, the BioBrick™ Public Agreement encourages open and responsible usage and contribution of BioBricks.[54] The stated expectations of the Registry, iGEM, and the BBF have been that users of BioBricks will contribute back both (1) new genetic parts, devices, and systems and (2) information and data on existing and novel genetic parts, devices, and systems, so as to expand the scope and improve the usefulness of research in the synthetic biology community.[55] Though patenting is not explicitly forbidden, strong community norms favoring openness and sharing have discouraged patenting parts derived from, or submitted to, the Registry.

Despite the goals of openness, sharing, and documentation of accurate information underlying the Registry, the reality has been messier. Many users have failed to give back their modified BioBricks to the Registry, and those who have made contributions have often supplied poor-quality samples described with incomplete or inaccurate

48 Requirements, *iGEM*, http://2016.igem.org/Requirements (last visited Apr. 6, 2016).

49 Labs Program, note 47. 50 Ibid.

51 Registry of Standard Biological Parts, *iGEM*, http://parts.igem.org/Main_Page (last visited Dec. 29, 2015).

52 Labs Program, note 47.

53 OpenWetWare, *iGEM Registry*, http://openwetware.org/wiki/CH391L/S12/iGEM_Registry (last visited Dec. 3, 2015).

54 Torrance and Kahl, note 25, at 220–21. See also *Biobrick™ Public Agreement*, https://biobricks.org/bpa/ (last visited May 20, 2016).

55 See, e.g., *Biobrick™ Public Agreement*, https://biobricks.org/bpa/ (last visited May 20, 2016).

information. This has likely stemmed, in part, from lack of enforcement capacity and a desire not to alienate participants by iGEM organizers. In addition, participants may intend, initially, to contribute their new parts to the Registry, but then they fail to do so because of apathy, forgetfulness, or insufficient commitment to the openness ethos. Despite these problems, the Registry has grown rapidly in size and sophistication, with the number of BioBricks in its catalog having grown more than twenty-fold from 2004 to 2015. To counter the leakiness of new Biobricks contribution by iGEM teams, the iGEM competition now requires each team to set up a webpage detailing all new BioBricks used in its project.[56] A technical development may also increase compliance. Previously, fragments of DNA were exchanged in physical form, with these fragments then amplified into large enough samples to be used by their receivers. However, the ease and cost of synthesizing DNA have improved rapidly to the point where only the sequence, rather than a physical sample, of a DNA fragment is needed to allow automated synthesis. Thus, costs of compliance with the iGEM rules have fallen considerably in a short period of time, boding well for increased compliance with the Get & Give principle.

9.2.4 *iGEM Competition*

Prizes, and reputational gains that accompany them, may be an effective means of fostering interest and innovation in a particular technological field. Synthetic biology has its own annual competition: iGEM. Held annually since 2004, the iGEM jamboree functions as the Olympic Games of synthetic biology.[57] The iGEM competition has been growing in popularity, with the number of iGEM teams expanding from 5, in its first year, to 245 teams, and more than 2700 attendees, from more than 32 countries, in 2015.[58] Originally, iGEM allowed only undergraduate teams to compete, in part to take advantage of the supervision and legal indemnification provided by their sponsoring home universities. Recently, undergraduate teams have been joined by teams composed of high school students.[59] In 2014, do-it-yourself biology (DIYbio) teams of amateur citizen scientists were also welcomed.[60] Originally, "The competition founders consciously decided to target undergraduates since, as Randy Rettberg, the director of iGEM puts it, "undergraduates don't know what you can't do."[61] As multiple iGEM competitions have been held without health or environmental consequences, it may be that the organizers have become comfortable enough with the competition's safety to expand participation.

[56] Requirements, *iGEM*, http://2016.igem.org/Requirements (last visited May 20, 2016).
[57] Learn About, *iGEM*, http://igem.org/IGEM/Learn_About (last visited Dec. 3, 2015).
[58] Press Kit, *iGEM*, http://igem.org/Press_Kit (last visited Dec. 3, 2015). [59] Ibid.
[60] *DIY BIO*, http://diybio.org/2013/11/06/diy-igem/ (last visited Dec. 3, 2015).
[61] E. Frow and J. Calvert, "Can Simple Biological Systems Be Built from Standardized Interchangeable Parts?": Negotiating Biology and Engineering in a Synthetic Biology Competition, 5 *Engineering Studies* 42 (2013).

The teams in the competition compete for different awards depending on the project they complete and their education level, separating undergraduate and overgraduate (graduate student–level) teams.[62] The first level of award is a medal, which is offered to every team that achieves certain criteria.[63] The better a team performs, the better medal that team will earn from bronze, to silver, to gold.[64] There are also Special Awards, open across all projects but separated by education level, such as Best New Basic Part, Best New Composite Part, and Best Innovation in Measurement.[65] These trophies are given "to honor specific innovative and unique contributions to iGEM."[66] Next, there are Track Awards, which are trophies awarded to the team that designs the best project in each category, such as Best Energy Project, Best Health and Medicine Project, and Best Manufacturing Project.[67] Finally, the most prestigious trophy goes to the grand prize winners for best undergraduate and best overgraduate project.[68]

Each registered team is given a kit containing biological parts from the Registry.[69] Teams use these parts, and new parts of their own design and fabrication, to build biological devices or systems and usually "operate" them in living cells.[70]

At the 2015 iGEM competition, a team from Delft University of Technology (TU Delft), in the Netherlands, was the grand prize winner in the Overgrad (i.e., graduate student–level) category. The project for which TU Delft won, entitled Project Biolink, involved "3D-printing of biofilms, linked together through nanowires."[71] The TU Delft team described its project as follows:

> Our printing system, called Biolink, can be summarized in the following sentence: biofilm producing bacteria are printed with the help of a flexible scaffold hydrogel. First of all, our homemade bacteria (modified to make biofilms) are mixed with a solution of sodium alginate and subsequently with calcium chloride. There, the Ca2+ molecules keep the structure fixed creating a stable gel. This hydrogel-bacteria mixture is then induced with rhamnose, a sugar specific for our promoter, which makes them synthesize CsgA, the linking molecule. CsgA proteins polymerize to an amyloid structure surrounding the cells and connecting them to each other through the scaffold. Once the cells are all attached in the structure defined by the gel scaffold, it is no longer necessary. Consequently, the hydrogel is dissolved with sodium citrate. But the cells are still connected due to the curli amyloid! So, we obtain a perfectly defined 3D structure made of bacteria.[72]

Not all projects entered into iGEM competitions are as scientifically sophisticated or technically successful as Project Biolink. However, many teams enter projects that

[62] Judging/Awards, *iGEM*, http://2015.igem.org/Judging/Awards#Medals (last visited Apr. 12, 2016).
[63] Medals, *iGEM*, http://2015.igem.org/Judging/Medals (last visited Apr. 12, 2016). [64] Ibid.
[65] Judging/Awards, *iGEM*, http://2015.igem.org/Judging/Awards#Medals (last visited Apr. 12, 2016).
[66] Ibid. [67] Ibid. [68] Ibid.
[69] Press Kit, *iGEM*, http://igem.org/Press_Kit (last visited Dec. 3, 2015). [70] Ibid.
[71] *Project Biolink*, http://2015.igem.org/Team:TU_Delft/Description (last visited Dec. 29, 2015).
[72] Ibid.

improve the scientific bases of synthetic biology, and, in aggregate, the many projects entered since 2004 have contributed not only the raw materials (i.e., more than 20,000 BioBricks) but also myriad devices and methods based on these raw materials that accelerated advances in the field.

All of this has been accomplished through an expressly open, not proprietary, model of innovation. As noted earlier, iGEM competition rules require teams to contribute back to the Registry all new BioBrick parts and devices they design, along with formal documentation of their structure, function, and methods of making and using if the team wants to compete for a medal or trophy.[73] But reality has been different, with many genetic parts either not contributed back to the Registry or submitted to it without full or accurate documentation.

9.3 SUSTAINABILITY OF THE BIOBRICKS KNOWLEDGE COMMONS: SOME EMPIRICAL EVIDENCE

The acknowledged difficulties in ensuring that those who use BioBrick parts make the expected contributions of their own work back to the commons raise the question whether the BioBrick institutions are collecting new knowledge sustainably, such that the commons-based approach will continue to be viable or whether, instead, it is threatened by free riding. One way to approach this question is to determine, as an empirical matter, the extent to which free riding dominates the behavior of those who have used BioBrick parts. This section describes such an empirical study, based primarily on BioBrick parts involved in the iGEM competitions spanning 2009 to 2013.

9.3.1 *Data and Methods*

iGEM categorizes team projects by their intended function. This study focused on the iGEM-determined Health and Medicine category. Health and Medicine projects were further classified in this study as follows: therapeutic (treatments for diseases and gene/drug therapy), diagnostic (disease and cancer detection), prevention (probiotics and nutrient delivery), and general (production of antibodies and peptides and elucidating certain pathways).

Competitions are organized on the iGEM competition website (igem.org).[74] The 2014 iGEM website, which was the source of the data for this study, included a series of world maps, each corresponding to a competition category, indicating which BioBrick parts were involved in each iGEM team's project and whether such parts were (1) derived from the Registry and simply used or (2) newly created and then contributed back to the Registry.

[73] Ibid.

[74] The IGEM website was reorganized in 2015. This study was performed using the website prior to the 2015 reorganization.

Every competition team is marked on the categorical map; each mark indicates a team's home location (e.g., BYU's team mark is Provo, UT).[75] Hyperlinked to each team's mark is the following information, if available: (1) every year the team competed, (2) corresponding documents submitted for each competition, and (3) the team website. Newly designed parts created by iGEM teams for the competition ("contributed parts") were described in each team's corresponding documents. Corresponding documents generally included a PowerPoint presentation and/or a research poster. Some team projects offered both, while other team projects offered neither on the iGEM website. The corresponding documents and team website offered the only online access points to each team's project information, specifically the synthetic parts the teams used from and contributed back to the Registry.

For the study, corresponding documents were examined when available, and each team's contributed parts were recorded. If a team did not have any corresponding documents linked to its mark on the iGEM map, the team's website was examined for project information. Any identified contributed parts were recorded.

Previously designed parts from the Registry that were used by iGEM teams for the competition ("used parts") were located and recorded using the same basic process as described. If used parts were not listed in the corresponding documents, which frequently occurred, the team's contributed parts were examined for used part components using the Registry. It is common that contributed parts are composed of, or based upon, several previously designed parts.

The Registry organizes parts in a variety of ways, including by curated collection, biological function, chassis, and category. The Registry categorizes parts into 13 main categories: coding, composite, generator, plasmid, promoter, protein domain, ribosome binding site (RBS), regulatory, reporter, RNA, signaling, tag, and terminator (Table 9.1). This study focused on part categories as the main way of organizing the analysis for both used and contributed parts.

9.3.2 *Results*

9.3.2.1 Characteristics of iGEM Competition Entrants

Teams from all over the world enter the iGEM competition every year to demonstrate the value of their synthetic parts and devices. This study specifically focused on the Health and Medicine track. Within this track were 100 entrants from 2009 to 2013. Entrants were divided geographically into major geographic or political units: United States, Europe, Asia, and Other (Figure 9.2). "Other" includes multiple continents, regions, and countries, including Canada, Central America, the Caribbean, South America, Africa, and Australia.

Overall, entries gradually increased for all geographic categories between 2009 and 2013. In 2009, the total number of teams was 13. In 2010, entries increased to 16.

[75] Competition, *iGEM*, http://igem.org/Competition (last visited Dec. 3, 2015).

TABLE 9.1 *Part categories with brief description and/or examples*

Part Category	Brief Description and/or Examples
Coding	Encompasses a variety of sequences (e.g., proteins, protein domain), BglII restriction enzyme
Composite	Composed of multiple other parts, such as a promoter, coding region, tag, and terminator
Generator	luxR protein generator
Plasmid	Any type of backbone
Promoter	Variety of promoters, Lac operon promoter
Protein Domain	DNA binding, reporter protein domains and special domains, cI – repressor from E.coli phage lambda
RBS	Ribosome binding protein
Regulatory	Proteins involved in activation or repression of transcription, lasR activator from P. aeruginosa PAO1(+LVA)
Reporter	Proteins used to measure gene expression, amilCP, blue chromoprotein
RNA	siRNA
Signaling	After stimuli, it produces a measurable product, $3OC_6HSL$ Sender Device
Tag	Green fluorescent protein (GFP)
Terminator	Encompasses a variety of terminators, T1 from E. coli rrnB

Entries slightly decreased in 2011 to 12 but then increased 20 in 2012. By 2013, entries had greatly increased to 39 teams. The number of entries in the United States, Europe, and Other categories each increased gradually from 2009 to 2013. The most dramatic increase of entries came from Asia, which grew from a mere 3 entries in 2009 to 13 in 2013 (Figure 9.2).

9.3.2.2 *Project Types*

Projects within the Health and Medicine track were divided into four categories: therapeutic, diagnostic, preventative, and general.[76] The majority of the projects from 2009 to 2013 were therapeutic (n=57). The remaining 43 projects fell into the following categories: diagnostic (n=19), preventative (n=14), and general (n=10) (Figure 9.3).

Therapeutic projects were the most prevalent category during each year from 2009 to 2013, while the other categories' prevalences varied from year to year (Figure 9.4). Indeed, there were at least twice as many therapeutic projects each year as there were projects in any other category (Figure 9.4).

[76] Although there was some overlap between categories, each part was assigned to the category in which that part's function was predominantly based.

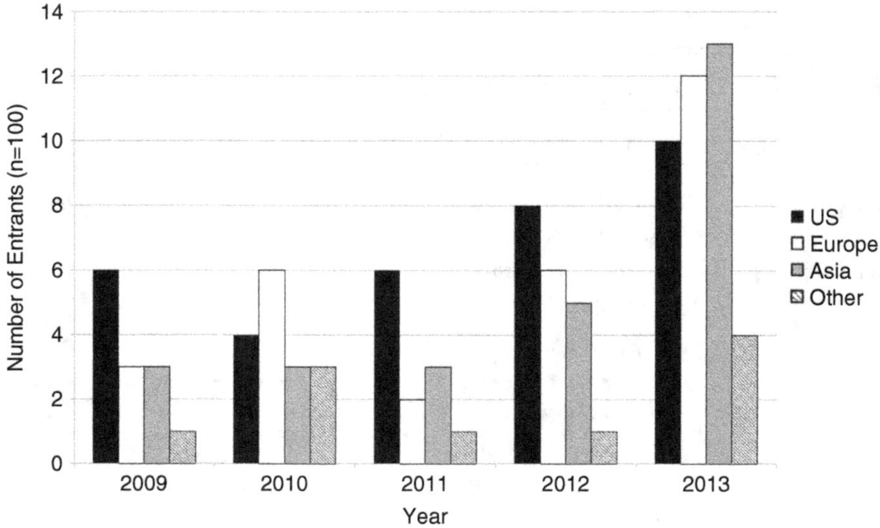

FIGURE 9.2 Number of entrants geographically divided from 2009 to 2013. Data was acquired from the iGEM competition website focusing on the Health and Medicine track. Entrants (n=100) are divided geographically (left to right: US (black), Europe (white), Asia (gray), and Other (diagonal pattern). The other category includes entrants from Canada (n=4), Central America (n=2), South America (n=2), Africa (n=1), and Australia (n=1).

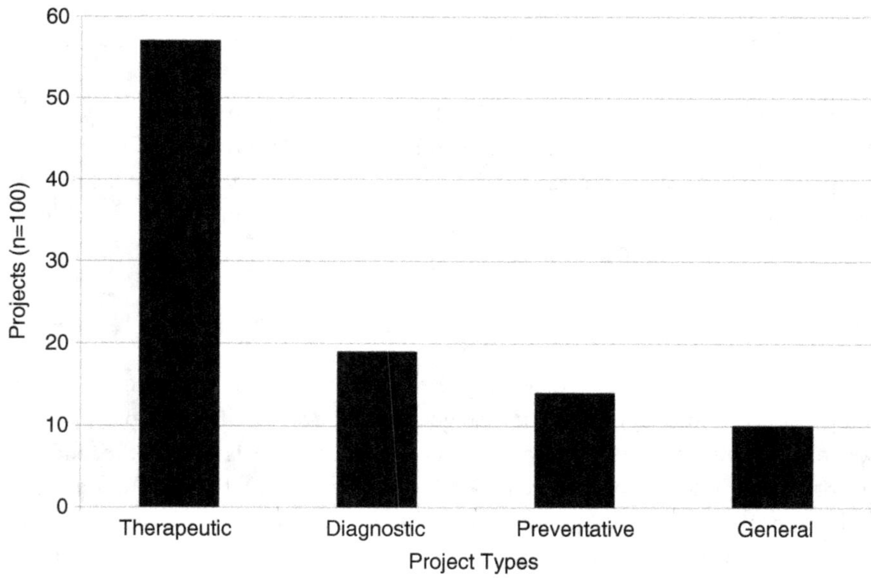

FIGURE 9.3 Project types. Data was acquired from the iGEM competition website focusing on the Health and Medicine track. Therapeutic categories include treatments for diseases and gene and drug therapy. Diagnostic projects include both disease and cancer detection. Preventative projects include probiotics and nutrient delivery. General projects include production of antibodies and peptides and elucidating certain pathways.

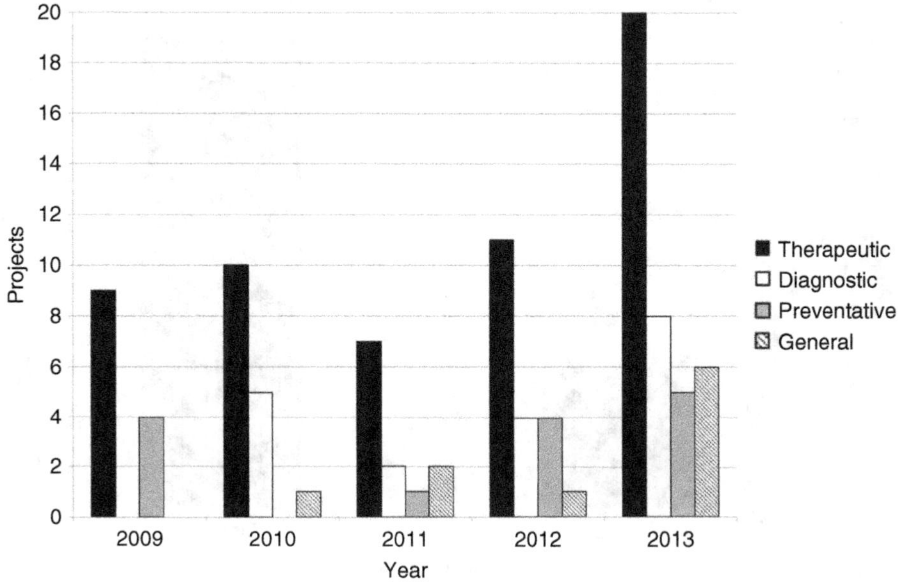

FIGURE 9.4 Project types from 2009 to 2013. Data was acquired from the iGEM competition website focusing on the Health and Medicine track. Therapeutic projects are indicated by black bars (n=57). Diagnostic projects are indicated by white bars (n=19). Preventative projects are indicated by gray bars (n=14). General projects are indicated by diagonal pattern bars (n=10).

The therapeutic category includes projects focused on treatments for diseases (n=43) and projects focused on gene and drug therapy (n=14) (Figure 9.5). The number of gene and drug therapy project entries stayed steady from 2009 to 2013, while the number of disease projects dramatically increased over the same period of time (Figure 9.6). Gene and drug therapy is a relatively new area of biological research as opposed to research concerning the general treatment of disease, which may help explain this discrepancy. Another possible explanation for the discrepancy in project numbers is that the disease category encompasses a much wider variety of projects, including projects focused on bacterial and parasitic disease, heart and autoimmune disease, and cancer.

The diagnostic category is the second-largest category and was divided into subcategories based on what the project aimed to diagnose: bacterial disease, cancer, or other (which includes diseases that are not bacterial). Project numbers for each subcategory were similar, with bacterial disease projects comprising a slightly larger group than those of the cancer and other categories (Figure 9.7). Diagnostic projects focused on bacterial disease were a slightly larger group, and this subcategory had entries each and every year diagnostic projects were present in the competition (i.e., 2010–2013). The other subcategories were not represented every year. Cancer

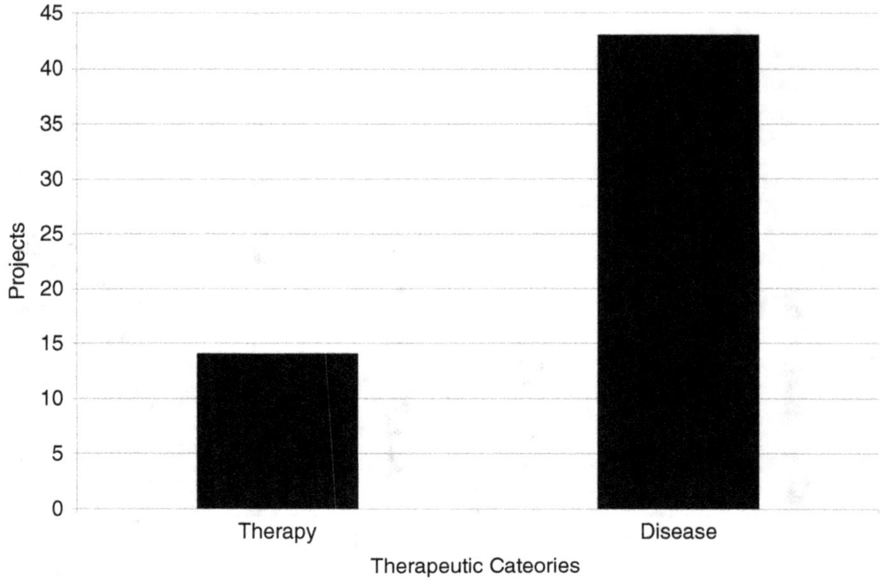

FIGURE 9.5 Therapeutic projects categories. Data was acquired from the iGEM competition website focusing on the Health and Medicine track. Therapeutic projects were divided into two categories: therapy (n=14) and disease (n=43).

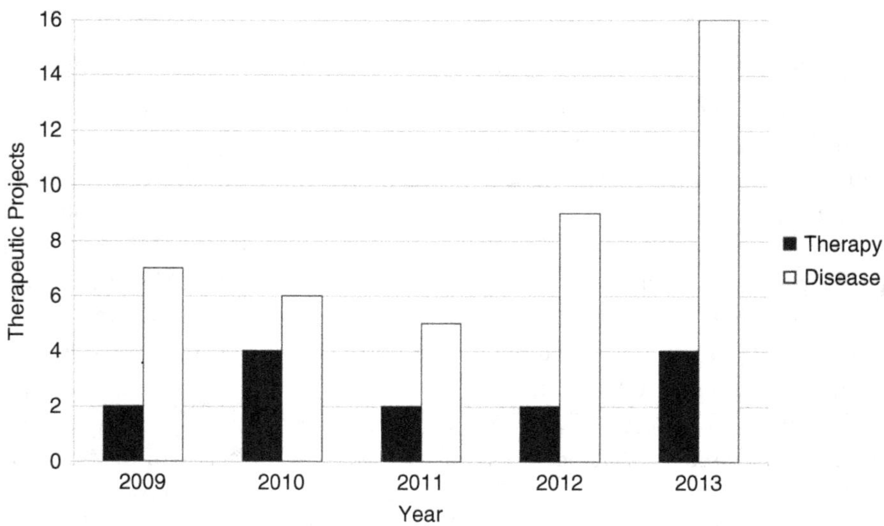

FIGURE 9.6 Therapeutic projects categories from 2009 to 2013. Data was acquired from the iGEM competition website focusing on the Health and Medicine track. Therapy projects are indicated by a black bar (n=14). Therapy projects include gene and drug therapy. Disease projects are indicated by a white bar (n=43). Disease projects include bacterial, heart, autoimmune, and parasitic disease and cancer.

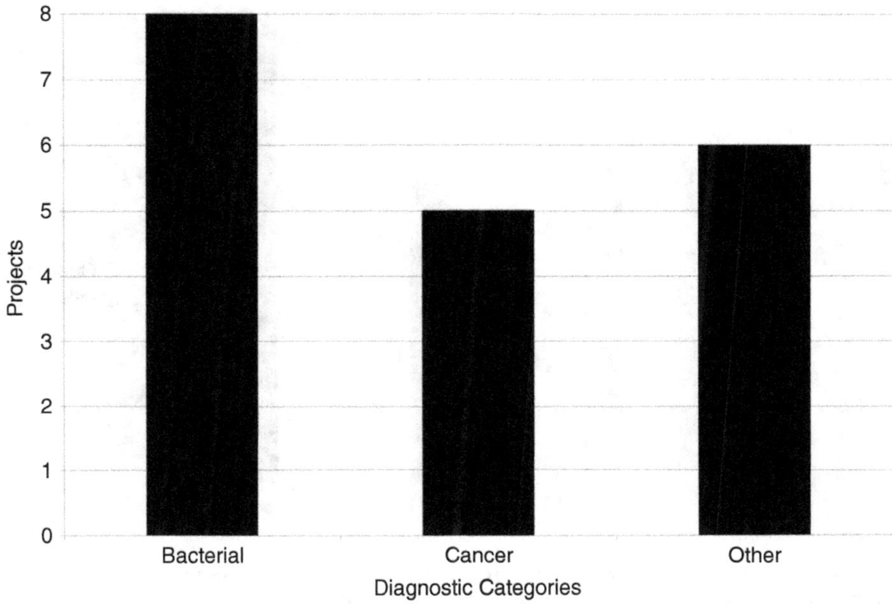

FIGURE 9.7 Diagnostic projects categories. Data was acquired from the iGEM competition website focusing on the Health and Medicine track. Diagnostic projects were divided into three categories: bacterial, cancer, and other. Other includes diseases that are not bacterial infections.

projects were absent in 2011, and other projects were absent in both 2011 and 2012 (Figure 9.8). This data may indicate a slight preference among teams for carrying out bacterial diagnostic research using synthetic parts.

9.3.3 *Numbers of Parts Used and Contributed*

In general, the quality of Biobricks and the information describing them vary widely, with some BioBricks functioning as described in their documentation, but many neither functioning nor well described.[77] Comprehensive examination was made of the numbers and categories of parts used and contributed by iGEM teams from 2009 to 2013 within the Health and Medicine track. Given that much scientific research builds on previous scientific results, it is not surprising that iGEM teams used many parts from the Registry to build new parts that performed new functions. However, it is remarkable, particularly in light of the concerns about inadequate contribution discussed earlier, that iGEM teams contributed far more new parts to the Registry than they used from the Registry, especially in the years 2011 and 2012 (Figure 9.9). Although the number of parts used by iGEM teams remained relatively steady from 2009 to 2012

77 Christina Vilanova and Manuel Porcar, iGEM 2.0 – Refoundations for Engineering Biology, 32 *Nature Biotechnology* 420, 423 (2014).

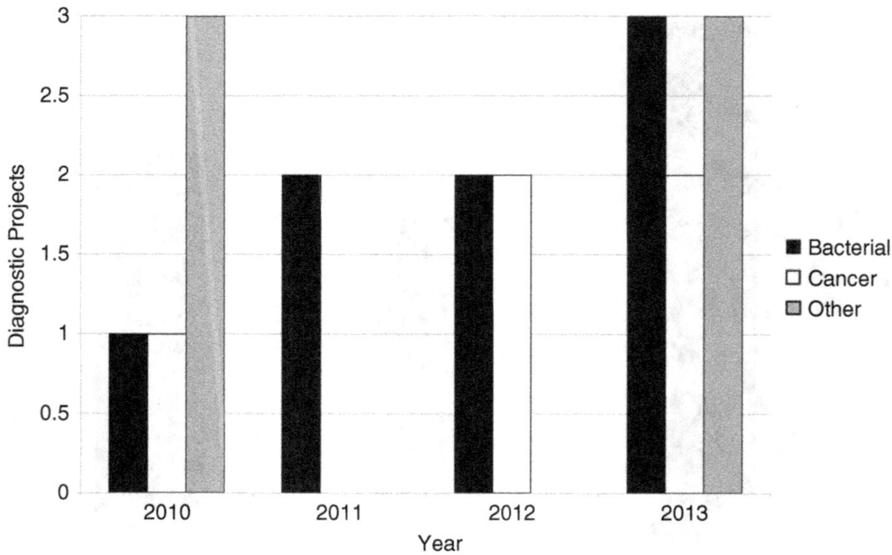

FIGURE 9.8 Diagnostic projects categories from 2009 to 2013. Data was acquired from the iGEM competition website focusing on the Health and Medicine track. There were no diagnostic entries in 2009. Bacterial diagnostic projects are indicated by a black bar (n=8). Cancer diagnostic projects are indicated by a white bar (n=5). Other projects are indicated by a gray bar (n=6).

(Figure 9.10), there was a large increase in parts teams contributed back to the Registry in 2011 and 2012. For example, in 2011, iGEM teams used 27 parts and contributed back 104 parts, a ratio of about 1:4, and, in 2012, iGEM teams used 16 parts and contributed back 130 parts, a ratio of about 1:8. Not all teams contributed back significantly more parts than they used, however. Rather, contributions back to the Registry can be accounted for by specific teams that contributed large numbers of parts (Figure 9.11). The teams accounting for a higher number of contributions typically had a higher chance of reaching the finals.[78]

The 2013 iGEM competition warrants special discussion. Parts used and contributed decreased dramatically during this year (n=14) (Figure 9.9). However, it is highly likely that this observation is explained by a lack of full data for this year having been posted to the iGEM website. This limitation should be corrected once full data become available for the 2013 iGEM competition. In addition, this study will be expanded to include the 2014 and 2015 iGEM competitions once data for these years has similarly become available. It is predicted that data from these years will bolster the finding that iGEM teams tend to contribute parts back to the Registry at much higher rates than they use parts taken from the Registry.

Overall, from 2009 to 2013, iGEM teams used 94 parts and contributed 287 parts, which is a more than threefold difference. It provides vivid evidence that synthetic

[78] Ibid. at 423.

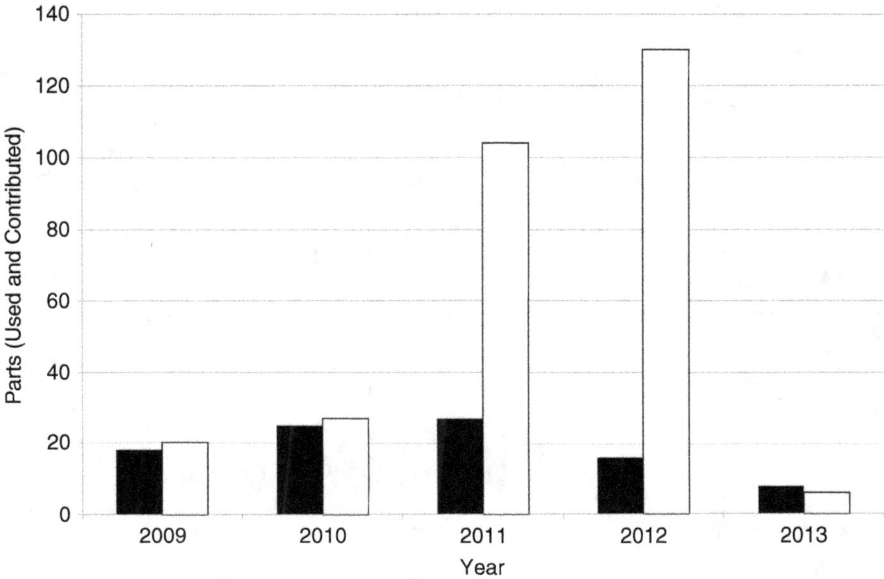

FIGURE 9.9 Number of used and contributed parts from 2009 to 2013 by entrants (n=381). Data was acquired from the iGEM competition website focusing on the Health and Medicine track. Used parts are indicated in black (n=94), and contributed parts are indicated in white (n=287).

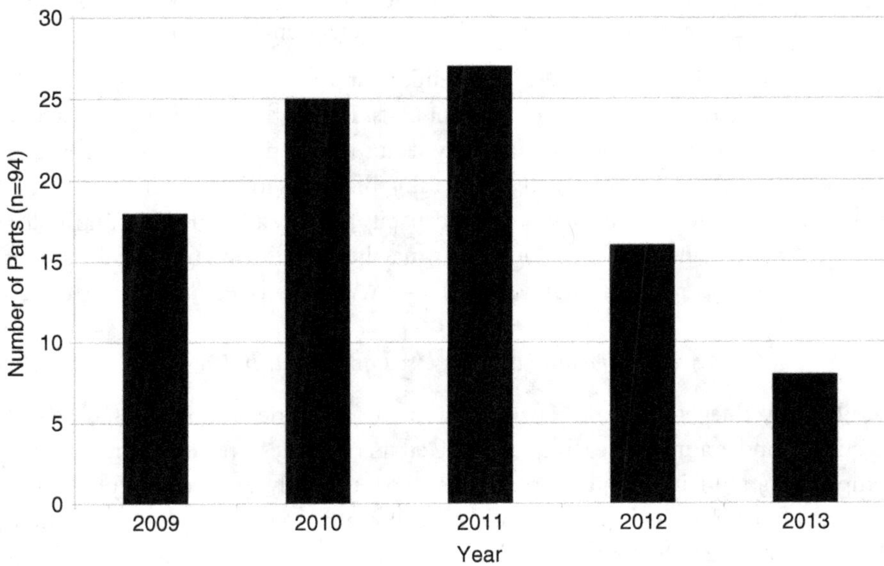

FIGURE 9.10 Number of used parts from 2009 to 2013 by entrants. Data was acquired from the iGEM competition website focusing on the Health and Medicine track. Only parts used (n=94) are indicated on this graph.

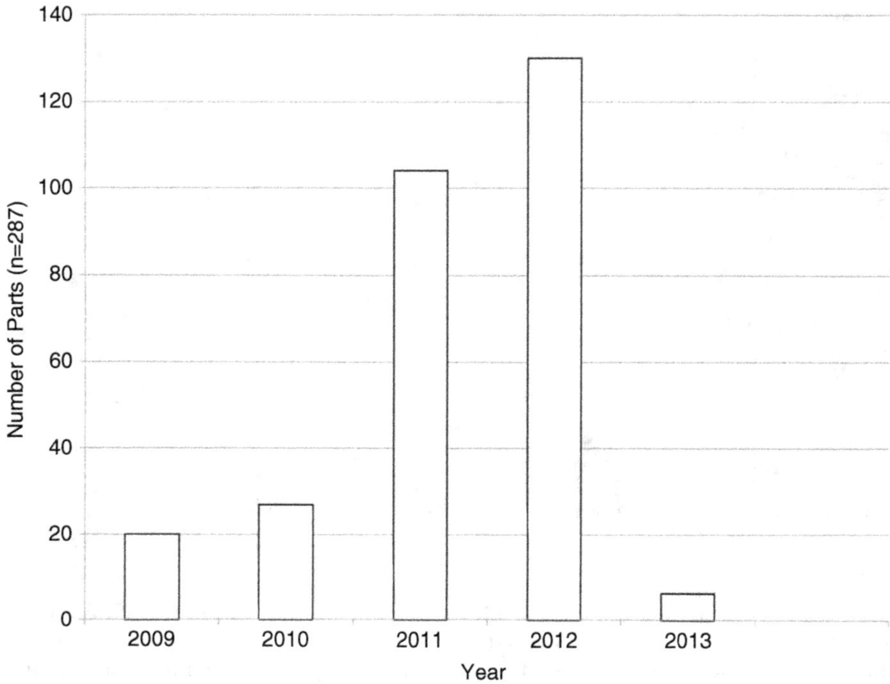

FIGURE 9.11 Number of contributed parts from 2009 to 2013 by entrants. Data was acquired from the iGEM competition website focusing on the Health and Medicine track. Only parts contributed (n=287) are indicated on this graph. This data represents two large contributions: from MIT in 2011; and from Slovenia in 2012.

biologists involved in the iGEM competition appear to prefer contribution of BioBricks to the Registry over mere usage of parts. Rather than taking free rides, this portion of the synthetic biology community seems to give free rides to future iGEM teams and any other biologists interested in using BioBricks in their research. There is evidence that iGEM increasingly lacks the capacity to verify all BioBricks contributed by iGEM participants.[79] In addition, teams may be synthesizing more and more of their own parts as a result of improvements in DNA synthesis technology.

9.3.4 *Categories of Parts Used and Contributed*

The Registry categorizes parts. There are 13 main categories (Table 9.1 has a brief description and example for each category). Certain categories tend to encompass more complexity, and their constituent parts often serve relatively specific physiological or structural functions. Such parts include generator and composite parts. In contrast, other categories tend to contain simpler synthesized parts serving more general functions, such as RBS, promoters, and terminators. iGEM teams frequently use simpler

[79] Ibid.

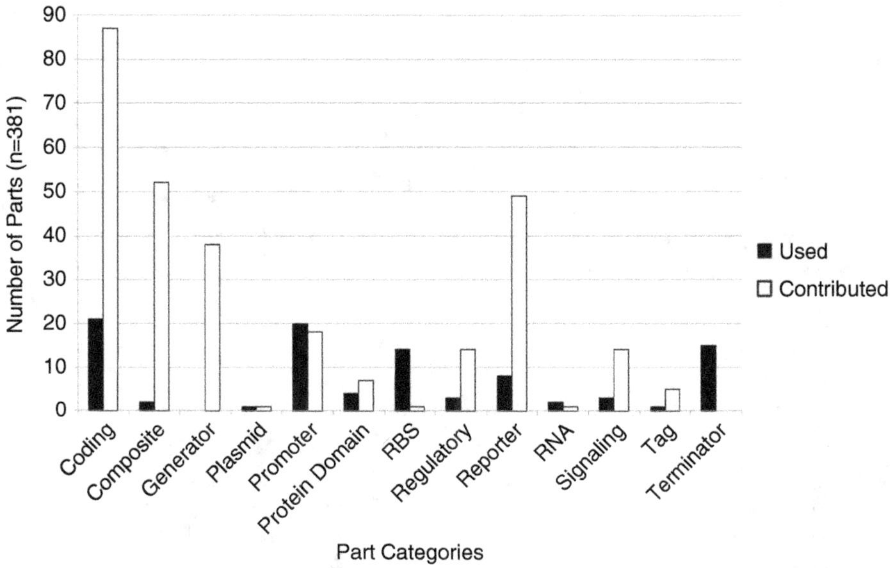

FIGURE 9.12 Categories of used and contributed parts. Data was acquired from the iGEM competition website focusing on the Health and Medicine track. Used parts are indicated by black bars and divided into 12 categories. There are no used parts categorized as a generator. Contributed parts are indicated by white bars and divided into 12 categories. There are no contributed parts categorized as a terminator. There are 13 total categories and 381 parts.

parts to build more complex composite parts. This tendency is reflected in the relative frequency of contribution and use for parts in various categories.

This study analyzed the use and contribution of parts by category. Contributed parts most often fell into the categories of coding (n=87), composite (n=52), generator (n=38), and reporter (n=49) parts. Used parts most often were taken from the coding (n=21), promoter (n=20), RBS (n=14), and terminator parts (n=15) categories (Figure 9.12).

Some part categories showed similar levels of use and contribution, including promoters (20 parts used and 18 parts contributed), protein domains (4 parts used and 7 parts contributed), and plasmids (1 part used and 1 part contributed) (Figure 9.12). In some categories, however, parts were much more frequently contributed than they were used; in other categories, parts were much more frequently used than contributed. For example, more than four times as many coding parts were contributed (n=87) as were used (n=21), more than 25 times as many composite parts were contributed (n=52) as were used (n=2), and 6 times as many reporter parts were contributed (n=49) as were used (n=8). Indeed, while 38 generator parts were contributed, none were used (Figure 9.12). In other categories, the converse was true. Thus, many more RBS parts were used (n=14) than were contributed (n=1), and there were no terminator parts contributed but 15 terminator parts were used (Figure 9.12). This data suggests that teams often use

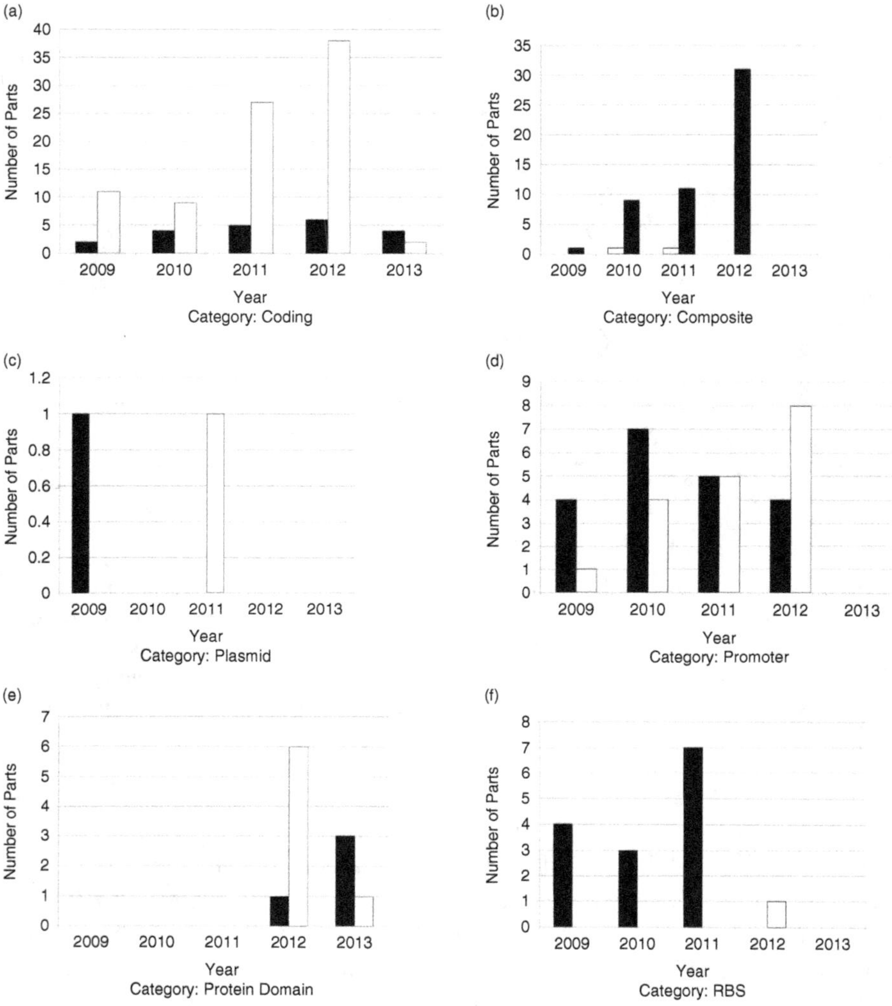

FIGURE 9.13 Categories of used and contributed parts compared from 2009 to 2013. Data was acquired from the iGEM competition website focusing on the Health and Medicine track. Black bars indicate used parts and white bars indicate contributed parts. Parts are divided into 13 categories. The generator category is not graphed because all 38 parts were contributed in 2011.

simple, more generalized parts, many of which are considered "antiquity" parts by the Registry, to construct complex, more specific parts.

Each category of parts was also individually analyzed for the 2009 to 2012 time period. (Data from 2013 is excluded from consideration, because of likely lack of data availability.) Dramatic increases in coding, composite, protein domain, regulatory, reporter, and signaling parts contributed were observed by 2012, even though project numbers had not increased at nearly the same rate (Figures 9.13a–9.13l); in 2009, there

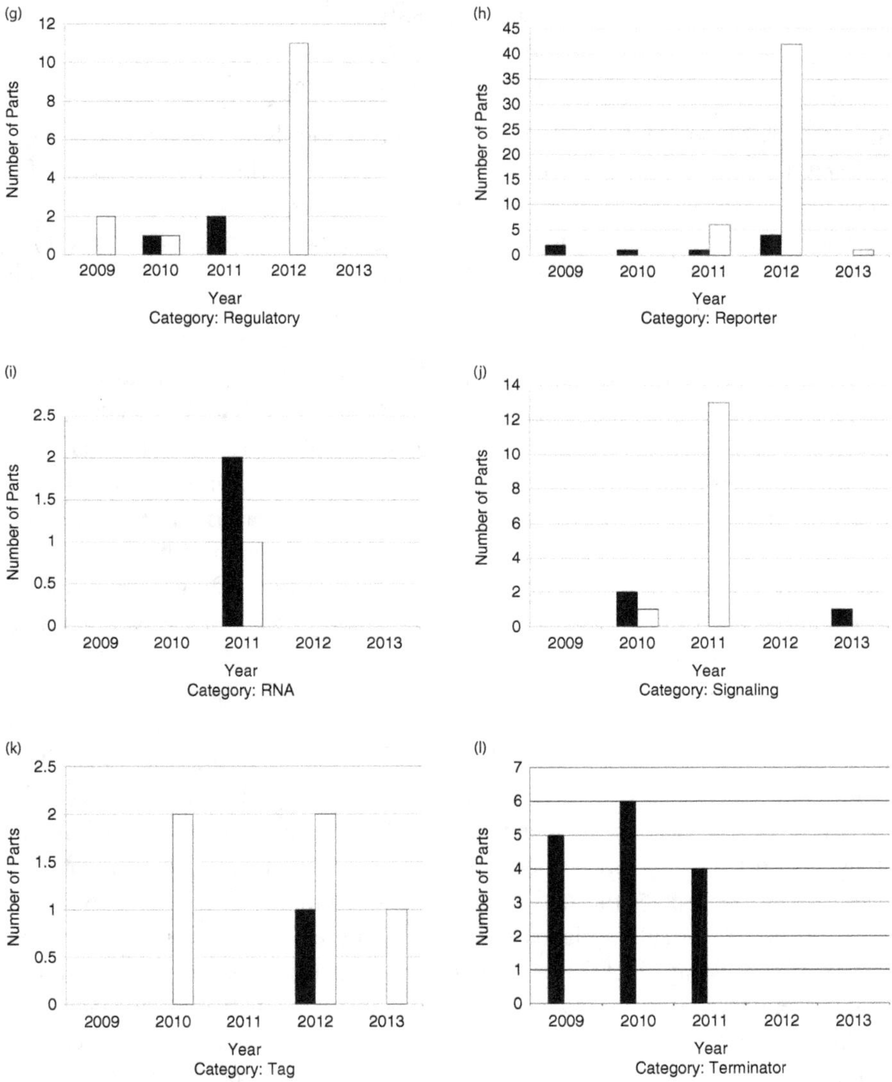

FIGURE 9.13 (cont.)

were 13 entries, and by 2012 there were 20 entries (Figure 9.2). Teams were certainly utilizing modestly more parts over this time period, but they were also synthesizing, and subsequently contributing, brand new parts at a markedly faster rate.

9.3.5 *Reuse of Parts Contributed by Previous iGEMs Teams*

Though not illustrated in a graph, it was found that iGEM teams often used parts previously contributed by teams that had competed in prior iGEM if their projects had similar goals.

9.4 DISCUSSION

9.4.1 *Open versus Proprietary Innovation*

For most of its modest history, the field of biotechnology has innovated in a largely proprietary manner. Trade secrecy and patents have been standard approaches for protecting inventions relating to new vaccines, genes, polypeptides, cells, and organisms. In fact, a major impetus for the biotechnology industry was the 1980 landmark US Supreme Court patent decision *Diamond v. Chakrabarty*, which confirmed the availability of patent protection for "anything under the sun that is made by man," and specifically biotechnological inventions.[80] Since *Chakrabarty*, patents have generally been considered crucial to biotechnological innovation.[81]

The case that patent protection drives innovation and has positive social utility is strongest for the pharmaceutical and biotechnological industries.[82] The standard narrative suggests that patent protection for biomedical inventions is necessary for attracting capital to research and development projects that must not only produce working inventions but also successfully navigate these inventions through expensive and time-consuming regulatory approval by the Food and Drug Administration (FDA). It has been widely assumed that without patents, such efforts would not be sustainable by private firms.

Synthetic biology has begun to challenge these assumptions. As noted earlier, an ethos of openness pervades the field. Many synthetic biologists view patents with suspicion, at best, and as substantial impediments to innovation, at worst. The assumption that patents claiming molecular building blocks, such as DNA sequences, or basic molecular techniques, such as the polymerase chain reaction (PCR), cause a "tragedy of the anticommons"[83] is widely believed within synthetic biology. The concept of the tragedy of the anticommons envisions an excess of patent rights creating substantial barriers to innovation because any making or using of molecular building blocks or techniques risks triggering expensive, even ruinous, infringement litigation.[84] Consequently, open access to such building blocks or techniques, akin to the model provided by open source software, is viewed as crucial for ensuring that biological innovation avoids impediments and thrives.[85]

Theory and assumptions notwithstanding, little empirical evidence exists with which to evaluate whether or not proprietary or open modes of innovation lead to more innovation. Several experimental studies have suggested that innovations in

80 *Diamond v. Chakrabarty*, 447 US 303 (1980).

81 E.g., Sheila Jasanoff, *Designs on Nature: Science and Democracy in Europe and the United States* (2005).

82 James Bessen and Michael J. Meurer, *Patent Failure: How Judges, Bureaucrats, and Lawyers Put Innovators at Risk* (2008).

83 See, e.g., Michael A. Heller and Rebecca S. Eisenberg, Can Patents Deter Innovation? The Anticommons in Biomedical Research, 280 *Science* 698 (1998).

84 Ibid. 85 von Hippel, note 19.

open systems lacking patent protection outperform those in which patent protection is available.[86] In addition, historical analyses of technologies and industries, across different time periods and countries, have suggested that patent protection does not tend to be associated with greater levels of innovation than does the lack thereof.[87] However, definitive evidence has yet to accumulate.

One of the key claims made by supporters of patent protection is that, without the availability of property rights in inventions, innovation will suffer because of a preference for free riding upon existing innovations. However, Wikipedia, open source software regimes, and the Associated Press are all examples of communities forming knowledge commons without formal property rights.[88] Each of these communities offers different incentives to its members, from interest in the subject to the ability to use shared knowledge.[89] Synthetic biology offers another challenge to this view. Together, the BioBricks Foundation, Registry of Standard Biological Parts, and iGEM have generated substantial data on whether participants in iGEM simply avail themselves to preexisting BioBricks or, alternatively, generate new BioBricks and then contribute those new BioBricks back to the Registry for future use by others. Contrary to the assumptions of those in the proprietary innovation camp, data from iGEM competitions presented in this study strongly suggests that the generation and contribution of new BioBricks far outweigh any free riding on existing BioBricks.

9.4.2 *Open Culture of Synthetic Biology*

As noted, synthetic biology, from its conception as a distinct field, has been characterized by a strong commitment to open innovation, including openness with respect to the participants in synthetic biology innovation. Biological knowledge tends to be viewed within the synthetic biology community as something that should be made widely available to anyone with interest, with the hope that interested individuals will not only learn about and benefit from the output of the research enterprise but also contribute to it. Contrast this to the more traditional approach of academic biology, in which, despite open publication of research results, access to knowledge, expertise, and laboratories has tended to be limited to those possessing the correct credentials. These credentials include PhDs, postdoctoral fellowships, and professorships, as well as ancillary staff, such as undergraduate students and laboratory technicians who work under the supervision of the former. In synthetic biology, knowledge is made available not only in published journal articles but also

86 See, e.g., Andrew W. Torrance and Bill Tomlinson, Patents and the Regress of Useful Arts, 10 *Colum. Sci. & Tech. L. Rev.* 128 (2009).

87 See, e.g., Josh Lerner, 150 Years of Patent Protection, 92 *Am. Econ. Rev.* 221 (2002).

88 Frischmann, Madison, and Strandburg, Governing Knowledge Commons, in *Governing Knowledge Commons* 1–5.

89 Frischmann, Madison, and Strandburg, Governing Knowledge Commons, in *Governing Knowledge Commons* 477–79.

in more accessible forms, such as comic books,[90] blogs,[91] and wikis.[92] Expertise can be gained from mentors, such as iGEM team faculty supervisors, from laboratory technique wikis, and even from the many biotechnique video tutorials available from sources such as YouTube. Perhaps most distinctly, aspiring synthetic biologists have access to community laboratories, such as BioCurious, or even to used laboratory equipment (often from failed biotechnology companies) available inexpensively on online auction sites, such as eBay. In principle, anyone can now obtain access to the myriad BioBrick DNA building blocks available from the Registry simply by participating in iGEM, or registering as an iGEM academic research lab – and the number of these free BioBricks has been rising rapidly for a decade. As a cognate of "Maker" culture, synthetic biology thus is relatively democratized, but this has led to one major problem with the Registry: some parts are not fully characterized.[93] Many research groups end up moving from the public Registry to other professional registries that fully characterize parts and how they are supposed to be used.[94]

The data presented in this chapter confirms at least one part of the story that synthetic biology is characterized by open innovation. As part of iGEM competitions, participating teams not only receive free access to thousands of BioBricks from the Registry, but there is also a prevailing normative expectation that any new parts teams develop should be contributed back into the Registry. Such contributions have helped the Registry grow rapidly in the number of BioBricks. If iGEM participants behaved in conformance with simplistic versions of conventional economic theory, one would expect free riding to have stunted growth in the Registry. The truth is stranger, at least as judged from a traditional economic perspective. Far from free riding, our data (e.g., in Figures 9.9–9.13), suggest that iGEM participants give back to the Registry at a much higher rate than they use existing BioBricks originating in the Registry.

Why would iGEM participants contribute back to the Registry more BioBricks than they receive from it? There may be several reasons. Teams competing at iGEM want to do well and hope to win a prize in one of the several competition categories (e.g., Best Health and Medicine Project, Best Environment Project). To do this, and to distinguish their projects from those of similarly striving competitors, it is likely necessary for them to design new BioBrick parts. In fact, several prizes are explicitly awarded for new BioBricks (e.g., Best New Basic Part, Best New Composite Part). Nevertheless, for most competition categories, it is possible to design a new system or organism relying only on BioBricks already available from the Registry simply by remixing multiple existing individual parts into new combinations.

90 See *Nature*, note 20. 91 E.g., www.nature.com/subjects/biobricks (last visited Jan. 16, 2017).

92 *Open Wetware*, http://openwetware.org/wiki/Main_Page (last visited Dec. 29, 2015).

93 Richard Kitney and Paul Freemont, Synthetic Biology – The State of Play, 586 *FEBS Letters* 2029, 2032 (2012).

94 Ibid.

The prevailing ethos of synthetic biology may also influence the contribution of new parts to the Registry. As discussed earlier, the founding culture of synthetic biology emphasized openness and sharing as important community values. High rates of contribution of parts back to the Registry may suggest that those values are widely shared among iGEM participants. Though difficult to document, stories have circulated within the synthetic biology community of violations of openness and sharing norms leading to shaming of alleged violators. For example, in 2009 when a team competing in iGEM announced to the crowd that it had applied for three patents, loud boos were heard throughout the audience.[95]

Traditional assumptions about free riding and tragedies of the commons have been forcefully challenged in recent years, most notably by Nobel Prize–winning economist Elinor Ostrom[96] and, in the context of scientific knowledge and information, via the related knowledge commons research framework proposed by Brett Frischmann, Michael Madison, and Katherine Strandburg.[97] Among other insights, Ostrom demonstrated that particular norms and institutions appear to explain openness and sharing within some communities, such as Maine lobstermen and high-alpine Swiss cattle grazers.[98] Synthetic biologists attracted to iGEM, the BBF, and the Registry may tend to be influenced to be more open and sharing by the founding cultures of these institutions. The incentive of winning prizes may act to promote some contribution of BioBricks parts. However, most prizes are awarded for projects in which the overall result, not individual BioBrick parts, matters to success. Although the rules have become stricter recently, in previous years, it may have been possible to win without contributing back truly new or well-functioning BioBrick parts to the Registry. This large surplus of contribution over usage may suggest that the synthetic biology community shares predominantly contributory norms. However, the give-more-than-get pattern observed in iGEM may also have resulted, at least in part, from the extensive infrastructure the founders of the BBF, iGEM, and the Registry carefully planned and carefully put in place to encourage participation in synthetic biology and the contribution and usage of genetic parts.[99]

These predominantly contributory norms are substantially aided by the ease with which users of the Registry can contribute back their parts. Knowledge commons tend to depend on the ease of sharing knowledge by members of the community.[100] If it was difficult to edit a Wikipedia page or share jamband recordings, fewer people would contribute to those communities and they would be much less successful.[101]

95 Frow and Calvert, note 61, at 53.

96 Edella Schlager and Elinor Ostrom, Property-Rights Regimes and Natural Resources: A Conceptual Analysis, 68 *Land Econ.* 249, 257–59 (1992).

97 Frischmann, Madison, Strandburg, Governing Knowledge Commons, in *Governing Knowledge Commons* 1.

98 Ibid.

99 See generally Michael J. Madison, Brett M. Frischmann, & Katherine J. Strandburg, Constructing Commons in the Cultural Environment, 95 *Cornell L. Rev.* 657 (2010).

100 Ibid. at 683–704. 101 Ibid. at 662–64.

The Registry has dedicated pages on how to contribute parts including tutorials for adding basic parts, adding composite parts, and improving existing parts.[102] Further, participants in iGEM are provided with a submission kit to facilitate the process of sending DNA samples to the Registry.[103]

9.4.3 *Relevance to Other Areas of Innovation*

Evidence that the synthetic biology community – at least that portion of it that competes in iGEM – tends to share genetic inventions, rather than free riding on what is available or keeping their inventions secret, has precedents in other areas of innovation. The open source software community has long shared computer code, whether freely and without restrictions or within the context of open source software licenses. Far from stifling innovation, open source software has thrived, even becoming dominant for applications such as Apache, for server management. Similarly, the Nightscout community has demonstrated that substantial innovation in medical devices that matter tremendously to their users can take place without patents, copyrights, or trade secrecy.[104] Even in the face of firm worries and FDA resistance, innovation in continuous glucose monitoring has improved rapidly under the auspices of Nightscout.

Traditional pharmaceutical and biotechnological research has a very different approach. In these industries, strong patent rights have tended to be sought and vigorously enforced against competitors. One of the prominent justifications for this proprietary approach involves the need for FDA approval, which can take years, and, during which, patents may help companies attract the large amounts of capital necessary to develop, test, and propagate new biopharmaceutical inventions.[105] Even otherwise critical assessments of the net benefits of patents often cite the biotechnology industry as being especially dependent on patents, which can be used to attract investment. Synthetic biology, at least in its current incarnation, appears to offer an intriguing challenge to this proprietary paradigm.

9.4.4 *Future Directions*

The field of synthetic biology has been strongly influenced by attempts to establish an ethos of openness and sharing deliberately differing from the proprietary ethos that tends to prevail in the existing fields of biotechnology and pharmaceutical research. As recently as 2005, the synthetic biology community consisted of a handful of founding researchers well known to, and in close cooperation with, one another. Their deliberate efforts led to the iGEM competition, which has witnessed

102 Help:Submission Kit, *iGEM*, http://parts.igem.org/Help:Submission_Kit (last visited Apr. 11, 2016).

103 Add a part to the Registry, *iGEM*, http://parts.igem.org/Add_a_Part_to_the_Registry (last visited Apr. 11, 2016).

104 *Nightscout*, www.nightscout.info/ (last visited Dec. 23, 2015).

105 *Patent Failure*, note 82.

rapid growth in participation. In 2015, the number of people competing at iGEM approached 3000 and warranted a move in venues from the MIT campus to the Hines Convention Center in Boston. The number of biologists who describe themselves as synthetic biologists, scientific publications describing synthetic biological research, and students taking classes in synthetic biology are all on a sharply upward trajectory. Synthetic biology is a field experiencing a rapid increase in popularity, participation, and influence.

It is possible that such growth will occur without weakening the prevailing ethos of openness and sharing. Perhaps these principles will bleed into other fields of biology, leading to erosion of the traditional emphasis on proprietarity. On the other hand, the ethos of synthetic biology may itself be challenged and eroded by the proprietary practices of the wider field of biology that encompasses it. It is too early to know how this clash of ethos will resolve itself. Nevertheless, the evidence discussed in this chapter suggests the openness and sharing characteristic of synthetic biology remains robust more than a decade after the founding of the field. As the field continues to growth in participation and influence, it is likely that the rest of biology will absorb at least some of the practices that have made synthetic biology so successful in such a short time. Free riding may continue to be challenged by the voluntary giving of free rides.

10

Governance of Biomedical Research Commons to Advance Clinical Translation: Lessons from the Mouse Model Community

Tania Bubela, Rhiannon Adams, Shubha Chandrasekharan, Amrita Mishra, and Songyan Liu

INTRODUCTION

The translation of laboratory and clinical research into interventions that improve individual and population health is an iterative process with systemic directionality from basic research through preclinical research, clinical research, clinical implementation, and population health outcomes research (National Center for Advancing Translational Sciences 2015). Engaged in translation are patients and patient advocacy organizations, researchers from public and private sectors and from multiple disciplinary backgrounds, clinical practitioners, as well as a myriad of ancillary support professionals, from business executives, accountants, and marketing/sales staff to venture capitalists and public and philanthropic fund administrators to health and safety regulators.

New models of collaboration within this complex ecosystem are required to overcome waste and inefficiencies in current research and development (R&D)

Tania Bubela is Professor and Dean at the Faculty of Health Sciences, Simon Fraser University, Burnaby, British Columbia, Canada. At the time this work was completed, she was Professor at the School of Public Health, University of Alberta, Edmonton, Alberta, Canada. Rhiannon Adams was a researcher with the School of Public Health, University of Alberta, Edmonton, Alberta, Canada. Shubha Chandrasekharan is Assistant Research Professor, Duke Global Health Institute, Duke University, Durham, North Carolina, USA. Amrita Mishra was a researcher at the School of Public Health, University of Alberta, Edmonton, Alberta, Canada. Songyan Liu is a researcher in bioinformatics at the Research Institute in Oncology and Hematology, University of Manitoba and CancerCare Manitoba, Winnipeg, Manitoba, Canada.

Many individuals have participated and supported this research over the years. Most prominently, with respect to data and patent analyses, have been Dr. Andreas Strotmann, Dr. Sean Morrison, and Mr. Mark Bieber. Expert advice has been provided most notably by Dr. Lauryl Nutter, Dr. Ann Flenniken, Mr. David Einhorn, Dr. Edna Einsiedel, and Dr. Paul Schofield as well as the nearly 100 interviewees, internationally, who generously gave their time to inform and comment on our research. Research assistants and staff have additionally included Dr. Cami Ryan, Ms. Noelle Orton, Mr. Amir Reshef, and Ms. Lesley Dacks. Funding for the research has been provided by Genome Canada and Genome Prairie for the NorCOMM I Project (PI: Dr. Geoff Hicks; co-PI Dr. Janet Rossant); Genome Canada and the Ontario Genomics Institute for the NorCOMM II (Project Co-Lead Investigators: Colin McKerlie and Steve Brown); the Canadian Stem Cell Network funding to Dr. Tania Bubela.

within pharmaceutical or larger biotechnology companies (Hunter 2014; Munos 2009). Despite substantial increases in R&D investments to US$50 billion per year, the number of new drugs approved annually in the United States has remained constant over the past 60 years – the US Food and Drug Administration (FDA) has approved approximately 1200 new drugs (Munos 2009). The high cost of therapies is in part driven by the cost of failures in clinical development; only 15.3 percent of drugs traverse the pipeline from Phase 1 to market authorization for lead indications, a percentage that drops to 10.4 percent for all indications (Hay et al. 2014). Despite billions of dollars of investment, new cancer drugs developed between 2002 and 2014 have produced median gains in progression-free survival of only 2.1 months and median gains in overall survival of only 2.5 months (Fojo et al. 2014). This expenditure of time, money, and resources on marginal therapeutic benefits is "promoting a me-too mentality that is stifling innovation and creativity" (Fojo et al. 2014).

Some argue that precompetitive research partnerships can overcome the innovation and creativity gap by drawing on the respective strengths of different sectors to facilitate R&D of new therapies and diagnostics in the translational environment. Research commons can provide infrastructure to support such precompetitive collaborations between academia, government, industry, nongovernmental organizations, and patients (Bubela et al. 2012a; Edwards et al. 2009; Friend 2010). Precompetitive collaborations can facilitate sharing of data and materials without limiting the ability of commercial actors to appropriate knowledge that is closer to practical application. They aim to raise the knowledge levels for all R&D actors to avoid duplicative research while facilitating replication for validation, and to promote the use of standard research tools and methods.

Resources governed as research commons may be informational (e.g., databases), material (e.g., biorepositories and biobanks), or a combination of the two. Commons governance of information is especially important if one accepts the argument that the principal output of clinical translation is information, defined as including "information about the coordinated set of materials, practices, and constraints needed to safely unlock the therapeutic or preventive activities of drugs, biologics, and diagnostics" (Kimmelman and London 2015). Commons governance of materials allows researchers to share quality-controlled, standardized research tools (Schofield et al. 2009). Most importantly, the value of commons governance increases as more people use the shared resources. Pooled resources must therefore "be managed to facilitate use, but also re-contribution from the user community, creating a feedback loop between withdrawal, value-added research, and deposit" (Bubela et al. 2012b: 107).

Here we focus on one of the most established biomedical research commons – the mouse commons – that is composed of both biorepositories and databases, which we collectively refer to as archives (Einhorn and Heimes 2009; Schofield et al. 2009). The mouse model community established this commons in response to the challenge of coordinating the sharing of data and research reagents generated by high-throughput 'omics' technologies (Bubela et al. 2012a). We ask what lessons may be learned from this model organism community for others seeking to develop governance structures that will sustain long-term access to international research resources. We address the history and development of the mouse commons and key challenges in its development using Elinor Ostrom's Institutional Analysis and Development (IAD) Framework as modified for the study of knowledge commons (Frischmann, Madison, and Strandburg 2014). We focus on the role of formal intellectual property rights and contracts in promoting or impeding research commons as well as on rules development and implementation relevant to incentivizing, dis-incentivizing, and sanctioning participation in the commons. Finally, we discuss governance mechanisms that promote the long-term sustainability of the commons, especially with respect to the high costs associated with sustaining archives that house the resources.

Our analysis is based on a decade of work with the mouse model research community – we conducted nearly 100 interviews with a variety of international stakeholders, including managers of mouse commons infrastructure, high-throughput resource generators, funders, and research users (Bubela et al. 2012a; Bubela, Guebert, and Mishra 2015a; Mishra and Bubela 2014; Mishra, Schofield, and Bubela 2016). In addition, we participated in community-level infrastructure planning workshops, analyzed the patent landscape up to 2007, and analyzed contractual agreements that govern sharing by repositories and databases up to 2013.

10.1 APPLICATION OF THE IAD FRAMEWORK TO THE MOUSE MODEL RESEARCH COMMONS

Elinor Ostrom's IAD Framework enables the systematic study of the governance of commons, whether these be natural resource commons such as forests of fisheries (Ostrom 1990, 2005) or research commons where the goal is to share research reagents, know-how, and data (Dedeurwaerdere 2010a, 2010b; Hess and Ostrom 2006, 2007). Since research commons are a type of knowledge commons (knowledge in this context refers to "a broad set of intellectual and cultural resources" (Frischmann et al. 2014), the adapted knowledge commons framework provides the appropriate mechanism to study commons governance that aims to achieve broad-based participation and sharing of data and materials for research (Frischmann et al. 2014). This sharing is dependent on the accepted norms and behaviors of the research community – in this case, researchers who use mouse models to study human disease. These norms and behaviors may be impacted by the heterogeneity of the community, which creates challenges in managing differing sets of norms and behaviors about sharing versus withholding of data and materials (Bubela et al. 2012a). The main concern of individual researchers that contributes to the low 35 percent sharing rate for mice is the "free-rider" problem – that is, the prevention of users benefiting from the commons without contributing to it (Schofield et al. 2009). A further problem is the simple logistical burden of sharing mouse-related research materials with other researchers, one overcome by the one-stop deposit to a repository that then takes on the burden of onward distribution to the research community (Einhorn and Heimes 2009; Schofield et al. 2009). In addition, current trends toward commercialization of publicly funded outputs from research institutions have led to a plethora of intellectual property rights (IPRs), mostly patents, over mouse-related research materials. Ironically, the development of the mouse research commons is, in part, a reaction to commercialization policies of the same governments, funders, and research institutions that now promote the research commons (Caulfield et al. 2012; Popp Berman 2012).

A successful commons requires rules and governance structures to overcome some of these challenges (Ostrom 2005). Rules, ideally developed with the participation of community members; need to incentivize creation of the commons; contribution to the commons; use of the commons; and, most importantly, re-contribution of value-added data and materials to the commons. Rules need to provide a graduated system of sanctions for noncompliance; but in a complex ecosystem, debate occurs as to which entities should develop and enforce these sanctions and what mechanisms to employ for conflict resolution (Ostrom and Hess 2007). In a research commons, the hierarchy of rules usually ranges from national-level laws that govern IPRs, regulatory approval processes, and animal welfare to policies and guidelines for contractual arrangements, funding, and collaborative research. At their simplest, commons governance rules may include norms and practices within a community around citation, attribution, reciprocity and sharing, and form and timing of publication. In addition, governance models need to ensure the long-term sustainability of the commons, while remaining versatile and responsive to technological change (Mishra et al. 2016).

In the following sections, we first describe the background environment and history of the mouse model research commons, including its heterogeneity. We then discuss IPRs as impediments to the development of the mouse commons, the rules that have been put in place to incentivize participation in the commons, and the governance structures to support the long-term sustainability of the commons.

10.2 THE COMMONS ENVIRONMENT FOR MOUSE MODEL RESEARCH

The mouse is the quintessential biomedical research tool. With its genetic similarities to humans, it is an efficient and effective model system to assist researchers in understanding links between genes and disease states (Kim, Shin, and Seong 2010). Knockout mice are genetically manipulated to lack one or both copies of a specific gene (or portion thereof), with corresponding impact on the protein the gene encodes. Knockin mice carry engineered copies of genes that may still be functional. For example, knockin mice may be genetically manipulated to carry human genes that make them susceptible to cancer or that “humanize” parts of their immune system for drug testing. The scientific significance of mouse models was recognized by the 2007 Nobel Prize in Physiology or Medicine awarded to Dr. Mario R. Capecchi and Sir Martin J. Evans and Dr. Oliver Smithies for their early work on knockout mice.

In the 1980s, the generation of genetically modified mice was technically challenging, required highly skilled personnel, and it was costly in terms of time and research funds. The mice themselves, as mutants, were physiologically fragile and difficult to breed. Generation of mutant mouse models that were the bedrock of biomedical research was therefore beyond the skills and resources of many research laboratories, and those laboratories with model generation capabilities were reluctant to share these valuable resources. Since public funding agencies invested considerable resources into the generation of the mouse models, it became imperative to develop infrastructure capable of receiving strains from generating laboratories and distributing the strains to other users in the research community.

The Jackson Laboratory (JAX) was the first international mouse repository. It was created in the 1930s to distribute community-generated mice in addition to its own strains (Einhorn and Heimes 2009). JAX became a frozen embryo repository in 1979 and is now the world's largest repository of live research mouse strains (Jackson Laboratory 2014). JAX and other repositories promote and facilitate access to research tools and are at the epicenter of the mouse research commons. Such repositories accept deposit of mouse-related resources from individual research laboratories and then archive and distribute the resources using conditions of use or material transfer agreements (MTAs) that promote research use (Mishra and Bubela 2014). More recently, the commons resources have come to include mouse embryonic stem cell lines (mESCs) and gametes (mainly sperm), which are more efficient to store and distribute and can be used to generate live mice. They also now collect derivative cell lines, vectors for genetic manipulation, and associated genotyping and phenotyping data (Brown and Moore 2012a, 2012b; Collins et al. 2007; Skarnes et al. 2011). Collectively, these materials and associated data comprise a comprehensive mutant mouse resource.

Despite this robust international sharing infrastructure, only approximately 35 percent of generated mouse strains are made available to the research community (Schofield et al. 2009). Partly in response to this statistic, the international community launched the International Knockout Mouse Consortium (IKMC) in 2007 (Collins et al. 2007; Skarnes et al. 2011). The IKMC is generating a mutant resource for all protein-coding mouse genes that can be archived and distributed by repositories affiliated with the IKMC (Bradley et al. 2012). It has the added benefit, as a high-throughput pipeline, of enhancing efficiency and reducing the costs of developing mouse models, which formerly were funded through individual research grants. Those individually developed mouse models also may not have been of high quality, were non-standardized with respect to background strain of the mouse, and may or may not have been shared.

A second international consortium, the International Mouse Phenotyping Consortium (IMPC) was established in 2011 to add standardized phenotyping data to the IKMC resource, thereby generating an encyclopedia of mammalian gene function (Brown and Moore 2012a, 2012b). The user community could nominate genes to be prioritized for both production (IKMC) and phenotyping (IMPC). The IMPC is expanding to include additional data from secondary phenotypers, who will contribute additional specialized screens, and from experienced end users, who will re-contribute tertiary phenotyping data, working in collaboration with the IMPC centers (Adams et al. 2013). This ability to accept data from secondary phenotypers creates the network effect (the re-contribution of value-added resources) that promotes research commons.

The IKMC and the IMPC are both international consortia of mouse genetics centers, supported by national and regional funding bodies in North America, Europe, and Asia-Pacific. Each relies on government-funded infrastructure for archiving and sharing mouse strains and associated data. For example, IKMC resources are available from the Knockout Mouse Project (KOMP) Repository housed at University of California, Davis (www.komp.org/) and the European Mouse Mutant Cell Repository (EuMMCR) at Helmholtz Zentrum in Munich, Germany (www.eummcr.org/). Phenotyping data generated by the primary IMPC centers are processed, housed, and made available via the NIH-funded KOMP Data Coordination Center and the European Commission–funded International Data Coordination Center. These data coordination centers provide common semantics for comparing and integrating imaging, text-based, and numerical data (Mallon et al. 2012; Ringwald and Eppig 2011).

In summary, the mouse research commons is composed of (1) individual researchers who produce and/or use mouse models; (2) repositories and databases where individual researchers may deposit or access mouse models or data, such as JAX and Mouse Genome Informatics (MGI), the international database resource for the laboratory mouse (www.informatics.jax.org); (3) the high-throughput production centers for community resources that form the IKMC and IMPC consortia; (4) the high-level end users that contribute data to the IMPC; and (5) the national and regional funders that support the commons. The functioning of this commons is premised on rules and governance structures that promote the sharing of mouse research tools and associated data for biomedical research.

10.3 LEGAL ISSUES THAT IMPACT THE COMMONS ENVIRONMENT

10.3.1 *Historical Context*

In creating the mouse model research commons, the community confronted a number of well-known controversies over access to mice as research tools. Researchers at Harvard University created the OncoMouse, a knockin mouse with a predisposition to develop cancer. The OncoMouse strains and associated methods were covered by broad patents that were exclusively licensed to DuPont, which funded the research (Murray 2010). DuPont imposed restrictive licensing terms that were contrary to community norms for sharing valuable mouse strains that were emerging in the 1980s. The licenses restricted third-party distribution of novel strains developed in individual laboratories from oncomice. They required annual disclosure of research findings using the mice and imposed reach-through rights on future discoveries that entitled DuPont to "a percentage share in any sales of proceeds from a product or process developed using an OncoMouse, even though the mice would not be incorporated into the end product" (Murray 2010: 362).

Community resistance to these restrictions necessitated a negotiated compromise between DuPont and the National Institutes for Health (NIH), which signed a memorandum of understanding (MOU) in 1999. The MOU enabled academic researchers to share strains under simplified conditions of use. These conditions of use no longer included reporting requirements or reach-through-rights. JAX and other public repositories then made the strains widely accessible to academic institutions that had funding agreements with the Public Health Service of the US Department of Health and Human Services (DHHS). Researchers at institutions not so funded, including those outside of the United States, were advised to seek a license for use from DuPont (Mishra and Bubela 2014).

The NIH also intervened to enable access to *cre-lox* technology that was developed in DuPont's life sciences division in 1987. *Cre-lox* technology generates conditional mutants with genetic modifications expressed only in specific tissues (Sauer and Henderson 1988). Restrictive licensing agreements also limited access to this patented, powerful research tool for studying gene function. In 1998, NIH negotiated an MOU to allow JAX and institutions with funding agreements with the Public Health Service of the DHHS to distribute and share *cre-lox* mice, subject only to simple conditions on use. In light of these two NIH negotiated MOUs, follow-on research, measured through citations, increased (Murray et al. 2009). The MOUs also encouraged new authors at a greater diversity of institutions to conduct research using the mouse technology in a broader range of fields (Murray et al. 2009). Thus the development of institutional mechanisms for generation and distribution of mouse strains promoted sharing of these valuable research tools, one of the goals of a research commons.

These cases, however, also suggest that the seeking and rigorous enforcement of intellectual property rights may impede the creation and successful functioning of research commons. Since the 1980s, government and funding agency policies have incentivized the seeking of formal intellectual property rights by researchers receiving public funds, while promoting the sharing of data and research materials (Caulfield et al. 2012). The mouse-model research community was no exception, and our analysis of patents covering mouse-related research reagents, described in Section 10.3.2, demonstrates the extent to which incentives for academics to patent research tools have been effective. Such patents, with a few exceptions, are, in a practical sense, largely worthless in that they generate little to no revenue for the patent holder relative to the cost of patent acquisition and maintenance. Commons are a more effective mediator of exchanges of research tools because they reduce transaction costs associated with sharing, especially for research tools that are largely generated using public research funds and then used by other publicly funded researchers. The premium that may be charged for patented research tools makes limited sense from a social perspective because it represents a research tax from others within the same community, with public research dollars simply flowing from one institution to another. Indeed, our interviewees clearly stated the uselessness of patenting mouse-related research tools and expressed dissatisfaction with the entities that mediated such practices, namely, their technology transfer offices (Bubela et al. 2012a).

10.3.2 *Do Intellectual Property Rights Impede the Creation and Functioning of Research Commons?*

In analyzing the mouse patent landscape, we asked whether a legacy of basic research patents created under current laws and practices hindered the establishment of public sector commons infrastructures. Specifically, we (1) explored the characteristics of mouse genes that had been patented prior to September 2007 compared to a control set of unpatented mouse genes and (2) compared research activity based on patented mouse genes with research activity based on non-patented mouse genes. Briefly, on September 27, 2007, we searched the Thomson database, Delphion, for granted US patents that (1) had variants of the terms "mouse" or "mammal" in claims, (2) matched a modified Ade/Cook-Deegan Algorithm for RNA/DNA patents, and (3) did not have variants of "plant" in the claims. The search identified 7179 granted US patents, from which we extracted standard patent information from the database and which we then read and coded to identify the 1144 patents that claimed gene sequences, by SEQ ID (DNA/RNA/amino acid) or a gene name prior to 1996. In the Appendix, we describe our methods for analyzing our patent data set.

Contrary to the beliefs of many of our interviewees in the mouse model community, there was considerable patenting of mouse-related research reagents, especially during the heyday of "gene" patenting in the late 1990s through 2001 (Bubela et al. 2012a; Carbone et al. 2010; Cook-Deegan and Heaney 2010a, 2010b). Not only were such patents sought and granted, but most were maintained over the course of their patent terms (Figure 10.1).

The majority of mouse DNA and mouse patents were held by public and private universities and other nonprofit entities, which reflects a considerable investment by those organizations in maintaining a patent portfolio covering low-value research-related subject matter (Figure 10.2). By contrast, pharmaceutical and biotechnology companies were more strategic in their patent filing and maintenance. These companies dominated ownership of broad DNA claims that overlapped mouse DNA but were

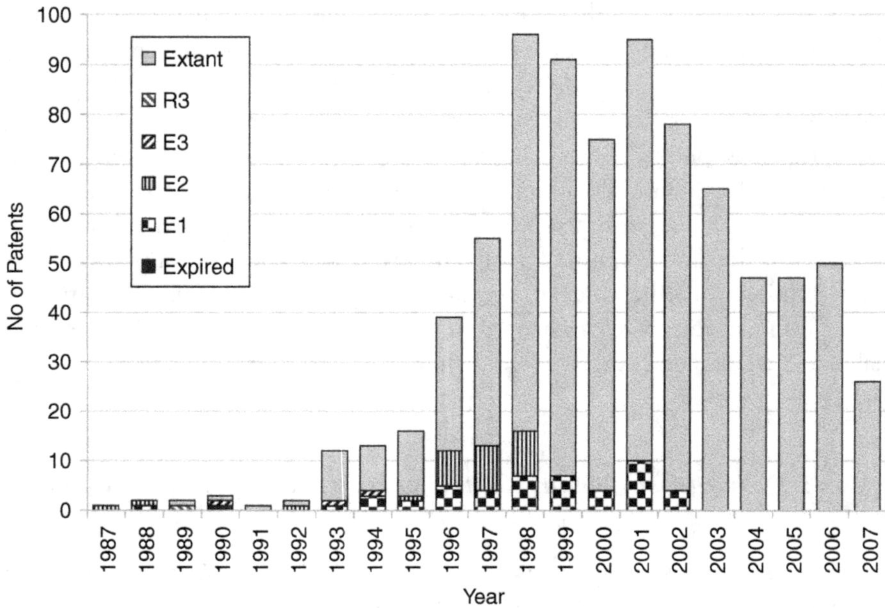

FIGURE 10.1 Maintenance status and filing date of 816 mouse gene patents (US) between 1987 and 2007. Maintenance codes are assigned by the USPTO: E1 – expired 4 years after the initial issue date; E2 – expired 8 years after the initial issue date; E3 – expired 12 years after the initial issue date; R3 reinstated after E3.

worded to include DNA from other mammals. They also dominated ownership of patents that claimed cell lines. Mice as research tools were claimed by all sectors.

To answer our question on the impact of patents on follow-on mouse model research, we identified each of 951 patented genes based on gene name or a blast analysis of the DNA sequences listed in the patents (see Appendix for a detailed explanation of the analysis). Using Online Mendelian Inheritance in Man (OMIM), the Mouse Genome Database (MGD), and the Mouse Genome and Informatics (MGI) databases, we detailed the characteristics of patented mouse genes. We compared these to a set of 1354 randomly selected unpatented genes identified from the same databases. The 951 patented genes were twice as likely to be listed in the OMIM database, 30 percent more likely to have a human orthologue, and nearly three times as likely to have a defined phenotype (Table 10.1). These are all indicators of research importance to human health – in other words, patented genes had more indicators relevant to research on the genetics of human diseases than our sample of unpatented genes.

We then examined the impact of gene patents on research outputs. Of the 108 mouse genes with greater than 100 associated research publications in PubMed, 86 (79.6%) were patented (Figure 10.3). Since number of publications is a metric for

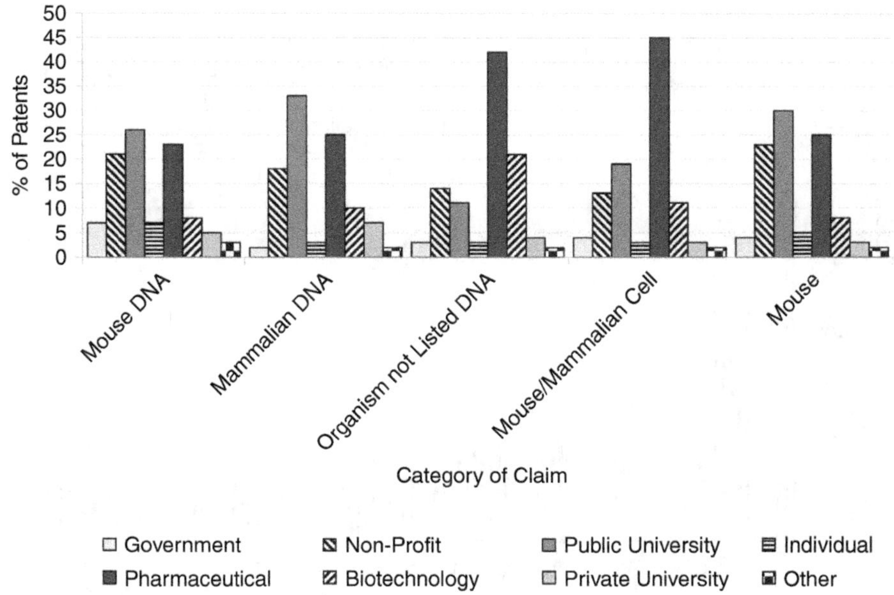

FIGURE 10.2 Percentage of 7179 US granted patents with claims that fell into five categories of mouse-related subject matter by type of assignee. Note that claims within one patent could fall within multiple categories of subject matter.

TABLE 10.1 *Characteristics of patented versus unpatented genes*

	Patented Genes (n=951)	Unpatented Genes (n=1397)
Gene Traps	600	1354
Genes on Targeting List	86.3% (821)	76.4% (1068)
Total Number of Targeting Designs	632	808
OMIM ID	64.7% (615)	39.4% (550)
OMIM Description	20.0% (190)	10.0% (141)
Gene Phenotypes	51.0% (485)	19.0% (266)
Human Orthologue	99.4% (945)	61.3% (856)

research intensity, the high level of research by groups of authors in addition to the named inventors likely represents broad community ignorance or knowing infringement of the identified patent portfolio (see also Walsh et al. 2005a, 2005b, 2007). Our interviews confirmed that the research community pays little attention to patents and/or believes that there is a broad-based research exemption. In the United States, especially after the law was clarified in *Madey v Duke*

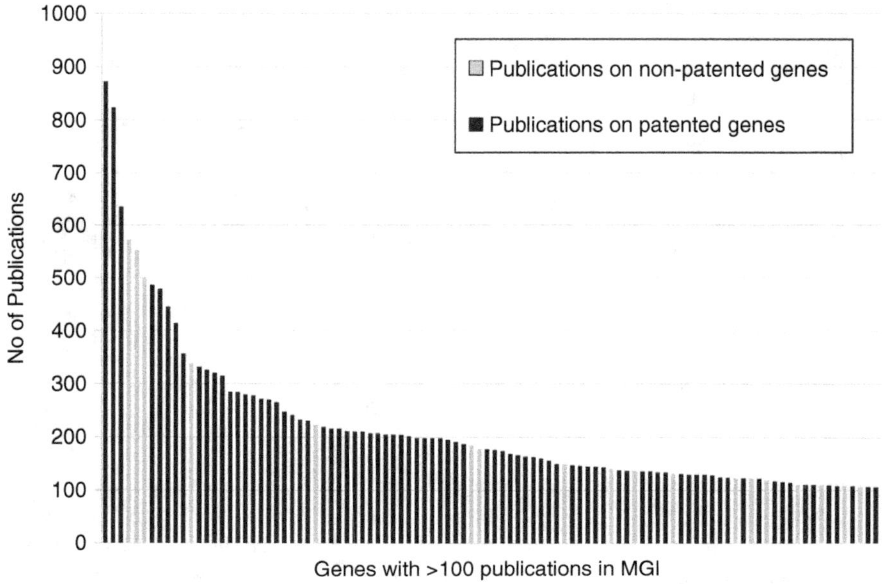

FIGURE 10.3 Genes with more than 100 associated publications in the Mouse Informatics and Genomics (MGI) database illustrating genes that are patented in the United States (black) versus those that are not patented (grey). Each bar represents one gene.

University,[1] there is a very limited research exemption in law. Nevertheless, a de facto research exemption operates because most preclinical researchers are simply not worth suing (Cook-Deegan and Heaney 2010a; Heaney et al. 2009). This further supports our contention that this patent portfolio over mouse-related research tools is of limited commercial value and merely muddies the waters for any researchers who attempt in good faith to ascertain their freedom to operate.

This conclusion could be encouraging even though it is based on broadly infringing research activity. However, our analysis further indicated that the *rate* of publications on mouse genes, based on annual rate of change, began to decline one year after a patent was granted. Publication rates for patented genes significantly decreased three years post–patent grant compared to the same time period prior to patent grant (Table 10.A2). The publication rates of our comparator set of unpatented genes remained constant over time, with no significant fluctuations in publication rate (Table 10.A4). Indeed, the publication rate for patented genes was significantly reduced compared to non-patented control genes three years post–patent grant. While the publication rate for patented genes increased to pre-patent publication levels five to seven years post–patent grant, it remained lower than publication rates on the comparator set of non-patented genes – a reversal from the pre-patent period (Figure 10.4; Tables 10.A6 and 10.A7). Prior to patent grant,

[1] 307 F.3d 1351 (Fed. Cir. 2002).

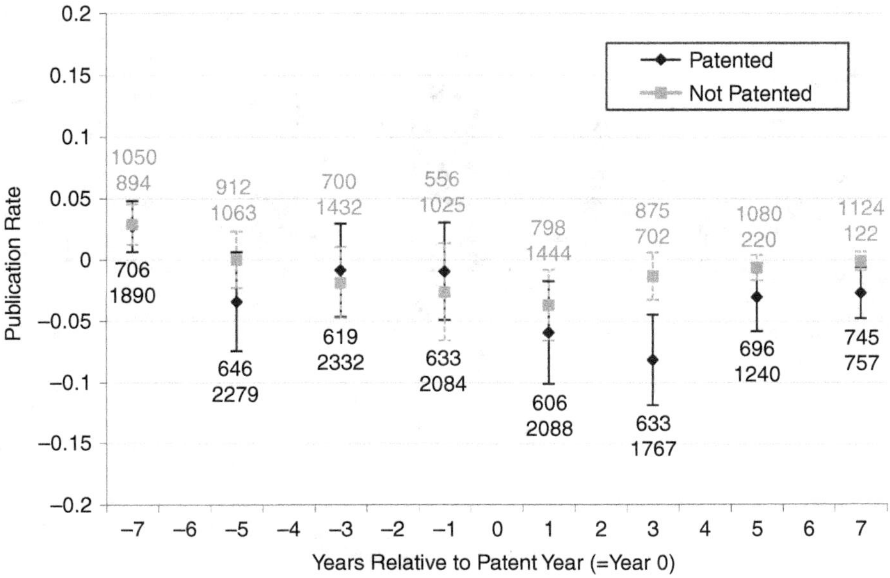

FIGURE 10.4 Publication rates of patents versus unpatented genes relative to the year of patent issue. See Appendix for methods of calculation.

publication rates for patented genes were non-significantly higher than for non-patented genes, also reflected in the fact that patented genes were among those with the highest numbers of associated publications.

For citations, which indicate follow-on research, the citation rate of patented genes declined significantly three years post–patent grant compared to similar time periods prior to patent grant (Table 10.A3); however, this trend likely reflects expected patterns of citation that rise to a peak and then decline over time – unpatented genes demonstrated the same trend of declining citation rates over time (Table 10.A5). Citation rates to publications over unpatented genes were significantly higher than publications on patented genes in six out of eight time periods (Table 10.A7). Taken together, our results imply that patenting had a negative impact on the contribution of knowledge in the scientific literature on mouse genes relevant to human health.

Our analyses imply that patenting of mouse genes had a discernible negative impact on follow-on research that used mouse models to study human disease. However, in our view, composition of matter patents were not the major impediment to the development of a mouse research commons, especially to that portion of the commons driven by high-throughput initiatives to build an international knockout mouse infrastructure. In this context, the creation of a high-throughput pipeline to generate standardized research reagents and associated data requires the aggregation of platform technologies used to generate the resource. The greatest

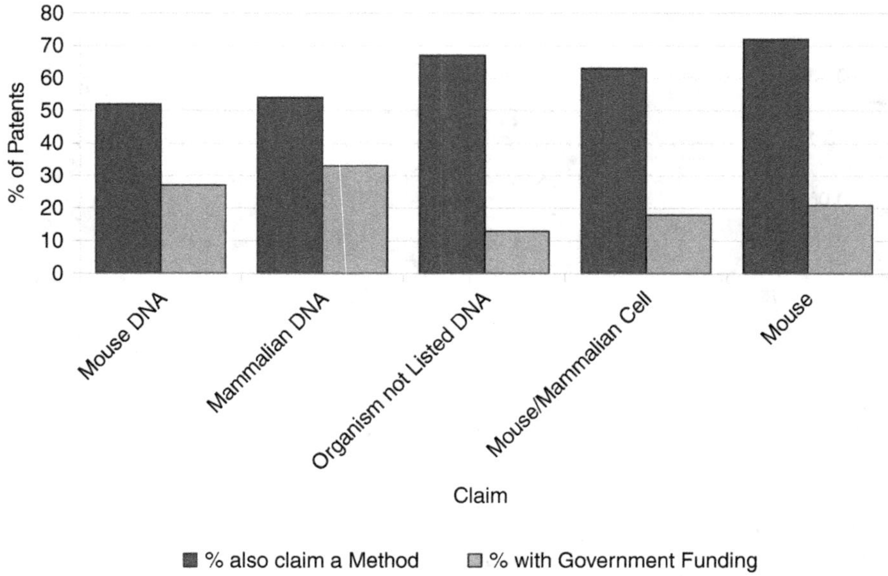

FIGURE 10.5 Percentage of 7179 US granted patents with claims that fell into five categories of mouse-related subject matter that indicated government funding and that claimed a method.

impediment to such aggregation was therefore the patenting of broad-based methods used to generate the resource. While we found that the majority of patents that claimed mouse-related compositions of matter also claimed a method for generating those materials (Figure 10.5), the most problematic 105 patents covered methods to generate the resource, held by a combination of industry and research institutions (Table 10.2).

Our conclusions on the impact of patenting of mouse-related research reagents may be summarized as follows. Our analysis identified a large number of overlapping patents on both compositions of matter and methods. Patents over mouse genes were associated with other indicators of research indicating relevance to genetics of human diseases. Most DNA patents were held by the public sector, while most cell lines and mouse-model patents were held by the private sector, reflecting their respective value to commercial and noncommercial sectors. We question the utility and expense to research institutions in maintaining this low-value patent portfolio, and this finding is likely indicative of increasing incentives to patent research outputs combined with a lack of resources within technology transfer offices to manage (i.e., prune) patent portfolios over their lifespan. Since preclinical mouse-related research is far from clinical application (timelines from Phase 1 clinical trials in humans to market authorization range from 10 to 14 years for small molecule drugs (Hay et al. 2014)), such patents are unlikely to generate

TABLE 10.2 *Mouse-related granted US methods patents by assignee as of 2007. The most problematic of the 105 methods patents covered BAC, positive/negative selection, FLP/FRT recombonase, isogenic DNA, recombineering, electroporation, PhiC31, Cryopreservation, Gateway technology,* Cre-lox, *inverse PCR, Vector construction, and homologous recombination. See table footnotes for company mergers and name changes current to 2016.*

Assignee	No. of Patents
None	9
Lexicon Genetics, Inc.	9
Institut Pasteur	7
Regeneron Pharmaceuticals, Inc.	6
University of Utah Research Foundation	6
The Salk Institute for Biological Studies	5
The Regents of the University of California	4
Invitrogen Corporation[1]	4
Genpharm International, Inc.[2]	4
Amgen, Inc.	3
Wisconsin Alumni Research Foundation	3
Artemis Pharmaceuticals, GMBH[3]	2
Deltagen, Inc.	2
Europaisches Laboratorium fur Molekularbiologie (EMBL)	2
Idec Pharmaceuticals Corporation[4]	2
Institut Curie	2
Roche Diagnostics, GMBH	2
The Institute of Physical and Chemical Research	2
The Jackson Laboratory	2
The University of Edinburgh	2
Biogen Idec, Inc.[5]	2
Centre National de la Recherche Scientifique	2

[1] Acquired by Thermo Fisher Scientific, Inc.
[2] Acquired by Bristol-Myers Squibb Company.
[3] Renamed Taconic Biosciences, Inc.
[4] Merged with Biogen, Inc.
[5] Renamed Biogen, Inc.

revenues from clinically available therapies. In addition, the patent portfolio covers preclinical *research* tools that are widely infringed, making it unlikely that a university will generate any licensing revenue. Nevertheless, any revenue is most likely to come from sister research institutions (the main users of mouse models for research), comprising a tax on public research resources.

While it appears that most researchers ignore this patent landscape, there are measurable impacts on publication and citation rates. Based on our key-informant interviews, the biggest impact lies in cultural shifts toward proprietization within the research community, which negatively impacts efforts to incentivize sharing of research reagents and associated data. Finally, broad-based methods patents may impede the generation of high-throughput resources, designed to increase research efficiency and create a research commons. We discuss the impact, based on interviews, of methods patents on high-throughput resource generation and the impediments posed to rules development and governance in the next sections.

10.4 RULES TO INCENTIVIZE AND FACILITATE PARTICIPATION IN THE COMMONS

Rules to incentivize and facilitate participation in the mouse research commons are promulgated by varied actors. As stated earlier, we use Ostrom's definition of rules-in-use as consisting of "shared normative understandings of what a participant in a position must, must not, or may do in a particular action situation, backed by at least a minimal sanctioning ability for noncompliance" (Ostrom and Hess 2007: 50). Ostrom outlines a hierarchy of rules as including formal laws; constitutional laws; policies and guidelines; and informal rules, community norms, and practices. In the previous section, we outlined the impacts of one set of formal laws – national intellectual property laws. Such generic laws are often out of sync with new capabilities, community norms, and technological advances (e.g., the development of technology platforms for high-throughput generation of research reagents). Other relevant formal laws include those associated with animal welfare standards and preclinical research requirements for regulatory approvals to advance to clinical trials. The former are closely tied to the development of the resource-generation projects, which aim to avoid duplication in the generation of live-animal models, thereby reducing the number of mice used in research (Russell and Burch 2014).

Earlier we also suggested that the policies and guidelines of funding agencies and research institutions that incentivize commercialization activities, including the seeking intellectual property rights over research outputs and partnerships with industry, may dis-incentivize participation in the commons. These policies result in an increase in secrecy and data withholding that may be contrary to the goals of open science (Walsh et al. 2005a, 2005b). Other policies and guidelines from funders, however, are broadly supportive of a research commons. Indeed, public funders internationally supported the resource initiatives of the IKMC and the IMPC, as well as existing biorepositories that are central to the mouse research commons, such as JAX.

Beyond funding, however, policies and guidelines supportive of the commons need to incentivize contributions to the commons, use of the commons, and activities that add value to the commons. These policies and guidelines codify community norms and practices for the sharing of mouse-related research tools and data. Many such guidelines exist. For example, most funding agencies require the deposit of publications and associated data into public databases (Van Noorden 2012; Whitfield 2011), and the NIH even has guidelines on the sharing of bioresources developed using NIH funds (Field et al. 2009).[2] There is, therefore, no shortage of policies and guidelines to promote sharing, but there is limited enforcement of these policies and guidelines, especially as they relate to deposit of mouse-related biomaterials (Schofield et al. 2009). Enforcement could include a denial of funding to researchers who cannot provide evidence of deposit for research tools into a recognized archive as is being contemplated by the NIH for researchers who cannot provide evidence of deposit of publications into open access archives within one year of publication (Grant 2012). Similarly, journals could deny publication without such evidence; some journals already require, for example, an accession number (evidence of deposit into GenBank) for sequence data prior to publication.[3] In terms of incentives, researchers are driven by publications and citations to those publications. The expansion of accession numbers to mouse-related research tools could provide a mechanism for attribution of effort and a means for citation to resources generated in addition to publications. These could then be recognized by research institutions in respect to assessments of researcher merit, tenure, and promotion. In other words, mechanisms for incentivization and enforcement exist but are yet to be fully implemented (Schofield et al. 2009).

In addition to policies and guidelines, MTAs and Data Transfer Agreements (DTAs) mediate the exchange of materials and data, respectively. In our case study, MTAs covered exchanges for mouse-related research reagents. As evidenced by the private sector MTAs initiated by DuPont in the 1980s, MTAs may be used to extend and protect proprietary interests over both patented and unpatented technologies. MTAs are almost universally despised by academic researchers in relation to research tools (Bubela et al. 2015a). Our interviews suggest that most academic researchers find MTAs problematic in their complexity. When mediating exchanges among collaborating researchers at different institutions, institutions insert overly onerous terms that delay negotiations and the transfer of materials (Mishra and Bubela 2014). This is especially problematic for low-value research tools in the precompetitive environment that are far from clinical application.

As types of licensing agreements (contracts that grant a permission to use), MTAs may also be used to embody the policies of funders and practices of the community with respect to the creation, maintenance, and functioning of a commons (Bubela et al. 2015a; Mishra and Bubela 2014). In other words, MTAs may be structured in such

[2] National Institutes of Health. 1999. Principles and Guidelines for Recipients of NIH Research Grants and Contracts on Obtaining and Disseminating Biomedical Research Resources. 64 *Federal Register* 72090. Retrieved from http://grants.nih.gov/grants/intell-property_64FR72090.pdf

[3] NCBI GenBank. 2015. How to Submit Data to GenBank. Retrieved from www.ncbi.nlm.nih.gov/genbank/submit/

a way that they simplify and promote sharing of research reagents rather than imposing limits on use of the materials and generating revenue and other benefits. We analyzed the extent to which the MTAs that cover mouse research tools embody sharing policies in Mishra and Bubela (2014) and found that the MTAs used to distribute mouse-related resources are generally supportive of the creation of a mouse research commons, at least among nonprofit researchers and their institutions. Since MTAs are also part of the broader governance structure of a research commons, we considered the role of repositories as mediators of exchanges between resource generators (whether individual laboratories or high-throughput resource generation programs such as members of IKMC).

In 1995, the National Institutes of Health published the Universal Biological Materials Agreement (UBMTA) and a Simple Letter Agreement for the Transfer of Non-Proprietary Biological Material (SLA) as general models for transfer of biological materials.[4] For research tools, the NIH and the Association of University Technology Managers (AUTM) recommend use of the SLA because the UBMTA is more complex and provides additional protections for patented materials (though it may also be used for unpatented materials). The KOMP repository uses an MTA largely based on the UBMTA for the distribution of its mouse resources, except that, under the terms of its funding, it additionally enables distribution to commercial entities – this additional requirement to distribute to industry means the KOMP repository cannot use the SLA (Mishra and Bubela 2014).

MTAs are used by repositories, central actors within research commons, to govern both the terms under which resources are deposited into the repository and the terms under which those resources are distributed to users. Issues arise when the deposit terms limit or otherwise impact the distribution terms. Variable terms in deposit MTAs, such as differential restrictions on commercial versus noncommercial research, need to be tracked, attached to the materials as metadata, and transferred to the distribution MTA. The operations of the repositories, and accordingly the operation of the commons, would be made more fluid by consistent, simplified terms governing both deposit and distribution. Highly variant MTAs create an

[4] The SLA provides that the material to be transferred (1) remains the property of the provider; (2) will not be used in human subjects; (3) will be used only for teaching and nonprofit research purposes; (4) will not be further distributed to third parties without permission from the provider; (5) the material will be acknowledged in publications; (6) standard warranty and liability provisions; (7) use of materials will be in compliance with laws and regulations; and (8) the material is provided at no cost beyond those associated with preparation and distribution (Retrieved from www.autm.net/resources-surveys/material-transfer-agreements/nih-simple-letter-agreement/. Accessed Dec. 12, 2015). General information is provided at www.autm.net/autm-info/about-tech-transfer/about-technology-transfer/technology-transfer-resources/ubmta/. Accessed Dec. 12, 2015.

The Association of University Technology Managers (AUTM) holds the UBMTA Master Agreements from research institutions that wish to use the UBMTA for some or all of their exchanges of biological materials (Retrieved from www.autm.net/resources-surveys/material-transfer-agreements/uniform-biological-material-transfer-agreement/. Accessed Dec. 12, 2015).

administrative burden for repositories and impose friction on commons-based sharing of mouse resources (Mishra and Bubela 2014).

Despite the existence of simplified mechanisms for materials exchanges, the use of complex, individually negotiated MTAs for research reagents is still common. Variable and negotiated MTAs rarely reflect the monetary value to the institution of the materials; indeed, they reflect a philosophical divide between institutionalized technology transfer professionals, tasked with institutional risk management and monetary returns on investment, and many researchers who wish to share their data and materials (Walsh et al. 2005a, 2005b; Walsh et al. 2007). In terms of risk management, research institutions are notoriously risk averse, but in reality, little litigation exists over exchanges for precompetitive research reagents compared to the volumes of MTAs negotiated each year (Bubela et al. 2015a). Indeed, our analysis of litigation found only 23 cases related to MTAs in the United States, of which only 4 concerned breaches of the terms of an MTA. Of interest to this chapter, although not directly relevant to mice, was an action brought by a biorepository – the American Type Culture Collection.[5] A researcher at the University of Pittsburgh was unsuccessfully prosecuted for mail fraud for using his institutionally approved account on behalf of a fellow researcher at an unapproved institution; the MTA prohibited transfer of materials to third parties. In our analysis, we do however recognize that more complex MTAs sometimes may be warranted, especially concerning exchanges of confidential information, when the contemplated transfers involve materials near clinical application or transfers to industry (Bubela et al. 2015a).

In the case of individually negotiated MTAs, AUTM and other innovation-focused institutions have further promulgated best practice guidelines that discourage some practices, such as reach-through terms that extend proprietary interests to derivative materials.[6] However, ironically, such terms were included in an effort to *promote* the research commons by the European component of the international knockout mouse project – EUCOMM. The clause in question entitled the Helmholtz Zentrum Munchen (the legal entity behind the EUCOMM Repository) "to a worldwide, nonexclusive, royalty-free, sublicensable and fully paid-up license to use, for noncommercial and teaching purposes, any IPRs that arise from the recipient's use of the EUCOMM material" (Mishra and Bubela 2014). In other words, if the recipient developed a drug based on its research using EUCOMM material, then it was obligated to grant a license to the Helmholtz Zentrum Munchen on the terms specified in the EUCOMM MTA, which were broadly supportive of research commons. In our analysis, we concluded that such

5 Order in *United States of America v. Steven Kurtz*, No. 04-CR-0155A (W.D.N.Y. Apr. 21, 2008), available at 2008 WL 1820903.

6 Organisation for Economic Co-operation and Development. 2006. Guidelines for the Licensing of Genetic Inventions. Retrieved from www.oecd.org/sti/biotech/guidelinesforthelicensingofgeneticinventions.htm; Association of University Technology Managers. 2007. In the Public Interest: Nine Points to Consider in Licensing University Technology. Retrieved from www.autm.net/Nine_Points_to_Consider1.htm

reach-through terms are equally problematic whether used to promote the nonprofit research or commercial interests because "the ability of repositories to monitor and then enforce this clause is questionable, and its complexity and presence may serve as a disincentive for potential users" (Mishra and Bubela 2014: 267).

The final complexity in materials sharing we wish to highlight is the transfer of materials to commercial entities, which raises the question of the extent to which private actors are part of the commons. In the mouse commons, commercial vendors, such as Charles River Laboratories, distribute research reagents to the pharmaceutical and biotechnology industries, as well as to nonprofit researchers. The biotechnology company Regeneron Pharmaceuticals Inc. was part of the Knockout Mouse Consortium because of its advanced capabilities in producing mouse models for pharmaceutical research.[7] Because of this commercial engagement in the development of the consortium in the United States, the KOMP repository does not restrict the distribution of its resources to the private sector. However, the situation was different in Europe, and here we tie back to the issue of background intellectual property rights over mouse-related materials and methods. The high-throughput resource generation centers needed to aggregate intellectual property rights over methods and processes used in their pipeline to construct the resource. Because of the complexity of the pipeline, however, it was not possible to identify all of the underlying IPRs and negotiate licenses for their use. The risk, therefore, was that the pipeline may have infringed IPRs, thereby making the resource-generating institutions vulnerable to patent infringement suits. It also limited the utility of the resource for industry use because in using a resource generated by infringing patents or incorporating patented materials, industry users faced patent infringement liabilities. Indeed, license negotiations over the underlying technologies continued until 2014 when a mechanism for distribution to industry was agreed upon by way of a French biotechnology company, genOway, which had aggregated identified underlying IP and took on the risk of distribution.[8]

The US members of the IKMC (the KOMP) were not so limited because of legal mechanisms available in that country (Bubela and Cook-Deegan 2015; Bubela et al. 2015b). In funding KOMP, the NIH employed a powerful legal tool commonly found in defense contracts – authorization and consent. The clause applies to patents and copyrights when use is "for and on behalf of the US

7 Regeneron's VelociMouse technology "enables the immediate generation of genetically altered mice directly from modified embryonic stem (ES) cells created by VelociGene, thereby avoiding the need to generate and breed chimeras (mice derived from a combination of modified and unmodified ES cells). This technology is faster and less expensive than other approaches currently being used. VelociMouse technology also enables the rapid creation of mice in which multiple modifications have been made in the same ES cells. This approach greatly reduces or eliminates extensive cross-breeding of mice that alters one gene at a time." Retrieved from www.regeneron.com/velocimouse

8 geoOway. 2016. Knockout and Reporter Mouse Catalogue. Retrieved from www.genoway.com/services/eucomm/eucomm-conditional-knockouts.htm?utm_source=google&utm_medium=cpc&utm_campaign=america

government."[9] When used in a research and development contract, its application means that the US government does not need to seek or negotiate a license to practice the patented invention. Moreover, 28 USC §1498 limits the government's liability for patent infringement. While the patent holder is entitled to reasonable compensation, it cannot seek an injunction, damages, or lost profits against the government or a government contractor (in this case the members of KOMP) for patent infringement.[10] In effect, the US members of KOMP, unlike their European counterparts, were protected from potential patent infringement suits, enabling KOMP to distribute the mouse-related resources to industry. We argue in the next section that distribution to industry is essential for the sustainability of the research commons.

10.5 GOVERNANCE FOR LONG-TERM SUSTAINABILITY OF THE COMMONS

The final issue we discuss here is the governance models needed to ensure that the mouse commons is sustainable over the long term, while remaining versatile and responsive to technological change (Mishra et al. 2016). The number and scale of repositories and databases supporting the mouse research commons to the global research community have expanded beyond their base, exemplified by JAX, that responded to need to share and distribute mice between individually funded research projects. The commons now includes archives that support high-throughput resource-generating initiatives. These initiatives, the IKMC and the IMPC, are international in scope, with member institutions in Austral-Asia, Asia, Europe, and North America and require sustainability of the mutant mouse resources developed by the IKMC and the IMPC (described earlier) beyond initial funding terms (Mishra et al. 2016). Here, we discuss three issues with respect to sustainability of the commons as it grows and undertakes additional tasks beyond sharing and distributing mouse models developed by individual research projects: (1) legal agreements that enable resources to be shared among and distributed by multiple archives within international consortia, (2) funding for archives, and (3) responsiveness to disruptive technologies.

The distribution of resources to researchers requires some mirroring/duplication of resources between repositories in different jurisdictions, both to ensure the security of the resource (e.g., against contamination or loss of funding for a repository) and to ease potential restrictions over the shipping of research materials to researchers across international borders. The sharing of resources across repositories within consortia remains problematic, however, because MTAs are required for such transactions (Mishra and Bubela 2014). Different drafting conventions and differences in ability to distribute to industry as opposed to only for noncommercial

[9] Judiciary and Judicial Procedure Act of 1948, 28 U.S.C. § 1498 (2016).

[10] The wording for and procedures relevant for granting authorization and consent are outlined in Federal Acquisition Regulations 52.227–1 and 27.2012–2, respectively.

research (discussed earlier) lead to difficulties in negotiating consortium agreements for the sharing of resources among repositories (Mishra and Bubela 2014). Long negotiations lead to delays, which have implications for the utility of the resources. Technological advances in this area of science are rapid, and new gene-editing technologies (Singh et al. 2015) may have superseded the utility of some aspects of the resources, in particular, the archive of mouse embryonic stem cells (Mishra et al. 2016).

The second challenge is the lack of sustained public funding. Funders commonly provide seed funding to establish archives, but such funding rarely provides a long-term investment to ensure sustainability of the resource (Mishra et al. 2016). Financial shortfalls, even if temporary, are problematic because they threaten the development and retention of highly qualified personnel and the maintenance of physical infrastructure and equipment. While there are economies of scale for larger archives, these also have higher operating costs, making them vulnerable to fluctuations in funding. Funders of archives generally demand a revenue-generation business model that transitions from outside funding to self-funding. Such models might incorporate differential pricing between noncommercial and commercial users, with the latter charged at a cost-recovery rate and the latter charged a premium rate that can be reinvested to support the operations of the archive. As discussed earlier, however, IP and other barriers to distribution to industry thus pose a problem for the financial sustainability of archives. In any event, given the realities of funding for the bulk of noncommercial users (and their decisions to allocate their research grants to purchasing research tools from archives), it is unlikely that archives will ever be self-sustaining; therefore, public funds will be needed to continue to subsidize archive operations (Mishra et al. 2016).

A further funding challenge is the lack of transnational funding models. In other words, archives operate transnationally, both in terms of depositors and distribution, but funding is national. In the context of archive consortia, national funders "find it difficult to harmonize policies and priorities to support archives in distinct jurisdictions but with networked operations" (Mishra et al. 2016: 284). Some European initiatives aim to develop new governance models to address the limitations of short-term national funding for research infrastructures, but such models are more difficult to implement across continents (Mishra et al. 2016). Thus the scale of transnational research commons limits their sustainability because of the lack of appropriate governance models that can facilitate long-term funding and prioritization of national funding agencies.

Finally, archives need to remain responsive to the utility of their resources and to technologies that may disrupt their business models. Mouse commons archives not only receive materials from small- and large-scale resource generators, store those materials, and distribute them, they also provide value-added, specialized services, such as in-depth phenotyping. Recent developments in gene-editing technologies, such as CRISPR (Clustered Regularly Interspersed Short Palindromic Repeats)

(Singh et al. 2015) are becoming increasingly cost effective and accessible to laboratories with expertise in molecular biology and use of animal models. Gene-editing technologies enable manipulation of genes in experimental organisms, such as mice, and allow for genomic alterations directly in embryos. They enable researchers to "avoid the lengthy and unpredictable process of genetically modifying [embryonic stem] cells, developing them into embryos and then into adult organisms, which may or may not be able to transmit the alterations to offspring" (Mishra et al. 2016: 287). This ability will likely reduce the reliance of researchers on archived mutant embryonic stem cell archives. Some repositories have already responded by providing gene-editing services to researchers who lack in-house capabilities, demonstrating the need for archives to adapt to new technologies to ensure long-term sustainability.

Ironically, gene-editing technologies may return the mouse-model research community to the conditions that the high-throughput resource generation projects and associated archives were designed to address, namely, non-sharing and non-standardization of mouse-related research reagents developed in individual research laboratories. As we explained in Mishra et al. (2016: 287–88):

> Despite enthusiasm for genome-editing technologies, off-target effects (unwanted mutations elsewhere in the genome) are a serious issue and may make the reagents irreproducible [(Editorial 2014; Lin et al. 2014)] … In the aggregate, the increased use of individualized "cottage industry" methods [namely gene-editing technologies] has several potential negative effects. It could divert already scarce research funds to the costly and piecemeal task of making reagents, which may have diminished quality and standardization in comparison with reagents produced using standard protocols in large resource-making efforts. Second, there are potential costs and losses from storing those reagents in ill-monitored and unstandardized small institutional freezers associated with contamination and damage.

In other words, these technologies may return the community to the "bad old days" when research groups were slow in depositing individualized reagents in archives because of the lack of incentives for doing so, or of consequences for not doing so. These conditions resulted in funder policies on data and materials sharing as well as funding for the high-throughput generation of standardized, high-quality community resources and support for associated archives. "Lessons learned are that widely dispersed resources lead to increased direct and marginal costs for funding agencies for the distribution of reagents associated with publications, duplication of resources, and increased mouse usage. The latter two effects counter the ethical experimentation aims of reduction, replacement and refinement, or '3 R' (Russell and Burch 2014). Thus, these novel technologies may be disruptive not only to archives but also to norms of open, reproducible and ethical science" (Mishra et al. 2016: 288).

CONCLUSION

In this chapter, we have discussed the lessons we have learned from the mouse model for human disease research community about rules and governance structures that sustain long-term access to international research infrastructures. With respect to rules, we focused on formal intellectual property rights and contracts in promoting or impeding research commons as well as rules development and implementation relevant to incentivizing, dis-incentivizing, and sanctioning participation in the commons. With respect to governance, we focused on policies that promote participation in the commons and funding and business models for long-term sustainability of the research commons.

The mouse research commons is international in scope and has a heterogeneous membership that varies in scale from small-scale laboratories, which develop individual mouse lines, to large-scale high-throughput generators of mouse-related research tools. This heterogeneity poses problems in facilitating the sharing of mouse-related research tools and an associated network effect, whereby resources are used and new knowledge and material are developed and re-contributed to the commons. Despite the development of archives that facilitate the sharing of mouse-related research tools through simplified rules for both sharing and relieving the logistical burdens of sharing for individual research laboratories, only 35 percent of new mice lines are shared. A plethora of policies that promote sharing are promulgated by funders and other research institutions; however, these are not accompanied by adequate enforcement strategies or incentive structures.

Contributing to the issue of incentives is the increased focus of funders on promoting the commercialization of publicly funded research outputs. Our analysis of the patent landscape indicated that the success of these incentives has contributed to the phenomenon of patenting of mouse-related research tools. While such patenting over compositions of matter has a small negative impact on follow-on research, the patenting of broad-based methods impacts the ability to develop high-throughput resource generation platforms that require the aggregation of multiple intellectual property rights. Protracted post hoc negotiations over such rights have delayed the distribution of resources, particularly to industry, a user-group that is essential to the financial sustainability of archives.

In conclusion, rules need to be put in place to incentivize use of and contributions to the commons. Where possible, MTAs and DTAs that mediate the exchange of materials and data, respectively, should be as simple as possible and avoid overly onerous terms that delay negotiations and the transfer of materials. This is especially problematic for low-value research tools in the precompetitive environment that are far from clinical application. Further governance structures are needed to address the international nature of the mouse commons. In reality, archives for research tools will require sustainable public funding to ensure their ongoing operations, utility, and ability to adapt to changing technologies and the needs of the user community. In our opinion, the issues facing the mouse commons, and the solutions that have so far driven its evolution, are not unique. The advanced nature of the mouse commons in terms of rules-in-use and governance structures as well as the debates within the community related to these issues serve as models for other biomedical research commons that aim to support the translation of research from bench to bedside.

REFERENCES

Adams, D., R. Baldock, S. Bhattacharya, A. J. Copp, M. Dickinson, N. D. Greene, M. Henkelman, M. Justice, T. Mohun, S. A. Murray, E. Pauws, M. Raess, J. Rossant, T. Weaver, and D. West. 2013. Bloomsbury report on mouse embryo phenotyping: Recommendations from the IMPC workshop on embryonic lethal screening. *Disease Models & Mechanisms* 6 (3):571–79.

Bradley, A., K. Anastassiadis, A. Ayadi, J. F. Battey, C. Bell, M.-C. Birling, J. Bottomley, S. D. Brown, A. Bürger, C. J. Bult, W. Bushell, F. S. Collins, C. Desaintes, B. Doe, A. Economides, J. T. Eppig, R. H. Finnell, C. Fletcher, M. Fray, D. Frendewey, R. H. Friedel, F. G. Grosveld, J. Hansen, Y. Hérault, G. Hicks, A. Hörlein, R. Houghton, M. Hrabé de Angelis, D. Huylebroeck, V. Iyer, P. J. Jong, J. A. Kadin, C. Kaloff, K. Kennedy, M. Koutsourakis, K. C. Kent Lloyd, S. Marschall, J. Mason, C. McKerlie, M. P. McLeod, H. Melchner, M. Moore, A. O. Mujica, A. Nagy, M. Nefedov, L. M. Nutter, G. Pavlovic, J. L. Peterson, J. Pollock, R. Ramirez-Solis, D. E. Rancourt, M. Raspa, J. E. Remacle, M. Ringwald, B. Rosen, N. Rosenthal, J. Rossant, P. R. Noppinger, E. Ryder, J. Z. Schick, F. Schnütgen, P. Schofield, C. Seisenberger, M. Selloum, E. M. Simpson, W. C. Skarnes, D. Smedley, W. L. Stanford, A. F. Stewart, K. Stone, K. Swan, H. Tadepally, L. Teboul, G. P. Tocchini-Valentini, D. Valenzuela, A. P. West, K.-I. Yamamura, Y. Yoshinaga, and W. Wurst. 2012. The mammalian gene function resource: The international knockout mouse consortium. *Mammalian Genome* 23 (9–10):580–86.

Brown, S. D., and M. W. Moore. 2012a. The International Mouse Phenotyping Consortium: Past and future perspectives on mouse phenotyping. *Mammalian Genome* 23 (9–10):632–40.

Brown, S. D., and M. W. Moore. 2012b. Towards an encyclopaedia of mammalian gene function: The International Mouse Phenotyping Consortium. *Disease Models & Mechanisms* 5 (3):289–92.

Bubela, T., J. Guebert, and A. Mishra. 2015a. Use and misuse of material transfer agreements: Lessons in proportionality from research, repositories, and litigation. *PLoS Biology* 13 (2):e1002060.

Bubela, T., S. Vishnubhakat, and R. Cook-Deegan. 2015b. The mouse that trolled: The long and tortuous history of a gene mutation patent that became an expensive impediment to alzheimer's research. *Journal of Law and the Biosciences* 23: 1–50.

Bubela, T., P. N. Schofield, C. Ryan, R. M. Adam, and D. Einhorn. 2012a. Managing intellectual property to promote pre-competitive research: The

mouse as a model for constructing a robust research commons. *Journal of Law and Information Science* 20 (2):98–121.
Bubela, T., and R. Cook-Deegan. 2015. Keeping score, strengthening policy and fighting bad actors over access to research tools. *Nature Biotechnology* 33 (2):143–48.
Bubela, T., G. A. FitzGerald, and E. R. Gold. 2012b. Recalibrating intellectual property rights to enhance translational research collaborations. *Science Translational Medicine* 4 (122):122cm3.
Carbone, J., E. R. Gold, B. Sampat, S. Chandrasekharan, L. Knowles, M. Angrist, and R. Cook-Deegan. 2010. DNA patents and diagnostics: Not a pretty picture. *Nature Biotechnology* 28 (8):784–91.
Caulfield, T., S. H. Harmon, and Y. Joly. 2012. Open science versus commercialization: A modern research conflict? *Genome Medicine* 4 (2):17.
Collins, F. S., R. H. Finnell, J. Rossant, and W. Wurst. 2007. A new partner for the International Knockout Mouse Consortium. *Cell* 129 (2):235.
Cook-Deegan, R., and C. Heaney. 2010a. Gene patents and licensing: Case studies prepared for the Secretary's Advisory Committee on Genetics, Health, and Society. *Genetics in Medicine* 12 (4 Suppl):S1–2.
Cook-Deegan, R., and C. Heaney. 2010b. Patents in genomics and human genetics. *Annual Review of Genomics and Human Genetics* 11:383–425.
Dedeurwaerdere, T. 2010a. Global microbial commons: Institutional challenges for the global exchange and distribution of microorganisms in the life sciences. *Research in Microbiology* 161:407–13.
Dedeurwaerdere, T. 2010b. Self-governance and international regulation of the global microbial commons: Introduction to the special issue on the microbial commons. *International Journal of the Commons* 4:390–403.
Editorial. 2014. Still much to learn about mice. *Nature* 509 (7501):399.
Edwards, A. M., C. Bountra, D. J. Kerr, and T. M. Willson. 2009. Open access chemical and clinical probes to support drug discovery. *Nature Chemical Biology* 5 (7):436–40.
Einhorn, D., and R. Heimes. 2009. Creating a mouse academic research commons. *Nature Biotechnology* 27 (10):890–91.
Field, D., S. A. Sansone, A. Collis, T. Booth, P. Dukes, S. K. Gregurick, K. Kennedy, P. Kolar, E. Kolker, M. Maxon, S. Millard, A. M. Mugabushaka, N. Perrin, J. E. Remacle, K. Remington, P. Rocca-Serra, C. F. Taylor, M. Thorley, B. Tiwari, and J. Wilbanks. 2009. Megascience. 'Omics data sharing. *Science* 326 (5950):234–36.
Fojo, T., S. Mailankody, and A. Lo. 2014. Unintended consequences of expensive cancer therapeutics – The pursuit of marginal indications and a me-too mentality that stifles innovation and creativity: The John Conley Lecture. *JAMA Otolaryngology Head Neck Surgery* 140 (12):1225–36.
Friend, S. H. 2010. The need for precompetitive integrative bionetwork disease model building. *Clinical Pharmacology and Therapeutics* 87 (5):536–39.
Frischmann, B. M., M. J. Madison, and K. J. Strandburg. 2014. Governing research commons. In *Governing Knowledge Commons*, B. M. Frischmann, M. J. Madison, and K. J. Strandburg eds., 1–44. Oxford: Oxford University Press.

Grant, B. 2012. NIH to enforce OA policy. *The Scientist*. November 20. www.the-scientist.com/?articles.view/articleNo/33327/title/NIH-To-Enforce-OA-Policy/

Hay, M., D. W. Thomas, J. L. Craighead, C. Economides, and J. Rosenthal. 2014. Clinical development success rates for investigational drugs. *Nature Biotechnology* 32 (1):40–51.

Heaney, C., J. Carbone, R. Gold, T. Bubela, C. M. Holman, A. Colaianni, T. Lewis, and R. Cook-Deegan. 2009. The perils of taking property too far. *Stanford Journal of Law, Science & Policy* 1:46–64.

Hess, C., and E. Ostrom. 2006. A framework for analysing the microbiological commons. *International Social Science Journal* 188:335–49.

Hess, C., and E. Ostrom. 2007. Introduction: An overview of the knowledge commons. In *Understanding Knowledge as a Commons: From Theory to Practice*, C. Hess and E. Ostrom eds., 3–26. Cambridge, MA: MIT Press.

Hunter, J. 2014. Collaboration for innovation is the new mantra for the pharmaceutical industry. *Drug Discovery World* Spring:9–15.

Jackson Laboratory. 2014. History of the Mouse Mutant Resource. Retrieved from mousemutant.jax.org/MMR-history.html.

Kim, I. Y., J. H. Shin, and J. K. Seong. 2010. Mouse phenogenomics, toolbox for functional annotation of human genome. *BMB Reports* 43 (2):79–90.

Kimmelman, J., and A. J. London. 2015. The structure of clinical translation: Efficiency, information, and ethics. *Hastings Center Report* 45 (2):27–39.

Lin, Y., T. J. Cradick, M. T. Brown, H. Deshmukh, P. Ranjan, N. Sarode, B. M. Wile, P. M. Vertino, F. J. Stewart, and G. Bao. 2014. CRISPR/Cas9 systems have off-target activity with insertions or deletions between target DNA and guide RNA sequences. *Nucleic Acids Research* 42 (11):7473–85.

Mallon, A. M., V. Iyer, D. Melvin, H. Morgan, H. Parkinson, S. D. Brown, P. Flicek, and W. C. Skarnes. 2012. Accessing data from the International Mouse Phenotyping Consortium: State of the art and future plans. *Mammalian Genome* 23 (9–10):641–52.

Mishra, A., P. N. Schofield, and T. M. Bubela. 2016. Sustaining large-scale infrastructure to promote pre-competitive biomedical research: Lessons from mouse genomics. *New Biotechnology* 33 (2):280–94.

Mishra, A., and T. Bubela. 2014. Legal agreements and the governance of research commons: Lessons from materials sharing in mouse genomics. *OMICS* 18 (4):254–73.

Munos, B. 2009. Lessons from 60 years of pharmaceutical innovation. *Nature Reviews Drug Discovery* 8 (12):959–68.

Murray, F. 2010. The oncomouse that roared: Hybrid exchange strategies as a source of distinction at the boundary of overlapping institutions. *American Journal of Sociology* 116 (2):341–88.

Murray, F., P. Aghion, M. Dewatripont, J. Kolev, and S. Stern. 2009. Of mice and academics: Examining the effect of openness on innovation. *Working Paper No 14819, National Bureau of Economic Research*.

National Center for Advancing Translational Sciences. 2015. Translational Science Spectrum. Retrieved from https://ncats.nih.gov/translation/spectrum

Ostrom, E. 1990. *Governing the Commons: The Evolution of Institutions for Collective Action, Political Economy of Institutions and Decisions*. Cambridge: Cambridge University Press.
Ostrom, E. 2005. *Understanding Institutional Diversity*. Princeton: Princeton University Press.
Ostrom, E., and C. Hess. 2007. A framework for analyzing the knowledge commons. In *Understanding Knowledge as a Commons: From Theory to Practice*, C. Hess and E. Ostrom eds., 41–82. Cambridge, MA: MIT Press.
Popp Berman, E. 2012. *Creating the Market University: How Academic Science Became an Economic Engine*. Princeton, NJ: Princeton University Press.
Ringwald, M., and J. T. Eppig. 2011. Mouse mutants and phenotypes: Accessing information for the study of mammalian gene function. *Methods* 53 (4):405–10.
Russell, W. M. S., and R. L. Burch. 2014. *The Principles of Humane Experimental Technique*. Maryland, MD: Johns Hopkins Bloomberg School of Public Health.
Sauer, B., and N. Henderson. 1988. Site-specific DNA recombination in mammalian cells by the Cre recombinase of bacteriophage P1. *Proceedings of the National Academy of Sciences USA* 85 (14):5166–70.
Schofield, P. N., T. Bubela, T. Weaver, L. Portilla, S. D. Brown, J. M. Hancock, D. Einhorn, G. Tocchini-Valentini, M. Hrabe de Angelis, and N. Rosenthal. 2009. Post-publication sharing of data and tools. *Nature* 461 (7261):171–73.
Singh, P., J. C. Schimenti, and E. Bolcun-Filas. 2015. A mouse geneticist's practical guide to CRISPR applications. *Genetics* 199 (1):1–15.
Skarnes, W. C., B. Rosen, A. P. West, M. Koutsourakis, W. Bushell, V. Iyer, A. O. Mujica, M. Thomas, J. Harrow, T. Cox, D. Jackson, J. Severin, P. Biggs, J. Fu, M. Nefedov, P. J. de Jong, A. F. Stewart, and A. Bradley. 2011. A conditional knockout resource for the genome-wide study of mouse gene function. *Nature* 474 (7351):337–42.
Van Noorden, R. 2012. Key questions in the UK's shift to open-access research. *Nature News Blog*. Retrieved from http://blogs.nature.com/news/2012/05/key-questions-in-the-uks-shift-to-open-access-research.html
Walsh, J. P., C. Cho, and W. M. Cohen. 2005a. Patents, material transfers and access to research inputs in biomedical research. *Final Report to the National Academy of Sciences' Committee Intellectual Property Rights in Genomic and Protein-Related Inventions*.
Walsh, J. P., C. Cho, and W. M. Cohen. 2005b. View from the bench: Patents and material transfers. *Science* 309 (5743):2002–3.
Walsh, J. P., W. M. Cohen, and C. Cho. 2007. Where excludability matters: Material versus intellectual property in academic biomedical research. *Research Policy* 36 (8):1184–203.
Whitfield, J. 2011. Open access comes of age. *Nature* 474 (7352):428. doi: 10.1038/474428a.

APPENDIX: METHODS FOR MOUSE PATENT LANDSCAPE AND IMPACT ANALYSIS

We searched the Thomson database Delphion on September 27, 2007, for granted US patents using the following search strategy. First we used a modification of the Ade/Cook-Deegan algorithm.[11] The algorithm restricts the search to relevant patent classes and searches claims for terms commonly associated with DNA/RNA patents: ((((((119* OR 426* OR 435* OR 514* OR 536022* OR 5360231 OR 536024* OR 536025* OR 800*) <in> NC)

AND ((antisense OR <case><wildcard>cDNA* OR centromere OR deoxyoligonucleotide OR deoxyribonucleic OR deoxyribonucleotide OR <case><wildcard>DNA* OR exon OR "gene" OR "genes" OR genetic OR genome OR genomic OR genotype OR haplotype OR intron OR <case><wildcard>mtDNA* OR nucleic OR nucleotide OR oligonucleotide OR oligodeoxynucleotide OR oligoribonucleotide OR plasmid OR polymorphism OR polynucleotide OR polyribonucleotide OR ribonucleotide OR ribonucleic OR "recombinant DNA" OR <case><wildcard>RNA* OR <case><wildcard>mRNA* OR <case><wildcard>rRNA* OR <case><wildcard>siRNA* OR <case><wildcard>snRNA* OR <case><wildcard>tRNA* OR ribonucleoprotein OR <case><wildcard>hnRNP* OR <case><wildcard>snRNP* OR <case><wildcard>SNP*) <in> CLAIMS))

AND (((mouse) OR (mus*) OR (mammal*) OR (musculus) OR (murine) OR (mice) OR (Mus musculus)))))

AND (((mammal*) <in> CLAIMS) OR ((mouse) <in> CLAIMS) OR ((mus*) <in> CLAIMS) OR ((murine) <in> CLAIMS) OR ((mice) <in> CLAIMS) OR ((musculus) <in> CLAIMS) OR ((Mus musculus) <in> CLAIMS)))

We then searched plant in claims (((Plant*) <in> CLAIMS)) and removed all patents from search one that were also found in search two.

We downloaded all available data fields for the 7179 candidate granted patent identified by our search, including title, publication date, original national class, publication number, publication country, number of claims, assignee/applicant name, assignee/applicant state/city, assignee/applicant country, USPTO assignee code, USPTO assignee name, application number, application date, application country, attorney name, domestic references, number of domestic references, forward references, number of forward references, foreign references, other references, designated states national, designated states regional, ECLA codes, Examiner – primary, Examiner – assistant, family patent numbers, inventor name, inventor city/state, inventor country, IPC-R codes, inventive IPC-R, IPC-7 codes, Main IPC-7, National class, Main national class, field of search, maintenance status code, number of pages, priority number, priority date, and priority country.

[11] The algorithm for identifying DNA patents is described at http://dnapatents.georgetown.edu/SearchAlgorithm-Delphion-20030512.htm

PATENT CODING

We read and coded all claims of all 7179 patents to (1) identify those patents that potentially claim mouse gene sequences; (2) identify the SEQ IDs of gene sequences actually claimed by patents; and (3) add additional codes, including: the assignee type (public/private university, government agency, pharmaceutical or biotechnology company, nongovernmental organization and individual inventor), any methods claimed, cell type(s) claimed, or transgenic animals claimed.

Included in our final analysis were 1144 patents that claimed mouse genes, mostly in the form of nucleotide sequences, but also amino acid sequences and a small number that claimed a gene by name. Prior to 1996, US patents did not require the genetic sequences to be listed with an associated SEQ ID.

LIST OF PATENTED MOUSE GENE SEQUENCES

The resulting list of patent number–sequence ID pairs was matched, using a simple Python script written by postdoctoral fellow at the University of Alberta, Dr. Andreas Strotmann, against the Cambia Patent Lens database of genetic sequences extracted from US patents retrieved in June 2008.[12]

We retrieved, in FASTA format, nucleotide sequences for 32,351 DNA SEQ IDs in 929 patents and 179 amino acid SEQ IDs in 105 patents for a total of 32,530 sequences or sequence patterns listed in 983 patents (note that some patents listed both nucleotide and amino acid SEQ IDs). This data set was then manually filtered to retain only those sequences that were actually claimed in patents. We collected patented sequences that were not matched to the Patent Lens database from the Entrez database (if only the gene name was specified), from the patent claims themselves, or from the Patent Analysis website.[13]

DETERMINING PATENTED MOUSE GENES

To determine the parts of the mouse genome that corresponded to the sequences in these patents, Dr. Songyan Liu, a bioinformatician, and his colleagues at the University of Manitoba performed a BLAST (basic local alignment search tool) analysis of all nucleotide and amino acid sequences identified earlier, using standard settings except for the following: Tag length ≥ 25; Expect < 0.001; Score ≥ 48 (Figure 10.A1). The Expect value setting means that there is a less than 1 in 1000 chance that the gene match is the result of pure chance. This is significantly lower than in the usual bioinformatics setting but higher than the Expect=0 exact match

[12] Bacon, N., D. Ashton, R. A. Jefferson, and M. B. Connett. 2006. "Biological sequences named and claimed in US patents and patent applications, CAMBIA Patent Lens OS Initiative." Retrieved from www.patentlens.net

[13] Patent Analysis. n.d. "Free databases." Retrieved from www.patentanalysis.com/index.php?pagetype=news_databases

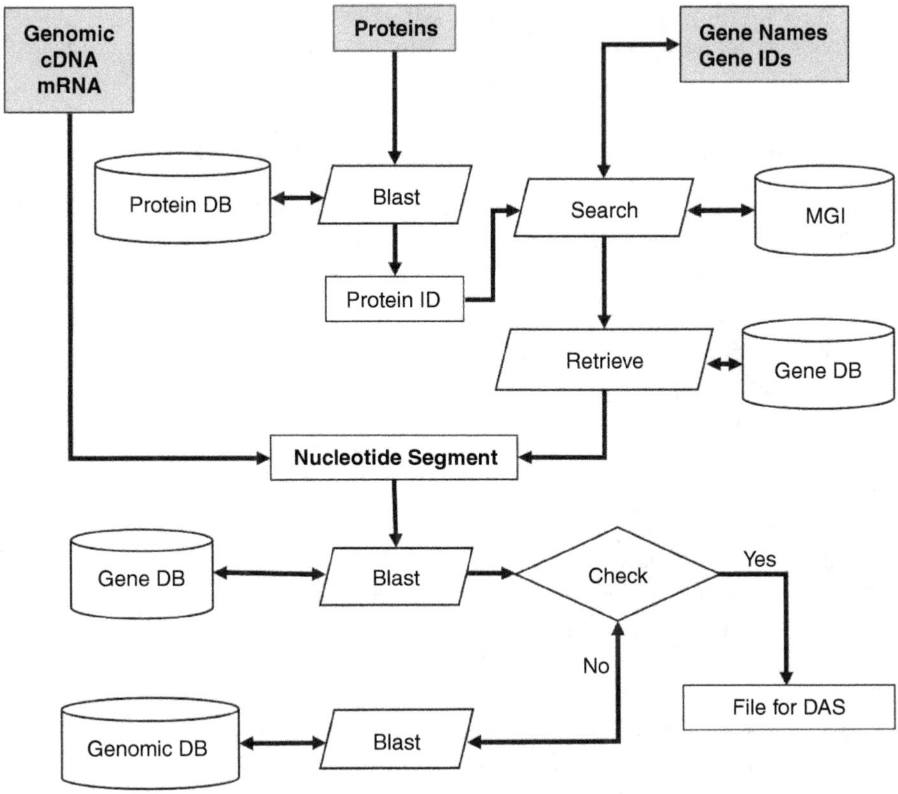

FIGURE 10.A1 Schematic of BLAST analysis – to match sequences identified from patents to the annotated mouse genome.

requirement in Murray and Jensen (2005).[14] The reasons for this choice are (1) most patent documents specifically state that they cover any genetic sequence *similar* to the one listed in the patent and (2) the sequence being patented and the corresponding sequence in the Ensembl database may be from different alleles of the same gene. In all cases, we retained only the best hit.

Using this method, we identified 1886 nucleotide sequences against the known mouse genome. An additional 62 entire genes were claimed by name or description rather than sequence. For the genes claimed by name or description, we searched the NCBI Entrez Gene database for entries matching their identifying description found in the patent claims. The resulting matches were added to the data set.

Our matching method identified 1692 genetic sequences from 952 mouse genes claimed, as a whole or in part, in 1049 US patent applications; including one mitochondrial gene (out of 37 known). This equates to 2.9% of the 32,480 mouse genes available in NCBI Mouse Build 37 against which we matched our sequences.

14 Jensen, K., and F. Murray. 2005. "Intellectual property. Enhanced: Intellectual property landscape of the human genome." *Science* 310 (5746):239–40.

Other sequences were from unknown species with low homology to the mouse genome, were for noncoding fragments (i.e., did not map onto known mouse genes) or were artificial sequences.

COLLECTING INFORMATION ON PATENTED MOUSE GENES

For each of the 952 identified genes, Dr. Songyan Liu, at the University of Manitoba, and his colleagues extracted the following information from bioinformatics databases in December 2008:

- Trap hit: how many known hits were available for this gene.
- Gene targeting status: 822 of the patented genes (86%) had a corresponding targeting request at one of the knockout mouse consortia.
- OMIM information on the gene: 616 patented genes (65%) had an OMIM ID, 191 (20%) an OMIM description.[15]
- OMIM disease descriptors for 952 – (649 + 6) = 297 patented genes (31%).
- MGI phenotypes available for each gene: 485 of the patented genes had some kind of phenotype listed (51%).[16]
- Detailed Gene Ontology information per gene – all functions, processes, and components where this gene is known to play a role; 888 of the genes (93%) had one or more gene ontology entries.
- 945 genes (99.2%) had entries for all three gene ontology components in the MGI Gene Ontology Slim Chart;[17] that is, seven of the patented genes were still classified as "novel genes" at MGI at the time the searches were run.
- PubMed IDs for publications relevant to the gene.
- For mouse genes, this information is hand-curated by MGI and uploaded to the NCBI Entrez Gene database; 906 of the genes (95%) had corresponding PubMed publications.
- Human orthologues for the mouse gene: 866 of the genes (91%) had a known human orthologue.[18]
- MGI information: 883 of the genes (93%) had an MGI identifier.
- Coordinates for the gene's position in the genome; this information is used for visualizations of the mouse gene patent landscape – it is available for all matched genes.

15 McKusick-Nathans Institute for Genetic Medicine, Johns Hopkins University (Baltimore, MD), and National Center for Biotechnology Information, National Library of Medicine (Bethesda, MD). 2009. "Online Mendelian Inheritance in Man, OMIM."

16 Bult, C. J., J. T. Eppig, J. A. Kadin, J. E. Richardson, J. A. Blake, and the members of the Mouse Genome Database Group. 2008. "The Mouse Genome Database (MGD): Mouse biology and model systems." *Nucleic Acids Research* 36 (Database issue):D724–28.

17 MGI. n.d. "MGI Gene Ontology GO_Slim Chart Tool." www.informatics.jax.org/gotools/MGI_GO_Slim_Chart.html

18 MGI. 2016. "MGI reports: Human and mouse orthology." Retrieved from ftp://ftp.informatics.jax.org/pub/reports/index.html#orthology

We also calculated statistics for genes using the MGI Gene Ontology Slim Chart Tool. These statistics were in addition to information specific to each genetic sequence mapped to each gene: Strand matched; Direction of match; Position of matched sequence in the genome; Chromosome (1-Y, mitochondrial); and Quality of match (score).

COMPARISON SET OF NON-PATENTED MOUSE GENES

For comparison purposes, Dr. Songyan Liu randomly selected a comparable number of unpatented genes. First, we randomly determined 2000 Ensembl Gene database entries for mouse genes. Of these, we removed 56 that were in the list of patented genes. Second, we searched for the remaining 1944 genes in MGI and identified 2012 hits. We removed 489 genes from this list if they did not have an official MGI symbol, 47 genes because they were in fact pseudogenes, and 96 genes because they were duplicates, including genes with multiple loci or Y chromosome genes that were a duplicate of X chromosome genes. In total, therefore, we selected 1397 genes for the control set to compare against our 952 patented genes out of a total of 32,480 possible genes (including mitochondrial genes) from NCBI Mouse Build 37.

As earlier, we extracted the following information in February 2009 on the genes from bioinformatics databases:

- 1069 genes (77%) had been investigated for targeting.
- All genes in this control set had hits in all three components of the MGI Gene Ontology Slim Chart (i.e., none were "novel genes").
- 144 genes (10%) had a corresponding OMIM ID; 133 (9.5%) had associated detailed disease identifiers.
- 266 genes (19%) had associated phenotype information.
- 1079 (77%) had at least one component of associated Gene Ontology information.
- 1211 (87%) had associated PubMed publications.

MOUSE GENE LITERATURE

We downloaded the full XML records for the MGI mouse gene associated PMIDs from PubMed, which resulted in 23,805 publications on patented mouse genes and 10,684 on non-patented mouse genes in December 2008. We then downloaded full records for literature that cited those publications from Thomson's ISI database. In detail, we

- Parsed XML PubMed records into an SQL database, using a Python script written by Dr. Strotmann, to extract (1) author names, affiliation; (2) article title, major MeSH codes; and (3) journal name, issue, year, number, pages.

- Located and downloaded full corresponding records in the Thomson ISI database so that we could download all citing literature. We located 98% of PubMed records in ISI.

STATISTICAL ANALYSIS

The goal of our statistical analysis, performed by consulting biostatistician Dr. Shawn Morrison, was to determine if the citation and publication rates for publications on mouse genes (1) changed after patenting and (2) differed between publications on patented and unpatented mouse genes. We considered eight time periods: ±1, ±3, ±5, and ± 7 years before and after patenting. For patented genes, date "0" was the date the US patent was granted. For non-patented genes, date "0" was the median time from the original publication to the date of the search. This gave us a distribution of publications that had from 0 to at least 14 years of publication and citation data. Given the length of time from scientific publication to patent grant, the two data sets had similar distributions around the patent date and the median publication date.

We retained only those articles that had sufficient data to estimate all year intervals for analysis. For example, if an article had ±4 years of data, it was included in the ±3 years analysis, but not the ±5 analysis. Some genes had sufficient data for the pre-patenting period but not the post-patenting period (and vice versa), and therefore sample sizes vary for each period.

Data in the original data set was on a per article basis (citations per year and per article). We re-summarized this information on a *per gene* basis rather than a *per article* basis. For example, in a given year, if one article about gene 'X' was cited 10 times, and another article about gene 'X' was cited 5 times, then the result was a total of 15 citations for that gene in that year. This per gene data was used to calculate citation rates and was the basis for summary statistics and t-tests (described later).

We calculated the publication and citation rates per gene for the eight periods. Calculation of citation rate requires information regarding the change in the number of publications/citations from one year to the next. For example, the citation rate in the first year post-patenting would be the rate from Year 0 to Year 1, the rate for the second year would be the rate from Year 1 to Year 2, and so on. More formally, the citation rate was the natural log of the ratio between the years of interest – this provides an estimate of the instantaneous rate of change at that point in time (i.e., the slope).

Some genes had a number of publications/citations in a given year but declined to zero citations in the next. This created difficulties in calculating rates (i.e., division by zero), and these genes were excluded from analysis. Fortunately, this only applied to a relatively small number of genes. The exception to this filtering rule occurs when both the starting and ending years had zero citations. In this case, the rate was unchanged (and calculated as a rate of change = 0.00).

TABLE 10.A1 *Rate calculations for publications*

Period of Interest (relative to patent year)	Year of Citation Data per Gene		
	From	To	Rate Calculation
–1	0	–1	ln(pubs in year-1/ pubs in year 0)
+1	0	+1	ln(pubs in year 0/ pubs in year+1)
–3	–3	–2	ln(pubs in year-3/ pubs in year -2)
+3	+2	+3	ln(pubs in year+2/ pubs in year+3)
–5	–5	–4	ln(pubs in year-5/ pubs in year-4)
+5	+4	+5	ln(pubs in year+4/ pubs in year+5)
–7	–6	–7	ln(pubs in year-7/ pubs in year-6)
+7	+6	+7	ln(pubs in year+6/ pubs in year+7)

Therefore, the years used in the calculation of publication rate for this analysis are shown in Table 10.A1 (note that the same rate calculation was applied to citations).

SAMPLE CALCULATIONS AND CONVERSIONS

If an article was cited 10 times in the year of patent grant (Year 0) and cited 11 times in the year following (Year 1), then the rate of citation during the first year post-patenting (Year 0 to Year 1) would be:

$$\text{Citation Rate} = \ln\left[\frac{11}{10}\right] = 0.09531$$

To estimate the percentage increase in citations over a given period, it is necessary to convert the instantaneous rate of change (r) to the finite rate of change (λ) as follows:

> $\lambda = e^r$, where "λ" is the finite rate of change and "r" is the instantaneous rate of change. λ may be thought of as a "multiplier" between years. In the previous example, one would have to have an increase of 10% for the number of citations to increase from 10 to 11. The multiplier in this situation is 1.1, or a 10% increase.

For example, if $r = 0.09531$, then the finite citation rate is calculated as $e^r = e^{0.09531} = 1.1$ per year, which is interpreted as a 10% increase in the number of citations. To convert back, the equation is as follows: $\ln(\lambda) = r = \ln(1.1) = 0.09531$.
The relationship between r and λ is shown in the accompanying table.

Citation Rate Is	r	λ
Decreasing	<0.0	<1.0
Stable	=0.0	=1.0
Increasing	>0.0	>1.0

Thus, the citation rate is increasing when r >0 and/or λ >1.0.

ANALYSIS AND RESULTS

Summary statistics for publication and citation rate per gene were calculated for each time period (Tables 10.A2–10.A5). Time periods were compared using Welch's t-tests[19] which are similar to the common Student's t-test but without the requirements for equal variances or equal sample sizes. A t-test was conducted for each period (±1, ±3, ±5 and ±7 years pre- and post-patenting) within publications and citations. Welch's t-tests were then used to compare each time period between patented and unpatented genes for both publication and citation rates. To compensate for false positive significance as a result of large sample sizes and multiple t-tests, we increased the significant P-value from 0.05 to 0.01. In the following tables, significant differences are bolded. In addition for each time period, we compared publication and citation rates between patented and unpatented genes using Welch's t-test (Table 10.A6).

TABLE 10.A2 *Summary statistics for publication rate per patented gene*

Period Relative to Patent Grant Year	Mean (r)	Std. Error	# genes	# publications	Years Compared	P-value	t-value	df
1 year prior	−0.009	0.020	633	2084	−1 to +1	0.091	1.691	4159
1 year post	−0.059	0.021	606	2088				
3 years prior	−0.008	0.019	619	2332	**-3 to +3**	**0.007**	**2.710**	**4043**
3 years post	−0.082	0.019	633	1767				
5 years prior	−0.034	0.021	649	2279	−5 to +5	0.873	0.160	3504
5 years post	−0.030	0.014	696	1240				
7 years prior	0.027	0.011	706	1890	−7 to +7	0.564	0.578	2386
7 years post	−0.027	0.011	745	757				

[19] Welch, B. L. 1947. "The generalization of 'student's' problem when several different population variances are involved." *Biometrika* 34:28–35.

TABLE 10.A3 *Summary statistics for citation rate per patented gene.*

Period Relative to Patent Grant Year	Mean (r)	Std. Error	# genes	# citations	Years Compared	P-value	t-value	df
1 year prior	0.417	0.028	680	118037	−1 to +1	0.052	1.94	237635
1 year post	0.344	0.024	738	144949				
3 years prior	0.473	0.032	490	73537	−3 to +3	<.0001	7.276	157969
3 years post	0.179	0.024	779	193711				
5 years prior	0.568	0.043	325	39525	−5 to +5	<.0001	7.965	66863
5 years post	0.179	0.024	740	222987				
7 years prior	0.572	0.063	184	21173	−7 to +7	<.0001	8.806	28759
7 years post	−0.030	0.026	647	236608				

TABLE 10.A4 *Summary statistics for publication rate per unpatented gene.*

Period Relative to Median Publication Date	Mean (r)	Std. Error	# genes	# publications	Years Compared	P-value	t-value	df
1 year prior	−0.026	0.020	556	1025	−1 to +1	0.668	0.429	1988
1 year post	−0.037	0.015	798	1444				
3 years prior	−0.018	0.015	700	1432	−3 to +3	0.770	0.292	2126
3 years post	−0.013	0.010	875	702				
5 years prior	0.0003	0.012	912	1063	−5 to +5	0.624	0.491	1280
5 years post	−0.006	0.005	1080	220				
7 years prior	0.029	0.008	1050	894	−7 to +7	0.038	2.086	261
7 years post	−0.001	0.004	1125	122				

TABLE 10.A5 *Summary statistics for citation rate per unpatented gene.*

Period Relative to Median Publication Date	Mean (r)	Std. Error	# genes	# citations	Years Compared	P-value	t-value	df
1 year prior	0.632	0.027	960	44835	−1 to +1	<.0001	15.801	98752
1 year post	0.696	0.023	1027	73640				
3 years prior	0.602	0.046	332	14329	−3 to +3	<.0001	11.593	17770
3 years post	0.040	0.016	1187	171824				
5 years prior	0.332	0.051	154	8652	−5 to +5	<.0001	4.047	10459
5 years post	0.116	0.016	1142	224631				
7 years prior	0.204	0.059	109	5287	−7 to +7	<.0001	16.046	7113
7 years post	−0.812	0.024	1119	235114				

TABLE 10.A6 *Summary statistics for comparison within each time period of publication rate for patented and unpatented genes Statistically significant differences are bolded.*

Period Relative to Year 0*	P-value	t-value	df
7 years prior	0.896	0.130	2731
5 years prior	0.147	1.451	3260
3 years prior	0.679	0.414	3760
1 year prior	0.560	0.584	2747
1 year post	0.389	0.862	3418
3 years post	**0.001**	**3.211**	**2407**
5 years post	0.114	1.583	1449
7 years post	0.023	2.284	873

TABLE 10.A7 *Summary statistics for comparison within each time period of citation rate for patented and unpatented genes Statistically significant differences are bolded.*

Period Relative to Year 0*	P-value	t-value	df
7 years prior	**<.0001**	**4.266**	**18451**
5 years prior	**0.0004**	**3.547**	**22556**
3 years prior	0.022	2.294	30776
1 year prior	**<.0001**	**5.467**	**133264**
1 year post	**<.0001**	**10.570**	**204122**
3 years post	**<.0001**	**4.851**	**325261**
5 years post	0.028	2.203	392287
7 years post	**<.0001**	**22.378**	**467887**

* Note that in Tables 10.A6 and 10.A7, year 0 is the year the patent was granted for patented genes and the median year for publications from first publication to date of search for unpatented genes (December 2008) for unpatented genes.

11

Constructing Interdisciplinary Collaboration: The Oncofertility Consortium as an Emerging Knowledge Commons

Laura G. Pedraza-Fariña

INTRODUCTION

In 2002, under the leadership of then-Director Dr. Elias Zerhouni, the National Institutes of Health (NIH) launched the Roadmap for Medical Research Initiative (Roadmap) with the goal of "reconfigur[ing] the scientific workforce by encouraging novel forms of collaboration."[1] The initiative was the result of several rounds of consultation with stakeholders, scientists, and health care providers, who were asked to identify major opportunities and gaps in biomedical research that no single institute at NIH could tackle alone.[2] One overarching theme emerged from these consultations: understanding the puzzle of complex diseases would require the expertise of nontraditional teams with divergent perspectives that cut across traditional disciplines.[3] Calling interdisciplinary science teams the "wave of the future,"[4] Zerhouni emphasized that assembling these nontraditional teams would require a paradigm shift in medical research.[5] The Roadmap initiative was launched to support this shift by identifying (and funding) potentially transformative research requiring collaboration and coordination across NIH institutes and across traditional scientific disciplines.[6]

Despite consensus among multiple stakeholders that interdisciplinarity is necessary to solve complex biological problems, conducting interdisciplinary team research

Laura G. Pedraza-Fariña is Assistant Professor of Law at Northwestern University Pritzker School of Law, Chicago, Illinois.

1 Elias A. Zerhouni, US Biomedical Research: Basic, Translational, and Clinical Sciences, 294 *JAMA* 1352, 55 (2005).

2 See, e.g., Elias A. Zerhouni, The NIH Roadmap, 302 *Science* 63 (2003).

3 See, e.g., Elias A. Zerhouni, The NIH Roadmap for Medical Research, presentation delivered on February 27, 2004, slide 13, www.webconferences.com/nihroadmap/ppt/02%202–27%20RM%20webcast%20EZ%20final%20v.4.ppt

4 Elias A. Zerhouni, A New Vision for the National Institutes of Health, *J. Biomed. Biotechnol.* 159 (2003).

5 Ibid. 6 See Zerhouni, note 2, at 63.

presents a number of important challenges related to coordination and information sharing across institutional and disciplinary boundaries – or what Frischmann, Madison, and Strandburg have called "boundary-spanning dilemmas."[7] Scientists are embedded in scientific "communities of practice."[8] Researchers who are part of the same community of practice usually share a common training trajectory and a set of assumptions and vocabulary to describe phenomena under study. They also interact with one another regularly, through scientific conferences, informal information exchanges, and collaborations. As a consequence, membership in a particular scientific community influences scientists' methodological approach to problems, the types of problems that they consider important, and the background assumptions made when addressing these problems.[9] In contrast, interactions between research communities can be fraught with obstacles. Scientists unfamiliar with the techniques or the body of knowledge of another field may not be able to evaluate that field's experimental designs and the quality of its results. Vested social interests in the set of skills and theoretical perspectives of their own community can lead to resistance to "outsider" approaches. In turn, this resistance can generate personal costs to crossing disciplinary boundaries, in addition to learning a new skill set, such as social isolation and loss of social standing.[10]

The Roadmap initiative represents an important opportunity to study the design of knowledge commons whose goals are to exchange information across disciplinary and institutional boundaries and to create new knowledge at their intersection. Fostering team science served as a guiding principle for all Roadmap grants.[11] But one subset of grants, the Interdisciplinary Research Consortia, was specifically designed to fund interdisciplinary research. This grant funded nine consortia for a period of seven years (2005–2012).[12] The consortia ranged in focus from the study of new ways to regenerate organ parts from stem cells (combining developmental biology, engineering, and computational approaches)[13] to research into fertility preservation techniques for young cancer patients through the Oncofertility Consortium (bringing together

7 Brett M. Frischmann, Michael J. Madison, and Katherine J. Strandburg, Governing Knowledge Commons, in *Governing Knowledge Commons* 1 (Brett M. Frischmann, Michael J. Madison, and Katherine J. Strandburg eds., Oxford University Press 2014), at 37.

8 Researchers have used different terms, such as "scientific social worlds" and "invisible colleges" to describe groups of scientists who share social networks. Importantly, these networks do not only track disciplinary lines. For example, communities can be formed around studying a particular disease, using a particular model organism, or focusing on understanding a particular organ. See Laura G. Pedraza-Fariña, Patent Law and the Sociology of Innovation, 2013 *Wisc. L. Rev.* 839 (2013) ("communities of practice," "scientific social worlds," or "invisible colleges," as they have alternatively been called, are defined by a core set of activities: accepted practices, techniques, legitimate research goals, training procedures, and relationships among a cluster of practitioners). See also Zerhouni, note 3, at slide 3.

9 Pedraza-Fariña, note 8, at 838–40.

10 Ibid. at 843–47.

11 NIH Roadmap Accelerates, *NIH News* (Mon. Oct. 4, 2004) ("Team science is an underlying current of the entire NIH Roadmap effort").

12 https://commonfund.nih.gov/Interdisciplinary.

13 https://commonfund.nih.gov/Interdisciplinary/consortia; https://commonfund.nih.gov/Interdisciplinary/consortia/syscode

reproductive endocrinologists, oncologists, molecular biologists, biological engineers, and cryobiologists).[14]

Each one of these consortia can be analyzed as a knowledge commons, since they all seek to institutionalize the sharing of resources among members of a new, interdisciplinary community. The resources shared all involve knowledge (including novel experimental techniques at the intersection of multiple disciplines), but some consortia also share rivalrous resources such as patient samples. All consortia were designed to lower the costs of conducting interdisciplinary research by creating an NIH-supported framework for the sustained co-creation and exchange of information, research protocols, samples, reagents, and ideas with the goal of addressing a well-defined research question at the intersection of multiple disciplines. Importantly, the Roadmap grant was designed to serve as a catalyst to collaboration – providing short-term, seed funding to enable cross-disciplinary connections. Because funding for all consortia has already ended, it is possible to study whether the grant enabled new relationships among fields that continued absent NIH funding and infrastructural support.

This chapter will focus on a particular commons nested within the Oncofertility Consortium: the National Physicians Cooperative (NPC). The Oncofertility Consortium was founded to address the unmet need of cancer survivors (and in particular female survivors) for fertility preservation options at the time of diagnosis. As cancer treatments have become more sophisticated and effective, the number of cancer survivors – and in particular childhood cancer survivors – has increased worldwide.[15] But research on the impact of cancer therapeutics on male and female fertility, as well as research on fertility preservation techniques for females, has lagged behind. So has the availability of fertility services for newly diagnosed cancer patients: at the time of the grant, the infertility industry was structured to deal exclusively with planned in vitro fertilizations but not equipped to offer emergency procedures. And despite the rising numbers of patients living cancer free, treating oncologists seldom discussed the treatment's effect on fertility or options for fertility preservation with their patients.[16] This was the case despite studies showing that cancer patients rank fears of losing their fertility second only to those of facing death.[17] As a result, many cancer survivors were confronted with a second devastating diagnosis: that of infertility resulting from their cancer treatments. One fundamental reason for this disconnect

14 https://commonfund.nih.gov/Interdisciplinary/consortia; https://commonfund.nih.gov/Interdisciplinary/consortia/oncofer

15 L. A. G. Reis, M. P. Eisner, C. L. Kosary et al. (eds.), *SEER Cancer Statistics Review, 1973–1999* (Bethesda, MD: National Cancer Institute 2002).

16 Oncofertility grant, at 134, on file with author.

17 Carrie L. Nieman, Karen E. Kinahan, Susan E. Yount, Sarah K. Rosenbloom, Kathleen J. Yost, Elizabeth A. Hahn, Timothy Volpe, Kimberley J. Dilley, Laurie Zoloth and Teresa K. Woodruff, Fertility Preservation and Adolescent Cancer Patients: Lessons from Adult Survivors of Childhood Cancer and Their Parents, 138 *Cancer Treat Res.* 201 (2007).

between the needs of cancer patients and research and treatment priorities was the lack of communication and collaboration between oncologists and reproductive endocrinologists. The Oncofertility Consortium sought to remedy this "information, data, and option gaps"[18] and "serve as an authoritative voice for research, clinical practice and training that happens at the intersection of oncology, pediatrics, reproductive science and medicine, biomechanics, material science, mathematics, social science, bioethics, religion, policy research, reproductive health law, cognitive and learning science in a new discipline called ONCOFERTILITY."[19]

The Oncofertility Roadmap grant contained a series of sub-grants structured around an administrative core to support the members of the consortium by providing governance and a communication and data-sharing plan.[20] The NPC, funded through a P30 core grant, was an integral part of the consortium's roadmap for addressing the disconnect between reproductive endocrinologists' and oncologists. The NPC had several missions: first, to serve as a repository for testicular and ovarian tissue for scientific research; second, to provide a referral network and serve as a connector between oncologists and reproductive endocrinologists; and third, to serve as a forum to exchange ideas, develop and disseminate new clinical research methods and technologies for ovarian research, as well as patient education and advocacy tools.[21] The NPC also aimed to serve as a reproductive medicine network that enabled researchers to conduct longitudinal studies on ovarian tissue.[22] Ovarian tissue for basic research would be obtained from cancer patients who would be asked to donate 20 percent of their tissue for research (80% would be cryopreserved for fertility preservation).[23]

To succeed, the NPC needed to recruit reproductive clinics (most of which did not traditionally serve cancer patients), convince them that providing emergency procedures for cancer patients was a worthwhile endeavor, and train them in cryopreservation procedures. But recruiting reproductive endocrinology clinics was only half of the puzzle: without referrals from treating oncologists, few patients would find their way to these clinics. Thus the NPC also sought to enlist

18 The grant application describes the unmet needs of the cancer-survivor community in these terms. The "information gap" refers to the lack of information regarding cancer treatment's effect on fertility and fertility preservation options to newly diagnosed cancer patients. The "data gap" refers to the "paucity of data on the precise gonadotoxicity of cancer drugs," and the "option gap" refers to the lack of research into fertility preservation techniques for females, including prepubescent girls. Oncofertility grant, at 137–38, on file with author.

19 Oncofertility grant, at 134, on file with author.

20 In addition to the U54 administrative core grant, the consortium was comprised four R01 grants for basic research into female follicles, and for addressing emerging social issues in oncofertility, two P30 cores, one educational and three training modules.

21 http://oncofertility.northwestern.edu/NPC.

22 Oncofertility consortium conference, NPC Panel, comments by Teresa Woodruff, December 2007.

23 National Physicians Cooperative of the Oncofertility Consortium Letter of Agreement ("NPC Letter of Agreement"), item 6. ("With the remainder of the tissue the patient can donate approximately 20% of the remaining ovarian cortex to the NPC for research use and the remainder will be frozen for the patient's own use.")

major research centers with oncology providers and to build a referral corridor between those providers and reproductive endocrinology centers.

The NPC has been successful in achieving several of its main objectives. In particular, it has created a robust referral network between oncologists and reproductive endocrinologists in several of the 50 US states where none had existed beforehand; it serves as a forum to synthesize current research into fertility preservation options and research, and to provide easy access to research tools (through detailed, annotated protocols and video demonstrations). Finally, it facilitates the exchange of ideas among oncologists and endocrinologists through a series of monthly expert group meetings, and an annual conference.

My case study suggests that the following factors were key to the NPC's success. First, echoing findings from studies on successful scientific social movements, the involvement of a "high-status intellectual actor,"[24] in this case Dr. Teresa Woodruff, with a high degree of trustworthiness in the eyes of consortia members, and with a network of preexisting relationships that formed the core of the consortium, was crucial to the program's success and continuity. Second, the NPC transitioned from a relatively "closed" format, in which protocols, findings, and access to expertise were available only to NPC members to an "open" format. A closed format appeared necessary to generate buy-in for the initial NPC consortium members. Once the consortium was firmly established, and with a higher degree of institutionalization (as evidenced by the creation of several expert working groups, and a cadre of new medical graduates who prioritized oncofertility), the consortium became more open – sharing most of its research findings, protocols, and expertise with any interested researcher or clinician.

The remainder of this chapter is organized as follows. Section 11.1 explains the methodology of this case study. Section 11.2 explains in more detail the background context in which the NPC is embedded and the coordination and discipline-bridging challenges the NPC, and the Oncofertility Consortium more broadly, sought to overcome. Section 11.3 describes the types of resources that the NPC is tasked with administering and creating. Section 11.4 explores the NPC's transition from a closed to an open community model. This section also discusses the history of the NPC, focusing on how its founding members described the existing barriers to collaboration in the area of fertility preservation for cancer patients that the NPC sought to address. Section 11.5 analyzes the NPC's governance structure. Section 11.6 analyzes the costs and benefits of the NPC both to its members and to the public at large. Section 11.7 concludes by synthesizing a set of hypotheses about successful commons management, and comparing them to conclusions drawn through other existing studies of scientific consortia.

[24] See Scott Frickel and Neil Gross, A General Theory of Scientific/Intellectual Movements, 70 *Am. Sociol. Rev.* 204, 211 (2005).

11.1 METHODOLOGY

My approach follows the modified version of the IAD framework described by Brett M. Frischmann, Michael J. Madison, and Katherine J. Strandburg.[25]

Specifically, I did the following:

- ***Conducted a literature review***. I reviewed available public documentation about the Roadmap Grant and about the Oncofertility Consortium. In addition, I obtained access to the full Oncofertility Consortium application for a Roadmap grant, and additional grants that currently support the consortium's activities. I also obtained access to the NPC Letter of Agreement, which must be signed by those who wish to join the NPC.
- ***Reviewed stored video footage of all oncofertility conferences and virtual grand rounds; attended 2016 Oncofertility Conference***. The Oncofertility Consortium website makes available video footage of all yearly oncofertility conferences since the consortium was launched in 2007. It also makes available virtual grand rounds – presentations by researchers working in the area of oncofertility. I also attended in person the 2016 Oncofertility Conference.
- ***Conducted a series of semi-structured interviews.*** I interviewed 12 professionals involved with the Oncofertility Consortium – whom I determined to be key informants: the named principal investigators (PIs) in all of the Oncofertility Consortium grants and all past and present administrators of the NPC. Interviews were tailored to each individual's role within the consortium and structured to seek answers to the key questions in the IAD framework.

11.2 THE NATIONAL PHYSICIAN'S COOPERATIVE BACKGROUND ENVIRONMENT

The National Physician's Cooperative emerged out of a concerted effort by a group of basic science researchers and clinicians to meet the reproductive needs of cancer survivors. The NPC's work is thus fundamentally shaped by the background social norms and practices of four distinct groups of professionals: (1) treating oncologists who first diagnose and treat cancer patients; (2) reproductive endocrinologists who, until the consortium's coordinated efforts, largely treated cancer survivors for infertility long after cancer treatment; and (3) scientists conducting basic science research on ovarian follicles. The NPC is also nested within the Oncofertility Consortium and thus constrained by the terms of the initial Roadmap consortium

[25] See Michael J. Madison, Brett M. Frischmann, and Katherine J. Strandburg, Constructing Commons in the Cultural Environment, 95 *Cornell L. Rev.* 657 (2010), and Frischmann, Madison, and Strandburg, Governing Knowledge Commons, in *Governing Knowledge Commons*.

grant. Finally, the ability of the NPC to meet its goals is also influenced by the interaction among the different NIH institutes that make up the Roadmap grant.

11.2.1 *Three Distinct Communities of Practice: Oncologists, Reproductive Endocrinologists, and Basic Research Scientists*

11.2.1.1 Oncologists

Oncologists are the first group of practitioners who encounter cancer patients. Because they drive the referral pattern to reproductive endocrinology clinics, the oncology community is a key component of a successful oncofertility program. Despite advances in cancer treatment that dramatically increased the odds of surviving cancer, and in particular childhood cancer, oncologists seldom discussed fertility with their female cancer patients prior to the creation of the Oncofertility Consortium. The reasons for this are manifold, but three in particular represent a common thread across all interviewees. First, oncologists' *research priorities* into cell proliferation and cell death (the hallmarks of cancer) meant that there was scant research into the fertility effects of cancer chemotherapeutic agents for different populations – and thus little information to give patients as to the effect of chemotherapeutic drugs on their fertility.[26] There was also a widespread assumption in the oncology community that hormones that would be used to stimulate egg production for fertility preservation were counter-indicated for women with cancer. For example, a PI in the oncofertility grant described a key hurdle to getting oncologists interested in fertility preservation as follows: "Oncologists thought hormones cause cancer. So, there was this notion that hormones are bad. And, they're not. And they're not causing cancer. This was just this kind of zeitgeist."[27]

Second, oncologists had developed particular practice styles and protocols that had become entrenched. Fertility preservation required a significant modification of these established practice routines. For example, a clinician member of the NPC remarked,

> There are individuals who have styles of practice. The issue for oncologists is living or dying. From the outset you see patients for cancer, the team says so and so has this cancer, and it's very hard and you don't know how much they have to live . . . My colleagues in oncology, they are so busy and they are so much dealing with living and dying issues. How to treat the cancer, what kind of cancer is it. They are getting pulled in all different directions about taking the cancer out. Talking about fertility preservation is not in their agenda. They are not trained to do it. The questions that are going to come out they are not ready to answer.[28]

[26] "[M]edical oncologists are not aware of the precise reproductive threats of their treatments on reproductive outcomes and clinical reproductive endocrinologists do not routinely treat cancer patients." Oncofertility grant, at 137, on file with author.

[27] Interview with Oncofertility Grant Principal Investigator, basic sciences track.

[28] Interview with Oncofertility Grant Principal Investigator, clinical track.

Finally, oncologists held particular ideas about their patients' priorities, which did not include a focus on fertility preservation. A PI with a background in endocrinology described her experience speaking with oncologists as follows: "they would tell me, we don't worry about [fertility], [the patients] should really think about that later and they are not married so they are not even thinking about that."[29] Another interviewee similarly remarked:

> These physicians had in-bred biases about how to deliver care to these patients. And those biases ran again from "Don't bother her, she's got enough on her mind right now, my focus is on getting her well. Don't worry about the esoteric stuff, she can't afford this. Don't even bring it up," to my favorite "Adoption is always an option," which we knew from our research was not the case. But they had all these biases that came from old school kinds of treatment and the fact that they hadn't re-calibrated their thinking to the fact that these were diseases that killed people in the last generation so we didn't have to worry about them.[30]

11.2.1.2 Reproductive Endocrinologists

While oncologists drive the referral pattern for cancer patients to receive fertility preservation, endocrinologists must also be equipped to provide fertility preservation to cancer patients for a successful oncofertility program to emerge. And prior to the creation of the Oncofertility Consortium, the practice styles of reproductive endocrinology programs were built around healthy, informed patients – not sick patients with limited knowledge of fertility treatments. This meant that reproductive endocrinology centers were not set up for performing emergency procedures. They were also, according to several interviewees, "used to patients who are the smartest medical consumers on the planet"[31] because "they've read everything that they can read about infertility for the most part, they've already maybe even gone through some procedure."[32] In contrast, oncology patients "think they're going to die. No matter how good the prognosis is. So, reproductive endocrinology is not used to having that kind of complexity."[33] As a consequence, prior to the formation of the Oncofertility Consortium, reproductive endocrinologists only came in contact with cancer patients long after the completion of their cancer treatment, when damage to their fertility was often already irreversible.

11.2.1.3 Basic Research Scientists

The Oncofertility Consortium also sought to bring together several communities of basic scientists to work on developing techniques for maturing eggs in vitro (a

[29] Interview with Oncofertility Grant Principal Investigator, basic research track.
[30] Interview with Oncofertility Grant Administrator.
[31] Interview with Oncofertility Consortium Patient Coordinator. [32] Ibid. [33] Ibid.

technique that would allow fertility preservation for prepubescent girls). To do so, it brought together engineers, biologists working on primate models of ovarian development, reproductive scientists, and cryobiologists. Although these groups did not traditionally work together, the particular individuals who made up the initial oncofertility grant all had preexisting relationships with Woodruff, the PI who spearheaded the Oncofertility grant. In particular, a number of both clinicians and basic scientists were part of an NIH group that brought together scientists who studied the ovary. Despite knowing one another, and one another's work, these scientists had not previously collaborated to address the key research questions posed by the oncofertility grant application: how can we mature follicles in vitro? How can we best understand follicle dynamics? Interviewees uniformly attributed this previous lack of collaboration to the entrenched practice styles of basic science researchers that develop early in a doctoral student's career, and to an 'unspoken' penalty for this type of collaboration in basic research. For example, one PI remarked:

> So, you use bench science, you write the paper, your students . . . do their work, they get their grant, their PhD, you get a grant and you repeat and it's a vicious cycle, but it's the cycle that we've all established to be the way we're going to increase our fount of knowledge but the problem is that doesn't allow you to escape that gravitational force and move into broader spheres . . . Now, there's kind of a penalty for collaboration; it takes a little more from everyone and it takes a lot more from one person. Whoever is leading the effort, there's more of a kinetic energy loss. So, you have to put more in and I think that's okay, because I think that's when you succeed, that's when the program can go ahead. So, if you don't put that loss in, if you don't put that extra kinetic energy in, everything can really then fall apart, because there is no center; there is no gravitational force. Everybody will go back to doing what they do.[34]

11.2.2 *The Roadmap Grant and the NIH Institutes*

The Roadmap grant sought to fund interdisciplinary team research projects that required a trans-NIH funding mechanism where multiple NIH institutes would work together. Indeed, according to several principal investigators involved in the Oncofertility Consortium, it was particularly hard to obtain individual investigator grants (or Rzero1 grants) for work at the intersection of reproductive endocrinology and engineering because it did not fit squarely into the work of any one NIH institute.[35] The Oncofertility Consortium sat at the intersection of the National Cancer Institute (NCI), which funds cancer research; the National Institute of Child Health and Development (NICHD), which funds fertility research; the

34 Interview with Oncofertility Grant Principal Investigator, basic sciences track.

35 For example, one PI explained: "[We] were doing these projects together that were really striving to make momentum and the first time we sent our grant in, the NICHD said: 'Well this is really good, but it's really cancer'. . . We fell through the cracks, our work just couldn't really go anyplace."

National Institute of General Medical Sciences (NIGMS), which funds basic approaches to cellular mechanisms; and the National Institute of Biomedical Imaging and Bioengineering (NIBIB), which funds basic and applied biomaterials and tissue-engineering research. The Roadmap grant sought to combine the work of all of these institutes by creating an administrative core whose purpose was to "reduce barriers, encourage research, solve problems, maintain documents and provide a robust intellectual environment with shared vision and an altruistic approach to credit and results."[36]

11.3 RESOURCES

The NPC creates, manages, uses, and shares a number of resources, ranging from tangible patient samples to an intangible referral network. These resources can be organized into three distinct categories: (1) patient samples; (2) research tools, reagents, and experimental protocols (including Institutional Review Board (IRB) approval protocols), and related know-how; and (3) referral network and brand name. While the three categories are related, each one has specific characteristics and presents particular types of social challenges that warrant individual analysis. The Oncofertility Consortium also receives monetary and infrastructure resources crucial for its sustainability from the NIH in the form of grants, and from multiple research institutions in the form of office space and administrative support.

11.3.1 *Patient Samples*

One of the main goals of the NPC is to serve as a repository for the ovarian tissue of cancer patients. Patients who chose to have ovarian tissue cryopreserved had the option of donating 20 percent of their tissue for research purposes, and keeping 80 percent for their own fertility preservation.[37] The cryopreserved tissue could later be thawed and transplanted into the patient – a technique that at the time of the grant had resulted in live births but that carried the risk of reintroducing cancer cells into the patient.[38] The portion of the tissue reserved for research was meant to provide samples to support consortium research projects. In particular, the bulk of the research samples was used for studies on in vitro follicle maturation funded by the consortium Rzero1 grants, that is, how to take immature follicles present in ovarian tissue and transform them into mature eggs.[39] Mature eggs could then be used for in vitro fertilization. Unlike tissue transplantation, this technique did not run the risk of reintroducing cancer cells into the patient. Tissue samples were also used to optimize new cryopreservation techniques. NPC members could apply for access

[36] Oncofertility grant, at 159, on file with author. [37] NPC Letter of Agreement, note 23.
[38] Interview with Oncofertility Consortium Principal Investigator. [39] Ibid.

to research tissue by submitting their own research proposals for consideration by the steering committee.

Because any individual reproductive endocrinology clinic sees only a handful of cancer patients, developing a national repository for ovarian tissue and for patient information is a key step to gathering sufficient data to make important discoveries regarding the impact of chemotherapy and the success of fertility treatments on different patient subpopulations. Tissue samples are an inherently rivalrous resource; as a consequence, the largest challenges facing the NPC regarding these samples was how to collect sufficient tissue to carry out research, and how to prioritize distribution of the tissue among NPC members who wanted to carry out research studies. Recruiting fertility centers required that the centers be willing to apply for (and obtain) approval from their institution's IRB and set up a cryopreservation protocol at their institution. Because ovary tissue must be cryopreserved shortly after extraction, participating centers also needed to learn and apply standardized tissue cryopreservation techniques, using consortium-approved freezing media and protocols to ensure reproducibility.

The NPC was extremely successful in recruiting reproductive fertility centers to donate tissue to the repository, quickly exceeding its initial goals. The reason for its success lay in the lack of interest on the part of most reproductive fertility centers to carry out their own research projects (thus diminishing concerns about allocation of scarce tissue resources) coupled with the ability of the NPC to trade access to tissue for other resources of value to reproductive fertility centers. In particular, *access to know how and reputational benefits* were both crucial elements in obtaining buy-in from fertility centers. For the first three years of the consortium's existence, core members provided training in tissue cryopreservation, as well as access to cryopreservation media – critical know-how in the field – only to NPC members. One NPC administrator who personally delivered lectures and training modules to several NPC allied centers explained: "[Learning how to do] tissue freezing and the possibility of being part of research was a big one. We also had a commercial company manufacture all of the media and freezing solutions. And we provided that to them for a charge. So, they were getting the secret recipe that no one else was going to have. That set them apart."[40] In addition, being an active participant in oncofertility research, as well as being associated with the consortium, provided a reputational boost to fertility clinics. As a NPC member explained: "Some of these people [at reproductive endocrinology clinics] had an interest in research but they couldn't do it because they were in practice. People were part of this Oncofertility Consortium that had this cache of being academic science and research."[41] Similarly, a former NPC administrator noted:

> A lot of IVF in this country is done in small IVF centers. Those people don't do enough clinical work to generate research [but] they would really love to be

40 Interview with Oncofertility Consortium Administrator.

41 Interview with Oncofertility Consortium Principal Investigator, clinical track.

> involved in research. And so, we were able to go out and appeal to these people and say, look, if you'll take the ride with us and go through the IRB process . . . you'll be involved in the research side of things simply by having contributed.[42]

Finally, to capture the expertise and clinical data of those centers that were interested in following their own protocols for ovarian tissue cryopreservation and keeping their own tissue for research, the NPC developed the "clinical membership" tier. Clinical members had access to know-how developed by the Oncofertility Consortium and were also able to contribute their own experience to the common knowledge pool through participating in NPC monthly and annual meetings. An NPC administrator explained the rationale for the different membership tiers as follows:

> Just in the last handful of months we've had a call where it's a center interested in joining the NPC, but saying "we already have an ovarian tissue protocol open, that's been open already for five years and it's been successful, can we still be a member?" So in that case that's fine because otherwise if we say, "Oh well, you have to switch to our protocol," then we're going to lose them as an NPC member and we're going to have no data that we're gathering from them. Whether it's a survey study or participating in meetings. So that was a way to have another membership tier so we're not shoving people away... [We tell them that the NPC] is always here as a resource, if this is something that you would like to switch over to someday, we can discuss it. You're in the fold already. In that case, there's not been too much pushback.[43]

11.3.2 *Research Tools, Reagents, Experimental Protocols, and Related Know-How*

The core members of the Oncofertility Consortium (i.e., the named principal investigators in the original interdisciplinary research grant) pioneered a series of experimental protocols to grow follicles in 3-D matrices,[44] to translate technology developed in vitro and in mice to primates,[45] and to freeze ovarian tissue.[46] Although several of these experimental protocols were published in peer-reviewed journals, many required in-person training to be carried out successfully. In addition, while protocols were continuously refined, those improvements were not always reflected in printed publications. For example, at the NPC launch in 2007, Woodruff explained the informational benefits of NPC membership:

42 Interview with Oncofertility Consortium Administrator.

43 Interview with Oncofertility Consortium Administrator.

44 This technique resulted from a collaboration between Dr. Teresa Woodruff, a reproductive biologist and Dr. Lonnie Shea, a bioengineer. See, e.g., L. D. Shea, T. K. Woodruff and A. Shikanov, Bioengineering the Ovarian Follicle Microenvironment, 16 *Ann. Rev. Biomed. Eng.* 29 (2014).

45 Oncofertility grant, at 151, on file with author.

46 Ibid.

> The key is that there is a lot of real knowledge that is embedded that has not come out in vetting some of these tables [from published papers]. And as we go forward, as people are really looking at this in a new and different way, we are going to be able to substantively change those documents. We'd like to get not only those pdfs but we'd like to annotate those pdfs. Getting your paper and having you annotate that, and then saying, what we now need to know is X. Now you may have the opportunity to study 100 more patients.[47]

Through its website, the NPC created a library of up-to-date, annotated protocols and videos of key procedures.[48] These protocols were only available to NPC members during the first three years of the consortium. In addition, core members of the Oncofertility Consortium would often travel to new NPC sites to show them how to perform key procedures in person.[49] Finally, cryopreservation media was, until quite recently, available only to NPC members. Access to both know-how and key reagents was an important draw of the NPC – and one that, as described in the previous section, was often sufficient to incentivize centers to contribute research tissue to the Oncofertility Consortium. One NPC administrator summed up the importance of the informational resources aggregated and created by the NPC as follows: "You got access to all this information. You got support, so when you had your very first case, we would fly someone out to you, to show you how to dissect the tissue and how to freeze it appropriately. And we also pay for all of your media. So we send you all the media that you're going to need. It's totally free, you don't have to pay anything."[50] Another NPC member and administrator similarly remarked: "The interesting thing about it was there was a lot of training that they got. It was a lot of intangibles, but there was very little money exchanged . . . Unlike a drug study where money is usually the motivator, this was more, well, I'm on the waiting edge of something cool."[51]

A key social dilemma that would be expected to arise in a data-sharing commons, especially one that involves sharing of know-how that cannot be easily gleaned from publications, is that members of the NPC who were not actively generating data or important know-how would free-ride on this knowledge, potentially using it to make competing discoveries or disclosing it to active research competitors. This concern was somewhat mitigated by the fact that most NPC members were not themselves actively engaged in research, and that Oncofertility Consortium members were getting something in return – valuable research tissue for their exclusive use. Nevertheless, interviews reveal that researchers were certainly worried about the dangers of disclosure. In fact, although annotated protocols and know-how were

47 Presentation at NPC Launch, Dr. Teresa Woodruff.

48 See, e.g., video coaching on how to prepare ovarian tissue for transport, http://oncofertility.northwestern.edu/media/prepare-human-ovary-for-fresh-transportation

49 Interview with Oncofertility Consortium Patient Coordinator.

50 Interview with Oncofertility Consortium Administrator.

51 Interview with Oncofertility Consortium Administrator.

certainly widely shared, ongoing and unpublished research findings were only discussed among a small core group of oncofertility researchers – namely the principal investigators named in the initial grant (and members of their laboratories) who held monthly virtual meetings. As will be explored later, these researchers were part of a preexisting social network and enjoyed high levels of trust in one another.

11.3.3 *Referral Network and Brand Name*

A final type of resource created by the NPC was a referral network whereby oncology providers (and others whose patients required treatment that could endanger their fertility) could be readily put in contact with local IVF centers that could perform emergency ovarian tissue-freezing protocols. In addition, the Oncofertility Consortium has developed a brand name with positive reputational externalities attached to it. Indeed, as the consortium's website states, "the Oncofertility Consortium® logo is a trademarked advocacy ribbon that reflects the growing concern for the reproductive future of cancer patients."[52] Branding materials (including the Oncofertility Consortium's logo, and PowerPoint presentation templates) are available to all NPC members, and generally available to download from the Oncofertility Consortium's website. As with any trademark, the consortium faced the possibility of its logo and name being used by NPC and non-NPC members in a manner that would not be consistent with Oncofertility Consortium goals, or to claim credit inappropriately for discoveries made by the consortium as a whole.

11.4 TRANSITION FROM A CLOSED TO AN OPEN COMMUNITY: THE ROLE OF PREEXISTING SOCIAL NETWORKS, TRUST, AND PATENT RIGHTS

A key attribute of a research commons is whether the resources that it creates and manages are available to the larger public or whether they are kept within the commons. As of this writing, the NPC shares many of its resources with members and nonmembers. But this was not the case when the NPC was founded. This section places the history of the NPC's creation within the larger context of the Oncofertility Consortium's history and goals, charts the NPC's transition from a relatively closed community to an open access structure, and addresses the factors that contributed to the initial decision to restrict access to NPC members and those who influenced its transition to an open infrastructure. It also places the NPC's structure within the broader framework of the Oncofertility Consortium, analyzing how information sharing took place in the consortium as a whole.

The idea for applying for an NIH interdisciplinary grant to form a consortium to address fertility preservation in cancer patients originated with Teresa Woodruff. Herself a reproductive endocrinologist, Woodruff was, in 2001, the director of

[52] http://oncofertility.northwestern.edu/branding-materials

basic sciences for the Cancer Center at Northwestern University. Through her work as a center director, Woodruff came in regular contact with cancer researchers and oncologists. As she describes it, her conversations with oncologists – who downplayed fertility preservation concerns for cancer patients – did not resonate with her experience with cancer survivors. Prompted by this gap between oncologists' and patients' views of fertility, Woodruff began work on trying to close that gap. Seeking to address a key hurdle in fertility preservation for women at the time – the inability to transform immature follicles into eggs in vitro – she began a collaboration with an engineer who also worked at Northwestern University, Dr. Lonnie Shea.[53] Woodruff explains how she brought together the core grant members, and the crucial role that the Interdisciplinary Research Consortium grant played in advancing the project:

> Lonnie Shea and I were doing these projects together that were really striving to make momentum ... [Our project] was very good, but then the grants would fall between the cracks because the portfolio for the NIH had no way to understand fertility in a cancer setting ... It fit neither under the NCI nor the NICHD ... Zerhouni decided with the Roadmap grant ... to take that common fund and ... ask the biomedical community, tell us what your most intractable problems are and how will you solve them using teams. And I thought that that was the best thing ever because what that said was that we could take something like oncofertility, which didn't fit and just make it an unmet need. And it was an intractable problem because there were no women, zero, who were getting fertility counsels at the time.[54]

Following the request for applications (RFA) for the interdisciplinary consortium grant from the NIH, Woodruff brought together the researchers who would become the principal investigators in the grant. At the time of the RFA, Woodruff and several of the principal investigators in the oncofertility grant were members of the Specialized Cooperative Centers Program in Reproduction Research (SCCPRR) – a program that fosters translational research projects in the reproductive sciences. This program also provided a venue for interaction with other programs around the nation that focused on reproductive research. One such venue was the Ovarian Focus Group Meeting, which took place every six months. In one of these meetings in the fall of 2005, Woodruff brought up the idea of putting together an application for an interdisciplinary consortium grant that would focus on oncofertility. As explained by Dr. Richard Stouffer:

53 This initial interaction between Dr. Teresa Woodruff and Dr. Lonnie Shea was mediated by Dr. Steven Rosen, the then-Director of the Cancer Center at Northwestern University. Dr. Rosen also recognized the option gap for cancer patients, and for the pediatric population in particular. Interview with Dr. Steven Rosen.

54 Interview with Dr. Teresa Woodruff.

> At the end of our focus group, Teresa said, "Let's talk about this" and she also invited [an] NICHD representative. So at that point, we had a person there, Teresa Woodruff, who had been working on follicle development, primarily in rodent models. She and I had collaborated some before (in fact we had one patent at one point when she was with Genentech). I was working on the monkey ovary, so I was using a primate model. Christos Coutifaris and Jeffrey Chang were both clinicians, who were working with infertility patients – polycystic ovarian syndrome, etc. So, we sat around and talked about that area and various aspects and how to treat it and several of the options came up . . . The two interdisciplinary aspects that were added was one that Teresa was aware of at Northwestern, which was with Lonnie Shea, who was a bioengineer, where she had the suggestion that it was possible to take small follicles out of the ovaries of rodents, put them into these alginate-type beads, basically Jello-type beads, and grow the follicles until a point that you could get a mature egg. So, Lonnie Shea was added to develop matrices and to consider ways that we can improve matrices to allow follicles to grow in vitro. But we realized of course that probably the best way to do this would be as patients determine that they have cancer that they would either decide to bank their eggs [or freeze ovarian tissue] . . . It's very difficult to freeze individual eggs, although we've made quite a bit of progress in that . . . So we decided we needed to add a second interdisciplinary person, which was a cryobiologist.[55]

One element in the composition of the original group of researchers that stands out is that most of them were part of a preexisting research network. Several of the founding members of the Oncofertility Consortium had known one another for a long time and held high levels of trust (both in their individual integrity and in their scientific abilities) and in Woodruff, the principal investigator who spearheaded the grant. Several had also collaborated prior to the consortium grant.[56] For example, one of the principal investigators, Dr. Mary Zelinski explained her relationship with Richard Stouffer and Teresa Woodruff as follows:

> Because of our interest in follicles we had known of Teresa's work for a very long time . . . And then if you're in a similar area, you get invited to give presentations at their home institution. So, we had all done that. Dick and I at Northwestern earlier and Teresa had been at our Primate Center. Well, since the very beginning of her career in science. So, we had known her for a long time.[57]

Similarly, Lonnie Shea remarked:

55 Interview with Dr. Richard Stouffer.

56 See, e.g., S. A. Pangas, H. Saudye, L. D. Shea, and T. K. Woodruff, Novel Approach for the Three-Dimensional Culture of Granulosa Cell-oocyte Complexes, 9 *Tissue Eng.* 1013 (2003); J. D. Brannian, T. K. Woodruff, J. P. Mather, and R. L. Stouffer, Activin-A Inhibits Progesterone Production by Macaque Luteal Cells in Culture, 75 *J. Clin. Endocrinol. Metab.* 756 (1992).

57 Interview with Dr. Mary Zelinski.

> I like to think that I have a good lab and Teresa obviously has a great lab as well. And I think we happened to hit a situation where two people with great labs came together and I think it bought us some really exciting science and some really exciting progress. And I think that, ultimately, it's the people that connect. And the ability for those people to work together. And Teresa and I have just been incredibly fortunate that we've just both had the same vision for the long-term goals and really stuck to it.[58]

None of them, however, had embarked on a collaboration of this magnitude, or held a focused discussion on how to address fertility preservation questions in a concerted manner prior to applying for the Oncofertility Consortium grant.

Within this original group of collaborating principal investigators, raw data was shared with an openness that many noted was "uncharacteristic" of their field. All of the interviewees in this core group credit this uncharacteristic data sharing with both accelerating the speed of discoveries and enabling different types of discoveries. Stouffer describes the level of data sharing and its impact on his research as follows:

> I think what made it so exciting was we had monthly virtual lab meetings . . . We could sit there every month and show our data to the rodent people, and say, "Look, you can grow these follicles in 14 days. But look, it takes us 5 weeks." What we found for example was that some of the follicles would actually just sit there and just look at you . . . And then you had others that would grow over the five weeks and turn into these beautiful, gorgeous antral follicles. And you'd sit there and say, "You know, what's this heterogeneity? Do you see this in the rodent?" And they would go, "No". . . But then you sit there and think, "Well, so how does this relate to follicles from humans?" For example, we found if we took follicles from young, reproductive age monkeys, what would be considered 20 year olds in humans they did really well, would give us a lot of those large growing follicles. If we took them from animals that were over 15 years of age, we didn't . . . And we thought, "Well, what did this mean for the cancer patient that's 40 or 35 as opposed to 20?". . . It made us think on a much broader scale and made us think that immediately because we were having these tremendous and exciting virtual lab meetings every month.[59]

Others similarly remarked that the combination of unusual data sharing with high levels of trust among researchers became "infectious," giving rise to a virtuous cycle of more openness and collaboration:

> What I loved about it was the openness of the sharing of data. You can't make advances unless you can share what you found and Teresa is a perfect example of that. [She would often say] "Oh here's what we can do now. We'd love to see if it works in your system and we'll help you in every way." And then that is infectious

[58] Interview with Dr. Lonnie Shea. [59] Interview with Dr. Richard Stouffer.

among people who share a similar science personality and it makes it very, very fun as a part of your career and also is critical for advancing the field.[60]

Beyond this core group of researchers, members of the NPC – but not the public at large – also received broad access to resources (including know-how developed by core members). Indeed, according to some interviewees, having privileged access is what prompted NPC members to join the cooperative. A former NPC administrator explained the decision to restrict access to NPC members as follows:

> Everything was closed ... because I felt that we had to create an exclusive club, in order to get people to want to join it ... For the first three years, anything that we provided was for members only. We had an 800 number where any patient or provider in the United States could call and they would be triaged to a local IVF program that was staffed and set up at Northwestern. But only members of the NPC got the benefit of those referrals. The training was only provided to NPC members. The ability to get access to reagents and so on [was] only [for] NPC members. We had a password-protected website. And only the members had the passwords and all of the documentation that they would need to take care of their patients, best practices and so on. We went beyond that, we had templated letters that they could use for the insurance companies. So, it was all an integrated whole that was seen as very beneficial. But many of them still would ask, "Are you going to do this for my competitor across-town?[61]

After spending its first three years as a closed community, the NPC eliminated its password-protected feature and transitioned to a more open structure. This transition was likely enabled by a combination of factors. First, the pull exerted from the basic science research norm of openness in sharing protocols and reagents played an important role: whether to make data and resources freely available to the general public was a source of disagreement among several core group members, many of whom thought closeness was "against the spirit of research."[62] In addition, once the NPC became an established group with a core membership and recognized reputation, exclusivity lost its importance in achieving buy-in from potential members. Rather, being part of a recognized network provided a reputational boost sufficient to encourage membership. In fact, NPC administrators report a surprising increased interest in membership when protocols were made widely available. This likely happened for two reasons: first, the annotated protocols and videos served as a *signal* of the worth of the cooperative; second, some of the benefits of membership reside in acquiring important know-how and being part of a reference network – all of which are still more readily available to NPC members. As a current NPC administrator remarked: "People if they find our protocols, they'll reach out and they'll say, 'You know, I saw these protocols. What do we need to do if we want to be a member? How

60 Interview with Dr. Mary Zelinski.
61 Interview with Oncofertility Consortium Administrator.
62 Ibid.

do we get this implemented? Is this something you can help with?'"[63] Finally, not all resources are accessible to non-NPC members. Access to research tissue is open only to NPC members. And although some non-NPC members have been given permission to purchase culture media (necessary to freeze ovarian tissue) from the NPC's commercial manufacturer, media is much more readily available to NPC members.

Oncofertility Consortium research led to several patents, owned by different combinations of principal investigators. For example, principal investigators Lonnie Shea and Teresa Woodruff are co-inventors on patent applications regarding methods for growing follicles in engineered alginate beads.[64] Researchers had an ambivalent relationship to patents. On the one hand, most found patents important both for commercializing technological developments in oncofertility, and for securing credit for their inventions. On the other, researchers worried that patenting their inventions would send the wrong signal to patients that they were profiting from their contributions to the NPC. Because none of the technologies patented by Oncofertility Consortium researchers has yet been licensed to a commercial company, it remains to be seen whether and how the NPC and named inventors would address disputes over potentially conflicting objectives (e.g., profit maximizing vs. wide access).

11.5 GOVERNANCE STRUCTURE: TWO NESTED GOVERNANCE REGIMES

The governance structure of the NPC can be best understood as composed of two nested governance structures. The first is the largely informal governance structure of the Oncofertility Consortium and the NPC. The second is the formal administrative structure at the NIH that was put in place to manage interdisciplinary consortia grants, and the specific NIH institutes that were required to work together to monitor and manage the Oncofertility Consortium.

11.5.1 *Managing the NPC: Informal Structure and Reliance on Social Norms*

At the NPC, the Oncofertility Consortium's Steering (or Leadership) Committee is in charge of all major decisions, including allocation of resources and membership criteria. The committee was first constituted following consortia grant guidelines. It included principal investigators from each project, as well as a survivor advocate and a bioethics representative. Since then, the committee has expanded to include what, through experience, current committee members have identified as key stakeholders including patient liaisons (usually nurses or physicians' assistants) and physicians or researchers involved with specific subpopulations (such as pediatric patients). When the Leadership Committee was first constituted, decisions were often made

63 Interview with Oncofertility Consortium Administrator.

64 See, e.g., US Patent Application 13/382709, Interpenetrating Biomaterial Matrices and Uses Thereof.

informally, involving the NPC administrator and the lead PI Teresa Woodruff. Indeed, all key stakeholders interviewed were satisfied to delegate decision making on many administrative matters to Woodruff and her administrative staff. The governance structure evolved, however, to become more formalized and to include a series of subcommittees that meet once a month. The leaders of each subcommittee also sit on the Leadership Committee, which meets quarterly. The subcommittees evolved organically – out of NPC annual meeting break-out panels. For example, the NPC now has a pediatric subcommittee, and a male fertility subcommittee.

Decisions regarding who should sit on the NPC Leadership Committee, when and how to seek expert external advice for a particular decision, whether to put an issue up for a vote from the entire NPC, or when to seek advice from all of the NPC members are still made informally, that is, on a case-by-case manner by members of the Leadership Committee. For example, an NPC administrator described discussions regarding NPC Leadership Committee membership as follows:

> Once we've identified the leaders of the subcommittees, that streamlined our NPC leadership meetings. We have thought about asking for either votes or nominations for people to spearhead parts of the annual meeting ... So people can throw out names and then we can ask for ... other input and then invite so and so to be the chair of the meeting or participate in the panel or be a keynote or something like that, and at some point maybe if they're really participating in the subcommittee maybe they can sit in on some of the NPC Leadership meetings. So there is some room for working your way through the layers of the meetings and somehow making it to the NPC Leadership table. But it's not a formal nomination ... It's very informal.[65]

Similarly, the decision to put a particular issue to a vote to the entire NPC membership or to rely instead on a vote of the Leadership Committee alone is made by the Leadership Committee on an ad hoc, informal basis:

> We've done it a few other times where we've put it to a vote to the NPC overall: all of the centers, all of their support staff, their research coordinators, their nurses, their admins, their physicians, lab scientists, things of that nature and had them all vote for different topics. So it depends on what the topic is in terms of, whether it's worth having, or more or less waiting, to get responses from 600 people versus [deciding by Leadership Committee vote alone].[66]

In contrast to the relatively informal process for NPC governance, which became progressively formal as NPC membership increased, the process of becoming an NPC member was more formal from its inception. Prospective NPC members sign a letter of agreement that forbids them from sharing "Oncofertility Consortium® documents,

[65] Interview with Oncofertility Consortium Administrator. [66] Ibid.

protocols, procedures, logos, promotional materials, reagents, formulas"[67] with anyone outside of the NPC. NPC research members also agree to contribute research ovarian tissue to the consortium and to delegate decisions regarding research use of the tissue to the Steering Committee.[68] Some interviewees attribute this early formality with helping enroll initial NPC members:

> We had early success in getting cooperation and getting help because we behaved more like a business and less like a scientific project in the beginning. We learned that if we put forward an organized and templated approach ... that people saw that as appealing and they wanted to be involved. So, we put together procedure manuals that were written. We put together training programs.[69]

Interestingly, Leadership Committee members interviewed perceived the role of the formal contract more as a tool to make membership appealing and to streamline the onboarding process than as a document that provided safeguards against disclosure of NPC research findings or protocols. Committee members spent little time considering what to do if an NPC member failed to live up to its obligations, or considering enforcement mechanisms – assuming it would be impractical to enforce the contract, and that breaches would be rare if they happened at all. Their most important concern was that "people would use [the Oncofertility Consortium name] as a branding mechanism."[70] Indeed, only a single instance involved improper credit allocation. At that time, an organization that carried out its first ovarian tissue freezing had a "big media splash and made it seem as though they were the people that were driving the grant."[71] This misapprehension was handled informally: "we just had to gently remind them to please correct that impression."[72]

Informal norms can develop in at least one of two ways: first, they can emerge in a decentralized manner, from the "bottom up," reflecting the informal consensus of a particular group. This is the case with scientific social norms. Second, they can emerge in a hierarchical, "top-down" manner. This appears to be the case with NPC governance: the strong leadership of the NPC was ultimately in charge of creating new norms as novel situations emerged. This informal, centralized norm creation appears quite important in the success of the NPC: it allowed board leaders to act nimbly as new situations presented themselves. These informal norms functioned effectively, however, because they were consonant with and relied upon the underlying social norms of the research and clinical community.

67 NPC Letter of Agreement, note 23. 68 NPC Letter of Agreement, note 23.
69 Interview with Oncofertility Consortium Administrator.
70 Interview with Oncofertility Consortium Administrator. 71 Ibid. 72 Ibid.

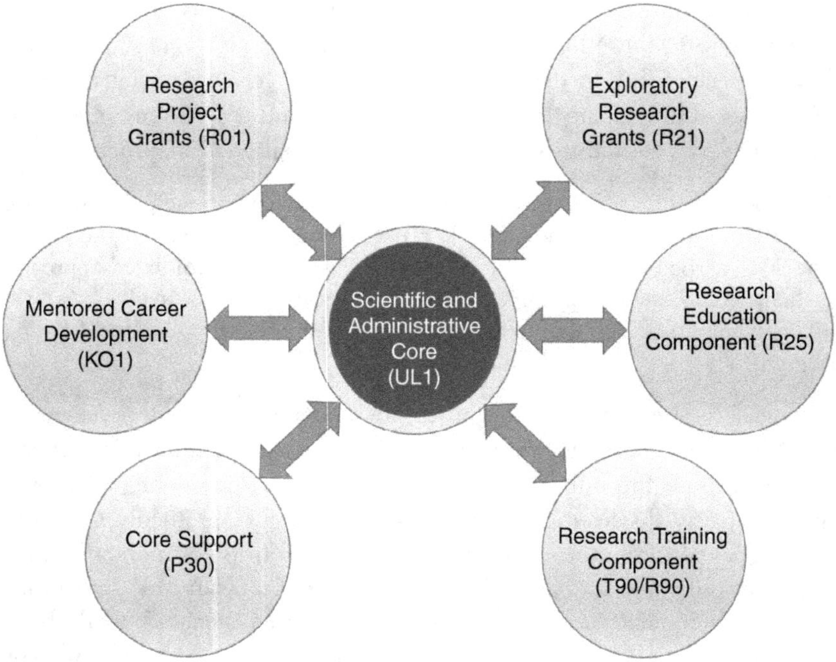

FIGURE 11.1 Grant structure of interdisciplinary research consortia (adapted from https://commonfund.nih.gov/Interdisciplinary/consortia).

11.5.2 *The NIH Governance Structure – Formal Structure, Expertise, and Coordination Challenges*

The basic structure of the interdisciplinary consortia grant is illustrated in Figure 11.1. The Oncofertility Consortium consisted of several individual NIH grant mechanisms, brought together through one administrative core funded by a U54 grant. The role of the administrative core was to organize and support the interdisciplinary team, develop scholarship on team interaction and function, and provide governance and a communication and data-sharing plan.[73] In addition to the administrative core, the Oncofertility Consortium contained four research grants given to specific principal investigators (Rzero1 grants), two P30 core grants – one to fund the NPC directly and a second one to fund a biomaterials core – one R25 grant to fund an educational module, and three "training mechanisms" (T90, R90, and K01 grants) to train oncofertility specialists.

Successful grant administration required coordinating the work of disparate communities at two distinct locales: first, within the Oncofertility Consortium and the NPC and, second, within the NIH itself. The latter required multiple

[73] Oncofertility grant, at 159, on file with author.

NIH institutes, with their own set of priorities and ways of organizing work, to come together to make joint decisions to evaluate Roadmap grantees' success. This proved very problematic. And although every single key informant interviewed highlighted how the grant process and award itself was crucial to the success of the consortium, each also emphasized the lack of coordination among NIH institutes as a key hurdle. One interviewee commented that NIH program officers did not fully incorporate the transdisciplinary goals of the consortium to their day-to-day operations: "they were still set in 'I'm in cancer and I'm in this department' and they just were very stuck to the rules of the ordinary road. It meant that we had a bunch of program officers that had different ideas about how the grant should be run."[74] Interviewees also pointed to the lack of expertise on the subject matter of the grant on the part of NIH officers in charge of making funding decisions as a constant source of friction between oncofertility researchers and NIH administrators. For example, one interviewee remarked: "they brought together program officers from different institutes at NIH, who had never touched anything like this before and were from backgrounds that really had no business overseeing some aspects of this grant. But they had to bring money together from different institutes within NIH to do these specialized grants."[75]

Many attributed this lack of expertise in reproductive endocrinology to an inflexible reading of what types of experiments could be performed under the terms of the grant. One member of the board of directors characterized his experience as follows:

> The overall project leader for the grant knew nothing about reproductive health and clinical medicine. And it showed when we had our meetings. At our oncofertility directors' meeting there were at least two or three people there from the NIH. One from NICHD who was aware of the reproductive health issues and was helpful but all decisions were made higher up. We would often get comments back like, "Well, those studies that you're doing are not in the grant. You can only do what's exactly in the grant." Well, you know, that's not the way research works. And you may put in there you're going to do this particular study. [But] we may culture follicles one way and it doesn't work, so we culture them in a different way. They basically expected us to follow the letter of the grant for everything we did. And it was a struggle.[76]

Another similarly described the relationship with some NIH officers:

> [The NIH officer] was very stuck in whatever was written in the original grant. It's what you were supposed to do and you could do no more. And I kept arguing that "this was a brand new field, what we wrote at the outset was what we thought we would do, but as soon as we started working together, there were many more things that came out of it." And those other things were not off target. They were on a trajectory that we could see, but we couldn't tell you what would be in there. So they

74 Interview with Oncofertility Consortium Principal Investigator, basic research track. 75 Ibid.
76 Ibid.

> were really stuck on the notion that, and I called it the old testament, that all we could do was what was in the old testament or the original constitution . . . So, that took a lot of my time just justifying the kind of science that was happening because science was happening very fast.[77]

Researchers who study when communities and individuals resort to formal, inflexible rules to reach a decision, as opposed to contextual, flexible standards, emphasize that novices in a field are much more likely to rely on rules to ground their judgment.[78] It is likely that a lack of familiarity with the subject matter of the grant gave rise to inflexible, textual decision making from NIH officers that hindered cooperation. This formalism in decision making stands in sharp contrast with the informal process used within the Oncofertility Consortium.

11.6 THE NATIONAL PHYSICIANS' COOPERATIVE: COSTS AND BENEFITS OF MEMBERSHIP

The major benefits of NPC membership accrue both to NPC members themselves and to the public at large. By pooling patient samples collected through standardized protocols, the tissue bank has the potential to generate reliable, reproducible data on patient populations that, as a result of the small size of patient tissue samples that could be collected at any one NPC site, would be impossible to generate otherwise. At a 2007 conference launching the NPC, Teresa Woodruff described the potential public benefits of the NPC as follows:

> We do fellows projects, for a short period of time, with available cohorts either through a computer database or whom they see in an 18-month rotation. But I think what that does is that cuts off the data on its knees and we get publications and abstracts that are not in the format where we can get authoritative data. The idea is that we will be that reproductive medicine network that allows us to do that kind of studies. We're hoping you all buy into the fact that we need to get our patients into this database. This will allow us to do longitudinal studies in a way we couldn't before.[79]

An additional benefit both to the public and to NPC members is the creation of an information exchange and clearinghouse – serving both to coordinate and to centralize data sharing. Through the NPC, members can quickly exchange information regarding best practices, and participate in discussions regarding important research questions that should be addressed by research consortium members. Because the website is no longer password protected, the public at large has the ability to access that information online.

77 Ibid.

78 See, e.g., Laura G. Pedraza-Fariña, Understanding the Federal Circuit: An Expert Community Approach, 30 *Berkeley Tech. L.J.* 90, 114–16 (2015).

79 2007 Oncofertility Conference, NPC Panel, http://oncofertility.northwestern.edu/media/npc-panel.

Finally, the NPC has created a bridge along two axes: first, it provided a mechanism for treating oncologists to refer their patients to reproductive endocrinologists who were equipped to perform emergency fertility preservation protocols. Second, it has fostered communication between basic scientists and clinical researchers and practitioners. This communication, in turn, influenced how basic scientists conducted their work. As a principal investigator remarked: "Then you get to this consortium where you have access to all of these people in different areas and even outside of the science . . . you get to hear from the people who are helping [the patients] make decisions about using your science. These are things you never get exposed to so in depth while you are doing your work."[80] According to several interviewees this in-depth, constant interaction with the clinicians who were seeing the patients who would ultimately benefit from their research not only motivated them to work but also influenced the types of questions they asked.

Despite this impressive set of benefits, one major cost to creating interdisciplinary research consortia is that a large monetary investment is required to bring them about. Creating infrastructure to facilitate coordination is costly, but creating infrastructure to facilitate coordination across entrenched practice styles and persistent boundaries is even more so. Indeed, interdisciplinary consortia grants given to each individual principal investigator were much larger than what those researchers traditionally obtained through the NIH's R01 mechanism. One factor, however, may mitigate this large upfront investment: several of the benefits described earlier have continued past the initial grant support, as the consortium gave rise to new and unexpected avenues of collaboration. For example, one researcher credits the consortium with starting a collaboration between cryobiologists and reproductive endocrinologists working on rhesus monkeys that dramatically advanced the field of ovarian cryobiology.[81]

CONCLUSION

As measured against its own stated goals (and those set forth in the Oncofertility Consortium grant), the NPC has been highly successful along at least two axes: creating a pathway for cancer patients to receive fertility counseling and treatment prior to starting cancer treatment, and advancing research on follicle development. The following six features of the NPC appear to have been important for its success. First, the core group of researchers and clinicians who spearheaded the NPC were part of a *preexisting social network with high levels of trust*. This enabled the core researchers to openly share raw experimental data and create a culture of openness that diffused to the broader NPC. Second, all of the researchers interviewed emphasized the importance of *monthly face-to-face research meetings* to maintain a high level of trust and excitement, and to sustain the fast pace of research

[80] Interview with Oncofertility Consortium Principal Investigator, basic research track. [81] Ibid.

that characterized the research arm of the NPC. Third, having a *relatively closed infrastructure*, where information and know-how were accessible only to group members, was important for the NPC to recruit members in its early stages – as it was trying to develop a reputation and a research culture. Once the NPC became an established commons, opening its protocols and know-how to the public at large did not negatively impact membership; to the contrary, it could rely on its reputation to attract more members. Fourth, the NPC employed a *hierarchical, centralized and informal governance structure* that was highly successful in large part because its decisions were consonant with and relied upon the underlying social norms of the research and clinical community. Fifth, the external, formal management structure of the NIH often clashed with the informal structure of the NPC leadership team, revealing *a particular type of coordination struggle involving nested governance structures*. Finally, the continued involvement of a *high-status intellectual actor* vested with a high degree of trust from the community, - Teresa Woodruff, was crucial to the success and cohesion of the project.

Several of these features echo findings made by Strandburg, Frischmann, and Cui in their research of the urea cycle research consortium.[82] In particular, both the NPC and the urea cycle research consortium have a close-knit core research group, strong principal investigator leadership, monthly research meetings, and an informal but hierarchical governance structure. Future studies of scientific research consortia are needed to establish whether these four key features are hallmarks of successful research commons governance.

[82] Katherine J. Strandburg, Brett Frischmann, and Can Cui, The Rare Diseases Clinical Research Network and the Urea Cycle Disorders Consortium as Nested Knowledge Commons, in *Governing Knowledge Commons* 155.

12

The Application of User Innovation and Knowledge Commons Governance to Mental Health Intervention

Glenn Saxe and Mary Acri

INTRODUCTION

User innovation has been applied in many fields (von Hippel 2005), including those related to health care. This chapter describes what is, to our knowledge, the first application of user innovation to the mental health field. We apply user innovation and knowledge commons governance to a mental health problem of considerable importance: child traumatic stress. As we detail, user innovation provides a unique opportunity to develop and adapt interventions that meet the needs of children with traumatic stress and their families. Knowledge commons governance provides a way to share, vet, and improve these user innovations. This approach provides a solution to a critical problem related to the delivery of effective interventions in the mental health field, where the development of effective treatments often is impeded by the inflexibility of evidence-based treatments (Saxe and Acri 2016). First, we describe the problem of child traumatic stress and the imperative to provide effective treatments for children who suffer from it. Second, we detail the problem within the mental health field about adapting interventions so that they meet the needs of individuals with mental health problems and can be delivered in a variety of typical care settings. Third, we describe how we encourage user innovation and harness it in a knowledge commons by creating an intervention model for traumatized children that is flexible enough to address their needs in a variety of typical care settings and by providing infrastructure for sharing and vetting the innovations made by users in adapting the model to their particular circumstances. This intervention model is called Trauma Systems Therapy. It is currently disseminated in 14 states and has been adapted to work in a wide variety of service settings via the process of user

Glenn Saxe is the Arnold Simon Professor and Chair of the Department of Child and Adolescent Psychiatry at New York University School of Medicine and the Director of the Child Study Center at NYU Langone Medical Center, New York, New York. Mary Acri is Research Assistant Professor, Department of Child and Adolescent Psychiatry, New York University School of Medicine, New York, New York.

innovation. These adaptations have been shared and vetted using a knowledge commons approach.

12.1 TRAUMA AND CHILD TRAUMATIC STRESS

Sadly, traumatic adversity has been a part of the human condition over the course of human history, and millions of individuals annually confront traumatic adversity in the form of wars, political violence, interpersonal violence, child maltreatment, community violence, injuries, and life-threatening medical illnesses in the United States and around the globe. The impact of trauma on children is revealed through the following facts:

- From the general public in the United States, 52.1 percent of adults have reported having at least one adverse childhood experience; 22 percent reported sexual abuse and 10.8 percent had experienced physical abuse (Felitti et al. 1998).
- In 2012, 4.5 children died *every day* across the United States due to abuse and neglect (US Department of Health and Human Services [HHS], Administration for Children and Families, Administration on Children, Youth and Families [ACYF], Children's Bureau 2013).
- Also in 2012, 3.2 million children received a child protective services response (HHS, ACYF, Children's Bureau 2013).
- In a nationally representative sample, 60 percent of children were exposed to violence, and 46 percent were assaulted within the past year (Finkelhor, Turner, Ormrod, Hamby, and Kracke 2009).
- Among New York City families receiving child welfare services, 92 percent of children have been exposed to at least one traumatic event, and *86 percent have experienced multiple traumatic events*. Among mothers, 92 percent have experienced a traumatic event, and 19 *percent have experienced five or more* types of traumatic events (Chemtob, Griffing, Tullberg, Roberts, and Ellis 2010).
- Childhood exposure to adverse experiences increases the risk for alcoholism, suicide attempts, depression, drug abuse, obesity, heart disease, and cancer (Felitti et al. 1998).

The most common response to traumatic exposure – post-traumatic stress disorder (PTSD) – involves responses to a traumatic event that include the following symptom categories (American Psychiatric Association 2013: 5–25):

Re-experiencing: Involves ongoing intense memories of the traumatic event, flashbacks, nightmares, and distress at reminders of the traumatic event.

Avoidance: Involves efforts to avoid thoughts and people, places, and things that are reminders of the trauma.

Negative cognitions and mood: Involves ongoing negative thoughts and feelings about the trauma such as persistent self-blame, diminished interest in activities, and inability to remember key aspects of the trauma.

Hyperarousal: Involves difficulty staying calm, startle responses, poor sleep, and vigilantly anticipating new traumas.

Obviously, there is a great need to develop effective interventions for traumatized children that will meet their needs and will be scalable in typical care settings. In fact, several interventions have been developed for children with traumatic stress that have demonstrated efficacy and effectiveness in clinical trials. A problem is that few have been able to be widely scaled in typical care settings with similar levels of fidelity or outcomes.

12.2 THE PROBLEM WITH EVIDENCE-BASED MENTAL HEALTH INTERVENTIONS

The problem with interventions for child traumatic stress is the same for other evidence-based mental health interventions. Most effective treatments do not reach those for whom they were intended (Mitchell 2011; Proctor et al. 2009). Dissemination efforts are slow (Proctor et al. 2009), and evidence-based treatments have been cited as inflexible and difficult to integrate into community clinics (Mitchell 2011). As a result, effective treatments for a host of mental health disorders, which costs taxpayers billions of dollars to study, fail to reach those in need to the detriment of millions of individuals currently experiencing psychiatric problems (Proctor et al. 2009).

A key part of the problem – and one that user innovation is ideally designed to address – relates to the great caution expressed within the mental health field about implementing an evidence-based treatment (EBT) in a way that deviates from the fidelity standard used in the clinical trial from which it gained its evidence base (Moore, Bumbarger, and Cooper 2013). A fidelity standard for a mental health intervention details the specific psychotherapeutic procedures that should be followed by a mental health provider with a person with a mental health problem for the improvement of that mental health problem. For example, a fidelity standard for an intervention such as cognitive behavior therapy for a psychiatric disorder such as depression would involve an assessment of the degree to which the clinician corrected distortions in thoughts (cognitions) about the self (e.g., "I am bad"), the world (e.g., "Everyone would be happy if I were dead"), and the future (e.g., "Nothing will ever change") since these types of thoughts/cognitions are believed to be central features of depression. Accordingly, cognitive behavior therapists are trained to correct such cognitive distortions as an essential part of their intervention approach, and the degree to which the correction of cognitive distortions is observed within cognitive behavior therapy is a primary way of assessing fidelity to this intervention model. Fidelity standards will often include details on the frequency and duration of sessions, the level of training of the clinician, as well as many details about how the central components of the intervention are to be delivered (e.g., for cognitive behavior therapy, details on how the cognitive distortions are to be corrected). Such procedures are written in a standardized format – often in great detail – so that they can be reliably delivered. The clinical trial that established the evidence base for the intervention employed its defined fidelity standard in the process of achieving the defined outcome.

An intervention's fidelity standard usually contains little information about how the procedures it specifies might be applied to the specific settings in which it would be implemented. Specific circumstances that might affect implementation include the complexity and diversity of a particular settings' clinical population; its providers, supervisors, and administrators; its organizational processes (including finances); and the specific service system in which that organization must operate. This rigidity seriously limits the effectiveness with which evidence-based treatments can be disseminated to those who need them. Successful implementation of an intervention would often necessitate adapting it to specific local circumstances via the development of new or adjusted procedures that would "accompany" the delivery of the given intervention (e.g., delivering the EBT with less frequent sessions, delivering the EBT to broader clinical populations). Under the standard approach to evidence-based treatment, however, such innovations would be considered fidelity violations.

Overly rigid fidelity standards also greatly limit the capacity of an intervention to be adjusted over time, based on experience. When a mental health intervention cannot be changed because any change becomes a fidelity violation (which then violates the evidence-basedness of the intervention), our interventions become fixed in time and the critical process of intervention improvement is stifled. The current standard paradigm for quality improvement in the mental health field, which requires the delivery of treatment in a way that adheres closely to a rigidly defined fidelity standard that was evaluated in the treatment's clinical trial excludes information from users of the treatment – including clinicians, clinic administrators, patients and their families – from the process of intervention development, innovation, and adaptation. We believe, however, that it is exactly the integration of this local information – which is held by users – that is required for an intervention to continue to improve in an evidence-based fashion.

12.3 WHY USER INNOVATION?

User innovation – by definition – integrates the needs of users into the process of developing products that will meet their needs. It incorporates their local knowledge of their particular problems and available resources that is not available to those traditionally expected to provide innovations – typically a manufacturer or expert. As described, there is usually no process for integrating users' local information into mental health intervention development, innovation, or adaptation. This is – in essence – a problem of the limitations of expertise that is analogous to the limitations of manufacturer knowledge typically explored in user innovation research. Mental health intervention developers may be expert in many areas. They may have a great deal of knowledge about the mental disorder in question and the research literature on interventions for the disorder. They may be experts on the standardization of interventions, the development and implementation of clinical trials, and the use of data from these clinical trials. Intervention developers – of whichever sort – do not have expertise about the specific settings in which their intervention will be implemented, however. Who has this expertise? The answer is the users of the intervention within these specific settings.

User innovation can leverage the expertise and knowledge of users in a variety of settings to expand the range of applicability of a treatment model and to improve it. To create an impactful and scalable mental health intervention for child traumatic stress, we designed our treatment model – Trauma Systems Therapy (TST) – with the user innovation process in mind, allowing us to leverage local user expertise in its development, innovation, and adaptation while preserving the value of the evidence-based approach. User innovation research also demonstrates that, to get the most out of the potential for user innovation, innovations must be shared, vetted, and improved upon by other users in a user community or knowledge commons. Our approach involved various measures aimed at facilitating such a knowledge commons for TST.

12.4 TRAUMA SYSTEMS THERAPY

As detailed in our book entitled *Trauma Systems Therapy for Children and Teens* (Saxe, Ellis, and Brown 2016), TST is both a clinical model for the treatment of children with traumatic stress and an organizational model for the successful implementation of the TST clinical model based on the way organizations work. It takes a defined position on the core clinical problems of traumatic stress in children and a defined position on how organizations can best support and sustain their TST programs. According to TST, traumatic stress occurs when a child is unable to regulate emotional states and in certain moments experiences his or her current environment as extremely threatening even when it is relatively safe. TST specifies interventions that address what is called a "trauma system," which emerges in response to disruption in the natural systemic balance between the developing child and his or her social environment. A trauma system is composed of the following:

1. A traumatized child who experiences survival states in specific definable moments. A survival state occurs when a child experiences her or his environment as threatening to survival when reminded of a past traumatic event.

2. A social environment and/or system of care that is not able to help the child regulate these survival states.

TST explicitly addresses these two core problem domains. Because the social environment (e.g., family, school, peer group, neighborhood) ordinarily has a core function of helping a child contain emotions or behaviors, we assume that a child's inability to contain emotions or behaviors reflects a diminished capacity of one or more levels of that social environment to help the child. Correspondingly, a child's inability to regulate emotional states presumptively implies some inadequacy in the system of care to help the child contain emotions or behaviors. The following two brief examples illustrate these issues:

1. A ten-year-old boy was repeatedly beaten by his father for reticence to engage in sports, and for his father's opinion about his poor performance on the sports field. The boy experiences severe anxiety prior to physical education class at school and has missed physical education repeatedly by visiting the school nurse for a variety of physical complaints. He experiences severe flashbacks about the assaults during the day and his grades at school have diminished because he cannot focus on his lessons.
2. A 15-year-old girl was sexually assaulted by her mother's boyfriend. She experiences a lot of pressure from her friends and from her mother to talk with and to date male classmates. She experiences severe anxiety and flashbacks about the sexual assault whenever she thinks about dating boys and whenever a male gets too close to her. The pressure from her friends and her mother also induces flashbacks. She has nightmares of the assault every night. Although she has told her mother about the assault, her mother continues be in a relationship with the man who assaulted her.

As can be seen from the brief descriptions of these children, their problems involve both the dysregulation of emotional states related to extreme threat/survival (e.g., severe anxiety, flashbacks, nightmares, avoidance) and problems within their environment for helping and protecting them (e.g., in the boy's case: how the school handles issues of attending physical education class and school performance, at home the ongoing threat from father. In the girl's case: the ongoing pressure from friends and mother to date boys, mother's continuing relationship with man who assaulted her daughter and lack of protection of her daughter).

To address these problems, TST provides a format for integrating interventions often provided within separate care settings, such as psychotherapy, psychopharmacology, and home-based care, and specifies how these modalities of intervention should be practiced. TST also specifies the processes by which mental health organizations should integrate and support the services they provide. These processes include the establishment of a multidisciplinary treatment team to collaborate on the assessment and treatment of children receiving TST, and the training and supervision process for ensuring TST is delivered with sufficient fidelity.

12.5 USER INNOVATION, KNOWLEDGE COMMONS GOVERNANCE AND TST

User innovation and knowledge commons governance were facilitated within the development and dissemination of TST via five commitments made and supported by the chief developers of TST:

1. ***A commitment to the public nature of intellectual property related to TST***. One obvious barrier to innovation is a concern that one will trespass on ownership claims by others in doing so. Indeed, developers of mental health interventions commonly do make ownership claims. We took a different approach. The TST book makes the waiver of our claim to intellectual property explicit. The waiver is accompanied by an invitation for users to feel free to adapt TST to their needs and to share their experiences with us, and with others. This commitment is a necessary step to facilitate user innovation by providing openness to change TST without concern for violating intellectual property laws. This commitment is also a necessary step to facilitate an informational commons by permitting complete openness to the sharing of information related to TST:
   TST is public property. It is designed to be used and is owned by its users. If you use TST, we consider you part of our innovation community and hope that you will use your skill and creativity to adapt it to best suit your needs, and more important, to the needs of the children and families you serve. If you make a useful adaptation to TST based on what will work in your organization, that is great and we hope you will share your innovation with us. It is our sincere hope that these innovations will continually work to create an ever-improved TST, and a model that users can feel they own (Saxe et al. 2016).
2. ***A commitment to a minimal fidelity standard***. In developing our fidelity standard, we have attempted to limit its restrictions to elements that we believe should minimally be in place for TST to be properly delivered, based on our experience – as user innovators ourselves – in delivering TST in many settings, over many years. Such minimal fidelity processes are conceptually similar to the goals of user "toolkits" in manufacturing fields (von Hippel 2001). A mental health intervention's fidelity standard is important. If it is not sufficiently well defined, then intervention cannot be specific enough to be effective. If it is over-defined then it is prohibitively difficult for users to fit the intervention to their local circumstances and needs. We believe that over-definition is a very big problem within the mental health interventions field. By developing a minimal fidelity standard that includes only the elements necessary to give us confidence that the treatment will be deployed appropriately, we aimed to encourage users to adapt TST to their needs in any fashion they want over and above the established minimal fidelity standard. (In truth, since we have not claimed intellectual property, nothing precludes a user from changing TST in a way that violates even the established minimal fidelity standard. In our experience, users have not

sought to do this.) The TST minimal fidelity standard thus becomes the platform on top of which all innovation occurs for the TST model.

3. ***A commitment to a community of innovators.*** User innovations are most effective when they are shared within a user community that can vet, improve upon, and disseminate them. There are barriers to such sharing, however. In the mental health arena, these barriers include concerns about possible ownership claims or issues of deviating from the fidelity standard and the time and other resources that such sharing may require of busy and resource-strapped local mental health providers. We have taken specific steps to overcome these barriers. Our initial commitment to encouraging users to innovate above the TST minimal fidelity standard removes potential concerns that sharing will attract negative reactions based on ownership claims. We have also created infrastructure to help overcome resource-based and other barriers to sharing. TST implementers are invited to join what we have called the TST Innovation Community to share their TST innovations and to learn from one another. The TST training team is based at the NYU Child Study Center and manages monthly conference calls for members of the TST Innovation Community to facilitate this sharing. A web-based portal located on the TST website is also available so that members can download the most current, official versions of all TST tools/forms, upload tools/forms created by member sites (with approval by the model developers) to be made available for all members to download and use, and communicate with one another via an interactive blog. Our continued involvement in supporting the TST Innovation Community makes it a more valuable resource and thus encourages users to join. It also helps assuage concerns that we, as the initial developers, or potential users might have about quality control. In this respect, our system functions much like most widely used open source software projects, which permit users to make and use their own modified versions of the code but maintain official releases of the software that are vetted and controlled by some coordinating body, usually including the initial developer of the code.
4. ***A commitment to the scientific process in standardizing and evaluating innovations.*** One of the reasons for over-specifying a fidelity standard for a mental health treatment is a concern by the initial developers that deviations from the standard will have adverse impacts on treatment effectiveness. Indeed, most users of TST are community-based providers who do not have the time, resources, or expertise to standardize or evaluate mental health intervention innovations. The standard approach to disseminating a treatment model provides no mechanism for addressing this concern. By adopting a community-based knowledge commons approach, we maintain contact with the TST user community and are in a good position to help users ensure that their innovations are effective. To that end, our NYU team provides technical assistance to user organizations so as to standardize and evaluate the utility of the innovations that they share with us. Thus, our process not only maintains a commitment to evidence-based

treatment based on our initial trials, but it also permits the continuing evaluation of the treatment's effectiveness as it is adapted for use in a range of local circumstances.

5. ***A commitment to the continual improvement of TST over time***. Our vision is for TST to develop as a platform for innovation in service delivery for traumatized children and families such that it grows with an ever-expanding set of standardized innovations developed by users to meet their specific needs and then implemented by other users with similar needs. In this way we have always seen the development of TST as a never-ending story of innovation with the continuing integration of new standardized and evaluated innovations based on their demonstrated utility. In our book we use the example of the release of the iPod by Apple in October 2001 to illustrate why this is so important.

TST has become a never-ending story based on a community of users. If we had stopped when we completed our manual in 2001, or when our first outcome study was published in 2005, or when our first book was released in 2006, it would have been like stopping the development of the iPod after its release on October 23, 2001 (we are not claiming that TST is as groundbreaking as the iPod – that's up to you to determine). We believe this tendency to stop improving a model has become a big problem in the field of psychotherapy development. A psychotherapy model gets developed and evaluated, a clinical trial gets published about the model's efficacy, and the development of the model then largely stops – because any change to the model becomes a fidelity violation and means that an implementation of the model, with this change, cannot be supported by the evidence base of the clinical trial. We are creating a field of 2001 iPods! (Saxe et al. 2016: 353–64).

12.6 RESULTS OF OUR USER INNOVATION AND KNOWLEDGE COMMONS–BASED APPROACH

Our user innovation and knowledge commons–based approach has been extremely successful in disseminating our treatment model. TST is now used within mental health agencies in 14 states and three nations. Moreover, establishing and maintaining our commitments to user innovation and knowledge commons governance as detailed earlier has led to the integration of many user innovations into TST, creating an intervention model that is much more flexible to responding to the needs of users than we could have possibly achieved without our community of users. Given the opportunity to innovate, users have adapted the model to settings and clinical problems that the developers never imagined when we set out to design TST. Here we briefly describe some of these innovations. For those who are interested, more details are given in our book.

None of the settings described here were considered in the initial design of TST. We designed TST at first as an outpatient mental health program within a hospital that served inner-city children and families (Boston Medical Center). It thus was designed as a treatment model for children with traumatic stress who receive care in outpatient mental health settings in urban environments. We never imagined that TST would turn out to be useful for programs outside this context. Providers in such programs imagined this use for us.

1. Residential Care Settings

What it is: Children in residential care settings cannot live with their families for periods of time that range from weeks to months. Usually, a child will be admitted to a residential care program because he or she has a significant mental health problem and his or her behavior poses a risk to the child, or others. Often the child has significant family problems that have contributed to his or her difficulties.

Why TST was thought to be a good fit: A large proportion of children in residential settings have mental health problems related to trauma and the dangerous behaviors are related to shifts to survival-laden emotional states described previously. Often the shift to these states is related to family problems. Once these children arrive in residential programs, shifts to a survival state occur within the programs and the child's providers want to do a better job helping the child regulate emotion. The trauma system of a child's dysregulation of emotional states within the social environment of the residential care setting and the child's home setting was thought to be an excellent fit for TST.

How TST was adapted to fit: Tools were created to assess survival states within residential settings:

- Residential care settings are managed by both clinical and nonclinical staff. Processes to integrate nonclinical staff were created.
- The TST organizational approach was adapted for the needs of administrators of residential care settings to address all services that interact with the child (e.g., psychology, social work, psychiatry, school, direct care, recreation).
- Residential care settings are usually affiliated with schools located on the site of the residential program. Processes to integrate schools were created.
- Many residential programs struggle with physically restraining children. Tools to help programs intervene without restraint were created.

2. Foster Care Settings

What it is: Children in foster care have been removed from their families because the child welfare authorities have determined sufficient maltreatment has occurred to mandate such removal and placement.

Why TST was thought to be a good fit: Traumatic stress reactions are common among children in foster care. The ongoing maltreatment, the removal from family, and the placement with a family that is usually unknown to the child set the stage for ongoing traumatic stress, survival-in-the-moment reactions. Agencies seeking TST for the foster care system have typically wanted a trauma-informed program that could prevent foster care placement disruptions and facilitate reunification with families, when appropriate.

How TST was adapted to fit:

- Teams are created that include mental health clinical providers and foster care case workers. Caseworkers and foster care staff provide the home-based component of TST intervention.
- Foster care placement disruptions are often driven by the child's repetitive shifts to survival in the moment. Foster families can be frustrated (and frightened) by the seemingly "out-of-the-blue" nature of the child's survival states. Accordingly, information about these states can be very helpful for foster families. A foster parent with a child who, for example, shifts to survival in the moment with specific struggles around food and mealtimes could be helped to understand how these struggles could be minimized and survival in the moment prevented.
- Placement decisions are informed by an understanding of a child's vulnerabilities defined by his or her propensity to shift into survival states. Some foster parents may have greater capacity than others to address a child's difficulties. In preparation for the placement of any foster child, the foster family should understand the child's specific vulnerabilities, as described, and needs to be supported by the foster care agency to manage them.
- Reunification decisions are informed by the understanding of the child's vulnerabilities defined by his or her propensity to shift into survival states. Before reunification is considered, the role of specific family members in the child's problem is examined with a view to whether there has been sufficient improvement. If a child's survival states typically involve suicidal or violent behavior, and these states have repeatedly been driven by specific interactions with family members, it is not surprising that they would recur upon reunification if there has been no effective intervention with those family members.

3. TST with Refugee Populations:

What it is: Refugee populations have a high prevalence of traumatic stress related to war and political violence in their nation of origin and the experience of displacement and resettlement. The cultural stressors related to resettlement present particular difficulties within the family context.

Why TST was thought to be a good fit: Agencies seeking TST for refugee populations typically are looking for trauma-informed programs that address the social environment, integrate the cultural context, and connect to the wider services system.

How TST was adapted to fit:

- The refugee child's home environment is shaped not only by the particular family members but also the larger culture of origin that influences the families' goals, behavior, and way of relating to the world beyond. Mental health clinicians typically cannot understand and appreciate the cultural nuances of cultures they are not a part of; cultural brokers, or members from the refugee community who have a deep understanding of their own culture, the resettlement culture, and mental health service systems culture, are integral members of the team. Cultural brokers can help with language translation and, perhaps more importantly, the translation of cultural meanings that relate to such factors as trauma, emotional disorders, and mental health intervention. The identified cultural broker is an integral member of the TST team.
- Broader community outreach provides a foundation from which the specific TST program can operate. Refugee communities can have great wariness about those in authority, and mental health providers are seen as those in authority. The engagement of the community, and a process of co-learning about both the community's primary concerns and the way trauma may be related helps engage whole communities in overcoming stigma and supporting their children in receiving the services they need.
- The inclusion of cultural and religious practices that children and family members find comforting and helpful can be important. The identification of these practices is assessed and integrated as strengths during the treatment planning and engagement process. They are included in the emotional regulation interventions. Partnering with religious leaders can be helpful here.
- The stigma of mental health problems and intervention can present large barriers to engagement with some refugee communities. Accordingly, it can be helpful to base TST refugee programs in less stigmatized settings such as within primary care or schools. In addition, non-stigmatized skill-building groups offered in a school setting allow families and children to begin engagement with TST ideas and team members in a way that does not single their child out as in need of services, but instead acknowledges the ubiquity of cultural stress and supports all refugee children's adjustment to a new cultural setting.

4. TST with Substance Abusing Adolescents:

What it is: The rates of trauma and victimization histories are high among adolescents presenting for substance abuse treatment. Childhood trauma exposure increases risk for later substance use, criminal activity, anxiety disorders, and so on. Youth who exhibit comorbid substance abuse and post-traumatic stress problems show greater clinical severity, increased functional impairment, and greater involvement with multiple service systems when compared to youth with only one of these conditions.

Why TST was thought to be a good fit: Agencies seeking TST for substance-abusing populations typically are looking for a treatment approach that can address how substance abuse may be related to traumatic stress reactions and that integrates the way the youth's social environment may contribute to these problems, across multiple services systems.

How TST was adapted to fit:

- Substance- abusing behavior is considered as an emotional regulation process related to survival states. Moment-by-moment analyses gather information about the patterns of these shifting states so that the contributors to the adolescent's substance abuse can best be understood.
- As the youth's substance abuse deepens, stimuli related to trauma diminish in importance as a result of the process of chemical dependency. Environmental cues related to substance abuse grow in importance. Trauma-related stimuli may continue to be contributors throughout but their relative importance diminishes. Accordingly, TST may be more effective earlier in the chemical dependency process than later.
- Psycho-education about substance abuse and its interaction with symptoms of traumatic stress are integrated in the treatment.
- Behavioral management techniques are particularly emphasized with substance-abusing adolescents. Behavior management strategies integrated into TST include increased substance abuse monitoring and appropriate limit setting, particularly around drug use and high-risk behaviors.
- The addition of substance abuse treatment strategies such as parent-teen communication skills, recognizing and planning for substance abuse cues or trigger situations, substance abuse cravings, cognitive and interpersonal problem-solving techniques, and other relapse-prevention techniques.

5. TST in Schools:

What it is: Children with traumatic stress can have particular problems in schools, and schools based in communities with high rates of trauma can have difficulties with a host of problems related to traumatic stress. Children who experience survival-in-the moment in schools can be highly disruptive in the classroom, and then they get suspended. These children can become quite avoidant of school and may have high rates of absenteeism. Children with traumatic stress may also be quietly dissociative in class and not learn at their intellectual capacity. Children with survival responses frequently are seen as discipline problems, unmotivated, or as children who are angry and over-reactive. This common, but inaccurate, interpretation of survival states by teachers often leads them to respond in ways that are not helpful and may even exacerbate the problem. A child who has been suspended for disruptive behavior, or who has a poor school attendance history, or who does not pay attention in class, is a child at high risk of school failure and/or dropping out.

Why TST was thought to be a good fit: Schools seeking TST typically are looking for an integrated treatment approach that can help with the children they are most worried about for reasons described earlier. They seek a program that can fully engage the social environment of the school and the teachers and other staff members of the school to better understand the school-related problems of traumatized children.

How TST was adapted to fit:

- The TST program in the school integrates within the school culture and performs a vital consultative role helping teachers and other school staff to see how traumatic stress can influence learning at school. Trainings should be offered by the TST team and direct classroom observations conducted to provide consultation to classrooms with particular difficulty.
- The organization plan within the school should be drafted with a leadership team that integrates representation from all specialties that will be involved in the care of children. This includes special education, physical education, security, and regular classroom teachers, as well as representation from the principal's office.
- There should be an evaluation plan that directly addresses the concern of the school (particularly the principal's office). Such a plan should track key educational indicators such as absenteeism, classroom disruptions, critical incidents, and school performance.
- The assessment of children should include classroom observation, particularly if there is concern about behavior in the classroom.
- Most schools do not have dedicated teams of mental health providers (although many have a small capacity for learning and behavioral consultation). Schools will typically refer to local mental health agencies for the children who cause concern, but that work then is usually quite disconnected from the school and does not address the social environment of the school. Successful programs have formed partnerships with local mental health agencies so that clinicians from those agencies join the TST team

and conduct the mental health intervention integrated with the work of the team and with fidelity to TST. Such providers, obviously, add to the mental health capacity of the TST program in the school. The interagency agreement between the school and the mental health clinic allows the mental health clinicians to "bill" for services, as usual, under the mental health clinic's license. This can be financially advantageous to the mental health clinic as providing intervention at the child's school reduces no-show rates.

- The child's family is integrated into care. If a child needs safety-focused treatment, there is a clear problem at home that needs to be addressed. Mental health agencies that provide home-based care for children and families with acute need should be integrated to the program and engaged through interagency agreement as described earlier. If a child needs safety-focused treatment, he or she may well be in danger at home. The child may also be highly disruptive in class. In such a situation, the situation will not improve without the integrated home-based services that are part of treatment. These are the children who are usually thought to be too difficult to handle in school. They get psychiatrically hospitalized and then lose their school placement.
- The TST team evaluates children's individualized education plans (IEP) for their suitability related to the impact of traumatic stress on the child's learning at school. TST providers attend the IEP meetings of the children they work with. There should be an agreement, reflected in the programs organizational plan, about how the situation will be handled if the TST team and the school's educational program disagree about IEPs.

As seen by these examples, an ever-broadening community of users and innovators adapted TST to their needs and became considerably, and increasingly, more useful than it was when first launched; it is now available to any organization that wants to use it. And it has been specifically adapted to a wide range of settings and for a diverse range of populations of traumatized children.

CONCLUSION

Undoubtedly, *user innovation* and *knowledge commons* governance have far-reaching potential to improve evidence-based treatments in the mental health field. To adopt this methodological approach, and the theory underlying it, however, developers will have to recognize the limitations of the standard paradigm, be willing to relinquish their "ownership" rights, and be open to allowing users to innovate in adapting a given treatment across settings and populations. Developers will also have to be ready to invest time and resources in maintaining a vibrant user community knowledge commons. While there are some costs and risks to adopting this approach, we believe the payoffs from wider employment of the user innovator community paradigm – to the field and to the well-being of children and adolescents with mental health problems – would be considerable.

REFERENCES

American Psychiatric Association, 2013. *Diagnostic and Statistical Manual of Mental Disorders*. 5th ed. Arlington, VA: American Psychiatric Publishing.

Chemtob, C. M., Griffing, S., Tullberg, E., Roberts, E., and Ellis, P., 2010. Screening for trauma exposure and posttraumatic stress disorder and depression symptoms among mothers receiving child welfare preventive services. *Child Welfare* 90(6):109.

Felitti, V. J., Anda, R. F., Nordenberg, D., Williamson, D. F., Spitz, A. M., Edwards, V. et al., 1998. Relationship of childhood abuse and household dysfunction to many of the leading causes of death in adults. The Adverse Childhood Experiences (ACE) Study. *American Journal of Preventative Medicin* 14(4):245.

Finkelhor, D., Turner, H., Ormrod, R., Hamby, S., and Kracke, K., 2009. *Children's Exposure to Violence: A Comprehensive National Survey*. Washington, DC: US Department of Justice, Office of Justice Programs, Office of Juvenile Justice and Delinquency Prevention.

Mitchell, P. F., 2011. Evidence-based practice in real-world services for young people with complex needs: New opportunities suggested by recent implementation science. *Children and Youth Services Review* 33:207.

Moore, J. E., Bumbarger, B. K., and Cooper, B. R., 2013. Examining adaptations of evidence-based programs in natural contexts. *The Journal of Primary Prevention* 34 (3):147.

Proctor, E. K., Landsverk, J., Aarons, G., Chambers, D., Glisson, C., and Mittman, B., 2009. Implementation research in mental health services: An emerging science with conceptual, methodological, and training challenges. *Administration and Policy in Mental Health and Mental Health Services Research* 36(1):24.

Saxe, G. N., Ellis, B. H., and Brown A. B., 2016. *Trauma Systems Therapy for Children and Teens*. 2nd ed. New York: Guilford Press.

Saxe, G. N. and Acri, M., 2016. Democratizing implementation and innovation in mental health care. *Administration and Policy in Mental Health and Mental Health Services Research*. doi: 10.1007/s10488-015-0714-1.

US Department of Health and Human Services, Administration for Children and Families, Child maltreatment. www.acf.hhs.gov/programs/cb/research-data-technology/statistics-research/child-maltreatment. Downloaded Nov. 10, 2015.

von Hippel, E., 2001. Perspective: User toolkits for innovation. *Journal of Product Innovation Management* 18(4):247.

von Hippel, E., 2005. *Democratizing Innovation*. Cambridge, MA: MIT Press.

13

Challenges and Opportunities in Developing and Sharing Solutions by Patients and Caregivers: The Story of a Knowledge Commons for the Patient Innovation Project

Pedro Oliveira, Leid Zejnilović, and Helena Canhão

INTRODUCTION

The Patient Innovation project is an initiative that aims to create a knowledge commons for patients and nonprofessional caregivers to share and further develop their innovative solutions to medical care–related problems through an online platform, https://patient-innovation.com. Patients and nonprofessional caregivers are the largest, and most important, group of stakeholders in the health care value chain. After all, the system exists for their benefit. Traditionally, however, they have been perceived as passive recipients of medical care, merely buying and consuming the solutions and products that "medical producers" create and provide. This perspective has influenced the development of an entire health care ecosystem that reinforces the passive position of patients and caregivers.

The assumption of passivity is highly flawed, as demonstrated by research aimed at studying innovation activity by "users" in health care and understanding the role of patients of chronic diseases (or their nonprofessional caregivers) in developing innovative solutions to help them cope with their health conditions (e.g., Oliveira et al. 2015; Oliveira and Canhão 2016). That collaborative and interdisciplinary research effort demonstrated that patients and their nonprofessional caregivers are major sources of health care product and service "user innovations" (e.g., Oliveira and von Hippel 2011; Oliveira et al. 2015; von Hippel 1988, 2005).

Most of the studies of innovation activity by patients build on several decades of "user innovation" research. This research demonstrated that ordinary users, not only commercial entities and research laboratories, are an important source of innovation. In his seminal work in this area, Eric von Hippel, defined user innovators as firms and

Pedro Oliveira is Associate Professor at the Católica Lisbon School of Business and Economics, Lisbon, Portugal. Leid Zejnilović is Assistant Professor at Nova School of Business and Economics, Nova University, Lisbon, Portugal. Helena Canhão is Professor, Nova Medical School, Nova University, Lisbon, Portugal.

individuals who innovate to benefit from using their innovation, rather than from selling it commercially (von Hippel 1988). Translating this definition to the health care domain, we define patient innovators as those who come up with novel treatments, strategies, and equipment that help them cope with their health disorders or the disorders of those to whom they give care. For years, failure to appreciate the potential importance of user innovation led to a lack of attention and support for the development and diffusion of these innovations, a situation that is only beginning to be addressed. The assumption of patient passivity may be even more firmly rooted in the health care context (Oliveira et al. 2015). Moreover, we anticipate that diffusion of patient and caregiver innovations to others who might benefit from them may pose particular problems. While patients and caregivers, especially those coping with chronic or rare diseases, are highly motivated to create solutions for their problems, for a variety of reasons many do not invest the time and resources that would be required to share their innovations with other patients. As a result, many valuable patient-generated ideas may never reach their potential to become solutions and many valuable patient innovations may disappear without a record.

Our findings of the prevalence of patient innovation (Habicht et al. 2012; Oliveira et al. 2015) motivated us to seek ways to help patients innovate and share their innovations more effectively. Eventually, this led us to build an online platform where patients and caregivers can share their innovations and learn about and suggest improvements to innovations shared by others. That online platform is the central piece of the Patient Innovation project. While our rationale for the Patient Innovation platform is fairly simple, setting up such a platform and governing it are far from simple. It is an ongoing endeavor, from which we are continually learning. By sharing our experience and some of what we have learned so far, we hope to encourage others to join our efforts and to develop their ways of addressing the issues related to patient innovation.

In this chapter, we begin by explaining what patient innovation is and what we know about it, based on the user innovation and medical literature. We then discuss some of the challenges that individuals are dealing with as they innovate, and why it is important to help them if we want to obtain their full social benefits. To inform that discussion, we employ a simple process model of patient innovation. Next, we discuss how platforms such as the Patient Innovation project can help innovating patients, and describe the benefits they can provide and the major obstacles to running them successfully. We end with a policy-level discussion that we hope will stimulate further action to help taking patients and caregivers to the front lines of research and development in medical care.

13.1 THE IMPORTANCE AND POTENTIAL OF PATIENT INNOVATION

13.1.1 *Do Patients and Caregivers Innovate?*

Studies have documented that, for some diseases, innovations by patients and caregivers have made a strong impact on medical practice; some even represent state-of-the-art technology for the relevant disease (Scherbatiuk 2012). To illustrate the patient innovation phenomenon, we begin by describing a few well-known examples of patients and caregivers who have created important medical innovations by building upon their deep intimate knowledge of their health disorders and the problems associated with them.

Tal Golesworthy, a process engineer, diagnosed with Marfan syndrome in 1992, is commonly referred to as a man who fixed his heart, for developing an external aortic root support to prevent its further dilatation (Treasure and Pepper 2015). Marfan syndrome is a rare inherited disorder that affects the aorta. The term labels the phenotype of several connective tissue disorders, or "fibrillopathies." Marfan syndrome results in decreasing functionality and resilience of the aorta, and progressive aortic root enlargement. Golesworthy's disease progressed to the point where valve replacement surgery was his only treatment option. Under the standard of care at that time, after the surgery he would have required a lifetime of anticoagulation therapy. Golesworthy considered both the surgery and forgoing treatment to be unattractive. Since he was an engineer, he decided to develop a more suitable solution for himself. He thought of the issue as a plumbing problem, and, given his engineering expertise, he believed that he could devise something to keep his aorta functioning without resorting to valve replacement surgery. He invented the external aortic root support (ExoVasc), a device designed to fit a patient's aorta exactly and reinforce it, thus avoiding both valve replacement and the lifetime anticoagulant drug regimen. In 2004, Tal became the first patient to have an ExoVasc implanted. In 2011, the External Aortic Root Support Project was the winner in the Medical & Healthcare category of the Engineer's Technology and Innovation Awards; in 2015, Golesworthy won one of the Patient Innovation Awards from our project. By the end of 2015, 56 patients had received the aortic support ExoVasc (Treasure and Pepper 2015).

Louis Plante, an electronics engineer with cystic fibrosis, developed a low-frequency waves-radiating device that helps clean mucus from the lungs (Shcherbatiuk 2012). Removing thick mucus from the lungs is a frequent necessity for cystic fibrosis sufferers. The standard approach to mucous removal involves a caregiver thumping a patient's chest for 20 to 40 minutes multiple times per day. Plante was attending a concert, seated near a large speaker when he was forced to leave the event because of a fit of coughing. His expertise in electronics helped him understand that low-frequency vibrations from the speaker had provoked his coughing (which had the effect of removing mucous from his lungs). He developed a device that generates similar vibrations without the accompanying loud sound. After developing the device for his use, he founded a firm (Dymedso) to commercialize his solution, thus becoming a user entrepreneur (Oliveira and Canhão 2016). Plante was one of the winners of the 2015 Patient Innovation Award.

In 2006, *The New England Journal of Medicine* published an article (Elkins et al. 2006) reporting on the benefits to cystic fibrosis sufferers of hypertonic saline therapy – inhaling sterilized salt water to clear the lungs of mucus – which has an interesting story behind it. Inhaling hypertonic saline was discovered by Australian surfer and cystic fibrosis patient Emily Haager (Peck 2006). Haager observed that she felt much better during and after surfing. She traced the effect to her inhalation of the salty seawater. She disclosed this epiphany to her doctor, who formalized the salt therapy and reported the results in *The New England Journal of Medicine*.

To skeptics, these examples may seem exceptional. They also may suggest that, if they are important, patient innovations will somehow find their way into medical practice within the existing system. Our research suggests, however, that well-known examples such as these are only the tip of the iceberg. There is also substantial reason to believe that important patient and caregiver innovations will fail to make their way to wider adoption without systematic efforts to assist their diffusion.

Survey studies in the United States, Japan, Finland, and the UK suggest that approximately 0.5 percent of citizens have modified or created health-related products or services for personal use (de Jong et al. 2015; von Hippel et al. 2012). In a study focusing on rare disease patients and their nonprofessional caregivers, whose needs tend to be underserved by the traditional medical innovation paradigm, we found a much higher occurrence of patient innovations: 8 percent of 500 survey respondents had developed innovations that were validated by two medical experts to be new to medical practice (Oliveira et al. 2015). These studies suggest that there may be large numbers of patient and caregiver innovators who are responding to pressing health-related needs by experimenting with new approaches and modifying existing solutions.

Of course, not all of these patient innovations are radical or sophisticated. (Indeed, radical innovation is rare even for well-supported professional researchers.) Even if it turns out that patient innovations are less likely to be radical than those made by professional medical researchers, that does not mean that they are insignificant. Good health is not merely the absence of disease or infirmity, but rather an overall well-being of an individual – physical, mental, and social well-being (WHO 1978). For individuals afflicted with a health disorder, radical treatments or cures thus are not the only important health care innovations.

The cumulative effect of various solutions that incrementally contribute to well-being can be extremely important. For those in need, a solution that alleviates the pressure of a disease or solves a practical problem is well worth having/using, be it simple or sophisticated.

13.1.2 *Why Do Patients and Caregivers Innovate?*

User innovation research has identified several factors driving users to innovate. One of the most important is "sticky information." Users and manufacturers have different types of information that influence the types of innovations they produce. Users have accurate and detailed information about their day-to-day needs and experiences. As a consequence, they – the users – often tend to develop innovations that are functionally novel, which tend to require a great deal of user-generated need information and context of use information for their development (Riggs and von Hippel 1994; Ogawa 1998). Commercial entities have detailed information about the needs of typical or average users, certain types of technical expertise, and expertise in marketing and diffusing profitable innovations. Synergies between innovative users and commercial entities are not uncommon, and producers sometimes even pick up user-developed solutions, improve them, and take them to the market (von Hippel 2010). These synergies tend to be sporadic, however, and the academic literature in management offers plenty of evidence of under-diffusion of impactful solutions developed by users (Baldwin et al. 2006; von Hippel et al. 2017).

Patient innovation and innovation by health care professionals may also be expected to proceed along different, but complementary paths because of the different information and expertise available to each, which is determined in part by the way in which the health care system operates. A typical encounter of a health professional – a medical doctor, for example – with a patient afflicted with a health disorder is of a short duration. The doctor usually considers an individual's medical history, information that the patient communicates about the reasons for the visit, and various other standard health indicators and bases treatment on that information. The doctor's goal is to identify the problem that brought the patient into the office and to recommend a solution to remove the problem (cure) or to manage it in a way that will minimize its impact. The appointment ends, the doctor moves on to the next case, and the patient is left to cope with any remaining problem(s). Doctors necessarily must address most of their attention to the most urgent issues confronting their patients. Nonetheless, problems related to independent functioning on a daily basis, social integration, and maintaining long-term functionality may have a significant impact on quality of life and individual well-being. Moreover, though a health disorder may manifest itself differently from case to case, and some patients may have idiosyncratic needs related to the disorder, doctors are unavoidably limited, in the short time available, in their ability to ferret out and address all but the most pressing of these idiosyncrasies. Patients also do not seem to believe that only their doctors appropriately address certain kinds of problems. Survey results from the Pew Internet & American Life project suggest that patients rely upon different sources to address different needs: health professionals are more important for accurate diagnosis, drugs prescriptions, and treatments, while peers, family, and friends are the dominant sources for finding solutions to cope with their diseases on a daily basis, and for emotional support – the peer network is especially important for people with chronic conditions (Fox 2011).

The paths of user innovation and seller innovation also may diverge because users and sellers have different motivations for innovating. In particular, commercial firms cannot be expected to invest in innovations that are not expected to produce significant profits. The mismatch of incentives can be acute in the medical arena. Consider the situation for those afflicted with one of more than 7000 rare diseases, whose sufferers constitute "orphan" markets. This designation means that patients can expect little help from producers in the form of specialized products to help them cope with their diseases, as the market incentives are perceived as too low to motivate vibrant research and development activity from commercial entities. Because many of these rare diseases are chronic and progressive, and particularly in light of the lack of commercial incentives, these patients and their caregivers have particularly strong incentives to develop their solutions – or to discover and adopt solutions developed by peers – to help them cope with their diseases and improve their daily lives. Consistent with this observation, our initial studies show an approximately 10 times higher rate of health related innovation among patients afflicted with rare diseases and their caregivers than among the public at large (Zejnilovic et al. 2016).

Our study of 500 patients with rare disease and caregivers provides further evidence of a correlation between innovative activity and patient/caregiver perception of need even among rare disease sufferers. The study also suggests, as have other user innovation studies, that innovative activity increases with level of education (Oliveira et al. 2015). Moreover, our data suggests that there may be an important subjective component to the perception of need and that it is an individual's subjective perception of need that drives innovative activity. Additional insight into this possible subjective factor comes from an epidemiological study of a representative sample of adult Portuguese (Branco, Rodrigues, Gouveia et al. 2016). In that survey study, individuals were asked to assess their general state of health. Some individuals were known to have multiple, clinically confirmed health disorders; nonetheless, they indicated that their health was very good, while others, who did not report any significant physical limitations or illnesses, reported mediocre general health status. While more research is needed to explore the factors driving patient innovation, it may be that individual perceptions of the severity of the need, the likelihood that it will be addressed by others, and their capability to address it all jointly influence the likelihood that a patient or caregiver will innovate.

In any event, though many questions about the extent and characteristics of patient innovation remain, the available evidence leads us to believe that a substantial amount of patient and caregiver innovation occurs. Unfortunately, there is also reason to believe that only a small fraction of patent innovations are ever shared with other patients and caregivers, adopted by physicians, or picked up by commercial providers. Given the fact that, globally, many individuals are innovating to cope with their health disorders, we believe it is important to consider how best to support patient innovation so that it will be as effective, safe, and socially beneficial as possible.

In the next two sections, we discuss the challenges and opportunities of patient innovation, from individual-level and platform-level perspectives and how the Patient Innovation project seeks to support it.

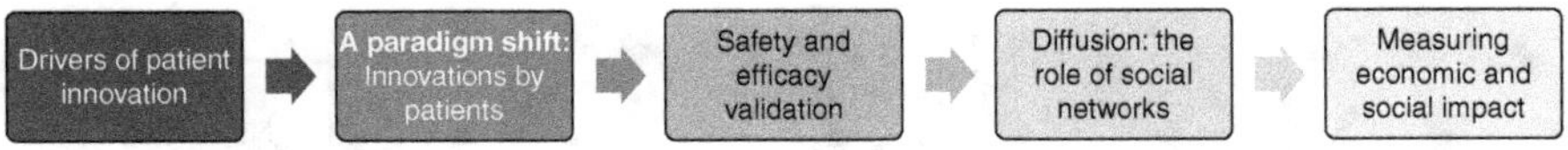

FIGURE 13.1 The Patient Innovation value chain.

13.1.3 *An Individual-Level Model of Patient Innovation*

To gain a better understanding of the innovation activity of patients and caregivers and identify ways to improve it, we model it with the Patient Innovation value chain shown in Figure 13.1. The underlying goal of this value chain is that the drivers of patient innovation will lead to the development of new treatments, therapies, and medical devices, which should be validated for safety and efficacy, and then diffused more broadly. Ideally, the economic and social impact of the output of the value chain should then be measured and evaluated. The integration of patient innovation into health care innovation represents a paradigm shift. While this shift is already happening, no studies yet assess its economic and social impact.

The Patient Innovation value chain starts with an identified need – a driver of patient innovation – that prompts the innovation itself. The process of patient innovation is easy to imagine, but it does not proceed according to the kind of structured process often implemented by commercial firms. The process of user innovation is likely to be an unstructured, iterative decision-making sequence, similar to the model proposed by Mintzberg et al. (1976), involving experiential learning, serendipitous jumps over the stages, and events that originate from the environment in which the users are embedded and which influence the process. Nonetheless, when considering how best to intervene in the Patient Innovation value chain, it will be helpful to devise an easy to interpret process model to help guide our interventions.

To develop our model, we conducted a qualitative study in Portugal, by interviewing 15 patients afflicted with chronic diseases or lesions (Oliveira 2014). From these 15 interviews, we identified 30 cases of patient innovation, adoption, or passive behavior by patients. Our analysis, grounded in the existing literature on user innovation and individual decision making, yielded a simple stylized develop-or-adopt process model of patient innovation (Figure 13.2). In Figure 13.2 we also show, in parallel, how this model compares to two other representations of the innovation process, the stages of development of a user innovation (Lüthje et al. 2005), and a decision-making model – the trichotomy identification-development-selection model (Mintzberg et al. 1976).

In this representation, the patient's problem-solving activity is a dynamic, iterative process that ends in either adoption or innovation. The linear representation of the stages is not meant to imply that every problem-solving activity by patients passes through all the steps in the order shown, as problem-solving is inherently an unstructured process embedded in a dynamic stochastic environment (Cooper 2008; Langley et al. 1995). Sometimes, for example, a patient may simply develop a solution, without any search. This simple model nonetheless provides a useful

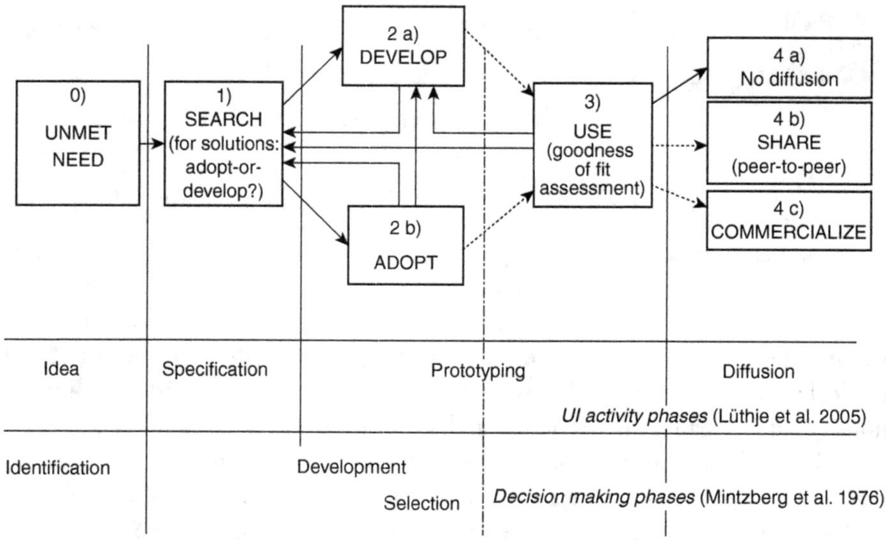

FIGURE 13.2 A stylized model of a patient's adopt-or-develop process with corresponding phases of user innovation activity and decision-making processes. The arrows indicate potential paths of problem solving – the transitions from one stage to another (UI - User Innovation).

structure within which potential interventions – aimed at helping patients make better decisions and obtain better outcomes from their innovation activity – may be considered. We will use this model to also describe our intervention, the Patient Innovation platform. However, before we move to the platform-related discussion, let us briefly describe the phases of the model, supporting them with selected interview excerpts.

13.1.3.1 Stage 0: Unmet need

As any problem-solving process starts with the identification of unmet need, this is the initial stage of the patient innovation develop-or-adopt process. There are two ways for individuals to become aware of a need: (1) through experiential learning – a form of learning-by-doing/using where a patient observes an unmet need and then attempts to formulate the problem informally (von Hippel 2005) or (2) by observing a solution simultaneously with identifying a need (von Hippel and von Krogh 2013). In 8 out of the 30 cases we analyzed, upon observing a problem, the patients immediately came up with a solution and pursued its development. A need may also be recognized by observing a solution (von Hippel and von Krogh 2015), and this was the case in 3 out of the 30 cases we analyzed; patients saw a solution and then realized that the solution was a match for a latent need or for a problem they had attempted to solve in the past:

> As I was watching TV, I saw a university professor talking about a software he developed to control computers with eye movements. He developed the software to help his wife in her work with people afflicted with cerebral paralysis. The software was free to use, and I thought about my difficulties to use computers. So, I gave it a try.
>
> (Tetraplegia, patient – interview D)

In this example, the patient was aware of difficulties when using a solution, but the need was latent as he was not actively pursuing or searching for a solution. Hearing about the software, the patient's latent need got activated and by adopting the solution, his quality of life has been improved. One takeaway from this example is that increasing the availability and salience of solutions may help people in unanticipated ways.

13.1.3.2 Stage 1: Search for information and solutions

If a solution does not immediately present itself upon recognition of unmet need, the next step is often to undertake a search for information and solutions. Real-life decisions are complex, and in response to a problem, people often do not search for the best possible solution, but for one that satisfices – fixes the problem to an extent that is satisfactory for their needs (Simon 1977). Descriptive models of decision making include a search for solution alternatives as part of a development phase. In decision-making procedures, the relevant subroutine or procedure (Mintzberg et al. 1976) employs an algorithm to develop alternatives that are subjected to a cost-benefit analysis against the previous best solution (Newell and Simon 1972). Having identified an unmet need, patient innovators may engage in a similar, though usually less formal, search process. The dynamics of the search for health-related information change as patients and caregivers gain experience about the health condition of interest:

> When she was diagnosed, I sought for support and information about epidermolysis bullosa. However, it is a rare disease, and with so few patients like her, it was difficult to find help. I searched everywhere, online fora, international associations, journals, pharmaceutical companies. I do it nowadays as well, but more to learn about a specific thing or to find new solutions. [Apart from innovating] I also adopted a solution developed by another patient, and I found it on an international online forum – to add table salt to bathing water, as skin contact with pH neutral or isotonic solution lessens the sting. I also experimented with sea salt instead of table salt, and it works even better for my daughter.
>
> (Epidermolysis bullosa, caregiver – interview F)

> In the beginning, I would search a lot for information about my condition, whereas nowadays I only search for specific information or solutions, when I feel it is needed. Usually, I search online (e.g., YouTube or scientific papers), but also, I ask other patients with spinal cord injuries and doctors.
>
> (Spinal cord injury – patient – interview I)

In the early stages, when an ailment is contracted, patients and caregivers search mostly for information about the nature of their ailment and the prospects of living with it. As they accumulate knowledge about their health condition and learn how to function with it on a daily basis, patients tend to engage more intensively in searching for specific solutions to their unmet needs.

It was obvious from our interviews that there is a stark contrast between active and passive patients. Active patients detailed about search behavior, solution development, tinkering, and adoption. Passive patients demonstrated strongly reliance on doctors only:

> I do not search for health-related information. All that I need, I get from health professionals in the rehabilitation center.
>
> (Spinal cord injury, patient – interview L)

We also asked the interviewees for their opinions about solutions that patients develop for themselves. We wondered whether patients' lack of confidence in their expertise would lead them to eschew solutions developed by other patients. The non-active patients we interviewed (such as the one from interview L) were not opposed – in principle – to the idea of adopting a solution developed by a patient. Rather, they expressed no need for such solutions, finding their existing medical care sufficient.

Not all patients who identify an unmet need begin their searches for solutions. In what is referred to as the "community push," patients may instead share the problem with others, who may then suggest solutions they know about or are using. We identified two such cases, which we elaborate upon in our discussion of the diffusion phase, since responding to inquiries from other patients is one mechanism for diffusing innovations.

13.1.3.3 Stages 2 and 3: Develop-or-adopt and then use a solution, an iterative trial-and-error process

The stage 1 search for a potentially satisfactory solution ends with a decision to adopt or develop a possible solution. This initiates a solution development (stage 2a), or acquisition of an existing solution (stage 2b). After obtaining the firsthand experience using the solution (stage 3), or even during the solution acquisition, the goodness-of-fit of the solution to the need is assessed (stage 3) based on the patient's personal cost-benefit assessment (e.g., Damanpour 1991; Rogers 2003). There is no guarantee that the outcome will be a satisfactory need-solution pair. In cases of mismatch, the patient may return to stage 2a for further development or to stage 1 for further search. Searching for a match is often a dynamic, iterative, trial-and-error process, both for solutions developed independently by the patient innovator or adopted from preexisting technology:

> Every time we encounter a new problem, we start by searching online to see if there is a solution, and we consider if we can come up with something by ourselves.

> … we were desperately trying to find a solution … something that would help KK to hold the dish when he places a spoon or a fork in it, or … in whatever he is eating. We searched everywhere and tried several things. For example, we tried available silicone adherent mats, but they were too big and did not hold well. However, once, when we bought a big bowl in a shop, I realized that it had a small silicone adherent mat inside, to hold the bowl, and it came to my mind that I should give it a try with KK … we used it and it worked so well for him. It holds whatever he is eating, he can eat by himself, and it is small, so he is OK to use it at school too (it is discrete). He now uses it for every meal.
>
> (Hemiparesis, caregiver – interview K)

> The guys in Brazil shared everything with me for free, about their surfboard, the chair attached to it, and how to make it. However, making it was a lengthy and costly process. It was even more difficult as their solution was custom made, and I decided that it was better to make a general purpose solution, something that anyone can use.
>
> (Poliomyelitis, patient – interview C)

If patients are not satisfied with the cost-benefit performance of potential solutions, they can conduct a new stage 1 search or return to stage 2 to refine or modify the solutions they have developed or adopted. In 8 of the 30 cases we analyzed, patients returned to stage 1 search after being dissatisfied with a potential solution, while in 11 out of 30 cases patients engaged in iterative refining or modifying the adopted or developed solutions. Patients, who initially attempted to solve their problems by adopting an available solution (stage 2b) uncovered during their search, may recognize the need to develop their innovative solution (shifting to stage 2a). This usually happens after a trial use of a recommended available solution, finding it to be inadequate:

> They [the doctors] gave us the orthopedic cast for my son's functional arm, but it was heavy, not practical, and did not quite do what we expected … I realized that I could just sew the sleeves on the functional arm, and that worked much better.
>
> (Hemiparesis, caregiver – interview K)

Rosenberg (1982) describes the trial-and-error process that we represent as iteration among stages 1, 2, and 3 as "learning-by-using." The accumulation of use experiences creates tacit knowledge, or what von Hippel (1994) refers to as sticky information. The cases we encountered show that users, based on their sticky information, may come up with more effective solutions than their commercial counterparts (Morrison et al. 2000; von Hippel 2010).

13.1.3.4 Stage 4: Diffusion of patient-developed solutions

Most patient innovations are potentially valuable to other, similarly situated patients and caregivers. Thus, the full social value of innovation is obtained only if it is shared with and used by other patients. Making solutions publicly available allows others to find solutions to problems they are attempting to solve (contributing to stage 1) and for need-solution pairs to arise (contributing to stage 0). In 13 out of the 22 cases that involved a developed or adopted solution, the patients made efforts to diffuse further the solutions. In diffusion efforts, solution developers may share information in a relatively passive way, such as by making an online post or preparing other types of written information. They can also actively suggest the use of a solution, a "market-push" approach, in which they bring the solution to the attention of people with whom they interact. We identified two such market-push cases. In such cases, we found that those who suggested a potential solution to a particular individual also provided help to reduce the solution's acquisition cost. The diffusion channel in these examples was a two-way interaction between peers, suggesting that social interactions with peers may increase the likelihood of adoption of patient-developed solutions.

At times, particularly when there is uncertainty about the safety and effectiveness of a potential solution, the patients may also involve medical doctors in the innovation process:

> We (the parents) exchange information about drugs, and the experiences with different combinations of drugs, what worked and for what. We experiment with different combinations of drugs to see which one works better. I did it at least once for my kid. First, I informed myself about a combination of drugs that other parents suggested. Then I went to my doctor and explained what I found, the reasons why I need it, and the doctor was enthusiastic and supportive about it. Therefore, I tried it, and it worked.
> (Child with Angelman syndrome, caregiver – interview E)

This example demonstrates the importance of the doctor-patient relationship. Namely, hazardous solutions can be identified with higher confidence if they are openly discussed with experienced professionals, and not solely within the community of patients.

Although most of the innovators in our sample made some efforts to share their solutions – after all, this is how we found them – in 2 out of 13 cases of developed solutions, the developers did not share their solutions, even though they were well connected to other patients and medical professionals. The patient innovators reported either that they had no time to engage in diffusion or simply that they did not share their solutions because no one asked. These observations are in line with the general arguments about potential market failure in the diffusion of user innovations presented by de Jong et al. (2015). It was very rational for some innovators not to share information about their solutions with others – after solving their problems they had no interest in investing time or money in diffusing the solutions. Where diffusion of a valuable solution does not occur, another patient or caregiver looking for a solution to a similar problem must replicate the whole development process. That replication is a waste of resources, and the patients may or may not succeed in finding or developing a solution. The cases of non-diffusion that we analyzed demonstrate that failure to diffuse may occur even when developers would be willing to share them for free – when patient innovators find sharing too burdensome or are unaware that others might be interested in knowing about them. The cases thus suggest that actively soliciting solutions from patients and educating them about the value of sharing the outcomes of their creative activity, as well as creating the infrastructure to reduce the costs of sharing, may be important to correct this market failure.

The model presented here provides an overview of the patient innovation process from the perspective of the individual innovator. In our design, implementation, and ongoing efforts to improve the Patient Innovation platform, we use this model to help us identify ways to move forward – in other words, to learn how an online platform can be used to address some of the challenges patients encounter in the process and to contribute to the development of patient innovation on a larger scale.

13.2 THE PATIENT INNOVATION ONLINE PLATFORM: INFRASTRUCTURE FOR A KNOWLEDGE COMMONS

Next, we discuss how the Patient Innovation platform can help overcome some of the barriers to successful patient innovation and diffusion of those innovations by providing the infrastructure for a knowledge commons.

13.2.1 *The Landscape of Health Care–Related Online Platforms*

Health care systems are under serious pressure to deliver good medical care despite capacity and budget constraints. Total spending on health accounted for 9.5 percent of GDP in the Organisation for Economic Co-operation and Development countries in 2012, and the cost is still rapidly rising, particularly because the population is aging and, relatedly, because more people are living longer with chronic diseases. Chronic diseases are the most common cause of death globally, accounting for 75 percent of direct health care costs in the United States, and taking a significant toll on the quality of life of the elderly (Thrall 2005; Vos et al. 2013). There is a common understanding that novel solutions and business models are necessary to help overcome constraints, contain costs, and unlock new opportunities. Technology, and especially digital platform-based business models, may be an important contributor to better and more cost-effective health care.

In the Merriam-Webster dictionary, a platform is defined as "a place or opportunity for communicating ideas and information." A "digital platform" is a set of components including a core, upon which third parties can build (Parker and Van Alstyne 2010). The value of a digital platform is characterized by network effects, meaning that it becomes more valuable when more third parties use and contribute to it. Popular examples of digital platforms include hardware and software environments such as Google Play Store, as well as websites where sellers and buyers are matched, such as Amazon, eBay, or Uber, which matches available amateur taxi drivers with people who need a ride. The Internet itself is a platform – an infrastructural platform. It enables the development of efficient, sustainable online resources that individuals can use to create and exchange knowledge, research pressing questions, communicate with one another, and even act upon their ideas.

In the health care arena, patients have been empowered by the resources available on the Internet to assume more responsibility for their medical care. Greater involvement of patients in managing their health may also decrease the burden on the health care system (Hibbard et al. 2004). In recent years, patient organizations, providers, commercial entities, and nonprofit organizations have developed a variety of online communities and virtual fora where patients can not only discuss their health concerns but also capture, record, and exchange valuable health-related information. In a similar vein, the US Food and Drug Administration made an additional effort to bring closer to patients their existing platform for reporting adverse effects of medical devices and drugs, MedWatch (FDA 2013). It introduced an easy-to-understand report form that can be downloaded from MedWatch website, and a way to submit the report online, aiming at consumers with little medical knowledge. Other interesting examples of online fora include the Braintalk community for neurological diseases and Building User Involvement in Motor Neuron Disease (BUILD) for amyotrophic lateral sclerosis (ALS). Going beyond communication and knowledge exchange, pharmaceutical companies are also keen to organize virtual clinical trials, in which the data collected is self-reported by patients (Roehr 2011).

Major technology companies, such as Apple, Google, IBM, Microsoft, and Samsung, also have stepped in to offer health care–related initiatives. Their strategies include open source frameworks for creating health-related software applications, providing medical data storage and analysis, and processing large amounts of health-related scientific data. Connecting users to report and share health data is also a business model for platform-based companies, which are harnessing the increasing availability of Internet connectivity to assist patients in finding and interacting with other people suffering from similar conditions. For example, PatientsLikeMe is a for-profit health data-sharing platform that aggregates patient-contributed health data to perform observational studies. PatientsLikeMe has more than 150,000 active users sharing data on more than 1000 health disorders. A study performed using this platform disproved a previous scientific paper regarding the effects of lithium carbonate in amyotrophic lateral sclerosis (ALS), by systematically collecting and analyzing self-experimentation information provided by patients (Wicks et al. 2011). Genomera, another online project, is "crowd-sourcing health discovery by helping anyone create group health studies" (Genomera 2013). These new platforms seek to enable patients, caregivers, and others whose input to medical research previously has been limited to a passive role. They create and enable communities that can help in coming up with suitable designs for testing hypotheses or answering questions by connecting knowledge but also locating peers willing to serve as testers, implementing the test design and sharing their symptoms and outcomes. These existing efforts demonstrate the potential for the Internet and related technology to enable the engagement of patients and patient associations, nonprofessional caregivers, health professionals, and even medical doctors who have, so far, been considerably excluded from the health innovation process.

13.2.2 *The Patient Innovation Platform*

The Patient Innovation initiative differs from prior online health platforms in that it aims to recognize and enhance the capacity of users – patients, caregivers, and collaborators with complementary skills who are intrinsically motivated to help people in need – to contribute to innovation in medical care. To that end, we developed and deployed the Patient Innovation platform, https://patient-innovation.com, a non-profit digital platform designed to provide infrastructure to support a knowledge commons for identifying, sharing, commenting on, improving, and diffusing the work of these medical user innovators. The Patient Innovation platform is international, multilingual, open, and free for use by patients and caregivers dealing with any disease. The platform was launched in February 2014 and relies on partnerships with numerous patient associations and medical research centers in the five continents to reach international audiences.

To increase public awareness of the potential benefits of patient innovation, we established the Patient Innovation Award. Each year we invite patient innovators to submit their best innovations to the competition. A jury composed of six highly reputable scientists reviews the proposed solutions and selects the innovator of the year in three categories – patient, caregiver, and collaborator. The awards are presented at a ceremony, which provides an opportunity to raise awareness of the Patient Innovation project. At the same time, this is an excellent occasion to gather individual patients, patient associations, health professionals, innovation experts, entrepreneurs, media, companies, and health authorities to discuss patient and caregiver innovation.

The Patient Innovation platform design invites patients and caregivers to submit their self-developed solutions as video files, sets of pictures, textual narratives, or a combination of these media. Other members of the network are free to evaluate each proposed solution, make their judgments about its applicability, safety, and to which problems it could usefully be applied. Also, members may engage in a co-creation process and upload modified versions of others' solutions, so that the path of development can be traced by users of the site. Tagging mechanisms and advanced search capability allow efficient search by patients and interested parties and may enable cross-pollinating of solutions across health disorders. The platform has the potential to become a unique repository of open knowledge, created and co-developed in a patient-to-patient trusted environment, about innovations to enhance the health and quality of life of chronic disease patients.

The Patient Innovation platform is intended to enable patients to assume more responsibility for the collaborative development and diffusion of their innovations, and to allow patients to contribute more knowledgeably to medical care. To further that goal, we designed the Patient Innovation platform to mesh strategically with the stages of patient innovation mapped out in the process model presented in Figure 13.2. The relationships between the design of the Patient Innovation platform and the stage of innovation activity are summarized in Table 13.1.

We see Patient Innovation and similar initiatives as useful efforts to bring health care closer to the patients, to enhance the participation of patients in the management of their health, to incorporate the patients' and caregivers' valuable use-based knowledge into the improvement of medical care, and to provide conduits for practical learning about how to improve struggling health care systems on a global scale. Because such initiatives involve humans and their well-being, they are embedded in complex legal, regulatory, and social environments. In such a landscape, new approaches to medical innovation may be in some tension with existing legal and social norms. We believe that such tensions, where they arise, should not discourage us from seeking means to incorporate patients and caregivers into the medical innovation ecosystem. Rather, they highlight the need to adapt health care systems and public policies to provide a meaningful framework for integrating patients and caregivers (and their important use-based local knowledge) more fully in the development of safe and effective health care solutions.

13.2.3 *Challenges and opportunities in developing the Patient Innovation platform*

We encountered (and continue to encounter) many challenges in designing and maintaining the Patient Innovation platform. Here, we discuss a few of the most significant challenges, and our response to overcome them. The most basic challenge for any digital-platform business is the creation of a community of users. The community supplies the content, without which the platform has no value. In the case of the Patient Innovation platform, the content consists of information about health-related patient innovations and the record of improvements to these solutions made by other patients. The community also plays the role as the demand side of the Patient Innovation platform. Those with health disorders may use the platform to learn about potential solutions to their needs by browsing descriptions of existing solutions developed by their peers. As they browse, community members can provide new content, feedback, and validation of usefulness (or not) of the posted solutions. As more community members participate as content providers or users of the content provided by a platform, the community becomes stronger, and the platform that supports the community becomes more valuable.

We engaged in developing the Patient Innovation platform in the face of substantial evidence that users – and in this case, the patients, caregivers, and

TABLE 13.1 *Stages of innovation activity by patients and the associated challenges and opportunities for the Patient Innovation platform*

Stage	The function provided by patient innovation	The expected improvements in the patient innovation process
UNMET NEED Need identification	Solution tagging and search by tags: disease, symptom, location, and activity tags	Faster identification of potential problems/solution
SEARCH Search for solutions		Faster and more successful search for a solution Spillover of knowledge from different diseases/solution categories; e.g., solutions for digestive problems as a primary health disorder can serve to those who have it as a side effect of a cancer treatment
ADOPT Adoption	Safeguard mechanism for obviously dangerous solutions Descriptions of the solutions: textual, audio, and visual	More solutions/versions to choose from Low investment in the acquisition of a solution
DEVELOP Development	Social networking feature: commenting	Comparison with the existing solutions, and incremental buildups
USE Goodness-of-fit assessment	Reviewing and updating use-related information /experiences from the users	Collection of evidence about solutions
DIFFUSE Sharing and/or commercializing	Free-of-charge and easy to use/post solutions platform Promotion	Higher rate of diffusion of patient-developed solutions

collaborators – often do not have strong enough incentives to share their content, given the time, effort, and resources that sharing requires. By creating a specialized venue for sharing peer-developed solutions, Patient Innovation lowers the barriers to diffusing patient innovations. An equally important role of the platform is to increase awareness about the potential importance of the patient innovation phenomenon, thereby bolstering patient innovators' intrinsic motivations to help others by sharing their innovations. During Patient Innovation's three years of operation so far, more than 700 solutions have been posted on the platform.

When we began developing the Patient Innovation platform, we had to make decisions about the governance of the platform. We desired to maintain as much openness as possible in light of our overall goals. We also hoped to create a sustainable knowledge commons based on the platform. Sustainability is dependent on maintaining a vibrant community and also on the mechanisms for funding and supporting the platform itself. We believed that sustainability would be enhanced by aligning the intended identity of the community with the mechanisms used to fund its development and maintenance The goal of sustainability thus had implications for our decisions about the platform provider, its legal structure, and the platform sponsors. We believed that a commons based on our fundamental commitment to openness and free peer-to-peer sharing would only be viable in an environment of trust. To encourage a trusting environment, we decided to structure Patient Innovation as a not-for-profit organization and to fund platform development and maintenance only through research grants and donations. Maintaining trust also requires that we keep the commons governance free of conflicts of interest, by working only with partners who share the same values and are dedicated to and invest efforts in better empowering patients within the health care system.

We also confronted decisions about the type and degree of openness to employ in governing the Patient Innovation platform. The openness of a platform (and the knowledge commons it supports) is multidimensional. For Patient Innovation, decisions had to be made about *who* could contribute content, *what types* of content could be contributed, and *which* contributed content would be displayed. (It went without saying that the content of the platform would be available for anyone to explore and use.) In line with our primary goal of promoting better medical care, we imposed some limitations along various dimensions of openness.

Patient Innovation is completely open about *who* can contribute, but we had to decide whether to allow anonymous participation or to employ some means of authenticating the identities of those who post on the site. There are benefits and weaknesses to authenticating participants in a virtual community versus allowing anonymous participation, including questions about the quality and value of anonymous peer-review feedback mechanisms. Trust among those who create and use the content of the knowledge commons supported by the Patient Innovation platform is also important for sustainability. Inappropriate or otherwise deleterious posts could easily erode this trust. User authentication is one means of discouraging disruptive (and, in this case, potentially dangerous) contributor behavior and incentivizing higher-quality participation. However, we did not want to discourage patients from participating, even if they preferred to remain anonymous. We thus decided to permit anonymous contributions, while incorporating other mechanisms of quality assurance to address our concerns about sustainability, trust, and safety.

We address the issue of quality assurance primarily by imposing some limits on *what types* of content can be posted and *which* particular contributed content is displayed. Like many other online communities, we employ community ratings and feedback to identify disruptive or otherwise inappropriate contributions. The medical context raises additional quality control concerns, and specifically related to safety, that we feared might not be adequately addressed by relying only on community feedback. We employ two additional mechanisms to alleviate these concerns. First, because of the particular difficulty in assessing the safety and efficacy of drugs and other ingestible treatments, Patient Innovation's terms of service simply forbid the posting of solutions involving drugs or other ingestible products. Second, each post is reviewed by a medical professional before it becomes visible on the site. This review ensures that contributions comply with the terms of service and satisfy the basic requirements of safety. The involvement of medical professionals in reviewing posts serves the additional purpose of beginning to bridge the gap between patient innovation and the medical professions. Bridging this gap is a worthwhile goal, given the important role that medical professionals play in validating and diffusing medical innovations.

Another dimension of openness relates to the potential uses of the content available on the site. One way to enhance the value of the content pooled in a knowledge commons is to permit third parties to design tools that interface with that content. A pertinent example of such a tool might be an application that allows users to report their health indicators before and after using a specific solution posted on the platform. Patient Innovation is open so that third parties can create tools that interface with the platform to enable collection and sharing of evidence about the effectiveness of the solutions. Our decision to make the platform open along this dimension was guided by our commitment to advancing paradigm change in health care in the direction of distributed innovation and patient-centric medical care.

Validating the safety and efficacy of patient innovations remains a major challenge, and we continue to consider ways in which a platform such as Patient Innovation might contribute to that task. The usual path for bringing medical innovations to the market requires clinical trials, defined as sets of tests that generate data on the safety and efficacy of health interventions. The merits of the clinical trial procedure are undoubted, but traditional clinical trials have serious drawbacks as well (e.g., Appel 2006). One major issue is the delay in patient access to newly developed treatments caused by regulatory constraints and clinical trial practices. Another related concern stems from the fact that safety and efficacy questions are most easily answered when a disease is common, and the outcome of interest has a high chance of occurring. In the case of rare diseases, the challenges are great, as trials of sufficient size are often impossible because of the difficulty of recruiting a sufficiently large sample of patients with a rare disease of interest (Hayes 2012).

This discussion suggests a need for developing new methods and more pragmatic practices for validating the safety and efficacy of at least some types of medical innovations, including (1) treatments, therapies, or medical devices developed by patients, who lack incentives to diffuse their innovations and do not have access to the resources needed to perform standard clinical trials and whose innovations may be tailored to circumstances encountered by relatively small numbers of patients and (2) innovations aimed at rare diseases, for which it is very hard to apply common methods of clinical trials for uncommon medical conditions.

Experiences with the complementary and alternative medicine (Ernst 2000) market may be informative. Even for complementary medicine, where out-of-pocket payments generated are measured in billions of dollars annually (Dodds et al. 2014; Harris et al. 2012; Xue et al. 2007), no satisfactory mechanism ensures that adequate efficiency and safety evidence is made available to consumers (Harvey 2012). Instead, patients often rely on anecdotes provided by laypeople, peers, or relatives or acquired over the Internet in deciding to try a health-related solution, despite the fact that these stories do not represent reliable evidence and the solution has not been endorsed by any expert authority (Harvey 2012; Williamson et al. 2008). The safety problem is perhaps even more complex regarding solutions developed for personal use by patients which, if they diffuse at all, usually spread for free through informal peer-to-peer networks. The existing literature and practices do not offer reliable answers to the question of how to validate the safety and efficacy of patient-developed solutions.

In light of this situation, we hope to extend the role of the Patient Innovation community to include both the roles of innovator and tester of the self-developed innovations. We are exploring innovative ways of collecting safety and efficacy data that might create new opportunities for validating new treatments, therapies, or medical devices. We are currently considering two possible approaches: the idea of a "toolkit" for patient self-management of chronic medical conditions and the potential to implement observational trials of innovative treatments using our platform.

User innovation toolkits are integrated sets of specialized tools that enable end users of a product or service to develop or modify products for themselves (von Hippel 2005). Shifting a problem-solving task to users via a toolkit lowers costs when users possess the information required to solve the problem in raw form and when it is less expensive to transfer the tools needed to process that information to the user than it is to transfer the user's information to an expert.

This same economic logic may apply to medical toolkits devised for specific purposes. Here we consider the possibility of toolkits for patient self-management of chronic medical conditions. Such toolkits would offer patients the tools needed to process their personal "raw" disease-related data into information that helps them manage their illnesses. The toolkit would give patients the information needed to (1) appropriately recognize when to apply a prescribed or over-the-counter medical treatment, (2) apply the treatment, (3) receive feedback on the results of the treatment, and (4) make appropriate treatment adjustments without the involvement of a health care specialist (DeMonaco et al. 2006). We are currently working on developing toolkits for allowing patients of some selected chronic diseases to test their self-developed treatments, therapies, or medical devices. Such toolkits, interfacing with the Patient Innovation platform, might help overcome the difficulties faced by clinical trials of rare disease treatments: the need to "recruit" patients spread across different areas and follow them for a longer period than typically needed for clinical trials aimed at more common diseases. To enable better collection of data, we aim to attract developers of cross-platform (Android, iOS, Windows) mobile applications, which would be integrated with the Patient Innovation solution-sharing platform, for patients to record vital health indicators and associate the recordings with the solutions shared in the platform. Shifting the validation of user-developed treatments, therapies, or medical devices to patients spread across different areas, using a toolkit for data collection, would significantly lower the costs of generating data on the safety and efficacy of the innovation.

Simply by providing an infrastructure for reporting patient innovations and centralizing information about patient innovations in an easily accessible location, Patient Innovation lowers barriers to the diffusion of innovation. The Patient Innovation platform also lowers the barriers to diffusion because it facilitates the patient-initiated search for solutions. Health needs often are heterogeneous, even among different patients suffering from the same disease. Patients and caregivers know their circumstances and needs better than anyone else and are well aware of when their needs are addressed by conventional health care and health systems and when they must adopt or discover solutions to fill in the gaps. By using an open platform, Patient Innovation helps diffuse solutions proposed by patients and caregivers, after careful screening for compliance with our terms of service. We are currently exploring ways to develop an ecosystem, which would enable even wider diffusion of solutions that have been proven to be of clinical efficacy.

CONCLUSIONS

The global sharing of innovative solutions and treatments developed by patients and their caregivers can potentially be a "game changer" in the health industry. The innovation efforts by patients and their valuable solutions can potentially save significant resources, reduce costs, promote the exchange of knowledge among target stakeholders, and ultimately have an important social and economic impact. Recognition of patient innovation also has the potential to enable patients to assume more responsibility for the collaborative development and diffusion of medical innovations. We have approached patient innovation along two complementary paths: an interdisciplinary scholarly research effort aimed at understanding the patient innovation phenomenon and the design and launch of the Patient Innovation online platform to encourage and facilitate the development and diffusion of patient innovations. Our academic research helped frame the development of the Patient Innovation platform. Implementing the platform has raised new research questions in turn.

Feedback between scholarly research and practical application in the patient innovation arena has the potential to produce great societal benefit. Consider how a similar virtuous cycle has operated in the recently developed field of "entrepreneurship." Individuals have always created new firms. However, only recently have researchers started studying entrepreneurship and firm creation in a systematic way. The topic has become so popular that schools now offer courses on the topic. The "buzz" has motivated people to become entrepreneurs, while the improved understanding of entrepreneurship can be employed to empower them to do so. Something similar can perhaps happen with patient innovation. With technology and guidance, we can empower patients to innovate, and this is Patient Innovation's mission.

We have shown that patients are innovators, and we have developed the basic infrastructure for a patient innovation knowledge commons, but much remains to be done. Many patients do not even understand that they have the potential to create valuable innovations – even if they are already doing so. Greater awareness of the potential for patient innovation might motivate patients who have various potentially relevant skills to become deeply involved in using those skills to improve their health care – just as Tal Golesworthy employed his engineering skills to design his aortic root external support. Numerous interesting questions for researchers in many disciplines remain. Our experience implementing the Patient Innovation platform uncovered questions lacking clear-cut solutions concerning intellectual property, legal responsibility, medical ethics, and the methodology for assessing safety and efficacy, just to name a few. We are only at the beginning of understanding patient innovation and realizing its potential to benefit society. We invite those with the skills and will to join our efforts, helping us understand and enable patient innovators and to level the field for meaningful patient participation at all levels of integrated health care.

REFERENCES

Appel, L. J., 2006. A primer on the design, conduct, and interpretation of clinical trials. *Clin. J. Am. Soc. Nephrol.* 1(6):1360–1367.

Baldwin, C. Y., C. Hienerth, and E. von Hippel, 2006. How user innovations become commercial products: A theoretical investigation and case study. *Res. Policy* 35(9):1291–1313.

Branco, J. C., A. M. Rodrigues, N. Gouveia et al. 2016. Prevalence of rheumatic and musculoskeletal diseases and their impact on health related quality of life, physical function and mental health in Portugal: Results from Epireumapt–A National Health Survey. *RMD Open* 2:e000166.

Cooper, R. G., 2008. Perspective: The Stage-Gates Idea-to-Launch Process – Update, what's new, and NexGen systems. *J. Prod. Innov. Manag.* 25:213–232.

Damanpour, F., 1991. Organizational innovation: A meta-analysis of effects of determinants and moderators. *Acad. Manag. J.* 34(3):555–590.

de Jong, J. P. J., E. von Hippel, F. Gault, J. Kuusisto, and C. Raasch, 2015. Market Failure in the Diffusion of Consumer-Developed Innovations: Patterns in Finland. *Res. Policy* 44(10):1856–1865.

DeMonaco, H. J., A. Ali, and E. Von Hippel, 2006. The major role of clinicians in the discovery of off-label drug therapies. *Pharmacotherapy* 26(3):323–332.

Dodds, S., S. Bulmer, and A. Murphy, 2014. Consumer value in complementary and alternative medicine (CAM) health care services. *Australasian Marketing J.* 22 (3):218–299.

Elkins, M. R., M. Robinson, B. R. Rose et al., 2006. A controlled trial of long-term inhaled hypertonic saline in patients with cystic fibrosis. *N. Engl. J. Med.* 354 (3):229–240.

Ernst, E., 2000. Prevalence of use of complementary/alternative medicine: A systematic review. *Bull. World Health Organ* 78(2):252–257.

FDA, 2013. *Medwatch Voluntary Report.* www.ncbi.nlm.nih.gov/pmc/articles/PMC2560678/

Fox, S., 2011. *Peer-to-Peer Healthcare.* Washington, DC: Pew Research Center.

Genomera, 2013. Genomera. Heal the World. http://genomera.com/.

Habicht, H., P. Oliveira, and V. Shcherbatiuk, 2012. User innovators: When patients set out to help themselves and end up helping many. *Die Unternehmung* 66 (3):277–294.

Harris, P. E., K. L. Cooper, C. Relton, and K. J. Thomas, 2012. Prevalence of complementary and alternative medicine (CAM) use by the general population: A systematic review and update. *Int. J. Clin. Pract.* 66(10):924–939.

Harvey, K., 2012. The evidence for complementary medicines. *Heal. Voices* (11).

Hayes, S., 2012. The Potential of Patient Initiated Research in Studying Rare Diseases. KevinMD.com blog. www.kevinmd.com/blog/2012/07/potential-patient-initiated-research-studying-rare-diseases.html.

Hibbard, J., J. Stockard, E. R. Mahoney, and M. Tusler, 2004. Development of the Patient Activation Measure (PAM): Conceptualizing and measuring activation in patients and consumers. *Health Serv. Res.* 39:1005–1026.

Langley, A., H. Mintzberg, P. Pitcher, E. Posada, and J. Saint-Macary, 1995. Opening up decision making: The view from the black stool. *Organ. Sci.* 6 (3):260–279.

Lüthje, C., C. Herstatt, and E. von Hippel, 2005. User-innovators and "local" information: The case of mountain biking. *Res. Policy* 34(6):951–965.

Mintzberg, H., D. Raisinghani, and A. Theoret, 1976. The structure of "unstructured" decision processes. *Adm. Sci. Q.* 21(2):246–275.

Morrison, P. D., J. H. Roberts, and E. von Hippel, 2000. Determinants of user innovation and innovation sharing in a local market. *Manage. Sci.* 46(12):1513–1527.

Newell, A., and H. Simon, 1972. *Human Problem Solving*. Englewood Cliffs, NJ: Prentice Hall.

Ogawa, S. (1998) Does Sticky Information Affect the Locus of Innovation? Evidence from the Japanese Convenience-Store Industry. *Res Policy* 26: 777–790.

Oliveira, P., and H. Canhão, 2016. Users as Service Innovators: Evidence from Banking to Healthcare, in K. Lakhani and D. Harhoff (eds.), *Revolutionizing Innovation*. Cambridge, MA: MIT Press.

Oliveira, P., and E. von Hippel, 2011. *Users as service innovators: The case of banking services. Res. Policy* 40(6):806–818.

Oliveira, P., L. Zejnilovic, H. Canhao, and E. von Hippel, 2015. Innovation by patients with rare diseases and chronic needs. *Orphanet J. Rare Dis.* 10.

Oliveira, R., 2014. Patients and caregivers as sources of innovative ideas and solutions: A multiple-case study approach. Master Thesis. Universidade Catolica Portuguesa.

Parker, G. G., and M. W. Van Alstyne, 2010. *Innovation, Openness & Platform Control*, in EC '10 Proceedings of the 11th ACM Conference on Electronic Commerce.

Peck, P., 2006. Studies look to sea for cystic fibrosis treatment. *CNN Health, MedPage Today*, Jan. 19, 2006, http://edition.cnn.com/2006/HEALTH/conditions/01/18/cf.saltwater/index.html.

Riggs, W. and E. von Hippel, 1994. The impact of scientific and commercial values on the sources of scientific instrument innovation, *Res. Policy* 23 (July): 459–469.

Roehr, B., 2011. Pfizer launches virtual clinical trial. *BMJ. Br. Med. J.* 342 (d3722), www.ncbi.nlm.nih.gov/pubmed/21672995.

Rogers, E. M., 2003. *Diffusion of Innovations*. 5th ed. New York: Free Press.

Rosenberg, N. Learning by Using, in *Inside the black box: Technology in economics* (N. Rosenberg, ed., 120–140. New York: Cambridge University Press, 1982).

Shcherbatiuk, V., 2012. *Users as Developers and Entrepreneurs of Medical Treatments Treatments/Devices: The Case of Patients and Their Families and Friends*. Catholic University of Portugal.

Simon, H., 1977. *The New Science of Management Decision*. Rev. ed. Englewood Cliffs, NJ: Prentice Hall.

Thrall, J. H., 2005. Prevalence and costs of chronic disease in a health care system structured for treatment of acute illness. *Radiology* 235:9–12.

Treasure, T., and J. Pepper, 2015. Personalised External Aortic Root Support (PEARS) compared with alternatives for people with life-threatening genetically determined aneurysms of the aortic root. *Diseases* 3:2–14.

von Hippel, E., 1994. "Sticky Information" and the Locus of Problem Solving: Implications for Innovation. *Manage. Sci.* 40(4):429–439.

von Hippel, E., 1988. *The Sources of Innovation*. New York: Oxford University Press.

von Hippel, E. 2005. *Democratizing Innovation*. Cambridge, MA: MIT Press.

von Hippel, E. 2010. Open User Innovation. *Handb. Econ. Innov*. Vol. 1. Elsevier B. V.:411–427.

von Hippel, E. A., and G. von Krogh, 2015. Identifying viable "need-solution pairs": Problem solving without problem formulation. *Organization Science* 27(1): 207–221.

von Hippel, E., J. P. J. de Jong, and S. Flowers, 2012. Comparing business and household sector innovation in consumer products: Findings from a representative study in the United Kingdom. *Manage. Sci.* 58(9):1669–1681.

von Hippel, E., H. J. DeMonaco, and J. P. J. de Jong, 2017. Market failure in the diffusion of clinician-developed innovations: The case of "off-label" drug discoveries. *Science and Public Policy* 44(1): 121–131.

Vos, T., A. Flaxman, M. Naghavi, and R. Lozano, 2013. Years lived with disability (YLDs) for 1160 sequelae of 289 diseases and injuries 1990–2010: a systematic analysis for the Global Burden of Disease Study 2010. *Lancet* 380(9859):2163–2196.

WHO, 1978. Alma Ata Declaration. www.who.int/publications/almaata_declaration_en.pdf

Wicks, P., T. E. Vaughan, M. P. Massagli, and J. Heywood, 2011. Accelerated clinical discovery using self-reported patient data collected online and a patient-matching algorithm. *Nat. Biotechnol.* 29(5):411–414.

Williamson, M., J. Tudball, M. Toms, F. Garden, and A. Grunseit, 2008. Information Use and Needs of Complementary Medicines Users. National Prescribing Service, Sydney, October 2008.

Xue, C. C. L., A. L. Zhang, V. Lin, C. Da Costa, and D. F. Story, 2007. Complementary and alternative medicine use in Australia: A national population-based survey. *J. Altern. Complement. Med.* 13(6):643–50.

Zejnilovic, L., H. Canhão, and P. Oliveira, 2016. Development, adoption, and attitudes towards health-related solutions developed by citizens – A representative survey in Portugal. *Open and User Innovation Society Meeting Proceedings*.

14

Chronic Disease, New Thinking, and Outlaw Innovation: Patients on the Edge in the Knowledge Commons

Stephen Flowers

INTRODUCTION

The gap between the innovations some people really want and the innovations that can be supplied by the standard practices of mainstream innovators can sometimes be extreme. This gap may result from a variety of factors, including regulation, lack of scientific knowledge, the inflexibility of suppliers, and inadequate market size. Whatever the reasons for its existence, such a gap creates a demand that will not be met within normal channels, creating a space for new thinking and innovative activity outside the mainstream. One documented response to needs that are unmet by market innovators, is "user innovation," in which users, often banding together in user communities, create their own innovative solutions to their needs. Innovation by users of all types (including patients) is a widespread phenomenon within modern economies (e.g., de Jong and von Hippel 2009; Flowers et al. 2010a; Schaan and Urbach 2009).

Chronic disease is one context in which market innovation fails to meet the needs of users. In this context the unmet demand of patients for a cure, or simply for effective symptom relief, meets a slow and inflexible medical industry that is unable to adequately respond. While industry in all fields often fails to meet the needs of some consumers, the medical context is particularly problematic because of the urgency of patients' unmet needs along with the fact that innovation is highly regulated. Medical innovations must go through a series of large-scale trials and tests to make sure that they are "safe" to offer for sale. For reasons of public safety, new drugs and therapies are subject to a series of trials, tests, and approvals that often last for many years with the result that the relatively fast diffusion of innovations from users to the mainstream cannot take place.

Stephen Flowers is Professor of Management (Innovation), Kent Business School, University of Kent, Canterbury, Kent, UK.

This regulatory environment, though intended for consumer protection, often creates tensions between the patient – the user of the treatment – and the medical professional, who may be discouraged or forbidden from offering promising experimental therapies that have not gone through the full regulatory process. This tension may be particularly serious in the context of chronic diseases, in which therapies may require a decade or more of research before they can begin the process of regulatory approval, which may itself take many more years.

Confronted with this situation, some patients decide that they simply cannot afford to wait. They determine to sidestep regulated processes, draw on published scientific research, and attempt to create their own therapies. These activist patients engage in what we term "outlaw innovation," which differs from much of the user innovation studied in prior research in its relationship to mainstream innovation. Newly created knowledge obtained by outlaw innovation is widely shared with other patients, but mainstream medical research is unable to draw upon it. The picture that emerges from our analysis is of a medical research system whose inflexibility means that it is unable to draw on vibrant sources of new knowledge that are being created by activist patients – the users of medical therapies – who have taken their treatment into their own hands.

This chapter explores the implications of outlaw innovation in the context of Crohn's disease, a chronic form of inflammatory bowel disease, a type of autoimmune disorder. Autoimmune diseases present a particular challenge to medicine as their causes are not fully understood, no cures are currently available, and they are very hard to treat. To explore the rich and complex territory of patient activism, medical innovation, and chronic disease, this chapter draws on a diverse range of medical practitioner, medical research, and innovation literatures.

It begins by exploring existing literature about patient innovation, before going on to examine how innovation in mainstream medical therapy typically proceeds. The chapter goes on to explore some of the scientific research that provides a backdrop for patient innovation for Crohn's disease: the use of helminths (a form of intestinal parasite) in treating autoimmune diseases. At the core of this chapter is the examination of the research and knowledge creation activities of a small group of activist patients as they work together, forming a knowledge commons, to try to develop an effective treatment for their Crohn's disease. The part played by such patients in adding to the medical knowledge commons in this area, and the challenge their outlaw innovation poses to the mainstream, is explored in the final part of this chapter.

14.1 PERSPECTIVES ON PATIENTS AS INNOVATORS

The contributions made by patients (as users) in the treatment of disease have been explored across a range of literatures, each with its own preoccupations and framing. The development of the broad discussion has tended to be driven by emergent empirical phenomena, as those afflicted with (often serious) medical conditions mobilize and deploy a range of resources to improve their diagnosis, treatment, and prognosis. The role of the Internet, and of social media in particular, emerges as an important theme in this literature. The Internet both enables the development of online communities, which create and govern knowledge commons to pool resources and advance the treatment of chronic conditions, and also makes these efforts highly visible.

The first part of this review will draw on conceptual approaches in the innovation studies (IS) and science and technology studies (STS) literatures to better understand the challenges faced by users who wish to innovate on their own account, rather than act as partners to mainstream professional actors. It argues that the conceptual approaches developed within the IS and STS literatures are complementary and throw new light on the evolving phenomenon of patient involvement in health care. To provide a wider context, the review will also draw on the health care practice literature to outline the growing importance of online user communities in the treatment of medical conditions.

14.1.1 *Patient Innovation: Insights from Innovation Studies*

An important thread of innovation studies examines the processes, motivations, and outcomes of "user innovators," who benefit directly from using the novel things they create and distribute, rather than from selling them. Innovation by users is prevalent when it is aimed at satisfying a local niche, rather than a broader market need (von Hippel 1986). The phenomenon was first noted in the field of scientific instruments by von Hippel (1976) and has since been observed in many other contexts, including medical devices (e.g., Oliveira et al. 2014) and surgical instruments (e.g., Lettl 2007). This large body of work is reviewed by von Hippel (2005) and shows the significant proportions of users who innovate in many diverse fields. The literature also has explored a series of features of user innovation, including horizontal networks (von Hippel 2007), how firms make use of open source (Dahlander and Magnusson 2005) and hacker communities (Flowers 2008), and the role of users as co-developers (Jeppesen and Molin 2003). The observation that many users will freely reveal their innovations has also been explored (von Hippel and von Krogh 2003), as have the voluntary information spillovers that emerge (Harhoff et al. 2003), and the social welfare gains that result from user innovation (Henkel and von Hippel 2004).

User innovation often occurs when users have needs that are not satisfied by the products and services available to them from the market and are able to mobilize the resources required to meet those needs (von Hippel 1986). Users possess extensive local (sticky) information concerning their specific needs, something that is often hard for producers to access (von Hippel 1994. Users who innovate are often "lead users," whose use is at the leading edge in a given arena and whose innovations thus point the way to the shape of a future market and are a valuable source of ideas for commercial firms (von Hippel 1986). The literature on lead users has been elaborated over a series of contributions that have refined our understanding of how they may be defined (e.g., von Hippel 1986), their motivations (e.g., Urban and von Hippel 1988), and how the mainstream may seek to collaborate with them (e.g., Lilien et al. 2002). Lead users are of interest to producers because they experience their needs in advance of the typical user and can act as "a need-forecasting laboratory for marketing research" (von Hippel 1986), such that their innovative activity can point the way to future market demand, a key producer concern. User innovation thus is often depicted as synergistic with innovation by mainstream firms. A key assumption of this framing is that producers should be in a position to benefit from the work of lead users, for example, by developing relevant in-house capabilities (e.g., Berthon et al. 2007).

While much user innovation, including much patient innovation (see, e.g., Chapter 13, this volume) is complementary to mainstream commercial innovation, some user innovators, including the patient innovators described in this chapter, consciously set aside mainstream practices, including formal rules and regulations, to free themselves to engage in certain types of innovation (Flowers 2008). These "outlaw users," whether working alone or in groups, actively oppose or ignore the limitations imposed on them by mainstream practices, setting up parallel, user-led innovation systems that are in tension with the mainstream system. They will generate outlaw innovations differing from those produced by mainstream practices (Flowers 2008). Because the mainstream is either unwilling or unable to work with outlaw users, they are a kind of doppelganger lead user, with a different kind of relationship to mainstream commercial players than the symbiotic relationship envisioned in much of the user innovation literature. While there is now a considerable literature concerning the interactions between lead users and commercial producers, we understand far less about how producers deal (or could deal) with the challenges of absorbing the outlaw innovations that are developed by outlaw users.

14.1.2 *Patient Knowledge: Insights from Science and Technology Studies*

The science and technology studies literature also offers a series of insights that will be useful in understanding the outlaw innovation explored here. The importance of patient knowledge and experience has been emphasized in this literature and active and informed patient associations (e.g., Barbot 2006) and "concerned groups" (Callon and Rabeharisoa 2003) are viewed as important innovation actors. The role of nonscientists in medical science – be they concerned citizens, patients, caregivers or (in the broadest terms) "users" – is also an important theme in this literature (e.g., Epstein 1996; Wynne 1996). Experimentation with the incorporation (or co-option) of these groups into professional scientific endeavors has led to the emergence of a new form of hybrid science, termed research "in the wild" (Callon and Rabeharisoa 2003). This form of research has been widely explored in the context of patient organizations focused on chronic disease, and their importance as partners in seeking improved outcomes has been clearly established. This STS literature focuses primarily on ways in which patient knowledge and experience can be drawn upon and valued within the more traditional (and mainstream) system of science involving laboratory and clinical trials. A few STS studies also document that patient groups may move beyond standard approaches and construct new forms of scientific community based on patient experiments and a broader palate of scientific approaches (Barbot 2006). However, there are few accounts of such (potentially outlaw innovation) activity and this form of innovative patient behavior remains largely unexplored.

14.1.3 *Patient Activism: Insights from Practice*

Complementary insights into the phenomenon of medical innovation by patients (as users) may be obtained by drawing on the practice literature in health care. This literature tends to be concerned with reporting and debating developments in medicine and is aimed at (and often written by) medical professionals. One feature that has been widely documented in this literature is the growing importance of online information sources. The practice literature contains many accounts of patients who benefited from advice and guidance found in online patient communities (e.g., deBronkart 2013) or who helped others by creating their own online communities (e.g., Seres 2013). Research has shown that the use of social media within health care is now widespread (e.g., Pew Internet 2010), and a wide range of approaches are employed, including discussion forums, blogs, and social networking (e.g., Hamm et al. 2013). This phenomenon continues to evolve and new forms of "crowd-sourced" clinical research have begun to emerge based on patient involvement in social media (e.g., Swan 2012a, 2012b).

This practice literature has long recognized that the core of this activity is the often detailed and in-depth knowledge that patients can possess: "[Patients] will typically know only about their one disease, but since they can devote a great deal of time to it, their knowledge within that single narrow niche can be impressive" (Ferguson 2000: 1130). The growing recognition within the practice literature of the valuable knowledge, experience, and expertise that are possessed and shared by some patients has also led to an exploration for new labels for these empowered groups. Terms that have been employed include "medical end user" (Ferguson 2002) and "e-patient" (Ferguson 2004; deBronkart 2013), but the term "patient" is still mainstream in discussions concerning the impact of social media on health care (e.g., Richards et al. 2013). Although within this literature is a recognition that the relationship between clinical professional and some patients is changing, the contribution of such groups is clearly positioned as an adjunct to mainstream medical practice and the issue of outlaw innovation remains mostly unexplored.

14.2 THE DRIVERS OF PATIENT INNOVATION FOR CHRONIC DISEASE TREATMENT

Chronic disease presents a particular set of circumstances within which the role of user innovators may be explored. User innovation theory proposes that when possessed by a need not met by the market, users with the resources to do so will innovate (von Hippel 1986), although the nature of the need and the level of resources required for innovation to occur are left unspecified. The theory also suggests that users will innovate based on their sticky local knowledge of their particular circumstances. Individuals suffering from a chronic condition, especially one that is relatively rare, are likely to have a strong need to obtain something that the market is unable to provide (a cure, remission, reduction in symptom burden). They also are likely to possess extensive and detailed experience-based knowledge concerning the "local" circumstances and the impact the disease has upon them. Individuals with chronic medical conditions thus are likely to possess many of the common characteristics of user innovators. It might be anticipated that, as a group, they could be a strong source of innovation relating to their specific afflictions.

Patients with chronic medical conditions differ from user innovators in other fields in a number of important respects, however, which may dampen their ability to innovate. To begin with, it is important to recognize that patients who suffer from a chronic medical condition are ill and may lack those most valuable of resources required to innovate – time and energy. The high rate of innovation reported in the surveys of rare disease patients and their caregivers discussed by Oliveira et al. (Chapter 13, this volume) suggest, however, that urgent and persistent need can overcome these barriers, at least in some disease contexts.

Some types of medical innovation, particularly those involving drug-based treatments, seem particularly unlikely to result from patient innovation, since patients might be expected to lack the scientific expertise and other specialized resources required both to develop such treatments and to assess their safety and efficacy. Indeed, barriers to patient innovation in this arena arise not only from lack of scientific expertise but also from the regulatory systems that were designed with the goal of ensuring that patients receive safe and efficacious treatments.

The regulated nature of the medical innovation system, with its rigorous standards for safety and efficacy means, however, that it can take a long time for a new treatment to be approved, and still longer for it to become widely available to patients. From the point of view of a patient diagnosed with a serious chronic disease, the future in the interim may appear bleak, potentially filled with ongoing periods of illness, and a series of more or less unpleasant holding strategies, including drugs and surgery with unpleasant side effects and no long-term relief. The sufferer is largely excluded from the standard medical innovation system and is expected simply to wait for new and better treatments to emerge. In this situation, extreme need may provide motivation for patients to seek solutions that lie outside the control of the regulated medical system, through a process of outlaw innovation. The next section explores one such case: the commons-based user innovation of helminthic therapy for Crohn's disease.

14.3 OUTLAW INNOVATION AND THE COMMONS-BASED PATIENT INNOVATION OF HELMINTHIC THERAPY FOR CROHN'S DISEASE

This section describes in detail how a small group of patients who suffer from Crohn's disease – a chronic disease for which there is no cure and no satisfactory long-term treatment for many patients – worked together to try and develop an effective therapy to treat the disease outside of mainstream medical processes of innovation and regulation. The case throws new light on what may drive users (in this case, patients with a chronic condition) to take a knowledge commons approach to pooling their knowledge and ideas. It illustrates how sufficiently strong user need, coupled with dissatisfaction with the pace of strongly regulated medical innovation, can facilitate the emergence of outlaw user communities (Flowers 2008) willing to innovate outside regulated processes. It also illuminates how this outlaw innovation process interacts with the standard scientific and medical research paradigms.

The case study involves the user-led development of helminthic therapy for Crohn's disease. In helminthic therapy, users ingest tiny worm larvae to develop the viable community of parasitic worms that will act to reduce the impact of their immune condition. The therapy is based on the firm foundation of mainstream scientific and medical research that suggests its potential safety and efficacy as a means of relieving serious and chronic symptoms of the disease, but it has been largely developed by a group of patients experimenting on themselves and pooling their knowledge and experiences in a form of outlaw innovation.

14.3.1 *Prologue: Crohn's Disease, Treatment, and Emerging Research Directions*

To set the scene, a brief overview of Crohn's disease and the scientific research into autoimmune disease is provided as background for the application of helminths in a therapeutic context.

14.3.1.1 Crohn's Disease and Its Treatment

Crohn's disease is a chronic condition whose cause is not fully understood and for which no cure is currently available (Van Assche et al. 2010a). The disease affects around 690,000 people in Europe (90,000 in the UK) (Cummings et al. 2008) and 1.4 million people in the United States (CCFA 2011). Crohn's tends to occur in the second or third decade of life and, although the precise cause remains unclear, it is currently believed to result from an inappropriately vigorous immune response in the intestinal lumen (Weinstock and Elliott 2009).

Crohn's disease was first described in 1932 (Crohn et al. 1932) and is named after Dr. Burrill Crohn, a gastroenterologist who encountered patients with inflammation in the part of their gut that lies between the small and large intestine (the terminal ileum). The science around the development of helminthic therapy draws on a series of different aspects of the disease that point to a causal relationship between its prevalence and the presence (or absence) of intestinal parasites. The research in this area provides evidence on five main aspects of the disease: the incidence and distribution (epidemiology) of autoimmune diseases such as Crohn's, the role of pathogens in developing the immune system, the role of microorganisms such as intestinal worms in moderating immune reactions, specific chemical and biological mechanisms that moderate the disease, and safety.

The chronic nature of Crohn's disease means that many patients with this condition have to live their lives with ongoing symptoms that may include weight loss, abdominal pain, diarrhea, anemia, and fatigue (Van Assche et al. 2010a). Given that there is no cure for Crohn's, mainstream treatments focus on inducing and maintaining remission or dealing with the complications of earlier interventions (Dignass et al. 2010). The main treatment regimens are corticosteroids, immunosuppressants, and antibiotics (Dignass et al. 2010). The need for surgery to resection intestines to eliminate blockages arising from internal scarring is historically very high, with around 80 percent of patients undergoing surgery at some point (Van Assche et al. 2010b). Medical treatment has advanced significantly in recent years, but Crohn's remains a deeply unpleasant chronic disease.

14.3.1.2 The Research Foundations of User-Led Helminth Therapy

The epidemiology of Crohn's disease displays what has become termed a North-South gradient in that, in common with many autoimmune diseases, prevalence is higher in North America and Europe than in more southerly, often developing, countries (Hutt 1979; Shivananda et al. 1996). Related evidence concerns the role of pathogens (i.e., a bacterium, virus, or other microorganism that can cause disease) in assisting in the development of the human immune system. This evidence, which led to the development of what came to be termed the Hygiene Hypothesis, proposed a link between exposure to pathogens while young and the development of allergic diseases (Strachan 1989). This hypothesis proposes that some of the increased prevalence of allergic and other autoimmune diseases is the result of poor regulation of the immune system as a result of reduced exposure to pathogens during childhood (Rook 2008). This hypothesis is linked to the Old Friends Hypothesis that suggests a mutually beneficial (symbiotic) relationship between ourselves and the fauna (e.g., intestinal parasites such as helminths) that have coevolved to inhabit the human gastrointestinal tract (Rook and Brunet 2005).

In addition to this contextual work, helminthic therapy also draws on extensive research that has explored the link between intestinal worms and immune responses. Animal trials have shown links between helminths and the prevention or treatment of intestinal infection (e.g., Elliott et al. 2000, 2003; Khan et al. 2002). Research has also examined the efficacy of different types of helminth, focusing on the pig whipworm (Trichuris suis) and the human hookworm (Necator americanus). As these helminths inhabit different parts of the gastrointestinal tract, their use in treatments is targeted at different forms of an autoimmune disease and, it is hypothesized, will have different effects according to the condition of the user, the scale of infection, and a host of other factors. To date, mainstream scientific research has explored the effects of both human and porcine (pig) helminths and their impact on immune responses in people.

Small-scale, experimental trials to study the safety and effectiveness of the pig whipworm Trichuris suis demonstrated that they were safe and were able to reduce the symptoms of Crohn's and also help with remission, with no side effects or complications (Summers et al. 2003, 2005a, 2005b). Since it has evolved to inhabit a different organism, Trichuris suis does not cause human disease and can only persist within humans for a relatively short period of time (Beer 1976). As a result, the application of these particular worms as "treatment" requires regular reinfection to maintain the required immune response, a feature that makes it potentially attractive from a commercial perspective.

In the context of human helminths, research on the application of human hookworm Necator americanus has also explored clinical responses to low doses of the helminths (Maxwell et al. 1987) and what appropriate levels of infection might be (Scrivener et al. 2001). This work revealed that small populations of helminths were supportable and examined the role of helminths in the suppression of asthma symptoms. Other research also found evidence to suggest that individuals who have previously been infected with human helminths have reduced immune responses (Borkow et al. 2000; Elliott et al. 2000) and that this effect may persist after infection has ceased (e.g., Bentwich et al. 1996).[1] In the context of autoimmune diseases such as Crohn's and colitis, this finding is encouraging and may suggest that the human autoimmune system can be "trained" to react in a more moderate fashion.

Thus a significant body of mainstream scientific research now points to the presence of a possible therapeutic link between helminths and Crohn's disease. This evidence has led to the question of whether the systematic elimination of all human helminths in modern developing countries may be responsible for the subsequent increased prevalence of Crohn's (Elliott et al. 2000) and the proposal of the IBD Hygiene Hypothesis (Weinstock and Elliott 2009) in which the absence

[1] A large body of research has also examined the problems caused by the heavy infestation with intestinal parasites (such as helminths) in developing countries and work is underway to develop a hookworm vaccine (e.g., Diemert et al. 2008).

of intestinal parasites in the human gut may be a contributing factor in the rise in the incidence of autoimmune diseases like Crohn's and colitis. However, despite the large body of careful scientific research that has examined a wide range of issues associated with helminths, and the promising results obtained from small-scale experimental trials, at the time of writing no large-scale clinical trials to examine their therapeutic effect are underway, with the first such trial being cancelled in 2013.

14.3.2 *User-Led Development of Helminthic Therapy*

The foundation for the application of human helminths as a therapy for a range of autoimmune diseases was laid down by the results of the mainstream scientific research outlined earlier. However, the translation of this research into an unlicensed therapy based on human hookworm, Necator americanus, has been primarily driven by patients, who have created an online community to pool their knowledge and efforts to develop a workable helminthic therapy for Crohn's disease. This section explores the way in which the online patient community formed and governs itself in working toward the goal of a safe and effective helminthic therapy for Crohn's disease.

The primary action arena for the helminth therapy community's innovative activity are the blogs on which community members post their activities, results, and comments, which are the personal accounts of patients who have made the decision to explore the use of helminths to seek remission from Crohn's and colitis. Analyzing this material provides detailed insights into the activities of these users and the governance of this highly specialized knowledge commons.

14.3.2.1 The Helminthic Therapy User Community: Formation and Membership

This setting is an entirely open community in which experiences are published on blogs and "membership" is achieved by a shared need, an openness to experiment with helminths, and the willingness to share the results of one's activities. In common with many open source groups, this is a self-organizing community in which membership is open to all, but one's place is earned by the hard "work" of contribution. In general, users are all driven by the strong need to find relief from the often extreme symptoms that arise both from autoimmune afflictions such as Crohn's, colitis, multiple sclerosis, asthma, and psoriasis and from the side effects of the standard treatments they have receive. The blogs offer an insight into the shape and nature of unmet need that drives this form of user to participate. The overwhelming and extreme desire for a cure for Crohn's or colitis or for a means to obtain remission is a recurrent theme within the blogs, as is the loss of, and need for, hope that an end is in sight for their suffering. The following is a typical example:

> My symptoms present as abdominal pain, rectal pain, diarrhea, fecal incontinence and malabsorption. And that's on a good day.
>
> Orin Twist: May 7, 2013

The membership and narrative of the community are also strongly influenced by its "outlaw" approach. Members label themselves as "citizen scientists," "experimental subjects," or "pioneers" in the field and recognize that they are operating outside the regulated health care environment. A blog post that captures this position follows:

> I can't see this ever being a mainstream . . . treatment that a doctor could prescribe. As a living organism, it's not something any drug company could ever patent, so it's unlikely to get all of the trials and testing it would need to get to that stage. But I've seen enough from the few trials that have taken place, and the anecdotal evidence I've read, for me to be certain that it's worth giving it a go. And whilst it may be experimental and therefore inherently risky, the types of risks we're talking about pale in to insignificance compared to the risks associated with the conventional treatments my consultant was proposing.
>
> Hookworm for Crohn's: September 22, 2010

14.3.2.2 Resources Shared and Created by the Community

The commons-based development of helminth therapy draws heavily on the current scientific understanding of the role and impact of human intestinal parasites on immune responses of people with an autoimmune condition. Infecting oneself involves swallowing parasite larvae with the intention of creating a viable, if small, colony to produce the required reduction in symptoms. However, although there is clear evidence for the therapeutic use of human helminths, there is little knowledge on how the treatment may be optimized. As a result, the treatment depends on the creation and sharing of a variety of knowledge resources, including relevant information from the mainstream scientific literature, the personal accounts of trial and error "experiments" conducted by members in treating their own disease, and collective discussion and critique of both. It also depends on the availability of hookworms, which are obtained from a small network of commercial suppliers or by "harvesting" them from those with viable helminth communities.

14.3.2.2.1 MAINSTREAM MEDICAL RESEARCH PUBLICATIONS

Despite the fact that this is an outlaw user innovator community, in the sense that participants are content to accept the risks associated with stepping outside the regulated health care system and experimenting with their own treatment, it is also a well-informed community that draws on the results of research published by the mainstream scientific community in this area, as well as on a wide range of additional scientific sources. This patient innovator community relies heavily on publicly available knowledge obtained from formal scientific studies to provide insights into the mechanisms and effects of helminths in regulating autoimmune diseases. As a result, the helminth therapy patient community is not fully outlaw in the sense of rejecting the results of mainstream medical research, and the main body of underpinning science is clearly outlined and the "case" for the therapeutic application of helminths is explored. For example:

> More specifically, this blog is about the pursuit of a new, relatively untested treatment for UC: helminthic therapy. Also known as whipworm parasite, I'm planning to introduce 1,000 ova of these little fellas to my system in January in hopes they will be a game changer in my ongoing slog against this stupid disease. I'll be using this space to document my progress on this treatment for other folks who are thinking of pursuing this course of action. Please note that under "For your information" I've included some links to what I think are some really good resources on the topic of IBD, including a couple of folks who are also keeping blogs about their experiences with helminthic therapy.
>
> The UC Chronicles: December 17, 2010

Moreover, members of this community help one another stay abreast of the ongoing work of the mainstream researchers active in the field and routinely share (and critique) findings from the latest published helminth studies and discuss and evaluate the results of associated research, for example:

> A new "biological fingerprint" – the bacterial enterotype – has recently been discovered which may eventually become as important as blood types and tissue types are today, with many implications for understanding and improving health . . . I suspect that this line of research will produce many more fascinating developments, and perhaps a few more surprises, along the way. This is definitely one to watch!
>
> gut_buddies: April 27, 2011

The helminth therapy community thus provides an example of a user innovator community that assimilates and shares specialized knowledge derived from scientific research and combines it with members' local experience and personal evidence. Indeed, to be fully effective and make informed decisions, these users must make substantial investments to obtain and understand this specialized scientific knowledge.

14.3.2.2.2 SHARING USER ACCOUNTS WITHIN THE COMMUNITY

At the heart of the development of the creation of experimental helminth therapy is users' willingness to engage in informed trial-and-error experimentation with their own treatments and to share personal accounts of their experiences with the group. To that end, members of this group shared detailed information concerning their own symptoms, treatments, dosages, test results, adverse reactions, side effects, and any interactions with mainstream medicine. Evidence of the experimental therapy's effects is examined in great detail through postings on the website and extensive debates among community members.

14.3.2.2.3 SOURCING HUMAN HELMINTHS

The user-created therapy is based on the application of human helminths, which can be obtained from commercial organizations. Such firms supply both the human hookworm (Necator americanus) and the human whipworm (Trichuris trichuria) and offer guidance on how these helminths may be applied therapeutically. Access to these human helminths is a vital part of engaging with this therapeutic approach, and although these firms are important sources of supply some users have taken a do-it-yourself (DIY) approach.

The DIY approach to sourcing human helminths is at the more extreme end of user activity and involves harvesting human helminths and incubating them so that they are viable for ingestion. The DIY approach also provides information on helminth egg counts (to obtain evidence of hookworm infection in a human host) and explanations on culturing different types of helminth. The information that is shared is both published scientific research and straightforward instructions written by users that combine scientific knowledge and personal experiences. Groups like Incubating Hookworm and the Helminthic Therapy Open Source Wiki are excellent examples of this aspect of the wider DIY phenomenon.

14.3.3 *Norms and Governance*

Though the helminthic therapy patient innovator community is not part of the mainstream medical research system, it has adopted norms aimed at importing the standards of scientific rigor into the process of patient innovation to the extent possible. For example, the website is designed such that each member has an opportunity to comment on each post made by another member. Though the detailed systematic review found within mainstream medical research is not observed, blog reports were subject to a form of "peer" review and vigorous debate was common. Moreover, blog comments were used not only for substantive discussion about the disease and the experimental therapy but also to emphasize and enforce norms of good user "science," as illustrated in the following extract:

> One note: as bloggers writing about an experimental therapy, we all have a responsibility to be careful about what we write ... Also, please be clear about the details of your therapy – how many helminths or ova you took, what date(s), which provider, etc., always useful. I get emails every week from interested readers, and am nearing 10,000 hits, so I do take my responsibility seriously with this blog.
>
> Colon Comrades: June 4, 2011

However, in the context of the scale of those suffering with autoimmune diseases, this is a small self-organizing community of individuals who decided to take action to try and find some form of remission for their conditions. This loose group coalesced around a shared commitment to experimenting with human helminths and sharing their results. What catalyzed the emergence of this community was press coverage exploring the role of helminths in alleviating autoimmune conditions (something that is still ongoing, e.g., Kohn 2016) and the ability to access these organisms from the commercial suppliers. These commercial suppliers were two of the nodes in the information network that emerged around this treatment. The information network that developed was more organic, respectful, and challenging with the most prominent sites reflecting the effort, knowledge sharing, and value provided by the individual involved.

14.3.4 *Relationship to Mainstream Medical Researchers*

Though the helminth therapy community draws heavily on the output of mainstream medical research, its outlaw character is reflected in the way it is perceived by mainstream researchers. Thus, the creation of such a user-led therapy has been controversial and has attracted negative reactions from researchers in the field who view their work as having been "bootlegged" (Weinstock 2009), and the therapy as "too risky" (Hotez 2008). In contrast, the following provides an alternative perspective concerning the negative reactions of mainstream researchers to the use of human helminths as an experimental therapy:

> I would like these researchers to think about this deeply. How many years away is your medicine that mimics the worms' effects? ... If research could just move a little faster ... Please don't be so dismissive. We are suffering horribly. And you are taking far too long.
>
> Waiting for the Cure: September 2009

14.4 USERS, CHRONIC DISEASE, INNOVATION, AND OUTLAW KNOWLEDGE

The application and development of helminths within a therapeutic context has largely taken place within the user-led outlaw innovation system that produced and shared outlaw knowledge (Flowers 2008). Because of its outlaw status, this small community consciously operated outside normal channels and avoided hostile jurisdictions. As a patient-led community to which mainstream resources and processes were unavailable, it developed and required different forms of evidence and recognized different forms of legitimation (e.g., Ferguson 2000). The outlaw status of this effort distinguishes it from previously studied user innovator communities in several interesting ways.

First, patients facing chronic needs that are unlikely to be met by the market may engage in significant, long-term efforts to try to innovate to improve their lives. Chronic disease is a context in which need is likely to persist for a long period of time. Patients are driven to engage in their own outlaw innovation because of the slow pace at which medical discoveries are translated into available treatments under current regulatory paradigms.

Second, the great need experienced by these patients drove them to make extensive efforts to acquire specialized knowledge that is not of the local experiential sort usually associated with user innovation. Their ongoing, persistent, and possibly urgent need stretching over many years provides a powerful platform for the development of the knowledge and network resources required both to innovate and to assess the merits of proposed innovations. Knowledge resources – the capability to understand medical mechanisms, the appreciation of breadth and depth of current research in the area, observations concerning clinical trials, knowledge of the benefits and limitations of the drugs available (including side effects), and understanding of the wider discourse over treatment options – may form an important part of the resources needed for innovation. Such knowledge is likely to be developed over many years and, as the case has shown, will be diffused through a network of blogs, fora, patient groups, and associations that are created around chronic diseases and may themselves act as focusing devices for the efforts of innovative users. Crucially, the mainstream medical knowledge on which the patient innovation here was based was publicly available in published form. The knowledge resources pooled and deployed by the patient innovator community thus included both the results of mainstream scientific investigation and the results of the patients' user experiences, permitting them to draw on both sets of resources in developing the experimental helminthic therapy.

Third, the outlaw status of this innovator community had significant effects on the potential for producer adoption and dissemination of the results of this user innovation. Within much of the user innovation literature, producers are observed to benefit from the activities of innovative users, with knowledge spillovers traveling from user to producer. As producers adopt lead user innovations and make them available on the market, a wider group of users also benefits. Such producers will also either appropriate lead user ideas or typically contribute to the innovation's dissemination to a wider body of users by using their expertise in areas such as quality control, user-friendly design, distribution chains, and so forth.

In contrast, the development of Helminthic therapy provides an example whereby the knowledge spillovers have flowed, in the first instance, from producers to users. The findings from the basic research undertaken within universities and other public bodies provided the initial hypothesis, proof-of-concept, and evidence of effect and risk that formed the basis for the experimental helminthic therapy developed by users. The synergy emphasized in lead user innovation studies, in which producers adopt and disseminate user innovations to a wider group of users, has not occurred in this context. Arguably, it is likely that such synergies can never take place in such contexts.

The regulated nature of health care innovation, along with the strict standards for demonstrating safety and efficacy, preclude the direction of knowledge spillovers found elsewhere in the user innovation literature – knowledge created by users spilling over to producer firms (e.g., Jeppesen and Molin 2003) – to be appropriated by the mainstream. The nature of the human helminth therapy experimentation conducted within the user community is such that it is not recognized as an authoritative data source for the mainstream medical innovation system. Within the patient community, legitimation flows from the personal accounts of those who have taken the helminths and from other users' discussion of their reports. The questions that drive this activity are not "Do we fully understand how this works?" but more simply "Does it work at all?" and "How do we make it work better?" These users freely reveal their experiences, and, much like users of poorly understood technologies in past times (e.g., Allen 1983; Nuvolari 2004), the community shares outlaw knowledge and experience as it attempts to optimize its activities. While this knowledge is not in the form demanded for mainstream adoption, it is unquestionably a potentially valuable trove of clinical data.

However, the mainstream medical innovation system has no mechanism for learning from this outlaw knowledge or incorporating it into the ongoing stream of research. As a result, while benefits may be obtained (or lessons about risks learned) by the small group of patient innovators participating in the community, potentially beneficial spillovers are blocked. Full understanding, optimization, and validation of these patient innovations would require detailed scientific enquiry, which would take time, expertise, and resources that a group of patients afflicted with a chronic disease does not have. Moreover, the lack of any mechanism for absorbing the lessons of outlaw innovation within mainstream medical innovation can create tensions between users and clinicians and between the regulated medical system and the informal user-driven system that discourage patients even from discussing these efforts with medical professionals. One result of this is that the scale, scope, and depth of user activity in this area are obscured, and a great deal of potentially informative clinical data – outlaw knowledge – is lost to science.

Even when producers are open to adopting promising user innovations, there is always some time lag between user innovation and mainstream appropriation of that innovation. Factors that will have an influence on the scale and nature of any time lag include regulation, investment cycles, capital intensity of the innovation context, structure of the business model employed, tractability of the technological context, type of user involved (business or consumer), and the part played by online communities. In some environments the physical nature of the product and the investment cycles associated with capital equipment may limit the ability of suppliers to quickly respond to user activity, with the result that there may be extensive time lags. In highly regulated environments (such as medicine), the lag would likely be even longer. Mainstream adoption may demand extensive scientific evidence and long-term programs of testing and require detailed certification processes for doctors and other medical professionals. The lack of any accepted mechanism for transferring knowledge for patient outlaw innovators to the mainstream makes the lag even longer – to the extent that spillovers from patient innovators to medical professionals occur at all. Patients are in great need, however, and many will simply be unwilling to wait. As a result, there may be a large gulf between the outcomes of "official" innovation processes and what users are doing on the ground. This may result in a disconnect between official and user activity and the evolution of quite different, and potentially conflicting, innovation trajectories.

From a knowledge commons perspective, this case demonstrates not only the potential importance of public domain knowledge as a resource for commons-based innovation but also the potential need for mechanisms for disseminating socially beneficial knowledge beyond the innovative community. Innovation researchers have recently begun to recognize that user innovators may lack incentives or face barriers to diffusing their innovations to a socially desirable degree. This case demonstrates that user innovator communities may have similar difficulties and that social value may be lost unless mechanisms are in place to ensure the appropriate level and type of synergy between a knowledge commons and the wider society.

CONCLUSIONS

This chapter has explored the way in which a certain form of user – individuals with a chronic medical condition – has led the development and application of a novel experimental medical therapy based on human intestinal parasites. The case provided the basis for an exploration of the role of users in medical innovation, and the difficulties that organizations may face in appropriating the outlaw knowledge that emerges from user communities was also explored.

The users active in the development of helminthic therapy possessed four shared characteristics: absence of effective long-term solutions from the mainstream medical system for their particular problems, a strong need to ameliorate their medical condition, access to the resources required to develop the medical therapy, and freedom of action unconstrained by medical regulations surrounding the development of new therapies. These shared characteristics meant that user innovation in this area was likely to be far faster, more responsive to new scientific insights, and quicker to close down lines of enquiry that are apparently unpromising. However, mainstream appropriation of the knowledge generated and shared in this process – outlaw knowledge – is likely to be difficult or impossible.

REFERENCES

Allen, R. C., 1983. Collective invention. *Journal of Economic Behaviour and Organization* 4:1.

Barbot, J., 2006. How to build an "active" patient? The work of AIDS associations in France. *Social Science and Medicine* 62:538.

Beer, R. J., 1976. The relationship between Trichuris trichiura (Linnaeus 1758) of man and Trichuris suis (Schrank 1788) of the pig. *Research in Veterinary Science* 20:47.

Bentwich, Z., Z. Weisman, C. Moroz, S. Bar-Yehuda, and A. Kalinkovich, 1996. Immune dysregulation in Ethiopian immigrants in Israel: Relevance to helminth infections? *Clinical & Experimental Immunology* 103:239.

Berthon, P. R., L. F. Pitt, I. McCarthy, and S. M. Kates, 2007. When customers get clever: Managerial approaches to dealing with creative consumers. *Business Horizons* 50 (1):39.

Borkow, G., Q. Leng, Z. Weisman, M. Stein, N. Galai, A. Kalinkovich, and Z. Bentwich, 2000. Chronic immune activation associated with intestinal helminth infections results in impaired signal transduction and energy. *Journal of Clinical Investigation* 106:1053.

Callon, M., and V. Rabeharisoa, 2003. Research "in the wild" and the shaping of new social identities. *Technology in Society* 25:193.

CCFA, 2011. Estimate published by Crohn's and Colitis Foundation of America, www.ccfa.org/info/about/crohns.

Crohn B. B., L. Ginzburg, and G. D. Oppenheimer, 1932. Regional ileitis: A pathologic and clinical entity. *Journal of the American Medical Association* 99 (16):1323.

Cummings, J. R. F., S. Kehave, and S. P. L. Travis, 2008. Medical management of Crohn's disease. *British Medical Journal* 336:May 10.

Dahlander L., and M.G. Magnusson, 2005. Relationships between open source software companies and communities: Observations from Nordic firms. *Research Policy* 3(4):481.

deBronkart, D., 2013. How the e-patient community helped save my life: An essay by Dave deBronkart. *British Medical Journal* 346:April 2.

de Jong, J., and E. von Hippel, 2009. Transfers of user process innovations to process equipment producers: A study of Dutch high-tech firms. *Research Policy* 38(7):1181.

Diemert D. J., J. M. Bethony and P. J. Hotez, 2008. Hookworm vaccines. *Clin. Infect. Dis.* 46(2):282.

Dignass A., G. Van Assche, J. O. Lindsay, M. Lémann, J. Söderholm, J. F. Colombel, S. Danese, A., D'Hoore, M. Gassull, F. Gomollón, D. W. Hommes, P. Michetti, C. O'Morain, T. Öresland, A. Windsor, E. F. Stange, and S. P. L. Travis, 2010. The second European evidence-based consensus on the diagnosis and management of Crohn's disease: Current management. *Journal of Crohn's and Colitis* 4(1):28.

Elliott, D. E., J. F. Urban Jr., C. K. Argo, and J. V. Weinstock, 2000. Does the failure to acquire helminthic parasites predispose to Crohn's disease? *FASEB J.* 14:1848.

Elliott, D. E., J. Li, A. Blum, A. Metwali, K. Qadir, J. F. Urban Jr., and J. V. Weinstock, 2003. Exposure to schistosome eggs protects mice from TNBS-induced colitis. *American Journal of Physiology – Gastrointestinal & Liver Physiology* 284:G385.

Epstein, S., 1996. *Impure Science: AIDS, Activism and the Politics of Knowledge*. Berkeley: University of California Press.

Ferguson, T., 2000. Online patient-helpers and physicians working together: A new partnership for high-quality health care. *British Medical Journal* 321:November.

Ferguson, T., 2002. Quality online patient networks need more attention than quality of online health information. *British Medical Journal* 324:March 9.

Ferguson, T., 2004. The first generation of e-patients. *British Medical Journal* 328: May 13.

Flowers, S., 2008. Harnessing the hackers: The emergence and exploitation of Outlaw Innovation. *Research Policy* 37:177.

Flowers, S., J, de Jong, T. Sinozic, and E. von Hippel, 2010a. *Measuring User Innovation in the UK*. London: NESTA.

Hamm, M. P. et al. 2013. Social media use among patients and caregivers: A scoping review. *BMJ Open* 3:e002819.

Harhoff D., Henkel J., and von Hippel E., 2003. Profiting from voluntary information spillover show users benefit by freely revealing their innovations. *Research Policy*. 32:1753.

Hotez, P., 2008. Quoted in S. Svoboda, The worms crawl in. *New York Times*, July 1, www.nytimes.com/2008/07/01/health/research/01prof.html.

Hutt M. S., 1979. Epidemiology of chronic intestinal disease in middle Africa. *Isr. J. Med. Sci.* 15:314.

Jeppesen, L. B., and M. J. Molin, 2003. Consumers as co-developers: Learning and innovation outside the firm. *Technology Analysis and Strategic Management* 15(3).

Khan, W. I., P. A. Blennerhasset, A. K. Varghese, S. K. Chowdhury, P. Omsted, Y. Deng, and S. M. Collins, 2002. Intestinal nematode infection ameliorates experimental colitis in mice. *Infection & Immunity* 70(11):5931.

Henkel, J., and E. von Hippel, 2004. Welfare implications of user innovation. *The Journal of Technology Transfer* 30:73.

Kohn, D., 2016. Why a diet of worms could be good for you. *The Guardian*, Feb. 8, online edition, www.theguardian.com/lifeandstyle/2016/feb/08/why-a-diet-of-worms-could-be-good-for-you

Lettl, C., 2007. User involvement competence for radical innovation. *Journal of Engineering and Technology Management* 24(1–2):53.

Lilien, G., P. D. Morrison, K., Searls, M. Sonnack, and E. von Hippel, 2002. Performance assessment of the lead user generation process for new product development. *Management Science* 48(8):1042.

Maxwell, C., R. Hussain, T. B. Nutman, R. W. Poindexter, M. D. Little, G. A. Schad, and E. A. Ottesen, 1987. The clinical and immunological responses of normal human volunteers to low dose hookworm (Necator americanus) infection. *American Journal of Tropical Medicine and Hygiene* 37:126.

Nuvolari, A., 2004. Collective invention during the British Industrial Revolution: The case of the Cornish pumping engine. *Cambridge Journal of Economics* 28 (3):347.

Oliveira, P., L. Zejnilovic, H. Canhão, and E. von Hippel, 2014. Innovation by Patients with Rare Diseases and Chronic Needs. Available at SSRN, http://ssrn.com/abstract=2456580.

Pew Internet, 2010. More than half of e-patients living with chronic disease consume user-generated health information, *Social Media and Health*, Pew Internet & American Life Project, www.pewInternet.org/2010/03/24/social-media-and-health/

Richards, T. et al. 2013. Let the patient revolution begin. *BMJ* 346:f2614.

Rook, G. A., 2008. Review series on helminths, immune modulation and the hygiene hypothesis: The broader implications of the hygiene hypothesis. *Immunology* 126(1):3.

Rook, G. A., and L. R. Brunet, 2005. Old friends for breakfast. *Clin. Exp. Allergy* 35 (7):841.

Schaan, S., and Urbach, M., 2009. Measuring User Innovation in Canadian Manufacturing 2007. Statistics Canada.

Scrivener, S., H. Yemaneberhan, M. Zebenigus, D. Tilahun, S. Girma, S. Ali, P. McElroy, A. Custovic, A. Woodcock, D. I. Pritchard, A. Venn, and J. Britton, 2001. Independent effects of intestinal parasite infection and domestic allergen exposure on the risk of wheeze in Ethiopia. *Lancet* 358:1493.

Seres, M. J., 2013. Re: Patient powered health. *British Medical Journal* 346:April 13.

Shivananda S., J. Lennard-Jones, R. Logan, N. Fear, A. Price, and L. Carpenter, 1996. Incidence of inflammatory bowel disease across Europe: Is there a difference between the north and south? Results of the European Collaborative Study on Inflammatory Bowel Disease (EC-IBD). *Gut* 39:690.

Strachan, D. P., 1989. Hay fever, hygiene, and household size. *British Journal of Medicine* 299:1259.

Summers, R. W., D. E. Elliott, K. Qadir, J. F. J. Urban, R. Thompson, and J. V. Weinstock, 2003. Trichuris suis seems to be safe and possibly effective in the treatment of inflammatory bowel disease. *American Journal of Gastroenterology* 98:2034.

Summers, R. W., D. E. Elliott, J. F. Urban Jr., R. Thompson, and J. V. Weinstock, 2005a. Trichuris suis therapy in Crohn's disease. *Gut* 54:87.

Summers, R. W., D. E. Elliott, J. F. Urban Jr., R. A. Thompson, and J. V. Weinstock, 2005b. Trichuris suis therapy for active ulcerative colitis: A randomized controlled trial. *Gastroenterology* 128:825.

Swan, M. 2012a. Health 2050: The Realization of Personalized Medicine through Crowdsourcing, the Quantified Self, and the Participatory Biocitizen. *J. Pers. Med.* 2:93.

Swan, M. 2012b. Scaling Crowdsourced Health Studies: The Emergence of a New Form of Contract Research Organization. *Personalized Medicine* 9(2):223.

Urban, G.L., and E. von Hippel, 1988. Lead user analyses for the development of new industrial products. *Management Science* 34(5):569.

Van Assche, G., A. Dignass, J. Panes, L. Beaugerie, J. Karagiannis, M. Allez, T. Ochsenkühn, T. Orchard, G. Rogler, E. Louis, L. Kupcinskas, G. Mantzaris, S. Travis, and E. Stange, 2010a. The second European evidence-based Consensus on the diagnosis and management of Crohn's disease: Definitions and diagnosis. *Journal of Crohn's and Colitis* 4(1):7.

Van Assche G., A. Dignass, W. Reinisch, J. C. van der Woude, A. Sturm, M. De Vos, M. Guslandi, B. Oldenburg, I. Dotan, P. Marteau, A. Ardizzone, C. Daniel, D. C. Baumgart, G., D'Haens, P. Gionchetti, F. Portela, B. Vucelic, J. Söderholm, J. Escher, S. Koletzko, K. Kolho, M. Lukas, C. Mottet, H. Tilg, S. Vermeire, F. Carbonnel, A. Cole, G. Novacek, M. Reinshagen, E. Tsianos, K. Herrlinger, B. Oldenburg, Y. Bouhnik, R. Kiesslich, E. Stange, S. Travis, and J. Lindsay, 2010b. The second European evidence-based Consensus on the diagnosis and management of Crohn's disease: Special situations. *Journal of Crohn's and Colitis* 4(1):63.

von Hippel, E., 1976. The dominant role of users in the scientific instrument innovation process. *Research Policy* 5(3):212.

von Hippel, E., 1986. Lead users: A source of novel product concepts. *Management Science* 32(7):791.

von Hippel, E. 1994. "Sticky information" and the locus of problem solving: Implications for innovation. *Management Science* 40(4):429.

von Hippel, E., and von Krogh, G., 2003. Open source software and the "private-collective" innovation model: Issues for organization science. *Organization Science* 14(2):208.

von Hippel, E., 2005. *Democratizing Innovation*. Cambridge, MA: MIT Press.

von Hippel, E., 2007. Horizontal innovation networks–By and for users. *Industrial and Corporate Change* 16(2):293.

Weinstock, J. V., 2009, quoted in Cox, L., Allergy desperation: I'll take a parasite, please. *ABC News Medical Unit*, July 20, http://abcnews.go.com/Health/AllergiesNews/story?id=8114307

Weinstock, J. V., and D. E. Elliott, 2009. Helminths and the IBD Hygiene Hypothesis. *Inflammatory Bowel Disease* 15(1):128.

Wynne, B. 1996. SSK's Identity Parade: Signing-Up, Off-and-On. *Social Studies of Science* 26(2):357.

SUGGESTED ADDITIONAL READING

Adams, T., 2010. Gut instinct: The miracle of the parasitic hookworm. *The Observer*, May 22, www.theguardian.com/lifeandstyle/2010/may/23/parasitic-hookworm-jasper-lawrence-tim-adams

Alvesson, M., and Skolddberg, K., 2000. *Reflexive Methodology*. London: SAGE Publications Inc.

Braun, V., and Herstatt, C., 2009. *User Innovation: Barriers to Democratization and IP Licensing*. Routledge.

Coronado, 2011. Filing for registration of securities, Amendment No. 1 to Form 10, Submission to United States Securities and Exchange Commission, July 2011.

Duncan, D. F., White, J. B., and Nicholson, T., 2003. Using internet-based surveys to reach hidden populations: Case of non-abusive illicit drug users. *American Journal of Health Behavior* 27(3):208.

Flowers, S., 2010b. User innovation: The developing Policy Research Agenda, in Flowers, S., and F. Henwood (eds.), *Perspectives on User Innovation*. London: Imperial College Press.

Franke, N., and von Hippel, E., 2003. Satisfying heterogeneous User Needs via Innovation Toolkits: The Case of Apache Security Software. *Research Policy* 32 (7):1199.

Klein S. J., and Rosenberg, N., 1986. An Overview of Innovation, in Landau, R., and Rosenberg, N. (eds.), *The Positive Sum Strategy: Harnessing technology for economic growth*. National Academy of Engineering.

Lüthje, C., Herstatt C., and von Hippel E., 2002. *The Dominant Role of Local Information in User Innovation: The Case of Mountain Biking*. MIT Sloan School. Working Paper #4377–02.

Lüthje, C., Herstatt C., and von Hippel E., 2005. User-innovators and local information: The case of mountain biking. *Research Policy* 34(6):951.

Luthje, C., 2004. Characteristics of innovating users in a consumer goods field: An empirical study of sport-related product consumers. *Technovation* 24(9):683.

Meyer, P. B., 2003. *Episodes of Collective Invention*, BLS Working Papers, Office of Productivity and Technology, US Department of Labor.

Morrison, P. D., Roberts, J. H., and Von Hippel, E., 2000. Determinants of user innovation and innovation sharing in a local market. *Management Science* 46 (12):1513.

NESTA, 2006. The Innovation Gap: Why policy needs to reflect the reality of innovation in the UK. Research Report, October.

Sonnenberg A., McCarty D. J., and Jacobsen, S. J., 1991. Geographic variation of inflammatory bowel disease within the United States. *Gastroenterology* 100:143.

von Hippel, E., and Katz, R., 2002. Shifting Innovation to Users via Toolkits. *Management Science* 48(7):821.

von Hippel, E., DeMonaco, H., and Oliveira, P., 2011. *Patients as Health Care Innovators: The Case of Cystic Fibrosis*, Open and User Innovation Workshop, June 4–6, Vienna.

15

The North American Mitochondrial Disease Consortium: A Developing Knowledge Commons

Katherine J. Strandburg and Brett M. Frischmann

INTRODUCTION

Rare diseases number between 5000 and 8000.[1] Each affects fewer than 200,000 individuals,[2] but in the aggregate, they affect millions. As summarized in a National Academies Report, *Rare Diseases and Orphan Products: Accelerating Research and Development*:

> Because the number of people affected with any particular rare disease is relatively small and the number of rare diseases is so large, a host of challenges complicates the development of safe and effective drugs, biologics, and medical devices to prevent, diagnose, treat, or cure these conditions. These challenges include difficulties in attracting public and private funding for research and development, recruiting sufficient numbers of research participants for clinical studies, appropriately using clinical research designs for small populations, and securing adequate expertise at the government agencies that review rare diseases research applications or authorize the marketing of products for rare conditions.[3]

Information sharing, collaboration, and community building among researchers, doctors, and patients are critical to rare disease research. The Rare Disease Clinical Research Network (RDCRN) is an NIH program aimed at developing infrastructure and methodologies for rare disease clinical research by creating a network of research consortia. Each RDCRN consortium (RDCRC) involves researchers,

Katherine J. Strandburg is the Alfred B. Engelberg Professor of Law and a Faculty Director of the Engelberg Center for Innovation Law and Policy at the New York University School of Law, New York. Brett M. Frischmann is the Charles Widger Endowed University Professor in Law, Business and Economics at Villanova University Charles Widger School of Law, Villanova, Pennsylvania. Professor Strandburg acknowledges the generous support of the Filomen D'Agostino and Max E. Greenberg Research Fund.

1 Marilyn J. Field and Thomas F. Boat (eds.), Committee on Accelerating Rare Diseases Research and Orphan Product Development; Institute of Medicine of the National Academies, *Rare Diseases and Orphan Products: Accelerating Research and Development* 1 (2011).

2 Federal Food, Drug, and Cosmetic Act, 21 U.S.C. § 360bb (A)(2)(A).

3 Field and Boat (2011): 1.

other health care professionals, and patients at a group of geographically dispersed clinical sites.

Medical knowledge is a nonrivalrous resource, which can be used to treat any number of patients without diminishing its value to others. RDCRCs nonetheless face resource governance challenges, including (1) managing rivalrous inputs, such as research funding and researcher time; (2) managing rivalrous incentives and rewards, such as authorship credit; (3) overcoming incentives to hoard scarce access to patients and their data; (4) reducing the transaction costs of cooperation between widely dispersed researchers; and (5) managing interactions with outsiders, such as pharmaceutical companies.

All scientific research confronts tensions between the need to apportion scarce, rivalrous resources and the value of sharing nonrivalrous research results and certain infrastructural data[4] and tools broadly. Mechanisms for managing this tension include public funding, reputation-based systems of peer review and publication, and scientific community norms. In clinical research, additional tensions between the value of the research and potential risks to research subjects are addressed by informed consent regulation, professional ethics prioritizing duty to patients, and institutional review boards (IRBs). These form part of the backdrop for the RDCRN and its associated consortia.

We previously studied the Urea Cycle Disorder Consortium (UCDC).[5] Here we focus on the North American Mitochondrial Disease Consortium (NAMDC). The next chapter in this book studies the Consortium for Eosinophilic Gastrointestinal Disease Research (CEGIR).[6] While there are many similarities between these consortia, which face common rare disease research problems and are structured by the RDCRN, there are also significant differences in the underlying challenges the groups face and the approaches they take to those challenges. The UCDC is much better established than the NAMDC and emerged from a history of greater previous cooperation. CEGIR is very new, but, like the UCDC, emerged from a close-knit group of researchers. Mitochondrial disorders are complex, varied, and difficult to diagnose, much less treat. The diseases studied by UCDC and CEGIR are comparatively well understood, with relatively well-accepted diagnostic criteria and targets for treatments. The consortia also have leaders with different styles and personalities and different governance structures.

4 See OECD, *Data-driven innovation for growth and well-being* (Oct. 6, 2015) (extensive discussion of "infrastructural data"); see generally Brett M. Frischmann, *Infrastructure: The Social Value of Shared Resources* (Oxford University Press 2012).

5 Katherine J. Strandburg, Brett Frischmann, and Can Cui, The Rare Diseases Clinical Research Network and the Urea Cycle Disorders Consortium as a Nested Knowledge Commons, in *Governing Knowledge Commons* 155 (Brett M. Frischmann, Michael J. Madison, and Katherine J. Strandburg eds., Oxford University Press 2014) [hereinafter, "UCDC Study"].

6 See Chapter 16 of this volume.

15.1 METHODOLOGY

Our study follows the *Governing Knowledge Commons* (GKC) framework described in Chapter 1. Specifically, we

- Reviewed public documentation about NAMDC and were provided access to some internal documents, including minutes of consortium meetings and monthly reports.
- Interviewed 22 individuals including NAMDC's two consortium principal investigators (PIs), project manager, biostatistician, data manager, and budget administrator, site PIs from 9 of the 16 other clinical sites, a researcher consultant working with NAMDC on issues of diagnosis, NAMDC's two assigned NIH officers, the executive director and scientific director of the United Mitochondrial Disease Foundation patient advocacy group, one NAMDC study coordinator and one unassociated mitochondrial disease practitioner and researcher. The semi-structured interviews ranged in length from 45 minutes to more than an hour. We used the GKC framework to structure the interviews.[7]
- Attended NAMDC's first half-day Face-to-Face Meeting, held in June 2015 in association with a conference sponsored by the United Mitochondrial Disease Foundation (UMDF) patient advocacy group. We were silent observers throughout the meeting, although we introduced ourselves and our project and spoke with participants informally during the breaks.
- Conducted an online survey designed to supplement our interviews, both by obtaining additional perspectives and by testing some of our observations. We emailed survey links to a list of potential respondents, including 24 active NAMDC researchers (the two consortium Co-PIs, 18 site PIs, a researcher consultant, a research fellow, the NAMDC biostatistician, and the director of the biorepository); NAMDC's project manager and data manager, 2 NIH representatives, a Data Management and Coordinating Center (DMCC) representative, two UMDF representatives, and 13 study coordinators at 10 NAMDC sites. We received responses from 12 active researchers, representing 9 out of the 17 clinical sites,[8] and 7 others. Only one study coordinator completed the survey in full. Because the number of survey respondents was too small for meaningful statistical analysis, we treated the survey responses primarily as additional input to our qualitative analysis.

[7] We maintain an archive of interview transcripts, which we rely on and quote from throughout. To preserve confidentiality as much as possible, we ordinarily do not cite particular interviewees. Throughout, readers may assume that unattributed quotations are taken from our interviews.

[8] For comparison, we received survey responses from 15 out of 20 PIs associated with 10 out of 15 clinical sites in our UCDC study.

- Analyzed the information we obtained using the GKC framework. With the exception of the study coordinators, we believe that our interviews and survey responses combined provide quite comprehensive coverage of NAMDC's participants. We received at least some input to the study from virtually the entire leadership/administrative team at Columbia University, from PIs at 13 out of 17 clinical sites, from the single consultant researcher and from the NIH and UMDF representatives.

15.2 NAMDC'S BACKGROUND ENVIRONMENT

NAMDC's larger context includes the biological realities of mitochondrial disorders, the cultural contexts of medicine and academic research and the more specific contexts of rare disease research and the RDCRN.[9] We refer the interested reader to that case study for more detail.

15.2.1 *The Basic Biology of Mitochondrial Disease*

Mitochondrial disease medicine and research have developed mostly over the past 25 to 30 years. Mitochondria are responsible for creating more than 90 percent of the energy our bodies need to sustain life and growth. When mitochondria fail, cells are injured and can die, and if this process repeats itself through the body, various systems can fail and life can be compromised. While mitochondrial diseases mostly affect children, adult onset is increasingly common.

As the NAMDC website explains:

> Mitochondrial diseases are a challenge because they are probably the most diverse human disorders at every level: clinical, biochemical, and genetic. Some are confined to the nervous system but most are multi-systemic, often affecting the brain, heart, liver, skeletal muscles, kidney and the endocrine and respiratory systems. Although severity varies, by and large these are progressive and often crippling disorders. They can cause paralysis, seizures, mental retardation, dementia, hearing loss, blindness, weakness and premature death.
>
> Because of the range of symptoms and the frequent involvement of multiple body systems, mitochondrial diseases can be a great challenge to diagnose. Even when accurately diagnosed, they pose an even more formidable challenge to treat, as there are very few therapies and most are only partially effective.[10]

9 For more detail about the RDCRN, see the UCDC Study, note 5.

10 www.rarediseasesnetwork.org/cms/namdc/About-Us. Mitochondrial replacement therapy is one promising, though controversial, potential treatment. See Rebecca Jacobson, Why the term 'three-person baby' makes doctors wince, *PBS Newshour*, Feb. 10, 2015 (interviewing Chuck Mohan, director of UMDF, and Dr. Bruce Cohen, NAMDC member and PI).

Because mitochondria affect the functioning of virtually every bodily system, mitochondrial disease research is particularly important.

As one of our interviewees explained, because of the diversity and heterogeneity of mitochondrial disorders, "establishing a diagnosis often remains challenging, costly, and, at times, invasive":

> [For the urea cycle disorders] yes, there is a variable presentation, but . . . the spectrum is . . . defined. Whereas with mitochondrial disease, any system, any organ, anything. If you have no diagnosis at all, you could be possibly mitochondrial. There's so much ambiguity in the physicians' minds and the patients' minds, and the general community's minds about these diseases. I think it's a very different kettle of fish.

Diagnosis may be controversial, as reflected in highly publicized incidents in which parents who believe their children are suffering from mitochondrial diseases have been accused of "medical child abuse" or Munchausen by proxy.[11]

New rapid genomic sequencing technologies hold out hope of providing a "single test to accurately diagnose mtDNA disorders"[12] in patients who exhibit symptoms.[13] It is possible for a patient to have a genetic mutation without having a disorder, however, potentially leading to misdiagnosis.

15.2.2 *The Mitochondrial Medicine Society and the Interplay between Diagnosis, Treatment, and Research*

Mitochondrial disease presents two broad, overlapping categories of knowledge problems. First, physicians must decide how to treat their patients, given the difficulty in diagnosing mitochondrial disease and the lack of definitive treatments. Second, clinical researchers must develop generalizable knowledge that can be used to improve diagnosis and develop new treatments. The line between these categories is somewhat artificial, given that clinical research revolves around existing patients but is an important constraint on NAMDC's goals and activities. As one NIH official explained: "NIH draws a line. NIH doesn't train physicians to take care of patients. NIH trains physicians to do research with patients."

The gold standard approach to treatment is to use robust clinical trial evidence to develop "clinical practice guidelines."[14] When available evidence is insufficient to

[11] Julie Gortze, a registered nurse, provides a useful explanation and survey in Rare Disease Caretaker vs. Munchausen Syndrome by Proxy/Medial Child Abuse Perpetrator: A Comparison of Psychological Profiles, *MitoAction*, Mar. 12, 2015, www.mitoaction.org/files/CaretakerProfileComparison.pdf. See Brian Palmer, Mitochondrial disease of medical child abuse?, *Slate*, Apr. 1, 2014, www.slate.com/articles/health_and_science/medical_examiner/2014/04/justina_pelletier_s_mitochondrial_disease_boston_children_s_hospital_suspects.html (describing Justina Pelletier's case).

[12] Parikh et al., Diagnosis and management of mitochondrial disease: A consensus statement from the Mitochondrial Medicine Society, 17 *Genetics in Medicine* 689, 691–92 (2015).

[13] Ibid.

[14] See Institute of Medicine, *Clinical Practice Guidelines We Can Trust* (2011), www.nationalacademies.org/hmd/Reports/2011/Clinical-Practice-Guidelines-We-Can-Trust/Standards.aspx

meet that standard (as is often the case for rare diseases), professional societies often develop multi-expert "consensus statements," which are "derived from a systematic approach and a traditional literature review where randomized controlled trials and high-quality evidence do not commonly exist"[15] and "synthesize the latest information, often from current and ongoing medical research."[16] Consensus statements aim to "help standardize the evaluation, diagnosis, and care of patients" until they can be "superseded by clinical trials or high-quality evidence that may develop over time."[17]

The Mitochondrial Medicine Society (MMS),[18] a practitioner organization, focuses on educating clinicians and developing materials to assist them with diagnosis and treatment. Citing "insufficient data on which to base [clinical practice guidelines]," "notable variability [] in the diagnostic approaches used, extent of testing sent, interpretation of test results, and evidence from which a diagnosis of mitochondrial disease is derived" and "inconsistencies in treatment and preventive care regimens," MMS sponsored the process leading to a 2015 consensus statement for mitochondrial diseases.[19]

Many NAMDC researchers also are heavily involved in the Mitochondrial Medicine Society. Indeed, 13 of the 2015 Consensus Statement's 19 coauthors are NAMDC members. Moreover, all of the past presidents of MMS, along with its current president and two of its five other officers and board members, are NAMDC PIs. As one of our interviewees explained, "I'm the president of the Mitochondrial Medicine Society and I'm also a PI in NAMDC, I run a NAMDC site. I have been a trustee for the UMDF, and I am about to join the Scientific and Medical Advisory Board. I kind of have all three hats on at the same time."

15.2.3 *The Rare Disease Clinical Research Network*

The RDCRN aims "to advance medical research on rare diseases by providing support for clinical studies and facilitating collaboration, study enrollment and data sharing."[20] As explained in the 2008 request for consortium proposals:

> Rare diseases pose unique challenges to identification and coordination of resources and expertise for small populations dispersed over wide geographic areas. Rare diseases research requires collaboration of scientists from multiple

15 www.chestnet.org/Guidelines-and-Resources/Guidelines-and-Consensus-Statements/Methodology/Consensus-Statements (an often-cited overview). See also F. Ingravallo, C. F. Dietrich, O. H. Gilja, F. Piscaglia, Guidelines, clinical practice recommendations, position papers and consensus statements: Definition, preparation, role and application, 35 *Ultraschall in Med.* 395 (2014).

16 R. Graham et al., *Clinical Practice Guidelines We Can Trust* (Institute of Medicine, National Academies Press 2011), http://nap.edu/13058.

17 Parikh et al., note 12.

18 The MMS is an international group of physicians, researchers and clinicians working toward the better diagnosis, management, and treatment of mitochondrial disease. See http://www.mitosoc.org/.

19 Parikh et al., note 12.

20 www.rarediseasesnetwork.org/about/index.htm. Basic research also continues to be key to understanding mitochondrial diseases but is outside the scope of our study.

> disciplines sharing research resources and patient populations. Rigorous characterization and longitudinal assessment is needed to facilitate discovery of biomarkers of disease risk, disease activity, and response to therapy. In addition, systematic assessment could resolve controversies concerning current treatment strategies. Well described patient populations will be important to bring promising therapies to the clinic.[21]

RDCRCs are selected through a competitive peer-review process and must have the following components:

- a minimum of two clinical research projects (at least one of them must be a longitudinal study)
- a training (career development) component
- at least one pilot/demonstration project
- a website for educational and research resources in rare diseases
- collaboration with patient support organization(s)
- an administrative unit.[22]

RDCRCs work closely with NIH scientists, through the "multiproject cooperative agreement (U54)" mechanism, in which a program coordinator from the Office of Rare Diseases and at least one NIH project scientist have "substantial scientific/programmatic involvement during the conduct of this activity through technical assistance, advice and coordination above and beyond normal program stewardship for grants."[23]

NIH also funds a centralized RDCRN Data Management and Coordinating Center (DMCC), which provides "coordinated clinical data integration of developed and publicly available data sets for data mining at RDCRCs, web-based recruitment and referral [of patient research participants], and a user-friendly resource site for the public" and manages the "collection, storage, and analysis of RDCRC data." It also is tasked with "monitor[ing] [protocol] compliance while addressing privacy and confidentiality issues related to database management, distributed computing, and multilevel data sharing."[24] The DMCC maintains the RDCRN Contact Registry, where patients can indicate interest in participating in clinical research or trials.

15.2.4 *The United Mitochondrial Disease Foundation*

NAMDC partners with the largest patient advocacy group focused on mitochondrial diseases, the UMDF, which was founded in 1996 by its current executive director. In 2013, it hired a full-time science/alliance officer with a PhD in chemistry. UMDF's mission is "to promote research and education for the diagnosis, treatment, and cure of mitochondrial disorders and to provide support to affected individuals and

[21] See, e.g., Rare Diseases Clinical Research Consortia (RDCRC) for the Rare Diseases Clinical Research Network (U54) – RFA-OD-08–001, http://grants.nih.gov/grants/guide/rfa-files/RFA-OD-08–001.html#SectionI

[22] Ibid. [23] Ibid. [24] Ibid.

families." UMDF attacks it mission through patient support groups, funding research, educating patients and physicians about mitochondrial disease, and advocating public policies supporting mitochondrial disease patients and researchers. UMDF sponsors an annual national symposium that includes both a scientific component for basic researchers, clinical researchers, and clinicians and a component for patients and families, affording them opportunities to learn about the latest research, meet with mitochondrial disease specialists, and participate in Q&A sessions. UMDF also sponsors "grand rounds" about mitochondrial disease at various medical schools.[25]

Compared to many other rare disease patient advocacy groups, UMDF is large, with a paid staff of 20 and a total budget of US$3.4 million. It has provided more than US$13 million in research grants, usually to pilot projects or beginning researchers. UMDF supports NAMDC's project manager out of its research budget.

Recently, UMDF inaugurated a patient-populated Mitochondrial Disease Community Registry aimed at "collecting the patient voice: quality of life issues, opinions on various matters," and "symptoms, extent of symptoms, what are the symptoms most important to you?" so as to "help drug developers whether they be in academia or in industry to understand the patient better, as opposed to just their medical condition."

UMDF was described by interviewees as a "hub of activity" related to mitochondrial disease or the "glue" holding different components of the effort together. An interviewee told us that UMDF is known for doing a good job of "getting on the radar screen of NIH." UMDF's science/alliance officer described his job as "connecting dots" with "UMDF in the center of this very complex process called therapeutic development, that has all kinds of bubbles around it. It's the patient community, it's the research community, it's the pharmaceutical community, it's the government, government agencies, clinical research network like NAMDC . . . all of these things overlap with UMDF in the middle, serving as a clearinghouse."

Most of NAMDCs researchers have long-standing relationships with UMDF that precede NAMDC's formation. Consortium PI Salvatore DiMauro, for example, was involved with UMDF from its inception. Currently, seven NAMDC members are on UMDF's Board of Trustees or Scientific Advisory Board. NAMDC researchers also have been involved in planning and participating in the UMDF annual symposia and grand rounds. NAMDC schedules its annual face-to-face meeting of its researchers to coincide with the UMDF symposium, which many or most of them attend regularly.

15.3 THE NAMDC CONSORTIUM

NAMDC is shaped by its own particular goals and history, by the individuals who make up the community, and by its governance structure, which are described in this section.

[25] Information taken from www.UMDF.org.

15.3.1 *Goals and Objectives*

NAMDC's makeup, the resources it creates and employs, and its governance structure center on its goals and objectives, which also provide metrics for assessing its success. NAMDC shares many of its overarching goals with other RDCRN consortia, though its specific objectives are tailored to the mitochondrial disease context. As NAMDC's mission statement explains:

> The challenge for the NAMDC is the extraordinary clinical spectrum of mitochondrial diseases, which all too often leads practitioners to either underdiagnose ("What is this complex disorder?") or overdiagnose ("This disorder is so complex that is must be mitochondrial!"). Yet mitochondrial diseases cause similar metabolic defects and presumably share – albeit to different extents – the same mechanisms. Thus, the availability of a mitochondrial patient registry and of a consortium will have a powerful impact in multiple ways, as already documented by similar organizations operating in Europe.[26]

In light of this mission, NAMDC articulates the following objectives:

- First, NAMDC will make these rare and still unfamiliar diseases known to practitioners and to the general public.
- Second, it will facilitate correct diagnosis by making "centers of excellence" available to physicians and affected families alike.
- Third, it will offer affected families the comfort and advice of a patient support group, the United Mitochondrial Disease Foundation (UMDF).
- Fourth, it will foster clinical research, such as natural history, that would be otherwise impossible because it requires relatively large cohorts of patients.
- Fifth, it will also foster more basic research by revealing unusual patients, leading to the discovery of new genetic defects.
- Finally, NAMDC will conduct rigorous and innovative therapeutic clinical trials.[27]

NAMDC approaches these goals and objectives through specific activities:

- Create a network of all clinicians and clinical investigators in North America (US and Canada, with the hope of including Mexico in the future) who follow sizeable numbers of patients with mitochondrial diseases and are involved or interested in mitochondrial research.
- Create[] a clinical registry for patients, in the hopes of
  - standardizing diagnostic criteria,
  - collecting important standardized information on patients,

[26] www.rarediseasesnetwork.org/cms/NAMDC [27] www.rarediseasesnetwork.org/cms/NAMDC

- facilitating the participation of patients in research on mitochondrial diseases.
- Establish[] a repository for specimens and DNA from patients with mitochondrial diseases, in order to make materials easily available to consortium researchers.
- Conduct clinical trials and other kinds of research. The consortium makes biostatisticians, data management experts, and specialists in clinical research available to participating physicians, so that experiments conducted through the NAMDC can make the most efficient and innovative use of the generous participation of patients.

15.3.2 *NAMDC's History*

When the RDCRN program began in 2003, NAMDC's consortium PIs, Salvatore DiMauro and Michio Hirano of Columbia University, proposed a mitochondrial disease consortium, to be called MAGIC. According to one of our interviewees: "The group in Columbia is a very well established and reputable group in the US, for the study of mitochondrial disorders. At some point it was the only one. It was the first one. It was good that very traditional and well-established leaders in the field started with the concept of having NAMDC and bringing people together." Several interviewees also emphasized the UMDF's important role as a catalyst for that initial proposal.

MAGIC was not funded in either of the RDCRN's first funding rounds. PI Hirano attributes the early funding failures primarily to the relative immaturity of the field and the consortium PIs' lack of clinical research expertise. In 2010, NAMDC received partial funding for two years through an American Recovery and Reinvestment Act of 2009 (ARRA) grant,[28] which focused on setting up basic infrastructure for the consortium:

> This application aims at establishing the infrastructure needed to launch a mitochondrial disease patient registry, biorepository, and a North American Mitochondrial Disease Consortium (NAMDC) with the support of [patient advocacy group] UMDF. The NAMDC will feature advanced data management systems and statistical design capabilities provided by the Statistical Analysis Center (SAC) in the Department of Biostatistics at Columbia University. This structure will be the indispensable basis for future collaborative studies of epidemiology, natural history, therapeutic trials, as well as in-depth research on pathogenesis.[29]

[28] The American Recovery and Reinvestment Act of 2009 (ARRA) provided a two-year infusion of money to the NIH as part of a general effort to shore up the economy after the 2008 financial crisis.

[29] Abstract, NIH Project No. 1RC1NS070232-01, https://projectreporter.nih.gov/project_info_description.cfm?aid=7830838&icde=29805686&ddparam=&ddvalue=&ddsub=&cr=45&csb=FY&cs=DESC

In 2011, NAMDC transitioned to a standard RDCRN grant, which was renewed during the RDCRN's 2014 funding cycle.

During the ARRA grant period, NAMDC's PIs decided to work closely with biostatistician John (Seamus) Thompson at Columbia's Statistical Analysis Center (SAC), which still provides primary data services for NAMDC:

> The [ARRA] money was absolutely necessary because it allowed us to work with Seamus Thompson and his statistical analysis center. We had never worked together before. They had all the database capacity and clinical trial expertise ... I was mainly, you know, a lab person at the time. I had not done this kind of clinical research. I needed their complementary expertise and tools. This allowed us to do it. This grant really funded us and put us together.
>
> This is obviously greater than the sum of its parts because Seamus had the expertise in statistics and database management and [] clinical trials and all of the things that we lacked, and we had the clinical expertise ... Billy DiMauro and I sat down and we created all of the ... information that we wanted. And Seamus was then able to turn that over to [data manager] Richard Buchsbaum who was then able to put it all into a data management system.

The choice to work with Thompson and Columbia's SAC appears to have had several important consequences for NAMDC's institutional development. NAMDC has a relatively loose relationship with the RDCRN's Data Management and Coordinating Center (DMCC), as compared to other RDCRCs. Though NAMDC provides copies of its data to the DMCC, data from NAMDC sites is collected, stored, and handled primarily through Columbia's SAC.[30] NAMDC's Project Manager Johnston Grier and Data Manager Richard Buchsbaum both came to NAMDC from the SAC. Finally, as we will discuss later, NAMDC's site funding model was grounded in Thompson's experience with clinical trials.

15.3.3 *NAMDC's Participants*

15.3.3.1 Columbia-Based Leadership Team

Consortium PIs DiMauro and Hirano are well-established mitochondrial disease clinicians and researchers, with large numbers of publications and a history of NIH grant support. DiMauro was described by another researcher as "the leading light founding father of modern mitochondrial disease." Hirano currently provides most of NAMDC's day-to-day leadership, spending about 40 percent to 50 percent of his time on consortium activities. Hirano has been working in the field of mitochondrial diseases since 1990, having received his MD at Columbia and completed a residency and a fellowship with DiMauro. He describes the subject as his "passion." Like all

[30] This decision caused some initial friction between NAMDC and the DMCC, but a satisfactory working arrangement is now in place.

NAMDC researchers, Hirano divides his time between treating patients and research. Prior to setting up NAMDC, he was a laboratory researcher, without clinical research experience.

Biostatistician Thompson's educational background is in sociology, but his time is now devoted entirely to providing biostatistics expertise and services to clinical researchers. He spends about 20 percent to 25 percent of his time on NAMDC.

Project Manager Grier is an integral part of the leadership team at Columbia and plays the central part in interfacing between the Columbia team and other clinical sites on virtually all nonscientific issues, such as organizing meetings and conference calls, overseeing the IRB process, and training site coordinators to enter data into NAMDC's database. He also had primary administrative responsibility for NAMDC's 2014 renewal proposal.

Data Manager Buchsbaum acts as "an interface between researchers, mostly clinicians, but researchers of all kinds, and the people who deal with the data" for NAMDC and many other Columbia projects. He provides

> a back-end IT infrastructure for research as an enterprise. Which means ... designing systems to collect or integrate research data, but it also means everything from scheduling to billing to other things where data systems can be of use. I program them, I supervise other programmers who program them, I do what might be equivalent to management consulting in terms of people will come with a protocol and I say, well, yes, but what happens when the patients don't behave the way you expect them to?

He "like[s] to be involved in the later stages of protocol development because [his] point of view is primarily a logistical one, which is not often represented in designing [protocols]."

The Columbia team also includes a site study coordinator and administrators who deal with budget and finance issues and spend only a fraction of their time on NAMDC work.

15.3.3.2 Other NAMDC Researchers

NAMDC's membership includes 18 active principal investigators (site PIs) associated with the 16 other clinical sites, as well as a researcher consultant unaffiliated with a clinical site, whose work has focused on the diagnosis action arena described later in Section 15.4.2.1. All site PIs are specialists in treating patients with mitochondrial disease and have medical degrees. About half also have PhDs. Their backgrounds are primarily in genetics, pediatrics, and neurology. Most were engaged in mitochondrial disease research before their association with NAMDC. NAMDC's PIs are extremely busy and hardworking people, who see patients; do research; and, in many cases, shoulder significant administrative responsibilities at their institutions. The effort that they are able to devote to research varies widely, depending largely on their clinical responsibilities, with some devoting about 80 percent of their time to research and others struggling to free up 20 percent of their time for research. All site PIs are responsible for enrolling patients in the NAMDC Patient Registry and Biorepository, which is NAMDC's version of the requisite longitudinal study. Some also conduct other NAMDC-sponsored studies.

15.3.3.3 Study Coordinators

Study coordinators perform many of the nitty-gritty tasks of clinical research, such as entering data into the NAMDC databases correctly, completely, and in accordance with protocols; obtaining informed consent from patients and ensuring IRB compliance at their study sites; and handling general administrative duties. They also often have major responsibilities for patient contact, arranging appointments, and so forth. Study coordinators have a variety of backgrounds. In the United States, they often are geneticists or nurses. Some, especially outside of the United States, have MD or PhD degrees. About half of NAMDC's clinical sites have at least one regularly affiliated study coordinator. At other sites, study coordinator duties are either assigned on a task-by-task basis or are performed by the site PI.

15.3.3.4 NIH and UMDF Representatives

NAMDC interacts closely with two NIH officials, a program officer and a scientific officer, as required by the U54 grant mechanism. The scientific officer is effectively "embedded" in the research community, participating in monthly telephone calls, helping develop research protocols, and even assisting with grant proposals. The program officer's role focuses mostly on administrative oversight, though it also involves assisting the consortium with its interactions with the NIH. These NIH representatives work with multiple consortia and are sources of broad-based expertise in dealing with issues that commonly arise. One interviewee noted that they "have a really wide view of what's happening in other consortia" and are able to contribute "very positively" based on that experience.

The UMDF's executive director and science/alliance officer are active NAMDC participants, with the executive director serving on NAMDC's executive committee.

15.3.4 *NAMDC Governance*

Our study identified three NAMDC governance institutions: (1) consortium-wide meetings, including monthly conference calls and an annual face-to-face meeting; (2) a committee structure; and (3) the Columbia leadership team.

15.3.4.1 Consortium-wide Meetings

NAMDC holds monthly conference calls and annual face-to-face meetings. Early conference call minutes reflect considerable discussion of NAMDC's evolving policies and activities. Perhaps because many decision-making functions have been assigned to the committees described in the next section, interviewees described current conference calls as "more of update calls than . . . decision-making calls" and as "somewhat repetitive but necessary." Large majorities of survey respondents agreed that conference call participation "contributes to my research" and disagreed that participation "takes too much time from my other responsibilities."

In 2015, at the recommendation of its NIH representatives, NAMDC held its first half-day face-to-face meeting, in conjunction with UMDF's annual conference, expanding an earlier practice of holding very short get-togethers at the event. Attendees included the Columbia leadership team, site PIs, several NIH representatives, two UMDF representatives, and the NAMDC fellow. Few study coordinators attended. The meeting covered many topics including the diagnostic criteria, issues with data entry and collection of biospecimens, data access policy, and selection of pilot studies. Several interviewees told us that the extended face-to-face discussion was valuable. As one put it, "I think most of the monthly meetings are pretty perfunctory. It makes me feel part of the community and you get updated. But I don't think there's a whole lot of time for discussion. [But the longer face-to-face meeting] was actually really good because I think it's healthy to get together and see people and really just focus on the details. So that was a really valuable kind of unique experience, relative to the [] monthly phone calls." Another interviewee commented that "of all the things, [the half-day face-to-face meeting] was the most productive, of all the sessions I've attended."

15.3.4.2 Committee Structure

NAMDC's committee structure, depicted in Figure 15.1, was established in 2014: "The overall goal of establishing NAMDC Committees is to distribute the workload of running the consortium and ensuring that everyone is participating actively." On the whole, NAMDC's committee structure was viewed positively by study participants. For example, strong majorities of survey respondents agreed that it "improves cooperative among researchers," "improves NAMDC decision making," and "makes NAMDC decision making less hierarchical," and disagreed that it "adds unnecessary bureaucracy."

The Executive Committee "is responsible for supervising the progress of NAMDC programs . . . setting the long-term strategic goals for the Consortium, and defining the terms and rules by which the Consortium interacts with outside entities . . . review [ing] all proposed NAMDC protocols . . . [and] review[ing] and either approv[ing] or

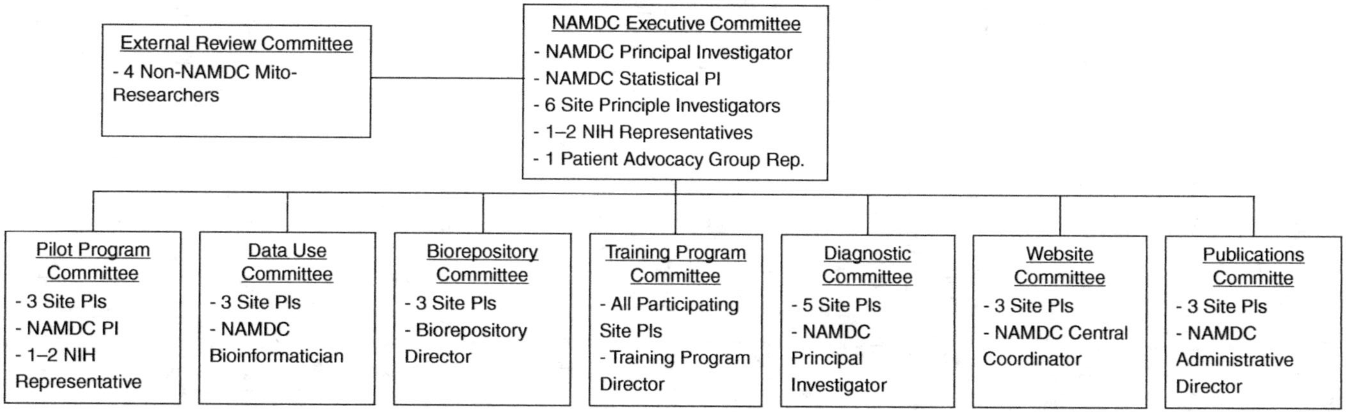

FIGURE 15.1 NAMDC Committee structure.

deny[ing] the addition of future NAMDC Clinical sites."[31] Prior to January 2014, the Executive Committee had been composed of every NAMDC site PI. The number of site PI members was reduced to six in 2014 because "with 18 different sites, some with multiple site PIs, this structure has been unwieldy." Our interviews suggested that the balance of decision-making authority between the Columbia team and the Executive Committee structure was still a work in process. While interviewees who served on the Executive Committee reported active participation in decisions such as "voting in and out new clinics," deciding whether NAMDC should publicly support activities of other organizations, final approval of pilot project funding, setting general research priorities for the consortium, and setting procedures for outsider access to NAMDC data, some interviewees were skeptical or unclear about the extent to which the Executive Committee really differed from the Columbia leadership group. One interviewee expressed the view that the Executive Committee "really is just leadership," while another was of the opinion that the "Executive Committee has so far only been a committee in name. They haven't really done anything. It really has been Michio as being the lead PI." Some interviewees also reported a desire for more "transparency" in NAMDC decision making, particularly as to allocation of funds.

The Diagnostic Committee has been dealing with one of NAMDC's greatest challenges: the establishment of research diagnostic criteria "to categorize patient's mitochondrial disease diagnosis . . . for research purposes and to provide feedback to NADC site investigators about the evaluations and diagnoses of each patient enrolled in the NAMDC Clinical Registry." The Diagnostic Committee is expected to "reevaluate and, if necessary, revise the NAMDC research Diagnostic Criteria on an annual basis." The development of NAMDC Diagnostic Criteria is an important action arena discussed in Section 15.4.2.1.

The Pilot Program and Training Program Committees are responsible for activities familiar to most academics: reviewing grant proposals and selecting and supervising fellows. The Pilot Program Committee makes recommendations to the Executive Committee, which finalizes funding decisions, though finalists present their proposals at the face-to-face meeting, suggesting that broader input from site PIs also is taken into account. The Training Program Committee reviews applicants for NAMDC's fellowship and runs the "curriculum" for the program.

The Data Use and Biorepository Committee is tasked with reviewing requests to use NAMDC data and specimens. NAMDC has formal data-use policies and procedures, but the committee appeared to be relatively inactive at the time of our study, perhaps because NAMDC's data and specimen collections were at a relatively early stage. For similar reasons, NAMDC had not yet established a publication policy. The Website Committee, tasked with maintaining NAMDC's public-facing website, also was not yet active. An interviewee explained that the website is administered by the RDCRN, so that changes would require NAMDC to "wait a

[31] 1/7/2014 Committee White Paper, on file with authors.

long time and make the request to the RDCRN." The relatively low priority apparently afforded to the public website is consistent with our UCDC observations. Perhaps this is because, beyond specific information about RDCRN studies, much of the information about rare diseases that would be of general public interest is available through patient advocacy group websites, for which public education is a priority.

15.3.4.3 Leadership

Leading an RDCRC is challenging. Consortium PIs are ultimately responsible for ensuring the success of the enterprise, but success depends on establishing norms of collaboration and cooperation. In an echo of our UCDC survey, survey respondents overwhelmingly selected "dedicated," followed by "trustworthy" and "determined" as among the best descriptors of current NAMDC leadership.[32] Interviewees also described NAMDC's leadership as "dynamic" and passionate. Interviewees consistently praised PI Hirano's success in bringing researchers together and forging cooperative relationships, "winning the confidence of the group and bringing them together in these enterprises," and instituting a "different model" from earlier times in which "there was a head guy, and he led the charge and that's how science was done." Interviewees described Hirano's leadership style as "very collaborative in drawing people in," "winning the confidence of the group and bringing them together," "not ... top-down," "hav[ing] a very light touch and ... working with [people] in any way he can," "consensus building," "reassuring ... and not confrontational." Several noted that they viewed these leadership traits as key to NAMDC's success, particularly given the challenges of forming a consortium in mitochondrial disease research when there was not much prior history of collaboration between researchers at different institutions.

While most survey respondents who expressed a view agreed that NAMDC's decision-making process is "fair" and "transparent," several interviewees were concerned that both authority and responsibility were concentrated too heavily in the Columbia group. One described NAMDC as "rather centralized," suggesting that it could be "a little more open in terms of soliciting suggestions and listening to the suggestions of others." Another suggested that perhaps "Columbia itself, just as a business institution, [is] used to having PIs make decisions," while a third was concerned that "site PIs may not necessarily feel like we have ownership ... that we're on the bus, but we're not helping drive it." Some believed that there should be more delegation of responsibility from consortium leadership, with one offering the following thoughts:

[32] Respondents were asked to select the best three descriptors among articulate, confident, decisive, dedicated, determined, friendly, outgoing, trustworthy, perceptive, and persistent. Only two respondents took the opportunity to suggest other descriptors.

> I suspect, as the lead PIs, they always feel like all the burden's falling on them. They may not realize it's because they may not have given the other PIs authority. We don't feel like we have authority to take things on . . . I suspect that's where things may fall apart, just because . . . it's too much of a burden for one or two individuals in the group to carry it. After a while the rest may end up getting disengaged, and then things move down the wrong path.

In apparent tension with these comments, some interviewees expressed concern that NAMDC's leaders were not sufficiently "directive" or demanding of consortium members, when "hold[ing] people's feet to the fire . . . may be necessary." One discussed the need for "setting goals, setting priorities, making this work, while capturing the creativity of the individual people," suggesting that in some other consortia "it's much more clear cut what they're working on, how they're moving forward, there is much more structure, and a personality to drive them to work together."

These somewhat opposing views of NAMDC leadership were also mirrored in our survey results. Strong majorities of survey respondents who expressed a view agreed or strongly agreed with the statements "NAMDC decisions are based on consensus" and "NAMDC decisions are made by majority vote," but strong majorities also agreed or strongly agreed that "Most NAMDC decisions are made by the leadership," "NAMDC is hierarchical," and "Site researchers should have more say in NAMDC decisions." Often, the same individuals expressed both sorts of views.

We observed a similar tension between perceptions of (and desire for) both shared, consensus-based governance and strong leadership in the UCDC study, despite important differences between the two consortia. For example, the UCDC is much better established, emerged from a closer-knit community, deals with a less complex set of disorders, and appears to rely much less on a formal committee structure.

15.4 NAMDC'S PRIMARY ACTION ARENAS

An action arena is "the social space where participants with diverse preferences interact, exchange goods and services, solve problems, dominate one another, or fight (among the many things that individuals do in action arenas)."[33] Each action arena involves a particular set of actors; employs, produces, and/or maintains a set of resources; and, in most cases, confronts a set of challenges or dilemmas. Overcoming these challenges or dilemmas generally requires some form of informal or formal governance. Meeting NAMDC's objectives requires cooperative efforts among NAMDC members, who may differ as to how best to accomplish those objectives, how to apportion responsibility and credit, and so forth. Moreover, constraints on

[33] Elinor Ostrom, *Understanding Institutional Diversity* 14 (Princeton University Press 2005). For further explanation of the "action arena" concept, which is central to our GKC framework, see Chapter 1 of this volume.

funding, time, and attention mean that NAMDC must prioritize and make trade-offs between efforts addressed to the various objectives.

In this section, we discuss eight primary NAMDC action arenas observed in our study, identifying the actors and resources involved, and discussing the challenges or dilemmas that must be overcome. These action arenas can be grouped loosely into three categories: (1) creating and sustaining a collaborative research community; (2) developing and managing a shared pool of research subjects, patient data, and biological specimens; and (3) managing relationships with preexisting mitochondrial disease organizations. We do not discuss NAMDC's interactions with pharmaceutical companies related to its objective to conduct rigorous and innovative therapeutic clinical trials. While this action arena is important, we found it too preliminary to delve into at this stage.

15.4.1 *Creating and Sustaining a Collaborative Research Community*

A research consortium's success may depend significantly on the extent to which members form community relationships of mutual trust and responsibility. Nearly all NAMDC researchers responding to our survey listed "participating in a research community" as very important or essential to their decisions to join NAMDC and agreed that "NAMDC is a close-knit community." One interviewee explained, "I really think that [there] is something beyond the practical aspects of it. There is something that improves your efficiency when you are part of a group." We discuss three community building action arenas: (1) determining NAMDC's membership, (2) promoting knowledge sharing and collaboration, and (3) recruiting and training mitochondrial disease clinical researchers.

15.4.1.1 Determining NAMDC's Membership

To create a network of mitochondrial disease clinical researchers, NAMDC must motivate researchers to join; their expected benefits must outweigh their anticipated costs. While participation costs begin to accrue immediately, many benefits are only potential so far. Costs include time and money invested in obtaining IRB approvals and consenting patients for NAMDC studies; data entry; preparing samples for submission to the biorepository; and participating in NAMDC meetings, conference calls, and committees. NAMDC participation also has significant opportunity costs for busy clinician researchers. NAMDC continues to receive requests to join, suggesting that many researchers anticipate substantial benefits such as, most importantly, the possibility of improving patient treatment, as well as opportunities for challenging and interesting research and a competitive edge with respect to publications and professional status. More immediately, membership may foster productive and enjoyable collaboration and knowledge sharing.

Like any knowledge commons, NAMDC must balance inclusiveness against difficulties that accompany growth, some – such as limited resources, growing transaction costs, and difficulties in building community and avoiding shirking and free riding in a larger group – related directly to size, and others related to potential members' compatibility with the group's goals in terms of expertise, dedication, or other factors. Whether NAMDC can (or should) include "all" mitochondrial disease clinical researchers depends on the costs and benefits of growth.

One can conceptualize NAMDC's "members" either as clinical research sites or as individuals. With the exception of the NIH and UMDF representatives and a few others, each individual member is affiliated with a NAMDC clinical research site. Expansion decisions are made on a site-by-site basis. We thus begin by considering the issues NAMDC confronts in determining which, and how many, clinical sites should be included and then briefly discussing some issues relating to members as individuals.

15.4.1.1.1 SELECTING CLINICAL SITES

NAMDC began with 9 clinical centers. By June 2014, it had expanded to its current 17 sites. Adding clinical sites allows NAMDC to reach more patients and increase its pool of research subjects, data, and specimens, but it puts more strain on limited resources. Setting up and maintaining a site involve significant overhead, including the costs of obtaining IRB approval and of training clinicians and study coordinators to follow NAMDC protocols, as well as ongoing management and participation costs. When sites are added, current members benefit from increased collaboration and knowledge sharing and from the availability of a larger pool of data and specimens, but funding, and eventual publication and reputational credit, may be spread more thinly, while group decision making and interaction become more time consuming and complex.

NAMDC members are aware of these trade-offs. Nearly all survey respondents were moderately or very concerned that funding would be stretched too thin if more sites were added, while more than half were similarly concerned about increased bureaucracy and difficulty in making decisions. As one interviewee explained:

> We're very scattered. We already have, I think, 18 centers, and sure there are other people who are seeing patients that have mitochondrial problems, but the question is should we have 18 centers for a rare disease? The downside of having fewer centers is the lack of convenience for families and patients ... The downside from the rare disease research side of things is that ... if you're not part of NAMDC, those patients aren't necessarily getting enrolled into the database, their data is not coming to us ... I think from the selfish side of things, I would opt for fewer centers ... There would be more money to go around to those centers and allow for better development of those centers as opposed to many different centers getting a tiny amount of funding and just scraping by.

Another interviewee noted: "It's already hard to manage the people that are present ... [If you expand the consortium] how do you have a face to face ... how do you even do monthly phone calls?" Indeed, some interviewees already often missed monthly conference calls because of scheduling conflicts.

NAMDC describes its target membership as those "who follow sizeable numbers of patients with mitochondrial diseases and are involved or interested in mitochondrial research." This suggests four distinct aspects of inclusiveness, two of which – geographical coverage and patient numbers – focus on *patients*, while the other two – clinical expertise and research interest and experience – focus on *researchers*.

Broad geographical coverage makes it easier for patients to access a site. Focusing on patient numbers favors locating NAMDC sites at clinics that see the largest numbers of patients, which may be of no help to isolated patients but would reduce overhead costs.

Sites could also be selected based on clinical expertise. Given the difficulty of diagnosing and treating mitochondrial diseases, clinical expertise may be important to identifying, enrolling, and following patients over time. Sites with research interest and experience may be more efficient and may have access to experienced study coordinators and other clinical research professionals.

NAMDC explicitly takes patient numbers into account by requiring each site to enroll at least 15 patients during its first three years. At least two sites have been dropped because they failed to meet that requirement after a start-up period. As of October 1, 2015, two continuing sites had not met the requirement, however, suggesting that the enrollment requirement is not dispositive.

Geographical coverage appears to have played a more secondary role. NAMDC's sites are concentrated roughly in the Northeast and on the West Coast, with additional sites in Florida, Texas, Colorado, and Minnesota.[34] This geographic distribution is probably a collateral consequence of focusing on researcher expertise and patient numbers, given that major academic medical institutions and population centers are similarly distributed. Nonetheless, NIH "wants the sites to be geographically diverse." NAMDC's most recently added site, in Denver, filled a coverage gap in the center of the country. Except for Cleveland, where the inclusion of two sites was "questioned by NIH," NAMDC has only one clinical site per city and recently declined a request to add a second site in Houston.

NAMDC has attempted "from the outset [] to incorporate all of the, or most of the, mitochondrial disease experts in this country." While opinions differed, our study participants mostly agreed that NAMDC is reasonably inclusive of active mitochondrial disease clinical researchers. According to interviewees, NAMDC has "captured most of the people who are seeing most of the patients" and "has

[34] For a graph showing the locations of NAMDC's sites, see the MMS website at www.google.com/maps/d/viewer?mid=1pzaRlALggxqNShL-n8F2hk6tEPg

been quite effective at getting most of them in," and active clinical researchers outside of NAMDC are "increasingly few."

Still, "there are many doctors who are clinically seeing patients, involved in clinical research, that are not NAMDC sites." The Mitochondrial Medicine Society's webpage displays a map of mitochondrial medicine specialists globally; several are in the United States, at academic medical centers, and not in close proximity to an existing NAMDC site. NAMDC must decide whether, how quickly, and where it should expand in light of the trade-offs involved.

NAMDC also must create a process for making those decisions. Its consortium PIs selected the sites included in the original NIH proposals. Subject to RDCRN approval,[35] based on general considerations including a proposed site's commitment and the DMCC's workload, NAMDC exercises considerable discretion about site expansion. Formally, NAMDC's Executive Committee is now empowered to make decisions about adding and, when necessary, removing sites, but NAMDC leadership was considering whether to "make this a little more democratic and make sure that everyone has a vote and has a say in who's in and who's out."

15.4.1.1.2 NAMDC AS A COMMUNITY OF INDIVIDUALS

Adding sites means integrating newcomers into the NAMDC community. Community building among NAMDC's clinician-researchers is facilitated by the fact that they already belong to a relatively small community of practice[36] and have a shared dedication to improving patient health. As one interviewee pointed out, "there aren't that many people that have a focused desire and expertise to work in mitochondrial disease," and many know one another through their training and other prior interactions. The mitochondrial disease research community overall was described as "a really congenial group, a really lovely group of people" and "very collegial," and its members as "very committed" and "driven." Nonetheless, when a relationship-based community grows, some strain on informal norms and trust relationships is likely.

Community building also means deciding how individuals at each site are incorporated into the NAMDC, which functions primarily as a community of site PIs. One PI observed that NAMDC has been a "pretty PI-driven group" and not "overly open to support staff." Though study coordinators and other support personnel at some NAMDC sites see themselves as "very active participants" in NAMDC's work, their interactions with the broader NAMDC community are PI-mediated "NAMDC communicates mainly through the PIs, perhaps the web list, the email invites go out to other people. But, like, at the face-to-face meeting, that was really just PIs who were welcome. I think you could take one research coordinator with you

[35] DMCC, Policies, Procedures & Standards: Rare Diseases Clinical Research Network (August 6, 2013) § I.F, on file with authors.

[36] See Chapter 11, this volume.

if you wanted to." As a study coordinator interviewee explained, "I have nothing in my job description that makes me need to contact anybody else."

This PI-mediated community model contrasts with that of the UCDC. UCDC study coordinators regularly attend consortium-wide meetings and have study coordinator telephone conferences. Study coordinator response rates to our survey may reflect this difference in community model. While 17 out of 25 UCDC study coordinators, representing 14 out of 15 sites, responded to our UCDC survey, only one NAMDC study coordinator responded.

Each model has advantages and disadvantages. Greater study coordinator cross-site interaction and direct involvement add both financial and transactional costs. UCDC employs consortium resources to fund dedicated study coordinator efforts at each clinical site and to finance study coordinator meetings. NAMDC does not "support anybody funding-wise. All they do is pay you back for putting in some patients." Indeed, only about half of NAMDC's sites had designated study coordinators at the time of our study. Recently, NAMDC has been taking steps to involve study coordinators more directly. At the 2015 face-to-face meeting, one of the few study coordinator attendees suggested involving study coordinators in protocol development to better anticipate practical implementation issues. A more general discussion of the study coordinator role in NAMDC ensued and the group voted to create a study coordinator committee.

15.4.1.1.3 RESOURCES, CHALLENGES, AND DILEMMAS

Deciding whether to add a site involves judgments about how best to use both NAMDC's limited available funding and the time and energy of NAMDC members. Study participants favored inclusiveness but were well aware of these trade-offs.

Limited funding was the most pressing concern reflected in our study. For example, a large majority of survey respondents were moderately or very concerned that funding would be stretched too thinly if sites were added. Because the governance dilemmas posed by funding constraints are also relevant to the patient registry and biorepository action arena, we discuss them in Section 15.4.2.2.

Majorities of our survey respondents were also moderately or very concerned that adding sites would increase bureaucracy and make decision making more difficult. These problems can be mitigated through institutional design. The challenge is to cut down time spent in meetings and other administrative and decision making activities, while maintaining a highly collaborative and participatory community. NAMDC's committee structure is one approach to this challenge. Though not fully implemented at the time of our study, the committee structure is designed to delegate tasks, encourage participation, and prepare topics for consideration by the group as a whole. The active Diagnostic, Pilot Project, and Training Program Committees appeared to be performing such functions effectively. Committee participation may also serve more general community-building purposes. A large majority of survey respondents agreed that NAMDC's committee structure improves cooperation among researchers, while an interviewee described a particular example of a collaboration that emerged as a side benefit of working with another NAMDC member on a committee.

15.4.1.2 Promoting Collaboration and Knowledge Sharing

Interviewees emphasized the importance of pooling efforts to make progress on rare disease research. Informal knowledge sharing is easiest when researchers are in physical proximity or have preexisting relationships. NAMDC's challenge is to promote collaboration and knowledge sharing among researchers at widely dispersed institutions, only some of whom know each other well.

Mitochondrial disease medicine is a small field, and most of NAMDC's researchers were somewhat acquainted with one another before joining NAMDC. Nonetheless, one interviewee described the pre-NAMDC environment as "fragmented" and observed that "you would hardly ever see even two people work together," while another observed that "in the old days … there seemed to be competing factions depending on where someone was situated in the country."

While some interviewees remained dissatisfied that "much of the mitochondrial research is still single investigator driven and not community driven," most study participants believed that NAMDC had improved knowledge sharing and collaboration significantly. As one interviewee put it, "what's really different with NAMDC is there is much more collaboration rather than individual work." Interviewees described NAMDC as a "very cohesive" and "congenial" community, in which members "have very healthy arguments, very healthy disagreements" without "the old-school mentality, like, 'If I share my data, I'm going to get scooped and then I'm not going to get my pubs and then I'm not going to get tenure and then I'm going to die under a rowboat, poor'" Survey respondents also generally agreed that NAMDC is a "close-knit community" and that they collaborate and share research ideas with other NAMDC members more often since joining.

As a rough check on these impressions, we tabulated cross-institutional coauthorship between NAMDC members before and after 2011, when NAMDC was established. Before 2011, currently active NAMDC PIs had coauthored more than once with an average of only about two members outside their own institutions. That average rose to approximately six for the period after 2011 consistent, at least, with participants' qualitative observations. Consortium membership may be particularly important for researchers at relatively less-known institutions. One PI reported that, "When the mitochondrial medicine society sent out a survey of which labs do you use we were not even listed. When I asked why we're not listed they said, well we don't know that you exist." That PI had not previously coauthored more than once with any other NAMDC member but had done so with nine NAMDC members since 2011.

NAMDC's members, at least, do not think that the enhanced cooperation and sharing among NAMDC members comes at the expense of cooperation with outside researchers. Not a single survey respondent agreed that NAMDC has made cooperation between members and nonmembers more difficult.

While some interviewees suggested that pre-NAMDC "fragmentation" among mitochondrial disease researchers was due to competitiveness, competitiveness does not seem to have created serious governance problems for NAMDC. As one interviewee put it:

> I found that in the old days when I used to go to the meetings that not all [mitochondrial disease researchers] worked well together. That's changed on a number of levels. So I think there seemed to be competing factions depending on where someone was situated in the country, and I think it was pretty obvious like a decade or so ago ... [but now] it's getting better ... [because] people realize they have to work together on these rare disorders. That you can't really be a silo out there because you don't have the access to the patients and the funding is always an issue so it's always better to work in a group to get these things accomplished.

An NIH representative concurred that competitiveness has not been a major hurdle for NAMDC. Rather, "the biggest issue for them is getting the data, seeing the patients, having the personnel to enter the data, having the [quality control]." Another interviewee similarly observed, "I haven't seen a lot of backstabbing. I see them more as competing as a group against other areas of research."

NAMDC appears to have increased collaboration and knowledge sharing primarily by providing infrastructure and coordination to facilitate it. One interviewee described NAMDC as

> a mechanism that's really very helpful in moving all of our goals forward. It's ... been synergistic because it's helped pull us all together and it's encouraging more research ... It's [provided] government funding to develop a longitudinal database which then can lead to all sorts of things because you can follow patient disease courses and you have a supply of patients for research. That just wouldn't happen otherwise.

Another described NAMDC's importance as a forum for building the mutual trust required for collaboration:

> Coming to meetings like NAMDC is building those personal connections; there are a number of people here I now have collaborations with that are really not as much based on the formal structure of NAMDC, but the informal meeting and finding people and talking about things. I think that's actually more effective than the formal structures. You can have formal structures and rely on everybody there, then you have a number of outliers who just don't do what they say, that does not work. When you want to work with people that you know, when they say they'll do something they actually will do it.

15.4.1.3 Recruiting and Training Mitochondrial Disease Clinical Researchers

RDCRN consortia are required to make efforts to "train[] investigators in clinical research of rare diseases."[37] Members see these efforts as critical to NAMDC's mission:

> You have to train the next generation, because a lot of people in our consortium are in their seventies, and many are still practicing, but eventually they're going to stop seeing patients. Then who is going to take care of these patients clinically and carry the mission forward?
>
> There has to be a strong investment in training the next generation and attracting them to do rare-disorder research because the funding's not as good. So, doing [pilot] projects within this [program,] I see as a benefit to get people interested in rare disorders. Because they can be more successful doing it as part of a consortium then trying to get R01, R21 on their own. They have the support of a group, and they have access to the patients. Once you get people interested in rare disorders, I think you can move the other things forward. If you can't get them interested, then it's not going to move forward.

NAMDC's Training Program Committee oversees its formal fellowship program and is responsible for the design and execution of its training program curriculum. The NAMDC fellowship is unusual in that fellows complete coursework at University of California–San Diego and then rotate among several NAMDC sites for clinical and research practice, rather than training with a single group at one location. PIs at all participating sites belong to the Training Program Committee and participate in a monthly webinar during which trainees discuss their research and members make presentations about the research going on in their groups. Multiple interviewees emphasized the value of these webinars. The NAMDC community also facilitates informal training and mentoring. Many of our interviewees related stories of how senior researchers provided critical guidance and support at early stages of their careers. As one interviewee put it, "I wish I had this when I was a fellow . . . If there was NAMDC before, I wouldn't have had to do a lot of things, just reinvent the wheel for myself all of the time."

Recruiting new mitochondrial disease researchers can be challenging. NAMDC has received only about two to four fellowship applicants a year and would like to receive more. Moreover, NAMDC's fellowship program is relatively new and still evolving. Some members questioned whether the rotation approach, despite its educational benefits, might deter potential applicants because of its disruption of the fellows' personal lives. There was also a possibly related concern that a recent fellow had spent too much time doing data entry and not enough time creating "a body of work that can help this person's career move forward."

[37] 2003 RFA, http://grants.nih.gov/grants/guide/rfa-files/RFA-OD-08–001.html#SectionI

15.4.2 *Developing and Managing a Shared Pool of Research Subjects, Patient Data, and Biological Specimens*

NAMDC's primary vehicle for overcoming the barriers posed by small numbers of geographically scattered rare disease patients is the NAMDC Patient Registry and Biorepository Study (7401 Protocol). All NAMDC sites take part, at least to some degree. The 7401 Protocol "is not itself a study, but rather a project to create infrastructure resources for laboratory studies, clinical trials, natural history studies, and other research endeavors."[38] It consists of two related efforts, one collecting patient data and the other collecting biospecimens. As described in NAMDC's 2014 renewal proposal, the Patient Registry

> gathers baseline clinical, biochemical, and molecular genetic data as well as tracks the natural histories of the patients through the NAMDC Clinical Longitudinal study. The overall missions of the NAMDC Clinical Registry are to: better understand the spectrum and overlap of phenotypes for specific mitochondrial diseases; enable genotype/phenotype correlations; facilitate enrollment into clinical studies under NAMDC and other entities; and characterize the natural histories of mitochondrial diseases . . . Samples of blood, skin, and other tissues are being deposited into the NAMDC Biorepository.[39]

Every RDCRN consortium is required to conduct a longitudinal study to characterize how its focal diseases develop over time.[40] The term "registry" is often used to indicate a database, such as the DMCC's RDCRN Contact Registry,[41] where patients can indicate interest in being contacted to participate in clinical trials or other research. UMDF maintains a Mitochondrial Disease Community Registry, which is intended not only for that purpose but also to collect patient-reported data about symptoms, quality of life, and so forth.[42] While titled a patient registry, NAMDC's 7401 Protocol is intended also to collect data for NAMDC's longitudinal study.

DMCC PI Jeffrey Krischer explains that while both longitudinal studies and contact registries are used to "identify populations for interventional studies," longitudinal studies are "physician enrolled with informed consent," "hypothesis driven," and "describe phenotypic variation," while contact registries are "patient/family enrolled with online informed consent; collect "limited data" and may be used to provide information and as a "vehicle for epidemiological studies."[43]

[38] NAMDC Patient Registry and Biorepository Study Protocol, p. 3 (2012) (on file with authors) (quote occurs twice, under "Study Design" and "Primary Outcome Measures").

[39] Abstract for NIH Project 5U54NS078059-05, Sub-Project 5771.

[40] See, e.g., the RFA for the 2014 round of RDCRN grants, http://grants.nih.gov/grants/guide/rfa-files/RFA-TR-13–002.html

[41] www.rarediseasesnetwork.org/registry/

[42] www.umdf.org/site/c.8qKOJ0MvF7LUG/b.9135169/k.D604/Registry.htm

[43] Slides from presentation on June 16, 2011, The Rare Disease Clinical Research Network: Registries and Longitudinal Studies, www.nbstrn.org/sites/default/files/Krischer-RDCRN-Registries-6–5-11.pdf

Longitudinal study data feeds directly into research, ordinarily without further patient contact. Thus, care must be taken with data collection at the outset. Most basically, collection should reflect agreed-upon diagnostic criteria for determining whether to include a given patient's data in a study. Thus, NAMDC has attempted to "create[] NAMDC Research Diagnostic Criteria for mitochondrial diseases with strict benchmarks for definite, probable, possible, or unlikely levels of diagnoses."

In this section we discuss three important NAMDC action arenas related to creating a pool of patients, data, and biospecimens for NAMDC's longitudinal study and other potential research: (1) developing the NAMDC Research Diagnostic Criteria, (2) recruiting patients and collecting the relevant data and biospecimens, and (3) managing and using the pooled research resources.

15.4.2.1 Diagnostic Criteria

"One of the great problems in our field is diagnosing mitochondrial disease. It's not one disease but many, probably hundreds or more. It's a dilemma." Diagnosis has been a major action arena for NAMDC. Even for *clinical* purposes, diagnosis remains a work-in-progress, as reflected in the MMS Consensus Statement. Moreover, these criteria may differ from what NAMDC requires for *research* purposes:

> Frankly, I think among rare diseases, mitochondrial diseases are among the most over-diagnosed and under-diagnosed because they're so diverse. They're under-diagnosed because people just don't recognize them, and then they're over-diagnosed because whenever there's a patient with a complex multi-systemic disease, people throw up their hands and say, "Must be a mitochondrial disease." We felt obliged to really set up criteria for our sake, for stratifying the registry, the patients in a registry. Also for research purposes, because we take the possible and probable patients and we may do additional genetic or molecular studies to define them better. And also just to say that there are a couple of patients that are very unlikely to have mitochondrial disease even though they were diagnosed by supposed experts who entered all these patients into the registry. [W]e're trying to use that as an educational tool so that when we put the patients through the diagnostic criteria, or their information through the criteria, we send back a letter to the site investigators and inform them what their NAMDC diagnosis is and level of probability. We're actually going through this exercise, and we're having people reevaluate their original diagnosis to see if they agree with the NAMDC criteria or not and if not why, and we're revising our diagnostic criteria. It's a back-and-forth activity here that's in progress.

Because mitochondrial disease research is still at an early stage, clinical diagnoses can be controversial, as one interviewee explained:

> Why do you need diagnostic criteria [when] you have experts diagnosing people? There's two [reasons]: One is . . . there's very few of these experts, and so if they feel that mitochondrial disease is under diagnosed, you want to give [the diagnostic criteria] to people who aren't experts so they can check off the checklist and say, "Oh, you've got mitochondrial disease," or, "You don't." But the other, which goes unsaid, is that there's very little agreement between these experts . . . I mean some of them are unambiguous; the very syndromes are unambiguous, but a lot of them are ambiguous, and there've been long, not fights, but vigorous conversations about how to define each one. And still, we had . . . a version that we came up with and then we ran it against the actual patient population, and the results of that were very controversial.

Ultimately, the value of the NAMDC patient registry as an *input* for research is contingent on the quality of the data included and the reliability of the diagnostic criteria. Thus, as one interviewee explained, "You want as clean a population as you can study, and so the diagnostic criteria are much tighter. That's one thing that NAMDC [focuses] on. That's why you have this issue of research diagnosis."

An initial set of NAMDC Diagnostic Criteria was developed by a committee of NAMDC's initial members[44] and programmed into NAMDC's online data collection system. A significant number of disagreements with clinical diagnoses were uncovered, leading to a concerted effort to uncover the sources of discrepancy and validate or revise the NAMDC Diagnostic Criteria. The validation effort involved surveying NAMDC investigators for feedback and tasking a consultant researcher with detailed review of cases where clinical diagnoses disagreed with NAMDC's automated diagnoses.

The consultant uncovered several disagreement scenarios. Sometimes the NAMDC criteria were "too strict," for example, when patients with a particular phenotype were not assigned the correct diagnosis because some data, such as age of onset, was not recorded. NAMDC attempted to address this problem by structuring the data entry process to "inform the physician what fields in the eCRF must have data entered" to obtain a particular NAMDC Criteria Diagnosis. Ambiguities or misunderstandings during data entry also could cause disagreement:

> In my head, if I have liver disease, I would check off hepatopathy, or something. But if a person who does not understand the term hepatopathy is entering the data for you, he or she sees a spreadsheet, the liver enzymes are abnormal, all the liver functions are abnormal, but there is no place to enter the liver enzymes are abnormal. So he/she does not mark that column there is liver involvement. The computer looks at it and says how can you call it Alpers when you don't have liver involvement? I am rejecting it.

[44] This committee preexisted the establishment of NAMDC's formal committee structure.

The NAMDC criteria were also sometimes "too rigid," making it hard "to factor in the evolution of the disease in some patients." Sometimes, the automated algorithm was simply missing "that sixth sense" that clinicians develop through experience.

Even as NAMDC works to improve and validate its diagnostic criteria, the science continues to evolve. As one interviewee explained: "So one of the inherent catch-22s in all this is that you set up criteria based upon what you know. But if you only know 15 percent of the causes of diseases then your criteria are only going to let you capture that 15 percent. It's not going to let you capture the unknown." Moreover, the data fields chosen for the NAMDC Diagnostic Criteria, though many, are a small fraction of possible choices and were likely to reflect historical bias: "For example, the new mito disease that we just discovered it's showing to affect the bones. We don't ask one question about bones [in the Diagnostic Criteria]. Zero. Zip ... So we would never capture the disease that involved the bones because we never asked." Scientific evolution is particularly rapid with respect to genetic markers, where there is "just an ever-changing landscape ... Even as we wrote the criteria four years ago until now, we've had at least probably another 50 genes added." The bottom line, in the opinion of one interviewee, is that mitochondrial disease diagnosis is "never going to be a perfect science."

NAMDC's experience highlights how unanticipated layers of knowledge dilemmas can emerge in a consortium setting. NAMDC's Diagnostic Criteria were developed as a research tool for constructing the patient data pool and enabling NAMDC's planned research, yet the development of accurate and workable criteria has itself become a dynamic and complex action arena facing many challenges. NAMDC has grappled with the diagnosis dilemma through formal and informal governance institutions. NAMDC's Diagnostic Committee was formed as an ad hoc group but integrated into the formal committee structure when it was instituted. The validation process evolved informally. For example, when asked who decided on the process that NAMDC's consultant would use to conduct her evaluation and who picked her to do it, one interviewee responded, "It just is one of these things that just evolved organically."

15.4.2.2 Creating a Pool of Research Subjects, Patient Data, and Biospecimens

NAMDC's Patient Registry aggregates medical and family histories, diagnostic test results, and other information from patients who enroll in the study. Clinical sites collect and enter the data, which is pooled using Columbia's data management facilities and shared with the DMCC, as NIH requires. Biorepository samples of blood, skin, and other tissues are collected by site researchers and submitted to and maintained at the Mayo Clinic.

15.4.2.2.1 THE NAMDC PATIENT REGISTRY

NAMDC initially set a goal of enrolling 15 patients per month in its registry, aiming eventually for a total of 1000 patients. The first patients were enrolled in June 2011. By

April 2012, four NAMDC sites had enrolled a total of 121 patients. NAMDC has exceeded its monthly recruitment goal since May 2012. By October 2015, 844 patients had been enrolled from 17 sites. Recruitment numbers vary substantially among sites, with cumulative enrollments as of October 2015 ranging from 136 to 7, and average monthly enrollments ranging from 2.6 to 0.2.

Enrollment numbers do not tell the whole story. For NAMDC's data pool to function as intended, each patient's data must be sufficiently complete to confirm a diagnosis using the NAMDC Diagnostic Criteria. By August 2012, that was the case for only about half the enrolled patients, while at four sites data was incomplete for every patient. Over time, this picture improved dramatically. By October 2015, data entry was sufficient for nearly 90 percent of enrolled patients, average site compliance rate was 90 percent, and the lowest compliance rate was 62 percent.

If NAMDC's patient registry data is to be used for a longitudinal study, patients also must be followed over time and data entered at appropriate intervals. The 7401 Protocol calls for yearly follow-up visits. By December 2014, however, only 17 percent of scheduled follow-ups had been completed, the average site follow-up rate was 25 percent and only about half of the sites had completed any follow-ups. By October 2015, things had improved only slightly; only 25 percent of scheduled follow-ups had been completed overall and the average follow-up rate was 36 percent.

15.4.2.2.2 THE NAMDC BIOREPOSITORY

The NAMDC Biorepository took some time to get up and running because of logistical difficulties. It first went "live" in January 2013 and its current director came on board in October 2014. The contribution rate has been low. By October 2015, nine sites had submitted specimens for 109 patients, representing about 13 percent of enrolled patients; nearly half of NAMDC's sites had submitted no biospecimens.

NAMDC's leaders believe that the biorepository is very important and the small number of contributions was critiqued during NAMDC's 2014 renewal review. To encourage participation, NAMDC covers the costs of shipping specimens to Mayo and in February 2014, the Mayo Clinic began distributing biorepository specimen collection kits, complete with shipment paperwork and instructions. In October 2015, the biorepository also began to accept "virtual" submissions of fibroblasts, effectively creating an index of cell lines without the need to submit and manage physical samples.

15.4.2.2.3 RESOURCES, CHALLENGES, AND DILEMMAS

Many aspects of NAMDC's Patient Registry have been successful. Nonetheless, challenges remained, particularly regarding follow-up rates and biorepository participation. Patient enrollment rates, follow-up rates, and biorepository participation rates also vary widely across sites, which may or may not be cause for concern depending on whether access to patients varies similarly. The diversity of mitochondrial diseases also poses data collection challenges because of the sheer number of data fields needed to capture relevant data. Some interviewees suggested that there is a trade-off between collecting data for a wide variety of diseases and collecting all relevant data for each disease.

Enrolling patients in the registry, entering data, and submitting biospecimens are time-consuming and costly activities.[45] While interviewees told us that most of the data requested by NAMDC's registry is already collected for clinical purposes, entering data regularly and accurately is a problem for some. As one explained:

> We probably have a couple hundred [patients] with primary confirmed mitochondrial disease, but most of them have not made their way into the database because of time constraints ... The problem is [that] [w]e're barely able to put data in for that initial patient, for the patients we're seeing in follow-up, they're usually going by the wayside and we're not getting follow-up data.

Another commented regarding the biorepository: "It's just been time consuming. We have samples on many, many people and so it's just a matter of sitting down one week and getting them all together and shipping the ones who have the proper access. That's just a manpower issue." Moreover, interviewees noted difficulty not only in finding time to prepare and submit specimens but also in finding ways to pay for biomaterial collection that is not covered by patients' health insurance.

Many study participants complained that their sites received insufficient funding to cover the costs of enrolling patients in the registry, entering data, collecting and submitting samples to the biorepository, and so on. Funding not only goes toward these direct costs but can also alleviate researcher time constraints in two ways. First, many researchers are required to account to the funding sources for their activities. If they cannot point to a funding source for NAMDC data input or specimen collection, their participation in the patient registry and biorepository essentially comes from their personal time.[46] As one interviewee explained, "Some doctors are having to enter the data themselves ... That's happening at 9:00 at night. There's homework to be done. That's going to happen after their homework." Second, while there are some things that researchers must do themselves,[47] they can be relieved of many tasks, such as obtaining informed consent from patients and entering data, if they have access to trained study coordinators. Coordinators also can assist with retaining patients and arranging follow-up visits for a longitudinal study.[48]

45 "One of the problems we have with this database is that it's like a four-hour job to fill out all of the questions." Data entry for "a single patient takes 30 to 60 minutes." "When I tried to do it myself, it really took me two to three hours to finish and it's very labor intensive."

46 "My boss, for many of us, our bosses say don't do it. It's a time suck, it's an energy suck. You are not making any money for yourself to protect your time."

47 "[A]t most centers, the MD position is doing the data extraction [from the chart], because ... [i]t's too complex, the diseases are too niche that there aren't other people who understand them."

48 See the UCDC Study, note 5.

Consortia face two interrelated funding issues: total funding constraints and questions about how to allocate available funding among consortium activities and among sites. NAMDC's NIH funding totals about US$1.25 million per year,[49] comparable to NIH funding for other RDCRN consortia. Consortia may also seek additional outside funding. UCDC reputedly has been successful in obtaining private donations and also raises money by charging pharmaceutical companies for its assistance in selecting and recruiting clinical trial participants using its longitudinal study data and in providing technical expertise for such studies on a consulting basis. NAMDC also has sought outside funding, so far with modest success: UMDF pays Project Manager Grier's salary, while a private foundation supplements the funding provided to NAMDC sites for their participation in the NAMDC registry. NAMDC also seeks to follow the UCDC's lead with regard to pharmaceutical companies. Designing the necessary structure for vetting pharma company studies and ensuring that NAMDC's participation complies with legal and IRB obligations has been quite time consuming, but a mechanism was finally put into place in late 2014. At the time of our study, it was too soon to tell whether it would bring in significant additional funds.

Many interviewees told us that NAMDC's funding for sites' registry and biorepository efforts is insufficient to cover study coordinator effort. Only about half of NAMDC's sites have designated NAMDC study coordinators. Those that do rely on institutional or other funding to support them. As one interviewee explained:

> In my world, it's been very successful because my work has an incredible organization built to do it and do it right ... I have an incredibly qualified research coordinator who does 90 percent and she has a partner that does about the other 10 percent ... Other sites don't have that. Some sites don't have a research coordinator. The money coming from NAMDC ... is probably not enough to support the actual hourly work that they do.

Another mentioned that "the biggest challenge he is having with recruitment is coordinator support as the funds from NAMDC do not adequately cover coordinator time."

The presence of a NAMDC-affiliated study coordinator appears to be quite strongly correlated with better patient recruitment. On average, sites with affiliated study coordinators recruited more than three times as many patients, both in total and on a per month basis, and completed nearly twice as many of their scheduled follow-ups, as sites without. Of course, study coordinator access may not be driving better enrollment numbers. The correlation could have some other cause. Perhaps, for example, sites with affiliated study coordinators have more mitochondrial disease patients to enroll. Given the importance that interviewees ascribed to study

[49] To facilitate comparison between consortia, all budget numbers are taken from NIH RePORTER, https://projectreporter.nih.gov/reporter.cfm

coordinators, however, it seems likely that study coordinator support would allow some sites to recruit more patients.

NAMDC's approach to allocating funding is quite different from that of UCDC and CEGIR in two respects: first, NAMDC budgets substantially less of its annual grant to its Patient Registry and Biorepository than the other consortia allocate to their longitudinal studies. Second, NAMDC allocates funds among sites using a per patient payment model, while UCDC and CEGIR allocate a roughly equivalent annual sum to each site.

In 2015, NAMDC budgeted about 20 percent of its NIH funds for the Patient Registry and Biorepository, while UCDC and CEGIR devoted 52 percent and 40 percent of their funds, respectively, to their longitudinal studies.

Because NAMDC has more member sites than either UCDC or CEGIR, this difference is magnified on a per site basis. Thus, while UCDC 's and CEGIR's 2015 longitudinal study budgets averaged about US$44,000 and US$56,000 per site, respectively, NAMDC's Patient Registry and Biorepository budget averaged only about US$15,000 per site.[50] The amounts potentially available for distribution to sites are lower than these averages, of course, as a result of institutional overhead and other expenses of running the studies. Thus, without supplementary funds from other sources, NAMDC's overall budget allocation is not designed to provide substantial study coordinator support.

NAMDC's choice to allocate less of its grant to its registry/longitudinal study means it can devote a larger fraction of its grant funds to other aspects of its work. In 2015, for example, 60 percent of NAMDC's grant was allocated to a combination of other research projects, pilot projects, and training, while UCDC and CEGIR budgeted only 27 percent and 43 percent, respectively, to these activities. (The three consortia each budgeted about 20 percent for central administrative costs.)

NAMDC also differs from UCDC and CEGIR in that it pays its sites "per work unit" for contributing to the patient registry, "as opposed to paying for say half a coordinator in every site where you don't really know what the person is necessary for." NAMDC provides each site a US$2,000 start-up payment, primarily to cover the costs of obtaining IRB approval for the study, pays the US$50 payment when each patient is initially enrolled, US$200 when data entry for a patient is sufficient for diagnosis using the NAMDC criteria, and US$50 for each annual follow-up. The data entry payments were instituted in February 2013 using supplemental funds obtained from a foundation. The US$50 follow-up payments were announced in February 2014. As of October 1, 2015, NAMDC sites had enrolled 844 patients, 754 of which had sufficient data entered for diagnosis, and completed 317 follow-up visits, corresponding to total site payments of about US$240,000 between June 2011, when the first patients were enrolled, and October 1, 2015.[51] Payments thus averaged about

[50] The amounts actually distributed to sites are lower than these averages, since not all funds budgeted for these studies are distributed to sites.

[51] NAMDC Monthly Report, Oct. 1, 2015, on file with authors.

US$14,000 total per site over this period. Because some sites recruited many more patients than others, however, the payments due to each site varied from about US $32,000 to about US$4,000.

Interviewees suggested three reasons for adopting the per patient payment model: insufficient total funds to support dedicated study coordinator time, deterring free riding, and fairness. As already discussed, NAMDC's total budget for the patient registry is largely a question of how its grant funds are allocated between the patient registry and other aspects of its activities.

Potential free-riding issues arise when community members have equal access to pooled resources regardless of how much they contribute. As one interviewee explained, "I think in the old days, they would say, 'We're going to pay 10 percent of a patient and of a coordinator's time.' Then, what happens when they don't deliver? [Give them] another 10 percent on the hopes that next year they'll put some data in?" In principle, per patient payments can mitigate free riding by giving sites direct monetary incentives to enroll more patients. Other mechanisms, both direct – such as quotas – and indirect – such as reputation, social norms, or a sense of community responsibility – also can reduce the likelihood of free riding. Indeed, NAMDC itself discourages free riding directly with its 15-patient minimum enrollment requirement and indirectly by reporting monthly to the group on each site's recruitment, data completion, biorepository contribution, and follow-up numbers.

Do NAMDC's per patient payments incentivize sites to enroll more patients? If the incentive effects were substantial, one might have expected patient enrollment to accelerate when the US$200 per patient payments for data completion began in early 2013, but NAMDC's patient enrollment appears to have increased roughly linearly over time, suggesting that there were no large incentive effects. If, as some interviewees suggested, the per patient payment does not cover the costs of enrolling an additional patient, the absence of a strong incentive effect is not surprising.

Some interviewees also suggested that giving each site an equal funding allocation would simply "not [be] fair because some sites will record no patients ... some of them will recruit four hundred patients, and they shouldn't get the same resources" and that "It just makes more sense to me is pay us for what we do." Counter to this view, some study participants suggested that the per patient model favors sites with alternative sources of study coordinator support, in a kind of rich-get-richer effect. As one interviewee put it, "Without a coordinator, I would have been dropped [for insufficient enrollment]. There's no way to enter all that data." It seems possible, at least, that per patient funding cannot effectively incentivize patient enrollment until a site has some threshold level of study coordinator assistance.

The question of funding allocation seemed to generate a modest amount of discontent with NAMDC governance, in rather sharp contrast to members' otherwise positive views of NAMDC, its leadership, and its decision making. For example, researchers responding to our survey nearly all agreed generally that NAMDC's decision-making process is "fair" and "transparent," but, when asked directly about the allocation of NAMDC resources, nearly all agreed that "NAMDC members should have more say in how NAMDC resources are allocated." Similarly, when asked about how NAMDC funding is allocated, one interviewee responded:

> I think some of it has been a little bit cryptic in the first funding cycle. It sounds like most of the time the funds are just used to pay for the administrators at Columbia and then the big funding decisions have come to how to pay for patients to be entered into the registry – that seems to be the number one priority . . . So I think those decisions were made out of Columbia. I think maybe together with the NIH and based on available funding. So I think the managing site still probably makes most of those decisions.

On the whole, our study suggests that designing a better mechanism to fund study coordinator tasks may be a significant challenge for NAMDC going forward, especially as it seeks to increase participation in the biorepository and complete follow-up data collection to support its longitudinal study.

15.4.2.3 Sharing and Using the Pool of Data and Biospecimens

NAMDC's pool of patient data and biospecimens has tremendous potential for use not only for NAMDC's longitudinal study but also as sharable input into other knowledge-generation activities, including other data-mining research, development of diagnostic tools and treatments, clinical trials, and other interventional research. Yet there are some challenges and governance dilemmas.

First, these infrastructural resources need to be fit for the research purpose and ready for use. At this stage of its development, NAMDC's primary focus seems to be on building rather than using the resources.

Second, access to and use of these resources require governance. For example, NAMDC's patient registry collects a variety of personal health information. Accordingly, NAMDC restricts direct access to the NAMDC system administrators. NAMDC sites get immediate access only to their own patients' data; access to other sites' data is granted only pursuant to a research protocol, approved by both the NAMDC Data Use Committee and the relevant IRB.

NAMDC's Data Use and Biorepository Committees review requests to use NAMDC data and specimens. According to the data-use request instructions (which are very similar to the instructions for biospecimen requests):

> To access NAMDC data an academic researcher or industrial representative must submit a proposal to the NAMDC Data Use Committee (NAMDC Data Use Request Form) detailing the data requested and how they propose to use them. Prior to data distribution, the researcher/industrial representative must also submit proof that the protocol has either IRB approval or has been granted an exemption by the IRB. The Data Use Committee will make its recommendation to the NAMDC Executive Committee who will make the ultimate decision as to what data may be

shared. If approved, the investigator must submit a full protocol for approval by NAMDC, RDCRN, NIH, and an IRB.

To standardize data and biospecimen use requests, and perhaps to encourage them by making the process a little easier and more transparent, NAMDC developed forms for NAMDC members' use as well as forms for two levels of review – by the relevant resource committee and the Executive Committee. Yet one interviewee critiqued this approach as "very 1985":

> The better way to do it would be to have all the information there and let people, kind of like chain of thinking. Like ask a question see what they find; ask another question. So we're really more in line with how people search the web now. If you really want somebody to really delve in and find what's there, they have to know what's there, right? Right now they can just ask questions like "how many patients in the database have an arrhythmia?" Or "what medications are they on?" But that's not really dynamic and live and it's time limited and it's clunky. Really, the data just needs to be put into a way that it could be interactively searched. Because, again you have different ways you'll see the data, if you do or don't know the diagnosis of if you do or don't have a drug that treats something, right? You might be having something very different that you see in the data. And I think you want people to make those connections. You want those new lines to be drawn and new ideas and you don't want to create it so artificially controlled. That's my opinion.

At this stage of NAMDC's development, while several relatively small-scale pilot projects and natural history studies piggyback on and complement the patient registry, the data pool is only beginning to be large enough for data-mining–type research and to pool patients for clinical trials. One interviewee explained:

> The registry itself in its existence is a huge thing. In that it's attracting drug companies to us, as they see it as a huge resource. It's attracting other researchers. It's only in the past year [2014–2015], reached that number where people are okay we can start mining this and start using the information in this to push, to sort of figure out where we should be going in studies. I think that's the biggest thing that's come out of the consortium and certainly would not be possible without the consortium existing.

Under NAMDC's data-use policy, both NAMDC members and outsiders can submit proposals, provided they comply with the procedures noted earlier. Permitting outsider access to the data might raise free-rider concerns for members. We did not encounter any such concerns in our study, though perhaps they will arise once the pool is fully ready for use. Interestingly, the interviewee who advocated allowing more direct mining of NAMDC data suggested that direct access to the data should be restricted to NAMDC researchers:

> That should be the value of membership, right? Is that you can actually look through the data. And of course you would cite it, right? And you would cite the

people who put the data in and all that good stuff, you would respect the data. But you would be able to use it. Like, let it breath and use it to make new discoveries which is what the patient community wants . . . In terms of access? I would say right now nobody has access to anything. You have to ask a question on a form and then get a written report . . . It's not exactly the same as searching Amazon.

15.4.3 *Managing NAMDC's Relationship with UMDF*

The UMDF and NAMDC were described by one interviewee as "intertwined." UMDF supports NAMDC in a number of concrete ways. It uses its website and other communications with patients to help explain NAMDC's activities and recruit patients for NAMDC's research. As a UMDF representative put it, "Who better to engage patients to register for a clinical trial than the patient advocacy group that can explain, that can engage, and can promote that type of registration?" UMDF also funds NAMDC's project manager, hosts NAMDC's monthly conference call meetings, helped resolve some issues relating to setting up NAMDC's biorepository, provides start-up grants for some NAMDC members' research projects, and has assisted NAMDC in making connections with pharmaceutical companies. In the other direction, a UMDF representative noted that NAMDC's status as an NIH-funded consortium provides a reputational boost for UMDF in its dealings with the agency.

Overall, our interviewees described the relationship between NAMDC and UMDF in positive terms, calling it a "partnership," and describing UMDF as a "huge part" of the consortium and its involvement as "indispensable" to NAMDC's success. As one interviewee explained, "I think there's a strong initiative at the NIH that you hear constantly. Engage the patient. Engage the patient. I think it's starting to filter down. I think there's a higher level of respect for the patient perspective and I think it certainly is driving research in a way that's necessary and in a way that's going to be more beneficial and valuable." A patient advocacy group representative suggested that one factor leading to a productive relationship between NAMDC and the UMDF was the fact that there is a dominant patient advocacy group dealing with mitochondrial diseases so that NAMDC leadership "doesn't have to look at trying to communicate, collaborate, or coordinate effort with 20 other groups."

Some interviewees noted tensions stemming from the different backgrounds and perspectives of researchers and patients that may sometimes make the relationship "collegial but strained." As one interviewee put it, "NAMDC has to answer to the NIH but the UMDF has to answer to patients who are sick now." Patients and researchers often have different views about the trade-offs between speed and quality control. An interviewee described it as a "matter of priority, transparency, communication, and also speed" in which "UMDF wants 20,000 patients in the NAMDC registry," while "NAMDC would rather have [fewer] patients that are better characterized, with more data on them." Patient advocates also find the bureaucracy associated with academic research (such as the IRB approval process) frustrating. In response, UMDF proposed to hire some individuals to help with data entry. So far, NAMDC has not implemented the idea because of regulatory and privacy concerns.

Diagnosis is another potential point of conflict, about which several interviewees expressed concern. While differences between clinical and research diagnostic standards do not necessarily result from clinical misdiagnosis or over-diagnosis, the issues are hard to disentangle. NAMDC's necessarily strict research diagnostic criteria may exclude some patients who will later turn out to have been correctly diagnosed. Several interviewees noted that some patients affiliated with UMDF, perhaps even a substantial number, will have diagnoses that are not certain enough to meet NAMDC's criteria. These interviewees anticipate – and are concerned about – the possibility that the diagnostic criteria adopted by NAMDC may exclude some significant number of UMDF members from NAMDC's studies, which "may not be news that they want to hear." The subject of diagnosis is particularly fraught for parents, given the fear that diagnostic ambiguities might lead to accusations of medical child abuse or Munchausen by proxy.[52]

NAMDC mitigates tensions between researchers and patients by fostering regular communication and improved understanding between researchers and patient representatives. One interviewee told us that NAMDC has "really cemented the relationship between researchers and the UMDF," while another explained that "[UMDF is] learning about how academics work, we're learning about what's important to . . . patients, so it's been great." Moreover, some interviewees observed that UMDF's "pushing and prodding [are] helpful and useful to say you could be better [at recruiting research participants]." Interviewees emphasized the important role of NAMDC's science/alliance officer, who interacts with NAMDC's leadership "on a weekly basis, we're always on the phone with him, or emailing, or something," participates in conference calls, is part of NAMDC's common data elements committee, and otherwise serves as "a communicator, a facilitator."

UMDF's Community Registry provides a good example of how NAMDC encourages cooperation between researchers and patient advocates. Neither group appears to see the UMDF Community Registry as competitive with NAMDC's physician-populated registry. Both researchers and patient representatives described the two registries as "complementary." The two registries collect "very different data," with UMDF's registry aiming to "add another layer on top of the deep medical information" being collected by NAMDC. They also serve different purposes. While one of UMDF's "main initiatives is to see [NAMDC] sites enroll patients into [NAMDC's] scientifically populated registry," UMDF's patient-populated registry provides "quantity, better engagement," and "a larger audience that [UMDF] can survey." In developing its Community Registry, UMDF worked closely with

[52] See, e.g., materials on UMDF website, note 25.

NAMDC researchers to "make sure that the databases can talk to each other" and "queries can be conducted in a uniform way." Researchers may also be able to make use of UMDF's registry. As one researcher interviewee explained, UMDF's Community Registry facilitates "direct to patient surveys with anonymized answers so it's a great way to get new questions answered pretty quickly" and provides "a great way to get information [about particular patients] that could eventually be used to supplement the information collected in NAMDC's structured database."

CONCLUSION

Our study of NAMDC revealed a consortium in the process of construction, grappling with the dual challenges of building a cooperative research community and combining resources to create a pool of research subjects, patient data, and biospecimens to provide a basis for successful mitochondrial disease research. The study also revealed both commonalities and differences in both challenges faced and governance approaches between NAMDC and the UCDC, which was the subject of our previous RDCRN case study.

Unlike the UCDC, which was built upon a preexisting "cohesive" clinical research community,[53] NAMDC began with a collegial, but "fragmented" group of researchers, with little history of inter-institutional collaboration. By all accounts, NAMDC has been successful in promoting cooperation and knowledge sharing among its researcher members. Study participants attributed this success in part to NAMDC's consortium PI's consensus-building leadership style, in part to a natural outgrowth of the regular meetings and other interactions required by the consortium structure, and in part to a growing realization among those in the field that cooperation was crucial to research progress. Notably, competitiveness between researchers does not seem to have posed a major barrier to such collaboration and knowledge sharing. NAMDC also appears to be successfully navigating the tensions that arise in the relationship between researchers and patient advocates, with study participants attributing this success in part to long-standing relationships between many NAMDC researchers and the well-established UMDF patient advocacy group and in part to the UMDF's recent hiring of a science officer who interfaces successfully with the researcher group. Unlike the UCDC, NAMDC had not, at least at the time of our study, integrated study coordinators and other site support personnel into the community directly; their relationships with NAMDC were mediated by the site PIs. We were unable to determine whether the choice between this PI-mediated model and UCDC's more participatory model is likely to have any bearing on long-term consortium success.

The primary goal of RDCRN consortia is to build a pool of research subjects, data, and biospecimens across dispersed institutions. The consortium structure is

[53] UCDC Study, note 5, at 171–72.

designed to overcome a presumed tendency for researchers to hoard these resources in search of publications and reputational credit. RDCRN consortia provide infrastructure for longitudinal study of the progression of rare diseases. In pursuing this goal, NAMDC has faced two major challenges, both of which illustrate how differences between disease contexts can affect consortium governance.

First, standardizing research diagnostic criteria has been a particularly difficult challenge for NAMDC because of the complexity and early stage of scientific understanding of mitochondrial disease. NAMDC's struggles with this issue highlight potential tensions between expert clinical diagnosis, which is the basis for patient treatment, and the need for standard, replicable diagnostic criteria for research purposes, especially when data from many patients is to be pooled across clinical sites. Given the limited scientific understanding of many rare diseases, other RDCRN consortia may face similar challenges. NAMDC has used a three-pronged approach to the diagnostic challenge: it designated a consulting researcher unaffiliated with any site to study the issue in detail, used a consensus-based iterative approach to update the criteria, and acknowledged that diagnosis poses a continuing challenge by creating a permanent Diagnostic Criteria Committee.

Second, NAMDC, like all RDCRN consortia, faced the challenge of allocating limited funds among its clinical sites. NAMDC opted for a per patient funding approach, while the UCDC opted to fund a fraction of study coordinator time at each site. NAMDC's choice was driven in part by concerns about shirking and free riding and in part by a lack of sufficient overall funds to pay for dedicated study coordinator time at each site. The UCDC was able to fund dedicated study coordinator time in part because it has somewhat fewer sites, but primarily because it has obtained substantial private funding. Some NAMDC sites had access to dedicated study coordinator time through institutional funding. We observed that those sites tended to be much more successful in enrolling patients and following them up over time. Though differences between sites can have many causes, these observations at least suggest that dedicated study coordinator time may be important to the success of consortium sites. Further investigation of this question seems warranted as the NIH continues to hone its consortium approach.

NAMDC's overall approach to governance, in dealing with these and other issues, has both similarities to and differences from the UCDC's approach. Participants in both consortia ranked dedication, trustworthiness, and determination as the most important characteristics of successful consortium leaders and attributed those characteristics to their leaders.[54] In both cases, there was some apparent tension in participants' views of consortium governance as both hierarchical and consensus based and, in NAMDC's case, both overly centralized and insufficiently directive. It seems possible that such tensions emerge naturally from the research consortium structure, in which leaders must find some way to navigate members' desires both to

[54] UCDC Study, note 5, at 186–87.

have control over decision making and to avoid time-consuming interactions. NAMDC recently established a formal committee structure, which is one means to increase delegation and sharing of responsibility and authority without the overhead of full participation in every decision. It is too early to tell whether the committee structure will successfully negotiate between participation and bureaucracy. NAMDC's approach differs from that of the UCDC, which appeared to rely almost entirely on informal governance.

Overall, this second RDCRN consortium case study finds both support for some of the hypotheses that emerged from our UCDC study and intriguing differences that appear to reflect the different histories of the two communities, the different biology of the diseases, different leadership styles, and other contextual factors.

16

The Consortium of Eosinophilic Gastrointestinal Disease Researchers (CEGIR): An Emerging Knowledge Commons

Katherine J. Strandburg and Stefan Bechtold

INTRODUCTION

This chapter reports our study of the Consortium of Eosinophilic Gastrointestinal Disease Researchers (CEGIR), which is part of the NIH Rare Diseases Clinical Research Network (RDCRN). CEGIR addresses eosinophilic gastrointestinal diseases (EGIDs), the most common and well studied of which is eosinophilic esophagitis (EoE).[1] Strandburg, Frischmann, and Cui (2014) previously studied the Urea Cycle Disorder Consortium (UCDC), while the North American Mitochondrial Disease Consortium (NAMDC) is the subject of the previous chapter in this book. While there are many similarities between the goals of these consortia and their general structures, there are also significant differences in the underlying challenges they face and the approaches they take to those challenges. These studies also provide snapshots at different stages of consortium development: The UCDC, funded in 2003, was among the first RDCRN consortia and was well into data collection at the time of our study. NAMDC began operations in 2011 and is engaged in constructing its pool of research subjects, patient data, and biospecimens. CEGIR was funded in 2014 and had been in operation for less than a year at the time of this study.

Katherine J. Strandburg is the Alfred B. Engelberg Professor of Law and a Faculty Director of the Engelberg Center for Innovation Law and Policy at the New York University School of Law, New York, New York. Stefan Bechtold is Professor of Intellectual Property at ETH Zurich, Switzerland. The authors are grateful for support from NYU's Engelberg Center on Innovation Law and Policy and would like to thank Arthur Argall, Himanshu Jain, Helen Reinhart, and Whitney Wadman for excellent research assistance. Professor Strandburg also acknowledges the generous support of the Filomen D. Agostino and Max E. Greenberg Research Fund.

[1] EoE is about 10 or 15 times more prevalent than the other EGIDs, eosinophilic gastritis and eosinophilic colitis (Jensen et al. 2016).

16.1 METHODOLOGY

Our study follows the *Governing Knowledge Commons* (GKC) framework described in Chapter 1. Specifically, we

- Reviewed public documentation about CEGIR and other materials about EGID research.
- Interviewed 23 individuals representing various CEGIR constituencies and other relevant groups, including 10 out of 22 CEGIR clinician researchers representing six out of nine CEGIR clinical sites (including CEGIR's consortium principal investigator (PI) and administrative director), a non-US-based CEGIR-affiliated clinician researcher, a dietician and biostatistician at CEGIR's lead site, two CEGIR study coordinators, three representatives of the two major patient advocacy groups, three pharmaceutical company representatives, one non-CEGIR-affiliated researcher and one non-CEGIR-affiliated study coordinator. The semi-structured interviews ranged in length from 45 minutes to more than an hour;[2]
- Attended Digestive Disease Week 2015, the "world's largest gathering of physicians and researchers in the fields of gastroenterology, hepatology, endoscopy and gastrointestinal surgery."[3]
- Analyzed the documents and interview transcripts using the GKC framework.

16.2 CEGIR'S BACKGROUND ENVIRONMENT

CEGIR, and the research community from which it emerged, are nested within a background environment that includes the biological realities of EGIDs as well as the general context of rare disease medical practice and research in the United States and internationally. Patients, represented by patient advocacy groups, are also important actors in this environment. The first three parts of this section briefly describe the EGID research context. The final part discusses relevant patient advocacy groups.

16.2.1 *EGID Basics*

Eosinophilic gastrointestinal diseases cause inflammations involving eosinophils (a type of white blood cell) that affect the esophagus (eosinophilic esophagitis, EoE),

[2] We maintain an archive of interview transcripts, which we rely on and quote from throughout this chapter. To preserve confidentiality as much as possible, we ordinarily do not cite particular interviewees. Readers may assume that unattributed quotations are taken from our interviews.

[3] www.ddw.org

the lining of the stomach (eosinophilic gastritis) or the colon (eosinophilic colitis). Adult EoE patients usually have difficulties swallowing, which may become so severe that the esophagus is physically obstructed. Food refusal and failure to thrive are common manifestations in children. If left untreated, EoE can result in fibrosis, esophageal dysfunction, and permanent changes to esophageal tissue. EoE is a chronic disease that nearly always recurs if treatment is discontinued. While the exact causes of EoE are unknown, many patients also have other atopic diseases, such as asthma, food allergies, or atopic dermatitis, suggesting that EoE is allergy related (Cianferoni and Spergel 2016: 160).

EoE was first observed in the 1980s and appears to have been a truly new disease at the time (Schoepfer, Simon, and Straumann 2011: 632). The first systematic scientific descriptions of EoE, by Stephen Attwood of the UK and Alex Straumann of Switzerland, were published in 1993 and 1994 (Attwood et al. 1993; Straumann et al. 1994). Initially, EoE researchers encountered significant resistance from other medical professionals. One interviewee recalled giving a conference presentation on the disease in the early 2000s: "The chairman introduced me as follows: 'Now we hear a contribution about a disease which does not exist.' I can understand. It was new. It was from his own area." Today, EoE's existence is accepted, but questions about what causes it and how best to diagnose and treat it remain open (Straumann 2013).

Studies estimate that between 50 and 100 per 100,000 persons have EoE (Dellon 2014: 203). A study using 2009–2011 data estimated 150,000 US cases (Dellon et al. 2014). Annual incidence[4] is estimated at 6 to 13 new cases per 100,000 persons per year (Dellon 2014: 206). EoE has now been reported in children and adults across the globe, although it is more prevalent in Western countries than in Asia and no cases from sub-Saharan Africa or India are known (Dellon 2014, Cianferoni and Spergel 2016: 160). EoE affects three times as many males as females and is most common in Caucasians (Cianferoni and Spergel 2016: 160).

Both prevalence and incidence of EoE have increased dramatically over the past two decades (Dellon 2014: 207–210, Giriens, Yan et al. 2015: 1636). A Swiss study found a 10-fold increase in EoE incidence when comparing the period from 2010 to 2013 with the period from 1993 to 2009 (Giriens et al. 2015: 1633, 1637). A Minnesota study found a 27-fold increase in incidence between the 1993–1995 and 2001–2005 periods (Prasad et al. 2009). These increasing numbers cannot be fully explained by increasing awareness of the disease and improved diagnosis, but they appear to reflect a true increase in affected individuals (Giriens et al. 2015: 1636; Dellon 2014: 667).

EoE's increasing prevalence, combined with the nascent scientific understanding of the disease, has generated an active research effort. As Figure 16.1 illustrates, the number of EoE publications has skyrocketed in recent years. Entire academic careers can now be built on research into EGIDs.

4 *Prevalence* indicates the total number of individuals exhibiting the disease at a given time. *Incidence* indicates the number of *new* cases occurring during a given time frame (Dellon 2014: 206).

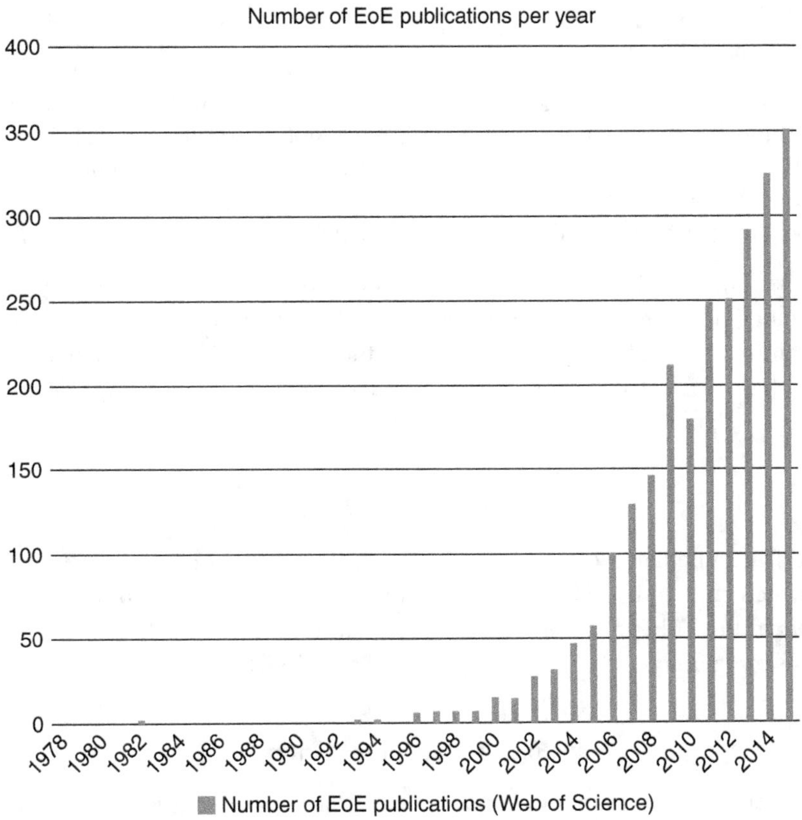

FIGURE 16.1 Number of EoE publications per year.
Note: These figures are based on a citation report for articles identified in a September 2016 Web of Science (Core Collection) search for the topic "eosinophilic esophagitis" (September 2016 EoE Articles).

16.2.2 *EGID Research and Treatment: An Interdisciplinary Endeavor*

EGID research is interdisciplinary in at least two respects: it involves specialists from medical disciplines spanning allergy, gastroenterology, pathology, and other fields, and it afflicts both pediatric and adult patients. To be effective, and take advantage of potential synergies, CEGIR must bridge these potential divides.

16.2.2.1 Allergy, Gastroenterology, and Pathology

The interdisciplinary nature of EGID clinical research brings both challenges and opportunities. Specialists from different backgrounds may have different expectations and view similar phenomena differently, which could lead to conflict.

Interdisciplinarity also creates opportunities for synergies, however. As one interviewee explained:

> I think the field of EoE has gotten close to where IBD [inflammatory bowel disease] has in 20 years, as opposed to almost 100. That, I think, is directly attributable to the collaborative nature about it, and part of it is the disease itself. You need the pathologist. You need the gastroenterologist. You need the allergist . . . The cross-disciplinary nature has, I think, led to much quicker insights.

Interdisciplinary interactions also can be intellectually stimulating, as one gastroenterologist interviewee told us: "I have learned a lot of things and I'm still learning about immunology, things that happened in the tissue, cytokines, all these mechanisms. I have learned a lot about allergy . . . If I attend any session, I always learn new things. It's challenging."

16.2.2.2 Pediatric and Adult

EGIDs affect both adults and children, so that clinical researchers come from both adult medicine and pediatrics. In the United States at least, "a lot of the major players in the EoE world came from the pediatric world." Pediatricians and adult doctors bring different training and perspectives to EGID research.

16.2.2.3 Diet versus Drugs

One place in which these disciplinary divides have played out is in the choice of treatment. Currently, there are two alternative standard treatment options for EoE: daily topical steroids and strict food elimination diets (Cianferoni and Spergel 2016). According to our interviewees, treatment preferences have tended to split along the allergist-gastroenterologist and pediatric-adult divides. The elimination diet approach requires knowledge about nutrition and, because compliance is difficult for patients, support from a dietician, as an interviewee explained:

> You need a dietician at the back end to enforce the diet, to explain to them clinical contamination, how do I avoid milk, . . . what are the foods that contain it, processed foods and all these contaminants. It requires an effort, whereas steroids are very easy. The majority of the physicians go the steroid route because they don't understand diet.

Allergists are more inclined to use diet-based treatments, in part because they have more training in nutrition and in part because they ordinarily have better access to the dietician and nutritionist resources necessary to implement them effectively. As one gastroenterologist told us:

> I think the issue is for practicing docs with GI [gastrointestinal] training, we literally learn nothing about nutrition on the adult GI side. Literally, nothing. That's not true, obviously in pediatric GI; nutrition's a huge part of what they do. But even so,

> trying to direct the patient yourself, as a gastroenterologist, as to these food elimination diets, they won't work. You just can't answer the questions ... I think most practices with GI docs don't have any access to nutritionists, and so many will use the topical steroids. And of course, you look at the diets, they're not that easy. You have to be a very motivated person to try to do those diets.

Pediatricians, whether they specialize in allergy or gastroenterology, are more inclined toward the diet approach because of concerns about long-term use of steroid drugs by children and because parents "care more about their kids than themselves, so they take their therapies more seriously" and "enforce compliance with their kids a lot better, than they would otherwise do for themselves."

At one time, these differences in training and perspective were exacerbated by skepticism about the effectiveness of the diet approach on the part of many steroid proponents. Most of our interviewees told us that these divisions have lessened over time, as the effectiveness of elimination diets has become more clearly established, and because it appears that less draconian dietary approaches may be effective. Standard dietary treatment eliminates all milk, eggs, soy, wheat, nuts, and fish products (six-food elimination diet). Adhering to such a restricted diet is difficult and has a significant impact on quality of life. Ongoing research is isolating the foods most likely to cause eosinophilic esophageal inflammation, in the hope that more palatable dietary treatments, such as the elimination of cow's milk alone, will be effective for most patients (Kagalwalla et al. 2012).

Several interviewees thus told us, in essence, that food elimination diets and steroid drugs "both work, so I let the patient decide," based on the patient's willingness and ability to comply with the necessary dietary restrictions. Nonetheless, interviewees agreed that clinicians' preferred treatments continue to vary, largely along the disciplinary lines discussed earlier.

16.2.3 *Patient Advocacy Groups*

CEGIR partners with several patient organizations, the two largest of which, the American Partnership for Eosinophilic Disorders (APFED)[5] and the Campaign Urging Research for Eosinophilic Disease (CURED)[6] are described here. APFED and CURED representatives are heavily involved in CEGIR.

16.2.3.1 APFED

APFED was formed in 2001 by a group of mothers of EGID patients. Early on, APFED focused primarily on education and advocacy. Beginning in 2008, it began to fund some research. From 2012 to 2014, about half of its expenditures of about US$500,000 per year were devoted to research, primarily through pilot grants.

[5] http://apfed.org/ [6] https://curedfoundation.org/

APFED has a paid executive director and both the chair and president of its board of directors are physicians. It is part of the lay organizations committee of the American Academy of Allergy, Asthma & Immunology (AAAAI). In 2013, APFED launched the Eosinophil.Connect Patient Registry to "capture self-reported, de-identified demographic and medical information for patients who have eosinophil-associated diseases into a central database so that it could be shared among researchers" (American Partnership for Eosinophilic Disorders 2014: 10). APFED has long-standing relationships with EGID researchers. About half of the members of APFED's medical advisory board are CEGIR investigators and several CEGIR investigators have been associated with APFED since its founding. APFED currently provides US$50,000 per year to CEGIR.

16.2.3.2 CURED

CURED was founded in 2003, also by parents of a child suffering from eosinophilic disease. One of its founders still serves as president of its executive board and as a volunteer executive director. Like APFED, it is part of the lay organizations committee of AAAAI. Though CURED organizes and participates in some educational and advocacy activities, it is dedicated primarily to raising money for research. Virtually all of its annual expenditures, averaging about US$370,000 for 2012 to 2014, go to research grants. CURED also has long-standing relationships with CEGIR researchers, particularly with Dr. Marc Rothenberg's group at the Cincinnati Children's Hospital Medical Center. Initially, all of CURED's research funds went to the Cincinnati center. In 2008, CURED began making smaller grants to a few additional institutions, nearly all of which are now CEGIR sites. Five CEGIR investigators serve as members of its honorary board, which includes medical professionals and others. CURED currently provides US$25,000 per year to CEGIR.

16.3 THE CEGIR CONSORTIUM

As explained in the previous chapter, the RDCRN aims "to advance medical research on rare diseases by providing support for clinical studies and facilitating collaboration, study enrollment and data sharing."[7] Each consortium must have two clinical research projects (including a longitudinal study), a training program for junior researchers, at least one pilot project, a website, and a collaboration with a patient advocacy group.[8] Though CEGIR shares its general structure and goals with other RDCRN consortia, it is shaped by its own particular goals and history, by the

7 www.rarediseasesnetwork.org

8 See, e.g., Rare Diseases Clinical Research Consortia (RDCRC) for the Rare Diseases Clinical Research Network (U54) – RFA-OD-08–001, http://grants.nih.gov/grants/guide/rfa-files/RFA-OD-08–001.html#SectionI

individuals who make up the community, and by its own governance structure and choices, some of which are described in this section.

16.3.1 *Goals and Objectives*

CEGIR[9] is dedicated to "improving the lives of individuals with eosinophilic gastrointestinal disorders through innovative research, clinical expertise and education via collaborations between scientists, health care providers, patients, and professional organizations." CEGIR pursues its mission through its clinical research projects, pilot study program, and training program. CEGIR also plans to "partner with industry in order to improve the lives of patients with EGIDs, including conducting clinical trials."

CEGIR's goals for its longitudinal study are both typical and tailored to the particular diagnostic and evaluation challenges posed by EGIDs. The study aims to "determine the correlation of clinical outcome measures (COMs), including patient-reported outcomes (PROs), with the histological disease activity as measured by mucosal eosinophil counts"; "test a series of related hypotheses concerning secondary histological parameters that may correlate with clinical and phenotypic measurements, potentially leading to a new gold standard for EoE, EG, and/or EC diagnosis and monitoring"; and "determine the correlation of the molecular profile for EoE, EG, and EC with COMs and mucosal eosinophilia."

CEGIR's second major project is an interventional study comparing the efficacy of the standard six-food elimination diet with that of a milk elimination diet and studying whether patients who experience diet failure remain responsive to swallowed glucocorticoids therapy. Eventually, CEGIR hopes "to develop a personalized medicine approach based on a biomarker analysis that can predict the best treatment for individual patients." All nine CEGIR sites are expected to participate in these major clinical research projects.

16.3.2 *CEGIR's History*

CEGIR's leaders, Drs. Marc Rothenberg and Glenn Furuta, were among the first researchers in the US to study EoE after it was identified in the 1990s. In October 2006, they were instrumental in organizing the First International Gastrointestinal Eosinophil Researcher Symposium (FIGERS), convened under the auspices of the North American Society of Pediatric Gastroenterology and funded by the NIH. The patient advocacy organizations also played a part in encouraging the researchers to meet.

[9] Information about CEGIR quoted in this section is taken from www.rarediseasesnetwork.org/cms/cegir/About-Us

FIGERS instituted the production of so-called consensus guidelines for diagnosis and treatment, which review and evaluate the state of the art based on the available literature. The first set of EoE consensus guidelines was published in 2007 (Furuta et al. 2007). Coauthors of the 2007 consensus guidelines formed a group of about 13 senior researchers, which eventually became known as TIGERS. TIGERS was described by one of our interviewees as "essentially [an] unfunded consortium of concerned people who really wanted to work together and identify areas of need and so on. We work well together. It was quite natural." TIGERS "maintained monthly meetings to talk about things relevant to the field and perform small research projects, had collaborations, participant education, advocacy efforts." Though TIGERS received some private funding beginning in 2008, it has not had significant research funds but has served mostly as a forum for discussing scientific issues and organizing collaborative efforts.

TIGERS was instrumental in the development of updated consensus guidelines in 2011, though the group of coauthors for those guidelines was substantially larger (Liacouras et al. 2011). Over time, the consensus guidelines have become important references for the EoE community.[10]

Consensus guidelines, while useful for both clinicians and researchers, do not provide sufficiently standardized diagnostic and efficacy metrics for use in large-scale, multi-site clinical research or to provide clinical end points for FDA assessment of potential drug therapies. To address these needs, TIGERS also "engage[d] with the FDA to say, 'How do we talk about getting new treatments in place?'" and began to work to develop end points for clinical trials. TIGERS organized the development of both pediatric (Franciosi et al. 2011, Martin et al. 2015) and adult (Schoepfer et al. 2014) assessment tools incorporating laboratory tests and patient-reported outcomes (Nguyen et al. 2015).

To validate the tools, "people who were leading the efforts enrolled subjects at their own institutions as well as at TIGERS institutions" for a "multi-institutional effort that required a couple hundred patients." Validation was accomplished "without much backing, but [with] a lot of unfunded efforts on people's parts."

The decision to apply for NIH funding to create CEGIR was "simply an evolution" of this history of collaboration between senior researchers in the field: "Basically, we took the expertise from TIGERS, laid it into the grant application of what we had been doing for a while, teamed with the patient advocacy groups we were pretty engaged with already, and put the application in."

Many CEGIR investigators, including CEGIR's two primary leaders, are TIGERS members or were otherwise involved in the consensus process. Nearly every CEGIR site has at least one TIGERS member. Moreover, 15 of CEGIR's 22 investigators were coauthors of the 2007 consensus guidelines, FIGERS participants,

[10] This is evidenced not only by our interviews but also by citation patterns. The consensus recommendations are the most heavily cited EoE-specific articles on Web of Science (Core Collection). By September 2016, the 2007 and 2011 publications had received 692 and 561 citations, respectively.

or coauthors of the 2011 consensus guidelines. In this respect, CEGIR resembles the UCDC, which also grew out of a close-knit community of researchers.

16.3.3 *CEGIR's Participants*

16.3.3.1 Consortium Leadership

CEGIR has two primary leaders: Marc Rothenberg, of Cincinnati Children's Hospital, who serves as overall consortium principal investigator and hosts consortium administration at his institution, and Glenn Furuta, of Children's Hospital Colorado, who serves as consortium administrative director and is the named principal investigator for CEGIR's longitudinal study. Rothenberg and Furuta were the initiators of the 2007 consensus process and the primary founders of TIGERS. Their leadership of the consortium flows directly from these earlier leadership roles.

Rothenberg, a specialist in pediatrics, allergy, and immunology, is the founder and director of the Cincinnati Center for Eosinophilic Disorders, the first US center dedicated to eosinophilic disorders. Rothenberg spends about 80 percent of his time on research, much of which is basic, rather than clinical, about 5 percent of his time seeing patients, and the rest of his time on administrative duties. As he explained: "Now, if someone asks me, 'What do I do?' I don't consider myself a clinician. I consider myself a professional researcher so I'm coming to work every day to do research." Rothenberg is the most highly cited researcher of eosinophilic diseases; the next two most cited are also at the Cincinnati Center.[11] In addition to Rothenberg, the Cincinnati Center includes four other CEGIR investigators (including CEGIR's lead pathologist), CEGIR's lead study coordinator (effectively, a project manager) and other administrators, two biostatisticians, an informatics analyst and CEGIR's lead dietician.

Furuta, a pediatric gastroenterologist, is director of the Gastrointestinal Eosinophilic Diseases Program at the University of Colorado School of Medicine. One of CEGIR's three pathologists, a CEGIR study coordinator, and the recipient of CEGIR's first pilot project funding are also located at Colorado. Furuta is the fifth most highly cited researcher in the field, following the Cincinnati researchers and pioneer Straumann. Furuta views himself as "mostly [a] physician" and his program at Colorado focuses primarily, though not exclusively, on clinical research.

11 In December 2015, we searched Web of Science (Core Collection) for the topic "eosinophilic esophagitis." We used HistCite to calculate how often these "December 2015 EoE Articles" by a particular author are cited by other articles (a "Global Citation Score" (GCS)). According to this calculation, the most important EoE authors are Marc Rothenberg (Cincinnati, GCS: 6909), Philip Putnam (Cincinnati, GCS: 4759), Margaret Collins (Cincinnati, GCS 4439), Alex Straumann (Switzerland, GCS: 3967), and Glenn Furuta (Colorado, GCS: 3202). The high scores of the three Cincinnati Children's Hospital authors reflect their frequent coauthorship. For some general information on HistCite and other bibliometric software tools, see van Eck and Waltman (2014).

16.3.3.2 Other CEGIR Investigators

CEGIR's investigators are located at nine NIH-funded sites at US academic medical centers. All but one of CEGIR's 22 clinician researchers have medical degrees, while the other has a PhD. Three of the MDs also have PhDs. CEGIR investigators range in experience from those who obtained their medical degrees in the 1970s to those who obtained their degrees in the 2000s. Fourteen are gastroenterologists, six specialize in allergy and immunology (one with a dual specialization), and three are pathologists. About two-thirds are pediatricians. As one interviewee explained:

> We all play in the sandbox really well together. It's adult. It's pediatric. It's allergy, GI, pathology. It's basic and clinical researchers ... At the end of the day, we're mostly physicians. We're mostly people who are looking at how can we take care of patients better. What are new treatments and how are we going to get those treatments in place?

16.3.3.3 Study Coordinators

Study coordinators do much of the day-to-day implementation of clinical research projects. They obtain informed consent from patients, ensure that the appropriate tests are done and specimens collected, and enter data. They also "get to know the patients well, because they're seeing them for the study visits, they're on the phone with them to coordinate stuff. They're recruiting them, explaining the studies, the whole nine yards. Their job is really valuable." Study coordinators also bring a practical perspective to study design:

> They will go through and edit and write protocols that make sense. If they don't have the buy-in, then nothing is going to work. I think the group of coordinators, especially the ones who are really running logistics, they're so engaged in doing everything. It's not the usual thing that you find, I think ... To this point, they've been involved in the logistics of the study design, and the instruments, and they'll be like, "Look, we have all these instruments, do we really need every single one of these questions and data points?" We've gone through on a very painful call, and multiple forms, and like, nope, nope, nope, yes, nope, this has to be changed ... If you have a study that you did by yourself, and you're like, "Okay, here it is, implement it," it wouldn't go well.

16.3.3.4 Dieticians

Consistency in diet protocol between sites is crucial to the success of CEGIR's study of the comparative efficacy of six-food versus one-food elimination diets. CEGIR employs a coordinating dietician at the Cincinnati lead site and a dietician at each site to administer and monitor the protocol. As one interviewee put it, food elimination diet therapy requires "a very talented dietitian."

16.3.3.5 Patient Advocacy Group Representatives

Patient advocacy group representatives are full-fledged members of CEGIR and are involved in CEGIR activities in many ways, such as serving on committees, reviewing the CEGIR website, attending meetings and conference calls, and commenting on study protocols and other issues. They are expected to be pivotal in recruiting patients to participate in CEGIR's studies.

16.3.3.6 NIH and DMCC Representatives

RDCRN grants are so-called U54 grants, meaning that NIH representatives take an active role in consortium activities, participating in conference calls and meetings and providing input at various stages. Because CEGIR is funded through three NIH institutes, several NIH representatives are regularly involved with its activities. NIH also funds a centralized RDCRN Data Management and Coordinating Center (DMCC), which provides various services related to collecting and managing consortium data. DMCC representatives also work closely with CEGIR. Interviewees called the DMCC "a huge, huge resource" of "enormous" value, describing it as "unbelievably responsive," "very helpful," and noting that it "operate[s] pretty quickly." Even though some observed that DMCC involvement "add[s] one extra layer of review and time involved," they concluded that "the value that it adds is probably quite significant."

The DMCC has assisted CEGIR in setting up a central Institutional Review Board (IRB). IRBs review and monitor study compliance with ethical requirements for human subject research. Traditionally, each institution's IRB reviews each study protocol, perhaps suggesting revisions, and then decides whether to approve it. Central IRBs are intended to make this process more efficient for multi-site studies. Most interviewees were convinced that the central IRB approach would "streamline things . . . in the end," but getting the necessary inter-institutional agreements in place to the satisfaction of all local IRBs can be a complicated matter. The DMCC "ha[s] all sorts of experience with setting up IRBs and central IRB models and just working with a lot of different groups with a lot of different types of study structures. In a lot of ways they can provide a lot of creative solutions to different things you want to try to do."

16.3.4 *CEGIR Governance*

16.3.4.1 Leadership

As in our previous studies, interviewees confirmed the importance of consortium leadership to consortium success. One interviewee described the importance of Rothenberg and Furuta's leadership in getting CEGIR started:

> It would've been difficult for any of the other ones in the group to have pulled this off. I mean, they've had the NIH funding the longest in the group. They've made really seminal discoveries in the field. They're incredibly collaborative. Glenn [Furuta] has a wonderful personality of bringing people together and developing consensus, in a very understated way. I think probably everybody who is involved recognizes those would be the two natural people to do it. They foster the collaboration and stuff, but they also have the connections. They were able to work back door, and find out all the details and the whole nine yards, and get the thing put together. It was an enormous undertaking. They also have the infrastructure administratively to help to do that.

Having leaders who are so well known in the field also will be important to CEGIR's future interactions with pharma companies. Pharma sector interviewees explained that once a company identifies EoE drug development as a business opportunity, it begins reaching out to well-established experts in the field to get their input and advice on study designs, drug development, and regulatory approval:

> First, there is the compound and the business development opportunity. Then starts the networking with [the] experts ... We work with well-known experts in the field who are very well connected, who are thought leaders, and who are either treating patients themselves or are connected with investigators and physicians who have very good knowledge and experience with treating this disease.

Their input is also influential in discussions with the FDA about suitable end points for the drug approval process (Fiorentino et al. 2012).

Interviewees described CEGIR's leaders as "great mentors," "pioneers in the field," "generous," "delegative, "passion[ate]," "motivating," "goal oriented" and "a great team." One noted: "[The research] means so much to them that they make everybody so interested in it or so excited about it. They pull everybody in. They listen to everybody. It's not just their way or the highway. It's they want input from every single person who's on the call." Another interviewee was of the view that CEGIR's leaders were adapting well to the transition from running a single lab to leading a multi-site consortium:

> I think like everybody else they're learning as they go and going from a one-man show to incorporating opinions from a lot of people I think has been a learning experience for all of them. They have done a really good job at it and they are seeing the value in the team ... They do a very good job of making people feel included, making sure opinions are heard, do their best, of course, to ensure things are fair ... I think they've been very open and open to new ideas, open to looking at things differently.

Interviewees also noted that "personality-wise, [CEGIR's two leaders] are very different people" with distinct leadership roles. They emphasized Rothenberg's devotion to scientific productivity and to "getting the job done in the right way" and his "analytical mind," while emphasizing Furuta's role in "bringing people together and developing consensus," in taking "a global view of things" and "making sure [all the various projects in the consortium] are actually moving forward." Interviewees saw Furuta's community-building skills as essential. As one interviewee put it:

> I think it's the strength of his personality and his charisma, if you will, which is very quiet. It's not showy, it's not flashy, it's very steady and his ability to navigate choppy waters and smooth things over when they need to be that has resulted in a very long ongoing relationship among a lot of us . . . I'm not sure there would be a consortium if there hadn't been a Glenn [Furuta].

Another explained: "Dr. Furuta, he's a great leader. He's very open for discussion, very appreciative for everybody's input. I'm literally talking from the secretaries up to the pathologists."

Despite these generally very positive views of CEGIR's leadership team, a few interviewees expressed concern that CEGIR's leadership "is not inclusive, it's exclusive" with regard to those outside the inner circle, suggesting that the criteria for determining insiders and outsiders lacked transparency and that NIH's funding of CEGIR might serve to "validate that structure, that hierarchy that we have" in the field.

16.3.4.2 Conference Calls, Committees and Decision Making

CEGIR's primary governance institutions are regular conference calls and committees. Many interviewees commented on the sheer number and frequency of calls involved in getting CEGIR up and running. Bimonthly conference calls involve all CEGIR participants. Because these calls involve so many participants, they serve mostly for updates, for providing feedback, and for final approval of proposals hashed out in smaller working groups and committees. There also are monthly study coordinator calls and calls involving participants in particular committees and activities. For example, dieticians from the various CEGIR centers have been in frequent communication to work on standardizing the diet instructions for the food elimination comparison study.

Interviewees generally believed the calls were well run and served important purposes. As one interviewee explained:

> I think the calls . . . keep you on your toes. It's like a built-in deadline. There's a CEGIR call coming up, I better get this thing . . . straightened out before the next CEGIR call, because they're going to ask me about it. It's a reminder to keep the ball rolling about what needs to be set up next and so on. It's a good way to keep informed of what's happening, how many subjects have been enrolled and where the various studies are in the IRB process and the NIH review process, and so on. I think they're generally informative. The CEGIR-all call, certainly the advocacy

> groups are called on to voice what their meanings, desires, or wishes are. They're very helpful in terms of helping to recruit people to sign up for registries, and from registries we potentially can recruit people into clinical trials. That aspect is very helpful. I think [the calls] serve a good purpose. They are numerous, but I don't miss them – if I'm here, I'm on the call – so it's not like they're that painful to have that I'd do anything to not be on the call.

CEGIR has a number of committees, including a Steering Committee and committees focusing on each of the main research projects, the pilot projects, the training program, the contact registry, data monitoring, publication policy, and various other aspects of CEGIR's activities. An ethics committee eventually will deal with issues such as intellectual property and cooperation with pharmaceutical companies. These committees include not only researchers but also, depending on the committee, may include patient representatives, dietitians, study coordinators, statisticians, or other administrators. Most committees are composed of volunteers.

The expectation is that, for most issues, the PIs and the Steering Committee will serve primarily as a "red stamp," so that, in essence, "decisions are being made locally by the committee." As one interviewee described the process:

> It's hard, I think, to make major decisions in [the large conference call], so I think what happens is that there are a lot of smaller working groups that bring preliminary decisions to the bigger groups for discussion, and basically it's not, "Does everybody agree?" but "Does anybody have a problem with this?" is the way that it's usually presented. I'll give you an example for the Publication Committee. They said there's going to be a Publication Committee, who wants to do it ... [Several people volunteered, then the committee] had multiple calls and hashed out some of the details, and then [drafted] guidelines ... [that] got sent out to the group. They said, "Here's a draft. Give comments." [There were] no comments, and so [it was] like, "Okay. Here it is" ... [S]ame thing for protocol design, there are smaller working groups for the protocols ... One or two of the people drive the bus. Those are PIs. They do the initial protocol, and then a smaller group gets on the phone to review it, and go through it ... [Changes are made based on that small group discussion] and then that goes back out to the group. Sometimes ... when you get a lot of feedback, it's just too many cooks in the kitchen for stuff. There's no way that a real major decision can be made on a call with 120 people, but it is a place [where] people ... can voice their opinions, and everybody gets a chance to get heard.

16.4 CEGIR'S PRIMARY ACTION ARENAS: FORMING A CONSORTIUM COMMUNITY

As discussed in the previous chapter, an action arena is "the social space where participants with diverse preferences interact, exchange goods and services, solve problems, dominate one another, or fight (among the many things that individuals do in action arenas)" (Ostrom 2005: 13).[12] Because CEGIR was at such an early stage at the time of our study, it was too soon to observe how some of its action arenas would function in practice. We thus focus here primarily on action arenas related to CEGIR's start-up: community building within CEGIR and interactions between the CEGIR community and "outsiders."

16.4.1 *Building the CEGIR Community*

Clinical research requires the participation and cooperation of clinical researchers, supporting research personnel, such as site coordinators, dieticians, administrators, and patients. To be most successful, an RDCRN consortium must leverage the motivations of these various participants to build trusting, effective collaborative relationships.

16.4.1.1 Motivating Participation

Clinical researchers generally have both intrinsic and extrinsic motivations for their work. Researchers' extrinsic motivations, such as career incentives and reputation among colleagues (rewarded, e.g., by invitations as keynote speakers or invited contributions in prestigious journals) are somewhat competitive and may thus have ambiguous implications for community building. Interviewees emphasized how the intrinsic rewards of engaging in EGID research motivate collaboration. The satisfaction of solving a complex medical problem is one such reward. As one interviewee explained: "The main driving force is enthusiasm. We need money for all these research projects. We cannot work without any money, but it is not the main motivation ... My main motivation is to improve the understanding of this disease." The desire to help patients is also an important motivator. Several interviewees suggested that the prevalence of pediatricians in the EGID community in the United States played a role in facilitating and encouraging cooperation because "in general, pediatricians can collaborate and come together in things like a consortium, more easily than adult physicians can"[13]:

> Well, there are children involved. It's easier to let go of one's ego or at least to keep it under a little tighter rein when you've got a sick kid, then when you've got an adult who won't stop smoking, or an adult who won't take the blood pressure medicine. Noncompliance among adults is a large part of internal medicine whereas in pediatrics, they didn't do anything wrong, just got sick by bad luck or bad genes or whatever and you really want to help and make a difference. The motivation is a little different in pediatrics than in adult medicine generally. It shows in the ability to collaborate and then to get results.

[12] For further explanation of the "action arena" concept, which is central to our GKC framework, see Chapter 1 of this volume.

[13] UCDC interviewees made a similar observation (Strandburg et al. 2014).

Supporting research personnel also will be driven by a mix of intrinsic and extrinsic motivations. With some exceptions, their career incentives are likely to be concentrated primarily on their local sites and less concerned with reputation and status within the larger EGID research community. Their intrinsic motivations may depend on how much impact they perceive their efforts as having on research progress and on whether they find their social interactions with other consortium participants rewarding.

Patients will be motivated to participate in clinical studies if they believe that the studies are designed with their needs in mind and will lead to progress in treatment and that participation is not too burdensome. Sometimes, the community can take active steps to shape the factors motivating participants. As a patient advocacy group representative who organizes meetings between researchers and patients explained:

> It's ... amazing for the researchers to get to meet the patients, to get to see the patients' families and actually see the tears of those families and to know the pain those families are suffering ... One of the things we said at our conference, we want to have a tour of the lab. I want the lab workers to be part of the tour. I want them to meet the patients. I want the patients to meet the lab workers. They're like, "No, it's a Saturday. They don't really work that much on Saturdays." I'm like, "It's going to work both ways. It's going to drive your people to work harder and it's going to drive the patients and families to help fundraise so please" ... When they meet us and they hear stories, they're floored. They have no idea. It's all that they know; it's a blood slide or a rat or a mouse or whatever they're doing. They don't know the emotions.

A researcher made a similar observation:

> Meeting with patients also gives you perspective about why you're doing all the research. It's easy to kind of get lost in who's going to be on the paper; who's going to do this; who's going to do that. Then when they're like, "We've got these kids, and we don't know what to do with them, we don't know what the treatments are." That's actually the goal for all this stuff, and it kind of keeps everybody grounded, I think.

16.4.1.2 CEGIR's TIGERS Roots

CEGIR builds upon the collaborative relationships already established in the relatively small, close-knit TIGERS research community. The community was described by interviewees as "generous," "friendly," and "incredibly collaborative." As one interviewee explained:

> We're very lucky in that most everyone in this community is very collaborative and productive and wants to see the field move forward and wants to help patients, wants to improve their lives. So I think it's been very effective ... I don't know what it is

> about the EoE community. I do think it is very, very unique, because I hear some of my colleagues experiences with other areas of GI where it might be much more competitive and not as collaborative.

The trust among researchers that has been established through preexisting cooperation plays an important role. As one interviewee put it: "In my personal experience, I don't know a colleague before I have done a project with him. Working together, you get familiar with his personality. Once you can trust this person, then I don't need many legal rules."

As CEGIR expands out from TIGERS, it confronts two primary challenges. First, it must integrate its non-TIGERS researchers into the community. Second, it must transition from a community of researchers to a community that also includes patient representatives, dieticians, study coordinators, and others. In addition, since the NIH funding for CEGIR must be renewed every five years and may eventually be discontinued (whereas TIGERS is a collaborative project with no clear time limit), CEGIR has to maximize collaboration within a given time period so that the collaborative research network is stable enough to survive in post-CEGIR times.

16.4.1.3 Integrating Non-TIGERS Researchers

Our study suggested four strategies that may help extend the TIGERS collaborative culture to additional CEGIR researchers. First, CEGIR has expanded slowly from its TIGERS foundation, attempting to select participants with strong intrinsic motivations who "are really committed and the amount of ego is on the low level" so that they can "appreciate each other's strengths and weaknesses and not get too aggressive." Second, CEGIR has attempted to provide a high degree of transparency into decision making, including budgetary matters. Third, CEGIR attempts to be fair and transparent in various ways, the most salient of which at this early stage is its approach to allocating funding between sites. Fourth, CEGIR is focusing its research efforts on two projects that involve all of its sites in presumptively equal roles and, particularly in the case of the elimination diet/steroid interventional study, cross specialty boundaries and exploit the synergies of its interdisciplinary group of investigators.

16.4.1.3.1 A CAUTIOUS APPROACH TO SITE EXPANSION

On the whole, while CEGIR has expanded somewhat from its TIGERS roots, it has not expanded very far: most CEGIR's researchers are either TIGERS members or colleagues at the same institutions as TIGERS members. As one interviewee explained:

> It's a bigger group in CEGIR. [W]e all pay in the sandbox really well together. It's adult. It's pediatric. It's allergy, GI, pathology. It's basic and clinical researchers. To have that synergy in people who work well together, we really wanted to make sure we had that synergy. When we were going to do the [CEGIR proposal], we said "All

right, this is going to change some of the dynamics a little bit and we need to think about what that's going to do, but we need to [expand], and we will, but we also are going to be a little bit particular about how that happens." There are more people involved in it now, but it's worked out well.

Interviewees foresaw the need for further expansion but noted the potential trade-offs involved and the importance of "keeping it in centers that . . . would be able to accomplish the research and also work well together," and "focus[ing] on success from within," rather than "expanding it too broadly." Some were concerned about "overextending and diluting out the efforts" given the consortium's limited resources and about having the infrastructure needed to handle a larger effort. Others worried about the potential difficulty of finding additional researchers willing to put in the necessary effort, in light of the limited funding associated with CEGIR participation: "I think the people involved [so far] are willing to do it without getting much money. I think if we expand out more, I'm not sure what the willingness is to do things. Maybe some, but not a lot."

Unlike our interviewees in the NAMDC and UCDC studies, CEGIR interviewees did not generally articulate a goal of including all or nearly all EGID researchers in the consortium. This difference may stem from the growing prevalence of EoE. Higher prevalence generally means that each site sees more patients, reducing the need to aggregate patient participants from many centers to obtain a useful sample size. Indeed, one of our interviewees mentioned that CEGIR might need to add more sites if it intensifies its focus on the rarer forms of EGIDs. Increasing prevalence also attracts more researchers to the field, making the goal of incorporating all active researchers in a single consortium less feasible. As one interviewee explained:

> I don't think it's feasible that there's just one single massive research network that controls every researcher in the world . . . There's just not enough funding to support that type of structure. So for that reason it's absolutely necessary that people do small little things or even large-scale things on their own separate from the consortium, because competition is always good. Competition drives ingenuity and invention. That is just a fact of life.

While interviewees generally viewed it as "very positive that more people are engaged" in EGID research, one interviewee expressed concern that an influx of money related to growing prevalence would attract more competitive individuals to the field. Many interviewees emphasized the advantages of the currently small size of the EGID research community, which promotes "collegiality" and "friendliness" and helps "break down what could be contentious rivalries." The small size also gives younger researchers "the opportunity to get to know the big players, as opposed being a small fish trying to wade through the really big ocean." CEGIR's cautious approach to growth reflects an appreciation of the trade-offs involved in expansion.

16.4.1.3.2 TRANSPARENT DECISION MAKING

CEGIR's leadership has attempted to put a thumb on the scale toward transparency, even at the cost of a potentially overwhelming number of conference calls:

> We're exhausted from the number of calls, but we said, "The first year is the hardest because we got to get everything together." We kind of overdid the communication almost because we wanted to make sure that people felt at least engaged, they weren't excluded, that there was a good synergy of people. If people said it's too much, that's okay, but we don't want them to say, "What's going on? We don't have access."

Our interviewees generally seemed satisfied with their level of engagement in consortium decision making, at least so far. As one told us:

> Usually, when Glenn [Furuta] and Marc [Rothenberg] run the meetings, they're actually good at being, "Okay, NIH, anybody want to say anything?" "Patient advocacy groups, want to say anything?" I think it's a way that everybody feels like they're included, and there's certainly no shortage of phone calls for people to be included in the first year of planning. It's nothing but phone calls. I think the decision making has been working okay, and they've made an attempt to be transparent with budget stuff, and decision making, and who theoretically is in charge of the different subareas and everything.

16.4.1.3.3 ALLOCATION OF CONSORTIUM FUNDS AND OTHER POLICIES

RDCRN consortia must allocate grant funding among sites and researchers, manage publication credit and access to and use of data collected through its longitudinal and other studies, and eventually may need to make decisions about intellectual property. The perceived fairness and transparency of a consortium's approach to allocating resources and rewards may affect its success in forming a collaborative community. While CEGIR had developed a publication policy, tasked a committee with managing data use, and formed an ethics committee to deal with intellectual property questions and other matters, these issues had yet to attract much attention from CEGIR members at the time of our study. Thus, the most salient allocation question concerned the distribution of consortium funding among CEGIR sites.

CEGIR's budget was determined through a proposal-writing process in which members from all current CEGIR sites were involved. While the Cincinnati and Colorado sites receive larger funding allocations because of their administrative responsibilities, funding is otherwise divided roughly evenly among sites. As an interviewee explained:

> Basically, there's a number of different models that one could use for [allocating funds among sites]. You can have pay as you go or pay as you perform – you do some work, you get some money. Or you can divide it up, equal divisions depending upon what you're expected to do. We've taken the latter model.

About 20 percent of CEGIR's US$1.25 million grant is allocated to the administrative costs of the lead site, consistent with the administrative budgets for the two other consortia we studied.[14] Additional moneys, totaling about 20 percent of CEGIR's grant, are allocated to pilot projects and the training program for junior researchers. The remaining 60 percent or so is divided between CEGIR's two primary clinical research studies, in which all of the sites participate. On average, CEGIR's budgets for the longitudinal and food elimination/steroid comparison studies amount to about US$50,000 and US$35,000 per site, respectively.[15] The majority of CEGIR's funding allocation for each site goes toward "the salary of the investigators and the clinical research coordinators and a couple of other people like the statisticians. We divide [the funding] up so each site is going to get the same approximate amount of effort for each [category of] individual. It's a 5 percent effort of an investigator, 20 percent effort on a CRC [study coordinator]." The remaining site allocations support "the clinical processes that are basically just for research purposes and the research procedures and assays and the biochemical and molecular analyses that are done," as well as "a small amount of money for administrative issues like travel and meetings and things like that." None of our interviewees voiced complaints about CEGIR's funding allocation model, suggesting that the allocation was perceived as reasonably fair and transparent.

16.4.1.3.4 MULTI-SITE STUDIES THAT BRIDGE DIVIDES

Both of CEGIR's primary research studies involve all of its sites in relatively equal roles. The UCDC study noted that "the longitudinal study formed a backbone for . . . developing collaborative practices" (Strandburg et al. 2014: 206) simply by providing a structured platform requiring group interactions. We hypothesize that the same will be true for CEGIR's two major projects. Indeed, the standardizing of diet instructions for the studies seems already to have played a community-building role for CEGIR's dieticians. Moreover, CEGIR's interventional study comparing treatment options across disciplinary perspectives not only exploits the possible synergies of CEGIR's interdisciplinary membership but may also promote community cohesion across specialization lines.

16.4.1.4 Integrating Other CEGIR Participants

Building a trusting and committed community that extends beyond researchers to include patient advocacy group representatives and site personnel such as study coordinators and dieticians is likely to enhance CEGIR's effectiveness. Beyond

[14] Budget information quoted here was obtained from NIH RePORTER, https://projectreporter.nih.gov/reporter.cfm, to facilitate comparison between consortia.

[15] The UCDC consortium, which adopts a similar funding approach, budgets a similar amount per site for its longitudinal study, while the NAMDC consortium, which employs a "pay as you perform" model, budgets less than a third as much.

mandating the involvement of patient advocacy representatives, who generally sit on consortium steering committees, the RDCRN framework does not address this issue, so each consortium must determine how it will go about integrating its non-researcher participants.

16.4.1.4.1 PATIENT ADVOCACY GROUP REPRESENTATIVES

Our interviews suggest that CEGIR has been successful so far in integrating patient advocacy group representatives into the community. Though most CEGIR researchers were involved with the patient advocacy groups before CEGIR was established, interviewees of all stripes stressed the benefits of the RDCRN patient participation model, which one interviewee described as "a whole different level of collaboration in terms of planning studies and sort of the back and forth."

Researcher interviewees emphasized the value of patient advocacy group input in designing and conducting studies that will successfully recruit and retain patient participants. As one explained:

> I think the patient advocacy groups are actually incredibly important, and a very unique aspect of [CEGIR]. First of all, there's several reasons. There's the obvious one where they can say, "This is important to our patients. It's not important to patients." That really can help drive some of the stuff, and actually some of the major study decisions, they were giving feedback on, so for [the interventional study] there was debate about which of the eliminations diets we were going to use. It came down to . . . asking them, "Is this something that a patient would agree to be randomized to? Is this realistic?" It's a real practical input that you don't get when you're just designing this stuff theoretically in a room. If you can't get patients into it, you're kind of hosed.

Suggestions from patient representatives already have led CEGIR to change a study protocol "in a dramatic way." The changes made the dietary information provided to patients "much easier to follow and read and much more patient friendly" and gave "practical advice" about "ensuring adherence" to study protocols."

From a researcher perspective, patient advocacy group involvement does "have its challenges in terms of we all tend to speak a common language, and then you bring somebody in who doesn't and that's hard. Sometimes there may be things that don't seem worthwhile or equitable or whatever that are scientifically necessary, and that can be a hard discussion to have, but probably still a valuable one." Nonetheless, the overwhelming view expressed by interviewees was that the advantages of patient advocacy group involvement make it well worthwhile to deal with the challenges.

For their part, patient representatives emphasized how participating in CEGIR had connected them to into the community in a way that their association with TIGERS had not. As one interviewee explained:

> For me, I think it's a lot like . . . a collaboration because . . . there's so many different committees and we're part of every one of them, and there's a different mix of

> physicians at each committee . . . The patient advocacy groups are eligible to be on every one of those committees. We're just very fortunate.

Another told us that "I saw minds change after listening to me. I'm totally impressed with the way they care about what the patients feel."

CEGIR faces one potential challenge in dealing with patient advocacy groups that we did not encounter in our two earlier studies: the two major national patient advocacy groups dealing with EGIDs. As discussed earlier, the two groups take different approaches, with CURED emphasizing that it is volunteer run and that "Only CURED Donates 100% of Profits to Research for CURE,"[16] and APFED emphasizing its "future and long-term vision . . . to become an all-encompassing eosinophilic advocacy organization."[17] These groups generally do not work cooperatively and compete for funding and volunteer time. In 2014, the Coalition of Eosinophil Disease Patient Advocacy Groups (C-EOS) was formed,[18] in part to support CEGIR's application for RDCRN funding. The coalition now meets on a monthly basis.

It is not yet clear what effect, if any, the patient advocacy group coalition, or CEGIR itself, will have on relationships between the patient advocacy groups. Both CURED and APFED are devoted to CEGIR's success, however, believing that "at the end of the day, everybody's got to work together or we're not going to get anywhere." As a result, differences between the patient advocacy groups had not led to "any complications to date" for CEGIR:

> In general, [any differences between patient advocacy groups haven't] stalled out the research. It's just like in patient care what we always try to come back to is what's best for the patient, what's best for making those decisions. In this, it's what's best for the research and completing the mission of the grant. That usually works. People are able to come back to the mission and say, "Okay, yep."

16.4.1.4.2 SITE PERSONNEL

There are at least two possible participation models for supporting personnel. In a hub and spoke model, site personnel interact primarily with others at their sites, as they would during a single-site research project, and occasionally with the project manager or others at the lead site. They may also sit in on monthly consortium conference calls. In a more thickly connected model, site personnel interact more directly and more often with members at other sites. Cross-site interactions between the personnel responsible for the nitty-gritty of running consortium studies may benefit a consortium in various practical ways, for example, by helping ensure uniform implementation of study protocols and surfacing practical problems at an earlier stage. Less tangibly, cross-site relationships between site personnel may benefit the consortium by fostering a sense of

16 http://curedfoundation.org 17 http://apfed.org 18 www.c-eos.org

belonging and responsibility to the larger community and enhancing intrinsic motivations. CEGIR's dieticians already appear to relate to the consortium through the more connected model, while it is too early to assess how CEGIR study coordinators will relate to the consortium.

16.4.1.4.2.1 Dieticians

By the time of our study, CEGIR's dieticians had already engaged in significant cross-site interactions in preparing for CEGIR's elimination diet study, in consultation with CEGIR's researchers and patient advocacy group representatives. While much of the work was carried out by email and teleconference, CEGIR's dieticians also met in person for a daylong session at CEGIR's annual meeting. As a dietician interviewee explained:

> Of course, one big issue of the study is that we all need to give the same advice. That's something interesting, because if you put 10 dietitians in a row . . . and you say, "What do you say about wheat avoidance? How do you handle 'may contain traces'? What do you say about milk avoidance?" you get ten different answers . . . I knew that one of the biggest issues of this trial would be that we have a standardized approach. It may be not exactly what you would do in clinical practice, but we all need to do exactly the same thing. Otherwise, we can't compare outcomes across the different sites.

The sites' geographical dispersion created challenges because "people eat very differently in different states. We had to take all of that into account, which once again was why it was so good to have dietitians from all the sites on board."

Like CEGIR's researchers, most of CEGIR's dieticians already knew one another reasonably well, which presumably facilitated community building. Many were involved in a working group aimed at producing standardized dietary recommendations to implement the EoE consensus guidelines. Most also had worked closely with CEGIR's researchers in the past. As a result, "There were never contentious issues. We all like each other. We know each other. It wasn't a big deal to make a decision."

16.4.1.4.2.2 Study Coordinators

CEGIR's funding allocation approach means that each site has a study coordinator who dedicates a fraction of his or her time to CEGIR activities. In principle, CEGIR study coordinators can form cross-site relationships through CEGIR's monthly consortium-wide conference calls and study coordinator calls. At the time of our study, however, only the lead coordinators at Cincinnati and Colorado had been significantly involved in CEGIR teleconferences and other cross-site activities. Study coordinators at other sites generally had not yet participated regularly. Interviewees anticipated that their participation would pick up, however, once patient enrollment for CEGIR's studies, in which coordinators play a major role, kicked into gear.

Even after patient enrollment and participation begins, however, eliciting study coordinators' full participation in cross-site dialog may be challenging, in part because they may be more reticent than investigators and dieticians about speaking up:

> I think, in general, study coordinators are a little bit less vocal than the investigators. For example, if you're on a big conference call when you have investigators and coordinators, you're going to hear primarily from the investigators and not as much from the coordinators. Even when we're on just a coordinator call, they're just a lot less vocal than the investigators are.

Unlike CEGIR's researchers and dieticians, study coordinators generally do not have preexisting relationships with CEGIR participants at other sites, which may exacerbate this reticence.

Cross-site interaction between study coordinators may be valuable, however, and thus worth facilitating. As one interviewee explained:

> I do think it would be helpful sometimes for the coordinators to have a better opportunity to be able to work together besides the email and the conference call . . . Every site is different, and the way things are done at every site is a little bit different. Sometimes it's hard when you're not talking with them face-to-face to figure all those things out; to design the study in a way that really accommodates all of the idiosyncrasies of how each site has to do things.

This interviewee suggested that occasional face-to-face meetings might help strengthen bonds between study coordinators.

16.4.2 *Relationships with Outsiders*

In addition to building its community from within, CEGIR must manage its relationships with non-CEGIR research entities and researchers. Two aspects of this management task surfaced during our interviews: relationships between TIGERS, CEGIR, and US-based outsiders, and relationships between CEGIR and the international EGID research community. We discuss these issues briefly here, with one important caveat: most of our interviewees were CEGIR members, which means that our view of these boundary matters is unavoidably one sided.

16.4.2.1 CEGIR, TIGERS, and other US-Based EGID Researchers

When the TIGERS group of a dozen or so EGID researchers was formed in the mid-2000s, the EGID research community was considerably smaller than it is now. At that time, the group may have included all the most active US researchers in the field. That is no longer the case. TIGERS has added only a few new members over the years, intentionally opting to remain a small, self-selected, close-knit group. While there are obvious advantages to such an approach, our interviews suggested that TIGERS may be perceived by some as exclusive and clique-ish, particularly because the criteria for membership are, as one of our interviewees described them, "nontransparent."

Though CEGIR is distinct from and larger than TIGERS, its membership also is limited. Even though 19 of the top 23 US-based EoE researchers are at CEGIR institutions[19] and 8 out of the 10 most influential EoE research centers in the United States belong to CEGIR,[20] many EGID researchers are not included. Thus, when asked what fraction of US EGID researchers were included in CEGIR, one interviewee responded: "If you'd asked me that five years ago, it probably would have been the majority. If you ask me that now, I would say probably less than half, but it's hard to know." CEGIR's cautious approach to expansion, along with its deep roots in TIGERS, may lead to perceptions of exclusion. As one interviewee put it:

> From my perspective, there is a trade-off. It's going to be the ins and the outs and the haves and the have-nots. There would be groups, you surmise, that are going to be wanting to get in and maybe feel that they should be in and maybe deserving to be in but aren't in and then they can say, "That's an elite group," or, "They didn't give us a chance. They don't have a fair policy to spread it out."

To some degree, such trade-offs are endemic to consortia that do not incorporate essentially all active researchers in a field. EoE's increasing prevalence may put CEGIR in a particularly tricky position, however. When a disease has a small researcher base, as is the case for most rare diseases, it may be possible to include nearly "everyone" (in some sense of the term) in a single consortium. Both UCDC and NAMDC adopted that goal, at least in principle. When a disease is sufficiently common to have a large patient and researcher base, including everyone in a single consortium is both impractical and unnecessary. Instead, multiple research groups compete with one another for funding and publication credit in the traditional way. As EoE prevalence increases, CEGIR may find itself uncomfortably in the middle, in that the EGID patient and researcher base may grow too large for a single consortium but remain too small to support multiple effective research groups.

As CEGIR becomes more established, it will face additional boundary management questions related, for example, to data access and sharing. Despite the substantial overlap in membership, CEGIR is distinct from TIGERS and from the preexisting close-knit EoE community. For example, our interviews suggested some tension over the scope of CEGIR's rights to use assessment tools developed at particular sites and validated with TIGER participation. These tools consist, in part, of questionnaires addressed to patients, in which questionnaire developers may assert copyright. As one interviewee explained: "It's a property. It's a five-year

19 To determine the most-cited authors, we used HistCite to calculate how often December 2015 EoE Articles by each author had been cited by other articles in the group. We then checked whether the institutions associated with the top 30 authors were CEGIR members. Seven of the top 30 authors were from institutions outside of the United States, which are not eligible for RDCRN funding.

20 Here, we identified the most influential institutions in EoE research as those institutions as those with the highest GCS based on our December 2015 EoE Articles.

process. You have shed blood, sweat, and tears for that. It's like your baby and you're going to keep a little bit track of your little baby, I guess." The norm seems to be to make the assessment tools available for free or at low cost to academic researchers, while charging considerably higher fees to commercial companies. The scope of CEGIR's rights to these assessment tools (as a matter of community norms, if not as a legal matter) is a potential source of conflict, particularly if CEGIR seeks to use an assessment tool for clinical trials involving pharmaceutical companies.

16.4.2.2 The International EGID Research Community

CEGIR's members are US institutions. EoE research has international roots, however, and cross-border cooperation may be important for research progress. Europeans authored the first articles documenting EoE. Soon after, the center of gravity for EoE research shifted mostly to the United States, which played an important coordination and catalyst role in the medical community's recognition of the disease. While pioneering EoE research was performed in Europe, acceptance in the United States apparently served as a worldwide credibility signal.

Though Swiss pioneer Straumann has been a part of TIGERS since the beginning, his relationship with the US EGID research community is unique. Straumann's clinic is CEGIR's only "collaborating site" abroad.[21] When asked whether TIGERS was an international group, one of our interviewees explained: "To be honest, Alex [Straumann] was the international group. Now, we're starting to expand out a little bit more from that, but he was the international part." Indeed, Straumann was the only non-US EoE researcher that some of our interviewees could name.

If this US myopia was ever excusable, it certainly is no longer appropriate. An active, high-quality research scene exists outside the United States. About 45 percent of all EoE publications are authored in other countries,[22] some of which have significant EoE research programs. Average citation rates for papers produced in Switzerland, Belgium, and Canada are higher than the average for US papers,[23] and interviewees mentioned important work being done in Spain and Australia. One interviewee suggested that international collaboration may be particularly important for EoE research because differences in diet across the globe could provide interesting avenues of investigation. Moreover, there seem to be fewer pediatric EoE patients in Europe than in the United States. Such cross-country differences may provide important clues to understanding and treating the disease.

[21] www.rarediseasesnetwork.org/cms/cegir/Learn-More/Participating-Clinical-Centers

[22] A total of 1448 of the 2624 (55%) September 2016 EoE Articles were written by US-based authors. Other important countries include Spain (6%), Switzerland (4%), Canada (3%), Australia (3%), Germany (3%), as well as the United Kingdom and Japan (2% each).

[23] The average December 2015 Article from Switzerland, for example, is cited 36.5 times, while the average US publication is only cited 19.6 times. The Swiss result may be largely driven by Alex Straumann's prolific publication record. Other countries with high average citation rates include Canada (21.2) and Belgium (26.2), although the number of papers originating from these countries is smaller.

While CEGIR's leaders recognize the importance of global research cooperation, international research collaborations face distinctive organizational problems. Several interviewees pointed out that funding structures may impede international collaboration. As one interviewee put it:

> I think it would be a good thing to collaborate, I think logistically the way that the funding is developed it's for US centers, and that's the issue here. I don't think that [the smaller amount of international collaboration] is because there are questions about research integrity, or research quality. Logistically, I will tell you, in terms of just conference calls, it's very hard with time zones to get it all organized.

Data sharing across national borders also was reportedly more rare than sharing between US centers.

While funding structures and logistical difficulties may impede transatlantic collaboration, competition with research centers in the United States may incentivize collaboration among European researchers. European single-site studies are typically smaller than those administered by US centers. Cross-site collaboration among European sites is a way to compete more effectively. As one interviewee explained:

> Switzerland is relatively small … For a long time, that was recognized as a disadvantage because you were never able to have large patient sets to publish. This was really a limitation if you are located at an institution in Switzerland. You never reach the large scale of US size. Of course, you also publish less well, because it's the large patient numbers that give your results more creditability. I think that was one additional motivator to draw all together, basically to also have the possibility to publish better.

The smaller sizes of hospital teams and patient cohorts in smaller countries generally limit specialization. It is much harder for Swiss physicians to dedicate themselves only to the esophagus than it is for physicians at large US academic hospitals. Whether this lack of specialization is an advantage or a disadvantage remains unclear. On the one hand, researchers in smaller countries run the risk of superficiality, given the lack of opportunities for deep specialization. On the other hand, working with patients with a wider spectrum of diseases may produce beneficial research spillovers.

CONCLUSIONS

CEGIR is a new RDCRN consortium that focuses primarily on EoE, an eosinophilic gastrointestinal disease discovered in the early 1990s whose prevalence and incidence have increased substantially since then. In the past, a relatively small, close-knit interdisciplinary community that has tackled the disease with great motivation and enthusiasm and achieved remarkable progress has driven EoE research. As research on EoE advances, the research community grows and the prevalence of EoE increases, CEGIR is attempting to move the EoE community from a loose network of researchers in which personal connections provide the only social glue necessary for collaboration to a more formal way of collaborating at a larger scale.

Like the UCDC, the CEGIR research community evolved from a consensus recommendation process. The consensus process not only served its intended purpose of standardizing definitions, diagnostic tools, and treatment options but also catalyzed ongoing cooperative activity, in the form of TIGERS. TIGERS, in turn, was instrumental in CEGIR's creation.

CEGIR benefits, as did the other consortia we studied, from the ongoing leadership of pioneers in the field. It differs from the other consortia in the way that it divides leadership between individuals with different strengths. As one interviewee described it, the CEGIR community functions well because of its members' diverse skill sets. Some community members are incredible for their publications and scientific productivity; some can engage well with people and are charismatic; some are doers who make sure that things get done; and some have particularly novel ideas. So far, at least, CEGIR seems to have mostly avoided, or successfully dealt with, the conflicts that one might anticipate from such a divided leadership structure.

Various aspects of CEGIR's governance appear to contribute to community cohesiveness and stability. As with the UCDC, CEGIR's multi-site projects seem likely to serve as an infrastructure for community building. Limiting consortium growth may also help build a cooperative culture among CEGIR members.

While both the EGID research community in general and CEGIR in particular look like success stories so far, they may face various hurdles in the future. First, as the EGID research and patient communities continue to grow, CEGIR may find it increasingly difficult to balance inclusiveness with manageability. Second, as the EGID research community becomes more global, research activities concentrated in the United States will become less and less comprehensive. Third, while intellectual property issues have not been very important so far, they may become more contentious in the future. Indeed, some of our interviewees raised concerns about maintaining ownership interests in assessment tools in the consortium context. Finally, and especially if EoE continues to increase in prevalence, new players – including pharma companies – may enter the field. When more money is on the line, social ties and norms that successfully managed collaborative activity in the historically small community of highly determined, intrinsically motivated researchers may be put under stress. Conversely, if EoE eventually loses its official status as a rare disease, but remains relatively uncommon, pharma company interest in developing EoE treatments may decrease again, as pharma companies would lose the benefits governments grant developers of rare disease drugs (such as smaller patient groups in phase 3 clinical trials, tax incentives, or orphan drug exclusivity). Only time will tell whether and how a transition of EoE into a non-rare disease will impact the EGID research environment.

We close by noting how efficient the RDCRN approach appears to have been in promoting large-scale collaboration, in light of the relatively small size of RDCRC grants, which must be shared among many sites. The RDCRN approach seems to reduce barriers to cooperation primarily by providing institutional infrastructure that leverages physicians' intrinsic motivations to advance science and treat patients and builds on preexisting community relationships to catalyze large-scale collaboration.

REFERENCES

American Partnership for Eosinophilic Disorders (2014). Annual Report. http://apfed.org/wp-content/uploads/2014/12/APFED_AnnualReport2014_Final.pdf

Attwood, S. E., T. C. Smyrk, T. R. Demeester, and J. B. Jones (1993). Esophageal Eosinophilia with Dysphagia: A Distinct Clinicopathologic Syndrome. *Digestive Diseases and Sciences*. 38: 109–116.

Cianferoni, A. and J. Spergel (2016). Eosinophilic Esophagitis: A Comprehensive Review. *Clinical Review of Allergy & Immunology*. 50: 159–174.

Dellon, E. S. (2014). Epidemiology of Eosinophilic Esophagitis. *Gastroenterology Clinics of North America*. 43: 201–218.

Dellon, E. S., E. T. Jensen, C. F. Martin, N. J. Shaheen, and M. D. Kappelman (2014). Prevalence of Eosinophilic Esophagitis in the United States. *Clinical Gastroenterology and Hepatology*. 12: 589–596.

Fiorentino, R., G. Liu, A. R. Pariser, and A. E. Mulberg (2012). Cross-Sector Sponsorship of Research in Eosinophilic Esophagitis: A Collaborative Model for Rational Drug Development in Rare Diseases. *Journal of Allergy and Clinical Immunology*. 130: 613–616.

Franciosi, J. P., K. A. Hommel, C. W. DeBrosse, A. B. Greenberg, A. J. Greenler, J. P. Abonia, M. E. Rothenberg, and J. W. Varni (2011). Development of a Validated Patient-Reported Symptom Metric for Pediatric Eosinophilic Esophagitis: Qualitative Methods. *BMC Gastroenterology*. 11: 126.

Furuta, G. T., C. A. Liacouras, M. H. Collins, S. K. Gupta, C. Justinich, P. E. Putnam, P. Bonis, E. Hassall, A. Straumann, and M. E. Rothenberg (2007). Eosinophilic Esophagitis in Children and Adults: A Systematic Review and Consensus Recommendations for Diagnosis and Treatment. *Gastroenterology*. 133: 1342–1363.

Giriens, B., P. Yan, E. Safroneeva, M. Zwahlen, A. Reinhard, A. Nydegger, S. Vavricka, C. Sempoux, A. Straumann, and A. M. Schoepfer (2015). Escalating Incidence of Eosinophilic Esophagitis in Canton of Vaud, Switzerland, 1993–2013: A Population-Based Study. *Allergy*. 70: 1633–1639.

Jensen, E. T., C. F. Martin, M. D. Kappelman, and E. S. Dellon (2016). Prevalence of Eosinophilic Gastritis, Gastroenteritis, and Colitis: Estimates from a National Administrative Database. *Journal of Pediatric Gastroenterology and Nutrition*. 62: 36–42.

Kagalwalla, A. F., K. Amsden, A. Shah, S. Ritz, M. Manuel-Rubio, K. Dunne, S. P. Nelson, B. K. Wershil, and H. Melin-Aldana (2012). Cow's Milk Elimination: A Novel Dietary Approach to Treat Eosinophilic Esophagitis. *Journal of Pediatric Gastroenterology and Nutrition*. 55: 711–716.

Liacouras, C. A., G. T. Furuta, I. Hirano, D. Atkins, S. E. Attwood, P. A. Bonis, A. W. Burks, M. Chehade, M. H. Collins, E. S. Dellon, R. Dohil, G. W. Falk, N.

Gonsalves, S. K. Gupta, D. A. Katzka, A. J. Lucendo, J. E. Markowitz, R. J. Noel, R. D. Odze, P. E. Putnam, J. E. Richter, Y. Romero, E. Ruchelli, H. A. Sampson, A. Schoepfer, N. J. Shaheen, S. H. Sicherer, S. Spechler, J. M. Spergel, A. Straumann, B. K. Wershil, M. E. Rothenberg, and S. S. Aceves (2011). Eosinophilic Esophagitis: Updated Consensus Recommendations for Children and Adults. *Journal of Allergy and Clinical Immunology*. 128: 3–20.e26.

Martin, L. J., J. P. Franciosi, M. H. Collins, J. P. Abonia, J. J. Lee, K. A. Hommel, J. W. Varni, J. T. Grotjan, M. Eby, H. He, K. Marsolo, P. E. Putnam, J. M. Garza, A. Kaul, T. Wen, and M. E. Rothenberg (2015). Pediatric Eosinophilic Esophagitis Symptom Scores (PEESS v2.0) Identify Histologic and Molecular Correlates of the Key Clinical Features of Disease. *Journal of Allergy and Clinical Immunology*. 135: 1519–1528.e8.

Nguyen, N., G. T. Furuta, and C. Menard-Katcher (2015). Recognition and Assessment of Eosinophilic Esophagitis: The Development of New Clinical Outcome Metrics. *Gastroenterology & Hepatology*. 11: 670–674.

Ostrom, E. (2005). *Understanding Institutional Diversity*. Princeton University Press.

Prasad, G. A., J. A. Alexander, C. D. Schleck, A. R. Zinsmeister, T. C. Smyrk, R. M. Elias, G. R. Locke III, and N. J. Talley (2009). Epidemiology of Eosinophilic Esophagitis over Three Decades in Olmsted County, Minnesota. *Clinical Gastroenterology and Hepatology*. 7: 1055–1061.

Schoepfer, A. M., D. Simon, and A. Straumann (2011). Eosinophilic Oesophagitis: Latest Intelligence. *Clinical & Experimental Allergy*. 41: 630–639.

Schoepfer, A. M., A. Straumann, R. Panczak, M. Coslovsky, C. E. Kuehni, E. Maurer, N. A. Haas, Y. Romero, I. Hirano, J. A. Alexander, N. Gonsalves, G. T. Furuta, E. S. Dellon, J. Leung, M. H. Collins, C. Bussmann, P. Netzer, S. K. Gupta, S. S. Aceves, M. Chehade, F. J. Moawad, F. T. Enders, K. J. Yost, T. H. Taft, E. Kern, M. Zwahlen, E. Safroneeva, and the International Eosinophilic Esophagitis Activity Index Study Group (2014). Development and Validation of a Symptom-Based Activity Index for Adults with Eosinophilic Esophagitis. *Gastroenterology*. 147: 1255–1266.e21.

Strandburg, K. J., B. M. Frischmann, and C. Cui (2014). The Rare Diseases Clinical Research Network and the Urea Cycle Disorders Consortium as Nested Knowledge Commons. In *Governing Knowledge Commons*. B. M. Frischmann, M. J. Madison, and K. J. Strandburg (eds.). Oxford University Press: 155–208.

Straumann, A. (2013). Eosinophilic Esophagitis: a Bulk of Mysteries. *Digestive Diseases*. 31: 6–9.

Straumann, A., H. P. Spichtin, R. Bernoulli, J. Loosli, and J. Vogtlin (1994). Idiopathic Eosinophilic Esophagitis: A Frequently Overlooked Disease with Typical Clinical Aspects and Discrete Endoscopic Findings. *Schweizerische Medizinische Wochenschrift*. 124: 1419–1429.

van Eck, N. J. and L. Waltman (2014). Visualizing Bibliometric Networks. In *Measuring Scholarly Impact*. Y. Ding, D. Rousseau, and D. Wolfram (eds.). Heidelberg: Springer: 285–320.

Governing Knowledge Commons: An Appraisal

Katherine J. Strandburg, Brett M. Frischmann, and Michael J. Madison

How, where, and why do innovation and creativity occur? What influences the design and development of productive and sustainable knowledge production and preservation institutions? And what lessons, if any, should public policy and law derive from answers to these questions? These are the macro questions that inform empirical research on knowledge commons, including the 15 case studies gathered in *Governing Medical Knowledge Commons* and the 11 case studies published in 2014 in *Governing Knowledge Commons* (GKC).

Knowledge commons governance is one strategy for overcoming social dilemmas regarding the production, stewardship, preservation, distribution of, access to, and consumption and other use and re-use of knowledge and information resources. That strategy may often be as important and powerful as strategies grounded in law and related public policy, including intellectual property law, competition law, communications law, and security and privacy law. For its potential to be realized, "knowledge commons" should be more than a rallying cry for the public domain or a piece of rhetoric deployed in political battles about access to knowledge and information. Empirical investigation, of the sort reported in this book, is a critical prerequisite for sound knowledge commons policy.

The social dilemmas encountered in deploying knowledge commons governance are extremely diverse. Moreover, knowledge commons governance is intertwined, in varied and context-specific ways, with publicly enacted law and other government initiatives. As a result, empirical research must be modest. The world of knowledge commons governance is too diverse, both today and in historical context, to permit

Katherine J. Strandburg is the Alfred B. Engelberg Professor of Law and a Faculty Director of the Engelberg Center for Innovation Law and Policy at the New York University School of Law, New York. Brett M. Frischmann is The Charles Widger Endowed University Professor in Law, Business and Economics at Villanova University Charles Widger School of Law, Villanova, Pennsylvania. Michael J. Madison is Professor of Law and Faculty Director of the Innovation Practice Institute at the University of Pittsburgh School of Law, Pittsburgh, Pennsylvania. Professor Strandburg acknowledges the generous support of the Filomen D'Agostino and Max E. Greenberg Research Fund.

drawing firm conclusions or generating forceful policy guidance based on the empirical work done so far, both in these books and elsewhere.

Nonetheless, some patterns and themes have begun to emerge. Here, we update and refine the tentative substantive conclusions that we offered in the Conclusion to *GKC*. In most respects those conclusions remain viable in light of the evidence collected here; in some respects, added nuance is important. The recurrence of many themes in this new body of evidence encourages us to believe that the GKC framework provides a valid and useful basis for generation and testing of hypotheses that eventually will establish a firm foundation for policymaking.

C.1 RECURRING THEMES

The following are themes that we have identified as particularly important to date, given the research included in GKC and in this book. In Section C.1.1 we discuss themes that emerged from the GKC case studies and remain salient and important, though sometimes in slightly revised form, in light of the additional cases presented here. We also note specific ways in which these themes appear to play out in the medical context. In Section C.1.2, we discuss two additional themes that have emerged from the studies in this book. The first is a modification of the theme of trusted leadership discussed in GKC, while the second identifies the important role that the state often plays in structuring medical knowledge commons. Readers and researchers may and likely will derive their own conclusions and identify additional themes in the case studies in this book and in GKC. That is absolutely as it should be.

C.1.1 *Themes Identified in GKC*

C.1.1.1 Knowledge Commons Confront Diverse Obstacles or Social Dilemmas, Many of Which Are Not Well Described by or Reducible to the Simple Free-rider Dilemma

As with the case studies in GKC, here, the most obvious "goals and objectives" of commons governance often were to organize the sharing of knowledge resources to facilitate the creation of new knowledge. Sometimes – though not always – such sharing had been stymied, as traditional intellectual property theory would predict, by concerns that competitors would free ride on shared knowledge resources without compensating the contributors. But to stop there would be to miss the forest (or worse, the complex ecosystem) for the trees. Here, as in the earlier studies, closer analysis tended to reveal multiple dilemmas and obstacles that shaped action arenas and created demand for governance institutions. Among these were (attribution is to the authors of chapters in this volume):

- *Dilemmas attributable to the nature of the knowledge or information production problem.*
  In most arenas, the production of knowledge and ideas is constrained by the nature of the community's substantive goals. Often, and especially in the medical arena, this is a matter of the "biophysical characteristics," not of the non-rivalrous knowledge resource, but of the question at hand. For example:
  - The rare disease research consortia studied here and in GKC face institutional dilemmas stemming from the fact that the diseases they study are so rare that cooperation across a number of geographically scattered sites is necessary to make progress (Strandburg and Bechtold; Strandburg and Frischmann; Strandburg, Frischmann, and Cui (in GKC)).
  - Many medical problems are so scientifically complex that studying them requires the participation of specialists from a variety of different backgrounds, who may have different norms and practices (Strandburg and Bechtold, Pedraza-Fariña).
  - Some medical conditions manifest themselves in sufficiently various and complex ways that cooperation requires resolving and managing difficult and potentially contentious questions about how and with what granularity a particular disease or treatment should be defined (Frischmann and Strandburg, Saxe and Acri).
  - The most promising approach to a given medical issue often requires the aggregation of data produced by many sources and stored in many ways, creating a coordination dilemma about how best to standardize formats and definitions (Lee, Evans, Abbott, Strandburg and Bechtold, Strandburg and Frischmann, Larson and Chon, Mattioli).
  - Productive research may require access to particular biological materials or research tools, which are not easily substitutable because of the biophysical characteristics of the medical issue at hand (Torrance, Bubela et al.).
- *Dilemmas arising from the interdependence among different constituencies of the knowledge commons.*
  The traditional free-rider story focuses attention on the need for cooperation among competing researchers or physicians, who are presumed to have similar skills and objectives. Medical research and treatment often involve a much wider variety of participants, however. Patients, long viewed as essentially passive recipients of the output of medical innovation, are increasingly understood to be crucial participants in the creation and sharing of medical knowledge, whose perspectives must be taken into account in knowledge commons governance (Evans, Boggio, Strandburg and Bechtold, Strandburg and Frischmann). Indeed, patients,

nonprofessional caregivers, and the public at large are beginning to take new and much more central roles in governing and conducting cooperative medical innovation (Oliveira et al., Flowers, Torrance). Dilemmas arising from differences in perspectives, norms, and goals of critical constituencies thus are endemic in the medical context and often pose crucial governance issues. Besides patients, important constituencies may include the following:

- Researchers or physicians from disparate specialty backgrounds (Pedraza- Fariña, Strandburg and Bechtold).
- Clinicians working in very different treatment contexts (Saxe and Acri).
- Study coordinators, informatics specialists, and administrators (Strandburg and Bechtold, Strandburg and Frischmann).
- Insurance carriers, institutional health care providers, and pharmaceutical companies (Abbott, Bubela et al., Larson and Chon).
- Private and public funders (Larson and Chon, Strandburg and Bechtold, Strandburg and Frischmann, Contreras).
- Third-party custodians of health records, data, and tissue samples (Lee, Boggio, Bubela et al., Strandburg and Bechtold, Strandburg and Frischmann).

- *Dilemmas arising from the need to manage rivalrous resources that are necessary inputs into production and use of the shared knowledge resources.* As noted in GKC, knowledge commons governance often must manage the allocation and deployment of rivalrous inputs, such as attention, time, labor, and funding (Contreras, Pedraza-Fariña, Strandburg and Bechtold, Strandburg and Frischmann, Abbott) and rivalrous outputs, such as attribution/authorship credit and associated status (Evans, Larson and Chon, Mattioli, Bubela et al., Saxe and Acri). Governance mechanisms for rivalrous resources routinely must cope with scarcity. Those who manage access to a shared pool of tissue samples or other biomaterials may also need to anticipate and take account of the risk that samples might be damaged during use or transport or simply degrade over time (Bubela et al., Boggio, Pedraza-Fariña).
- *Dilemmas arising from (or mitigated by) the broader systems within which a knowledge commons is nested or embedded.*

All of the knowledge commons examples studied in this book are facilitated by, constrained by, and simply embedded within a much broader social system of medical research, practice, and regulation. General regulations, such as those from the FDA or HIPAA, provide top-down hierarchical constraints with which most knowledge commons must comply. In studying natural resource commons governance, Ostrom and her collaborators noted the potential benefits of "nested governance," in which one (smaller, more limited) governance system is embedded within a hierarchically higher (larger, broader) governance system, as a way of ensuring that community governance of a commons resource is appropriately tailored to the expertise and interests of local constituents. Nesting of this sort plays a role in a few of the cases reported here (Strandburg and Bechtold, Strandburg and Frischmann, Saxe and Acri). In many cases, however, the relationship of a medical knowledge commons with the larger universe of medical institutions is one of overlapping participants and functions, rather than of hierarchy. These overlapping relationships are often both facilitative and generative but can also produce governance dilemmas, in part because of their non-hierarchical nature. (Strandburg and Bechtold, Strandburg and Frischmann, Saxe and Acri, Lee, Larson and Chon, Oliveira et al., Flowers).

C.1.1.2 There Often Were Complex Relationships between Knowledge Commons and the Systems within Which They Operate and/or Are Nested and Embedded

We noted in the Conclusion to GKC that we had not fully anticipated how strongly broader background contexts would influence the shape of commons governance and/or interact with other framework inquiries. In the current collection, researchers' attention to these background constraints pays important dividends. As already discussed, these contexts often give rise to governance dilemmas, both by providing external constraints much as the biophysical characteristics of the resource do in the natural resource context and because of overlapping membership and functions between knowledge commons and other institutions. But the impact of the background context often went well beyond these effects. Background contexts shaped goals and objectives, participants' roles and motivations, behavioral norms and social relationships, and other important features in much more dynamic ways. Background context and systems matter significantly to the opportunity to develop commons governance in the first place and to the ability of knowledge commons governance to respond to the complex social dilemmas it confronts. History, whether of general practices in the medical field or of social relationships among knowledge commons participants, also matters. It may be more difficult to establish commons governance if historical patterns push in countervailing directions (Bubela et al., Larson and Chon, Saxe and Acri, Mattioli), while preexisting cooperative relationships or norms may promote the emergence of knowledge commons governance (Strandburg and Bechtold, Torrance, Lee). Indeed, where historical patterns suggest an opportunity for commons governance to take root, those patterns may be useful assets for institutional designers and policymakers.

C.1.1.3 Close Relationships Often Exist between Knowledge Commons and Shared Infrastructure

The theme as we expressed it in GKC was "knowledge commons often depended on shared infrastructure." It may be more appropriate to say that infrastructure and knowledge commons are often related, because shared infrastructure often appears to be central to the success of the knowledge commons, because it is often appropriate to identify shared infrastructure – whether technical (e.g., computing resources) or social (data schemas, or community culture on which commons governance is constructed) – as a type of knowledge commons resource that often helps resolve a social dilemma or overcome an obstacle to cooperation. Shared infrastructure may be created by the commons community (Torrance, Mattioli) or constructed or funded by the state (Contreras, Strandburg and Bechtold, Strandburg and Frischmann, Abbott) or contributed by a private benefactor or "commons entrepreneur" (Oliveira et al., Flowers, Lee, Larson and Chon, Saxe and Acri). It is important, however, not to simply equate knowledge commons governance with infrastructure. Instead, the theme that emerges from the case studies is that knowledge commons governance and shared infrastructure are often closely aligned, with each tending to enable and reinforce the success of the other.

C.1.1.4 Commons Governance Often Evolved over Time, and Commons Seemed to Play an Especially Important Role in the Early Stages of Some Industries

In GKC, we observed that several cases illustrated the proposition that commons governance may evolve as the number of participants grows or as innovation affects the nature of the shared knowledge or the balance between competition and cooperation within the group. This theme appears with less frequency in the current collection of cases in the medical research domain, perhaps because none of the cases in the present book deals with a knowledge commons with a sufficiently long historical track record. While there are examples of knowledge commons governance emerging in relatively nascent medical arenas (Torrance, Pedraza-Fariña, Larson and Chon, Saxe and Acri, Strandburg and Bechtold), we do not yet know whether these arrangements will change as these arenas evolve. There is no instance here of a knowledge commons evolving or maturing into something else.

C.1.1.5 Knowledge Commons Governance Often Did Not Depend on One Strong Type or Source of Individual or Institutional Incentives or Motivations or Cooperation

As we noted in GKC, knowledge commons entail cooperation in the building, sharing, and preservation of knowledge resources, but the reasons individuals cooperated in particular knowledge commons varied. Not only did different individuals cooperate for different reasons, but sometimes a single individual had multiple motivations for cooperating, partly intrinsic and partly social. Participants often had both competitive and cooperative motives, and the balance between the two often varied among individuals or changed over time. Motivations often varied according to participants' roles as creators, maintainers, and/or users of shared knowledge resources. Yet the overall contrast to the traditional free-rider story, in which individuals are assumed to compete for resources as a result of self-interest, is striking. This variety of motives is partially responsible for the variety of social dilemmas that arise in governing knowledge commons.

This theme, like the earlier ones, carries over from GKC, but limiting the present collection of cases to medical and life sciences research leads inevitably to narrowing the scope of the diversity of motivations. Improved scientific and medical knowledge, improved clinical outcomes, and improved public health outcomes are, in general terms, motivations common to each of the case studies here. Pursuing those goals is complicated by motivations to protect patient interests of other sorts, such as patient anonymity and privacy, and motivations linked to professional and personal advancement, such as attribution and authorship credit for research results. The variety of institutional actors involved in medical innovation introduces further diversity of motivations and incentives, since many of these cases involved participants from public (i.e., the state), not-for-profit (some clinical care institutions and knowledge repositories), and for-profit (some electronic health information providers, some clinical care institutions, many individual clinical providers) institutions.

C.1.2 *New and Modified Themes*

C.1.2.1 While Informal Governance Institutions, and Especially Trusted Leadership, Sometimes Played Key Roles in Knowledge Commons Governance, Other Modalities for Stabilizing Commons Governance, including Preexisting Cultural or Community Norms, Formal Governance, and the Creation of Infrastructure to Facilitate and Structure Relationships by Commons Entrepreneurs

The commons cases studies in GKC appeared to point to the idea that informal governance, premised on trusted leadership, often plays a critical role in knowledge commons. Based on the data collected in this book, that theme may need to be revised. While trusted leadership as an informal governance mechanism emerged as a central theme in some of the case studies in this book (Pedraza-Fariña, Strandburg and Bechtold, Strandburg and Frischmann, Larson and Chon), the importance of leadership was muted or absent in others. In some cases, the need for strong leadership appears to have been mitigated by the way in which commons governance can usefully inherit and build upon preexisting cultural or community norms (Lee, Evans, Torrance, Flowers). Trust relationships and norms about sharing and cooperation are parts of community or group fabrics, and those preexisting cultural fabrics are often extremely helpful in the evolution of governance institutions. While strong leadership may be one effective way of promoting the trust relationships that can stabilize knowledge commons governance, preexisting group dynamics play a similarly stabilizing role. In other cases, formal governance appeared to play a far more important role than we had observed in the previous set of cases (Contreras, Abbott, Mattioli, Bubela). In still others, knowledge commons sharing was promoted not so much by trusted leadership as by what one might call "commons entrepreneurship," in which promoters of a commons-based approach facilitated knowledge commons formation (and set up at least some of the rules of commons governance) by providing infrastructure to reduce the obstacles to knowledge sharing (Saxe and Acri, Contreras, Oliveira et al.). Of course, many knowledge commons arrangements combine one or more of these modalities. Moreover, trusted leadership or commons entrepreneurship may be important in establishing the community norms and relationships that later appear to stand on their own (Evans, Lee, Torrance). Future work may provide insights into the circumstances under which a particular modality can successfully sustain knowledge commons governance.

C.1.2.2 Knowledge Commons May Be Intertwined with State-Supplied Resources in Complex Ways

Whether or not Ostrom intended researchers to infer that the state plays or should play a relatively nominal role in commons governance, that conclusion often has been implicit in commons research in the natural resources domain. In GKC, while we included case studies in which the state played an important role, the state's direct role in many of the examples studied was minimal. In this book, however, we observe that the state often plays a critical role, or more than one critical role, in developing and sustaining knowledge commons governance in the medical arena. This theme is most directly and forcefully recognized in Contreras (Chapter 2), but the many ways in which the state regulates, supports, and otherwise influences the domain of life sciences and medical research are illustrated in a number of the other chapters (Lee, Evans, Boggio, Abbott, Mattioli, Bubela, Pedraza-Fariña, Strandburg and Bechtold, Strandburg and Frischmann). While a positive role for the state is illustrated in these studies, some of the cases in this book raise interesting questions about the potentially negative impact of top-down rules and regulations in this arena. Flowers explores a knowledge commons devoted to what he terms "outlaw innovation" by patients for whom the pace of mainstream medical research seems unduly constrained by regulation. Though not dealing with the role of the state per se, Saxe and Acri discuss the way in which overly risk-averse understandings of the requirements of evidence-based medicine can stymie the adjustment of treatment methods to better fit particular contexts. Evans discusses the weaknesses of a top-down approach to aggregating genomic data, proposing that groups of individuals join together to create their own data pools, to be deployed as they see fit. These studies echo the traditional argument by commons proponents against overly uniform approaches and in favor of local control.

C.2 LOOKING AHEAD

We closed *Governing Knowledge Commons* by noting that the book was both a tribute to Elinor Ostrom's landmark book *Governing the Commons* (1990) and the beginning of a new research program and journey, inspired by Ostrom's work but with hypotheses and hopes of its own. We are encouraged that in the space of roughly a decade, the ideas that animate knowledge commons research have moved from being an intuition that there is more to knowledge production than patent and copyright law to being the subject of a research program with participants and adherents around the world. The researchers included in this book are part of an emerging knowledge commons of research and researchers sharing their results. We believe that this additional collection of case studies, supplementing the group presented in GKC, affirms the utility of the research framework described in Chapter 1, as both a design for investigating a knowledge commons case and a device for interpreting and beginning to synthesize data from multiple cases.

As additional theoretical and empirical work on social dilemmas involving knowledge and information resource expands, and as that research is shared and interpreted, its normative implications, and its role in public policy and law, will take on more importance. Throughout this book and its predecessor, we have tried as rigorously as possible to explore knowledge commons governance with an eye to its weaknesses as well as its strengths and to maintain our roles as researchers rather than becoming advocates. What becomes of knowledge commons research in the future, however, will depend critically on how, when, and where it is engaged by legal institutions and public policy in general. That is so for at least two critical reasons: (1) because the character of the knowledge and information resources that are governed as commons (or otherwise) is specified in the first place by those very same legal and public policy institutions and (2) because as the work in this book shows, the state is often a crucial actor in successful commons institutions.

We look forward to continuing along the research pathway identified and illustrated by the work here, and we also look forward eventually to engaging with existing and new colleagues – students, faculty researchers, public policy analysts, participants in legal institutions, and activists and practitioners around the world – to determine whether, when, how, and why knowledge commons may become a better acknowledged and accepted part of the ecology of knowledge and information.

For EU product safety concerns, contact us at Calle de José Abascal, 56–1°,
28003 Madrid, Spain or eugpsr@cambridge.org.

www.ingramcontent.com/pod-product-compliance
Lightning Source LLC
LaVergne TN
LVHW011531200926
848484LV00001B/232

* 9 7 8 1 1 0 7 1 4 6 8 7 7 *